Insurgent Terrorism

International Library of Criminology, Criminal Justice and Penology – Second Series
Series Editors: Gerald Mars and David Nelken

Titles in the Series:

Gender and Prisons
Dana M. Britton

Quantitative Methods in Criminology
Shawn Bushway and David Weisburd

Detecting Deception
David Canter and Donna Youngs

Offender Profiling
David Canter and Michael Davis

Insurgent Terrorism
Gerald Cromer

Criminal Courts
Jo Dixon, Aaron Kupchik and Joachim Savelsberg

Crime and Security
Benjamin Goold and Lucia Zedner

Crime and Regulation
Fiona Haines

Recent Developments in Criminological Theory
Stuart Henry

Gun Crime
Richard Hobbs and Robert Hornsby

The Criminology of War
Ruth Jamieson

The Impact of HIV/AIDS on Criminology and Criminal Justice
Mark M. Lanier

Burglary
Robert Mawby

Domestic Violence
Mangai Natarajan

Women Police
Mangai Natarajan

Crime and Immigration
Graeme Newman and Joshua Freilich

Surveillance, Crime and Social Control
Clive Norris and Dean Wilson

Crime and Social Institutions
Richard Rosenfeld

The Death Penalty, Volumes I and II
Austin Sarat

Gangs
Jacqueline Schneider and Nick Tilley

Corporate Crime
Sally Simpson and Carole Gibbs

Green Criminology
Nigel South and Piers Beirne

Crime and Deviance in Cyberspace
David Wall

Insurgent Terrorism

Edited by

Gerald Cromer

Bar-Ilan University, Israel

ASHGATE

Published by
Ashgate Publishing Limited
Gower House
Croft Road
Aldershot
Hampshire GU11 3HR
England

Ashgate Publishing Company
Suite 420
101 Cherry Street
Burlington, VT 05401-4405
USA

Ashgate website: http://www.ashgate.com

British Library Cataloguing in Publication Data
Insurgent terrorism. – (International Library of
criminology, criminal justice and penology. Second Series)
1. Terrorism 2. Terrorism – Philosophy 3. Terrorism –
Religious Aspects
I. Cromer, Gerald, 1944–
306.6′25′

Library of Congress Cataloging-in-Publication Data
Insurgent terrorism / edited by Gerald Cromer.
p.cm. – (International library of criminology, criminal justice and penology–Second Series)
Includes bibliographical references.
1. Terrorism. 2. Political violence. I. Cromer, Gerald, 1944– II. International library of criminology, criminal justice & penology. Second Series.

HV6431.I755 2006
363.325– dc22

2006042724

ISBN 0 7546 2583 4
ISBN 978-0-7546-2583-4

Printed in Great Britain by TJ International Ltd, Padstow, Cornwall

Contents

PART IV IN THE NAME OF GOD

PART V IN COMPARISON

Acknowledgements

The editor and publishers wish to thank the following for permission to use copyright material.

Blackwell Publishing for the essay: Quintan Wiktorowicz and John Kaltner (2003), 'Killing in the Name of Islam: Al-Qaeda's Justification for September 11', *Middle East Policy*, **10**, pp. 76–92.

Cambridge University Press for the essays: Albert Bandura (1990), 'Mechanisms of Moral Disengagement', in Walter Reich (ed.), *Origins of Terrorism: Psychologies, Ideologies, Theologies, State of Mind*, Cambridge: Cambridge University Press, pp. 161–91. Copyright © 1990 Woodrow Wilson International Center.

Comparative Politics for the essay: David C. Rapoport (1988), 'Messianic Sanctions for Terror', *Comparative Politics*, **20**, pp. 195–213.

Greenwood Publishing Group for the essay: Richard W. Leeman (1991), 'The Rhetoric of Terrorism', in Richard W. Leeman (ed.), *The Rhetoric of Terrorism and Counterterrorism*, New York: Greenwood Press, pp. 45–69.

Taylor & Francis for the essays: Bonnie Cordes (1987), 'When Terrorists Do the Talking: Reflections on Terrorist Literature', *Journal of Strategic Studies*, **10**, pp. 150–71; Khachig Tololyan (1987), 'Cultural Narrative and the Motivation of the Terrorist', *Journal of Strategic Studies*, **10**, pp. 217–33; Mark Juergensmeyer (1987), 'The Logic of Religious Violence', *Journal of Strategic Studies*, **10**, pp. 172–93; Paul Sant Cassia (1999), 'Martyrdom and Witnessing: Violence, Terror and Recollection in Cyprus', *Terrorism and Political Violence*, **11**, pp. 22–54. Ehud Sprinzak (1991), 'Violence and Catastrophe in the Theology of Rabbi Meir Kahane: The Ideologization of Mimetic Desire', *Terrorism and Political Violence*, **3**, pp. 48–70; Jeffrey Kaplan (1995), 'Absolute Rescue: Absolutism, Defensive Action and the Resort to Force', *Terrorism and Political Violence*, **7**, pp. 128–63; Raphael Israeli (2002), 'A Manual of Islamic Fundamentalist Terrorism', *Terrorism and Political Violence*, **14**, pp. 23–40; C.J.M. Drake (1998), 'The Role of Ideology in Terrorists' Target Selection', *Terrorism and Political Violence*, **10**, pp. 53–85; Garrett O'Boyle (2002), 'Theories of Justification and Political Violence: Examples from Four Groups', *Terrorism and Political Violence*, **14**, pp. 23–46; Hanspeter van den Broek (2004), '*BORROKA* – The Legitimation of Street Violence in the Political Discourse of Radical Basque Nationalists', *Terrorism and Political Violence*, **16**, pp. 714–36.

Westview Press a member of Perseus Books Group for the essay: Begoña Aretxaga (1993), 'Striking with Hunger: Cultural Meanings of Political Violence in Northern Ireland', in Kay

Warren (ed.), *The Violence Within: Cultural and Political Opposition in Divided Nations*, Boulder: Westview Press, pp. 219–53. Copyright © 1993 Westview Press.

Every effort has been made to trace all the copyright holders, but if any have been inadvertently overlooked the publishers will be pleased to make the necessary arrangement at the first opportunity.

Preface to the Second Series

The first series of the International Library of Criminology, Criminal Justice and Penology has established itself as a major research resource by bringing together the most significant journal essays in contemporary criminology, criminal justice and penology. The series made available to researchers, teachers and students an extensive range of essays which are indispensable for obtaining an overview of the latest theories and findings in this fast changing subject. Indeed the rapid growth of interesting scholarly work in the field has created a demand for a second series which like the first consists of volumes dealing with criminological schools and theories as well as with approaches to particular areas of crime criminal justice and penology. Each volume is edited by a recognised authority who has selected twenty or so of the best journal articles in the field of their special competence and provided an informative introduction giving a summary of the field and the relevance of the articles chosen. The original pagination is retained for ease of reference.

The difficulties of keeping on top of the steadily growing literature in criminology are complicated by the many disciplines from which its theories and findings are drawn (sociology, law, sociology of law, psychology, psychiatry, philosophy and economics are the most obvious). The development of new specialisms with their own journals (policing, victimology, mediation) as well as the debates between rival schools of thought (feminist criminology, left realism, critical criminology, abolitionism etc.) make necessary overviews that offer syntheses of the state of the art.

GERALD MARS
Visiting Professor, Brunel University, Middlesex, UK

DAVID NELKEN
Distinguished Professor of Sociology, University of Macerata, Italy;
Distinguished Research Professor of Law, University of Cardiff, Wales;
Honourary Visiting Professor of Law, LSE, London, UK

Introduction

In Words and Deeds

Modern terrorists have tended to minimize the effect of words. Peter Kropotkin (1978, pp. 93–95), for instance, contended that they get lost in the air like the empty chiming of bells. Actions, on the other hand, awaken the spirit of revolt. He therefore sang the praises of those men of courage who are not satisfied with words and are ever searching for the means to transform ideas into actions. Just one daring deed of theirs, Kropotkin insisted, may in a few days make more propaganda than one thousand pamphlets.

Notwithstanding their preference for the propaganda of the deed (Laquer, 1987, pp. 48–51), Kropotkin and his fellow anarchists by no means abandoned the realm of discourse. In fact, many of them insisted that it was of vital importance to their cause. Johannes Most (1978, p. 106), for instance, argued that once an action is carried out, the most important thing is that the world hears about it from the revolutionaries. He therefore urged his colleagues to put up posters setting out the reasons for their actions in order to make them palatable to the people and to encourage them to join the fray.

This ambivalence about the power of words has been commented upon by a number of scholars. Miller (1983), for instance, argued that terrorists have a 'love-hate relationship with language', and Leeman (Chapter 6), drew attention to their 'rhetorical tension between communication and action'. Both of them, however, were at pains to point out that terrorist movements have no choice but to engage in propaganda. As Miller (1983, p. 10) rather clumsily put it: 'It is vital to the articulation of the political justification for their violent methods'.

The terrorists' verbal strategy is designed to justify the resort to violence in their own eyes as well as in the eyes of others. They are engaged in propaganda and auto-propaganda (Cordes, Chapter 3) at one and the same time. While scholars may differ about the extent to which these two kinds of persuasion overlap, they all agree that terrorists use a wide variety of mechanisms of moral disengagement (Bandura, 1990), to try to convince themselves of the rightness of their actions. Doing so is a necessary prerequisite for taking up arms against the enemy.

Despite the ubiquity of terrorist literature and the fact that 'it gives us our best, and sometimes, only inside view of terrorist life and thinking' (Cordes, p. 63), it has not attracted a great deal of scholarly interest. The present volume therefore brings together the most important studies in what is still a largely unexplored field. The introductory essay that follows constitutes an attempt to summarize the major findings. In doing so, it draws attention to both the different kinds of terrorist propaganda and the underlying similarity between them.

In the Name of the Cause

Writing at the end of the 70's, Leites (Chapter 1) bemoaned the fact that the 'numerous writings' on modern terrorists only dealt with what they do and which environments and personalities dispose them to do it, and paid no attention whatsoever to how they viewed their resort to violence. In an attempt to redress this imbalance, Leites analysed the writings of the terrorists themselves to see 'what they thought they were doing and precisely what good it would do'. He found that they focused on the supposed impact of their actions on both the powers-that-be and the public at large. Terrorists were convinced or, to be more precise, tried to convince themselves, that the use of violence is the best, and even the only way to further their cause.

Leites' pioneering essay – he himself called it 'a very first approximation' – concentrated on how terrorists relate to the effectiveness of their actions rather than on their moral status. It paid only scant attention to how they try to justify the resort to violence. Subsequent studies, in contrast, have adopted a different approach. While they do relate to the oft-made claim that terrorism is the only kind of action that stands a chance of success – a strategy of last resort (see Cordes, Chapter 3) – the emphasis is clearly elsewhere. A series of essays published in the late 80's and early 90's focused on the different techniques of neutralization (Sykes and Matza, 1957) and/or accounts (Scott and Lyman, 1968) that terrorists use to justify their resort to violence in their own eyes and the eyes of others, rather than on their ruminations about the efficacy of doing so.

The studies draw attention to the fact that terrorists occasionally resort to the language of non-responsibility (Bandura, Chapter 4). In particular, they use the agentless passive form in order to portray their actions as the work of impersonal social forces rather than as the result of human choice. However, this kind of response is the exception rather than the rule. Terrorists, in common with other political criminals, use justifications (Scott and Lyman, 1968, p. 47) or acclaiming tactics (Schlenker, 1980, pp. 162–64) rather than excuses. They deny the pejorative quality associated with their actions, and accept, or even try to maximize responsibility for them.

All the readings in Part II of this volume indicate that terrorists of all kinds make an appeal to higher loyalties (Sykes and Matza, 1957, p. 669). They argue that engaging in violence, although illegal, is legitimate because it complies with a more important norm. Bringing down the capitalist system, fighting for national independence, or obeying the will of God each provide a moral justification for violating the law and using terror against external and internal enemies alike.

But terrorists do not only appeal to higher loyalties; they also engage in the condemnation of condemners (Sykes and Matza, 1957, p. 668). Each of the studies seems to confirm Miller's (1987, p. 392) finding that the positive depictions of self are outnumbered by negative images of the other. This is due to the fact that all four waves of terrorists (Rapoport, 2004) have cited the misdeeds of their enemies as a justification of their actions. Terrorist propaganda is replete with provocation stories about particular acts of violence (Picard, Chapter 5) or/and critiques of the structural violence of the system as a whole (Leeman, Chapter 6) in support of their claim that the movement in question is simply reacting to the prior crimes of omission and commission of the enemy.

Both the appeal to higher loyalties and the condemnation of the condemners find linguistic expression in what Cordes (Chapter 3) called a war of labels. Terrorists invariably refer to themselves as freedom fighters, guerillas, or an army, and vilify their adversaries in exactly the same way as they themselves are disparaged – as terrorists, criminals, and even as being less than human. They, in common with the enemy, adopt a reflective strategy (Leeman, Chapter 6) in order to convince themselves and others of the rightness of their cause.

Each of the essays in Part II of this volume show how terrorists 'constructing a bipolar world which clearly divides between good and evil' (Leeman, p. 132). Tugwell (Chapter 2), however, drew attention to an additional theme of terrorist propaganda and auto-propaganda that the other authors overlooked. He pointed out that they do not simply pit the forces of light against the forces of darkness; they also relate to the result of the conflict between them. According to conventional wisdom might is right, but in reality, the terrorists argue, exactly the opposite is the case. Right is might, and they will therefore eventually prevail, despite the seemingly insurmountable odds against them. The battle may be a long and bitter one, but victory is assured.

Tugwell's observation suggests that terrorist propaganda meets what MacIntyre (1981, p. 456) singled out as the essential requirement of a narrative – 'an evaluative framework in which good or bad character help to produce happy or unfortunate outcomes'. It is, therefore, best understood and analysed as a story rather than as a series of techniques of neutralization or accounts. This is particularly so in the case of nationally and religiously inspired terrorism.

In the Mirror of the Past

The cultural specificity of each national liberation movement makes it difficult to generalize about the content of their terrorist tales. However, the articles included in the third section of this volume and other studies of the Irish Republican Army/IRA (Aretxaga, 1997; Arthur 1996), the Armenian Secret Liberation Army/ASALA (Tololyan, 1987), and the three movements that fought against the British mandate in Palestine (Schatzberger, 1985) indicate that there is a striking resemblance between them. In each case, the propaganda revolves around a reading or, to be more precise, a rereading of the history and meta-history of the nation, and the life histories of those who gave their lives in the struggle for independence.

Drawing attention to the profound impact that witnessing violence had on those who decide to take up arms against the British presence in Northern Ireland, Aretxaga (Chapter 8) argued that it has the force of self evidence that cannot be contested and needs no elaboration. However, as Scott (1991, p. 25) pointed out, experience does not exist outside the flow of discourse so personal experiences of violence are recalled in the individual accounts of those concerned (Sant Cassia, Chapter 9) and 'embedded in the discursive flow of collective memory that emerged as a frame of interpretation' (Aretxaga, Chapter 8).

The propaganda of national liberation movements is therefore replete with references to the past. All the contemporary protagonists – the freedom fighters and their external and internal enemies – are compared to figures from yesteryear. These analogies invariably take the form of narratives (Tololyan, Chapter 7) or story-like creations (Aretxaga, Chapter 8) about oppression and victimization and, when relevant, about the resistance they engendered. Telling these terrorist tales is not designed to simply transmit knowledge about the nation's past. As Aretxaga (Chapter 8) pointed out, history is 'condensed in key events that have become part of the cultural consciousness of people', and is therefore 'understood in existential terms as a predicament that gives meaning to peoples' lives legitimizing their politics and charging their actions with emotional power'.

The resort to history is meant to reactualize the past by engendering new feats of heroism. National liberation movements hail past acts of bravery in order to encourage similar actions in the present. Their collective memory therefore consists of a series of projective narratives that are descriptive and prescriptive at one and the same time. 'They not only tell a story of the past but also ... tell individuals how they would ideally have to live and die in order to contribute properly to their collectivity and its future' (Tololyan, Chapter 7).

These narratives of the ideal life and death are backed up by regulative biographies (Tololyan, Chapter 7) or mythbiographies (Sant Cassia, Chapter 9) of those who did, in fact, personify them. The life histories of freedom fighters who fell in the struggle for independence are constructed in such a way that they can be portrayed as examples of the national ideal. They relate to how those who took up arms against the enemy first learnt, then lived, and finally became part of the movement's projective narrative (Cromer, Chapter 10). Members are therefore depicted not as outcasts from society but as paradigmatic of its deepest values.

The different terrorist tales – present and past, individual and collective – form an intricate network of nested narratives (Gergen and Gergen, 1983, p. 263) that reinforce each other because they all assume the same basic form. Every story foretells that the nation and/or those who take up arms on its behalf will eventually defeat the evil enemy and emerge victorious. Even if the liberation movement has suffered defeats and continues to do so, its members transmit the love of freedom to their contemporaries and future generations, who will continue the struggle until it is crowned with success and independence is achieved.

The articles in the third section of this volume draw attention to the fact that all the national liberation movement's narratives – history, meta-history, and life histories – are very different from or, to be more precise, directly opposed to those of the religious authorities. Their preoccupation with divine intervention is replaced by an emphasis on human action, or what Schatzberger (1985, p. 57) referred to as the motif of an active deed. Paradoxically, however, nationalist stories are replete with symbols made effective by centuries of ecclesiastical rhetoric. Because of the centrality of religion in the national consciousness, the leaders of liberation movements often couch their criticism of it in sacred terms. They use the language of the faith to attack its most basic tenets.

As a result of this process of dialogic narration (Bruner and Gorfain, 1984) with the prior religious discourse, traditional models are rarely discarded; they are rather transformed and infused with new meanings. Thus the three movements that fought against the British mandate in Palestine reinterpreted the most sacred prayers and precepts of Judaism in their attempt to undermine the traditional understanding of them (Schatzberger, 1985, pp. 38–46). Rereading the commandments and rewriting the liturgy in this way enabled them to attack the religious worldview and benefit from its sacred aura at one and the same time.

A similar process has occurred in the ASALA and IRA. In each of these cases, however, the figure of the martyr is the major instrument and site of the struggle for cultural legitimacy. Although the concepts of sacrifice and martyrdom are as central to the rhetoric of national liberation as they are to church sermons and other forms of religious discourse, the message conveyed is exactly the opposite. Writing about the IRA, O'Doherty (1998, p. 20) pointed out that Republicanism and Catholicism are both about the recompense for sacrifice. However, while 'for the Catholic the promise is of an eternity of bliss, for the republican the promised land is ... a new Ireland which is imagined to be the restoration of a pure and ancient Ireland, uncontaminated by British influence'. The reward is in this world rather than in the world-to-come.

In the Name of God

This kind of appropriation of religious language makes it imperative to distinguish between terror justified by religion and religious or holy terror. As Juergensmeyer writes (1991, pp. 111–12): 'It is one thing when the moral sanction of religion is brought to bear on such worldly and non-spiritual matters as political struggles. It is quite another when the struggles themselves are seen primarily as religious events ... and are perceived by the faithful as facets of a more fundamental confrontation'. In such cases, the current conflict between good and evil is not just nested within a historical and meta-historical one; it is portrayed as the latest, and hopefully the last, round of a cosmic struggle between the forces of light and darkness.

All the essays in Part IV of this volume draw attention to this aspect of religious terror. It is most clearly seen, however, in Kaplan's analysis of the gradual evolvement of a theology of violence in the United States anti-abortion movement. According to the leaders of the Rescue Movement, all those who took part in the abortion holocaust or even passively acquiesced to it were the contemporary embodiment of the devil's timeless evil and President Clinton was the Antichrist himself. Translating the current situation into theological terms, the members of Defensive Action saw them as part of the End Times scenario of the Book of Revelations. In their view, the temporal confrontation with the abortion culture and the cosmic struggle between the forces of good and evil have become one.

This belief that the transcendental conflict is played out in history is widely regarded as one of the conditions under which the faithful are more likely to resort to violence. However, both Juergensmeyer (Chapter11) and Rapoport (Chapter 12) contend that it is not enough for them to believe in this juxtaposition of the worldly and other-worldly struggle; they must also be convinced that the latter is at a decisive stage and that their actions are crucial to the consummation of the process. The true believers must hold that they have it in their power to force the hand of God and bring the redemption.

Looked at from the perspective of this volume, the two necessary conditions for resorting to terror – immanence and human agency – can be seen as justifications for doing so. True believers claim that these prerequisites do, in fact, exist, and that is therefore permissible, and even obligatory to take up arms against the enemy. Failure to do so constitutes a breach of faith and a deviation from the true path.

The debate over the permissible conditions for the use of violence (*jus a bellum*) and the form it should take (*jus a bello*) is not just a conflict of ideas; it is also a struggle for sacred authority within a particular textual community (Martin, 1986). In their attempt to convince themselves and others of the rightness of their cause, advocates of what Kaplan (Chapter 14) aptly referred to as a theology of violence are at pains to point out that it derives from a, or to be more precise, the correct reading of the sacred sources. They are engaged in a constant war of verses (Cromer, 2001, pp. 167–69) with those who favour a more conservative and traditional interpretation of the privileged texts (Kirk, 1979. p. 96).

The essays included in Part IV of this volume indicate that this always has been, and still is the case in both monotheistic and non-monotheistic religions. In recent years, however, scholarly interest has focused on the conflict within Islam because of the fierce debate about the status of suicide bombings in Muslim law. A number of studies have drawn attention to the extent to which religious authorities cite fatwa and Hadith stories to legitimate their stance and delegitimate that of their opponents about both the idea of active death in martyrdom (Israeli, Chapter 15) and the targeting of civilians (Wiktorowicz and Kaltner, Chapter 16).

Advocates of a theology of violence are also at pains to explain their opponents' stance. Resorting to what Young (1974, pp. 247–51) referred to in a rather different context as a corrupter-corrupted model, they often attribute it to the deleterious influence of unbelievers. Nevertheless, the faint at heart are criticized for adopting a hierarchy of priorities that places personal ambition and aggrandizement above obedience to the divine will. Their weak and diluted belief is compared to the authentic faith of those who actually engage in or even just support holy terror (Sprinzak, Chapter 13).

A careful reading of terrorist propaganda indicates that religiously inspired terrorists and their theological mentors sometimes take this argument a stage further. They relate to both the current confrontation and the cosmic struggle between the forces of light and the forces of darkness as an ongoing battle within each and every individual (Juergensmeyer, Chapter 11). According to this view of things, even the staunchest warriors must always be on their guard because the evil inclination is constantly trying to make them stray from the true path and lay down their arms.

Whether the enemy is depicted as being beyond the confines of the faith, amongst coreligionists, or within the true believer, the narrative is always essentially the same. The propaganda and auto-propaganda of religiously inspired terrorists, like that of their secular counterparts, assumes the form of a morality play in which the forces of good eventually defeat the forces of evil. This is not altogether surprising. After all, in their minds at least, God is on their side.

In Comparison

Earlier studies took the form of an analysis of the propaganda of a single terrorist movement, a particular kind of organization, or of terrorist groups in general. It is only since the end of the 90's that scholars have begun to carry out comparative research within (van Den Broeck, Chapter 19) and between movements (Drake, Chapter 17; O'Boyle, Chapter 18), and until now, at least, their findings have been rather inconclusive.

Drake (Chapter 17), in his study of the role of ideology in terrorists' target selection, argued that the process is never indiscriminate. However wide the range of legitimate victims, it is always anchored in an ideology that 'sets out the moral framework within which they operate'. Building on this initial premise, Drake showed that an analysis of the ideologies of opposing terrorist organizations (republican and loyalist terrorists in Ireland) and even essentially similar ones (the Red Brigades in Italy and the Red Army Faction in Germany) leads to an understanding of the marked differences in their selection of targets.

Rather than looking at one specific aspect of terrorist discourse, van Den Broek (Chapter 19) and O'Boyle (Chapter 18) attempted to make a general comparison of terrorist propaganda within a particular group and between groups respectively. However, they found it difficult to delineate any significant differences. As a result, van Den Broek's conclusions related to the aims of the discourse of legitimation rather than to its content, and O'Boyle felt the need to cite a number of reasons such as the need to address diverse audiences at one and the same time, and the internal logic of certain moral justifications for the difficulty in disentangling consequentialist and deontological arguments in favour of terror.

These and other comparative studies have taken the form of an analysis of the techniques of neutralization and accounts used by the different movements. However, as has already been pointed out, terrorist propaganda is best understood as a narrative. This approach, it is suggested, does not only provide a more productive way of analysing particular examples of terrorist discourse; it also affords new opportunities for making comparisons between them. Each of the concepts developed in an earlier paper (Cromer, Chapter 10) and referred to briefly in this essay – narrative structure, nested narratives and dialogic narration – affords new opportunities for exploring the similarities and dissimilarities within a particular group (for example, material addressed to diverse audiences), between different organizations of the same kind (for example, the perceived threat of external and internal enemies), and between different types of movements (for example, revolutionary left, national liberation, and religiously inspired ones), and lead, in turn, to a deeper understanding of terrorist tales and those who tell them.

And this is not all. The terrorists' emphasis on the propaganda of the deed referred to at the beginning of this essay has led to a plethora of research on the mass media coverage of their actions. As Dobkin (1992) pointed out, this too is best understood as 'tales of terror'. Adopting a narrative approach therefore has an additional benefit. It makes it possible to compare the stories told to legitimize and delegitimize the resort to violence and to examine the dialogue between them. Contrary to what each side so vehemently claims, the enemy is human. In the theatre of terror, both the actors and their various audiences are exemplars of what Fisher (1987) so aptly referred to as homo narrans.

References

Aretxaga, Begona (1997), *Shattering Silence: Women, Nationalism and Political Subjectivity in Northern Ireland*, Princeton: Princeton University Press.

Arthur, Paul (1996), 'Reading Violence: Ireland', in David E. Apter (ed.), *The Legitimization of Violence*, New York: New York University Press, pp. 234–91.

Bruner, Edward M. and Phyllis Gorfain (1984), 'Dialogic Narration and the Paradoxes of Massada', in Edward M. Bruner (ed.), *Text, Play and Story: The Construction and Reconstruction of Self and Society*, Washington, DC: American Ethnological Society, pp. 56–79.

Cromer, Gerald (2001), 'The War of the Torah: The Israeli Religious Peace Movements' Struggle for Legitimation', *Jewish Political Studies Review*, **13**(3/4), pp. 159–87.

Dobkin, Bethami A. (1992), *Tales of Terror: Television News and the Construction of the Terrorist Threat*, New York: Praeger.

Fisher, Walter R. (1987), *Human Communication as Narration: Toward A Philosophy of Reason, Value, and Action*, Columbia: University of South Carolina Press.

Gergen, Kenneth J. and Mary M. Gergen (1983), 'Narratives of the Self', in Theodore R. Sarbin and Karl E. Scheibe (eds), *Studies in Social Identity*, New York: Praeger, pp. 254–73.

Juergensmeyer, Mark (1991), 'Sacrifice and Cosmic War', *Terrorism and Political Violence*, **13**(3), pp. 101–17.

Kirk, J. Andrew (1979), *Liberation Theology*, Atlanta: John Knox Press.

Kropotkin, Peter (1978), 'The Spirit of Revolt', in Walter Laquer (ed.), *The Terrorism Reader: A Historical Anthology*, New York: New American Library, pp. 90–96.

Laquer, Walter (1987), *The Age of Terrorism*, Boston: Little, Brown and Co.

MacIntyre, Alasdair (1981), *After Virtue: A Study in Moral Theory*, Notre Dame: University of Notre Dame Press.

Martin, Richard C. (1986), *Striving in the Path of Allah: Toward an Understanding of Religious Violence in Text and Context*, Paper Presented at the International Conference on Terrorism, University of Aberdeen, Aberdeen.

Miller, Bowman H. (1983), *The Language Component of Terrorist Strategy.* Unpublished PhD. Thesis, Georgetown University, Washington, DC.

Miller, Bowman H. (1987), 'Terrorism and Language: A Text-Based Analysis of the German Case', *Terrorism*, **9**(4), pp. 373–407.

Most, Johannes (1978), 'Advice for Terrorists', in Walter Laquer (ed.), *The Terrorism Reader: A Historical Anthology*, NewYork: New American Library, pp. 100–108.

O'Doherty, Malachi (1998), 'The Trouble with Guns', Belfast: Blackstaff.

Rapoport, David C. (2004), 'The Four Waves of Terrorism', in Audrey Kurth Cronin and James M. Ludes (eds), *Attacking Terrorism: Elements of a Grand Strategy*, Washington DC: Georgetown University Press, pp. 46–73.

Schatzberger, Hilda (1985), *Resistance and Tradition in Mandatory Palestine*, Ramat Gan: Bar Ilan University Press (Hebrew).

Schlenker, Barry R. (1980), *Impression Management: The Self-Concept Social Identity and Interpersonal Relations*, Monterey, CA: Brooks/Cole.

Scott, Joan (1991), 'The Evidence of Experience', *Critical Inquiry*, **17**(4), pp. 773–97.

Scott, Marvin B. and Stanford M. Lyman (1968), 'Accounts', *American Sociological Review*, **33**(1), pp. 48–62.

Sykes, Gresham M. and David Matza (1957), 'Techniques of Neutralization: A Theory of Delinquency', *American Sociological Review*, **22**(6), pp. 664–70.

Tololyan, Khachig (1987), 'Martyrdom as Legitimacy: Terrorism, Religion and Symbolic Appropriation in the Armenian Diaspora', in Paul Wilkinson and Alasdair M. Stewart (eds), *Contemporary Research on Terrorism*, Aberdeen: Aberdeen University Press, pp. 89–103.

Young, Jock (1974), 'Mass Media, Drugs and Deviance' in Paul Rock and Mary McIntosh (eds), *Deviance and Social Control*, London: Tavistock Publications, pp. 229–59.

Part I
In the Beginning

[1]

Understanding the Next Act

Nathan Leites
The Rand Corporation

Abstract The practitioner and analyst of Russian unconventional warfare in 1812, Denis Davydov, distinguished three levels of violence: (big) war, small war, and "burning one or two granaries" (Laqueur 1976, p. 46), for which he had no name and which I shall call small violence, or microviolence; even if passenger terminals of metropolitan airports or 747s were, in the near future, to be substituted for granaries. What differentiates microviolence—a mere quantity—is that with "small war" you may expect to impose substantial attrition on the enemy at least over the long run, and with "microviolence" not even that.

The numerous writings concerned with "urban guerrillas" and modern "terrorists" have focused on what they do, and—to some extent—on what makes them do it: which environments and personalities dispose to microviolence. Even the most sophisticated treatments, such as the recent analyses by J. Bowyer Bell and Walter Laqueur, do not systematically consider *what they thought they were doing, precisely what good it would do.*

To be sure, in some cases where microviolence occurs on behalf of a widely shared cause—usually an ethnic one, whether it be Basque, Palestinian, Irish—a large part of the answer is evident. But what about the Weathermen, the Japanese United Red Army, the Italian Brigate Rosse, the West German Rote Armee Fraktion and June 2 Movement? It is with these that I shall largely deal.

Data on their calculations are meager, and those extant are not easily available. Hence the following pages are a very first approximation, much in need of correction, amplification, further illustration. But as no piece of similar structure has, to my knowledge, been written, the present one might yet be useful. I am aware of the disproportion between the importance of the subjects addressed in many of the following sections on the one hand, and their brevity on the other hand. But, apart from the faults in what I am saying, this should incite rather than repel.

Not all of the microviolent ones with whom I deal show all of the characteristics I shall describe. It might be a subsequent task to establish major constellations.

Of the factual assertions that enter into the microviolents' calculations, many are, to put it mildly, dubious; often so clearly that I have left it to the reader to note the contrast with reality.

The microviolent ones inhabit a universe of estimates and preferences strikingly different from that of those who devise and execute countermeasures against acts of terror. If some of the latter gained from the following pages a more vivid understanding of their strange adversaries, this study might be of some use.

Sometimes I shall present reactions attributed to microviolent ones as if *they* had written this essay; the context will, I trust, convey this. Emphases, unless otherwise stated, are mine.

In analyses of "terrorists" in developed countries acting on behalf of a radicalism which is little shared, one question has often been slighted: how do they make it plausible to themselves that their acts serve the attainment of their goal? The pages to follow aim at drawing a first map of answers.

The essay was written in early 1977. No attempt has been made to incorporate the evidence which has become available since then.

I. Impacts

Section 1: Bombing into Awareness

"The urban guerrilla," "the first phase of revolutionary war," observes a leader (Renato Curcio) of a group (Brigate Rosse) engaging in microviolence in a developed country (Italy) in the seventies, "is indispensable . . . for enlarging the 'possible consciousness' of the European proletariat . . ." (*L' Espresso*, 2 March 1975, p. 33): a proposition widely accepted in groups of that kind. (They seem to be little aware of Bakunin already having thought so.) The "enlarging" of "consciousness" is to come about in a variety of ways.

First of all, as has very often been noted, by heightening attention to the users of microviolence—to their message.

If a large part of the population, in the belief of many partisans of microviolence, *should* be hostile to the present shape of things but *isn't*, it is also because a barrier is interposed between the revolutionary message and the people. Acts of microviolence may be intended to break down that barrier; most obviously by coercing the authorities to allow the revolutionaries themselves or their messages access to the media.

It requires, the microviolent ones may point out, an extreme event to induce the media to break silence about them. "As I am nothing," a French anarchist (Leon Lehautier) explained in the late nineteenth century, "if my protest does not entail a scandal which forcibly attracts attention to my grievances, it is as if I were not complaining at all" (Salmon 1959, p. 334). It was the death by hunger strike in prison of one of them (Holger Meins), the leaders of the West German Rote Armee Fraktion (the "Baader-Meinhof" group) point out (while engaged in the same conduct) to a left-of-center news magazine *(Der Spiegel)*, which "has broken up the news boycott against the strike." Therefore, "that there are many who wake up only when a person has already been murdered, understand only then what the issue is, is also due to you. Thus *Der Spiegel* has kept silence for eight weeks about the hunger strike of forty political prisoners. . . . Your first report came on the fifty-third day of the strike, five days before the death of Holger" *(Der Spiegel,* 20 January 1975, p. 54).

Convinced that the present order cruelly frustrates the interests of most, which could be gratified only by the profound changes they favor, the microviolent ones are apt to take it for granted—in contrast, for instance, to revolutionaries in the Bolshevik tradition—that exposure to their ideas commends conversion to them. Thus the Brazilian "urban guerrillas" in the late sixties found it, in the estimate of a critic-revolutionary (João Quartim), "easy to confuse . . . the publicity which the bombings received with a . . . building up of strength among the people" (Kohl and Litt 1974, p. 153). The authorities' high attention to us is undoubtedly accompanied by hostility and fear; surely, then, the people's interest in us goes with love and trust.

And it also goes with gratitude in those cases where microviolence leads to benefits bestowed on some among the people; when, for instance, land registers containing the titles of big owners are burned or the rich coerced into donations to the poor; unless the microviolent ones themselves, in the words of a Brazilian (Joaquin Camara Ferreira), "attack food warehouses and distribute the food among the people; kill cattle and distribute the beef among the hungry . . ." (Moss 1972, p. 200). "The guerrillas," Bernardine Dohrn remarks about the abduction of Patty Hearst, "have kidnapped the daughter of a rich and powerful man in order to provide food to the poor." The point of their actions is that it "has unleashed . . . a leap in everyone's consciousness . . ." (Letter of 20 February 1974, *The Berkeley Barb*, 1-7 March 1974). Microviolent ones may even aspire to instituting multiple reforms by permanent coercion. "The proletarian organization," explains Horst Mahler, "can impose upon the rich obligations to contribute to collective institutions (nursery schools, health care centers, youth hostels, etc.)"; and "urban real estate can be gradually deprived of its power, rents can be lowered . . ." (Mahler 1971, pp. 32–33).

Or the intention may be to arouse favorable sentiments by exercising vengeance and punishment against the people's enemies.

Again, microviolence may aim at obtaining documents or confessions compromising the established order (a prominent device of the Tupamaros).

If they are willing to go that far, the people may be expected to reason about those who commit microviolence, there must be much to their cause.

Look at the damage they are willing to *incur*. "By the attitude of the crowd" at the execution of Sofia Perovskaya for contributing to the assassination of Czar Alexander II in 1881, "she understood," Kropotkin surmised, "that she had dealt a mortal blow to the autocracy, and she read in the sad looks which were directed sympathetically towards her that by her death she was dealing an even more terrible blow from which the autocracy will never recover" (Joll 1964, p. 128). Having on 22 February 1974 sabotaged the meteorological tower at the nuclear plant site of Montague, Massachusetts, Samuel H. Lovejoy explained to a *New York Times* reporter: "I wanted people to think: 'that guy's willing to go to jail—these nuclear plants must be heavier than I thought.' " "The fact that . . . dozens of us are prepared to die . . . ," one of the Brazilians who had kidnapped the West German ambassador assured, "penetrates to the population" (Kohl and Litt 1974, p. 143).

And look at the damage the microviolent ones are willing to *inflict:* their targets must be bad indeed—so it may be hoped that the people will reason—to deserve such treatment. The "systematic sabotage of

American targets, from consulates to factories and officials'' would, to a Brazilian (Jamil Rodriguez) be ''actions whose function it is to unmask the enemy in the eyes of the masses'' and ''thus indirectly to transmit a political line'' (*Les Temps Modernes*, March 1971, p. 1611).

Here violence is presumed to be sensed as bad in itself. But it may also be believed to be valued for its own sake by elements of the people—people attracted to revolutionaries precisely because they neither respect the law nor cherish the word (another forgotten idea of Bakunin's). At the national council of the Students for a Democratic Society at Boulder, Colorado, 10-12 October 1968, ''the Mother-fuckers [the SDS chapter from New York's Lower East Side] argued that militant . . . action could capture the allegiance of . . . drop-outs living in hippie and working class communities who would be turned off by the 'intellectual bullshit' of traditional radicals'' (Powers 1971, 93). ''When I was at Ann Arbor,'' Bill Ayres reminisced in the fall of 1969, ''all the talk about revolution was in the abstract''; but ''since we have moved to Detroit, we have made the revolution real.'' Now ''the Grease come up to us and say, 'Hey, aren't you the guys who beat up the pigs at McDonald's last night? How come?' '' The point is that ''you understand the revolution when you make the revolution, not when you talk about it'' (Powers 1971, pp. 147–48). In fact, ''anybody who has been out to a high school, to a drive-in or to a community college in an aggressive and assertive way knows that the people out there loved the fuckin' action and thought that it was out of sight'' (Powers 1971, p. 201). In short, ''when you say SDS in Detroit, they say, 'Oh, they are those broads who beat up guys' '' (Powers 1971, p. 205).

Those who like nonpolitical violence may have fought *against* those who are prone to the political variety before fighting *with* them. ''One Saturday afternoon in the middle of July [1969] about forty members of Motor City SDS had gone to Detroit Metropolitan Beach, known as Metro Beach by the white working class youths who spent weekends there. The Weathermen . . . planted the [Red] flag in the midst of a crowd and began to argue aggressively with the white youths, many of them Vietnam veterans, who gathered around. At one point an angry veteran said, 'Let's get the flag' and a general brawl erupted.'' As it should, for ''the theory behind the Metro Beach riot . . . was that working class kids were turned off by sissy intellectuals who talked about fighting the ruling class, but always had some smooth reasons why the actual moment to fight had not arrived. By . . . proving their commitment by fighting the Weathermen would win the respect of working class kids. A punch in the nose, properly explained, would do more to radicalize the Grease (as working class kids were called) than years of patient explanation. 'It was great' Bill [Ayres] told one friend about the Metro Beach riot. '. . . The kids love it' " (Powers 1971, pp. 132–33). "At the Metro Beach action," the same participant-observer reports, "Motor City SDS got into a fight with a gang. But a week later the gang sent a message that they sure did dig beating up SDS, but they also did dig going to Chicago [for the Days of Rage] to beat up some pigs" (Powers 1971, p. 209).

Now that we have employed an extreme means, violence, on behalf of an extreme cause, we have even less than before the right to abandon that cause: in such fashion microviolence may be intended to commit.

It may commit, for instance, in a calculation often attributed to Palestinian "terrorists," fickle Arab governments and publics who may be disposed to abandon the goal of ending the State of Israel.

And it may commit, in the first place, the microviolent ones themselves. "Middle class in origin," an observer points out about "white radicals" in the United States of the late sixties, they "were sensitive to the charge that they could drop out of the movement at any moment and resume the . . . privileged lives they had left behind." Now, "realizing this, and perhaps defensive about their own revolutionary inertia, black militants took a certain pleasure in attacking white radicals as summertime soldiers playing at revolution." (Powers 1971, pp. 124–25.) Also, as Bernardine Dohrn recalled (in a statement of 21 May 1970), "the parents of 'privileged' kids have been saying for years that the revolution was a game for us" (Powers 1971, p. 213). "As," according to the observer who quotes this remark, "even the police and the courts seemed to share . . . [this] belief," "there was only one way white radicals could defend themselves against this charge: to become criminals for whom there would be no longer any choice of returning to straight society" (op. cit., 181).

They, by the very same acts, would also in their souls separate themselves even more from that society. They would be able to begin violence because they had already, to a perhaps only slight extent, reduced in themselves the sense that it was forbidden. But it would be the practice of violence that would—should—further enfeeble that inner obstacle, in a happy circle between violating waning prohibitions and feeling good about it. (Thus Pascal recommended to unbelievers that they start using holy water; thus Giovanni Gentile suggested to Italian fascists that "the act precedes the norm.")

Leaders may then be the ones who forbid themselves violence least and thus liberate their comrades. "They," a former member of the Rote Armee Fraktion (Peter Homann) observes about two prominent militants (Ulrike Meinhof and Horst Mahler), "again and again came up against a limit which they at first did not dare overstep: they had internalized bourgeois legality." But "then," as the journalist interviewing the former microviolent one remarks, "came Andreas Baader," who already had a penal record. Yes, "he transmitted the feeling that violating . . . laws is . . . a revolutionary act" (*Der Spiegel*, 25 November 1971, p. 62).

Such was a revolutionary act not only for the violator, but also for the people who will learn about—and from—such an act. For, as Horst Mahler explains, "education in bourgeois society cannot fully extinguish the spontaneous tendency to defend oneself against oppression by force"; "the potential for force of the oppressed is . . . merely tamed, always ready *(auf dem Sprung)* to appear once more in the right direction." Now "the universality of obedience is an essential condition for obedience being maintained." Hence, "if that obedience is . . . refused at length and demonstratively, with the claim to violate the law of the rulers in order to realize the higher right of the oppressed," then "the norm [of obedience] finally loses its general validity. . . ." But "to break the habit (*Entwöhnung*) of obedience with regard to the bourgeois legal order" is "an essential precondition for revolutionizing the masses." Once again, "it is not a question of theoretical understanding"; rather, "in order to overcome the reflexes of obedience the *repeated* violation of norms *in deeds* is required" (Mahler 1971, 45–46, emphases in the text). Therefore "we must attack in order to arouse the revolutionary consciousness of the masses," even though in "so doing we encounter the resistance . . . aiming at the preservation of the painfully acquired psychic equilibrium under oppression." For "this resistance is the representative *(Statthalter)* of the exploiting system in the heads of the oppressed." Thus "we throw the bombs aimed at the apparatus of oppression also into the consciousness of the masses" (Mahler 1971, pp. 58–59). "It was," a former member (Beate Sturm) of his group recalls, ''Andreas Baader's great idea: a criminal deed is already in itself a political deed'' (*Der Spiegel,* 7 February 1972, p. 60). ''The progressive element of putting fire to a department store,'' Ulrike Meinhof comments on Baader's first act, ''resides not in the destruction of the merchandise, but in the criminality of the deed, in the violation of the law. . . .'' (*Konkret,* 4 November 1968). According to the Tupamaros, ''the very act of . . . pursuing activities that violate bourgeois legality generates revolutionary consciousness . . .'' (Kohl and Litt 1974, 227). ''Everything,'' Kropotkin had remarked, ''which falls outside legality is good for us.''

Illegal acts are good, not only because they free one morally, but also because they suggest that the destruction of the present order is feasible; they raise a hope that permits desire for another life to unfold. ''The consciousness of the necessity to change conditions,'' Horst Mahler recalls, ''is only *one* element of revolutionary consciousness,'' the other being ''the awareness of the *possibility* of revolutionary change'' (Mahler 1971, p. 48. Emphases in the text). ''The demonstration of the vulnerability of the regime,'' a Brazilian (Jamil Rodriguez) discerns, ''is . . . very important for creating the subjective conditions for the revolt of the masses'' (*Les Temps Modernes*, March 1971, p. 1597). It may not matter so much, with regard to that effect, what the ratio between the losses of authority and rebellion in an encounter is. ''How would you evaluate,'' a Tupamaro is asked about the brief occupation of a town (Pando), ''the three dead, sixteen prisoners, the losses of arms and vehicles and the overrunning of your bases or hideouts by the other side?'' ''These blows,'' the answer comes, ''didn't detract from the fundamental objective achieved by the operation, which were: to demonstrate that there is a guerrilla movement capable of seizing a town . . .'' (Gilio 1973, p. 152).

Such a demonstration will also change beliefs about what the current relationship of *forces* between the authorities and the revolutionaries is, (see Section 2) and thereby affect the balance of *preferences* for and against the status quo: one of the several *indirect* ways in which microviolence, in the forecasts of its practitioners, may favorably influence attitudes.

Another indirect way is by rendering middle roads less practicable: adherents to an extreme are apt to be confident that if people only have the choice between their and an opposed pole, they will largely make the right decision. Within the SDS at the University of Michigan in the fall of 1968 those opposed to violence "insisted that premature action would simply alienate the vast majority," while those in favor "insisted that action was the only thing likely to create a situation in which radical solutions to American problems would be considered" (Powers 1971, p. 88). To a Montonero the killing of former President Aramburu is useful because it is "pointing up that the country has no . . . alternatives except Peronism or anti-Peronism" (Hodges and Abu Shanab 1972, p. 304). With a presumption of the potential favor enjoyed by one's own side it becomes reasonable to envisage "the creation of a climate of tension . . . to propose destroying power stations" (Jamil Rodriguez, *Les Temps Modernes*, March 1971, p. 1611): a possible rationale behind Giangiacomo Feltrinelli's death in the process of damaging a transformer near Milan.

A "strategy of tension" *(la strategia della tensione* has presumably been practiced by Italian fascists since the fall of 1969) may be accompanied by aspirations to reduce the established order's output of goods and services, always implying that the "system" rather than its saboteurs would be blamed. In a caricature of this orientation a West German (Ulrich Schmücker of the "June 2 Movement") rendered ticket vending machines of West Berlin subway stations inoperable by clogging up the slots into which coins were to be inserted *(Der Spiegel*, 10 June 1974, p. 33). But it is according to Carlos Marighella himself that "the urban guerrilla should endanger the economy of the country." Hence it is gratifying to recall that "industrial workers acting as urban guerrillas are excellent industrial saboteurs . . . doing far more damage than a fully-informed layman could do" (Kohl and Litt 1974, p. 121).

It is implied that "the people," or at least a substantial fraction of it, is about as ready to sacrifice income to radical change as are the microviolent ones; and that many ordinary persons perceive a self-inflicted damage to current income to be as unavoidable a means for a better life later as it seems to the revolutionaries. These are no doubt estimates distant from realities; and characteristic, in precisely that distance, for many beliefs of microviolent ones about the people to whom they want to be so close. In many respects, they seem to take it for granted that their actions will be understood as they are meant, while, to an observer, this may be far from certain. When on 4 September 1969, 12:30 P.M.

seventy-five Weatherwomen suddenly appeared on the grounds of South Hills High School in Pittsburgh, spray-painted "Ho Lives" and "Free Huey" on the school's main entrance door and then charged inside shouting "Jail Break!" and "Shut down the school!" the high school students, according to an observer, were "mystified . . . they had no idea who the Weatherwomen were or why their school was being invaded" (Powers 1971, p. 141). Brazilian microviolent ones kidnapped first the ambassador of the United States, then a consul of Japan, then the ambassador of the Federal Republic of Germany, and the envoy of Switzerland: "the diplomats were abducted in the order their countries ranked in investment in Brazil, a fact presumably believed by the kidnappers to be understood by the public, though, in the event "lost on most Brazilians" (Kohl and Litt 1974, p. 50). Similarly, on the occasion of the visit to Brazil of a U.S. secretary of defense (Robert McNamara), a bomb was set off at the entrance to the Sears Roebuck department store in São Paulo, in view of the secretary's alleged financial connection with that enterprise—again though "no one in Brazil, except the initiated few, knew that McNamara owned shares in Sears Roebuck" (João Quartim in Kohl and Litt 1974, p. 151) and though the microviolent group in question had neither the capacity nor, apparently, the intent to spread that information. Consider in contrast the first would-be assassin of Czar Alexander II, Karakozow, who was much worried lest his act be wrongly understood by the people and wrote a manifesto in simple language designed to explain an act surely less in need of such aid than the piece of microviolence mentioned before.

For the few to exaggerate so greatly how similar the many are to them borders on recognizing the difference, and being indifferent toward it, if not relishing it. British microviolent ones in the early seventies used for one of their groups the assumed name of an obscure nineteenth-century Irish rebel and called themselves The Moonlighters Cell. Presumably they did not care much about—indeed cared much for *not* being understood by those whom they idealized.

With calculations such as the ones described in the preceding pages one may buttress one's confidence that, in the words of Al Fatah, "we shall strike our enemy in order to win our people" (Yaari 1970, p. 113); strengthen one's estimate that, in the assessment of the Tupamaros, "in the Cuban revolution guerrilla war . . . constituted the principal instrument for the raising of the consciousness (*consientisaçion*) of the masses'' (Costa, 1972, p. 251); confirm one's intuition that, in Horst Mahler's formula, ''the practical revolutionary example is the only path toward revolutionizing the masses'' (Mahler 1971, p. 57).

Microviolence is as powerful as words are feeble (see Section 14). ''The guerrillas,'' a Brazilian discerns, ''show a method of struggle that raises consciousness more effectively than distributing leaflets'' (Kohl and Litt 1974, p. 391).

More particularly, violence inspires imitation more than words induce acceptance. While ''we realize that blowing up a bridge could not be a determining fact for liberation,'' a Palestinian observes, ''yet . . . [it] would recruit ten other people to join Fatah'' (Laffin 1973, p. 21). One of the ''objectives'' of ''urban guerrilla'' according to Carlos Marighella is ''to give proof of its combativeness . . . in order to permit all malcontents to follow our example and fight with urban guerrilla tactics'' (Kohl and Litt 1974, pp. 108–9). ''Armed actions'' for the Weather Underground ''are a great . . . example'' (*Prairie Fire* 1974, p. 4).

Armed struggle may be made even more attractive by applying high technology. With regard to the kidnapping of one who had prosecuted them (Mario Sossi), a member of a group of Italian microviolent ones (Brigate Rosse) explains that the group had felt ''the necessity to furnish to the vanguards an example of organizational capability at a high level'' (Gabriele Invernizzi, *L'Espresso*, 12 May 1974, p. 20).

Thus one can resolve the anguishing question whether, in Marxist-Leninist language, the ''subjective conditions'' for microviolence are present here and now: ''by beginning the armed struggle,'' the Weather Underground explains, ''the awareness of its necessity will be furthered'' (*Prairie Fire*, 1974, p. 3). ''It would be wrong to engage in armed struggle only when the 'consent of the masses' is assured,'' Horst Mahler elaborates; ''for this would mean to . . . renounce this struggle altogether as this consent can be obtained only by the struggle itself'' (Mahler 1971, p. 43). True, another West German partisan of microviolence recalls, ''an armed struggle can take place only when it is understood by the masses.'' ''But'' in its turn, ''the comprehension of the masses is only aroused through the armed struggle'' (*Agit 883*, 18 June 1970. Baader-Meinhof Report 1972, p. 152).

Any area is apt to be perceived by one disposed to small violence in the light in which his or her continent appears to a Tupamaro: as ''a Latin America with a vast explosive potential that had not as yet been touched off [and which] needed the presence of a . . . a fuse to trigger the explosion . . . all that was necessary was to create the fuse . . ." (Kohl and Litt 1974, p. 284). Then "a few dozen fighters . . . can unleash an avalanche" (Mahler 1971, p. 43). "The people of Quebec," a leader of the Front de Libération du Québec (Charles Gagnon) writes from prison in the late sixties, "are angry": perhaps he is sure they are as angry as he knows himself to be. "Their apparent indolence is but suppressed anger": the rise, in recent decades of the awareness that a human being can be more angry than he knows, makes it easier to see the other as equalling him in resentment despite the lack of overt evidence to such effect. "It needs only a spark to set [everybody's suppressed anger] on fire." And "it is precisely our role . . . to provide this spark" (Morf 1971, p. 91). Mac, who has provided the image, has done it; so have Ho and Fidel; so have the Algerians—so why not we?

Section 2: Altering Beliefs about the Relationship of Forces

"Was the show of strength," a Tupamaro was asked by a friendly interviewer about one of his group's sensational actions, "intended to impress your own side or the enemy?" "It was intended," he answered sagely, "to impress the public, the enemy and us, too" (Gilio 1973, p. 149).

The very fact of microviolence appearing where there was none may for some time reduce the estimate of the authority's power—and hence prospects—in all strata of the population. Thus microviolent ones may, to start with, set themselves the objective of proving to an often incredulous audience that microviolence is feasible: just that. "Expropriations," remarks an Argentinian, "serve as a demonstration of efficiency"; the very act of accomplishing them and surviving (in a measure at least) "reveals the effectiveness of a method of struggle" (Kohl and Litt 1974, p. 382), a "method" that had not seemed available before. "What we do and at the same time want to show," Ulrike Meinhof explains, "is: that armed conflict can be accomplished [*durchführbar sein*]" (*Der Spiegel*, 18 June 1970, p. 73). "In the first phase" of armed action, Horst Mahler observes, "the task is . . . to demonstrate that armed groups can form and maintain themselves against the apparatus of the State." In short, "the instrument of armed struggle has to be discovered practically'' (Mahler 1971, p. 43), so as to alter immediately perceptions of the relationship of forces between the authorities and their enemies. ''Although the enemy appears strong, he is weak: we are strong''—these words, which the Turkish People's Liberation Army adopted from Mao when it had captured four U.S. airmen, may have been thought and spoken by many microviolent ones in diverse times and places when they had destroyed or subdued a fraction, however small, of the enemy. As long as such an act had not often happened close by in time and space, as long as it had not yet ceased to evoke shocked surprise (delighted, horrified, curious), the astonishing quality of the event—authority struck down or coerced—suggests a sharp change in relative power between the Establishment and its enemies. There may then be a sense of a serious competitor to the existing order having suddenly emerged, awesome in its rapid rise from nothing; and vulnerable to return to nothingness if it can't continue delivering a high performance so as to live up to a suddenly acquired respect.

Also, a microviolent group, having committed a striking act, may be known to absorb, for some time at least, the attention and action of the authorities' top level: surely an organization producing this effect possesses high power. When a group such as the Russian ''terrorists'' of the late nineteenth century, in the words of an observer close to them (Stepniak), appears to have ''compelled the Government for many years to neglect everything and do nothing but struggle with them'' (Moss 1972, p. 40), the attribution of great strength to them is for many difficult to avoid.

Sometimes the microviolent ones intend to reinforce such a belief by stressing the very smallness of their resources. ''For the past month and a half,'' declares the Turkish People's Liberation Army, having captured four U.S. airmen, ''the police . . . has bowed to a handful of our fighters.'' At other times, however, a microviolent group may desire to have its resources and capabilities exaggerated (see below), as well as the population's favorable reactions to it. ''Helmut Schmidt,'' argue the leaders of the Rote Armee Fraktion, ''would not in his new year's allocution have included the actions of the RAF under the five most threatening facts/developments for imperialism in 1974—world inflation, the oil crisis, Guillaume, unemployment, RAF—. . . if revolutionary politics had only a very small basis. . . .'' (*Der Spiegel*, 20 January 1975, p. 56).

In any case, the quality of the microviolence committed may be unquestionably high (see Section 1), which by itself suggests power. "The action," says a left Peronist (Hector Victor Suarez) about an operation (occupying the town of Garin) of his group (FAR), "impressed the people because of the synchronization and technical resources involved" (Kohl and Litt 1974, p. 382).

Both the authorities and the media tend to exaggerate the capabilities and the future acts of a microviolent group under the impact of a blow struck by it. While the membership of the Quebec FLQ perhaps never exceeded 150, a federal minister claimed shortly after the group's two kidnappings of prominent persons that it had about three thousand members and two thousand pounds of dynamite, "enough to blow up the center of Montreal" (Moss 1972, p. 128). The group itself was of course eager to foster such exaggerations, suggesting no doubt to one of its hostages, a minister of the province, a letter to his prime minister according to which "we are facing a well-organized escalation. . . . After me there will be a third one, then a fourth, and a twentieth. If all political men are protected they will strike elsewhere, in other classes of society"—while in fact, of course, the FLQ never struck again.

When microviolent ones—to mention one factor fostering exaggerated forecasts about their deeds—expose categories of persons who had not felt before that they were living under risk, to even a *small* probability of *high* damage, they may arouse high anxiety—which in turn may induce an excessive estimate of the chance that one will in fact be hurt. "We have wanted to demonstrate to the nation," declares the right-wing Italian Ordine Nero, having bombed a leftist mass demonstration (in Brescia) "that we are capable of placing bombs where we want, at any hour, in any spot, where and when it pleases us" (*L'Espresso,* 11 August 1974, p. 6). The same formula was used a few months later with regard to the bombing of a passenger train. While such words are compatible with a low frequency of attacks (which turned out to be the case), they do suggest a high incidence (that is, a sharp change of the relationship of forces in disfavor of the status quo); and they are apt to activate the translation of the quality of fear into the quantity of risk.

Replacing unavailable quantity by suggestive quality, a microviolent group may engage in acts that one ordinarily expects only of government. They then intend to make believe that there is "dual power"; rapidly and easily achieved and hence rendering the next jump to dominance plausible. ''When we decide to raid the home of a political police agent,'' a Tupamaro explains, ''it's our way of showing them and the people that there are two powers . . . that just as our homes can be raided, so can those of the security agents'' (Kohl and Litt 1974, p. 281). In ''the building of dual power,'' another Tupamaro discloses, ''the first step . . . was to look for a type of military action that showed that we were a force able . . . to administer justice''; ''this was the origin of the People's Jail'' (Wilson 1974, p. 146). For ''the keeping of prisoners . . . implies a power equal to the regime'' (Wilson 1974, p. 142). Even more so when the latter seems to acknowledge that an unexpected equal has appeared within its domain: when the director of a major state-owned public utility enterprise was abducted, for the second time, by the Tupamaros and sentenced to life imprisonment in the People's Prison, the president, two months later, appointed a successor for the vacancy (Moss 1972, p. 229); the same Pacheco who had forced the media to sharply curtail mentions of the ''terrorists'' and had banned both the official name (MLN) and the popular one. In a move of the same order the Italian Brigate Rosse made it known that, having abducted a prosecutor (of them), they had interrogated him and obtained the names of penetration agents within their group (*L' Espresso,* 5 May 1974, p. 15).

Section 3: Destroying the Enemy through One Strike

''The chemist,'' a Weatherwoman recalls about a comrade, ''drove us to the mountains once a week. Anne and I planted our fertilizer under bridges and tree stumps, under rocks and beside streams. In the still mountain darkness we lit homemade fuses and detonators. Then we ran and hid. Great explosions rent the air, and big craters replaced the rocks and bridges and tree stumps. We had visions of IBM and Boeing going up in pieces . . .'' (Stern 1975, p. 262). As modern society appears more complex and fragile, modern weapons more impressive, and their application to the centers of developed countries surprising—as these several trends join—microviolent ones may permit themselves the idea of bringing down the existing order by one blow, the counterpart to the all-out strike of some planners of nuclear war. ''Through guerrilla struggle,'' in a rather moderate West German estimate, ''a few thousand—if necessary without the support of industrial workers—can considerably weaken the imperialist system in the metropoles . . ." (A leaflet of the group Rotzknast, 1971, Mahler 1971, p. 71). Striking at the enemy's head will increasingly incapacitate his entire organism: "we who live in the head [of world capitalism] must . . . confuse his nerve centers . . ." (ibid., p. 71). "Our intention," announces the Weather Underground, "is to disrupt the Empire . . . [ellipsis dots in the text–NL] to incapacitate it . . ." (*Prairie Fire* 1974, p. 1). "Now things must explode *(muss das krachen)*, society must go to pieces *(zerbrechen)*," resolves a West German given to picturesque formulations (Fritz Teufel) (*Der Spiegel*, 4 January 1971, p. 48). If the enemy's destruction won't come instantly, then by avalanche: according to Sam Melville's estimate of microviolence, "it will snowball and bring down the power structure" (Melville 1972, p. 140)—mined as it allegedly is by the latent hostility of most, perceived on the model of one's own flagrant aversion.

Section 4: Slowly Exhausting the Enemy through Attrition and Stress

"The mountain of the military potency of the bourgeois State," declares Mahler, alluding to a famous use of a Chinese legend by Mao, "must be levelled" (Mahler 1971, p. 28): it may, it is implied, take decades, but what does that matter? (This is a characteristic stress on "protracted" struggle, which, I would surmise, wards off the microviolents' impatience.) "We shall," a Palestinian declared in the mid-sixties, "burn citrus plantations, demolish factories, blow up bridges, and cut off communication lines. The revolution will last a year, two years and more, up to twenty or thirty years" (Yaari 1970, p. 53): look at Algeria, China, Vietnam.

There is no alternative. "It will," the Weather Underground declares, "require lengthy . . . armed struggle . . . to wear away at the power of the enemy" (*Prairie Fire* 1974, p. 2). According to a Montonero, "the enemy army . . . can't be defeated in frontal combat," but it "can be worn down over a long time" (Hodges and Abu Shanab 1972, p. 306). "The only way to destroy the enemy," George Habash discloses to Oriana Fallaci, "is to give a little blow here, a little blow there; to advance step by step, inch by inch, for years, for decades . . ." (*Life*, 22 June 1970). While there will be a "final state" of "general insurrection,'' it is only by a ''lengthy'' armed struggle that the enemy can be ''progressively enfeebled (*zermürben*)'' before he is ''finally smashed'' (Mahler 1971, p. 8).

But during such a protracted conflict, will the enemy not be able to replace the resources of which he is being deprived?

No, for physical attrition will be accompanied by an even more important moral one that, it is implied, can be achieved with even less force.

The personnel of the state, accustomed to dish it out, will be permanently demoralized by now *having to take it*—never mind (it is implied) how much and how often; and that from elusive attackers who ''harass'' the authorities, ''work on their nerves through . . . small damages'' (George Habash to Oriana Fallaci, *Life*, 22 June 1970).

These damages are also ''unexpected'' (ibid.); their ever-present possibility induces unremitting *anxiety*. One of the ''objectives'' of ''urban guerrilla,'' according to Carlos Marighella is ''to oblige the army and the police . . . to change the relative comfort and tranquility of their barracks and their usual rest for a state of alarm and growing tension in the expectation of attack.'' ''The government,'' too, will then be living with ''ever present fears of an attack on its strategic nerve centers, without ever knowing where, how and when the attack will come'' (Kohl and Litt 1974, pp. 108–9).

A very few attacks affecting but a minute fraction of the authorities' personnel will, it is implied, suffice to arouse high and protracted anxiety in the Establishment at large; whether its members are highly sensitive to even a small probability of high damage, or whether they exaggerate (also, driven by that sensitivity—see Section 2) how much their enemy will presently proceed to do. One way or the other, it seems feasible to produce with sparse resources a state in which ''nowhere will there be a pacified domain for officers and leading officials, a secure rear, a peaceful *Heimat*, a safe private life'' (Mahler 1971, p. 42). ''The execution of important members of the repressive hierarchy'' a Tupamaro observes, or alleges, ''created confusion . . . within the army whose members were accustomed to a non-militarized *civilista* role.'' For ''these army personnel were now faced with the possibility of . . . death . . .'' (Kohl and Litt 1974, p. 305).

In addition to anxiety, there is the effort and discomfort of the permanent *alert*, the defensive living that the microviolents expect to impose on the authorities. "You will sleep in your uniforms," the "Stern group" announced to the British military in Palestine, "you will bear your arms, your life here will be hell day and night . . ." (Hyams 1974, p. 160). "Already," the Turkish People's Liberation Front discerned upon having captured four U.S. airmen, "from the police to our president, no one sleeps easily in their homes; they cannot come and go comfortably to their homes."

Finally, there is the *frustration* that elusive microviolent ones expect to impose on their targets, whom they show to be powerless as much as they prove them helpless. One of the "objectives" of the "urban guerrilla," according to Carlos Marighella, is to engage the authorities permanently in "a search for tracks that vanish without a trace" (Kohl and Litt 1974, p. 109).

The combined effect of these various torments will be "a gradual attrition *(Auszehrung)* of the enemy's forces, degradation of morale *(Verschleiss)*" (Mahler 1971, p. 28), "the disorganization and demoralization of the oppressor's armed forces by a lengthy extenuating (*zermürbend*) small war" (Mahler 1971, 31).

Section 5: Practicing for the Final Battle

Agreeing with revolutionaries in the Bolshevik tradition that the "seizure of power" will require "armed struggle,"—"in the ultimate conflict between the classes only guns count" (Mahler 1971, p. 41)—the microviolent ones may affirm that this final encounter calls for protracted practice that should begin "here and now." According to Horst Mahler, "a fighting group can originate only in the fight itself" (Mahler 1971, p. 65). For the Weather Underground it needs "guerrilla action" to "lay the foundation for the decisive armed struggle" (*Prairie Fire* 1974, p. 23); "the mass armed capability which will destroy the enemy has its beginning in armed action" (Mahler 1971, p. 2), of initially, it seems implied, very small size. Conversely, it is "from the very beginning of guerrilla action" that "mass armed capability develops" (Mahler 1971, p. 141).

Thus the microviolent ones seem to apply to fighting the contemporary disposition to believe that so many acts, which were earlier regarded as capabilities available to human beings without previous practice, do in fact require just that. So much has to be learned, and one learns only by doing.

The new belief can be smuggled into formulations that at first sight resemble the conventional wisdom of, say, the Austrian social democrats. In the early twenties they created a military organization for possible defensive use (to occur in the following decade). But they did of course not maintain that an endemic civil war would be required from the start to have the Republikanische Schutzbund become efficient by virtue of permanent practice. In ostensibly similar fashion the Weather Underground observes that "the mass armed capability which will destroy the enemy . . . will not spring fullblown on the scene at the magical moment of insurrection" *(Prairie Fire* 1974, p. 2). "I am tired," a Venezuelan elaborates,

> "of hearing the . . . threats which the revolutionary parties make when limiting themselves to legal struggle: they would revert to violence if they were declared illegal. . . . Sooner or later they are declared illegal . . . and they don't do anything . . . ; or they try to do something and the enemy acts faster than they do. This is explainable. The enemy has counted on apparatuses trained in violence for many years. . . . One cannot suddenly defeat them. . . . One cannot think that when the revolutionaries resolve to use violence—those revolutionaries who until a short time ago were speaking of legality . . . the popular masses . . . are going to defeat such a powerful apparatus. Popular violence cannot be improvised. . . . It should be *organized* patiently" (Hodges and Abu Shanab 1972, pp. 240–41).

"To leave people *unprepared* to fight the State [in the final encounter] is to mislead about the inevitable nature of what lies ahead" *(Prairie Fire* 1974, p. 141). Commenting on the first proclamation of the Rote Armee Fraktion, *To Build the Red Army,* Ulrike Meinhof explained the new group: "Name: 'To Build the Red Army' . . . a sentence. It says what we do" (*Der Spiegel,* 18 June 1970, p. 73)—which, in the usual nonviolent sense of *aufbauen* (build) it precisely did not.

In an overt formulation, "it is," according to a West German, "our duty to begin already today *practicing* (*Einübung)* the armed struggle" (*Agit 883*, 24 December 1970. Baader-Meinhof Report 1972, p. 157). "There is a . . . necessity . . . to learn to fight through fighting" (*Prairie Fire* 1974, p. 10). If this truth is heeded, then, according to a Québecois (Pierre Vallières), "at . . . [the] point . . . of armed confrontation between the people and their enemy . . . the revolutionary forces will have had their training in their daily struggle" (Hodges and Abu Shanab 1972, p. 324).

Accordingly, early in September 1969 seventy-five Weatherwomen drove to Pittsburgh for an action "intended as a practice run for Chicago [the planned 'Days of Rage' in the first half of October]" (Powers 1971, p. 140). And on September 27 of the same year there was an SDS rally outside Detroit's public library "which, like the Pittsburgh High School raid was intended as practice for the 'Days of Rage' " (Powers 1971, p. 146).

Surely only live practice is effective against inhibitions. "This beginning [of guerrilla activity]," as the Weather Underground looks back at its own career, involving "a confrontation with . . . inhibition . . . was impolite, rough, destructive and disorderly" (*Prairie Fire* 1974, p. 10). When in February 1970 the Weatherwoman Diana Oughton went to see an old friend in Ann Arbor, "Mrs. Howes said the Chicago action [the 'Days of Rage'] had struck her as simple hoodlimism, which would only alienate potential allies. Diana admitted it might, but insisted it was a necessary step . . . 'People have to learn to confront violence' . . ." (Powers 1971, pp. 176–77).

Section 6: Setting Enemies to Fight among Themselves

Acts of microviolence, their proponents point out, are apt to become major occasions for conflict within the ruling group: its various factions, rather than closing ranks, may quarrel about what allowed such acts to occur, how they were handled, and how they should be: all of which may be both genuine issues and pretexts in struggles for power. Thus an objective of the Tupamaros at one point was "to sharpen the contradictions within the government" between the advocates of a "hard" and of a "soft" line toward them. A Brazilian recalls, "Every mistake of the regime [on the occasion of violence directed against it] is exploited by those who, within the ruling group, want to assume 'the responsibilities they merit'; this provokes multiple administrative and ministerial changes, and is useful to us in all respects: 'when two thieves fall out, the honest man can only gain,' says the proverb" (*Les Temps Modernes*, March 1971, p. 1597).

Section 7: Diverting Resources of the Enemy from a More Important Front

Even though it may be recognized that the enemy won't have to reallocate its resources noticeably as a consequence of one's micro-attack on it, one may feel a moral obligation to help "Vietnam" in this fashion to the maximum of one's capacity, be it only little above zero (see Section 11).

The same calculation may be applied to one's relationship with nonviolent revolutionaries. "For those who hold up to us as an example the successes of mass organizations in the working class" a Brazilian explains, "we recall . . . that their work is only possible because we, the armed organization . . . concentrate the forces of repression on us" (Jamil Rodriguez, *Les Temps Modernes*, March 1971, p. 1593).

Section 8: Showing How Harmless the Enemy Is

According to the extreme Zionists in late World War II and during the years of the British presence in Palestine following the war, the moderates overestimated the damage to Zionism that would follow from the British response to a sharpening of the Zionist line. One of the motives for the violence employed by Irgun/"Stern Group" against the British was to show the limits to the British response, thus to liberate mainstream Zionists of their excessive fears, and allow them to act more assertively.

Section 9: Showing How Bad the Enemy Is

"During the summer of 1970 the young men [of the Front de Libération du Québec who were to kidnap the British trade commissioner James Cross] discussed abducting several people, among them [Montreal] U.S. Consul General John Topping." But "the day before the planned kidnapping they chose Cross over Topping because 'we figured the English in Quebec would never identify with an American, but if we took the Englishman, we thought it would stir more *hostility* from the English in the province and across Canada . . ." [*Weekend Magazine*, supplement of *The Toronto Globe and Mail*, 22 January 1974, p. 2] hostility that would, it was hoped, lead to federal repression in Quebec and that would in turn stimulate Québecois separatism. For a "basic principle of revolutionary strategy" is, in the words of Carlos Marighella, "to release such a volume of revolutionary action that the enemy will be obliged to transform the political situation into a military one"; for "then dissatisfaction will reach all the strata of society" (Kohl and Litt 1974, p. 82). Prior to the provoking of microviolence the badness of the present order may have been fully visible only to the trained or passionate eye of a few; the reactions of the authorities, which that violence is intended to induce, will render their evil nature obvious to the many. The point is, in Ulrike Meinhof's calculation, as paraphrased by an associate, "to provoke the latent fascism of society, to bring it to the light, to force society to unmask itself" (Rühmkorf 1972, p. 228). Violence operates, in words circulated in prison by the leaders of the Rote Armee Fraktion so that "the pigs' true mug comes to the surface, they are forced to renounce their ideology themselves" (*Dokumentation* 1975, p. 163). Thus, according to a Brazilian, "the political value of the guerrilla's actions derives not from its popularity, but from the unpopularity of the ensuing repression" (Jamil Rodriguez, *Les Temps Modernes*, March 1971, p. 1597).

So sure are revolutionaries inclined to microviolence of that unpopularity and of the damage from it to the establishment that they are apt to neglect the persisting disposition of men in power to instigate small violence against themselves, so as to benefit from revulsion against it as well as from the repression with which they intend to respond to it. "The old strategy of tension [presumably followed by elements of the Italian Right from the fall of 1969 on]," an observer explains in the mid-seventies, "operated on the basis of three suppositions. First: Italy believed that it is the anarchist Valpredea who has placed a bomb in the Bank of Agriculture [in Milan, 12 December 1969]. Second: this conviction creates a mood hostile to the Left. Third: in this mood a coup d'etat from the Right, managed or supported by the military, is well received or at least provokes only limited reactions, which are easily controllable" (Fabrizio Dentice, *L'Espresso*, 11 August 1972, p. 4).

In contrast to such good sense—with the decisive exception of the belief that one will easily be able to impute one's own deeds to another—those tending toward microviolence may be convinced that many of the people will be unhappy with the government's response to microviolence and blame the authorities instead of the rebels for it; rather than, for instance, condoning or even welcoming restrictions on everyone's liberties in response to violence; or at least blaming the violent ones for having unleashed their enemies. If the aim of the Québecquois kidnappers of 1970 was to force the government to take extreme measures, then in that they succeeded—falsely predicting, however, a predominantly negative reaction of at least the francophone population to "extreme measures" against the terrorists.

Also, the microviolent ones may not consider whether the benefit to them from a popular revulsion against the extreme response they will have provoked might not be smaller than the loss to them from the repression included in that response. In several and well-known recent cases that loss has amounted to annihilation (e.g., in Brazil and Uruguay).

Finally, it might be overlooked that the authorities may limit themselves to repression directed against the microviolent ones without touching the rest of the population much and that this repression might be effective while not harsher, perhaps indeed less severe, than what "public opinion" demands. The West German microviolent ones may not have foreseen that the SPD-FDP government, on the occasion of the coercive hostage taking in the FRG embassy in Stockholm in 1976, would be moved to substitute a no-concessions policy for the former safe-release policy also from concern for the coming election: it is the voters who were believed to demand, in their majority, a hard line, which, they correctly perceived, would scarcely affect them. In contrast, the microviolent ones often take it for granted that they and the public at large cannot be separated as targets. When "the government," conforming to the intent of its enemies, "has no alternative except to intensify repression," then, according to Carlos Marighella, "the police networks, house searches, arrests of innocent people and of suspects, closing off streets, make life in the city unbearable" (Kohl and Litt 1974, pp. 131–32).

Those given to violence seem indeed apt to exaggerate in various ways the bonds between them and the population.

This is presumably what permits them to orient so much of their operations on their own concerns rather than responding to aspirations outside of themselves. It is rare to find a group such as the "Trotskyite" ERP in Argentina, which for a time concentrated on kidnapping business executives so as to coerce their companies to distribute food and clothing to the poor as well as exercise books and pencils to their children, to rehire discharged workers, and to improve the conditions of those employed. More frequently one finds in coercive hostage taking a set of demands such as that formulated in Communiqué No. 1 of the Montreal FLQ of 5 October 1970: the authorities should cease all efforts to liberate the hostage taken, give the kidnappers access to the media, release "political" prisoners, provide aircraft for conveying the kidnappers to sanctuaries, deliver cash, disclose informers—and rehire certain workers: the only demand not directly concerning the microviolent ones themselves, and also the one that they waived first in the ensuing negotiation with the authorities. When the Tupamaros' program consisted of six points, "the release of all imprisoned comrades" was the first, the "unfreezing of wages" arriving second (Kohl and Litt 1974, p. 276). On 31 January 1974, two Japanese belonging to the United Red Army and two Arabs of the Popular Front for the Liberation of Palestine tried to blow up a Shell Oil Company refinery in Singapore. They failed, and with this their interest in the world outside them ended, as far as their operation went. For they then seized eight hostages aboard a ferryboat and threatened to kill themselves as well as the hostages unless they were given *safe passage* to an Arab country. On February 6, five PFLP members took over the Japanese Embassy in Kuwait, seized about twelve hostages including the ambassador, and demanded that the Japanese government supply an airliner *to bring their comrades* from Singapore to Kuwait; which was done. After picking up the other five, who had released their hostages, the plane went on to Aden on February 8, where *everybody was freed*. When West Germans kidnapped a West Berlin politician (Peter Lorenz), their only approach to the interests of the public at large was the mailing of bank notes to the mother of a mongoloid child, with a note, "Dear Frau Busch, we are the abductors of Herr Lorenz. Now don't get scared" (*Der Spiegel*, 4 August 1975, p. 53).

A considerable fraction of the targets consists, to be sure, of persons who have damaged other microviolent ones.

The names of microviolent groups are apt to refer to incidents in their war with the authorities and hence be unintelligible to almost all: the West German "June 2" group alludes to 2 June 1967, when a student was killed by police in West Berlin; the Greek "October 1" group to the date on which Greece surrendered a West German fugitive to the FRG, while the Spanish group naming the same date (GRAPO) commemorates the execution of five in 1975.

That such self-centeredness becomes possible by a belief in one's small and secret group being the object of mass love is shown, for instance, when Ulrike Meinhof explains why the Rote Armee Fraktion chose as its first deed the liberation of Andreas Baader: "We believe that those to whom we want to make it clear what is politically at issue today have no problems whatsoever in identifying themselves with the liberation of prisoners." "That part of the proletariat of which we believe that it is potentially revolutionary," she repeats, "has no difficulty in identifying itself with the liberation of prisoners . . ." (*Der Spiegel*, 15 June 1970, p. 74). People at large, microviolent ones may manage to believe, care almost as much about the repression befalling "terrorists" as if it were inflicted on themselves. "Many," the leaders of the Rote Armee Fraktion advance, "[who] changed their attitude towards this State because of the measures of the government against us, begin to recognize it for what it is . . ." (*Der Spiegel*, 20 January 1975, p. 55). It is as if what happened to the few of us had been suffered by many. "Revolutionary terrorism," a statement by the Tupamaros explains, "is . . . the guerrilla's response to the terrorism the people daily receive from the hands of the servants of the ruling class. It is repayment for the people being harassed in the streets, having their homes invaded in the early morning hours, seeing suspects being tortured, raped and murdered during police questioning" (Wilson 1974, p. 76).

If indeed the microviolent ones are the center of the people's concerns, then the group's communications may be focused not on the aspirations of ordinary individuals, but rather on the special situation of these exceptional few. Item "I" in the "daily schedule" recommended by Ulrike Meinhof from prison for persuasion outside of it is "daily militant actions . . . for 'freedom for all imprisoned revolutionaries—an end to torture by isolation—away with all special measures in the prisons—long live the RAF!' " As if this were not enough, she continues for the case that "you want to say one more word": "then talk about what is just now timely: 'Berlin justice wants to assassinate the prisoners engaged in a hunger strike.' " Indeed, "the number of actions cannot be large enough and they cannot be militant enough as long as all prisoners are not liberated" (*Der Spiegel*, 2 June 1975, p. 29).

Naturally, then, the strength—even the existence—of ordinary interests may be overlooked (see Section 1). When Brazilians, on the occasion of Robert McNamara's visit, set off a bomb at the entrance of the Sears Roebuck store in São Paulo, not only did they credit the population with a knowledge of the secretary's personal portfolio (as I already remarked), they also perhaps forgot what a friendly critic (João Quartim) reminds them, namely that "Sears, like all the big stores, sells its goods cheaper than the small shops. Closing it down for a few days meant upsetting the local housewives . . ." (Kohl and Litt 1974, p. 152).

Section 10: Coercion to Reduce the Enemy's Resources and the Efficiency of Their Use

Attributing to themselves a capacity for unleashing the enemy to their own advantage (Section 9), the microviolent ones may also believe they know how to leash the enemy.

First, the enemy supposedly can be deterred through reprisals. When in late 1946 two members of Irgun were sentenced by the British to be flogged and one of them was, the Irgun in turn captured and flogged four British military men; the second Irgun prisoner was not flogged, nor was any subsequent captive of the British. When several Irgun members were sentenced to death, Irgun captured British officers and officials, and held them until the death sentences were in fact rescinded. When the British hanged two Irgun prisoners, the Irgun hanged two British sergeants, and the British hanged no more. One of the objectives of "kidnapping" according to Carlos Marighella is "to force the suspension of torture in jails" (Kohl and Litt 1974, p. 120). "Pereira Reverbel," declared the Tupamaros on 7 August 1968, having abducted that prominent personage, "with his person will guarantee the physical well-being of our comrades and of all those who are being persecuted. . . . The physical security and well-being of Pereira Reverbel will depend upon the conduct of the repressive forces and Fascist groups in their service; . . . we are attentive to the methods they employ" (Carlos Alonso in *Sucesos Para Todos*, Mexico, 18 July 1970, translated in JPRS 51529, p. 58). "We shall," announced a "commando" of the Rote Armee Fraktion, having wounded a judge and his wife, "execute attacks with explosives against judges and prosecutors as frequently and as long as they will not have ceased to violate the laws at the expense of political prisoners" (*Der Spiegel*, 24 June 1974, p. 29).

Second, those disposed to microviolence may direct their attention to the large number of persons who each make a small contribution to the enemy's strength (the total being considerable) and who are loath to accept even a *low* chance of *high* damage from their activities. But microviolence may produce just such a chance and thereby significantly (in the expectation of "terrorists") reduce both the amount of resources at the enemy's disposal and the efficiency with which they will henceforth be used. The microviolent ones may foresee that the persons thus exposed to novel risks will not, even with time, come to accept them; and/or that the operation for which the risks are created will be completed before the targets get accustomed to them.

These targets may be viewed as foreigners whose departure one desires to compel, such as colonials in a colony. "Because of the Fedayeen," an Arab statement foresaw, "Israelis will swarm to the sea and airports . . ." (Schiff and Rothenstein 1972, p. 74). An announced purpose of the Front de Libération du Québec was "to make them [the Anglophones] go home . . . to Ontario or Great Britain or the United States" (Saywell 1971, 134).

Microviolence may be intended to isolate the target area from the rest of the world. It is with this intention that Poder Cubano has committed thousands of microbombings of hundreds of travel agencies, airline and steamship line offices, consulates, and exhibits. And it is of course thus that Palestinians have acted to isolate Israel. In the words of George Habash, "Israel is an island. Its only connections are through the sea and the air. We must orient our strategy toward this" *(Der Spiegel,* 1970, no. 10, p. 106).

Within the target area, previously riskless activities favoring the status quo may be made risky so that they might be abandoned in some measure. "We ask of Springer," declared a group after an attack on that publisher's building in Hamburg, "that his newspapers stop his . . . campaign against the New Left, against strikes, against the Communist Party here and in other countries" *Der Spiegel,* 24 June 1974, p. 29). "In numerous German cities the police has recommended to cinema owners to cease showing Warner-Columbia's film on Entebbe in order to avoid . . . further arson and bombing on the part of unknown perpetrators who designate themselves in anonymous letters as 'Revolutionary Cells' and as 'Fighters for a Free Palestine.' Many cinemas, for example in Aachen, Düsseldorf, Duisburg, Essen, Köln, Stuttgart and Munich have followed the advice of the police and changed their program" (*Frankfurter Allgemeine Zeitung,* 7 January 1977, p. 3), two months before the showing of *God's Messenger* was temporarily interrupted in American cities.

Burdening the activities of the authorities' civilian and military personnel with fear is to suggest a negative answer to the question: "Where can the State find the tens of thousands of heroes ready to fight under such anxiety?'' (Mahler 1971, p. 42).

Resignations may then prevail over entries: ''those who see a cushy job in being a policeman or a soldier will increasingly understand the risk which this profession entails under the changed circumstances'' (Mahler 1971, pp. 33–34)—an appeal of the Tupamaros during their heyday.

Short of abandoning their posts, the servants of the state may prudently curtail their performance. The Greek-Cypriot EOKA made a point of picking off patrols moving in the country to discourage police from advancing outside of towns. ''It must be shown,'' dreams Horst Mahler, ''that each employment of the state apparatus . . . against actions of the workers in the enterprises inevitably entails sanctions against the property and the person of those responsible for it'' (Mahler 1971, p. 33). Colonel Grivas's intent to make Cypriot policemen ''turn a blind eye to our activities'' was to be brought about also by murdering highly efficient officials with much publicity (Moss 1972, p. 50). Examples could of course be multiplied, for this as well as the other variants of the calculation envisaged in this section.

II. The Act Itself

Section 11: Not Betraying

Some microviolent ones seem concerned with refuting the suspicion—entertained by others and perhaps also by themselves—that their dedication is limited. One ''reason'' for ''beginning [the activity of the Rote Armee Fraktion] with the liberation of a prisoner [Andreas Baader],'' Ulrike Meinhof explains, is ''to make it really clear that we are serious *(es ernst meinen)* . . . we are people for whom what we are doing is no game . . .'' (*Der Spiegel,* 15 June 1970, p. 74).

I am not falling short of doing what I possibly could. ''If we did not resort to violence,'' a West German recalls, ''this would show only our weakness and not at all that it would not be necessary to do so'' *(Agit 883*, 18 June 1970). But, precisely, ''we recognized . . . the terrible cost of not doing all we possibly can'' *(Prairie Fire* 1974, p. 7).

That it may be not much is no excuse for not doing it. ''This whole fall

[1969]," a Weatherman declares, "we begin to chip away at imperialism in the most concrete way that we can" (Powers 1971, p. 207). "It's a message passed on to the ruling class": thus the British "Angry Brigade" explained its decision to bomb. "Okay, your conspiracy will continue, and the bombs won't make that much difference to the way it operates." Yet, "it's going to be just a little bit more difficult for you," and "we're not just going to sit around and produce petitions against what you're doing" (Carr 1975, p. 64).

Employing violence, I am showing that I am not afraid of it (any more). "We are still scared of fighting. We have to get into armed struggle," observed Bernardine Dohrn in the fall of 1969 (Powers 1971, p. 170).

We will at least not be resigning ourselves to a lower order of action than that, say, the Vietnamese. "We made the choice to become a guerrilla organization," the Weather Underground recalls, "at a time when the Vietnamese were fighting a . . . heroic peoples' war, defeating half a million U.S. troops and the most technologically advanced military power" (*Prairie Fire* 1974, p. 2).

I shall not be untrue to my beliefs. "The intellectual Left," Ulrike Meinhof recalls about her first armed action, "has on the whole rejected this action. . . . The intellectuals . . . have come so far as to know that arming oneself is necessary . . .; but they are people who are not going to take the next step . . . namely to do that of which they talk" (*Der Spiegel*, 15 June 1970, p. 74). "We decided," the Tupamaros explained, "that our political line should be very simply stated, in restrained language. This was partly a reaction against the verbalism of the Left, but it also responded to a feeling of the people who were long tired of promises and proposals which never came to fruition. For this reason, too, we have never spoken before acting, preferring to communicate our line through action." (*Generals and Tupamaros* 1944, Introduction). "The hour of action and of commitment here and now," the same group advanced, "has begun. The hour of conversations of the theoretical enunciation of propositions and of promises which are never realized has ended" (Costs 1972, p. 102).

Engaged in violence, I shall show that I am not a sissy. "I wanted to give him pills," Andreas Baader's mother remembers about her twelve-year-old having a toothache, "and to go to the dentist with him. He refused. He said he wanted to test how much pain he could bear"

(*Der Spiegel,* 19 May 1975, p. 38). Recalling that a recolutionary in the underground is "under pressure, after all, to talk to somebody" and that "the effect then becomes cause, that is; the revolutionary considers somebody 'reliable' only because he can't himself keep his mouth shut," members of the Rote Armee Fraktion comment that "this is naturally related to this shit society which does not develop the force to resist, but rather such shit mechanisms [as the one described]." Indeed, "the devices for rationalizing, for finding the 'suitable' motivation for something like that are numberless . . ." [ellipsis dots in the text—NL]; (*Dokumentation* 1975, p. 82).

Employing violence, I prove that I am not unwilling to die for my cause. "The intellectual Left has on the whole rejected this action," Ulrike Meinhof recalls about the first armed enterprise of her group, "because . . . by virtue of their own class situation they are not capable of making the next step [from seeing the necessity of violence to applying it], . . . because by virtue of their class situation they still have very much to lose, very much of life to lose. Each of them, within his bourgeois existence, has a perspective of life so that there is no objective reason for them to take the step . . ." (*Der Spiegel,* 15 June 1970, p. 47). "That the [armed] struggle *(Kampf)* is . . . not feasible for us," other West Germans discern, "is an invention of our impulse towards self-preservation" (A leaflet of the group Rotzknast, Mahler 1971, p. 70). "Either pig or human being," writes a member of the RAF (Holger Meins) during the hunger strike in prison from which he is going to die. "Either survive at any price or fight unto the death. Everybody, after all, dies. The question is only how, and how you have lived. The matter is perfectly clear: fighting against the pigs" (*Der Spiegel,* 18 November 1974, p. 30).

Section 12: Not Submitting

" 'Action,' " an observer surmises, "was Andreas Baader's . . . defense against 'the danger of being eaten and digested by the system' " (Hermann Schreiber, *Der Spiegel,* 19 May 1975, p. 39). "Those who support us," Baader's group observes, "know that their petty personal interests (*Kram*) are not worth integration and adaptation for the duration of their life . . ." (*Der Spiegel,* 26 April 1971, p. 32).

"Every man who doesn't want to go down on his knees to you," a

British microviolent group addressed USG in the late sixties, "can only reply by . . . direct action to your world terrorist planning" (Carr 1975, p. 61). "We refuse," said Bernardine Dohrn, at the beginning of the Days of Rage, in an often-employed phrase, "to be good Germans" (Powers 1971, p. 155). "In a time when all actions seem meaningless, at least we won't be good Germans," wrote Sam Melville from prison (Melville 1972, p. 140). (The meaning of the phrase extends of course beyond Vietnam.)

Nor will we submit to the moral pressure of the whole of society, from reactionaries to pseudorevolutionaries. "Urban guerrilla," Ulrike Meinhof discerns, "presupposes . . . being sure that the methods of the *Bildzeitung* are without impact on one, that the syndrome antisemitism—criminality—sub-humanity—murder and arson which they apply to revolutionaries, that the entire shit which continues to influence many comrades in their judgment of us has no impact on one" (Baader-Meinhof Report 1972, pp. 82–83).

Section 13: Avoiding Petty Labor

What other kinds of revolutionary activity hold out some promise of *striking* results obtained by a *few* right *now?* What other methods are as far removed as microviolence from *Kleinarbeit*, petty work of imperceptible yield?

To the microviolent ones "a few dozen fighters . . . can fundamentally transform the political scene" (Mahler 1971, p. 43).

Less than in conventional political pursuits do I depend on others in microviolence: "Anybody can begin. He does not need to wait for anybody" (ibid., p. 43). "Armed struggle," the Weather Underground observes, "starts when someone starts it" (Moss 1972, p. 73). "We ask license of no one," declares Carlos Marighella, "to perform revolutionary actions" (Kohl and Litt 1974, p. 74).

While, as we have seen in Section 4, microviolent ones may stress the protracted character of their action—perhaps also so as to subdue impatience—the "notion" is widespread among them "that," in the words of a Weatherman, "if I don't . . . construct socialism within twenty years [securely within one's lifetime—NL], that is a defeat" (Powers 1971, p. 197). "Fire under the ass of all imperialists," Fritz Teufel inscribed on a poster, "shortens the long march" *(Der Spiegel*,

4 January 1971, p. 48). "The end of the pigs' rule is in sight!" foresaw the first proclamation of the Rote Armee Fraktion (*Der Spiegel,* 18 June 1970, p. 73); "the final moment has arrived (*jetzt ist Schluss*), now the battle starts (*jetzt geht es los*)" (*Der Spiegel,* 22 February 1971, p. 31). "The RAF," paraphrases an Italian microviolent one (Renato Curzio)—in the language of highbrows that he, characteristically, prefers to that of what used to be called the gutter cherished by those he praises— "is a precious patrimony of the entire European Left." For "it has posed . . . the question of the proletarian revolution in a technological-metropolitan society. The chapter seemed closed forever, antagonism eliminated beyond the sphere of politics, the conflict canalized and controlled. But the Baader group . . . combatting in the heart of the metropolis, where few thought it still possible, has put the narcotizing mechanism into crisis" (*L'Espresso,* 2 March 1975, p. 32)—has inspired, among other sequels, a group calling itself "We Want Everything (*Wir Wollen Alles*)"

Section 14: Escaping the Words

"Writing is shit, now let's make revolution," declared Ulrike Meinhof, abandoning her column in a radical-chic periodical (*Konkret*).

"It is not sufficient to talk," affirm the leaders of the RAF, "it is possible and necessary, necessary and possible to *act* [underlined in the text—NL]" (*Der Spiegel,* 20 January 1975, p. 55).

Once one has talked, not to act accordingly is a sin (see Section 11). "We have learned," explains a German minister's daughter (Gertrud Ensslin) at her trial for arson, "that talking without activity is wrong" (Baader-Meinhof Report 1972, p. 20).

As well as weak.

As are words by themselves. The first anarchist assassin in late nineteenth-century France (Louis Chaves) had already observed that "it is not with words or paper that we shall change existing conditions" (Woodcock 1962, p. 301). It is by "militant confrontation politics," the Weathermen recall, that "we broke with the powerless past" (*Prairie Fire* 1974, p. 7). "Our power," explains Communiqué No. 7 of Britain's Angry Brigade, "is the six Conservative offices petrol-bombed on January 13, [1971] the Altrincham generator which was blown out . . ." (Carr 1975, p. 102).

Words are worse than vain: while directed against the established order in what they affirm, they may strengthen it through what they effect. ''We lived in the fear,'' Gertrud Ensslin recalls in the statement from which I quoted above, ''that verbal protest against the war [in Vietnam] would only serve as an alibi for our society'' (Baader-Meinhof Report 1972, p. 20).

Section 15: Really Acting

''It is better,'' proposes Carlos Marighella, ''to err acting than do nothing for fear of erring'' (Kohl and Litt 1974, p. 30). Moreover, ''it is better to make mistakes doing something, even if it results in death'' (Kohl and Litt 1974, p. 29).

To be violent may be to prove to oneself and others that one is not bereft of power. ''There is,'' an American confides, ''a kind of ecstasy in knowing that you destroyed something, that you were effective. Because all of your life you are told you can't get away with it, you can't beat it, and we beat it'' (*Scanlan's Monthly*, January 1971, p. 19).

In fact, one may feel oneself omnipotent: creating microviolence where there was none. ''The partisan unit,'' Horst Mahler shows, ''emerges from nothingness *(entsteht aus dem Nichts)*'' (Mahler 1971, p. 43).

As the final battle will be a violent one, using violence is to be advanced (see Section 5). ''It is an indication of growth,'' the Weather Underground assesses, ''that we are learning [by practice] how to fight'' *(Prairie Fire* 1974, p. 3).

Section 16: What Remains But Violence?

''Back in Ann Arbor [at the beginning of the school year of the University of Michigan in the fall of 1968],'' an observer reports,

> ''[Bill] Ayres, Terry Robbins . . . and Jim Mellen made plans to capture control of the sober . . . SDS chapter at the University. . . . The group at first called itself the Lurleen Wallace Memorial Caucus . . . but finally settled on . . . the Jesse James Gang. At the first meeting of Voice-SDS . . . September 25, 1968, the James Gang launched a[n] . . . assault on the old leadership. . . . The gang ridiculed previous SDS campaigns, princi-

pally a year-long organizing attempt to discredit war research carried on at the University of Michigan under the aegis of the Institute for Defense Analysis (IDA). . . . Eventually the University's Students' Government Council took up the issue and sponsored a University-wide referendum on the war research affiliation with IDA. The result: a heavy turnout by the School of Engineering and decisive rejection of the SDS proposals. Where did that leave SDS? Ayres wanted to know. Was war research all right now that it had received democratic approval?"

And this Weatherman developed a formula expressing a stance of many a microviolent one: "We are tired of tiptoeing up to society and asking for reform, we are ready to kick it in the balls" (Powers 1971, pp. 87–88). The group that set fire to an ITT subsidiary near Paris on 1 March 1974 as a welcome to the new Chilean ambassador called itself We Must Do Something.

Section 17: One Can Say It Only with a Bomb

When—to take one case among many—on 13 September 1974, a bomb exploded at the office of the Algerian airline in Marseilles, no one claimed responsibility. Presumbly it would be clear to everybody concerned that the deed was done by or in the name of Europeans who had left Algeria twelve years before. Probably it was also evident that no nonviolent mode of expression would have seemed adequate to the strength of the feelings and judgments to be conveyed. When a number of American houses in Western Germany were assaulted by fire, unaccompanied by words, a radical student leader remarked that "these actions are not wordless *(sprachlos)*, everybody can understand them" (*Der Spiegel*, 29 May 1972, p. 27); as everybody, or almost everybody, could understand that less than violence would not have been adequate to express reactions to violence in Vietnam.

Presumably words today are felt to be a less strong medium than earlier in the century.

Much of the voluminous microbombing of recent years is probably of this expressive kind. The following are a few instances chosen at random:

- May 25, 1972, bombs exploded at the U.S. consulate and at offices of the American Legion, Pan-American World Airways and TWA in Paris.

- April 5, 1973, a bomb exploded in the garden of the U.S. embassy marine guard quarters in Rome, breaking windows and causing moderate structural damage.
- May 1, 1973, a member of the Pakistani Black December group shot at an assistant manager of the Indian Airlines office in Kabul.
- July 1, 1973, a small bomb destroyed the iron gate of the French embassy in Lima, Peru. The bombing was believed to be a protest against the planned French nuclear tests in the Pacific.
- December 15, 1974, bombs exploded outside TWA and Coca-Cola offices in Paris, causing slight damage. On December 16, another bomb exploded at the Minnesota Mining and Manufacturing Company, shattering windows. According to a French police statement, the extreme right-wing Youth Action claiming responsibility said that the blasts were a protest against the meeting in Martinique of the presidents of France and the United States.

Those having recourse to microviolence may exaggerate the degree to which the public shares their beliefs and tastes, and hence be all too sparing in their explanations (see Section 1). On 15 September 1974, two persons were killed and thirty-four wounded by a young man who threw a hand grenade into a crowd in the Drugstore Saint-Germain complex in Paris and then escaped. An extreme right-wing organization, the Group for the Defense of Europe, claimed responsibility but did not disclose, for instance, whether it believed American capital to be invested in the complex bearing an American name, or whether it viewed the establishment as a vehicle of the American way of life in France, or both, or something else.

Expressive violence of high intensity may be felt to be particularly appropriate to signifying one's perseverance with regard to an extreme aim that one is suspected (by others as well as oneself) to be tempted to abandon, given the obstacles in its path. "We carried out the operation at Qiryat Shemona," said the Palestinian PFLP-GC about its attack on an apartment house in Israel, "to underline that our liberation struggle is not limited to the West Bank or Gaza, but covers all Palestinian territory" (*Arab Report and Record*, 1–15 April 1974, pp. 138–39).

Section 18: *Écrasez l'infâme*

"You have nothing more to do with the law except to lay hands on it," said one of the orators (Sam Fielden) on that famous day in Haymarket

Square, "do everything you can to wound it." "When in 1882 a bomb was thrown in the early hours of the morning into a music hall in Lyon," a historian reports, "there were some people, including the police, who regarded this as the . . . fulfillment of an article in an anarchist paper, some months earlier, which said: 'You can see there, especially after midnight, the fine flower of the bourgeoisie and of commerce. . . . The first act of the social revolution must be to destroy this den' " (Joll 1964, p. 130). "I will at least have had the satisfaction," said one of the authors of spectacular violence in that period and country (Auguste Vaillant). "of having wounded existing society" (Guilleminault and Mahé 1963, p. 112). "There is so much to denounce in the system," declared a Québecquois (Pierre Vallières) in the late sixties, "so much to *destroy* [underlined in the text—NL] . . ." (Hodges and Abu Shanab 1972, p. 329): the earlier sentiments of violent anarchists have been revived.

Destroying may be felt as self-defense: "Wreck what wrecks you *(macht kaputt was euch kaputt macht).*" Or as loving: "love for human beings is today possible only in the death-dealing hate-filled attack on imperialism-fascism" (Ulrike Meinhof, *Der Spiegel,* 2 June 1975, p. 2). Or as an exercise of taste, as when a student coresponsible for burning a branch of the Bank of America in Santa Barbara points out that "it was . . . an ugly building. Esthetically, it was ugly. As one of my friends remarked: 'that fucking thing was so ugly it had to go anyway' " (*Scanlan's Monthly,* January 1971, p. 21). Or destruction may be felt as punishment. The crime sanctioned may be believed to be inevitably committed by anybody who occupies a certain position in society; as when a French anarchist of the late nineteenth century predicted that "when I strike the first bourgeois I encounter, I shall not be striking an innocent" (Joll 1964, p. 117); or as when a famous man of violence of the epoch (Émile Henry) more pithily declared: "Nobody is innocent." The punishment may, specifically, be inflicted on those who had previously damaged proponents of microviolence. "We decided," a Montonero reports on a certain moment in his group's history, "to leave our anonymous stage . . . behind. It was time to stop mourning our dead. It was time for the others to do some of the dying; it was time for the enemy to receive some of the grief" (Hodges and Abu Shanab 1972, p. 310).

All the more as some of the others are scarcely human. "People," declares Ulrike Meinhof about intellectual revolutionaries rejecting the

RAF, ''have no difficulty, when talking about the Panthers, to use their words for cops (*Bullen*), namely the word pigs (*Schweine*). But they do not apply this word to the police which they encounter themselves.'' As to Ulrike Meinhof, ''we say, naturally, the *Bullen* are *Schweine*. . . . The guy in uniform is a *Schwein*, that is, not a human being *(Mensch)*. . . .'' Hence ''we don't have to with him''; in fact, ''it is wrong'' to do so, but ''naturally one can shoot *(kann geschossen werden)*'' *(Der Spiegel*, 15 June 1970, p. 75). I have never heard that a policeman is a human being, the late nineteenth-century German Johannes Most had already observed (Laqueur 1976, p. 147).

Similar feelings may be entertained about the unpaid, indeed ''exploited'' supporters of the status quo in the lower-middle and lower strata of the population. The classical case here is the bombing, in the late nineteenth century, of a café near the Gare St. Lazare in Paris. ''One must strike the bourgeois,'' explained the author of the deed, ''but also all those who are content with the present order, those employees with a salary of 300 francs a month who applaud the acts of the government, who hate the people even more than the big bourgeois . . . the habitual clientèle of the Terminus. They all have rejoiced about the death of Vaillant. That is why I have hit them'' (Émile Henry at his trial, Guilleminault and Mahé 1963, p. 121).

Killing and wounding some fortunately entails spoiling the pleasures of many for long. ''I wanted to show the bourgeoisie,'' Émile Henry added, ''that their pleasures would no longer be complete . . . their triumphs would be disturbed'' (Joll 1964, p. 137). The Tupamaros destroyed Uruguay's only bowling club, Montevideo's golf club, and several fashionable night clubs.

Or the target may be one of the innumerable material vehicles of the exploitation/oppression to which the few supposedly subject the many. ''We set fire to department stores,'' Andreas Baader and Gertrud Ensslin explained in a note they had intended to leave in the places of their first deed (in Frankfurt, 2 April 1968), ''so that you cease buying.'' For ''the constraint to comsume (*Konsumzwang*) terrorizes you'' (*Der Spiegel*, 5 June 1972, p. 23)—the victim is the terrorist.

Section 19: It's Fun

''It's fun,'' exclaims Sam Melville at the thought of violence (Melville 1972, p. 140).

Perhaps the only fun left. "Brothers and sisters," asks Communiqué 8 of Britain's Angry Brigade, "what are your real desires? Sit in the drugstore, look distant, empty, bored, drinking some tasteless coffee? Or perhaps BLOW IT UP OR BURN IT DOWN . . . just kick it till it breaks" (Carr 1975, p. 104; capitals in the text).

In the late twentieth century, fun and duty are probably mingled as they were almost a hundred years ago among French anarchists:

> Danse, dynamite
> danse, danse vite
> dansons et chantons
> dynamitons, dynamitons
>
> Dansons la Ravachole
> vive le son, vive le son
> dansons la Ravachole
> vive le son
> de l'explosion
>
> Nos pères ont jadis dansé
> au son du canon du passé.
> Maintenant la danse tragique
> veut une plus forte musique:
> dynamitons, dynamitons

Section 20: If You Can Bring It Off, Do It

"We have established ourselves in the Left," observes a Brazilian about his group, "by proving the *possibility* of an armed organization in Brazil, but not yet the political *efficacy* of armed struggle" (Jamil Rodriguez, *Les Temps Modernes,* March 1971, p. 1589). How right this militant was to allude to the tendency toward "confusing," in the words of a friendly critic (João Quartim), "the military possibility of an action with its political correctness" (Kohl and Litt, 1974, p. 159) becomes apparent when we hear from the Rote Armee Fraktion that "the question whether it is correct *(richtig)* to organize armed . . . resistance groups in the Federal Republic and in West Berlin is the question whether it is possible to do so." It follows that "the answer can only be ascertained practically.'' That is, ''some comrades have resolved to engage in this enterprise. By this it will be shown whether there are enough persons, enough . . . energy, enough shrewdness, enough discipline . . . available . . . so as to be able actually (*tatsächlich*) to attack imperialism in the . . . Federal Republic and West Berlin.'' When affirming that ''only opportunists could dismiss the liberation of Baader as adventurous, putschist, anarchist,'' the Rote Armee Fraktion offers the novel proof we would now expect: ''success showed that the operation was executed with a correct evaluation of our own and the pigs' forces . . .'' (Baader-Meinhof Report 1972, p. 158).

Where so many doubt whether microviolence can be brought into existence at all in an environment in which it has been absent for some time, the very feat of producing that strange and striking means of production may suggest its high productivity for the consumer good intended, the Revolution. ''In the last analysis and contrary to the opinion of many,'' the Tupamaros exult upon having abducted the director-general of the telephone and power company, ''even in this country it is possible to counter the ruling sector's repression with direct action'' (Wilson 1974, p. 44).

It is possible, but it takes most of one's energy. When the sister of an imprisoned RAF militant (Gudrun Ensslin) objects to her that ''in comparison with the laborious work of the Left placing bombs is simple,'' she draws the retort: ''Do you have any idea of how difficult it was to place bombs?'' (*Der Spiegel*, 24 July 1972, p. 62). A statement of her group mentions the ''laborious, lengthy work on details (*Kleinarbeit*) of the urban guerrilla . . .'' (*Der Spiegel*, 24 April 1972, p. 83)—work that, as we have seen, also bears the opposite character (Section 13). ''His principal duty . . . to attack and survive'' (Carlos Marighella, in Kohl and Litt 1974, p. 89) may absorb him to the detriment of a continued inquiry into impacts. ''He told of lice [listening devices] which hang from the windows,'' a temporary militant of the RAF (Beate Sturm) reminisced about Andreas Baader. ''If one talks, then at best only in a moving car—that drowns out the lice. As in a real American detective story . . . what we really wanted, that question we did not put to ourselves clearly any more'' (*Der Spiegel*, 7 February 1972, p. 57). On the question ''where this armed struggle is leading,'' the prevailing opinion among the Tupamaros seems to have been that ''armed struggle thinks with its own head'' (Wilson 1974, p. 66).

III. Prospects

All the favorable forecasts about the impact of microviolence (Part I) and all its intrinsic attractions (Part II) may not quench the dismay aroused by the awareness that, in Bernardine Dohrn's words, "most of our actions have hurt the enemy on about the same military level as a bee-sting" (Moss 1972, p. 74). Focusing on the "here and now," the microviolent ones are also moved to go beyond it in space and time.

Section 21: Elsewhere

"You have hanged men in Chicago," a prominent microviolent one in late nineteenth-century France (Émile Henry) addressed the existing order at his trial, "cut off their heads in Germany, strangled them in Jerez, shot them in Barcelona, guillotined them in Montbrison and Paris . . ." (Joll 1964, p. 138). Similar words have been pronounced more recently to subdue the sense of the microviolent that they are small, perhaps insignificant.

"One small group"—such as the speaker's own—"is nothing," a Brazilian admits. "But we know that people are forming small groups all over the world . . ." (Kohl and Litt 1974, p. 146); the result, no doubt larger than the sum, is formidable.

All the more as some of these "groups" are big. When a newsmagazine queries the imprisoned leaders of the Rote Armee Fraktion whether "you want to . . . remain cadres and bring about the revolution by going it alone or whether you still believe that you will be able to mobilize proletarian masses," the answer is that "it is silly to attribute to us the intent to 'go it alone,' given the state of the contemporary anti-imperialist battle in Asia, Latin America, Africa, in Vietnam, Chile, Uruguay, Argentina. There are also in Western Europe not only the RAF but also the IRA, ETA, [and only now—NL] groups engaged in armed combat in Italy, in Portugal, in England" (*Der Spiegel*, 20 January 1975, pp. 55–56). Upon the question asked a Weatherwoman by her sister, "when blue collar workers are making $6 an hour, where is the support coming from?" the militant replied that "the revolution is already taking place. It's a worldwide thing" (Powers 1971, p. 163).

A small microviolent group in an advanced country can, in case of need, always view itself as a mere auxiliary, albeit a precious one, of a big group in a less-developed area (see Section 7). "In Hanoi," claim the leaders of the Rote Armee Fraktion, "there were fotos of us in the streets, because the bombing in Heidelberg, for which the RAF has taken responsibility, has destroyed the computer with which the U.S. bombing of North Vietnam was calculated and directed" *(Der Spiegel,* 20 January 1975, p. 57).

In this function of external support, a *positive* yield, however small, may seem assured to any microviolent group in an advanced country—a yield that, given the priority given to the big struggle elsewhere, may be believed to be certainly higher than a possibly negative impact at home. As a result, then, there is no risk of being counterproductive. "If . . . the basic struggle in the world today is the struggle of the oppressed people against U.S. imperialism," a Weatherman demonstrates, "then nothing we could do in the mother country could be adventurist" (Powers 1971, pp. 194–95).

Section 22: Later

We may be small now, but that is just because "we are at an early stage, going from small to large" *(Prairie Fire* 1974, p. 2). "We are all," an Argentinian declares about the several armed groups in the country, "embryos of the People's Army" *(Les Temps Modernes,* April 1972, pp. 1557–58). The Turkish People's Liberation Army admits, when capturing four U.S. airmen, that "today" it is "a handful of fighters" and predicts that "tomorrow" it "will become thousands and millions."

"I would like the glory," the first anarchist assassin in late nineteenth-century France confided, "of being the first to start" (Woodcock 1962, p. 301). What glory indeed, in our days, to make oneself into a first like the first in Ching Kan Shan (1927), the Aurès Mountains (1954), the Sierra Maestra (1956). "We are," the Rote Armee Fraktion announced its birth, "the first regular units of the Red Army . . ." *(Der Spiegel,* 31 January 1972, p. 59).

If we are fated to grow, it is, however, only because we start out with violence. "An armed group, no matter how small," the Tupamaros explain, "has greater possibilities for converting itself into a . . . popular army than a group that limits itself to revolutionary positions" (Wilson 1974, p. 57). "It is"—it is only—"revolutionary action" that, in a formula of the same group, "precipitates revolutionary action"

(Moss 1972, p. 218). When a spokesman of the group was asked to "give . . . [an] example illustrating the [Tupamaro] principle that revolutionary action generates revolutionary consciousness, organization and conditions," he of course replied that, "Cuba is an example. In place of the long process of forming a Party of the masses, a guerrilla foco of a dozen men was installed, and this deed generated revolutionary consciousness, organization and conditions" (Kohl and Litt 1974, p. 227).

It is not only compatible with eventual victory to start out tiny, it is indispensable to do so (see Section 5): in Raoul Castro's formula, the big motor of the Revolution requires a small motor to get started.

There may be a leap already tomorrow. The October Manifesto of the Front de Libération du Québec broadcast in Montreal on 8 October 1970 foresaw the imminence of "100,000 revolutionary workers, armed and organized, flooding into the streets of Montreal" (Moss 1972, p. 126).

Or it will take a long time, but we will get there—always on condition that there be at least some violence from the start. "Future actions, beyond the conspiracy level," the Tupamaros foresee, "will be but the first step in a revolutionary war. It won't be a quick war . . . but a slow . . . protracted struggle." Yet this "should not be a reason to postpone action until a quick victory is insured, for [in that case] it will never arrive." Therefore, without delay, "the 'little motor' must be started" (Wilson 1974, p. 70); and it must be little. "You start with one to reach a hundred, as the saying goes," the French anarchist quoted above recalled (Woodcock 1962, p. 301).

If you refuse starting tiny, you will never grow big. Considering the "contradiction" of the "system" that "affirms that there are no political prisoners, while they do of course exist," the imprisoned leaders of the Rote Armee Fraktion affirm "that" to be "the piece of ground . . . from which . . . we can do what we want to do: enlarge it." On the other hand, "if we do surrender this little piece of ground from . . . dismay *(Bestürzung)* about the fact that it is so small, then beautiful socialism will, naturally, always remain a beautiful cloud" *(Dokumentation* 1975, p. 163). The same holds true for violence.

Section 23: Soon

One may hide doubts about microviolence from oneself and others by presenting aspirations toward a capacity for small war; for that kind of war presents fewer problems except, alas, that of being strong enough to conduct one. "The only important point," observes Carlos Marighella (choosing a formulation that may suggest that the desirable is also feasible) "is to increase substantially the volume of urban guerrilla activity in order to *wear out* the government . . ." (Kohl and Litt 1974, p. 99)—to be sure, once you can do that, you have it made. But what if you can't? "It is necessary," Horst Mahler observes (again in a fashion that suggests realization and not only requirement, though the former be arduous and the latter obvious), "to develop numerous groups of partisans in all major population centers in order to force the enemy already in the phase of creation to disperse his forces and to overload his intelligence apparatus" (Mahler 1971, p. 31). From prison Andreas Baader demands that his shattered group revive, "if possible," in the shape of "eight to ten guys *(Typen)* in every major city" with "one center in the city and three to five apartments" (*Der Spiegel,* 25 November 1974, p. 33).

Aspirations may go beyond small war to big war. For Carlos Marighella "the armed struggle of the urban guerrilla points towards two essential objectives: 1. the physical liquidation of the chief and assistants of the armed forces and the police . . ." (Kohl and Litt 1974, p. 92). "Our next leap," declare the Tupamaros about to die, "is to destroy the living forces of the enemy . . ." (Wilson 1974, p. 159).

Beyond inflating one's aspirations one may magnify one's forces. While "you speak of the fact that some of us are imprisoned," the leaders of the Rote Armee Fraktion observe to hostile journalists, "you do not speak of the political cost to the . . . State of . . . the hunt for *only a small* RAF unit" (*Der Spiegel,* 20 January 1975, p. 57). When on 3 March 1968 six bombs went off within minutes of each other in six locations in Turin, The Hague, and London, the forces of the British Revolutionary Solidarity Movement, First of May Group (Carr 1975, p. 61) should perhaps appear larger than they were to the microviolent ones themselves as well as to whomever else paid attention. The "Chenier" cell of the Front de Libération du Québec, having kidnapped a province minister, also signed communications using the names "Vigier" and "Dieppe"; whereas each of the six bombings of the Rote Armee Fraktion in May 1972 was signed by a different name (*Der Spiegel,* 24 June 1974, p. 29). In more exacting fashion—and then probably also more for self-delusion—a microviolent group may painstakingly prepare for a scale of operations well beyond its foreseeable resources.

Thus the Rote Armee Fraktion established approximately 500 files on West German citizens to kill or abduct, with addresses, telephone numbers, indications about families and affairs, habitual bars and restaurants (*Der Spiegel*, 10 March 1975, p. 25). According to an attorney general of the state of California a captured SLA list of more than 900 targets showed that "they probably had a better library than many police departments . . ." (Evelle Younger, Hearing, Committee on the Judiciary, U.S. Senate, 23 September 1974, p. 22).

Beyond such disproportionate preparations, plans of operations may be exaggerated.

One may pretend to oneself and others that one is actually engaged in producing an attrition of the enemy force, as in small war. "Its purpose," the Tupamaros say in an internal document about "terror and sabotage," "is to lessen their [the enemy's] *capacity* for repression," which is to be achieved by "interrupting their communications, damaging their property . . ." (Wilson 1974, p. 76)—obviously, in considerable amounts. From prison Ulrike Meinhof orders a "*daily* schedule: I. Daily militant action against installations of the State, of the monopolies (industry, commerce, banks) and of the U.S. occupants . . ." (*Der Spiegel*, 2 June 1975, p. 29; emphasis in the text). Establishing a "small attack strategy for Northern Germany," a document of the Rote Armee Fraktion begins with a "first step," Hamburg: "Monday morning, setting two fires in each of the following department stores: Karstadt, Keta, Horten, Kaufhalle, Kaufhof"; then goes on to "Bremen: in the night from Monday to Tuesday one attempt with dynamite against the Spanish consulate." The "second step" still concerns Bremen: "Tuesday morning two attacks with fire in each of the following department stores: Hertie, Karstadt, Horten." Still within the "second step" is Kiel—and so on until the sixth (*Dokumentation* 1975, p. 84). While "to ambush and annihilate enemy contingents" is a difficult maneuver for a rural guerrilla," to do, the Tupamaros allege it "will be a simple and daily operation for the urban guerrilla" (Costa 1972, p. 252).

From an objective that is still of small war—"the principal task of the urban guerrilla is . . . to wear out . . . the military dictatorship"—one (in this instance, Carlos Marighella) may rise to a purpose of big war: ". . . and also to . . . destroy the wealth and property of the North Americans . . . and the Brazilian upper class" (Kohl and Litt 1974, p.

89). In the late nineteenth century in Paris, Ravachol—who acted alone and asserted, "We are one hundred, we are one thousand in Paris who can do as much"—having dynamited two houses inhabited by a prosecutor and a judge respectively, affirmed that "a provision of dynamite has been distributed which is sufficient for every house lodging a judge to explode in the near future" (Guilleminault and Mahé 1963, p. 69). "If one truck with Springer papers is set on fire," Horst Mahler observes, "that is arson." But "if all Springer trucks burn, that is a political action" (*Der Spiegel*, 22 February 1971, p. 28)—indeed, that is civil war; but *can* you make them all burn, or even many? It was at the very last of the six famous bombings by the Rote Armee Fraktion in May 1972 that the group asked "the militants in the Federal Republic and West Berlin to make . . . *all* American installations into targets of their attack" (*Der Spiegel*, 24 June 1974, pp. 29–30). "The suicide commandos of the FLQ," a notice to the population of Quebec announced seven and a half years before the kidnappings that made that group famous, "are aiming principally at the *complete* destruction by sabotage of the colonial institutions, of *all* means of communication in the colonial language, of *the* enterprises . . . practicing discrimination against the Québecois. The FLQ will proceed to eliminate *all* persons collaborating with the occupant" (Morf 1971, p. 4). "In summation," observed an internal document of the Tupamaros shortly before they were destroyed in 1972, "to commence hostilities directly and systematically must become the immediate concrete task on which we must concentrate all our energy. This must be calculated with military precision. WE MUST HAVE OUR 'D' DAY (this last sentence in capital initials—NL) . . . To succeed we must defeat the armed forces. We propose a systematic and selective attack on them . . . The [Organization's] Information Service about the Armed Forces can propose to the Organization . . . objectives for military action to destroy the moral and material forces of the enemy" (Wilson 1974, p. 163). "Our next leap"—and "we have been looking for the . . . possibilities of 'leaping' since 1970"—is "to destroy the living forces of the enemy" (Wilson 1974, p. 154)—rather than, as happened, having one's own living forces destroyed by the enemy. The reality of microviolence disappears behind the aspiration toward a big war, even a preamble to a plan for it.

Source Material

Alexander, Y., ed. *International Terrorism*. New York, 1976.
Baader-Meinhof Report. Mainz, 1972.
Carr, G. *The Angry Brigade*. London, 1975.
Costa, O. *Los Tupamaros*. Mexico, 1972.
Dokumentation über Aktivitäten anarchistischer Gewalttäter in der BRD. Bonn, 1975.
Gaucher, R. *Les terroristes*. Paris, 1965.
Generals and Tupamaros. London, 1974.
Gilio, M. E. *The Tupamaro Guerrilla*. New York, 1973.
Guilleminault, G., and Mahé, E. *L' épopée de la révolte*. Paris, 1963.
Hodges, D. C., and Abu Shanab, R. E. *NLF*. New York, 1972.
Hyams, E. H. *Terrorists and Terrorism*. New York, 1974.
Joll, J. *The Anarchists*. London, 1964.
Kohl, J., and Litt, J. *Urban Guerrilla Warfare in Latin America*. Cambridge, Mass., 1974.
Laffin, J. *Fedayeen*. New York, 1973.
Laqueur, W. *Guerrilla*. Boston, 1976.
Mahler, H. *Kollektiv RAF: Über den bewaffneten Kampf in Westeuropa*. West Berlin, 1971.
Melville, S. *Letters from Attica*. New York, 1972.
Morf, G. *Terror in Quebec*. New York, 1971.
Moss, R. *The War for the Cities*. New York, 1972.
Powers, T. *Diana*. Boston, 1971.
Prairie Fire. Printed Underground, 1974.
Ruhmkorf, P. *Die Jahre die ihr kennt*. Hamburg, 1972.
Salmon, A. *La terreur noire*. Paris, 1959.
Saywell, J. *Quebec 70*. Toronto, 1971.
Schiff, Z., and Rothstein, R. *Feyadeen*. New York, 1972.
Stern, S. *With the Weatherman*. New York, 1975.
Wilkinson, P. *Political Terrorism*. New York, 1974.
Wilson, C. *The Tupamaros*. Boston, 1974.
Woodcock, G. *Anarchism*. Cleveland, 1962.
Yaari, E. *Strike Terror*. New York, 1970.

Part II
In the Name of the Cause

[2]

Terrorism and Propaganda: Problem and Response

by
Maurice Tugwell

INTRODUCTION

Propaganda is defined by the North Atlantic Alliance as any information, ideas, doctrines or special appeals disseminated to influence the opinion, emotions, attitudes or behaviour of any specified group in order to benefit the sponsor either directly or indirectly.[1] Terrorism, in Grant Wardlaw's definition, is the use, or threat of use, of violence by an individual or a group, whether acting for or in opposition to established authority, when such action is designed to create extreme anxiety and/or fear-inducing effects in a target group larger than the immediate victims with the purpose of coercing that group into acceding to the political demands of the perpetrators.[2]

Propaganda and terrorism are identical insofar as they both seek to influence a mass audience in a way that is intended to benefit the sponsor. Yet while terror has a singular purpose — inducing fear and uncertainty — propaganda can and does serve every imaginable purpose from religion to politics to commerce. Terrorism is, as the nineteenth century anarchists claimed, 'propaganda by deed'; in Brian Jenkins more recent formulation, it is theatre.[3] Terrorism may be other things as well, but there is no doubting the very close links between these subjects. Indeed, terror might be seen as a sub-species of propaganda.

Terrorism is also a sub-species of revolution, which is a struggle for power. The key to that power is popular allegiance, whether given voluntarily or out of fear. Allegiance is transferred from regime to revolutionaries by shifts in the popular conception of relative credibility and legitimacy. Credibility rests on demonstrated ability to control events by being in command, running a government or an alternative power structure, or perhaps by winning small battles, while legitimacy is the public's conception of a right to rule based on whatever values the public may associate with that right. The legal definition of legitimacy, which sides with the incumbent regime, ceases to apply once the government's credibility is eroded. Consequently the fight for allegiance consists of myriad small battles over credibility and legitimacy, in which the two issues become inextricably mixed.

Clearly, in its revolutionary context, terrorism is very much more than a series of front page stories. The direct and obvious link between terrorism and propaganda is merely the visible tip of an iceberg. Whether terrorism is part of a wider campaign of revolution or a free-standing conflict form, its political objectives can only be reached by a complex psychological-military process in which propaganda and violence can be compared to a boxer's two fists. It is operational propaganda that needs to be better understood and countered, for without it terrorism would be fighting with one hand tied behind its back, and ought, therefore, to be more easily defeated.

REVOLUTION

Revolution's three key ingredients are leadership, organization and inspiration. Michael Elliott-Bateman calls the last ingredient the "cultural-spiritual," and regards it as the foundation of the struggle.[4] Terrorism, as a sub-species of revolution or as a component, also relies on these essential ingredients; it too elevates the cultural-spiritual element to pride of place.

The cultural-spiritual inspiration goes far beyond normal political persuasion. The latter is concerned with concrete issues; it is the stuff of ballot boxes and activities *within* the existing political and social dispensation. Revolutionary inspiration transcends conventional politics and demands the overthrow of the existing order, existing laws, existing beliefs and ways of thinking, and their replacement by some higher truth. Of course concrete issues may feature in this vision of the future, but they are reinterpreted within the new cultural-spiritual value system.

Revolutionary inspiration may come from religion, nationalism, racism or political ideology, or from a mixture of these and other sources. Whatever the cause, the cultural-spiritual element must fire the imagination by revealing the beauty of the promised land. It must justify the resort to violence by depicting the incumbent regime as deaf to reason and incapable of reform. It must cast the regime and its institutions as the incarnation of evil, because they stand between the people and the promised land. Finally, it must assure audiences that, with good on their side, they will surely overcome. These three themes of virtue, evil and inevitable victory dominate terrorist propaganda aimed at the convinced activists.

Because the regime and its institutions are evil, true believers are not bound by its laws, customs and moral codes, only by the higher truths and laws of the cause. This inspiration distinguishes the revolutionary, including the political terrorist, from the criminal. Whereas the profit-motivated activist may be amoral, and may commit crimes knowing them to be immoral, he or she expects to be judged by conventional standards. The true revolutionary, however, insists that violent crimes committed for the cause are just, and argues that he or she is answerable only to the revolutionary leadership, or to some higher authority such as God or history.

Revolutionary propaganda's first priority is to create such a circle of true believers. The objective is total, unquestioning loyalty. There is, therefore, a need for the totalitarian propaganda described by Jacques Ellul, which he insists can exist only within a tightly disciplined organization:

> Without organization, psychological incitement leads to excesses and deviation of action in the very course of development. Through organization, the proselyte receives an overwhelming impulse that makes him act

> with the whole of his being. He is actually transformed into a religious man in the psycho-sociological sense of the term; justice enters into the action he performs because of the organization of which he is a part.[5]

Ellul explains how action makes propaganda's effect irreversible, how he who acts in obedience to propaganda can never go back. To justify his past action, the recruit must now *believe* the propaganda because he has broken old rules, values and friendships. The deeper his actions carry him into the world of reversed morality, the more dependent he becomes on propaganda to sustain him.[6]

Baruch Hazan suggests that propaganda must first attract an audience's attention by penetrating the 'absorption screen,' a relatively easy task, and that, to be effective, it must then penetrate the 'personality screen.' During the latter process the beliefs, values, attitudes, concepts, expectations, etc. of individuals in the audience relate to the propaganda message, simplify, classify and label it, and produce an opinion. The individual acts because he has been influenced by the message and not because of his previous views. Eventually his personality is changed.[7] Families that have lost members to exotic religious cults will recognize this process. Clearly, Ellul's initiation of true believers, the terrorist's first priority, penetrates the personality screen. Without organization, such penetration is presumably rare.

A second task of revolutionary propaganda is to influence the general public and even the international audience. Although terrorists regard the regime, its institutions, and its agents as evil enemies to be destroyed without mercy, they look upon the general public as an audience whose allegiance is required. The purpose of all revolutionary activity is conversion. Elimination is reserved for symbolic or vengeance targets, those who threaten the movement, and those who refuse conversion. The objectives for this wider audience are complex. Because the target is not yet incorporated within an organization, complete allegiance is unlikely to be achieved, nor will the personality screen be penetrated. However, provided the absorption screen is pierced — and acts of terrorism are particularly effective in attracting attention — a climate of opinion can be created in which the cadre of true believers can increase in number and effectiveness, the government is restrained and hampered in its response, and the public is made confused, ambivalent, fearful and vulnerable.

The concept of organization may tend to conjure up an image of a physically compact group, isolated from society. This would be misleading. The group is psychologically compact but physically dispersed, infiltrating institutions, the media, even the armed forces and police. Some members may establish fronts or redirect existing ones. Only in the covert cells might a degree of isolation exist. Thus, in the physical sense, the two audiences are mixed. True believers dedicated to extreme objectives, who have secretly rejected the norms of society within the covert organization, may be seen and heard by the public arguing within the existing norms for seemingly reasonable objectives. Their agenda is hidden behind tactical reasonableness.

Spring 1986

THEMES OF TERRORISM

Whether terrorism is a component of a wider revolutionary strategy or stands on its own, the themes aimed at the general public seem fairly constant. These are some of the most common.

Guilt Transfer. Terrorists blame the consequences of all violence on the regime they are opposing. Naturally, all that the police and military do is presented in the worst possible light, and casualties are made into innocent victims or martyrs, regardless of whether or not such terms are appropriate. Having associated the regime with violence and death, this theme then goes an important step further, blaming terrorist violence on the authorities as well. This technique follows that of Napoleon Bonaparte, who, according to Clausewitz, insisted that his aggression was peaceful, war being the responsibility of victims who resisted.[8]

The El Salvadoran terrorists and rebels have been particularly successful in this theme. Western observers frequently attribute blame for the entire death toll to the regime, as if the FMLN had neither contributed nor participated.[9] Martin McGuinness, a senior Provisional IRA leader, explicitly blamed Britain for every death in Northern Ireland, including the deaths of his own victims.[10]

Guilt transfer frequently involves the rejection of the term 'terrorist' by the violent group and the transfer of the term to the regime. State-sponsors of terrorism are particularly adept in this regard.

Invulnerability. Whereas true believers accept the inevitability of victory as part of their ideological conditioning, the 'invulnerability' theme tries to rationalize the same message for the general public. It is said that liberal government is powerless in the face of clandestine attack, that security forces are ill-equipped to deal effectively with terrorism, that time is on the side of the revolutionaries. The purpose of this theme is to demoralize the government and its supporters and to neutralize the mass, counting on the fact that no one wishes to back a loser.

The notion that time is on the terrorists' side dresses a terrorist campaign in the clothes of full-scale revolution. It argues that, for the regime to win, the authorities must eliminate every last terrorist and extinguish the cultural-spiritual inspiration — which is obviously impossible. So long as one terrorist survives, the struggle continues. Eventually, protracted war will undermine the regime. Robert Taber wrote:

> Time works for the guerrilla both in the field — where it costs the enemy a daily fortune to pursue him — and in the politico-economic arena ₅₅₅. Protracted internal war threatens all of this [political and economic credibility], for no investor will wish to put his money where it is not safe and certain to produce a profit, no banks lend without guarantees, no ally wishes to treat with a government that is on the point of eviction.[11]

Latin American terrorists have often employed this technique.

The Provisional IRA exploited this theme in a novel way after their terrorists had bombed a Brighton hotel, narrowly missing the British Cabinet. In their communiqué, the Provisionals boasted: "Today we were unlucky. But remember, we have only to be lucky once. You will have to be lucky always."[12]

The invulnerability theme, of course, depends for its credibility upon the armed actions of the terrorist group. Daring acts, appropriately publicized, make authority appear powerless and the terrorists, invulnerable. The two fists must work together to accomplish desired psychological results.[13]

Spurious Justification. While the campaign as a whole endeavours to accumulate legitimacy for the organization, at a lower, day-to-day tactical level spurious justifications are devised to protect terrorists from the full force of public wrath — wrath which might find expression in tougher anti-terrorism laws and procedures. Perhaps the commonest ploy is to justify murder by reference to alleged and sometimes real political or social injustices. The apparent intention is to confuse ends with means and to produce an ambivalent or even supportive public attitude.

After the Provisionals killed 10 army bandsmen and cavalrymen in London in July 1982, their spokesman explained that "Britain's interference" in Ireland's affairs "makes bringing the war to Britain inevitable."[14] Sheik Mohammad Hussein Fadlallah, a senior Iranian official, spoke of "an open-ended war between the impoverished and deprived against the United States, Israel and all the enemies of Islam."[15] FALN, a Puerto Rican group, justified a spate of bombings in December 1982 with a long communiqué speaking of "fascist repressive actions of the FBI, U.S. courts and police" and the use of Puerto Rico as "a base of operations which will be used as a springboard to protect its interests in the Caribbean, Latin America...."[16]

Sometimes the appeal is much more seductive. When young Canadian terrorists fire-bombed pornographic video stores in Vancouver, it would have been easy for this writer to have said: "I cannot condone the violence, but I do understand why some people feel compelled to act." Yet, to have said this would have amounted to an attempt to profit from terrorism while evading moral responsibility. This is the reaction desired by terrorists, and confusion of ends and means arguably does more to keep terrorism alive than any other theme.

Television appearances by terrorist leaders and spokesmen also provide occasions for justification. On this medium, the 'presence' of the speaker influences audiences more than his or her words. By all accounts Josef Mengele was 'charming.' Had he been interviewed by BBC in 1944, would he have persuaded some allied viewers that his actions were justified?

Another argument within this theme explains that violence by the terrorists is a reluctant but inevitable reaction to violence by the state. Costa Gravas's film *State of Siege* (1973) portrayed Tupamaro violence as a justified reaction to United States political and economic domination of Uruguay, a domination which, the film alleged, introduced torture to that country.[17] Reinhard Hauff's film *Stammheim — The Trial* (1986) reportedly grants legitimacy to Baader-Meinhof atrocities by portraying the suicides of convicted terrorists as 'state terrorism.' In both cases the justification theme merges with guilt transfer, because audiences are required to see authority in a worse light than the terrorists.

Disarming Themes. Here the aim is to discredit and destroy any method, individual, police or military unit, weapon or policy that, because of its potential effectiveness, threatens the terrorists' integrity and freedom of action. Unlike spurious justification, which usually advances from the upside-down morality of terrorist logic, disarming themes are often argued within the norms of conventional morality. Consequently fronts are extensively used, and they appear to advance their causes *pro bono publico*, to save the government from blundering into error. Consequently this is a very difficult area, because many pressure groups operating in this field will be devoid of sinister motive. Moreover, public input is valuable to government decision-making. It would be extremely dangerous to label all appeals for restraint as terrorist propaganda. This difficulty is exploited by the terrorists through infiltration of innocent pressure groups and by burying demands of operational importance within a program of reforms assembled in good faith by concerned citizens.

Northern Ireland in the early 1970s provided a host of examples where government security measures drew fire from loyal critics and terrorist fronts alike. Internment, deep interrogation, rubber bullets, the 'paras,' army 'black propaganda,' CS smoke, the Ulster Defence Regiment, and many other real or imagined targets were made the subjects of investigations, exposés, legal actions and public agitation. Some were justified, many were understandable, some were parts of systematic disarming propaganda. It seems at least possible that a fearful anticipation of this type of propaganda deterred British governments from deploying units of the Special Air Service in Northern Ireland for about five years. In another setting, but contemporaneously, the United States 'Office of Public Safety' program for Latin America was destroyed by this form of propaganda, of which Costa Gravas's film was a part.[18]

Terror. It is easy to overlook that terror is itself a theme of propaganda. To every member of its audience it says: "oppose us, and you die!" The effect is hard to measure, because it is slow and unacknowledged. If someone begins to sympathize with the terrorist cause, he or she will seldom admit that fear is the reason. Many critics have alleged that Western reporting from Lebanon before and during the Israeli invasion was distorted by PLO intimidation tactics.[19] Journalists who decide to 'report from the other side' are almost inevitably going to slant their copy accordingly. Unless they are seeking martyrdom, how could they do otherwise? Terror can isolate the police and other security forces, because the judiciary, bureaucracy and general public fear to commit themselves to the fight. Frequently, police are singled out as targets, until they too cease to operate effectively.

Combined with a violent campaign, these themes can be instrumental in deflecting government responses until it is too late to reverse the shift of popular allegiance from regime to terrorist. That, at least, is the terrorist hope. Where terrorism is only a component of a wider revolutionary strategy, as in the decolonization campaigns of the 1940s, 1950s and early 1960s, rebel objectives have often been met. Success also crowned the efforts of Shia fundamentalists in Iran, Sandinistas in Nicaragua, and other movements where terrorism was a subordinate means. Free-standing terrorist campaigns have, however, been much less successful. It is as though the strategic component of their propaganda — their spiritual-cultural code — was unable to fire sufficient imagainations. The true believers remained a small group and mass mobilization never succeeded.

Yet many terrorist campaigns endure for decade after decade. A lack of strategic success does not seem to deter true believers whose commitment to the cause and the violent road cannot easily be rejected. Indeed, their whole reason for existing seems to be bound up in the struggle, which becomes an end in itself. Tactical success proves sufficient reward and the game continues. Survival themes such as guilt transfer, spurious justification, disarming and terror are often brilliantly deployed and their success may be a key reason why so many ill-starred campaigns seem capable of indefinite prolongation.

COUNTERING THE PROPAGANDA OF TERRORISM

If propaganda is half the terrorist's armoury, and perhaps the decisive half in terms of survival, there is surely a strong case for government counter-terrorist measures to contain a psychological component. The problem, of course, is public unease at any form of propaganda, and politicians' consequent unwillingness to touch the subject. This understandable squeamishness seems to have effectively deterred democracies from competing in the war of ideas and ideals on *any* front.

The question is too important, however, to be shunned much longer. Western publics are also becoming squeamish about massacres in airport terminals. If the subject were handled intelligently, informed publics might agree that in a choice of evils, terrorism was worse than government publicity to help control it.

In place of repressive state terror which for centuries provided the standard government response to challenges to its authority, and still does in many Third World and all Marxist-Leninist states, democratic countries have developed doctrines of counter-insurgency and counter-

Spring 1986

terrorism. These doctrines confine government, police and military to lawful reactions. No one likes such processes, but they are not necessarily regarded as a threat to democracy and are accepted as a counter-terrorism tool. What is needed, surely, is an acceptable doctrine of counter-propaganda to complement counter-insurgency.[20]

The controls suggested are that government counter-propaganda should operate within the accepted norms of publicity or public relations. It would reject 'black' and 'grey' operations, disinformation, deliberate untruth and all the manipulative characteristics associated with propaganda. Indeed, it would differ from publicity and public relations mainly in its operational aims and its close coordination with all other aspects of counter-terrorism.

Much of this coordination would be connected with the collection and analysis of terrorist propaganda. Another function of the counter-propaganda (CP) staff would be the provision of advice to all concerned with the planning and execution of counter-terrorist operations on what might be called the 'public opinion factor.' The grist for the terrorists' propaganda mill is always provided by blunders of policy or execution, by poorly briefed soldiers or policemen and by nonsensical, aggravating procedures. Proper attention to the public opinion factor could minimize this source of raw material. Another task would be to insure that the news media had access to all levels of responsibility, from the chief to the man on patrol, and that these individuals knew what they were doing, and why, and therefore were able (with training as necessary) to explain their functions convincingly to television, radio and newspaper audiences. If the media found the terrorists and their front spokesmen available, relaxed, articulate and seemingly well-motivated, and authority tight-lipped, tense, monosyllabic and seemingly paranoid, reporting would reflect the contrast. By no means should law-and-order people become excessively garrulous. Instead they should be, and be seen to be, in command, quietly confident, and on the side of the angels.

Only when authority's house was in order would CP staffs address the outside world. Existing PR staffs handle this function already, if they are doing their jobs properly, by providing accurate information and the government viewpoint. CP staffs would assist this process by their analysis of the terrorists' psychological strategy, by recognizing hostile themes and provocations as they emerged, so that they could be preempted or exposed, and by uncovering the topic of propaganda as a news story in its own right. Terrorist fronts could be challenged by being asked questions publicly over affiliations and motives. Naturally, CP's liaison with the intelligence staff would allow controlled release of 'hot' material damaging to the cohesion and esteem of terrorist groups. Driving wedges between hardcore terrorists and their circle of sympathizers and fronts is essential to success. Terrorist themes of guilt-transfer, spurious justification and disarmament could command priority attention by CP staffs, since these are the notions which permit even the most discredited and hard-pressed groups to survive.

To a large extent, contact with the public would be through the media. Media coverage of terrorism, while a subject for separate study, is closely linked to propaganda. CP's major challenge would be to persuade the media to recognize the role and importance of terrorist propaganda and the way that the media are often used as transmission belts.

CP could also go directly to the public by purchasing advertizing space and time, through ministerial and other speeches, conferences, seminars, film production and other means. If saving fuel, driving safely, avoiding drugs and moderating sex are appropriate subjects for publicity of this kind, so, one might think, is saving innocent life.

Remarkably, however, many may not agree. Opposition political parties are likely to object on the grounds that these measures are political and therefore improper topics for publicly-funded advertizing. In a democracy, counter-terrorist measures of all kinds as a rule have to be introduced slowly, at times when public opinion and opposition parties will tolerate them. All that has been suggested about CP, therefore, relates to a certain stage in a terrorist campaign when public and media are disillusioned with the groups and sickened by their violence. At this stage, a bi-partisan publicity policy can possibly be agreed between ruling and opposition parties. Indeed, if a government attempts to move too fast in this field it may polarize public opinion, providing the terrorist with a ready-made constituency of sympathizers.

CONCLUSION

Above and beyond the minor tactics of countering terrorist propaganda, the West must endeavour to arm itself psychologically to defend democracy. This is not a non sequitur. Terrorism directed at the democracies is an attack on democracy itself, because terrorism by its very nature proclaims that elected governments and their laws are subordinate to demands backed by violence or the threat of violence. Academics sensibly separate method from cause in their analysis of terrorism. Nevertheless, in endeavours to exclude value judgement, one ought not to overlook the method's inherently anti-democratic character, and this caution applies equally to politicians and opinion-formers.

Jorge Nef recognized the West's moral dilemma in respect of terrorism as early as 1979, when he wrote:

> There is an alarming psycho-cultural aspect to contemporary terrorism. This is the growing acceptance of violence as inevitable and legitimate ... In an echo of "the war to end all wars," we have even glorified violence as the solution to violence. It is this trend in our culture that makes the human tragedy of terrorism acceptable — tactically expedient in the short run, morally justifiable in the long run.[21]

The West's ambivalent attitude towards terrorism may be a manifestation of a wider spiritual-cultural malaise. Symptomatic are the notions that nothing in the Western heritage is worth defending, that the use of force to defend democracy is illegitimate, and that any amount of violence is justifiable in the hands of 'progressive' forces, because history is on their side, making victory inevitable. It is as though the totalitarian lurking inside each and every one of us is busy rationalizing and compromising, hoping that the human half of our being will capitulate.

Henri Bergson argued that time spent refuting a rival philosophy was time wasted. Instead, the good philosophy was "of itself able to displace the erroneous idea" becoming, "without our having taken the trouble of refuting anyone, the best of refutations."[22] At this cultural-spiritual level the battle against terrorism merges with the battle against totalitarianism. Political, spiritual and cultural leadership are in the end even more important than intelligence, response teams and firepower. Without surrendering objectivity and independence, scholars who value democracy may have a duty to help launch the ideas that will displace the erroneous philosophy.

Footnotes

An earlier version of this paper was given at the University of Aberdeen's April 1986 conference: Research on Terrorism, an International Conference.

1. NATO Glossary of Military Terms, p. 2-205.
2. Grant Wardlaw, *Political Terrorism: Theory, Tactics, and Counter-Measures* (Cambridge: Cambridge University Press, 1982), p. 16.
3. Concerning propaganda by deed, see Walter Laqueur, *Terrorism* (London: Weidenfeld and Nicolson, 1977), p. 67; concerning 'theatre', see Brian M. Jenkins, *International Terrorism: A New Mode of Conflict* (Santa Monica, Ca: Rand Corporation P-5261, 1974), p. 4.
4. Michael Elliott-Bateman, "The Battlefronts of People's War," in Michael Elliott-Bateman, John Ellis and Tom Bowden, *Revolt to Revolution: Studies in the 19th and 20th Century European Experience* (Manchester: Manchester University Press, Rowman and Littlefield, 1974), pp. 314-315.
5. Jacques Ellul, *Propaganda: The Formation of Men's Attitudes* (New York: Knopf, 1965), Vintage edition, 1973, p. 29.
6. *Ibid.*
7. Baruch A. Hazan, *Soviet Propaganda: A Case Study of the Middle East Conflict* (Jerusalem: Keter Publishing, 1976), pp. 19-25.
8. See Carl von Clausewitz, *On War* ed. and trans. Michael Howard and Peter Paret, (Princeton: Princeton University Press, 1976), p. 370; on guilt transfer generally, see Maurice Tugwell, "Guilt Transfer," in David C. Rapoport and Yonah Alexander (eds.), *The Morality of Terrorism: Religious and Secular Justifications* (New York: Pergamon, 1982), pp. 275-289.
9. In El Salvador the theme was given credibility by the brutal government and right-wing repression of the early 1980s. The notion that all deaths were attributable to the regime was therefore made easy to promulgate. See Liisa North, *Bitter Grounds: Roots of Revolt in El Salvador* (Kitchener, Ontario: Between the Lines, 1981), p. 108; Tommie Sue Montgomery, *Revolution in El Salvador: Origins and Evolution* (Boulder, Co: Westview, 1982), p. 191; Marcel Niedergang, "Death Squads back on the rampage in El Salvador," *Washington Post*, January 22, 1985.
10. Stated explicitly by Martin McGuinness, Provisional IRA leader in an interview during BBC television documentary *Northern Ireland: At the Edge of the Union* (Broadcast in U.K. in 1985 and in USA on Public Broadcast Service, February 18, 1986).
11. Robert Taber, *The War of the Flea: Guerrilla Warfare Theory and Practice* (London: Paladin, 1970), pp. 29-30.

12. Quoted *Time,* October 22, 1984, p. 38.
13. For an example of violence supporting propaganda, see Maria McGuire, *To Take Arms* (London, 1973), p 75.
14. Quoted *Globe and Mail* (Toronto), July 23, 1982.
15. Quoted *Philadelphia Inquirer,* June 16, 1985, p. 6.
16. Text of FALN communiqué, reissued by the Prairie Fire Organizing Committee (a Weather Underground front), January 8, 1983.
17. See Mark Falcoff, *Small Countries, Large Issues: Studies in U.S.-Latin American Asymmetries* (Washington, D.C.: American Enterprise Institute, 1984), pp. 13-33; see also, Thomas Lobe, "The Rise and Demise of the Office of Public Safety," *Armed Forces and Society,* vol. 9, no. 2 (Winter 1983), pp. 195, 211, n. 27.
18. *Globe and Mail* (Toronto), March 14, 1981, p. 10; Falcoff, *Small Countries; The National Reporter,* Winter 1986, pp. 18-21.
19. See Ze'ev Chafets, "Beirut and the Great Media Cover-Up," *Commentary,* September 1984, pp. 20-29.
20. This section is developed from Maurice Tugwell, *Revolutionary Propaganda and Possible Counter-Measures* (unpublished doctoral thesis, King's College, London, 1979), pp. 318-335.
21. Jorge Nef, "Reign of Terror," *Weekend Magazine,* May 5, 1979.
22. Henri Bergson, quoted Will Durant, *The Story of Philosophy* (Washington Square ed.; New York: Simon and Schuster, 1926), pp. 462-463.

[3]

When Terrorists Do the Talking: Reflections on Terrorist Literature

Bonnie Cordes

Introduction

Much research has been devoted to examining what terrorists have done in the past and to identifying trends for predicting what they might do in the future. Less attention, however, has been focused on terrorist motivations, mindset or indeed, on *terrorists'* self-perception. By using the primary materials provided by the terrorists themselves, that is, memoirs, statements, interviews, and communiqués, much information about the terrorist mindset and decision-making can be gleaned.

While sending a message of fear and intimidation through their violent actions, the terrorists must also use written and spoken language to legitimize, rationalize, and justify their actions. Although there are ample historic examples of appealing causes and precedents for terrorism,[1] the rationales for terrorism today frequently undergo severe strain. In the 1980s violence is directed against societies with more ample means than ever available to its citizens to express and redress grievances. Such a paradox requires extensive explanation by the terrorist to rationalize and justify his actions not only to an audience of perceived or potential sympathizers, but also to himself. Although terrorism is often described as a form of communication, terrorists are rather poor communicators. Like many poor writers, what they lack in clarity they often make up for in quantity. Yet what terrorists do say about themselves is often more revealing than they intend.

The fundamental contradiction the terrorists must deal with is that while they deliberately employ what we in fact regard as terrorist violence, they characterize their actions as something else.[2] While a criminal may accept that he is indeed a criminal, a terrorist goes to extraordinary lengths to deny that he is a terrorist. This denial may consist not only of semantic denial but of recharacterizing themselves as freedom fighters, revolutionaries, etc., and at the same time depicting the state and its representatives as the criminals and the terrorists.[3] This war of labels becomes terribly important in the contest between authorities and the terrorist challengers to win the sympathies of the public. Rather than be ignored, this terrorist 'name-calling' should be listened to carefully. Terrorist statements give us our best, and sometimes, only inside view of terrorist life and thinking within the group. To comprehend the terrorist mindset it is crucial to uncover the rationale, motivations, and mechanisms for denial. The rebels claim to be using terrorist violence as only a part of a larger, revolutionary strategy. Terrorism, they often claim, is merely one, necessary step in a broader struggle. Yet the revolution they propose is difficult to grasp – it demands that they communicate their own purpose, role, rationale, and legitimacy to the people for whom they claim to wage the battle. They must show that the violence is useful; thus they engage themselves in a necessary verbal, as well as violent strategy. And to convince others, they must themselves be convinced.[4]

In 1979 Nathan Leites recognized that, although much work of varied nature is being conducted on what terrorists do and some on what makes them do it, very little at all considers 'what they thought they were doing', or more precisely 'what good [they thought] it would do'.[5] There are several reasons for this gap. First of all, there is a paucity of relevant data provided by the rebels themselves. When terrorists write or speak about themselves it is often indirectly. Terrorist violence is meant to carry a message that is not always heard or understood as the terrorists would like it to be: rather than communicating 'mayhem and destruction' with a particular bombing, for instance, they would prefer that their audience read 'solidarity with the oppressed peoples of the Third World'. So, not only do they throw bombs, but they also have to write. Often unconsciously, it appears, the purposes of communiqués are not only to explain their actions to others but to persuade the terrorists themselves that what they have done was justified, was appropriate, and carried sufficient weight in the pursuit of their cause. Most material, however, is event-related, that is, written for or just after a particular terrorist action, or in the form of declaratory communiqués. Occasionally the terrorists will issue explanatory political tracts, give patchy interviews with often sympathetic journalists, or – on the *very* rare occasion when a terrorist lives long enough and has the inclination – write memoirs. What does exist of this sort of material is rarely published and even more difficult to obtain in the original. Last but not least, the terrorist literature that is available provides ponderous, and often repetitive, reading. Consequently, a valuable primary source is frequently neglected.

By listening to what some terrorists have to say, this analysis suggests how terrorists see themselves, what they think they are doing, and what they think their actions will accomplish; it also proposes a simple framework for a more systematic examination of the terrorists' view of themselves and their actions. Terrorist communications can be analyzed from two different aspects: how they persuade (or intend to persuade) others (what I call the *propaganda aspect*) and how they persuade themselves (the *auto-propaganda aspect*). Keeping these two ostensible purposes in mind when reading terrorist literature we can perhaps address Leites' question '... how do they make it plausible to themselves that their acts serve the attainment of their goal?'[6] It is the mechanics of such self-explanation that provide us with valuable insights into the workings and mindset of the group.

Focus

The existence of several different types of terrorist groups, many with differing aims and socio-political contexts, further complicates the study of terrorist literature and thwarts most attempts at generalization. Part of the complexity of terrorism is the fact that it is conducted by a variety of idiosyncratic individuals with widely divergent national and socio-cultural backgrounds. Efforts to provide an overall 'terrorist profile' is misleading, for as Jerrold Post cautions, 'there are as nearly as many variants of personality who become involved in terrorist pursuits as there are variants of personality'.[7] To mitigate the errors inherent in making generalizations, a study must necessarily limit itself to an examination of terrorists from a particular geographical area, and with similar ideological bent. Such categorization simplifies and minimizes error through over-generalizations. Eventually it may be possible to make useful cross-national, cross-cultural, and cross-ideological comparisons. In the cases taken for this study the assumption is that, although a number of nationalities are represented, they share the experience of being 'Western' and 'European' and claim similar ideological frameworks of the radical left.

Post makes a useful distinction between 'anarchic-ideologues' such as the Italian Red Brigades or the German Red Army Faction and 'nationalist-secessionist' groups such as the Spanish Basques of ETA or the Irish Republican Army, stating that

> There would seem to be a profound difference between terrorists bent on destroying their own society, the 'world of their fathers,' and those whose terrorist activities carry on the mission of their fathers. To put it in other words, for some, becoming terrorists is an act of retaliation for real and imagined hurts *against the society of their parents*; for others, it is an act of retaliation against society *for the hurt done to their parents* .... This would suggest more conflict, more psychopathology, among those committed to anarchy and destruction of society ... .[8]

To illustrate the proposed framework for examining terrorist literature, this study uses a variety of material written and spoken by European 'anarchic-ideologues' – specifically, the major left-wing groups found in France, West Germany, Italy, and Belgium, frequently categorized in very general terms as anarchist/millenialists or, more recently, 'Euro-terrorists'.[9] This analysis employs material from Belgian groups such as the Communist Combatant Cells (CCC) and the Revolutionary Front for Proletarian Action (FRAP); from French groups such as *Action Directe* (AD); from German groups such as *Rote Armee Fraktion* (RAF), Revolutionary Cells (RZ), and *Rote Zora*; and from Italian groups such as *Brigate Rosse* (RB) and *Prima Linea* (PL).[9]

Although these particular groups have different ages,[10] all trace their roots and initial inspiration to the student revolts in Europe in 1968, originating in the protest movement against the Vietnam War. Focusing most of their energies on changing or overthrowing the governments of their respective countries, they share a common hatred for the United States and claim allegiance to a revolutionary brotherhood dedicated to solidarity with Third World liberation movements. It was in 1981 that the Red Brigades, considered purely an Italian problem, first struck out at NATO with its kidnapping of US General Dozier. Periodically, thereafter, other anti-NATO attacks occurred throughout Europe, culminating in 1984 and 1985 with a declaration of unity announced by the German Red Army Faction and the French *Action Directe*. Joint actions by these groups, with implied Italian inspiration, along with continued and apparently co-ordinated attacks against American, NATO, and Israeli targets by the entire spectrum of radical left groups throughout Europe (from Greece, to Portugal, to Belgium), led to the coining of the phrase 'Euro-terrorism' and the suggestion that an international master cell was in place guided by a single objective of destroying the Western alliance. European terrorist groups enjoyed an increase in stature while European countries scurried to work together as cooperatively as they imagined the terrorist groups were already doing successfully.

Although these groups are particularly interesting because of their longevity and attempt at unification, the choice of these groups as illuminators of the framework is purely arbitrary. The conclusions to be drawn, however, about the usefulness of terrorist literature are by no means limited to these groups.

The Framework

Behavioral assessments have been made of terrorist literature, using psycho-linguistics, psychiatric assessments, psychologic analysis, propaganda analysis and even graphological analysis.[11] More appropriate for this type of literature is the use of traditional content analysis which examines the texts as a whole rather than breaking them down into phrases and words. Although the original work is the most valid object for study, much information of less specific nature can still be derived from translations. And for any such study a familiarity with the group and the political context is essential.

The problem is to organize such a general content analysis so as to reach beyond speculative surmising and make available information about the inner workings of the terrorist group. If one accepts Jerrold Post's argument that a key motivation for membership in a terrorist group is the sense of belonging and the fraternity of like-minded members, it follows that there will be enormous apprehensions that the group may fall apart. With little or nothing to belong to what does a terrorist do? This issue can be monitored through the consistent readings of terrorist literature with a view to specifically pinpointing the group's sensitivities, the internal disagreements, and moral weaknesses to ascertain vulnerabilities. First, the audience of a communiqué or tract must be delineated. Normally, the purpose of the writing is to reach more than one audience. The government is the most prominent one. The communiqué claims credit and offers justification for an action. It threatens further action, and often demands specific changes or moves to prevent their further use of violence. A second prominent audience is the group's 'constituency' – 'the people', 'the workers', or 'the oppressed peoples of the Third World'. Their purpose is to inform this audience of their purpose, their courage, and their selflessness; to proclaim their love and sacrifice for this people they no longer see, to engender support amongst them, to draw sympathy and perhaps, to mobilize them.

A third important and crucial, but less prominent audience is the members of other like-minded groups. Whether in competition or in cooperation with one another, terrorist groups nurture large, sensitive egos. Their pride requires that they transmit their worth to all others – acceptance into the 'terrorist community' is not only essential to their national and/or international standing but also generates a pool of sympathizers and potential recruits. Proclamations of solidarity for other groups enhance their image and buy them matched salutes of solidarity, creating the effect of a larger and more powerful organization.

The most important and least obvious audience is the terrorists themselves. To maintain morale, the members of a group must feel good about themselves. Writing is the expression of the group's immediate feelings and an attempt to adjust them constantly upward. Thus, the *auto-propaganda* effect of the communiqués is to applaud and glorify the terrorists, to justify and even to criticize their actions, as well as to motivate members for further activity, and, as described by Albert Bandura, to promote what he calls the 'moral disengagement' of the group.[12]

Assuming that terrorists are products of the society in which they live (setting aside for the moment psychopaths or otherwise disturbed persons who may be, but rarely are members) we can also expect that they have incorporated to some extent certain moral standards and rules of conduct. This assumption is further strengthened when we realize that terrorists are deliberately overstepping moral bounds and therefore *must* be aware of what they are doing.[13] Violating the rules brings social condemnation, but interestingly enough and more importantly, it also brings *self*-condemnation activated, Bandura asserts, by learned 'internal regulators'.[14] Bandura describes ways in which one can turn off these regulators and be 'disengaged' from inhumane conduct, and those mechanisms are particularly relevant in an examination of terrorist literature.

Although he points out that this act of 'disengagement' is not unusual (people frequently must rationalize actions they carry out that have or could have injurious effects) it appears that it is an overriding concern of the terrorists. It has long been known that an indoctrination process is necessary to prepare members of a terrorist group to carry out violent acts.[15] Bandura calls this the generation of 'self-exonerations needed to neutralize self-sanctions'[16] or what we might call rationalizing guilt.

Because so much of the 'Euro-terrorist' literature serves the auto-propaganda purpose and since the aim of this study is to show how terrorists understand themselves, the remainder of the essay elaborates auto-propaganda themes. One tends to picture terrorist activity as wholly extraordinary but ironically it is striking how often and how emphatically terrorists describe their activities in moral language ordinary society is accustomed to using. Euro-terrorists' pamphlets are written to support a 'war', and that term is used in a literal not a metaphorical sense. For it is in war, Franco Ferracuti says, that society permits violence, and 'The "normal" [not insane] terrorist is therefore like a soldier outside of time and space living in a reality of war that exists only in his or her fantasy'.[17] Comparing real war with the terrorists' war he argues that the terrorists are actually attempting to replicate certain conditions which must exist for a war we can justify to take place. The process involves identifying a crisis (or creating one), building an organized collectivity of opposition, transforming the 'enemy' into something 'alien and hostile', and building a reciprocal 'maniacal feeling of increasing power and invulnerability'. Elements such as these are abundant in terrorist literature with constant references to the 'armed struggle', 'war on imperialist war', and to characterizations of themselves as 'soldiers'.

> BUILD UP THE POLITICAL-MILITARY FRONT IN WESTERN EUROPE AS PART OF THE WORLDWIDE STRUGGLE BETWEEN THE INTERNATIONAL PROLETARIAT AND THE IMPERIALIST BOURGEOISIE.
>
> NEVER BE DETERRED BY THE ENORMOUS DIMENSIONS OF YOUR OWN GOALS.
>
> THE WEST EUROPEAN GUERRILLAS ARE CONVULSING THE EUROPEAN CENTER.[18]

To maintain the 'war footing' it is at the same time necessary to discredit legal or peaceful attempts to fight the battle. In the following excerpt, the italicized words (my emphasis) demonstrate this fascination with the image that the terrorists are 'at war' because of the imminence of war, and the futility of other non-violent means, in a declaration of responsibility for the bombing of a computer office of the French Ministry of Defense:

> *Wars, war economy*, a continuing economy based on *arms*: This is the central characteristic of the economy of imperialism, a question of *the two great wars, the cold war of the 1950s, the some 250 armed conflicts* the world experienced from 1945 to 1984, the intensification of *weapons* spending ... *militarism* clearly appears as the lifesaver to which capitalism systematically clings whenever the

> forces inherent in its own system risk sinking it in the abyss of *crisis*. Confronted with the need inherent in the system, *it is ridiculous to look to peaceful pacifism.*[19]

To the terrorists the time is long past for engaging the legal system of the state or using peaceful protest to change the system. The 'capitalists'' cards are stacked against them. The reigning system has built-in mechanisms for 'pacification of the antagonism of the masses'. While 'the bell jar of state security that is in place over society does not disappear, but rather is felt by increasing numbers of the people, the screw of impoverization that they have applied begins to take hold'.[20] The terrorist is not deluded.

It may be that violence, terror, *illegal* actions breed more satisfaction and *possible* results despite the higher risks. Always the terrorist effort is described, as any just war would be, as the strategy of last resort. It is not seen as a more expedient course, nor is there ever a limit outlined in the pamphlets, as contrasted with the memoirs, which indicate that the desire to act frequently determines the decision to take up arms.

> Our original conception of the organization implied a connection between the urban guerrilla and the work at the base. We would like it if each and all of us could work in the neighbourhoods and factories, in socialist groups that already exist, influence discussion, experience and learn. This has proved impossible .... Some say that the possibilities for agitation, propaganda and organisation are far from being eradicated and that only when they are, should we pose the question of arms. We say: it will not really be possible to profit from any political actions as long as armed struggle does not appear clearly as the goal of the politicisation, ...[21]

The auto-propaganda effect of these messages is to persuade the terrorist the enemy is real, the cause just, and the terrorist's existence not only justified, but called for due to the 'urgency' of the moment. It is very difficult but necessary to maintain this sense of urgency. For while they wait, discuss, and delay action the enemy is overtaking them: 'the period of small steps [by the imperialists] and of hitting individual targets is over; the acceleration of the process of reconstruction is now proceeding with the regularity of a steam roller ... [over the bodies of the workers].'[22] Indeed, the terrorists are endowed with particular qualities that allow them to carry on the struggle, 'to work towards a strategy of communist liberation of the proletariat' because they can 'regard the present with the insights of tomorrow ...' and recognize that the 'historic task of the communists – both as a faction and as an organized avant garde of the proletariat – is to understand the movement of capital in its entirety ... to understand ... the development of the revolutionary consciousness of the proletariat ...'.[23] Although the terrorist relies upon 'Marxist analysis in order to understand reality',[24] without violent action such 'Marxist methodology would deteriorate to a static theorizing about reality'. With both methodology *and* action, the terrorists feel they can 'really develop the dynamic of construction/destruction'.[25]

Although at times difficult to comprehend, terrorism is a rational strategy, one in which the benefits exceed the costs for its employers. The driving force and justifications for the group's existence are moral. Thus, the 'just' war is the battle against evil, and always in self-defense. Going against the prevailing system and mores, and using violence in a 'legitimate' fashion can provide individuals with personal satisfaction far beyond the stated 'cause'. Obviously, there are many motives for engaging in such unconventional activities.

When the media 'misrepresents our combat' by introducing 'questioning and suspicion'[26] and by labelling the combatants as 'anarchists', more explanations are needed, and more communiqués are generally issued. Terrorists treasure their commitment to the people, believe the feelings are reciprocal, and fashion themselves as adventurous young people who, with little trouble and much ingenuity, are able to make an impact on the state. Intrigue is the exciting part of the game and 'intelligence [covert action] is not a shameful disease ... but a necessary practice ...'.[27]

Memoirs of defectors and depositions given by repentant terrorists reveal that terrorists themselves have debated the issues of the morality of violence and just what constitutes 'terrorism'.[28] Living underground, such individuals slowly become divorced from reality, descending into a world in which they wage Ferracuti's 'fantasy way'. They can never rest or withdraw from the struggle, however. The German defector Klein describes the misery of his life after leaving the group still hiding underground, but this time without his comrades, living in fear of *them* as well as of the authorities. Klein has swapped one struggle for another.[29]

Because the abstract boundary between political terror and crime is not clear, there is a continuing need to elevate the terrorist motive above that of the criminal, a need that becomes elemental to the terrorist's perception of his success.[30] This need to justify and validate his violent actions becomes a consuming part of his existence, for the terrorist is *aware* of the moral, legal boundaries he oversteps which is why he must fashion himself to be a soldier.[31] But not only is he a soldier, he must also be a victim, one whose pain assures that he will prevail: 'Not those who cause the most suffering will be victorious, but rather those who suffer the most!'[32] Dying for the cause is the ultimate propaganda act and proof of one's dedication to others as well as to oneself. Turning the terrorist violence against the terrorist becomes an exquisite paradox – passively killing oneself so as to believe oneself.[33]

Apparently, the auto-propaganda aspect of words and actions can at times become too powerful and dominating, to the point that the group loses touch with reality. Popular support can hardly be gained by a group that does not become a symbol of justice and liberty. Between 1980 and early 1984, limited to avoiding arrest and running from police, and occasional seemingly meaningless bombings, the European terrorist groups lost what minor public support and interest they had previously enjoyed. There was a tendency to lose sight of their strategic need to mobilize the masses and to open up the 'path' to their goal. Condemning aimless violence (and a violence which must have appeared self-serving) AD, RAF, and new CCC communiqués tried to correct this situation in a stream of written material during the summer and fall of 1984 in the wake of the European peace movement and the addition of nuclear missiles to the continent.

The 'enemy' was now characterized on a grander, more evil scale, and its 'true character' was more evident than before. The time was right, according to the terrorist, to achieve some remarkable results:

> Attacks on the multinational structures of NATO, on its bases and strategies, on its plans and propaganda, are bringing about a transformation of the awareness and practices of the proletariat, going beyond its national characteristics and bringing about an international organizational advance.[34]

While 'this situation is understood by all workers ...' (it is tactfully added so as not to condescend to the prized constituency), the response to the terrorism provides a further augmentation of 'the capital of sympathy and unification which we were in the process of accumulating ...'.[35]

What has been called 'Euro-terrorism' actually developed as a concept years before its manifestations in joint communiqués and action. The shift from clearly indigenous groups to a 'West European guerrilla' was more an expansion of a state of mind than a radical change in type of operations. Terrorists in Italy and Germany have histories stretching back to the late 1960s, when as purely indigenous groups, they held programs to overthrow their respective establishments. Although they had all, to one extent or another, engaged in activities or at least in rhetoric, targeting 'imperialist' and US institutions, the focus had been on domestic targets. Concentrating on such actions now was to be considered 'utopian presumptiveness' since 'detaching one's own territory from the imperialist chain' is not only impracticable but selfish.[36] Within the new concept, it is admitted that each national struggle is equally necessary and must take place simultaneously, but that unity in the struggle should supercede. Yet the newly declared association of the French AD and German RAF (in January 1985) has not kept either group, or the newly formed Belgian CCC, from persisting in their purely national-minded attacks or statements. In practice, despite the talks of unity, the groups remain greatly concerned with anti-establishment actions, with political developments in their own countries, and particularly with the fate of their own comrades and the treatment of 'political prisoners'. Such concerns are reflected in page after page of communiqués explaining the failure of operations, and condemning actions by authorities against incarcerated comrades.

The 1985 announcement of unity had declared that 'It is now necessary and possible to open a new phase in the development of a true revolutionary strategy in the Imperialist Centers ...' with the purpose of creating 'a West

European guerrilla',[37] where each of the European groups was to continue acting on its own national program. Keeping in mind the shared struggle, although recognizing that 'Each one must fight in the sector where he has the most strength', the rebels would at the same time 'always offensively [link] the fight to those of other proletarians involved in other sectors of the same struggle'.[38] The apparent shift in strategy of several European terrorist groups simultaneously brought out a spontaneous reaction from government officials used to flirting with the notion of terrorist conspiracies. The media was full of talk of the need for European cooperation against the united terrorist front. The terrorist campaign of joint actions and communiqués was credited, and rightly so, with having tremendous impact:

> There is a specter going around in Europe: the specter of 'Euro-terrorism'. All forces of old Europe have aligned themselves in a holy crusade in order to hunt down this specter: the Pope and NATO, Paris and Washington, Scelfaro and Barrionuevo, Fabius and Kohl, etc. The entire repressive apparatus of old Europe, the Europe of the alliance, has placed itself in a state of emergency in view of the rise of revolutionary guerrillas.[39]

An educational process was necessary, they state, part of which would be effected through writings, part through joint actions. The union was envisaged by the terrorists as a requisite step in revolutionary strategy where 'Today it is important to regard Western Europe as a homogeneous territory, where the formation of a unified revolutionary pole is possible ...'[40] but not to be accomplished overnight. 'Concretely put: we regard the process of the new-formation of the totality of the European proletariat into one single proletarian faction as a process that has not yet been concluded'.[41]

This union of 'internationalization of the proletariat' is necessary *because* the *enemy* is unified. But the unification of the European terrorist groups into a 'metropolis proletariat' will not be 'a soup in which all experiences are blended ...'[42] but will recognize national differences. Although the very idea of a 'front' is called an 'open concept', it is insisted that there must be resistance to any purely independent structures.

Ironically, the union of revolutionary groups into an 'anti-imperialist front in Western Europe' is required to fend off the unification of Western Europe, which is considered the next step in 'imperialist domination'. The most 'aggressive of the capitalist factions' is the military-industrial complex, considered responsible for the impetus to militarize, homogenize, and 'Americanize' Western Europe into 'one counterrevolutionary bloc'.[43] The crisis is imminent and action, not pacifism, is necessary *now* because of 'the reality' of the coming 'imperialist war' and the risk of being 'damned to be "cannon fodder" in the coming conflicts and, until that point, to be "profit fodder" in the Near East, Africa, etc.'.[44] Exhorting to action is not to take the offensive, however. Revolutionary acts are in response to what is characterized as an offensive threat. Thus, an action is justified if it is accepted that, 'That which is destroying us must itself be destroyed ...'.[45]

To believe these words and be able to act on them is a whole process in itself. The techniques for the necessary 'moral disengagement' are heavily disguised and not easily recognized. Bandura suggests that part of the process is carried out by what he terms 'euphemistic labelling' and 'dehumanization'.[46] Renaming themselves, their actions, their victims and their enemies accords the terrorist respectability. What they say and what they do are actually two entirely different things. A May Day bombing, for instance, is an 'intervention on behalf of the works', or an 'affirmation of the proletarian value of the world holiday of the oppressed'. Much effort goes into characterizing the enemy. The David and Goliath theme is prevalent – there is nobility and honor in the courage and determination of an oppressed party who dares to strike out at the 'oppressor'.

The use of euphemisms or name-calling is profuse throughout the communiqués of every group (that is, 'pigs', 'imperialist exploiters', 'carrions and their consorts', etc.). Often the name-calling process degenerates to the point where, to further ascribe guilt and worthiness of punishment, the terrorists divest the enemy of human qualities. By imputing 'bestial qualities' to the targets they choose to attack makes them subhuman or even animals. 'Pigs' deserve nothing more than what the terrorists deliver them.

Frequently the state is labelled *terrorist*, particularly with regard to treatment of the rebels themselves (such as 'the terrorist program against the prisoners') and frequently with regard to actions seen as directed against the rest of the people in general: 'the major power of NATO has raised state terrorism against the anti-imperialist guerrilla groups, the liberation movements and the population, which are refusing their loyalty, to an official government policy'.[47] Some analysts would label this technique as projection on the part of the rebels, but they are not the only ones to do so:

> The demonizing of the guerrillas, the witch hunt, the *projection of terrorism* onto the guerrillas are losing their effectiveness, and no longer mobilize on behalf of the state. On the contrary, terror is the concept that clings like tar to a system that only destroys, suppresses and stands in the way of any kind of human development (emphasis mine).[48]

It was previously noted that a terrorist prefers to call himself a 'revolutionary' or a 'freedom fighter'. Often reference is made to historical moments and historical figures for validation, in what Bandura terms 'advantageous comparison'.[49] A technique used to elevate the terrorist sense of what he is and what he is doing, such comparisons frequently use quotes from illustrious revolutionary figures – Marx, as we have seen with the use of the Communist Manifesto, or Lenin, or Che – and are used to explain that 'The present belongs to the struggle; the future belongs to us. (Che)'[50] and that the terrorists are merely carrying on the struggle.

Again, through recitations of the cruelties carried out by the state, the terrorists appear relatively innocent. Often this technique is employed when terrorist members are arrested and held in prison. The RAF used such an occasion to spell out the atrocities (solitary confinement and 'sensory deprivation') committed against their comrades by the German authorities, resulting in their suicide/'murders'.

> As a symbol of the revolutionary potential that exists in every corner of W. German cities, the RAF had to be annihilated before they became heroes and examples for the malcontents to follow. And so on 18 Oct. 1977, Andreas Baader, Jan Carl Raspe and Gundrun Ensslin were murdered in Stuttgart-Stammheim prison.[51]

> The number of political prisoners suffering from the terrorist conditions of prisons are not limited to urban guerrillas, but include lawyers, authors, publishers and bookshop keepers.[52]

Such restructuring of their own behavior in contrast to that of the state provides not only self-exoneration but also, states Bandura, self-glorification and a source of self-pride.[53] Dehumanizing the enemy becomes automatic with practice. Klein, in an interview given from hiding after his defection from the RAF, spoke of his fear of having a weapon with him *now* because he was unsure of his control over it. Possession caused what he called an 'over-estimation of your opponent' and subsequent use became easily justified with little forethought.[54] When no one technique will satisfactorily transform or 'whitewash' a violent act, there is always a way to deny responsibility for it in the first place.[55] Unfortunately for them, the hard-sought exposure given to the terrorists is not to their liking. When actions have unintended consequences, groups have been known to withdraw their claims. In 1981, when *Action Directe* was still very young and as yet inexperienced in the fine arts of assassination, it found itself in a cooperative venture with a Lebanese group in Paris (the so-called Lebanese Armed Revolutionary Faction or LARF) which was involved in the elimination of American and Israeli diplomats and functionaries. A bomb placed under the car of Roderick Grant, then American diplomatic councillor at the embassy in Paris, was discovered, but not before AD claimed responsibility for placing it. LARF also claimed to have taken part in the action. Two members of the Paris bomb squad were killed instantly as they attempted to defuse the device. When news of their deaths hit the press, AD members, presumably dismayed by this turn of events, promptly telephoned authorities to disown their part in the action. Such a disclaimer is instructive of a number of possible tendencies: either the deaths were actually unintended or some or all of the members decided belatedly that they wanted no part of such violence; possibly there was disagreement within the group about the prudence or justification for such action; or, once the news was broadcast, the group feared the negative public reaction.

If a disclaimer is not practical, elaborate explanations may be required. The CCC May Day bombing, which claimed the lives of two firemen at the scene of the burning van containing explosives, prompted the group to displace responsibility for the deaths. To punctuate their accusation, they bombed the 'head financial and logistics office' of the Brussels gendarmerie. According to the CCC, 'The entire world will understand the selection of this target for attack because of the responsibility of the gendarmerie ...',[56] presumably for the firemen's deaths. The firemen were the first fatalities of the extensive bombing activity initiated by the CCC in October 1984. The media and government response was outrage, but communiqués suggest that the CCC experienced a severe reaction to the event as well. Rather than expressing remorse or guilt, however, they express their indignation: 'The deaths of these two men shock us deeply and arouse our rage at those responsible ...'.[57] Several pages are dedicated to explaining how the responsibility for the firemen's deaths could and should be placed at the doorstep of the 'gendarmerie' and not at their own. Their dismay lies more in the fact that 'the deaths of these public servants has destroyed and obviated the power of our initiative, has concealed the correctness of the attack ...' and that 'the police campaign which is being carried out in the media concerning our so-called "contempt for human life" is a despicable falsification of our political texts ...'.[58] Although they regret the deaths, they are convinced of the appropriateness of the target. It is the deaths that 'in a tragic way' made the act 'incomprehensible and inaccessible to the population as a whole'.[59] The explanation is that the 'pigs' sent the firemen to their deaths, probably because of the 'scorn that the bourgeoisie has for the workers ...' and so that the authorities could 'exploit' the accident.

It is difficult not to hear the remorse of the terrorists, particularly in one passage that nearly sounds like a plea for forgiveness: 'We bow down before the victims and respect the pain of their families and comrades. We understand their rage, but we ask them in view of our explanation to consider against whom this rage should be directed ...'.[60]

Much more difficult to detect in terrorist written works is the attempt to justify actions based on what Bandura terms the 'diffusion of responsibility'[61] where all members of the group share the onus of an action but at the same time no one individual is to blame. Presumably this could be revealed in terrorist confessions or when a group has fractured.[62] This technique is enhanced in groups with rigid hierarchical structures. Here, individual members relinquish personal control over their actions, while honoring their obligation to the group and their commitment to the cause. Group decision-making and collective action can also have the same effect, so that no one person need feel *he* made the choice or the move that brings moral condemnation.

What They Think It Will Accomplish

Most terrorist actions are perfectly suited to distancing oneself from the effects of one's actions. The majority of terrorist attacks are hit and run operations where the actual damage, destruction, and/or deaths need not be witnessed first-hand. As long as the terrorists keep themselves insulated from the effects of their violence, that is, leaving the scene, not dwelling on the news of the dead and injured but rather on the reactions of the authorities, they can avoid dealing with their moral anxieties.

Yet whatever the terrorists believe they will accomplish is fairly well hidden. That they believe they are successfully moving toward this unknown is often stated and with confidence. According to one imprisoned terrorist, 'It is fairly certain that the extent of the armed actions and the massive actions in solidarity with the revolutionary militant prisoners *justify the fear* that has been unleashed on the governments of the member states of NATO ... the success of all of this activity is undeniable.'[63] In piecing together allusions to this future a picture emerges of destroying one society so as to replace it with a new one. This new social system is to be based on the free development of the individual, the emancipation of the proletariat and 'can only come about through the destruction of capitalism and the opening of a path to communist liberation'.[64] Not one of the terrorist authors seems to be able or interested in specifying what the new social system will be like, but all are agreed that 'We want to destroy this society in order to build up' another, one that will be 'a just and classless society, in which production meets the needs of all, not only the needs of a privileged few, ... a society in which "equality for all" no longer has to be demanded, because it has already been realized'.[65] To justify acts of violence, the situation must be black and white, with little room for hesitation. Often using the claim of conspiracy, the groups build the evil enemy, explaining here why violence is necessary and why it is necessary *now*:

> We arrive at this step from the objective situation: The central importance of Western Europe for the reconstruction of imperialism which has become weakened as the result of the liberation struggle of the peoples of the South ... which in turn has resulted in a collision between the growing forces of productivity and the limitations of the world markets. This has led to a global political, economic, and military crisis in the imperialist chain of states, and has now touched the entire imperialist system.[66]

The tone of alarm communicates the necessity of the organization while the murky, sometimes confused explanation portrays the revolutionaries as dedicated, hard-working intellectuals who have clearly thought all of this out. It is hard to imagine the average man on the street getting this message from the widely distributed flyer. Instead, the tract impressed its writer, making him *feel* that this generation of the Red Army Faction had been created in response to a threat. Characterizing the enemy as a conspirator allows the terrorists to refuse to believe what is so apparent and obvious to everyone else. The terrorist plays the part of self-appointed detective with a superior ability to recognize and decipher the state's *real* intentions.

Although he may pose himself as particularly knowledgeable about the purposes of the 'imperialist conspiracy', it is evident that much internal group friction results over these debates. The discussions themselves can lead to disagreement and cleavage with factions following a new, self-determined rationale. All revolutionary groups – terrorist or guerrilla – have had their internal critics. Sometimes these critics, like Hans Joachim Klein and Michael Baumann of the German millenialist groups, for example, have left the underground and written or talked about how the clandestine life of terrorist violence had gone wrong. Debates over the justification for violence, the types of targets, the issues of indiscriminate versus discriminate killing, are endemic to a terrorist group. Such differences of opinion within terrorist groups have on occasion led authorities to believe that a schism existed. Because of the new 'internationalist' focus of AD communiqués, for instance, and the continuation of AD anti-establishment actions, French authorities are convinced of a group split.

Concluding Reflections

Terrorism entails the use of violence for effect, 'speaking with action' rather than with words. Yet the meaning of an act is not always clear, and therefore an integral part of most terrorist activity is the explanation later provided in written and oral forms. Although this explanation is ostensibly directed at the state authorities, or a constituency, or potential recruits, it has rarely been recognized that the explanations are developed to convince the terrorists themselves that what they are doing is correct and justified. An awareness of the auto-propaganda aspect brings a richer dimension to the information normally available to the analyst in terrorist communiqués.

Some groups write more than others. The Belgian Communist Combatant Cells (CCC) has been quite prolific since its inception, while the French *Action Directe* (AD) was never able to sustain a flow of written materials. Save for some interviews and a few short papers, AD's communiqués have often been rather short and brutally to the point, while the CCC will take five pages or more to explain a particular action. The Italian Red Brigades (RB) are known for their voluminous works and painfully detailed documents, while the German Red Army Faction (RAF) wrote about itself and its actions consistently in the early years, but only sporadically since then. Indeed, the absence of any significant declarations by the RAF since 1982 led authorities to believe this was one more indication that the movement was in disarray and weakened.

A necessary caution in analyzing written materials of terrorists is that, while we tend to attribute the declarations to the entire group, the individual author or authors certainly imbue the text with personal elements. It is usually unknown to what extent the texts are approved or censored by other members, although such practices undoubtedly exist. The frequency and quantity of writing may, as mentioned, indicate the health of the group, yet much written material is issued from prison cells by incarcerated members. More likely, it appears that the frequency, quantity, and style of writing depends as much on the availability of an intellectual member prone to written expression as on the overall condition of the group, although it may be this very lack of intellectual leadership that also indicates a group in decline.

Without the 'proper' justification and explanation of the group's violence, and periodic assessment and/or realignment of strategy, terrorist activity tends to deteriorate into mindless or self-serving violence. 'Communication and discussion are necessary because they are the prerequisites for all to learn ...'[67] but at the same time, 'Communism does not develop via radical positions in texts. It expresses itself in a precise analysis of the situation and in a transfer to actual practice ...'.[68] Similarly, during the early days of the RAF, then leader Ulrike Meinhof dedicated herself to espousing revolutionary doctrine for the group, concluding, however, that 'Writing is shit, now let's make the revolution'.[69] With Meinhof's death, Brigitte Monhaupt took over the pen as well as the intellectual leadership of the RAF rather effectively, but with her demise 'on the whole, at least toward the outside, the RAF has become less verbal, and the men and women now prominent in it make very few statements. For example, we have no statements at all ... from current co-leader Christian Klar. But that does not mean he is not a true fanatic.'[70] Klar has since written some rather unintelligible material from his prison cell in Germany, accompanied by some superficially theoretical tracts from Brigitte Monhaupt – it appears that some individuals simply choose to write more than others.

Certain personalities carry the weight and responsibility of writing for the group. Pierre Carette, presumed leader of the Belgian CCC and probable author of their extensive communiqués, has a history of radical activity and as a professional printer, has an intimate association with the written word. The Red Brigades owes its literary debt to figures such as Curcio and Moretti, and the Germans to Mahler, Monhaupt and Meinhof.

An additional caution is necessary in such an analysis of terrorist literature. Each type of material presumably has a particular purpose: policy papers are for internal as well as external consumption to outline strategy and rally support; communiqués are to explain and persuade a larger public and a perceived constituency; memoirs are personal therapeutic autobiographies to justify and evaluate the past. Yet all this material can be seen as focusing on several audiences. The very need, even compulsion, to explain and justify, works to deny the real appearance of the violent actions. And this denial is directed as much at an outer audience as it is to an inner one. Not only need they convince themselves, but other terrorist groups as well. They have a 'constituency' they must answer to, be it fringe sympathizers or potential recruits or the terrorists of other groups. A certain prestige and intellectual sophistication is required to be considered legitimate. The least important audience of all, perhaps, is the government, although the communiqués are often directed to the authorities. The group and the individual author(s) require the written and spoken exercise to build conviction amongst the members and in its audience. There is no greater fan of the terrorist, however, than the terrorist himself. Analyzing the material from these two different aspects should separate one fiction from another and perhaps even provide some useful facts.

Text analysis can be useful in a number of ways. Changes can be detected in the mood and thinking of the group, and at times disharmony can be illuminated. It can provide obvious clues to tactical procedures and changes. Most importantly, however, it can reveal the methods and level of 'moral disengagement' necessary to head off internal disagreements and disenchantment of individual members. Although the analysis should ideally be carried out using the original work, translations can provide a lot of otherwise unavailable information and insights.

Idiosyncratic differences emerge from group to group because of different writers, different nationalities, and different national programs, but the basic characteristics of the European 'anarchic-ideologues' are the same. The groups share (1) obviously, but importantly, a common use of terrorist violence; (2) denial that they are terrorists; (3) the need to portray themselves in a favorable light in order to attract support; (4) the need to rationalize and justify what they do; and (5) the need to feel good about themselves to maintain group cohesion.

A number of basic conclusions consequently emerge. According to the memoirs of defectors and the depositions of repentant terrorists, a life of violence tends to harden or defeat its adherents. Once in the underground it is nearly impossible to leave it intact. Those who do escape are more demoralized than renewed, as Klein indicates in his written work from hiding.

Another impression, but certainly not conclusion from terrorist literature, is that it may be true that European anarchists, unlike other terrorists, belong more to the 'province of psychologists than political analysts ...'.[71] Reality in their terms, is dramatically unreal to us; their continuing attempts to convince themselves and others of this abstract vision is remarkable in its energy and persistance.

A closer assessment needs to be made, but this brief look suggests that, difficult as it is to gauge systematically the frequency and quantity of writing by terrorists the impression is that not only do the groups appear to write less frequently as they age, but by deduction this suggests they may care less about the consequences of their acts. These observations are less evident in the communiqués than in the memoirs or statements of repentants.

The stress of life underground and the continuous struggle to survive often distorts the already 'strange' perceptions of terrorists, according to members of terrorist groups who have defected or recanted. Another form of 'underground life' – the prison – appears to have similar effects on the terrorists. After several years of incarceration, virtually cut off from the outside world, the images they conjure of the people and of the enemy become more and more bizarre.

What about 'Euro-terrorism?' Declarations of 'unity', 'comradeship', 'brotherhood', etc., do not disguise the fact that cooperation is elusive. The 'Western anti-imperialist front' is more a loose confederation of like-minded groups than an actual organizational structure. Intuitively, this failure to unite can be attributed to idiosyncratic group rationales and strong, uncompromising personalities. Attempts at cooperation with each other appear difficult to execute in practice and, if achieved, are often short-lived.

Despite the claims of union, the real focus of these groups is the problems they see in their own countries and political systems. It is not simply a matter of ageing as a group and expanding horizons. On the contrary, the older and more sophisticated the group, the stronger the realization appears to be that because of the inherent imbalance between the group and its chosen enemy the state, no notable changes can be forced into the international environment. The prospect for change at home can be nearly as futile, but time and again these groups have felt they made an impact, if only by the attention they generated from the security services of the state and media coverage. A recent document put out by remnants of the Red Brigades of Italy makes this sentiment clear when its author thanks all the other European revolutionaries for their actions and declarations of solidarity, but insists that the Red Brigades not be distracted and continue with the business at hand – the problems of politics at home. The union of the European groups remains more in the mind of authorities than in the minds of the terrorists, where there is actually more an absorption with self than with the enemy.

Text analysis can be useful if carried out with caution and consistency. Following the writings of a particular group can provide invaluable insights to the workings and mindset of the group, can detect changes in mood and thinking and illuminate disharmony amongst the members or with the members of other groups. Besides providing obvious clues to tactical procedures and changes, terrorist literature unintentionally reveals the methods and intensity of 'moral disengagement' that may be creating tension and conflict within the group. Only by reading and analyzing this material (or, of course, through the rare and difficult procedure of communicating with a successful plant in the group) can such information be obtained. Not only is the quantity and quality of such literature a measure of the health and cohesion of a group, but it also appears to be a most important window into their otherwise clandestine, underground life.

NOTES

An earlier version of this paper is being published in Paul Wilkinson (ed.), *Current Research on Terrorism* (Aberdeen: University Press, 1987).

1. Frequently cited are the examples of the French and American revolutions and successful colonialist revolts.
2. Issues of definition, of course, have presented a problem to many parties seeking a clear boundary for what should be considered terrorism. The label has become so burdened with value connotations that the actors themselves reject it, a distinct change from the turn of the century when anarchists and revolutionaries proudly adopted it. Terrorism in this essay refers to a definition first used by Thornton in 'Terror as a Weapon of Political Agitation', *Internal War: Problems and Approaches*, edited by Harry Eckstein (1964), p.73; 'Terror is a symbolic act designed to influence political behaviour by extranormal means, entailing the use or the threat of violence'. Additionally, it is determined by the nature of the act and not by the nature of the perpetrator. See also Brian Jenkins, *The Study of Terrorism: Definitional Problems* (The Rand Corporation, Dec. 1980).
3. For the purposes of this article, I will risk the criticisms of the rebels by labeling subnational groups employing violence as 'terrorists' throughout.
4. David Rapoport was, to my knowledge, the first to make such an assertion about the terrorist mentality. In his 1971 primer on *Assassination and Terrorism* he states, 'All terrorists must deny the relevance of guilt and innocence, but in doing so they create an unbearable tension in their own souls, for they are in effect saying that a person is not a person. It is no accident that left-wing terrorists constantly speak of a "pig-society"; by convincing *themselves* that they are confronting animals they hope to stay the remorse which the slaughter of the innocent necessarily generates, *Assassination and Terrorism*, (Toronto: CBC Merchandising, 1971), p.42.
5. Nathan Leites, 'Understanding the Next Act', Terrorism, Vol.3 (1979), p.1.
6. Ibid., p.2.
7. Jerrold Post, 'Notes on a Psychodynamic Theory of Terrorist Behavior', *Terrorism* (1984), p.242.
8. Ibid., p.243.
9. The sources enlisted in this study are representative, and not a comprehensive compilation of all such primary source material.
10. The French AD, for instance, was created in 1979, and the CCC not until 1984, while the Italian Red Brigades and the German RAF were well into their second generation by that time. Several current groups are the result of the decline, splitting, or 'regeneration' of previous groups.
11. See Joyce Peterson's *Using Stylistic Analysis to Assess Threat Messages* (The Rand Corporation, Oct. 1985), for a description of these techniques still being developed. She suggests using accepted literary tools as well. For other work on the psychological mechanisms, personality, and social backgrounds of those drawn to political violence, see works by Konrad Kellen, *On Terrorists and Terrorism* (The Rand Corporation, Dec. 1982), and A. Kaplan, 'The Psychodynamics of Terrorism', *Terrorism* (1978).
12. Albert Bandura, 'Mechanisms of Moral Disengagement', unpublished paper presented at the Interdisciplinary Research Conference on 'The Psychology of Terrorism: Behaviors, World-Views, States of Mind', Washington, DC, March 1987.
13. Again, this point has been suggested earlier by David C. Rapoport: 'To speak of the systematic use of terror for publicity and provocation purposes is to presume, of course, that the antagonists in some critical senses share a moral community.' See 'The Politics of Atrocity' in Yonah Alexander and Seymour Maxwell Finger (ed.), *Terrorism: Interdisciplinary Perspectives* (New York: John Jay Press, 1977), p.51.
14. Bandura, p.1.
15. See, for example, Menachem Begin, in his chapter on going underground 'We Fight, Therefore We Are', *The Revolt*, pp.26–46.
16. Bandura, p.1.

17. Franco Ferracuti, 'A Sociopsychiatric Interpretation of Terrorism', *The Annals of the American Academy of Political and Social Science* (Sept. 1982), p.136.
18. 'Communiqué of Action Directe', June 1985.
19. 'Communiqué from Direct Action', *Ligne Rouge*, 13 July 1984.
20. Brigitte Monhaupt from prison, 26 March 1985.
21. 'RAF Philosophy', *The German Guerrilla: Terror, Reaction, and Resistance* (Orkney, UK: Cienfuegos Press, undated), p.98.
22. 'Communiqué from Direct Action', *Zusammen Kaempfen*, July 1985.
23. *Zusammen Kaempfen*, July 1985, pp.3–6.
24. Ibid.
25. Ibid.
26. 'Concrete Answers to Concrete Question', CCC Communiqué, May 1985.
27. Ibid.
28. See, for instance, Menachem Begin's defence of the actions of the *Irgun* and denial that its members were terrorists in *The Revolt* (New York: Nash Publishing, 1978), pp.45–56 and 59–61.
29. Hans-Joachim Klein, 'Les Memoires d'un Terroriste International', *Liberation*, 8 Oct. 1978.
30. Early anarchist theory in Russia and Western Europe at the end of the nineteenth century and during the 1960s explicitly endorsed all criminal activity as revolutionary.
31. To further illustrate the relationship of military violence to terrorist violence see David C. Rapoport, 'The Politics of Atrocity', in Alexander and Finger (eds.), op. cit., p.59, footnote 14: 'When a war begins, each military act (as long as it stays within the boundaries of military convention) does not have to be justified morally. Precisely because conventions are always being violated, terrorists feel compelled to justify each successive action.'
32. Brigitte Monhaupt quoting Irish hunger striker Patsy O'Hara, 26 March 1985, cited in the Spring 1986 issue of *Open Road*, Vancouver, Canada.
33. This paradox is portrayed in Albert Camus' play *The Just Assassins*, in which Yanek, an imprisoned terrorist, hangs for his crime rather than accept a pardon.
34. 'Communiqué from Action Directe', claiming credit for the assassination of General René Audran, 25 Jan. 1985.
35. 'CCC communiqué', 6 May 1985.
36. Communiqué from FRAP, July 1985.
37. 'For the Unity of Western Europe's Revolutionaries', RAF communiqué early 1985.
38. 'Communiqué from Directe Action', *Ligne Rouge*, 13 July 1984.
39. This remarkable quote taken from *Zusammen Kaempfen*, July 1985, pp.14–16, is undoubtedly a conscious paraphrasing and restatement of Marx's Communist Manifesto which I cite here for comparison: 'A spectre is haunting Europe – the spectre of Communism. All the Powers of old Europe have entered into a holy alliance to exorcise this spectre: Pope and Czar, Metternich and Guizot, French Radicals and German police spies.' (Quoted from 'The Manifesto of the Communist Party', in Robert C. Tucker (ed.), *The Marx–Engels Reader* (New York: W.W. Norton, 1978, p.473.) It is clear that the author using Marx had a sense that his own movement was at a turning point and thus deserved this historic description.
40. Unknown author, 'Internationalization of the Struggle', *Zusammen Kaempfen*, July 1985, pp.3–6.
41. Ibid.
42. Ibid.
43. *Zusammen Kaempfen*, July 1985, pp.8–9.
44. Ibid.
45. 'Communiqué by FRAP', April 1985.
46. Bandura, pp.8–9 and 17–21.
47. 'Christian Klar from prison', 26 March 1985.
48. Ibid.
49. Bandura, pp.9–11.
50. *Zusammen Kaempfen*, July 1985, pp.28–31.

51. 'RAF Philosophy', p.100.
52. Ibid., p.101.
53. Bandura, p.10.
54. 'Interview with Hans Joachim Klein', *Liberation*, 8 Oct. 1978.
55. This Bandura terms simply as 'displacement of responsibility'. See his 'Mechanisms', pp.11–13.
56. 'CCC on 1 May Action', 6 May 1985.
57. Ibid.
58. Ibid.
59. Ibid.
60. Ibid.
61. Bandura, p.13.
62. The European groups in focus here did not provide such an example. Just such a split did take place in an Armenian terrorist group, however, in July 1983. The defectors subsequently wrote pages of accusations of their former leader and in many instances attempted to absolve themselves of the blame for terrorism conducted while they were members. See 'The Reality' presumably authored by Monte Melkonian.
63. *Zusammen Kaempfen*, July 1985, pp.14–16.
64. Ibid.
65. 'Communiqué of FRAP', April 1985.
66. 'For the Unity of Western Europe's Revolutionaries', RAF communiqué approximately early 1985.
67. Unknown author, 'Anti-Imperialist Front', *Zusammen Kaempfen*, July 1985.
68. 'Communique' of Action Directe', June 1985.
69. Quoted in Leites, p.32.
70. Konrad Kellen, Unpublished 'Primer' on the Red Army Faction, 1982.
71. Bowyer Bell, 'Old Trends and Future Realities', *Washington Quarterly*, Spring 1985.

PRIMARY SOURCE MATERIAL

Belgian Groups

Fighting Communist Cells Communiqué', dated 26 Nov. 1984, *Open Road*, Vancouver, Canada, Spring 1986.
'Concrete Answers to Concrete Questions', CCC Communiqué, May 1985.
'Communiqué to CCC', 1 May 1985
'CCC on May 1 Action', 6 May 1985, in *Zusammen Kaempfen*, July 1985.
'CCC Communiqué No. 3 from the Karl Marx Campaign', 4–5 Nov. 1985.
'CCC Communiqué and Addendum', 28 Jan. 1986.
'FRAP Communiqué', May 1985.
'Communiqué by FRAP', in *Zusammen Kaempfen*, July 1985.

French Groups

'Interview with "Action Directe" Leader Rouillan', *Liberation*, Paris, 17 Aug. 1982, p.3.
'Action Directe Leader Rouillan on Attacks, Goals', *Le Matin*, Paris, 5 Oct. 1982, p.19.
'Un Manifeste d'Action Directe', excerpts of lengthy AD communiqué, *Le Monde*, Paris, 21 Oct. 1982.
'Action Directe Communiqué, Anti-Apartheid Bombings', 4 Sept. 1985, *Open Road*, Vancouver, Canada, Spring 1986.

German Groups

RAF Texts, Bo Cavefors Publishers, Malmo, Sweden, 1977.
'RAF Communiqué', 8 Aug. 1985.
Baumann, Michael, *Terror or Love? Bommi Baumann's Own Story of His Life as a West German Urban Guerrilla*, Grove Press, NY, 1978.
Baumann, Michael, 'The Mind of a German Terrorist', *Encounter*, Vol. LI, No. 3 (Sept. 1978), pp.81–8.

Klein, Hans-Joachim, *La Mort Mercenaire: Temoignage d'un Ancien Terroriste Ouest-Allemand*, Editions du Seuil, Paris, 1980.

Klein, Hans-Joachim, 'Les Memoires d'un Terroriste International', *Liberation*, 8 Oct. 1978.

'Revolutionary Cells Communiqué', dated both 24 April 1985 and 2 Sept. 1985, in Spring 1986 issue of *Open Road*, Vancouver, Canada.

'Revolutionary Cells and Rote Zora, Discussion Paper on the Peace Movement', *Open Road*, Vancouver, Canada, Spring 1986.

Italian Groups

Court Depositions of Three Red Brigadists, ed. Sue Ellen Moran, The Rand Corporation, N–2391–RC, Feb. 1986.

'Document 142', excerpts of Red Brigades communiqué in *Le Point*, 2 April 1984.

Prima Linea, 'Des deserteurs du terrorisme temoignent', *Liberation*, No. 2072, Paris, 13 Oct. 1980.

[4]

Mechanisms of moral disengagement

ALBERT BANDURA

Self-sanction plays a central role in the regulation of inhumane conduct. In the course of socialization, people adopt moral standards that serve as guides and deterrents for conduct. Once internalized control has developed, people regulate their actions by the sanctions they apply to themselves. They do things that give them satisfaction and build their sense of self-worth. They refrain from behaving in ways that violate their moral standards, because such behavior would bring self-condemnation. Self-sanctions thus keep conduct in line with internal standards.

But moral standards do not function as fixed internal regulators of conduct. Self-regulatory mechanisms do not operate unless they are activated, and there are many psychological processes by which moral reactions can be disengaged from inhumane conduct.[1] Selective activation and disengagement of internal control permits different types of conduct by persons with the same moral standards. Figure 9.1 shows the points in the self-regulatory process at which internal moral control can be disengaged from destructive conduct. Self-sanctions can be disengaged by reconstruing conduct as serving moral purposes, by obscuring personal agency in detrimental activities, by disregarding or misrepresenting the injurious consequences of one's actions, or by blaming and dehumanizing the victims. The way in which these moral disengagement practices

Preparation of this chapter was facilitated by Public Health Research Grant MH-5162-25 from the National Institute of Mental Health. Some sections of this chapter include revised and expanded material from the book, *Social Foundations of Thought and Action: A Social Cognitive Theory* (Englewood Cliffs, N.J.: Prentice-Hall, 1986).

[1] A. Bandura, *Social Foundations of Thought and Action: A Social Cognitive Theory* (Englewood Cliffs, N.J.: Prentice-Hall, 1986).

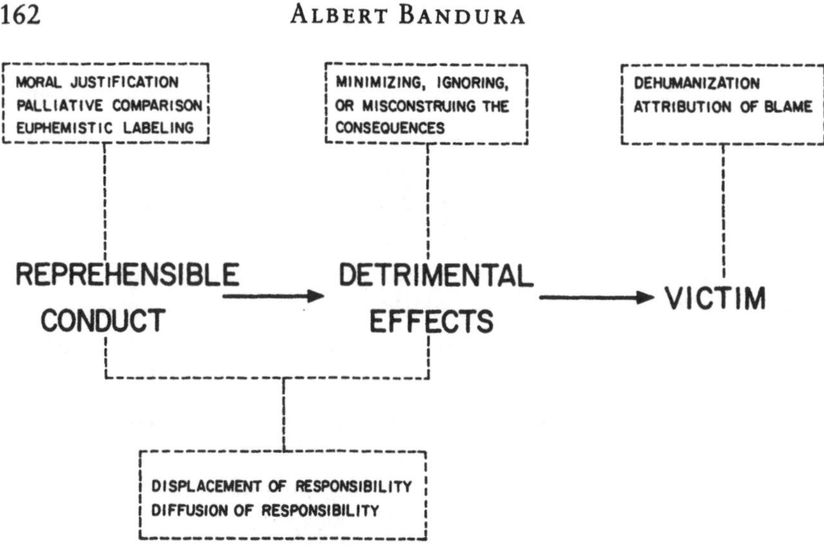

Figure 9.1. Psychosocial mechanisms through which internal control is selectively disengaged from detrimental conduct at three major points in the self-regulatory process. These include reconstruing conduct, obscuring causal agency, distorting consequences, and blaming and devaluating the targets.

operate in the execution of inhumanities is analyzed in considerable detail later in this chapter.

These psychosocial mechanisms of moral disengagement have been examined most extensively in relation to political and military violence. This limited focus tends to convey the impression that selective disengagement of moral self-sanctions occurs only under extraordinary circumstances. Quite the contrary: Such mechanisms operate in everyday situations in which decent people routinely perform activities that further their interests but have injurious human effects. Self-exonerations are needed to eliminate self-prohibitions and self-devaluation. This chapter analyzes how the mechanisms of moral disengagement function in terrorist operations.

Terrorism is usually defined as a strategy of violence designed to promote desired outcomes by instilling fear in the public at large.[2] Public intimidation is a key element that distinguishes terrorist violence from other forms of violence. In contrast to the customary violence in which victims are personally targeted, in terrorism the victims are incidental to the terrorists' intended objectives and are used simply as a way to pro-

[2] M. C. Bassiouni, "Terrorism, Law Enforcement, and the Mass Media: Perspectives, Problems, Proposals," *Journal of Criminal Law and Criminology* 72 (1981): 1–51.

voke social conditions designed to further their broader aims. Third-party violence is especially socially terrorizing when the victimization is generalized to the civilian population and is unpredictable, thereby instilling a widespread sense of personal vulnerability.

The term *terrorism* is often applied to violent acts that dissident groups direct surreptitiously at officials of regimes to force social or political changes. So defined, terrorism becomes indistinguishable from straightforward political violence. Particularized threats are certainly intimidating to the martial and political figures who are personally targeted for assassination and create some apprehension over destabilizing societal effects, but such threats do not necessarily terrify the general public so long as ordinary civilians are not targeted as the objects of victimization. (As is shown later, terrorist tactics relying on public intimidation can serve other purposes as well as a political weapon.)

From a psychological standpoint, third-party violence directed at innocent people is a much more horrific undertaking than political violence in which particular political figures are targeted. It is easier to get people who harbor strong grievances to kill hated political officials or to abduct advisers and consular staffs of foreign nations that support repressive regimes. However, to slaughter in cold blood innocent women and children in buses, in department stores, and in airports requires more powerful psychological machinations of moral disengagement. Intensive psychological training in moral disengagement is needed to create the capacity to kill innocent human beings as a way of toppling rulers or regimes or of accomplishing other political goals.

Moral justification

One set of disengagement practices operates on the construal of the behavior itself. People do not ordinarily engage in reprehensible conduct until they have justified to themselves the morality of their actions. What is culpable can be made honorable through cognitive reconstrual. In this process, destructive conduct is made personally and socially acceptable by portraying it in the service of moral purposes. People then act on a moral imperative. Radical shifts in destructive behavior through moral justification are most strikingly revealed in military conduct.

People who have been socialized to deplore killing as morally condemnable can be transformed rapidly into skilled combatants, who may feel little compunction and even a sense of pride in taking human life.

Moral reconstrual of killing is dramatically illustrated by the case of Sergeant York, one of the phenomenal fighters in the history of modern warfare.[3] Because of his deep religious convictions, Sergeant York registered as a conscientious objector, but his numerous appeals were denied. At camp, his battalion commander quoted chapter and verse from the Bible to persuade him that under appropriate conditions it was Christian to fight and kill. A marathon mountainside prayer finally convinced him that he could serve both God and country by becoming a dedicated fighter.

The conversion of socialized people into dedicated combatants is not achieved by altering their personality structures, aggressive drives, or moral standards. Rather, it is accomplished by cognitively restructuring the moral value of killing, so that the killing can be done free from self-censuring restraints.[4] Through moral sanction of violent means, people see themselves as fighting ruthless oppressors who have an unquenchable appetite for conquest, protecting their cherished values and way of life, preserving world peace, saving humanity from subjugation to an evil ideology, and honoring their country's international commitments. The task of making violence morally defensible is facilitated when nonviolent options are judged to have been ineffective and utilitarian justifications portray the suffering caused by violent counterattacks as greatly outweighed by the human suffering inflicted by the foe.

Over the years, much reprehensible and destructive conduct has been perpetrated by ordinary, decent people in the name of religious principles, righteous ideologies, and nationalistic imperatives. Throughout history, countless people have suffered at the hands of self-righteous crusaders bent on stamping out what they consider evil. Elsewhere, Rapoport and Alexander have documented the lengthy blood-stained history of holy terror wrought by religious justifications. Acting on moral or ideological imperatives reflects a conscious offense mechanism, not an unconscious defense mechanism.[5]

Although moral cognitive restructuring can easily be used to support self-serving and destructive purposes, it can also serve militant action aimed at changing inhumane social conditions. By appealing to morality, social reformers are able to use coercive, and even violent, tactics to force

[3] T. Skeyhill, ed., *Sergeant York: His Own Life Story and War Diary* (Garden City, N.Y.: Doubleday, Doran, 1928).

[4] H. C. Kelman, "Violence without Moral Restraint: Reflections on the Dehumanization of Victims and Victimizers," *Journal of Social Issues* 29 (1973): 25–61; and N. Sanford and C. Comstock, *Sanctions for Evil* (San Francisco: Jossey-Bass, 1971).

[5] D. C. Rapoport and Y. Alexander, eds., *The Morality of Terrorism: Religious and Secular Justification* (Elmsford, N.Y.: Pergamon Press, 1982).

social change. Vigorous disputes arise over the morality of aggressive action directed against institutional practices. Power holders often resist, by forcible means if necessary, making needed social changes that jeopardize their own self-interest. Such tactics provoke social activism. Challengers consider their militant actions to be morally justifiable because they serve to eradicate harmful social practices. Power holders condemn violent means as unjustified and unnecessary because nonviolent means exist to effect social change. They tend to view resorts to violence as efforts to coerce changes that lack popular support. Finally, they may argue that terrorist acts are condemnable because they violate civilized standards of conduct. Anarchy would flourish in a climate in which individuals considered violent tactics acceptable whenever they disliked particular social practices or policies.

Challengers refute such moral arguments by appealing to what they regard as a higher level of morality, derived from communal concerns. They see their constituencies as comprising all people, both at home and abroad, who are victimized either directly or indirectly by injurious social practices. Challengers argue that, when many people benefit from a system that is deleterious to disfavored segments of the society, the harmful social practices secure widespread public support. From the challengers' perspective, they are acting under a moral imperative to stop the maltreatment of people who have no way of modifying injurious social policies, either because they are outside the system that victimizes them, or because they lack the social power to effect changes from within by peaceable means. They regard militant action as the only recourse available to them.

Clearly, adversaries can easily marshal moral reasons for the use of aggressive actions for social control or for social change. Different people view violent acts in different ways. In conflicts of power, one person's violence is another person's selfless benevolence. It is often proclaimed that one group's criminal terroristic activity is another group's liberation movement fought by heroic freedom fighters. This is why moral appeals against violence usually fall on deaf ears. Adversaries sanctify their own militant actions but condemn those of their antagonists as barbarity masquerading behind a mask of outrageous moral reasoning.

Moral justification of counterterrorist measures

So far, the discussion has centered on how terrorists invoke moral principles to justify human atrocities. Moral justification is also brought into play in selecting counterterrorist measures. This poses more troublesome problems for democratic societies than for totalitarian ones. Totalitarian regimes have fewer constraints against using institutional power to control media coverage of terrorist events, to restrict individual rights, to sacrifice individuals for the benefit of the state rather than to make concessions to terrorists, and to combat threats with lethal means. Terrorists can wield greater power over nations that place high value on human life and are thereby constrained in the ways they can act.

Hostage taking has become a common terrorist strategy for wielding control over governments. If nations make the release of hostages a dominant national concern, they place themselves in a highly manipulable position. Tightly concealed captivity thwarts rescue action. Heightened national attention, along with an inability to free hostages independently, conveys a sense of weakness and invests terrorists with considerable importance and coercive power to extract concessions. Overreactions in which nations render themselves hostage to a small band of terrorists inspire and invite further terrorist acts. In contrast, hostage taking is stripped of functional value if it is treated as a criminal act that gains terrorists neither any coercive concessionary power nor much media attention.

Democratic societies face the dilemma of how to morally justify countermeasures that will stop terrorists' atrocities without violating the societies' own fundamental principles and standards of civilized conduct.[6] A set of critical conditions under which violent counterattacks are morally justified can be spelled out. It is generally considered legitimate to resort to violent defense in response to grave threats that inflict extensive human suffering or endanger the very survival of the society. But the criterion of "grave threat," while fine in principle, is slippery in specific application. Like most human judgments, gauging the gravity of threats involves some subjectivity. Moreover, violence is often used as a weapon against threats of lesser magnitude on the grounds that, if left unchecked, they will escalate in severity to the point at which they will eventually exact a high toll in loss of liberties and in suffering. Gauging potential gravity involves even greater subjectivity and fallibility of judgment than does assessment of present danger. Construal of gravity prescribes choice of options, but choice of violent options also often shapes construal of gravity. Thus, projected grave dangers to the society are commonly in-

[6]D. J. C. Carmichael, "Of Beasts, Gods, and Civilized Men: The Justification of Terrorism and of Counterterrorist Measures," *Terrorism* 6 (1982): 1–26.

voked to morally justify violent means that are used to squelch limited present threats.

It is hard to find any inherent moral rightness in violent acts that are designed to kill assailants or to deter them from future assaults but that inevitably risk the lives of some innocent people as well. Because of many uncertain factors, the toll that counterterrorist assaults take on innocent life is neither easily controllable nor accurately calculable in advance. To sacrifice innocent lives in the process of punishing terrorists raises fundamental moral problems. Democratic societies that happen to kill some innocent people in the process of counterterrorist actions find themselves in the vexing predicament of violating the values of their society in defense of those values. Therefore, the use of violent countermeasures is typically justified on utilitarian grounds—that is, in terms of the benefits to humanity and the social order that curbing terrorist attacks will bring. On the assumption that fighting terror with terror will achieve a deterrent effect, it is argued that retaliatory assaults will reduce the total amount of human suffering. As Carmichael notes, utilitarian justifications place few constraints on violent countermeasures because, in the utilitarian calculus, sacrificing the lives of some innocent persons can be greatly outweighed by the halt to repeated massacres and the perpetual terrorizing of entire populations.[7]

Public intimidation and judgments of retaliatory violence

Several features of terrorist acts give power to a few incidents to incite widespread public fear that vastly exceeds the objective threat. The first such feature is the unpredictability of terrorist acts. It is impossible to predict when or where a terrorist act will occur. When people are threatened by someone they know, their fears are circumscribed, because they can judge when they are safe and when they are at risk. In contrast, violent acts in which assailants pick victims and places of attack unpredictably instill the strongest phobic fear because everyone is continually vulnerable.[8]

The second feature is the gravity of the consequences. Terrorist acts maim and kill. People are unwilling to risk such threats even though the chance of being victimized by a terrorist attack is extremely low. Indeed,

[7] Ibid.

[8] L. Heath, "Impact of Newspaper Crime Reports on Fear of Crime: Multimethodological Investigation," *Journal of Personality and Social Psychology* 47 (1984): 263–76.

domestic crime takes an infinitely heavier toll on human life day in and day out than do the sporadic terrorist acts. But domestic crime arouses much less public fear because most homicides involve acquaintances. The incidence rates of terrorist acts, of course, increase substantially if the definition of terrorism is expanded to include state violence in which tyrannical regimes terrorize their own people.

A third feature of terrorist acts that renders them so terrorizing is the sense of uncontrollability that they instill. People believe that they can exercise no control over whether they might be victimized. Perceived self-inefficacy in coping with potential threats activates fear and self-protective courses of action.[9] The risk of being maimed or killed from driving an automobile is infinitely higher than from falling victim to a terrorist act. But people fear terrorists more than their cars, because they believe they can exercise personal control over the chance of injury by the care with which they drive. The combination of unpredictability, gravity, and perceived self-inefficacy is especially intimidating and socially constraining.

The fourth feature is the high centralization and interdependency of essential service systems in modern-day life. When people were widely dispersed in small communities, the consequences of a violent act affected mainly the persons toward whom the behavior was directed. In urbanized life the welfare of entire populations depends on functional communications, transportation and power systems, and safe water and food supplies. Because these service activities are controlled from centralized sources, they are highly vulnerable to disruption or destruction. A single destructive act that requires no elaborate apparatus to perform can instantly frighten or harm a vast number of people. Thus, for example, poisoning a few imported Israeli oranges aroused widespread alarm in the importing nations. Drugstore terrorism—the poisoning of a few packages of patent medicine—struck fear in an entire population and forced elaborate safeguards in packaging. People shun countries and airlines that have been the object of terrorist attacks. Airline hijacking and the development of sophisticated explosive devices have imposed escalating financial burdens on societies by requiring costly electronic surveillance and bomb detection systems. In short, the actual number of terrorist acts may be relatively few, but the fear of terrorism affects the lives of vast populations.

Efforts to reduce societal vulnerabilities with better counterterrorist

[9] Bandura, *Social Foundations of Thought and Action.*

technologies beget better terrorist tactics and devices. A security officer characterized such escalating adaptations well when he remarked, "For every 10-foot wall you erect, terrorists will build an 11-foot ladder." Technological advances are producing highly sophisticated terrorizing devices that increase societal vulnerability to attack. Supportive nations and former intelligence operatives who have become terrorism entrepreneurs—aided by international networks of former military officers, government officials, and weapons merchants—readily supply the world's terrorists with the most advanced lethal tools.

In coping with problems of terrorism, societies face a dual task: how to reduce terrorist acts and how to combat the fear of terrorism. Because the number of terrorist acts is small, the widespread public fear and the intrusive and costly security countermeasures pose the more serious problems. Utilitarian justifications can readily win the support of a frightened public for violent counterterrorist measures. A frightened and angered populace does not spend much time agonizing over the morality of lethal modes of self-defense. Should any concern arise over the taking of innocent lives, it can be assuaged by stripping the victims of their innocence by blaming them for not controlling the terrorists in their midst. The perturbing appearance of national impotence in the face of terrorist acts creates additional social pressures on targeted nations to strike back powerfully.

Extreme counterterrorist reactions may produce effects that are worse than the terrorist acts themselves. Widespread retaliatory death and destruction may advance the political cause of terrorists by arousing a backlash of sympathy for innocent victims and moral condemnation of the brutal nature of the counterreactions. To fight terror with terror often spawns new terrorists and provides new justifications for violence that are more likely to escalate terrorism than to diminish it. Indeed, some terrorist activities are designed precisely to provoke curtailment of personal liberties and other domestic repressive measures that might breed public disaffection with the system. Extreme countermeasures can, thus, play into the hands of terrorists.

Euphemistic labeling

Language shapes thought patterns on which people base many of their actions. Activities can take on a very different appearance depending on what they are called. Euphemistic language thus provides a convenient device for masking reprehensible activities or even conferring a respectable status on them. Through convoluted verbiage, destructive conduct is made benign and people who engage in it are relieved of a sense of personal agency. Laboratory studies reveal the disinhibitory power of euphemistic language.[10] Adults behave much more aggressively when given opportunities to assault a person when assaultive acts are given a sanitized athletic label than when they are called aggression. In an insightful analysis of the language of nonresponsibility, Gambino identifies the different varieties of euphemisms.[11] One form, palliative expressions, is widely used to make the reprehensible respectable. Through the power of hygienic words, even killing a human being loses much of its repugnancy. Soldiers "waste" people rather than kill them, intelligence operatives "terminate (them) with extreme prejudice."[12] When mercenaries speak of "fulfilling a contract," murder is transformed by admirable words into the honorable discharge of duty. Terrorists label themselves "freedom fighters." Bombing attacks become "clean, surgical strikes," invoking imagery of the restorative handicrafts of the operating room, and the civilians they kill are linguistically converted to "collateral damage."[13] Sanitizing euphemisms, of course, perform heavy duty in less loathsome but unpleasant activities that people are called on to do from time to time.

The agentless passive form serves as a linguistic device for creating the appearance that culpable acts are the work of nameless forces, rather than people.[14] It is as though people are moved mechanically but are not really the agents of their own acts. Gambino further documents how the jargon of a legitimate enterprise can be misused to lend an aura of respectability to an illegitimate one. Deadly activities are framed as "game plans," and the perpetrators become "team players" calling for the qualities and behavior befitting the best sportsmen. The disinhibitory power of language can be boosted further by colorful metaphors that change the nature of culpable activities.

[10] E. Diener, J. Dineen, K. Endresen, A. L. Beaman, and S. C. Fraser, "Effects of Altered Responsibility, Cognitive Set, and Modeling on Physical Aggression and Deindividuation," *Journal of Personality and Social Psychology* 31 (1975): 143–56.

[11] R. Gambino, "Watergate Lingo: A Language on Non-Responsibility," *Freedom at Issue* 22 (November–December 1973): 7–9, 15–17.

[12] W. Safire, "The Fine Art of Euphemism," *San Francisco Chronicle*, 13 May 1979, p. 13.

[13] S. Hilgartner, R. C. Bell, and R. O'Connor, *Nukespeak: Nuclear Language, Visions, and Mindset* (San Francisco: Sierra Club Books, 1982).

[14] D. Bolinger, *Language: The Loaded Weapon* (London: Longman, 1982).

Advantageous comparison

Whenever events occur or are presented contiguously, the first one colors how the second one is perceived and judged. By exploiting the contrast principle, moral judgments of conduct can be influenced by the expedient structuring of what it is compared against. Self-deplored acts can be made to appear righteous by contrasting them with flagrant inhumanities. The more outrageous the comparison practices, the more likely it is that one's own destructive conduct will appear trifling or even benevolent. Thus, terrorists minimize their slayings as the only defensive weapon they have to curb the widespread cruelties inflicted on their people. In the eyes of their supporters, risky attacks directed at the apparatus of oppression are acts of selflessness and martyrdom. People who are objects of terrorist attacks, in turn, characterize their retaliatory violence as trifling, or even laudable, by comparing them with carnage and terror perpetrated by terrorists. In social conflicts, injurious behavior usually escalates, with each side lauding its own behavior but condemning that of its adversaries as heinous.

Advantageous comparisons are also drawn from history to justify violence. Advocates of terrorist tactics are quick to note that the democracies of Britain, France, and the United States were born of violence against oppressive rule. A former director of the CIA effectively deflected, by advantageous comparison, embarrassing questions about the morality and legality of CIA-directed covert operations designed to overthrow an authoritarian regime. He explained that French covert operations and military supplies greatly aided the overthrow of oppressive British rule during the American Revolution, thereby creating the modern model of democracy for other subjugated people to emulate.[15]

Social comparison is similarly used to show that the social labeling of acts as terrorism depends more on the ideological allegiances of the labelers than on the acts themselves. Airline hijackings were applauded as heroic deeds when East Europeans and Cubans initiated this practice, but condemned as terrorist acts when the airlines of Western nations and friendly countries were commandeered. The degree of psychopathology ascribed to hijackers varied with the direction of the rerouted flights. Moral condemnations of politically motivated terrorism are easily blunted by social comparison because, in international contests for political power,

[15] Brief comment by Colby on television during the Irangate hearings.

it is hard to find nations that categorically condemn terrorism. Rather, they usually back some terrorists and oppose others.

Cognitive restructuring of behavior through moral justifications and palliative characterizations is the most effective psychological mechanism for promoting destructive conduct. This is because moral restructuring not only eliminates self-deterrents but engages self-approval in the service of destructive exploits. What was once morally condemnable becomes a source of self-valuation. After destructive means become invested with high moral purpose, functionaries work hard to become proficient at them and take pride in their destructive accomplishments.

Moral justifications and the media

The mass media, especially television, provide the best access to the public because of the media's strong drawing power. For this reason, television is increasingly used as the principal vehicle of social and moral justifications of goals and actions. Struggles to legitimize and gain support for one's causes, and to discredit the causes of one's foes, are now waged more and more through the electronic media.[16]

Terrorists try to exercise influence over targeted officials or nations through intimidation of the public and arousal of sympathy for the social and political causes they espouse. Without widespread publicity, terrorist acts can achieve neither of these effects. Terrorists, therefore, coerce access to the media in order to publicize their grievances to the international community. They use television as the main instrument for gaining sympathy and supportive action for their plight by presenting themselves as risking their lives for the welfare of a victimized constituency whose legitimate grievances are ignored. The media, in turn, come under heavy fire from targeted officials who regard granting terrorists a worldwide forum as aiding terrorist causes. Security forces do not like media personnel to track their conduct and broadcast tactical information that terrorists can put to good use, or to interpose themselves as intermediaries in risky negotiation situations. Social pressures mount to curtail media coverage of terrorist events, especially while they are in progress.[17]

[16] S. J. Ball-Rokeach, "The Legitimation of Violence," in *Collective Violence*, edited by J. F. Short, Jr., and M. E. Wolfgang (Chicago: Aldine-Atherton, 1972).

[17] M. C. Bassiouni, "Terrorism, Law Enforcement, and the Mass Media: Perspectives, Problems, Proposals," *Journal of Criminal Law and Criminology* 72 (1981): 1–51.

Displacement of responsibility

Another set of dissociative practices operates by obscuring or distorting the relationship between actions and the effects they cause. People behave in injurious ways they normally repudiate if a legitimate authority accepts responsibility for the consequences of their conduct.[18] Under conditions of displaced responsibility, people view their actions as springing from the dictates of authorities rather than from their own volition. Because they are not the actual agents of their actions, they are spared self-prohibiting reactions. In terrorism that is sponsored by states or governments in exile, functionaries view themselves as patriots fulfilling nationalistic duties rather than as free-lancing criminals. Displacement of responsibility not only weakens restraints over one's own detrimental actions but also diminishes social concern over the well-being of people mistreated by others.[19]

Exemption from self-devaluation for heinous deeds has been most gruesomely revealed in socially sanctioned mass executions. Nazi prison commandants and their staffs divested themselves of personal responsibility for their unprecedented inhumanities; they were simply carrying out orders.[20] Impersonal obedience to horrific orders was similarly evident in military atrocities, such as the My Lai massacre.[21] In an effort to deter institutionally sanctioned atrocities, the Nuremberg Accords declared that obedience to inhumane orders, even from the highest authorities, does not relieve subordinates of the responsibility for their actions. However, because victors are disinclined to try themselves as criminals, such decrees have limited deterrence without an international judiciary system empowered to impose penalties on victors and losers alike. In studies of the disengagement of self-sanctions through the displacement of responsibility, authorities explicitly authorize those who play the role of functionaries to carry out injurious actions and hold themselves fully accountable for the harm caused by those actions. However, in the sanctioning practices of everyday life, responsibility for detrimental conduct is rarely assumed so explicitly, because only obtuse authorities would leave themselves open to accusations of authorizing heinous acts. Actual

[18] Diener et al., "Altered Responsibility."

[19] H. A. Tilker, "Socially Responsible Behavior as a Function of Observer Responsibility and Victim Feedback," *Journal of Personality and Social Psychology* 14 (1970): 95–100.

[20] B. C. Andrus, *The Infamous of Nuremberg* (London: Fravin, 1969).

[21] Kelman, "Violence Without Moral Restraint."

authorities are concerned not only with adverse social consequences to themselves, should the courses of action they advocate miscarry, but with the loss of self-regard for sanctioning human atrocities in ways that leave blood on their hands. Therefore, authorities usually invite and support detrimental conduct in insidious ways that minimize personal responsibility for what is happening.

In the preceding chapter, Kramer described the great lengths to which Shi'ite clerics go to produce moral justifications for violent acts that seem to breach Islamic law, such as suicidal bombings and hostage taking. These efforts are designed not only to persuade the clerics themselves of the morality of the terrorists' actions but to preserve the integrity of the perpetrating group in the eyes of other nations. The religious code permits neither suicide nor the terrorizing of innocent people. On the one hand, the clerics justify such acts by invoking situational imperatives and utilitarian reasons, namely, that tyrannical circumstances drive oppressed people to resort to unconventional means in order to rout aggressors who wield massive destructive power. On the other hand, they reconstrue terrorist acts as conventional means in which dying in a suicidal bombing for a moral cause is no different from dying at the hands of an enemy soldier. Hostages simply get relabeled as spies. When the linguistic solution defies credibility, personal moral responsibility is disengaged by construing terroristic acts as dictated by the foe's tyranny. Because of the shaky moral logic and disputable reconstruals, clerics sanction terrorism by indirection, vindicate successful ventures retrospectively, and disclaim endorsing terroristic operations beforehand.

States sponsor terrorist operations through disguised, roundabout routes that make it difficult to pin the blame on them. Moreover, the intended purpose of sanctioned destructiveness is usually linguistically disguised so that neither issuers nor perpetrators regard the activity as censurable. When culpable practices gain public attention, they are officially dismissed as only isolated incidents arising through misunderstanding of what, in fact, had been authorized. Efforts are made to limit the blame to subordinates, who are portrayed as misguided or overzealous.

A number of social factors affect the ease with which responsibility for one's actions can be surrendered to others. High justification and social consensus about the morality of an enterprise aid in the relinquishment of personal control. The legitimacy of the authorizers is another important determinant. The higher the authorities, the more legitimacy, respect, and coercive power they command, and the more amenable are people to defer to them. Modeled disobedience, which challenges the legitimacy of the activities, if not the authorizers themselves, reduces the willingness of observers to carry out the actions called for by the orders of a superior.[22] It is difficult to continue to disown personal agency in the face of evident harm that results directly from one's actions. People are, therefore, less willing to obey authoritarian orders to carry out injurious behavior when they see firsthand how they are hurting others.[23]

Obedient functionaries do not cast off all responsibility for their behavior as though they were mindless extensions of others. If this were the case, they would do nothing unless told to. In fact, they tend to be conscientious and self-directed in the performance of their duties. It requires a strong sense of responsibility to be a good functionary. In situations involving obedience to authority, people carry out orders partly to honor the obligations they have undertaken.[24] It is therefore important to distinguish between two levels of responsibility, duty to one's superiors and accountability for the effects of one's actions. Self-sanctions operate most efficiently in the service of authority when followers assume personal responsibility for being dutiful executors while relinquishing personal responsibility for the harm caused by their behavior. Followers who disowned responsibility without being bound by a sense of duty would be quite unreliable.

Displacement of responsibility also operates in situations in which hostages are taken. Terrorists warn officials of targeted nations that if they take retaliatory action they will be held accountable for the lives of the hostages. At different steps in negotiations for their release, terrorists continue to claim that the responsibility for the safety of hostages rests with the national officials. If the captivity drags on, terrorists blame the suffering and injuries they inflict on their hostages on the officials for failing to make what they regard as warranted concessions to right social wrongs.

[22] W. H. J. Meeus and Q. A. W. Raaijmakers, "Administrative Obedience: Carrying Out Orders to Use Psychological-Administrative Violence," *European Journal of Social Psychology* 16 (1986): 311–24; S. Milgram, *Obedience to Authority: An Experimental View* (New York: Harper & Row, 1974); and P. C. Powers and R. G. Geen, "Effects of the Behavior and the Perceived Arousal of a Model on Instrumental Aggression," *Journal of Personality and Social Psychology* 23 (1972): 175–83.

[23] Milgram, *Obedience to Authority*, and Tilker, "Socially Responsible Behavior."

[24] D. M. Mantell and R. Panzarella, "Obedience and Responsibility," *British Journal of Social and Clinical Psychology* 15 (1976): 239–46.

Diffusion of responsibility

The deterrent power of self-sanctions is weakened when responsibility for culpable behavior is diffused, thereby obscuring the link between conduct and its consequences. Responsibility can be diffused in several ways, for example, by the division of labor. Most enterprises require the services of many people, each performing fragmentary jobs that seem harmless in themselves. The fractional contribution is easily isolated from the eventual function, especially when participants exercise little personal judgment in carrying out a subfunction that is related by remote, complex links to the end result. After activities become routinized into programmed subfunctions, attention shifts from the import of what one is doing to the details of one's fractional job.[25]

Group decision making is another common bureaucratic practice that enables otherwise considerate people to behave inhumanely, because no single person feels responsible for policies arrived at collectively. When everyone is responsible, no one is really responsible. Social organizations go to great lengths to devise sophisticated mechanisms for obscuring responsibility for decisions that will adversely affect others.

Collective action is still another diffusion expedient for weakening self-restraints. Any harm done by a group can always be ascribed, in large part, to the behavior of other members. People therefore act more harshly when responsibility is obfuscated by a collective instrumentality than when they hold themselves personally accountable for what they do.[26]

Disregard for, or distortion of, consequences

Additional ways of weakening self-deterring reactions operate through disregard for or misrepresentation of the consequences of action. When people choose to pursue activities that are harmful to others for reasons of personal gain or social inducements, they avoid facing or minimize the harm they cause. They readily recall prior information given to them about the potential benefits of the behavior, but are less able to remember

[25] Kelman, "Violence without Moral Restraint."

[26] A. Bandura, B. Underwood, and M. E. Fromson, "Disinhibition of Aggression Through Diffusion of Responsibility and Dehumanization of Victims," *Journal of Research in Personality* 9 (1975): 253–69; E. Diener, "Deindividuation: Causes and Consequences," *Social Behavior and Personality* 5 (1977): 143–56; and P. G. Zimbardo, "The Human Choice: Individuation, Reason, and Order Versus Deindividuation, Impulse, and Chaos," in *Nebraska Symposium on Motivation*, edited by W. J. Arnold and D. Levine (Lincoln: University of Nebraska Press, 1969), 237–309.

its harmful effects.[27] People are especially prone to minimize injurious effects when they act alone and thus cannot easily escape responsibility.[28] In addition to selective inattention and cognitive distortion of effects, the misrepresentation may involve active efforts to discredit evidence of the harm they cause. As long as the detrimental results of one's conduct are ignored, minimized, distorted, or disbelieved, there is little reason for self-censure to be activated.

It is relatively easy to hurt others when their suffering is not visible and when causal actions are physically and temporally remote from their effects. Our technologies for killing people have become highly lethal and depersonalized. Mechanized weapons systems and explosive devices, which can cause mass death by destructive forces unleashed remotely, illustrate such depersonalized action. Even a high sense of personal responsibility is a weak restrainer when aggressors do not know the harm they inflict on their victims.[29] In contrast, when people can see and hear the suffering they cause, vicariously aroused distress and self-censure serve as self-restraining influences. For example, in his studies of commanded aggression, Milgram obtained diminishing obedience as the victims' pain became more evident and personalized.[30]

Most organizations involve hierarchical chains of command in which superiors formulate plans and intermediaries transmit them to executors, who then carry them out. The further removed individuals are from the end results, the weaker is the restraining power of the foreseeable destructive effects. Kilham and Mann set forth the view that the disengagement of personal control is easiest for the intermediaries in a hierarchical system—they neither bear responsibility for major decisions nor are a party to their execution.[31] In performing the transmitter role, they model dutiful behavior and add legitimacy to their superiors' social policies and practices. Consistent with these speculations, intermediaries are much

[27] T. C. Brock and A. H. Buss, "Dissonance, Aggression, and Evaluation of Pain," *Journal of Abnormal and Social Psychology* 65 (1962): 197–202; and T. C. Brock and A. H. Buss, "Effects of Justification for Aggression and Communication with the Victim on Postaggression Dissonance," *Journal of Abnormal and Social Psychology* 68 (1964): 403–12.

[28] C. Mynatt and S. J. Herman, "Responsibility Attribution in Groups and Individuals: A Direct Test of the Diffusion of Responsibility Hypothesis," *Journal of Personality and Social Psychology* 32 (1975): 1111–18.

[29] Tilker, "Socially Responsible Behavior."

[30] Milgram, *Obedience to Authority*.

[31] W. Kilham and L. Mann, "Level of Destructive Obedience as a Function of Transmitter and Executant Roles in the Milgram Obedience Paradigm," *Journal of Personality and Social Psychology* 29 (1974): 696–702.

more obedient to destructive commands than are people who have to carry them out and face the results.[32]

Diverse functions and consequences of terrorism

The term *terrorism* is most commonly applied to surreptitious acts of violence in which dissidents attack a state by victimizing citizens. However, like other forms of coercive and aggressive conduct, terroristic violence involves varied targets and serves diverse functions. Variation in purpose alters the readiness with which causal responsibility is acknowledged and the way in which the consequences of terrorist acts are represented. Terrorism directed by states at their own people is designed to eliminate internal opposition and squelch peaceful dissent and social activism against the ruling cliques who use force to keep themselves in power. The punitive consequences for challenging the regime are publicized in order to deter potential opponents, but the mechanisms and brutality of tyranny are concealed. State-sponsored international terrorism seeks political gains through surreptitious underwriting of terrorist operations performed by surrogate groups. The sponsors go to great lengths to distance themselves publicly from the pernicious operations and the havoc they wreak. However, the public appearance of noninvolvement in international terrorism is difficult to pull off for states that provide the training sites and sanctuaries for known terrorist groups.

Politically motivated terrorism carried out against a state in the name of liberation movements is designed to gain widespread media dissemination of grievances. Terrorists therefore actively seek publicity for their cause in the effort to enlist popular support for the social or political changes they desire. They often attempt to minimize, or deflect attention from, the harm inflicted through their terrorist acts by centering attention on the inhumanities perpetrated on their compatriots by the state.

Some terrorist violence is carried out by self-appointed crusaders who act on behalf of oppressed people with whom they identify. They are motivated, in large part, by ideological imperatives and mutual reward of their efforts by fellow members. Their tactics are often calculated to expose the weaknesses of power holders and to provoke them to foolish actions and repressive security measures. Such counterreactions will presumably create widespread public disaffection and outrage, discredit the

[32] Ibid.

power holders' own leadership, and thus help bring about their own downfall and the regime over which they preside. Such groups readily take responsibility for their terrorist acts. Their eye is on the radicalization of the "consciousness of the masses" rather than on the carnage inflicted on those victimized by their actions.

Shared fervent belief sustains terrorist activities. The power of belief to sustain a program of political activism offering little hope of quick successes operates in virtually all groups seeking to effect social change and is not peculiar to terroristic groups that have little prospect of inciting the intended popular uprising.[33] Were social reformers to be entirely realistic about the prospects of transforming social systems during their operative period they would either forgo the endeavor or fall easy victim to despair.

A fair amount of terrorism is performed for financial gain that is justified on political grounds. Executives of foreign corporations and advisers of powerful and wealthy nations are favorite targets of terrorist acts. The particular victims are depersonalized as mere symbols of imperialism. People are more subject to self-reprimands for inflicting human suffering than for extracting money from prosperous, faceless corporations. Moral self-sanctions are therefore more easily disengaged from destructive conduct directed at a despised system than at a person. Lucrative ransom and extortion payments make this form of terrorism profitable.

Another tactic of terror that quickly spreads when it pays off involves the abduction of foreign advisers and diplomats in order to force release of jailed "political prisoners."[34] Abduction is a highly efficacious weapon for dissident groups as long as governments are willing to negotiate. Abductors view their action as a political bargaining tool rather than as an act of terrorism, especially if they gain release of their jailed compatriots without having inflicted physical injury on their captives.

Some people are motivated by bizarre and malevolent beliefs to commit acts that terrorize the public. Such idiosyncratically motivated acts are illustrated in recent incidents of drugstore terrorism, in which isolated individuals indiscriminately took the lives of several people by lacing bottles of patent medicine with poison. Once the idea of such an act is planted in the public consciousness, it is not uncommon for new variants of death threats involving food substances to appear. Through the

[33] Bandura, *Social Foundations of Thought and Action.*

[34] A. Bandura, *Aggression: A Social Learning Analysis* (Englewood Cliffs, N.J.: Prentice-Hall, 1973).

influence of modeling, terrorist acts that were originally politically motivated may be adopted by individuals for their own idiosyncratic purposes.[35] The rapid spread of airline hijacking internationally is illustrative of this modeling process.

As previously noted, the task of psychologically circumscribing and sanitizing destructive effects presents special problems for democratic societies when they resort to violent counterterrorist actions that take the lives of some innocent people. Counterattackers try to minimize the brutal aspects of such assaults by depicting them as "surgical strikes" that wipe out only terrorists and their sanctuaries. The targets of violent retaliation try to arouse worldwide condemnation of such attacks through graphic media portrayals of the carnage inflicted on women and children. Some nations pursue the policy that terrorist acts will be promptly answered with massive deathly retaliation, whatever the cost might be, on the ground that this is the price that must be paid to check terrorism. Opponents of such policies argue that overkill countermeasures only fuel greater terrorism by creating more terrorists and increasing public sympathy for the causes that drive them to terroristic violence. Vigorous verbal battles are fought over immediate results and long-range effects of such violent countermeasures.

Dehumanization

The final set of disengagement practices operates on the targets of violent acts. The strength of self-censuring reactions to injurious conduct depends partly on how the perpetrator views the people toward whom the harmful behavior is directed. To perceive another person as human enhances empathetic or vicarious reactions through perceived similarity.[36] The joys and suffering of similar persons are more vicariously arousing than are the joys and suffering of strangers or of persons who have been divested of human qualities. Personalizing the injurious effects experienced by others also makes their suffering much more salient. As a result, it is difficult to mistreat humanized persons without risking self-condemnation.

Self-sanctions against cruel conduct can be disengaged or blunted by

[35] Bandura, *Aggression: A Social Learning Analysis.*
[36] A. Bandura, "Social Cognitive Theory and Social Referencing," in *Social Referencing and Social Construction of Reality,* edited by S. Feiman (New York: Plenum, 1989).

divesting people of human qualities. Once dehumanized, the potential victims are no longer viewed as persons with feelings, hopes, and concerns but as subhuman objects. They are portrayed as mindless "savages," "gooks," "satanic fiends," and the like. Subhumans are regarded as insensitive to maltreatment and capable of being influenced only by harsh methods. If dispossessing antagonists of humanness does not blunt self-reproof, the self-reproof can be eliminated by attributing bestial qualities to the antagonists. It is easier to brutalize victims, for example, when they are referred to as "worms."[37] Studies of interpersonal aggression give vivid testimony to the self-disinhibitory power of dehumanization.[38] Dehumanized persons are treated much more punitively than persons who have not been divested of their human qualities. When punitiveness fails to achieve the desired result, the terrorists view this outcome as further evidence of the unworthiness of dehumanized persons, thus justifying their even greater maltreatment. Dehumanization fosters different self-exonerative patterns of thought. People seldom condemn punitive conduct—in fact, they create justifications for it—when they are directing their aggression at persons who have been divested of their humanness. By contrast, people strongly disapprove of punitive actions and rarely excuse them when they are directed at persons depicted in humanized terms.

Under certain conditions, the exercise of institutional power changes the users in ways that are conducive to dehumanization. This happens most often when persons in positions of authority have coercive power over other persons and when adequate safeguards for constraining the behavior of power holders are lacking. Power holders come to devalue those over whom they wield control.[39] In a simulated prison experiment, even college students, who had been randomly chosen to serve as either inmates or guards given unilateral power, began to treat their charges in degrading, tyrannical ways as guards.[40] Thus, role assignment that authorizes use of coercive power overrode personal characteristics in promoting punitive conduct. Systematic tests of relative influences similarly

[37] J. T. Gibson and M. Haritos-Fatouros, "The Education of a Torturer," *Psychology Today* (November 1986): 50–8.
[38] Bandura et al., "Disinhibition of Aggression."
[39] D. Kipnis, "The Powerholders," in *Perspectives on Social Power*, edited by J. T. Tedeschi (Chicago: Aldine, 1974), 82–122.
[40] C. Haney, C. Banks, and P. Zimbardo, "Interpersonal Dynamics in a Simulated Prison," *International Journal of Criminology and Penology* 1 (1973): 69–97.

show that social influences conducive to punitiveness exert considerably greater sway over aggressive conduct than do people's personal characteristics.[41]

The overall findings from research on the different mechanisms of moral disengagement corroborate the historical chronicle of human atrocities: It requires conducive social conditions rather than monstrous people to produce heinous deeds. Given appropriate social conditions, decent, ordinary people can be led to do extraordinarily cruel things.

Power of humanization

Psychological research tends to focus extensively on how easy it is to bring out the worst in people through dehumanization and other self-exonerative means. The sensational negative findings receive the greatest attention. Thus, for example, the aspect of Milgram's research on obedient aggression that is most widely cited is the evidence that good people can be talked into performing cruel deeds. However, to get people to carry out punitive acts, the overseer had to be physically present, repeatedly ordering people to act cruelly as they voiced their concerns and objections. Orders to escalate punitiveness to more intense levels are largely ignored or subverted when remotely issued by verbal command. As Helm and Morelli note, this is hardly an example of blind obedience triggered by an authoritative mandate.[42] Moreover, what is rarely noted is the equally striking evidence that most people steadfastly refuse to behave punitively, even in response to strong authoritarian commands, if the situation is personalized by having them see the victim or requiring them to inflict pain directly rather than remotely.

The emphasis on obedient aggression is understandable, considering the prevalence and harmfulness of people's inhumanities to one another. However, of considerable theoretical and social significance is the power of humanization to counteract cruel conduct. Studies examining this process reveal that, even under conditions that weaken self-deterrents, it is difficult for people to behave cruelly toward others when the potential victims are humanized or even personalized a bit.[43]

[41] K. S. Larsen, D. Coleman, J. Forges, and R. Johnson, "Is the Subject's Personality or the Experimental Situation a Better Predictor of a Subject's Willingness to Administer Shock to a Victim?" *Journal of Personality and Social Psychology* 22 (1971): 287–95.

[42] C. Helm and M. Morelli, "Stanley Milgram and the Obedience Experiment: Authority, Legitimacy, and Human Action," *Political Theory* 7 (1979): 321–46.

[43] Bandura et al., "Disinhibition of Aggression."

The moderating influence of humanization is strikingly revealed in situations involving great threat of violence. Most abductors find it difficult to harm their hostages after they have come to know them personally. Calm, patient negotiations with captors, therefore, increase the likelihood that captives will survive the ordeal. With growing acquaintance, it becomes increasingly difficult to take a human life cold-bloodedly.

Humanization, of course, is a two-way process. Captives may also develop some sympathy for their captors as they get to know them. Unfortunately, this phenomenon is sometimes called into question in analyses of terrorism by identifying it with the Stockholm syndrome. In the incident that spawned this "syndrome," people who were held hostage for six days by bank robbers began to sympathize with their criminal captors and sided with them against the police.[44] This hostage incident included several features that are conducive to the development of an affinity with the captors. The hostages were under extended siege by a horde of police seeking opportunities to shoot the robbers, depriving the group of food and other necessities to force their surrender, and poking holes in walls to gas the robbers into submission. The captors often acted as the hostages' protectors against the frightening maneuvers by the police. The refusal by the police to make concessions angered the hostages, who began to blame the police for their terrifying plight. ("It is the police who are keeping me from my children.")

As previously noted, construal of events is strongly colored by contrast effects. The chief captor in the bank-robbery case aroused strong feelings of gratitude in his captives by coupling brutalizing threats with seeming acts of considerateness. For example, he informed one of the hostages that he would forgo his plan to kill him to force police concessions, but instead would shoot him in the leg and have him pretend that he had been killed. This hostage expressed a strong sense of gratitude even long after the ordeal was over. ("How kind that he would shoot only my leg.") Another hostage was similarly overcome with gratitude over her captor's considerateness of her claustrophobic dread of sleeping in the bank vault. The "benevolent" gesture that won him good will consisted of placing a rope around her neck and letting her out of the vault on a thirty-foot leash. ("He was very kind to allow me to leave the vault.") The captors often consoled their captives when they were distraught, comforted them when they were physically miserable, and personalized

[44] D. A. Lang, "A Reporter at Large: The Bank Drama (Swedish Hostages)," *New Yorker* 50 (40) 1974: 56–126.

themselves by empathetic self-disclosures of their own human longings and feelings. The contrasting treatment led the hostages to perceive the police as the inhumane ones. ("I remember thinking, why can't the police be considerate like that?") Whether captivity produces sympathy for captors is determined by several factors—the extent to which captors personalize themselves and their plight, show some compassion toward their captives, portray the hostages' country as disregarding their welfare or jeopardizing their lives by reckless countermeasures, and act as their protectors.

Ideological terrorists are more likely to harass, browbeat, and degrade their hostages than to console them. Therefore, people who are subjected to terrifying political captivity rarely ally themselves with their abductors. But this does not mean that hostages never develop any sympathy for their captors' cause or plight, or that personalization never moderates captors' cruelty toward the people they hold hostage. When an important psychological phenomenon is linked to an example of questionable similarity, such as the Stockholm set of reactions, the aggression-restraining power of humanization may be inappropriately dismissed through improper comparison.

Attribution of blame

Imputing blame to one's antagonists is still another expedient that can serve self-exonerative purposes; one's own violent conduct can then be viewed as compelled by forcible provocation. For example, when power holders willfully disregard legitimate grievances concerning maltreatment, terrorists can easily persuade themselves that their actions are motivated by self-protection or desperation. Oppressive and inhumane social conditions and thwarted political efforts breed terrorists who often see foreign governments' complicity in their plight through support of the regime that they believe victimizes them. People who become radicalized carry out terrorist acts against the regime as well as the implicated foreign nations. When the social conditions breeding discontent and violent protest are firmly entrenched in political systems that obstruct legitimate efforts at change, governments readily resort to violent countermeasures in efforts to control terrorist activities. It is much easier to attack violent protesters than to change the sociopolitical conditions that fuel the protests. In such skirmishes, one person's victim is another person's victimizer.

Destructive interactions usually involve a series of reciprocally escalative actions, in which the antagonists are rarely faultless. A person can always select from the chain of events an instance of the adversary's defensive behavior and view it as the original instigation. Injurious conduct thus becomes a justifiable defensive reaction to belligerent provocations. People who are victimized are not entirely blameless, because, by their behavior, they contribute partly to their own plight. Victims can therefore be blamed for bringing suffering on themselves. Terrorists can achieve self-exoneration by viewing their destructive conduct as forced by circumstances rather than resulting from a personal decision. By blaming others or circumstances, not only can they excuse their own actions, but also they can even feel self-righteous in the process.

Terrorist acts that take a heavy toll on civilian lives create special personal pressures to lay blame elsewhere. In 1987, Irish Republican Army (IRA) guerrillas planted a large bomb that killed and maimed many family members attending a war memorial ceremony in a town square.[45] The guerrillas promptly ascribed the blame for the civilian massacre to the British army for having detonated the bomb prematurely with an electronic scanning device. The government denounced the "pathetic attempt to transfer blame" because no scanning equipment was in use at the time.

Observers of victimization can be disinhibited in much the same way as perpetrators are by the tendency to infer culpability from misfortune. Observers who see victims suffer maltreatment for which the victims themselves are held partially responsible leads observers to derogate the victims.[46] The devaluation and indignation aroused by ascribed culpability, in turn, provides moral justification for even greater maltreatment. The fact that attribution of blame can give rise to devaluation and moral justification illustrates how the various disengagement mechanisms are often interrelated and work together in weakening internal control.

Gradualistic moral disengagement

The aforementioned disengagement devices will not instantly transform a considerate person into a ruthless one who purposely goes out to kill other human beings. Terrorist behavior evolves through extensive train-

[45] "IRA 'Regrets' Bombing, Blames British for Civilian Toll," *San Francisco Chronicle*, 10 November 1987, p. 19.

[46] M. J. Lerner and D. T. Miller, "Just World Research and the Attribution Process: Looking Back and Ahead," *Psychological Bulletin* 85 (1978): 1030–51.

ing in moral disengagement and terrorist prowess, rather than emerging full blown. The path to terrorism can be shaped by fortuitous factors as well as by the conjoint influence of personal predilections and social inducements.[47] Development of the capability to kill usually evolves through a process in which recruits may not fully recognize the transformation they are undergoing.[48]

The disinhibitory training is usually conducted within a communal milieu of intense interpersonal influences insulated from mainstream social life. The recruits become deeply immersed in the ideology and role performances of the group. Initially, they are prompted to perform unpleasant acts that they can tolerate without much self-censure. Gradually, through repeated performance and repeated exposure to aggressive modeling by more experienced associates, their discomfort and self-reproof are weakened to ever higher levels of ruthlessness. The various disengagement practices form an integral part of the training. Eventually, acts originally regarded as abhorrent can be performed callously. Escalative self-disinhibition is accelerated if violent courses of action are presented as serving a moral imperative and the targeted people are divested of human qualities.[49] The training not only instills the moral rightness and importance of the cause for militant action, but also creates a sense of eliteness and provides the social rewards of solidarity and group esteem for excelling in terrorist exploits.

Sprinzak, in Chapter 5 of this volume, traces the gradual evolution of the Weatherman terrorist group. The process of radicalization began with opposition to particular officials and social policies; grew to increasing estrangement from, and eventual rejection of, the whole system, a process fueled by disillusionment, embittering failures, and hostile confrontations with authorities and police; and culminated in terroristic efforts to destroy the system and its dehumanized rulers. To inculcate the revolutionary morality and eliminate any residual self-censure and revulsion over ruthless behavior, the Weatherman group created small, isolated collectives where they eradicated their "bourgeois morality" with a vengeance.[50]

[47] A. Bandura, "The Psychology of Chance Encounters and Life Paths," *American Psychologist* 37 (1982): 747–55.

[48] Bandura, *Social Foundations of Thought and Action;* L. Franks and T. Powers, "Profile of a Terrorist," *Palo Alto Times*, 17 September 1970, pp. 26–28; and J. T. Gibson and M. Haritos-Fatouros, "The Education of a Torturer."

[49] Bandura et al., "Disinhibition of Aggression."

[50] Franks and Powers, "Profile of a Terrorist."

The preceding analyses have been concerned mainly with how disengagement mechanisms operate in removing moral impediments to terrorist violence and in combatting terrorism by violent means. These same mechanisms are also heavily enlisted by terrorist entrepreneurs, who supply militant states with the lethal tools to terrorize their own people or to equip the terrorist groups they sponsor. Frank Terpil, who became a terrorist entrepreneur after he fell from grace at the CIA, provides vivid testimony to these psychological mechanisms.[51]

Terpil shrouded his clandestine death operations in the euphemisms of a legitimate business fulfilling "consumer needs" under the appellation Intercontinental Technology. To spare himself any self-censure for contributing to human atrocities, he actively avoided knowledge of the purposes to which his weaponry would be put. ("I don't ever want to know that.") When asked whether he was ever haunted by any thoughts about the human suffering his deathly wares might cause, he explained that banishing thoughts of injurious consequences frees one's actions from restraints of conscience. ("If I really thought about the consequences all the time, I certainly wouldn't have been in this business . . . you have to blank it off.")

Efforts to probe for any signs of self-reproach brought self-exonerative comparisons. When queried concerning any qualms he might have felt about supplying torture equipment and tactical advice to Idi Amin in Uganda, Terpil countered with the view that the employees at Dow Chemical were not beset with guilt over the havoc wreaked on the Vietnamese population by the napalm they produced. ("I'm sure that the people from Dow Chemical didn't think of the consequences of selling napalm. If they did, they wouldn't be working at the factory. I doubt very much if they'd feel any more responsible for the ultimate use than I did for my equipment.") When pressed about the atrocities committed at Amin's "State Research Bureau" torture chambers, Terpil reiterated his depersonalized stance. ("I do not get wrapped up emotionally with the country. I regard myself basically as neutral and commercial.") To give legitimacy to his "private practice," he claimed that he aided British and American operations abroad as well.

The merchandising of terrorism is not accomplished by a few individuals. It requires a worldwide network of reputable, high-level operators who, by fractionation of function, perspective, and responsibility, amass

[51] D. Schorr, *Frank Terpil: Confessions of a Dangerous Man* [Film] (Boston: WGBH Educational Foundation, 1982).

arsenals of destruction, find places to store them, procure export and import licenses from different countries, obtain spurious end-user certificates that conceal the true destination of the shipments, and ship the arsenals around via circuitous itineraries. The cogs in this multifaceted network include weapons manufacturers, former government officials who have the useful political ties, ex-military and intelligence officers who provide valuable skills and contacts, weapons merchants, and shippers. By fractionating the enterprise, most of the participants see themselves as decent, legitimate practitioners of their own particular trade rather than as parties to a death operation.

Moral disengagement and self-deception

Does the disengagement of self-censure involve self-deception? Because of the incompatibility of being simultaneously a deceiver and the person deceived, literal self-deception cannot exist.[52] It is logically impossible to deceive oneself into believing something while knowing it to be false. Efforts to resolve the paradox of how anyone can be the agent and the object of deception at the same time have met with little success.[53] These attempts usually involve creating split selves and rendering one of them unconscious. The split-self conceptions neglect to specify how a conscious self can lie to an unconscious self without some awareness of what the other self believes. The deceiving self has to be aware of what the deceived self believes in order to know what kind of deceptions to concoct.

Different levels of awareness are sometimes proposed as another possible solution to the paradox. It is said that "deep down" people really know what they believe. Reacquainting the split selves only reinstates the paradox of how a person can be a deceiver and the person deceived at the same time. People, of course, often misconstrue events, lead themselves astray by their biases and misbeliefs, and act without first becoming informed. However, to be misdirected by one's beliefs or ignorance does not mean that one is lying to oneself.

Self-deception is often invoked when people choose to ignore possibly

[52] S. Bok, "The Self Deceived," *Social Science Information* 19 (1980): 923–36; T. S. Champlin, "Self-Deception: A Reflexive Dilemma," *Philosophy* 52 (1977): 281–99; and M. R. Haight, *A Study of Self Deception* (Atlantic Highlands, N.J.: Humanities Press, 1980).

[53] Bandura, *Social Foundations of Thought and Action.*

countervailing evidence. It could be argued that they must believe in its validity in order to avoid it, because otherwise they would not know what to shun. This is not necessarily so. Staunch believers often choose not to waste their time scrutinizing opposing arguments or evidence because they are already convinced of their fallacy. When confronted with evidence that disputes their beliefs, they question its credibility, dismiss its relevance, or twist it to fit their views. However, if the evidence is compelling, they alter their original beliefs to accommodate the discrepant evidence.

People may harbor some doubts concerning their beliefs but avoid seeking certain evidence because they have an inkling that the evidence might disconfirm what they wish to believe. Indeed, they may engage in all kinds of maneuvers, both in thought and in action, to avoid finding out the actual state of affairs. Suspecting something is not the same as knowing it to be true. Inklings can always be discounted as possibly being ill-founded. So long as a person does not find out the truth, what the person believes is not personally known to be false. Both Haight and Fingarette give considerable attention to processes by which people avoid painful or incriminating truth by not taking actions that would reveal the truth or not spelling out fully what they are doing or undergoing that would make it known.[54] They act in ways that keep themselves intentionally uninformed. They do not go looking for evidence of their culpability or the harmful effects of their actions. Obvious questions that would reveal unwelcome information remain unasked, so they do not find out what they do not want to know. Implicit agreements and social arrangements are created that leave the foreseeable unforeseen and the knowable unknown.

In addition to contending with their own self-censure, people are concerned about how they appear in the eyes of others when they engage in conduct that is morally suspect. This concern adds a social evaluative factor to the process. Haight argues that, in much of what is called self-deception, persons are aware of the reality they are trying to deny, but they create the public appearance that they are deceiving themselves.[55] Others are thus left uncertain about how to judge and treat persons who seem to be sincerely deluding themselves in efforts to avoid an unpleasant

[54] H. Fingarette, *Self-Deception* (New York: Humanities Press, 1969); and M. R. Haight, *A Study of Self Deception*.

[55] Haight, *A Study of Self Deception*.

truth. The public pretense is designed to head off social reproof. When people are caught up in the same painful predicament, the result may be a great deal of collective public pretense.

The mechanisms of moral disengagement involve cognitive and social machinations but not literal self-deception. In moral justification, for example, people may be misled by those they trust into believing that violent means are morally right because the means will check the human suffering of tyranny. The persuasive depictions of the perils and benefits may be accurate or exaggerated, or they may be just pious rhetoric masking less honorable purposes.

The same persuasion process applies to weakening of self-censure by dehumanizing and blaming adversaries. In the rhetoric of conflict, opinion shapers ascribe to their foes irrationalities, barbarities, and culpabilities that color public beliefs.[56] In these instances, people who have been persuaded are not lying to themselves. The misleaders and the misled are different persons. When the misleaders are themselves operating under erroneous beliefs, the views they voice are not intentional deceptions. They seek to persuade others into believing what they themselves believe. In social deception, public declarations by others may belie their private beliefs, which are concealed from those being deceived.

In reducing self-censure by ignoring, minimizing, or misconstruing the injurious effects of their actions, people lack the evidence to disbelieve what they already believe. The issue of self-dishonesty does not arise so long as people remain uninformed or misinformed about the outcomes of their actions. When moral disengagement is promoted by diffused and displaced responsibility, functionaries carry out the orders of superiors and often perform only a small subfunction of the enterprise. Such arrangements enable people to think of themselves merely as subordinate instruments, rather than as agents, of the entire enterprise. If they regard themselves as minor cogs in the intricate social machinery, they have little reason to believe otherwise concerning their initiatory power. This is not to say that disengagement of self-censure operates flawlessly. If serious disbeliefs arise, especially at the point of moral justification, people cannot get themselves to behave inhumanely. If they do, they pay the price of self-contempt.

[56] R. L. Ivie, "Images of Savagery in American Justifications for War," *Communication Monographs* 47 (1980): 270–94.

Conclusion

The massive threats to human welfare stem mainly from deliberate acts of principle rather than from unrestrained acts of impulse. The principled resort to destructiveness is of greatest social concern, but, ironically, it is the most ignored in psychological analyses of human violence. Given the existence of so many psychological devices for disengagement of moral control, societies cannot rely entirely on individuals, however righteous their standards, to provide safeguards against destructive ventures. Civilized conduct requires, in addition to humane personal codes, social systems that uphold compassionate behavior and renounce cruelty.

Monolithic political systems that exercise concentrated control over the major vehicles of social influence can wield greater justificatory power than pluralistic systems that represent diverse perspectives, interests, and concerns. Political diversity and toleration of public expression of skepticism create conditions that allow the emergence of challenges to suspect moral appeals. If societies are to function more humanely, they must establish effective social safeguards against the misuse of institutional justificatory power for exploitive and destructive purposes.

[5]

How Violence Is Justified: Sinn Fein's *An Phoblacht*

by Robert G. Picard

Political justification for IRA activity accounts for one-third of the content of this republican paper, with reports of provocations by security forces and others providing 25 percent and IRA-initiated violence less than 5 percent of the total.

What types of messages do politically violent groups send to their supporters? What importance do such groups place on different types of messages? This study considers communications of and about a terrorist group, the Provisional Irish Republican Army (IRA), in a newspaper controlled by its political wing, Sinn Fein. It thus provides a clearer view of the group's messages than studies of traditional media that generally support the status quo and are constrained by its social influence (3, 4, 39, 40).

Acts of confrontation, violence, and terrorism are as much forms of expression as is the language used to describe, justify, support, or oppose such acts. A growing body of literature has thus begun to explore the communication aspects of violent social and political conflicts (1, 3, 15, 16, 19, 32, 45, 46). As Scott and Smith (46) have argued, the messages of groups that employ confrontational strategies can help us understand and respond to the violence. Scholars need to "read the rhetoric of confrontation, seek understanding of its presuppositions, tactics, and purposes" (p. 8).

Larson (28, pp. 167–174) asserts that social movements have four major stages: (a) characterization—creating internal and external identities; (b) establishment of legitimacy—achieving the ability to support the identity the movement has created and exercising power; (c) achievement of participation—increasing strength of the movement, developing unity, and becoming institutionalized; and (d) penetration of society—gaining acceptance by others. A study of the history of the Palestine Liberation Organization has documented its twentieth-century evolution through the four stages, analyzed its changing violent and nonviolent rhetoric over time, and shown how its use of rhetoric has made it an important force in the Israeli-Palestinian conflict (8).

The subject of this study is *An Phoblacht/Republican News,* an English-language weekly newspaper published by Sinn Fein, the legal political wing of the republicans. In keeping with the cultural tradition of Ireland, the paper

Robert G. Picard is Professor in the Department of Communications, California State University, Fullerton.

AN PHOBLACHT

IRELAND'S BIGGEST SELLING POLITICAL WEEKLY

Republican News

Welcome home the Guildford Four

PAUL HILL & GERRY CONLON

Rally at GPO

DUBLIN

2.30pm Sat. 4th Nov.

Freedom of movement?

occasionally publishes an article in Gaelic. These articles appear infrequently and usually appear with no other Gaelic-language articles in an issue. The paper is distributed in Ireland, Northern Ireland, the United Kingdom, the United States, and other countries. The paper is available at newsstands willing to carry the publication, usually in areas with large Irish and Irish Catholic populations. It is also available at shops of large newspaper agents who carry a wide variety of publications from throughout the United Kingdom and Ireland.

The use of newspapers to support social movements and political violence is not a new phenomenon. The deliberate, tactical development of papers as tools for revolutionary propaganda began at the dawn of the twentieth century with Lenin's establishment of *Iskra* and his theorizing about the social-revolutionary role of the press in mobilizing the masses as propagandist, agitator, and organizer (30, 31). Lenin's views on the importance of media have been adopted by numerous social revolutionary, nationalist, and secessionist groups throughout the century, and many organizations have established or used newspapers to expose their views and promote their causes. Groups that gain significant popular support and an organizational infrastructure often are able to replace underground publications with public outlets, such as *An Phoblacht* (38).

The communications activities of the IRA and its supporters have been recognized for nearly three-quarters of a century as among the best organized and most effective of similar groups and have been credited with keeping the movement vital and active. Clutterbuck (10, p. 89) has noted that "its propaganda arm (Sinn Fein) has. . .always been more vital to its survival, and hence more effective, than its combat arm."

Irish desires for home rule and independence from the United Kingdom have promoted revolutionary efforts for two centuries. Following major insurrections in 1867 and 1916, the Irish Free State was established in 1921; it

Journal of Communication, Autumn 1991

included all but the six northernmost counties of the island. The desire to unite these counties with independent Ireland has remained strong among Catholics in those counties; Protestants there tend to favor continued allegiance to the United Kingdom. Relative peace existed in the six counties until the late 1960s, when a civil rights campaign was developed into a new effort for independence by the Provisional Irish Republican Army, using guerrilla and terrorist tactics (2, 5, 6, 26, 27, 29). The conflict now not only involves revolutionary desires but has elements of a sectarian civil rights conflict, as Catholics charge that they face social and economic discrimination in the six counties.

Sinn Fein has been a political voice throughout Ireland, arguing for unification of all Irish counties under the free Irish government and an end to economic and social disparities between Protestants and Catholics. It publicly lauds the efforts of the IRA, and many of its members are directly tied to the group. The party's major political views include socialist platforms involving housing, education, employment, and other domestic issues (14, 17).

Although a variety of significant essays and treatises have addressed media coverage of the IRA (7, 10, 20, 22, 48, 51), these have been almost wholly based on opinion and anecdotal evidence and involve the activities of dominant-culture media outlets. Even among them, few studies are based on social science research methods or large-scale serious analysis. Studies of television and newspaper coverage by Paletz, Ayanian, and Fozzard (36, 37) found that coverage of the IRA offered little information about the group's purposes or goals, was written in a tone designed to reassure audiences of government and social stability, and did not legitimize the IRA. Tan's (47) comparison of British, Irish, and U.S. newspaper coverage of the IRA over a 25-year period found little day-to-day coverage by the *Times* of London or the *New York Times.* When terrorism was mentioned, however, the coverage was clearly negative. A study of British information and entertainment media portrayals concluded that media do not provide excessive or supportive coverage of terrorists and that they do not uncritically accept official views (44).

This study considers the coverage of an interested and partisan voice—*An Phoblacht*, which carries Sinn Fein party and members' views of the Irish conflict. The paper is typically 16 pages in length, published in a two-color tabloid (11½" × 16¼") format. The cover price per issue is 30p in Ireland and 35p in Britain.

A significant body of research asserts that a primary purpose of terroristic acts is media coverage (3, 10, 33, 35, 45), that the media must be present for terrorists to have an effect and that terroristic acts are in fact created for such coverage (18, 52). Laqueur (quoted in 49), typifies this view when he says, "the media are the terrorist's best friend. The terrorist's act by itself is nothing; publicity is all." Given that *An Phoblacht* is a voice for the IRA, I expected news of IRA violence to be prominently displayed in the paper and to account for a significant portion of its coverage.

I further anticipated that Sinn Fein would make significant use of the paper to promote its candidates for office, put forth its political positions, and provide the political rationale and basis for the conflict. According to previous research, providing statements, issuing commentary about conflicts, and justifying violence are important parts of terrorists' media use, and violence is one means of gaining the attention of and access to media for this public, nonviolent discourse (12, 38).

In addition to social, economic, and political grievances, terrorists and their supporters cite "provocations" by security forces of Britain, Northern Ireland, and others as a factor in their rebellion against authorities (13, 23). I therefore expected coverage of violence by security forces to be prominently displayed in *An Phoblacht* and to account for a significant portion of the coverage. Similarly, I expected coverage of violence against republicans by members of organized and unorganized loyalist groups (made up predominantly of Protestants) to be prominently displayed and extensive.

The paper's standard five-column format yields 75 column inches per page; alternate layouts use four and six columns. To make measurements comparable, I created a conversion table for content in these formats. The four-column format required an upward calculation adjustment of 30 percent of its actual measurement, and the six-column format required a downward calculation adjustment of 22 percent of its actual measurement.

Fourteen of *An Phoblacht*'s 50 issues (28 percent) from 1989 were randomly selected for analysis. These issues comprise a reliable sample for that year but clearly do not necessarily reflect content in all other years.[1] The year was chosen because the issues were available to me; one year's issues provided a reasonable basis for assaying the efficacy of the types of analysis employed here.

Every article from the issues in the sample was measured and placed into 1 of 21 categories. For ease of computation, measurements were rounded upward to the nearest one-quarter inch. Photographs were included in the topical content analysis and the measurements of their space included in column inches devoted to the categorized topics.

To test for prominence of display, I recorded the page numbers of each article related to violence and provocations by the IRA, security forces, and loyalists. In addition, I recorded the number and page location of photographs of violence or destruction by the three groups.

Most category definitions listed in the accompanying tables are self-explanatory and were drawn from published content analyses of newspapers. Several operational definitions, however, are specific to this study.

"War news" refers to reports about IRA attacks. It takes its name from the logo used by *An Phoblacht* to report IRA violence and attempts at violence. In most cases these reports were two or three paragraphs long and grouped under a single headline as one story. On rare occasions, a particular attack was singled out for a separate story. "IRA nonwar news" refers to reports directly about the IRA, its leaders, and its activities that did not involve violence.

[1] Although 1989 was not an extraordinary or particularly unusual year for Sinn Fein and the IRA—political and armed ventures proceeded at a stable level relative to surrounding years—Sinn Fein's messages were likely to change over time because of social and political developments. The messages conveyed in 1989 therefore might not be the same as those in 1970, 1980, or 1995.

"Provocations—security forces" refers to actions of British military and domestic security forces, as well as those of the government of Ireland, that were reported as involving unnecessary violence or harm to individual rights, or reported as being outrageous, shocking, or harassing. "Provocations—loyalists" refers to similarly reported actions by groups and individuals loyal to the British government.[2] "Antirepublican nonmilitary government acts" refers to reports about judicial proceedings, hearings, government pronouncements, etc., against republicans or IRA members.

"Commercial ads" includes ads for products and services of a nonpolitical nature. "Political ads" are those urging votes on political issues and participation in political events. "Promotional ads" includes announcements for items offered for sale by *An Phoblacht* or Sinn Fein, including books, videotapes, and t-shirts with political slogans.

The analysis showed that, as expected, Sinn Fein's political activities accounted for close to a third of the paper's content. The several categories of political expression are shown in Table 1. "Electoral politics" provided 9.4 percent of total coverage (ranking third overall) and focused mainly on the electoral activities of Sinn Fein, contrasting Sinn Fein policies with those of other parties. "Political speeches/rallies" was devoted almost totally to Sinn Fein politicians and to rallies supporting the party and republican causes. It was the sixth-ranked category and accounted for 7.8 percent of the coverage.

"Editorials/opinion/columns" provided a platform for direct comment supporting the party and its views; this category was ranked seventh and provided 6.5 percent of the coverage. "Political ads" and "promotional ads" contributed 3.8 percent of the total coverage. "Calendar listings," which accounted for 1.6 percent of the total coverage, provided information devoted to party activities and events supporting causes endorsed by the party. Thus, 29.1 percent of the total coverage was directly devoted to political activities and interests of Sinn Fein itself.[3]

I had expected provocations by security forces and loyalists to be prominently displayed and to account for a significant amount of coverage in order to justify republican causes and IRA violence. And indeed, they accounted for 13.6 percent of all coverage, the single largest category. Although fewer stories reported loyalist provocations, together the two categories accounted for 16.1 percent of coverage. When these categories are combined with stories of nonmilitary government action, 25 percent of the coverage uses antirepublican acts to justify the existence of the IRA and its attacks.

[2] The labeling of acts in these categories as "provocations" would undoubtedly be disputed by supporters of the loyalists and the Crown forces. The use of the label here does not indicate a subjective judgment about the nature of the acts; it reflects how the acts were reported by the paper.

[3] Categories that do not appear to be directly political, such as "art/book/film/TV reviews" and "foreign news," almost always were addressed to the political interests of republicans and Sinn Fein. Thus, nearly all of the paper is regularly devoted to political journalism and support for the causes backed by the IRA.

Table 1: Topic areas covered in *An Phoblacht* by total percentage, total inches, and rank

	% of total	Total inches	Overall rank
Direct political expression			
Electoral politics	9.4	1,580	3
Political speeches/rallies	7.8	1,326	6
Editorials/opinion/columns	6.5	1,085	7
Political ads	2.3	381	15
Promotional ads	1.5	254	18
Calendar listings	1.6	262	17
Subtotal	29.1	4,887	
Expression of victimization			
Provocations—security forces	13.6	2,276	1
Provocations—loyalists	2.5	421	14
Antirepublican nonmilitary government acts	8.9	1,501	4
Subtotal	25.0	4,198	
Indirect political expression			
General domestic news	8.9	1,491	5
Foreign news	5.2	869	8
Economy/employment	4.0	672	11
Education	.5	88	19
Emigration/immigration	.2	48	20
Subtotal	18.8	3,168	
Expression of martyrdom			
Commemorations/remembrances/obituaries	10.8	1,807	2
Expression of IRA violence and effectiveness			
War news (IRA actions)	4.7	785	9
Expression of IRA unity, effectiveness, and legitimacy			
IRA nonwar news	3.1	514	12
Total	91.5[a]	16,882	

[a] Four of the 21 categories (commercial ads, reviews, letters, and others) are omitted here.

Multiple stories of security force provocations appeared in each issue but only infrequently on the first page. Stories of provocations by loyalists received greater prominence. Provocation stories tended to emphasize the victimization of Catholics, Sinn Fein members, and IRA members as suffering from occupation and abuse. The following excerpts are typical:

A British army undercover unit, some wearing masks and others with their faces blackened, smashed their way into several houses in the Springfield area of West Belfast late on Friday night, December 1st.

The people whose homes were attacked thought the gang were a loyalist murder squad. A woman had to be hospitalised with shock and a child needed medical attention such was her distress ("Residents Terrorised in SAS-Style Raid," December 7, 1989, p. 5).

A man who was so badly tortured in Castlereagh Interrogation Centre in 1987 that Belfast High Court ordered his release, has again been seriously assaulted, this time by British soldiers form [sic] the notorious Parachute Regiment.... Soldiers from the Parachute Regiment attacked Brian Gillen...after lying in wait for him near his home. He was beaten about the head with rifle butts and had to have eight stitches to the gashes over his eyes and his cheekbone was fractured ("Paras Ambush Man," April 20, 1989, p. 7).

In many articles and columns, security forces and their actions are ridiculed and stigmatized with such terms as "mangy Marines," "a pro-British death squad," "thugs," "a gang," "indiscriminately sprayed bullets," and "an orgy of destruction." Individuals who come into contact with such forces are described as "victims" or "innocents" who are "continually harassed" and "vulnerable," who "helplessly watched" or "suffered."

Previous studies of the symbolic control of portrayals in dominant media have revealed highly selective and politically motivated images of perpetrators of political violence. The language observed in this study indicates that media controlled by opposing organizations similarly control the portrayals of their adversaries.

Surprisingly, in comparison to the coverage of provocational acts, less than five percent of the paper's content was devoted to IRA violence. Such violence was given less coverage than foreign and domestic news, electoral politics, or reports on speeches and rallies. Weekly issues regularly reported a half-dozen to a dozen acts or attempted acts of IRA violence, but the individual reports were typically only about two or three paragraphs long.

Nevertheless, IRA violence was reported regularly and received prominent display. Typical of these reports is the following:

The main observation post fronting the massive British army base in Crossmaglen was badly damaged by the IRA on Thursday, October 26th.

In an operation described by the BBC as "undeniably daring," volunteers drove a mortar-laden tractor literally under the noses of Brit sentries just five yards outside the base's front gates ("Crossmaglen Barracks Blasted," November 2, 1989, p. 2).

Like other stories of IRA actions, this report emphasizes the power of IRA operations and evokes the heroism of the participants by emphasizing the danger of their activities. Even reports on unsuccessful operations took this tone. One noted that

Volunteers of the Belfast Brigade IRA managed to escape after British troops spotted a command wire leading to a 6lb landmine and made straight for the Volunteers' firing position.... The alertness of the Volunteers involved ensured that they were able to escape before being hemmed in by the British army patrols ("Landmine Uncovered," July 27, 1989, p. 2).

Such heroic images and descriptions are particularly useful in developing admiration and public support, promoting emulative behavior (see 34), and gaining new recruits for a cause. Media coverage plays a major role in building and conveying these images (24, 25).

IRA combatants were regularly portrayed as members of "brigades" or "service units," lending them the authority of organized opposition, and were most often referred to individually as "volunteers." Their opponents or targets were normally labeled as the "enemy." The coverage by this partisan publication thus portrays members of the combatant wing of the movement as heroic leaders who are trying to protect and save the people by correcting perceived wrongs and vanquishing their enemies.

Many articles justified violent acts by IRA members. An article on an IRA attack on the Shorts Brothers aerospace facility at Belfast Harbour Airport cited an IRA statement that "Shorts is a target because it is a major supplier of high technology military hardware to British forces" ("Shorts Blasted," July 6, 1989, p. 2). An article on the bombing of Royal Ulster Constabulary Superintendent Alwyn Harris justified the attack this way: "The Belfast Brigade said that Harris had been responsible for overseeing repressive crown forces operations throughout the North and the wrecking of nationalist homes" ("Top RUC Officer Executed," October 12, 1989, p. 2).

Although reports of IRA acts clearly were given import and were laudatory of participants, they were not given an unusual amount of coverage compared to how reports of violence are treated in the general press. This would seem to indicate that violence itself is not as important a part of terrorist groups' purposes as those who promote the "violence for the sake of violence" theory of terrorism believe.

An Phoblacht also carried reports about IRA activities that were not directly related to violence against political enemies (3.1 percent). These stories tended to promote institutionalization of the IRA, giving it legitimacy and promoting unity. An August 24, 1989, interview with IRA officials, for example, discussed the group's role in combating crime and its views on the political status of (southern) Ireland ("This Is the Final Phase," pp. 8–9). Other stories reported IRA reactions to British policies and pronouncements of government officials. Frequent representations of the acts as "hypocrisy," "disingenuous," or "a charade" were designed to denigrate or dissipate the effect of governmental activities. Such portrayals were used to simultaneously delegitimize dominant culture and legitimize IRA culture and activities.

Another way to understand how reports of IRA violence were treated is to compare them to reports of provocations by security forces and loyalists. As seen in Table 2, provocations by security forces were reported in nearly four times as many stories as were devoted to IRA attacks. Reports of authorities' provocations were most often published in the first half of the paper's pages (mean and median = page 6; mode = page 5). The average IRA "war news" story, however, was longer than the average story of security force provocations. It was also displayed more prominently near the front of the paper (mode and median = page 2; mean = page 3.2).

Table 2: Prominence of stories and photographs of violence in *An Phoblacht*

	IRA "War news" articles	Security forces "Provocations" articles	Loyalists "Provocations" articles
Stories of violence			
Number	17	63	16
Mean per issue	1.21	4.50	1.14
Mean size	46 in.	36 in.	27 in.
Photos of violence			
Number	6	14	7
Mean per issue	.43	1.00	.50

The number of articles about provocations by loyalists nearly equaled the number of IRA "war news" stories, but on average the former were about half the size of the latter (and one-third smaller than the "provocations—security forces" stories). Reports about provocations by loyalists, however, were more prominently displayed (mean = page 5.4; median = page 4; mode = page 2) than articles about security force provocations.

The use of photographs of violent acts or their aftermath was also analyzed. As had been the case for articles, there were more photos of security force violence than of IRA or loyalist violence, by a more than two-to-one margin. Again, however, photographs of IRA violence were more prominently displayed (mean = page 2.3; median and mode = page 2) than photographs of security force violence (mean = page 7.6; median = page 6; mode = page 4) or loyalist violence (mean = page 2.7; median = page 3; mode = 2, 3, 4).

An interesting and unanticipated finding is the importance of "commemorations, remembrances, and obituaries," in the pages of *An Phoblacht*. This was the second single largest category of content, providing more than one-tenth of the coverage (see Table 1). Almost all these stories concerned the martyrdom of IRA members and supporters killed or injured in action, imprisoned, or otherwise notable for their activities. Typical of this type of story is the following:

The families of several of the 1981 hunger-strikers were joined by several hundred local people as they gathered at the Republican Plot in Bellaghy, South Derry to commemorate the death eight years ago of Francis Hughes, perhaps the most renowned IRA Volunteer over the last 20 years of struggle. He died after 59 days on hunger-strike ("Francis Hughes Remembered," May 18, 1989, p. 10).

A regular feature included commemorative listings such as:

LOUGHGALL MARTYRS (2nd Anniversary) In proud and loving memory of eight gallant Irishmen who gave their lives at Loughgall, Co. Armagh on May 8th 1987. "From the graves of patriot men and women spring living nations."—Padraig Mac Piarais. From Liam, Mary and family, Manchester ("I nDil Chuimhne," June 1, 1989, p. 15).

This type of content may provide significant psychological rewards to those engaging in violence, potential participants, and their families. By ensuring that their actions, results, and participation are not forgotten, the paper promotes the importance of their acts, imbues them with heroic images, and lauds them for their participation. Creating a symbolic reality that keeps alive the meaning of dead or imprisoned partisans is one means of influencing the living and enabling them to express gratitude for sacrificial acts (21, 50). Thus, the commemorations in *An Phoblacht* may help assure members and supporters that sacrifices have not been meaningless and that they need to keep alive the struggle and the memory of its participants.[4]

The writing style and editorial processes used in media coverage of political violence are crucial in shaping public perceptions about perpetrators and acts of violence. Journalists amplify, arbitrate, and create rhetoric and representations about terrorism when they cover such violence for dominant media (41). This role is clearly duplicated by journalists writing for *An Phoblacht*.

The paper normally employs a traditional journalistic style, but with few linguistic subtleties to mask its social and political orientation. Its lack of bylines makes the identities of writers unclear. This also makes it difficult to study the processes and practices that guide how information is gathered, discussed, manipulated, and published. By observing the social acts that create *An Phoblacht* as a cultural product whose purpose is to create, develop, and maintain a distinct Irish Republican Army identity and culture, one would gain a clearer perspective of the meaning of the content and messages revealed in this study.

The extent to which writing, editing, and publishing the paper involves consultation within and outside the immediate staff is unclear. I suspect, however, that writers and editors are so committed to the cause and the purpose of the publication that they rarely disagree over the organization's general approaches to information processing and dissemination.

An Phoblacht offers intriguing possibilities for further study of the discourse of marginalized groups such as Sinn Fein and the IRA. Because the IRA embraces a social-revolutionary agenda that includes a classless, nongendered social order, studies of the paper's representations of class, power, and gender would provide insight into the extent to which those views are acted upon or are merely rhetoric. Analyses of symbolism and iconography, use of drama and creation of myth, and language and textual patterns would be appropriate here. Audience studies would also be useful, since clearly the meaning of the paper

[4] The commemorative functions of *An Phoblacht* extend the idea of commemoration in Catholicism. (IRA members and supporters are predominantly Catholic.) Catholic rituals preserve the memory of those held in affection and allow the living to give thanks for the deliverance of the dead from the sufferings of the material world and to appeal to God on their behalf. Martyrs receive special commemoration because it is believed that they may intercede with God on behalf of the living. The dead can thus be revered, appealed to, and appealed for in prayers and anniversary masses (11, 42).

and its content would differ among Catholics and Protestants, IRA supporters, nonsupporters, and opponents, Irish and non-Irish individuals, and residents and nonresidents of the six counties.

This study provides a unique view of what a mature terrorist group, with large popular support for its causes, will convey if it can control or highly influence a medium of communication. *An Phoblacht* is being operated as a vehicle designed to promote its cause. The themes and representations conveyed in the publication provide ways to understand the meaning of the violent acts surrounding the IRA.

Over 29 percent of the paper's content was devoted to social and political issues behind the conflict. This message seems to be aimed not only at republicans but at British officials and other observers of the conflict. The emphasis on social and political issues also may be intended to help downplay the public's reaction to IRA attacks so that the violence does not obscure the underlying reasons for the conflict.

The second largest category of stories, reports of provocations, conveyed the message that republicans are abused and fighting back, rather than initiating violence. This content comprised one-quarter of the coverage.

The third largest content category, apparently aimed at IRA members and supporters, takes the form of the commemorative listings and remembrances of those who have sacrificed life, limb, or liberty for the cause. These listings, which account for 10.8 percent of the total coverage, convey the view that the participation is important and recognized. Published letters often serve this purpose as well.

The message of IRA violence receives considerably less attention, accounting for only 4.7 percent of the total coverage. These stories convey the effectuality and abilities of those engaged in the conflict to their supporters and reward the risk-takers.

This analysis of the messages of *An Phoblacht* provides a view of the IRA's political violence within a broader framework of social and political movements and the desire of individuals and groups to assert self-determination. Cathcart (9) has argued that confrontation is central to social movements and is needed to establish identity and legitimacy. Scott and Smith (46) note that individuals who reject the social order seek confrontation as a means of asserting group identity and purpose. Once legitimacy is gained, however, some movements split into a struggle between moderates, who wish to engage in negotiation and political action, and radicals, who wish to continue a violent confrontational strategy.

These views fit well with Larson's stages of social movements (28). The communications and development of Sinn Fein show it to be a mature social movement, concerned with establishing its identity, legitimacy, participation, and penetration. The first three stages have been clearly reached by the group, and the paper carries messages designed to maintain and continue that development. The group has only partially developed in the fourth stage; messages about Sinn Fein leaders in Ireland, Northern Ireland, and Great Britain, and their worldwide travels to meetings with other groups and political personalities, are clearly designed to promote penetration and acceptance.

The IRA itself has not developed as much as its political wing because it does not enjoy above-ground status and directly perpetrates republican violence. Nevertheless, the messages about the IRA carried in *An Phoblacht* suggest that the group is capable of gaining support among part of the populace and exercising power toward achieving its goals. Although articles in the paper support the group's efforts toward institutionalization—especially through IRA nonwar news—the IRA has not achieved a significant degree of participation in Larson's scheme. Neither has it achieved significant penetration, the fourth stage in Larson's model.

This study suggests that supporters of IRA terrorism may be willing to separate themselves from terrorism or help end some violence if social and political grievances are ameliorated, as some authors have suggested (43). The independence of the six counties remains a separate issue, but the messages of the Sinn Fein paper suggest that support for violence might diminish if sectarian economic and social discrimination are addressed.

References

1. Alali, A. Odasuo and Kenoye Kelvin Eke (Eds.). *Media Coverage of Terrorism: Methods of Diffusion.* Newbury Park, Cal.: Sage, 1991.
2. Alexander, Yonah and Alan O'Day. *Terrorism in Ireland.* New York: St. Martin's Press, 1984.
3. Alexander, Yonah and Robert G. Picard (Eds.). *In the Camera's Eye: News Coverage of Terrorist Events.* Washington, D.C.: Brasseys, 1991.
4. Altschull, J. Herbert. *Agents of Power: The Role of News Media in Human Affairs.* New York: Longman, 1984.
5. Bell, J. Bowyer. *The Secret Army: A History of the IRA, 1916–1970.* New York: John Day, 1970.
6. Bell, J. Bowyer. *The Secret Army: The IRA, 1916–1979* (rev. ed.). Cambridge, Mass.: MIT Press, 1980.
7. "The British Media and Ireland." Campaign for Free Speech on Ireland, London, 1978.
8. Brock, Bernard L. and Sharon Howell. "The Evolution of the PLO: Rhetoric of Terrorism." *Central States Speech Journal* 39, Fall/Winter 1988, pp. 281–292.
9. Cathcart, Robert S. "Movements: Confrontation as Rhetorical Form." *Southern Speech Communication Journal* 43, Spring 1978, pp. 233–247.
10. Clutterbuck, Richard. *The Media and Political Violence* (2d ed.). London: Macmillan, 1983.
11. "Commemoration of the Dead." In James Hastings (Ed.), *Encyclopaedia of Religion and Ethics.* New York: Scribner, 1951, pp. 716–720.
12. Crelinsten, Ronald D. "Power and Meaning: Terrorism as a Struggle of Access to the Communication Structure." In Paul Wilkinson (Ed.), *Contemporary Research on Terrorism.* Aberdeen, Scotland: Aberdeen University Press, 1987.
13. Crenshaw, Martha. "The Causes of Terrorism." *Comparative Politics* 13, July 1981, pp. 379–399.
14. Day, Alan J. and Henry W. Deganhardt. *Political Parties of the World* (2d ed.). Detroit: Gale Research, 1984.

15. Decker, Warren and Daniel Rainey. "Terrorism as Communication." Paper presented to the conference of the Speech Communication Association, New York, November 1980.

16. Decker, Warren and Daniel Rainey. "Media and Terrorism: Toward the Development of an Instrument to Explicate Their Relationship." Paper presented to the conference of the Speech Communication Association, Louisville, Kentucky, November 1982.

17. Delury, George E. (Ed.). *World Encyclopedia of Political Systems and Parties.* New York: Facts on File, 1983.

18. Dowling, Ralph E. "Terrorism and the Media: A Rhetorical Genre." *Journal of Communication* 36(1), Winter 1986, pp. 12–24.

19. Dowling, Ralph E. "The Contributions of Speech Communication Scholarship to the Study of Terrorism and Media: Preview and Review." Paper presented to the conference on Communication in Terrorist Events, Terrorism and the News Media Research Project, Boston, March 3–5, 1988.

20. Elliott, Phillip. "Reporting Northern Ireland." *Ethnicity and the Media: An Analysis of Media Reporting in the United Kingdom, Canada, and Ireland.* Paris: UNESCO, 1977.

21. Foss, Martin. *Death, Sacrifice, and Tragedy.* Lincoln: University of Nebraska Press, 1966.

22. Francis, Richard. "Broadcasting to a Community in Crisis: The Experience in Northern Ireland." British Broadcasting Corporation, London, 1977.

23. Gurr, Ted Robert. *Why Men Rebel.* Princeton, N.J.: Princeton University Press, 1971.

24. Hadas, Moses and Morton Smith. *Heroes and Gods: Spiritual Biographies in Antiquity.* New York: Harper & Row, 1972.

25. Hook, Sidney. *The Hero in History: A Study in Limitation and Possibility.* New York: John Day, 1943.

26. Hyans, Edward S. *A Dictionary of Modern Revolution.* New York: Taplinger, 1973.

27. Janke, Peter. *Guerrilla and Terrorist Organisations: A World Directory and Bibliography.* New York: Macmillan, 1983.

28. Larson, Charles U. *Persuasion: Reception and Responsibility.* Belmont, Cal.: Wadsworth, 1973.

29. Lee, Alfred M. "The Dynamics of Terrorism in Northern Ireland, 1968–1980." *Social Forces* 59, Spring 1981, pp. 100–134.

30. Lenin, Vladimir Ilyich. "Draft of a Declaration of the Editorial Board of Iskra and Zarya." In *V. I. Lenin on Building the Bolshevik Party: Selected Writings, 1894 to 1905.* Chicago: Liberator Press, 1976.

31. Lenin, Vladimir Ilyich. "What Is to Be Done?" *Collected Works,* Volume 5. Moscow: Progress, 1977.

32. Martin, L. John. "Violence, Terrorism, Nonviolence: Vehicles of Social Control." In Joseph Roucek (Ed.), *Social Control for the 1980s: A Handbook for Order in a Democratic Society.* Westport, Conn.: Greenwood Press, 1978.

33. Miller, Abraham H. (Ed.). *Terrorism, the Media, and the Law.* Dobbs Ferry, N.Y.: Transnational, 1982.

34. Norman, Dorothy. *The Hero: Myth, Image, Symbol.* New York: World, 1969.

35. O'Neill, Michael P. *Terrorist Spectaculars: Should TV Coverage Be Curbed?* New York: Priority Press, 1986.

36. Paletz, David L., John Z. Ayanian, and Peter A. Fozzard. "Terrorism on TV News: The IRA, the FALN, and the Red Brigades." In William C. Adams (Ed.), *Television Coverage of International Affairs.* Norwood, N.J.: Ablex, 1982.

37. Paletz, David L., John Z. Ayanian, and Peter A. Fozzard. "The I.R.A., the Red Brigades, and the F.A.L.N. in the *New York Times.*" *Journal of Communication* 32(2), Spring 1982, pp. 162–171.

International Politics and the Press / Sinn Fein's An Phoblacht

38. Picard, Robert G. "Press Relations of Terrorist Organizations." *Public Relations Review* 15, Winter 1989, pp. 12–23.

39. Picard, Robert G. "The Socio-Institutional Context of Media in Terrorism." Paper presented to the conference on Media and Modern Warfare, Centre for Conflict Studies, University of New Brunswick, Canada, September 29–October 1, 1989.

40. Picard, Robert G. "Terrorism and Media Values: News Selection and the Distortion of Reality." In Y. Alexander and H. Foxman (Eds.), *The 1988–1989 Annual on Terrorism*. Amsterdam: Kluwer Academic, 1990.

41. Picard, Robert G. "The Journalist's Role in Coverage of Terrorist Events." In A. Odasuo Alali and Kenoye Kelvin Eke (Eds.), *Media Coverage of Terrorism: Methods of Diffusion*. Newbury Park, Cal.: Sage, 1991, pp. 40–48.

42. "The Prayer for the Dead." In *A Catholic Dictionary of Theology*. New York: Thomas Nelson, 1967, pp. 156-160.

43. Ross, Jeffrey I. and Ted R. Gurr. "Why Terrorism Subsides: A Comparative Study of Canada and the United States." *Comparative Politics* 21, July 1989, pp. 405–426.

44. Schlesinger, Philip, Graham Murdock, and Philip Elliott. *Televising 'Terrorism': Political Violence in Popular Culture*. London: Comedia, 1983.

45. Schmid, Alex P. and Janny de Graaf. *Violence as Communication: Insurgent Terrorism and the Western News Media*. Beverly Hills, Cal.: Sage, 1982.

46. Scott, Robert L. and Donald K. Smith. "The Rhetoric of Confrontation." *Quarterly Journal of Speech* 55, February 1969, pp. 1–8.

47. Tan, Zoe Che-Wei. "Media Publicity and Insurgent Terrorism: A Twenty-Five Year Balance Sheet." Paper presented to the conference of the International Communication Association, Political Communication Division, Montreal, May 25, 1987.

48. "Terrorism and the Media." In *Ten Years of Terrorism: Collected Views*. London: Royal United Services Institute for Defence Studies, 1979, pp. 87–108.

49. "Terrorism Is Likely to Increase." London *Times*, April 25, 1975.

50. Vernon, Glenn M. *Sociology of Death: An Analysis of Death-Related Behavior*. New York: Ronald Press, 1970.

51. Viera, John David. "Terrorism at the BBC: The IRA on British Television." *Journal of Film and Video* 40(4), Fall 1988, pp. 28–36.

52. Weimann, Gabriel. "The Theater of Terror: Effects of Press Coverage." *Journal of Communication* 33(1), Winter 1983, pp. 38–45.

[6]
The Rhetoric of Terrorism

Richard W. Leeman

Terrorism has occurred throughout human history and around the globe. Any generalization about terrorism and its rhetoric will not be universally applicable to every instance. Certain rhetorical features do recur, however, particularly among terrorists whose agendas are significantly anti-American. Specifically, I will argue that the terrorist's half of the dialogue typically consists of bipolar exhortation. Further, it is frequently marked by the presence of two significant rhetorical tensions.

Although the communication of terrorists can be studied in many ways, I am particularly interested in what M. Cherif Bassiouni has called its "socio-political message."[1] I will not be concerned with other types of terroristic communication, such as manuevering for publicity or negotiation. My concern in this study is with the message designed for a larger audience than network executives or government negotiators. The socio-political message attempts to inform the body politic of the terrorist's cause, and persuade them that the cause is just. Thus, this chapter describes not how terrorists procure the publicity by which their messages reach their audience, but the beliefs and actions those messages endeavor to secure.

The first section of this chapter describes the outstanding features of terrorists' rhetoric, features generated by the nature of terrorism. The second section outlines two rhetorical tensions which typically emerge.

TERRORIST RHETORIC AS BIPOLAR EXHORTATION

The rhetoric of terrorism is characterized by a bipolar, exhortative discourse. First, dividing the world into the good terrorist vs. the inhumane system portrays the terrorist's violence as a legitimate response. Second, given this stark division, the purpose of the terrorist's rhetoric becomes that of exhorting the body politic to action against that system. I examine each of these features in turn.

Legitimizing Terrorism through Bipolar Discourse

The outstanding feature of terrorism is its violence, whether actual or threatened. Typically, violence contravenes societal norms, arguing implicitly against the established order and against communication.[2] Whether the "system" is democratic or not, violence is antithetical to the "order" because violence is disorderly, and no "system" allows indiscriminate, unfettered violence.[3] In McLuhanesque fashion, the medium of violence *becomes* the message, suggesting by its very nature that the established order is illegitimate.[4] To use unsanctioned violence in a political setting thus invites the user to justify, or legitimate, that violence. Not surprisingly, justification is a primary concern of the terrorist speaker. Typically, terrorists defend their violence by constructing a bipolar world which cleanly divides good from evil. Terrorism is legitimate because it "responds" to an evil, illegitimate enemy.

Responding to an Inhumane System

Terrorists typically portray their violence as a *response*. That is, the existing violence to which they respond legitimates their actions. Terrorists characterize their acts as answers, a term implying not only that their violence is a response but that theirs is a response that *communicates*. Thus, the German *Rote Armee Fraktion* "Answers Bombs with Bombs" and the Angry Brigade "will answer their force with our class violence."[5] The "Squad of the Martyr Patrick Urguello" justified the 1972 Lod airport attack with this note:

> The raid launched today was a revolutionary *answer* to the Israeli massacre performed in cold blood by the butcher Moshe Dayan and his *devils* against the *martyr heroes* Ali Taha and Abdel Aziz Elatrash. . . . This revolutionary *answer* was a *tribute* to the blood of two *heroes* who fell as a result of a cheap trick.[6]

Amidst this language of praise and blame—tribute, martyr, heroes and devils—the terrorists' rhetoric sets forth the claim that this act is not only a response, but one that is measured and equitable in nature. Implicitly, the butchery of firing machine guns is equated with the acts of Moshe Dayan. If sneaking guns into an airport is a "cheap trick," so, too, is the Israeli takeover of a hijacked plane while they feigned negotiations. The terrorists' cold blooded killing simply answered cold blooded killing.

As the Lod note says so clearly, terrorism is not only a response, but an equivalent response. Terroristic violence is portrayed simply as a response to the violence of others, whether those "others" are Israel, the Federal Republic of Germany, or the military-industrial complex. George Habash, leader of the Popular Front for the Liberation of Palestine (PFLP), constructs the moral equation unequivocally: "after what has happened to us we have the right to do anything."[7] In parallel structure he creates a standard in which peace is equated with justice: "there will be no peace for them [Europe and America] until there is justice for Palestine."[8]

Terrorists argue that their violence is either balanced or outweighed by the violence of others, but in no case is the terrorists' the greater use of violence. The *Rote Armee Fraktion*, for example, justifies bombing an American military base because of the bombs dropped in Vietnam. Their measure of equity in one instance was to explicitly compare the firepower of their bomb with the firepower of those dropped on Vietnam. The numbers, they argued, revealed the justice of their action.[9]

If terrorists cannot find a specific violent action to legitimate their "answer," then their violence "responds" to the general violence of the opposition.

> The spontaneous and increasingly fierce violence of the people, . . . is the response called for [and obtained] by the violence that has been systematically practiced for centuries by the minority ruling classes. . . . Revolutionary violence is nothing but the organized and conscious violence of a people, a class, a national or multinational collectivity that has chosen to confront, combat and overcome the violence—it too, organized and conscious—of the established Order that is crushing it.[10]

"Violence," however, is not the only quality of the status quo which justifies the terrorists' violence. The inhumanity of the opposition similarly legitimates inhuman action in response, for example, violence. "As long as the economic conditions are not changed, a humane life is not possible. There is only one way out of our situation, and that is called social world revolution. . . . Destroy what destroys you!"[11] Terrorists frequently take upon themselves and "the people" labels of inhumanity to show what society has done to them. For example, according to the Quebecois polemecist Pierre Vallieres, the French Canadians are the *White Niggers of America*, a metaphor he develops extensively.[12] To live in such a society is not truly to live. The *Rote Armee Fraktion* claimed they were fighting for "living conditions"; not *better* living conditions, just *living* conditions.[13]

This bipolar division of the world into "us" versus "them" justifies the terrorists' violence via the evil to which they respond. Acts of terrorism may respond specifically to opponents' actions, or to the general violence and inhumanity of "them." Blaming is therefore a hallmark of terrorist discourse. Violent acts are justified less by what they may or may not accomplish than that to which they respond. Devil terms and invective pervade this blaming, similar to the use of scapegoating Haig Bosmajian describes in *The Language of Oppression*.[14]

For modern anti-U.S. terrorists, "the system" stands as a vague monolithic "other," a "summarizing symbol" which justifies terroristic violence.[15] *Rote Armee Fraktion* member Ulrike Meinhof wants to "hit the system in the face," while Order of the Aryan author Andrew MacDonald opens his narrative proclaiming "We are at war with the System."[16] Whether the terrorist is leftist or rightist, the system is very ambiguous, becoming what Murray Edelman calls a condensation symbol and gathering about itself many forms and many meanings.[17] The very ambiguity of the symbol provides much of its power. Vallieres argues that the system is difficult to perceive, partly because the system consciously deceives.

> The workers and all the clear-thinking people of Quebec must take *their* responsibilities in hand and stop relying on the Messiahs who are periodically thrown up by the system to fool the "ignorant." . . . [T]he workers, students, intellectuals, and the youth of the United States are beginning to recognize the true nature of the system, its *arbitrary* nature.[18]

For the British Angry Brigade, the hidden violence of the system can be discerned in "the shoddy alienating culture pushed out by T.V. films and magazines, . . . [and] in the ugly sterility of urban life."[19] Boutiques, which perpetuate that shoddy and sterile culture, are therefore legitimate targets for bombings.[20]

While ambiguous, the system is clearly inhuman, manifesting itself as an order, a program, a machine, a *thing*.[21] Workers are cogs in the "machinery of oppression," the "modern monopoly capitalist system of slavery."[22] Those who disrupt the machine, like the black militants and the Vietcong, are to be admired because "they're not cogs in the wheel anymore."[23] Those who run the machine are not themselves human because they are part of the machine as well; they are simply "types."[24] To argue that one should "smash the totality of this imperialist social order" extends the metaphor consistently.[25] One does not ordinarily "smash" a person, one "smashes" a machine, something material that has an "order" to be smashed.

In a metaphor related to "the machine," the "types" within the machine are not human because they are "puppets" wearing "masks." The machine makes of them something they are not, they become "actors."[26] The *Rote Armee Fraktion* coined the term *Charaktermaske* and applied it to one of their victims.[27] Interestingly, the victim did not *wear* a *Charaktermaske*, he *was* one.

The system is not consistently inanimate, but it is always inhuman. "World imperialism" is a "monster," the "bourgeois family is a social monstrosity," the United States is a "world-wide monster."[28] The state becomes such an unreasoning creature that "every move of the monster-state tightens the noose around its own neck."[29] One should not wonder that the monster will hang itself, because it obviously suffers from "insanity."[30]

The system is also not human because it belongs to the animal kingdom. One need sample only a small amount of the New Left terrorist rhetoric to discover their fascination with the term "pig." When opponents are so inhuman as to be "shit-pigs," then the announcement that "A Pig is a Pig . . . The Pig Must Be Offed!" gains legitimacy.[31] Killing animals, after all, is acceptable. In dogmatic bipolar fashion, "when a pig gets iced that's a good thing."[32] So pervasive is their use of the defamatory label, that Bowman Miller, studying the *Rote Armee Fraktion*, suggests that they may have believed their own rhetoric, and perceived the authorities *literally* as inhuman pigs.[33] The system is represented by other animals as well. Non-terrorist leftists are the "vultures who'll be flying to Clydeside to tell you what to do"; bourgeois capitalists are "rats and vermin," "parasites. . . . predators . . . [fond of cheap labor] the way wolves are fond of sheep."[34] Again, the system's inhumanity provides justification for the terrorist's violence. "Their bestial behavior shall drive the people to inevitable revolt."[35]

Sexual terms are also used to demean and dehumanize. The system is one in which "men have to alienate themselves, prostitute themselves."[36] If the laborer is the prostitute, then the capitalists are obviously the "poverty pimps."[37] The sexual act is also used in its vulgar sense to dehumanize, as when Jews are, for MacDonald, "Satan's spawn."[38] Whether the non-violent leftists are "bastards" in the sexual sense or simply in the less-than-human sense, according to the Angry Brigade, the bastards "will achieve bugger all."[39]

The discourse of terrorists relies heavily on this type of blaming, thus beginning the outline of a discourse of values.[40] The inhumanity of the system legitimates the act of terrorism, and terrorists then employ language connoting legitimacy to describe their own actions. Such language suggests that their actions are praiseworthy, a part of their discourse of values which achieves full measure with their exhortative praise of action. Terms of legitimacy are, in this instance, used to reinforce the bipolar discourse of terrorists.

Jurisprudential terms are one category of language terrorists use to imply the legitimacy of their actions and the illegitimacy of the system's. For example, the British police force commits "crimes against people," the *Rote Armee Fraktion* bombs a judge's car in retribution for his "crimes," and one who betrays the cause of white supremacy is a "race-criminal."[41] Colleagues are inevitably "tortured" and "murdered," words connoting illegitimate behavior by the system.[42] Because the system is illegal, and terrorists are the bipolar opposites, a kind of inversion is naturally implied. Laws and law enforcement are illegitimate while terrorism is legitimate. "In court it is we who defend legality, that is, the rules of the Criminal Code, and it is the Prosecution and the judge who are forced to resort to illegal manuevers."[43] Taking on their own trappings of legitimacy, the Tupamaros created "People's Prisons," Shi'ites hold trials of "CIA spies," and those found guilty are not murdered but "executed."[44]

Terrorists can, at times, weave their rhetoric of jurisprudential legitimacy with some measure of sophistication. In one communique, the Angry Brigade denounces the enforcement of a law as "'legal' lynching."[45] Placing the word "legal" within quotation marks implicitly questions the appropriateness of the word, a rhetorical device often employed by terrorists.[46] On paper, the enforcement of the law is legal, but the communique questions whether it is legal in the spirit of the law. The use of "lynching" reinforces that implicit claim. "Lynch" in this instance is metaphorical, as no one was killed or physically injured in the incident. "To lynch," of course, is to kill or hang unlawfully, by mob rule. The Angry Brigade thus twice renders law enforcement illegal, and illegitimate, in the space of two words.

A second family of terms used to implicitly and explicitly suggest legitimacy is "war." War is commonly considered "legitimate" violence, politics of the last resort. Thus, the Weather Underground entitled their first communique "A Declaration of a State of War."[47] Terrorists extend the argument by claiming they are "behind enemy lines," that prisons are "POW camps," and that they ought to be treated as prisoners of war.[48] Labelling terrorism as "war" means that it is a legitimate use of violence, that terrorists are not subject to ordinary criminal codes, and it renders legitimate previously illegitimate targets. Writes MacDonald in his fictional-theoretical work, "it is a terrible thing to kill the women of our own race, but we are engaged in a war in which all the old rules have been scrapped."[49] George Habash makes a similar argument in a practical, non-fictional instance. "El Al planes are a perfectly legitimate military target. . . . In a war it is fair to strike the enemy wherever he happens to be."[50]

The terrorists carry out their legitimate war against an illegitimate, inhuman enemy. West Germany is a U.S. "colony," while the Quebecois are resisting a "formidable American financial offensive . . . [which] had already undertaken the economic conquest of Quebec."[51] Terrorists fight for "the destruction of the empire," not against a true government, but a "regime."[52]

The rhetoric of anti-U.S. terrorists legitimates their violence via the inhuman evil to which they respond. The result is a world in which no neutral ground can exist. In this perspective, the body politic *must* choose to side with either the terorrist, or the system.

The Absence of Neutrality

Both Braden in his study of white supremacists and Scott in his essay on black militants found that these speakers primarily justified themselves by denouncing those they were against.[53] Similarly, for terrorists the "violence of the system" bipolarly balances the "violence of the terrorists." The choice becomes one of "either-or," either *for* the terrorist or *against* the terrorist. MacDonald summarizes this position directly. "More and more it will be a case of either being for us, all the way, or against us." For the Tupamaros West Berlin, violence against the system was the only escape from the system. "[You] cannot be neutral. Otherwise, you yourselves will be destroyed. You yourselves must beat and rob these pigs, burn their palaces, fight your oppressors, or you yourselves will be destroyed."[54]

In this zero sum game, neither passive agreement nor neutrality are possible. Not to act is to act against change, and therefore against the terrorist. "All who do nothing are equally guilty" presents the theory of collective guilt in slogan form.[55]

> After all, is not man essentially responsible for his condition, at least in a collective sense? . . . We can hardly consider ourselves blameless. We can hardly say we had no choice. . . . And are not folly, willful ignorance, laziness, greed, irresponsibility, and moral timidity as blameworthy as the most deliberate malice?[56]

For the *Rote Armee Fraktion* one is either a *Mensch* (person) or a *Schwein* (pig). For Vallieres, the "laggards" who will one day "reap the benefits" are "bloodsuckers," and the Angry Brigade calls the non-activist proletariat "the lump."[57]

Just as no compromise is available for the public, none is possible for the terrorist. Says Habash, "we don't want peace, we will never agree to any peaceful compromise."[58] Vallieres argues that "when I am willing to make compromises, I will have murdered *our* ideal in my mind and heart."[59] Rhetorically, Vallieres maintains that it is better to commit terroristic violence in response to the system's violence, than it is to "do violence" to one's ideals. The violence of terrorism is counterbalanced, and therefore justified, twice-over.

Legitimacy is thus established by constructing a bipolar world. Terrorism is a legitimate, equivalent response to an inhuman system. Because the world is so sharply divided into good and evil, no neutral ground is available. Acting against the "system" means to act for the terrorist, and therefore for "good." The remainder of the terrorist's discourse is thus devoted to that end: exhorting blows against the system.

Terroristic Rhetoric as Exhortation

Perceiving the struggle as a zero sum game, the terrorist exhorts the body politic to take *any* kind of violent action against the system. Praising "action" completes the discourse of values begun with blaming the system. "Violence" best represents the qualities of "action" and "against the system" which the terrorist seeks.

Antithetical to action and violence, in this perspective, is communication. Discourse serves an auxiliary function, merely illuminating correct action. Discourse can even be dangerous because it can siphon energy away from "action." The rhetoric which results from this perspective is one suspicious of communication itself.

Exhortation to Action

In *Rhetorical Criticism: A Study in Method* Edwin Black defines exhortative rhetoric as "that type of discourse in which the stirring of an audience's emotions is a primary persuasive force . . . and is extensively rather than incidentally used." Specifically, he argues that the process is one in which "emotion can be said to produce the belief, instead of the reverse."[60]

Observers of terrorism frequently note that terrorists begin by becoming frustrated with the system, that their politics is one of despair. The emotion of frustration and despair leads to the belief—and the accompanying rhetoric—which says that *something* must be *done*. Anger is one common emotion the terrorist seeks to inculcate in the audience.

> The politicians, the leaders, the rich, the big bosses, are in command, THEY control. WE, THE PEOPLE, SUFFER . . . THEY have tried to make us mere functions of a production process. THEY have polluted the world with chemical waste from their factories. THEY shoved garbage from their media down our throats. THEY made us absurd sexual caricatures, all of us, men and women. THEY killed, napalmed, burned us into soap, mutilated us, raped us.[61]

In a different communique, the Angry Brigade grounded rhetoric in the emotions of boredom and frustration.

> Life is so boring there is nothing to do except spend all our wages on the latest skirt or shirt. Brothers and Sisters, what are your real desires? Sit in the drugstore, look distant, empty, bored, drinking some tasteless coffee? or perhaps BLOW IT UP OR BURN IT DOWN. The only thing you can do with modern slavehouses—called boutiques—IS WRECK THEM.[62]

Other terrorists similarly base their appeals to emotion in the frustrations of daily life. The *Rote Armee Fraktion* coins new terms to represent the despair of every day living, especially using the suffix *terror* to balance their called-for violence. The terrorism of laboring simply to consume becomes *Konsumterror*, the terror of landlords is *Grundrechtsterror*, and *Leistungsterror* is the "terror of having to achieve." Bowman Miller, studying the *Rote Armee Fraktion*, makes a telling point as he argues that our assumptions about language help make this language effective. "Reality," we presume, requires a name. That is, we see objects around us and create for them labels, much as Adam named the animals in Genesis. We make this relationship symmetrical when we begin to assume that names must therefore indicate some existing reality. Thus, if people have a name *Konsumterror*, there "must be something there." Terrorists, Miller argues, play on this assumption by coining new words, often for emotions we "must" have.

To exhort the audience to act immediately, the terrorist must intensify the emotions as much as possible. Description is one rhetorical tool for increasing the boredom, frustration, anger, or hate the audience experiences. Habash, for example, appeals to sympathy and anger in his description of the Palestinian flight during the 1967 Six Day War.

> They [the Israelis] forced us to flee. It is a picture that haunts me and that I'll never forget. Thirty thousand human beings walking, weeping . . . screaming in terror . . . women with babies in their skirts . . . and the Israeli soldiers pushing them on with their guns. Some people fell by the wayside, some never got up again. It was terrible. One thinks: this isn't life, this isn't human.[63]

Similarly, MacDonald describes events from the 1960s in an attempt to evoke race hatred and anger at the system.

> There was a gang of armed, revolutionary Negroes who called themselves "Black Panthers." Every time they had a shootout with the police, the press and TV people had their tearful interviews with the families of the Black gang members who got killed—not with the cops' widows. And when a Negress who belonged to the Communist Party helped plan a courtroom shootout and even supplied the shotgun with which a judge was murdered, the press formed a cheering section at her trial and tried to make a folk hero out of her.[64]

Vivid description, according to Black, intensifies emotions, and in sufficient quantity signifies the exhortative nature of the discourse. Exhortation typically induces belief through visual, sensual language.[65]

A second device for intensifying emotions is to portray the opposition as a powerful, malignant force. Such an enemy justifies the powerful emotional response the terrorist desires, and the violence the terrorist advocates. Hyperbole and metaphor are frequently used to contribute to this portrait. The system, however termed, is generally depicted as conniving, conspiratorial, and pervasive, a "universe of cunningly organized dehumanization."[66] Thus, the Angry Brigade's enemy is "bureaucracy and technology [which are] used against the people . . . to speed up our work, to slow down our minds, to obliterate the truth."[67] Habash similarly perceives his opposition to be more than just the state of Israel.

> Our enemy is Israel, plus the Zionist movement that controls many of the countries which support Israel, plus imperialism. . . . [W]e have to stand against whoever supports Israel economically, militarily, politically, ideologically. This means the capitalist countries that have conceived Israel and are now using it as a bulwark to protect their interests in Arabia. They include the U.S., and almost every country in Europe.[68]

Such a powerful enemy makes immediate action imperative, which is the purpose of the terrorist's discourse.

Hyperbole also enhances the power of the enemy and the emotional sense of the rhetoric. Capitalism, for Vallieres, is the "stupidest, most anti-social, most inhuman enterprise conceivable."[69] The Angry Brigade asserts that "British democracy is based on more blood, terror, and exploitation than any empire in history."[70] Such hyperbole justifies the most extreme of actions. "Everything that has been and everything that is yet to be depend on us. We are truly the instruments of God in the fulfillment of His Grand Design."[71]

Metaphors are similarly employed to intensify the emotional response of the audience. The system is a parasitic, bestial, monstrous, perverted thing, easily meriting any disgust the discourse can evoke. A complementary metaphor, common in the discourse, is that of cancer. It suggests a powerful, malignant enemy which must be totally destroyed in order to be escaped. "[The System] is a cancer too deeply rooted in our flesh. And if we don't destroy the System before it destroys us—if we don't cut this cancer out of our living flesh—our whole race will die."[72] This emotional build-up culminates in violent action: "Our violence is the last outcry, the ultimate end of frustration of a people . . . [who] have tried in every way to fight their oppression, and they have been unsuccessful. Nothing remains but the violence."[73] Only action, for example, violence, can save the terrorist—and all of society—from the evil, inhuman system.

Action as a God Term

The terrorist's emotional exhortation finds its release in something called "action." The system's inhumanity, and the zero sum struggle that results, requires that the terrorist *act*. "Beware of emotion that finds no vent in action," writes Mrs. Pethwick-Lawrence, "translate every emotion, every feeling into deed, and act."[74] "Action" thus becomes a god term, as defined by Richard Weaver. "[A god term] is that expression about which all other expressions are ranked as subordinate. . . . Its force imparts to the others their lesser degree of force, and fixes the scale by which degrees of comparison are understood."[75] The rhetoric of terrorism routinely ranks all ideas by how they relate to "action."

Nechayev calls action the "propaganda of the deed." The specific act is immaterial, as long as it is against the system. Says Habash, "one must change the world, do *something*, kill if necessary, kill even at the risk of becoming inhuman in our turn."[76] The specific act is immaterial because the inhuman system must be destroyed first. By destroying the system, writes Vallieres, the Quebecois can "build on their ruins a new order and new values, which will take new men, create a new society and constitute true humanism, for the first time in history."[77] That "new order," but vaguely defined even in Vallieres's 300 pages, is reminiscent of Sorel's use of "the myth."

> Experience shows that the *framing of a future, in some indeterminate time*, may . . . be very effective, and have very few inconveniences; this happens when the anticipations of the future take the form of those myths, which enclose with them, all the strongest inclinations of a people, of a party or a class . . . which give an aspect of complete reality to the hopes of immediate action by which, more easily than by any other method, men can reform their desires, passions, and mental activity.[78]

Terrorists commonly argue that violence, coupled with such use of righteous myth, can "reform desires" and thus create "new men." Indeed, to act against the inhuman system defines one's person. For example, the Weathermen establish "levels" of armed struggle, differentiated by the type of weapon used. Almost like the ascent towards Nirvana, the "cadre" will lead the masses from the lower to the higher "levels" of conflict just as they themselves have progressed from one to the next.[79] The German *Rote Armee Fraktion* define a person by whether they had engaged in "propaganda of the deed"; those who commit acts of violence are *Mensch* (people).[80] An oft-used image is that of animals going to slaughter. "[Violence] show[s] that we're not just slaughter animals always getting the club over our heads."[81]

As a logical extension, the more wholly one *acts* against the system, the more fully he or she is a "*Mensch.*" Nechayev, for example, thinks of the robber as society's enemy *par excellence*: "we must unite with the adventurous tribes of brigands, who are the only true revolutionaries of Russia."[82] Likewise, Susan Stern views prostitutes and women criminals as the real pioneers of women's liberation.[83] Weatherman Underground Communique #4 sets the equation in strict parallel construction: "We are outlaws, we are free!"[84]

Action thus begins as the culmination of the emotional frustration and anger which the exhortation develops. Because it inevitably indicates one's membership in the correct half of the bipolar world, however, action comes to signal one's morality as well. Action, and usually violent action, becomes a moral good, praiseworthy in and of itself. Patrick Pearse justifies Irish terrorism metaphysically by echoing Frantz Fanon: "Blood is a cleansing and sanctifying thing."[85] Similarly, Timothy Leary writes that "to shoot a genocidal robot policeman in the defense of life is a sacred act."[86]

Quebecois terrorist Pierre Vallieres uses violence to distinguish between "men" and "sub-men," and his use of gender is arguably purposeful.[87] Scholars have noted that speakers frequently use masculinity to justify and goad audiences to violence.[88] One Weatherman joins the underground because, regarding protests and demonstrations, "I just see us doing the same, impotent things over and over again."[89] Not to "act" forcefully is "womanly hand-wringing."[90] Bernardine Dohrn admonishes the Left that "we've been wimpy on armed struggle."[91] Recriminations without action, after all, are "sterile."[92]

Terroristic violence, then, is an affirmation of one's courage and commitment to the values of the group.[93] Those values create intense emotions, and violent action is the appropriate conclusion for those emotions.

> "God Bless" those *courageous* young White Christians accused of the bombings. *They* are doing *God's work*, while other *so-called* Christians set back in their pews *like cowardly sheep* and refuse to even utter a whisper of protest.[94]

The terrorist act is thus portrayed as a logical, moral product of the inhuman system.

As action becomes the primary god term of terrorist discourse, communication evolves into an irrelevant, dangerous element because it detracts from such action. Those who talk do not act, writes Nechayev. They are "idle word-spillers . . . [and] the majority of these will leave nothing behind but a vast ruin."[95] Vallieres similarly portrays action and communication as polar opposites. "You are *all* accomplices in exploitation, obscurantism, and injustice as long as you do not perform ACTS. ACTS, not sermons!"[96]

Communication is also dangerous because, in the terrorist's perspective, it can be facile, unlike action. One either blows up the system's generator or one does not. In contrast, language is a slippery thing, easily misused by the system, and therefore not to be trusted. Typically, for example, the very use of the term "terrorism" is disputed. Just as Patrick Buchanan compares twenty-nine buildings bombed and "fifteen million children destroyed" and asks, "Now, what is the terrorism?", George Habash makes explicit the subjectivity of language. "We have the right to do anything, including what *you call* acts of terrorism. . . . one is forced to rely on terrorism, as *you call* it, to wage one's war."[97]

Because action is primary, communication is also largely irrelevant. Truth, therefore, can be asserted rather than demonstrated. Truth, in the terrorists' bipolar world, is obvious. Documentation is unnecessary, and to the extent that it detracts from action, even dangerous. Truth is therefore asserted. Miller notes that a typical *Rote Armee Fraktion* construction is "*es ist evident* (it is evident)."[98] Things "are," violence "is," terrorists "must" while the system "cannot" and "will never again." Qualifiers are notably absent, as their rhetoric speaks in superlatives: everything, nothing, never, always. Edwin Black argues that a preference for *is* and *will* over *ought* and *should be* is typical of exhortative discourse.[99] Roderick Hart discovers similar use of verbs and absolutes among true believers, "perhaps suggesting that stable entities, static relationships, and other certain and permanent phenomena are important . . . [such use] leaves no room for doubt about the facts of the matter."[100] In the discourse of terrorism, facts are asserted routinely. "Police computers cannot tell the truth."[101] "By 1967 we had understood the undeniable truth, that to liberate Palestine we have to follow the Chinese and Vietnamese examples. There is no escape from this logic."[102]

Because truth is obvious to those who will see, terrorists pay little attention to the use of documentation, or traditional standards of evidence. Most types of evidence—for example, testimonial and statistical—are rarely used at all. Documentation consists of "statistics and dry facts," so terrorists do not cite polls to show how many people feel bored, they do not discuss statistics of economic conditions, they do not quote authorities or give specific, actual examples of bored people.[103] As Klein puts it, "There is no need to cite a host of examples when referring to state terrorism."[104] Terrorists allude broadly to evidence, when they employ it at all. Typical of this tendency is the phrase "all of recent history shows us," used without mention of which events in all recent history "show us."[105]

This is not to say terrorist speakers never use history or other types of documentation more specifically. In fact, they can do so rather creatively. It is, however, usually an apocryphal use of evidence, relying more on popular conceptions of history or retelling second-hand accounts of repression. History, for example, is used more to confer upon the terrorist the revolutionary mantle, rather than to document. The Angry Brigade bombs a local Ford factory to celebrate "the hundred years of the Paris commune."[106] Habash refers to the European street revolts metaphorically, characterizing the PFLP and Al-Fatah as being on "the same side of the barricades."[107] Abortion clinic bombers compare themselves with John Brown, suggesting an analogical relationship between the status of slaves and unborn children.[108]

This use of history operates as what Edelman labels condensational symbols, as does the invective discussed in the previous section. In Edelman's discussion of hortatory, or exhortative, discourse he argues that condensation symbols are frequently used.[109] Black also argues that abstract nouns lend themselves to exhortative discourse in certain conditions.

> Abstract nouns . . . may, as a result of prior conditioning or prior persuasion, have become so deeply associated with a person's values and point of view that they have the ability to evoke in him an emotional response.[110]

Terrorists use condensational terms in just such fashion, strategically using ambiguity in an attempt to evoke an emotional response.

While the term "bipolar exhortation" summarizes this description of the terrorist's half of the dialogue, two important contradictions emerge which should be recognized. That is, when superficially discrete discourses are constructed in similar fashion, they often confront similar rhetorical obstacles. In this instance, two rhetorical tensions emerge in the discourse of terrorism. The counterterrorist's alternatives of response can only be fully appreciated when these contradictions are understood.

THE RHETORICAL TENSIONS OF TERRORISM

By "rhetorical tension" I mean that the speaker has contradictory impulses guiding the construction of the discourse. When, for example, a speaker wishes to tell the truth but also needs to shade that truth in order to present a "best case," rhetorical tension occurs. Such conflicting impulses, or motivations, are frequently, though not always, revealed in the rhetoric. I find two recurring tensions in the rhetoric: elitism versus populism and communication versus action.

Elitism versus Populism

Terrorists invest "the people" with a traditional, almost mystical, kind of power, perhaps best symbolized by the German concept of "the *Volk*," a popular symbol with the *Rote Armee Fraktion*. Terrorists' violence is justified because of how inhumanely the system treats the body politic. The terrorist wants to restore to "the people" power over their own destinies. By definition, however, terrorism commands the loyalty of few members of the body politic. Somewhere "the people" have erred, and must be "exhorted" to act upon the terrorist's dogmatic truth. A rhetorical tension arises for terrorists: to ground their legitimacy in "the people," yet to exhort that same "people" in the ways of the "Truth."

Like the *Rote Armee Fraktion*'s invocation of the "*Volk*," the Weather Underground locate their strength in the people: "political power grows out of a gun, a Molotov, a riot, a commune . . . and from the soul of the people."[111] "Power to the People" is an oft-used phrase, as well as concluding slogan for four of the Angry Brigade's communiques. "Let the working brothers and sisters be our jury" and "power to the people" they urge.[112] In her courtroom peroration, Susan Stern captures the sense of power with which terrorists invest the symbolic body politic.

> I can hear the chants of my people, of people who know where you are, where your head is at, where you stand, who know that you are on your last leg, that you are dying and that this country is dying with you; of people, young people, and a growing number of middle-aged and older people who are beginning to understand that there is a different kind of justice, that there is a different kind of law and order, that there is a new Renaissance, which we call the revolution that is going to create a new humanity.[113]

While Stern begins with very specific people, the demonstrators outside the courtroom, her meaning of "people" swells to become all of those who can participate in her vision of America.

By definition, however, within any given society terrorists are a select few who have chosen violence as their method of political change. Where the majority chooses violence, one finds war—guerilla or otherwise. Terrorists, therefore, have chosen as arbiters those who have explicitly opted *against* their method of political change, and hence rhetorical tension occurs. Within a single Weatherman document one discovers that the people are "brainwashed" and that their "movement [is] built on the basis of faith in the masses of the people."[114] George Habash illustrates a similar tension on an international scale as he explains why the PFLP is a proletarian party despite its insignificant numbers.

> The real people, the proletarian masses, follow our lead. . . . It is true that we aren't numerically strong; at least not yet. But . . . it is not enough to have many proletarians in a party to be a proletarian party. What counts is a proletarian ideology, a proletarian program.[115]

Note that Habash begins with an argument that contends that the PFLP has popular support. He then *dismisses* popular support as unimportant because the number of people does not matter, the ideology does.

Terrorists' commonly chosen path out of this dilemma is to claim that the people have been deluded into their passive acceptance of the system's inhumanity. Society is a "barren wasteland that has been imposed on this country by Democrats, Republicans, Capitalists and creeps."[116] MacDonald portrays Americans as passive cattle who simply want their three full meals, TV and funny papers. "Most Americans are still able to keep their bellies full today, and we must simply face the fact that that's the only thing which counts with most of them."[117] For that reason, he later argues that almost one hundred percent of the people could be justifiably hanged, because "they have been brainwashed; they are weak and selfish."[118] Because that would be an "entirely impractical task," however, he only recommends hanging for ten percent of the population.

Terrorists attempt to instruct these brainwashed masses into correct behavior which then permits a standard of popular support. The rhetorical tension is exacerbated, however, when popular support is not forthcoming. Susan Stern reflects the bitterness that arises when the terrorists' message falls on deaf ears.

> I suddenly felt enraged. Why wouldn't anyone listen? There was truth in what we said, our theories did mean something, Weatherman wasn't some idiot's dream. . . . But somehow, when we put our theories into practice, they disintegrated.[119]

She later answers her own question:

> The American people were already dead. They were past caring about freedom. Standing up there I suddenly felt that I had wasted my life, my youth; that as corrupt as my attempt had been, it had meant nothing. Nothing.[120]

The statement announcing Weatherman at the 1969 SDS convention declared in its title that "You Don't Need A Weatherman To Know Which Way The Wind Blows." After the Days of Rage, however, Weatherman Shin'ya Ono concluded just the opposite in his essay "You Do Need A Weatherman To Know Which Way The Wind Blows."[121] This change in attitude illustrates the tension between their exhortative position, revealed in their bipolar discourse, and their verbal support for a populist standard. The masses are simultaneously ignorant and the source of the terrorist's strength.

Communication versus Action

The second rhetorical tension common to the terrorist's discourse is that, as they dismiss communication as unimportant and even dangerous, they engage in that very act of communicating. Bowman Miller summarizes the second rhetorical tension well. "Theirs is a love-hate relationship with language. They would like to be effective without it, but it is vital to the articulation of the political justification for their violent methods."[122]

Those who talk but do not act are, for the terrorist, "idle word-spillers," not only ineffective but actively dangerous.[123] As documented above, communication is placed in a polar opposition to action. MacDonald again sharply contrasts the idle spilling of words with the confirmation of important values through violence.

> These were no soft-bellied, conservative businessmen assembled for some Masonic mumbo-jumbo; no loudmouthed, beery red-necks letting off a little ritualized steam about "the goddamn niggers"; no pious, frightened churchgoers whining for the guidance or protec-

> tion of an anthropomorphic deity. These were *real men*, *White* men, men who were now *one* with me in spirit and consciousness as well as in blood.[124]

MacDonald characterizes communication negatively: it is mumbo-jumbo, ritualized steam, pious and frightened whining.

In spite of their professed antipathy towards words and rhetoric, however, terrorists write books, issue communiques, and hold press conferences. Nor can their acts of rhetoric be seen as solely publicity-seeking. Terrorists want publicity which is rhetorical, that is, one which will influence the audience towards a particular socio-political point of view. For that reason the *Rote Armee Fraktion* demands the publication of their communiques in their entirety; similarly, the Iranians who took the American embassy negotiated with NBC to play *in full* a videotape produced by them.

Terrorists' communiques reflect this tension. Some are very short and cryptic, suggesting an impatience with language and mere words. Others go on at some length as they attempt to justify their actions. Although they disdain the norms of communication, they also rely on them. One of the more interesting examples of this use is the *Rote Armee Fraktion* communique issued after a bomb injured a number of workers. Their message ends with the formulaic "we are deeply distressed," a German phrase common in newspapers for expressing bereavement.[125] Ironically, while their violence was "smashing" the established order, their communique was using the language of that order.

Exhorting the body politic to act contains within itself the seeds of the contradiction. Terrorists are engaged in communication itself as they negatively contrast communication to action.

CONCLUSIONS

Political violence is, by definition, the hallmark of terrorism. Needing to justify their violence politically, contemporary anti-U.S. terrorists typically legitimate their violence by what it stands *against*: the inhumanity of their enemy. What emerges is a bipolar world in which the "system," frequently represented by America itself, constitutes all evil and the terrorist all good. Because it *responds*, the violence of the terrorist is legitimate in direct proportion to the system's inhumanity. Thus, the "system" is described variously as a machine, beast, monster, or perverse sexual act. In contrast, terrorism takes for itself the mantle of legitimacy, by using terminology which implies legitimate use of force, such as "criminal justice" and "war." Because the world is bipolarly divided into good versus evil, no middle, neutral ground is available, either for the terrorist or the body politic. What results, then, is a bipolar discourse, one primarily concerned with condemning the evil "system."

Once the terrorists' legitimacy is established, they exhort their audience to undertake correct action. They ground their discourse in the negative emotions of frustration, anger, and hatred of the system, then praise "action" as the morally correct outlet for those negative emotions. In contrast to "action," communication stands as an effeminate, irrelevant, and potentially dangerous alternative.

From this discourse two rhetorical tensions emerge. While terrorists ground their legitimacy in the system's inhumanity to "the people," theirs is the violence of a minority. Thus arises the first contradiction: elitism versus populism. The second rhetorical tension occurs because the terrorists praise action and condemn "mere rhetoric" while they simultaneously engage not in violent action, but in communication. Thus the second contradiction: communication versus action.

This summarizes the modern anti-U.S. terrorist's half of the dialgoue: bipolar, exhortative discourse containing, typically, two significant rhetorical tensions. As outlined in Chapter Two, the counterterrorist speaker has two primary choices for engaging the terrorist in dialogue. One strategy would be to reflect the terrorist, in which the counterterrorist would employ similar bipolar, exhortative discourse. Several important questions emerge. Would a reflective counterterrorist discourse lend legitimacy to significant elements of the terrorist's discourse? If so, which ones? Would a reflective counterterrorist discourse contain rhetorical contradictions similar to those of the terrorist's discourse? Most importantly, would a reflective discourse be a strategic one for the counterterrorist? Chapter Four will address these questions, concluding that, given the purpose of counterterrorism outlined in Chapter One, a reflective discourse is not a strategic choice.

Chapter Five will then examine a non-reflective strategy. Given the terrorist's part of the dialogue, what would constitute a non-reflective discourse? Second, would *that* discourse be a strategic choice for the counterterrorist speaker? Chapter Five will affirm that what may be termed "democratic rhetoric" would be a strategic alternative to the more traditional, reflective discourse of counterterrorism.

NOTES

1. M. Cherif Bassiouni, "Problems in Media Coverage of Nonstate-Sponsored Terror Violence Incidents," *Perspectives on Terrorism*, ed. Lawrence H. Freedman and Yonah Alexander (Wilmington, Del.: Scholarly Resources, 1983) 180–181.

2. See, for example, Dwight Van De Vate, Jr., "The Appeal to Force," and George Yoos, "A Critique of Van De Vate's 'The Appeal to Force'," *Philosophy and Rhetoric* 8 (1975): 43–60 and 172–176. Although the two authors have significant differences of opinion, both concur on the argument presented here. See also Cyril Welch, "Talking," *Philosophy and Rhetoric* 18 (1985): 216; and Rebecca Kay Carson, "From Teacups to Terror: The Rhetorical Strategies of the Women's Social and Political Union, 1903–1918," diss., U of Iowa, 1975, 163 and 193.

3. See, for example, Paul Wilkinson, *Terrorism and the Liberal State* (New York: New York UP, 1979) 23; and Richard W. Leeman, "Rhetoric and Values in Terrorism," *Multidimensional Terrorism*, ed. Martin Slann and Bernard Schechterman (Boulder, Colo.: Lynne Riener, 1986) 45–48.

4. Marshall McLuhan, *Understanding Media: The Extensions of Man* 2nd ed. (New York: Signet, 1964). See especially his discussion of weapons and modern war, 294–300.

5. Bowman Miller, "The Language Component of Terrorism Strategy," diss., Georgetown U, 1983, 213; and "Communique #4," *The Angry Brigade* (Port Galsgow, Scotland: Bratach Dubh, 1978) 5.

6. *New York Times* 31 May 1972: 27 Emphasis mine.

7. Interview of George Habash by Oriana Fallaci, "A Leader of the Fedayeen," *Life* 12 June 1970: 33. See also the *New York Times* 20 Sep. 1972: A12, regarding the justifications concerning the Munich Olympic slayings.

8. Habash, as quoted in Fallaci 33.

9. Miller 230–231.

10. Pierre Vallieres, *White Niggers of America* (New York: Monthly Review 1971) 223, 224.

11. Bommi (Michael) Baumann, *Terror or Love?*, trans. Helene Ellenbogen and Wayne Parker (New York: Grove, 1977) 82. See also Vallieres 10. Additionally, see Abraham Guillen, *Philosophy of the Urban Guerilla*, trans. and ed. Donald C. Hodges (New York: William Morrow, 1973) 246.

12. See, for example, Vallieres 21–22.

13. Miller 339.

14. Haig Bosmajian, *The Language of Oppression* (Lanham, MD: University Press of America, 1974).

15. A "summarizing symbol," in traditional rhetorical terms, operates synecdochically. That is, it comes to stand for, or summarizes, a more fully developed argument. For a good discussion of modern use of synecdoche, see Kathleen Hall Jamieson, *Eloquence in an Electronic Agè* (New York: Oxford UP, 1988) 90–117.

16. As reported in *The (London) Times* 15 December 1972; Andrew MacDonald, *The Turner Diaries* (Washington, DC: National Vantage, 1978) 1.

17. Murray Edelman, *The Symbolic Uses of Politics* (Urbana: U of Illinois P, 1964) 6–7, 134–138.

18. Vallieres 19, 76. Emphasis his.

19. "Communique #6," *The Angry Brigade* 4.

20. "Communique #7," *The Angry Brigade* 5–7; and "Communique #8," *The Angry Brigade* 7.

21. See, for example, Miller 220, 252; and "Communique #6," *The Angry Brigade* 5.

22. Respectively, "The Berlin Indomitables," (Interview with Ronald Fritzsch, Gerald Klopper, Ralf Reinders and Fritz Teufel), *The German Guerilla: Terror, Reaction and Resistance* (Minneapolis: Soil of Liberty, 1981) 74 and Central Committee of the Roaming Hash Rebels, "It is Time to Destroy," *Terror or Love?*, trans. Helene Ellenbogen and Wayne Parker (New York: Grove Press, 1977) 56. See also Miller 240.

23. Susan Stern, *With the Weathermen* (Garden City, N.Y.: Doubleday, 1975) 275.

24. Miller 282.

25. Shin'ya Ono, "You Do Need A Weatherman To Know Which Way The Wind Blows," *Leviathan* 7 (1969).

26. See, for example, "Communique #12," *The Angry Brigade* 10; and Miller 272–280.

27. Miller 121.

28. Miller 304; Vallieres 86; and Stern 275. See also Motor City SDS, "Break On Through to the Other Side," *New Left Notes* 23 Aug. 1969:4–5; Kathy Boudin, et al., "Bringing the War Home: Less Talk, More National Action," *New Left Notes* 23 Aug. 1969; "Washington, November 15, 1969," *Fire* 21 Nov. 1969; Stern 275; and "Inside the Weather Machine," *Rat* 2 (1970): 5. Additionally see Menachem Begin, *The Revolt* (Tel Aviv: Hadar, 1964) 204.

29. "Weatherground" (Communique #3) *Berkeley Tribe* 31 July 1970: 4.

30. "Weatherground" (Communique #1), *Berkeley Tribe* 31 July 1970: 4.

31. Baumann 34, 81. Elipses his. See also Karin Ashley, et al., "You Don't Need a Weatherman to Know Which Way the Wind Blows," *New Left Notes* 18 June 1969; Communique #7," *The Angry Brigade* 6; and Simma Holt, *Terror in the Name of God* (New York: Crown, 1964) 232.

32. Bill Ayers, "A Strategy to Win," *New Left Notes* 12 Sep. 1969. See also "Everyone Talks about the Weather . . . ," Jacobs 445.

33. Miller 56–57.

34. Respectively, "Communique #11," *The Angry Brigade* 8; Holt 149; and Vallieres 19. See also "Everyone Talks about the Weather . . . ," Jacobs 443. Additionally see Begin 36; and Holt 212–213.

35. S. Nechayev, *The Revolutionary Catechism*, reprinted in *Assassins and Terrorists*, ed. D. C. Rapoport (Toronto: Canadian Broadcasting Corp., 1972) 82.

36. Vallieres 141.

37. "Communique #7," *The Angry Brigade* 6.

38. MacDonald 199.

39. "Communique #11," *The Angry Brigade* 9.

40. In modern rhetorical terms, a "discourse of values" would be called "epideictic." That is, it is a discourse which celebrates and renews communally held values. See Chaim Perelman and L. Olbrechts-Tyteca, *The New Rhetoric*, trans. John Wilkinson and Purcell Weaver (Notre Dame: Notre Dame UP, 1969) 52.

41. "Communique #5," *The Angry Brigade* 4; Miller 216; MacDonald 168. See also Begin 337.

42. "Weatherground" (Communique #2), *Berkeley Tribe* 31 July 1970: 4. See also Holt 212–213.

43. Vallieres 263. See also Stern 320–323.

44. *New York Times* 4 March 1973: A30; Geoffrey Jackson, *Surviving the Long Night* (New York: Vanguard, 1974) 107, 179; and MacDonald 168. See also Begin 71; and George Grivas, *Guerilla Warfare and the EOKA's Struggle*, trans. A. A. Pallis (London: Longman, 1964) 65–66.

45. "Brothers and Sisters," *The Angry Brigade* 3.

46. Miller 158. See also Boudin, et al.

47. "Weatherground" (Communique #1), *Berkeley Tribe* 31 July 1970: 4. See also Habash, as quoted in Fallaci 32; and *The (London) Times* 16 August 1971: 3. Additionally see Begin 95; and Carson 165–166, 175.

48. "Weatherground" (Communique #1), *Berkeley Tribe* 31 July 1970: 4; and Miller 213, 229; "Weathermen Underground Statement," *Good Times* 18 Sep. 1970: 24; and Bowman Miller 253, 328. See also Linda Evans, "Letter to the Movement," Jacobs 463; and "Honky Tonk Women," Jacobs 317. Additionally see Begin 255; and Carson 215.

49. MacDonald 129.

50. Habash, as quoted in Fallaci 33. See also Grivas 68.

51. Miller 339; and Vallieres 36.

52. "Weatherground" (Communique #1), *Berkeley Tribe* 31 July 1970:4; and Miller 275. See also Begin 82, 205.

53. Waldo W. Braden, "The Rhetoric of a Closed Society," *Southern Speech Communication Journal* 45 (1980): 333–351; and Robert L. Scott, "Justifying Violence: The Rhetoric of Militant Black Power," *Central States Speech Journal* 19 (1968): 96–104.

54. Respectively, MacDonald 120; and "Open Letter to Eleonore K.," reprinted in Baumann 70.

55. Miller 223.

56. MacDonald 195–216.

57. Miller 242; Vallieres 89; and "The Brigade is Angry," *The Angry Brigade* 10–11.

58. Habash, as quoted in Fallaci 34.

59. Vallieres 197. Emphasis his.

60. Edwin Black, *Rhetorical Criticism: A Study in Method* (Madison: U of Wisconsin P, 1965) 142, 138.

61. Communique #7, *The Angry Brigade* 5. Ellipses and upper case theirs.

62. "Communique #8," *The Angry Brigade* 7. Upper case theirs.

63. Habash, as quoted in Fallaci 34. Ellipses in the original.

64. MacDonald 43.

65. Black 143, 144.

66. Vallieres 10.

67. Communique #9, *The Angry Brigade* 8.

68. Habash, as quoted in Fallaci 32.

69. Vallieres 29.

70. Communique # 5, *The Angry Brigade* 4.

71. MacDonald 71.

72. MacDonald 42.

73. Stern 276.

74. As quoted in Carson 163.

75. Richard M. Weaver, *The Ethics of Rhetoric* (Davis, CA: Hermagoras, 1985) 212.

76. Habash, as quoted in Fallaci 34.

77. Vallieres 86. See also Boudin, et al.; "National War Council," *Fire* 6 Dec. 1969; and "Revolution in the 70's," 30 Jan. 1970. See also Carson 42; Guillen 247; and Jackson 65, 183.

78. Georges Sorel, *Reflections on Violence*, trans. T. E. Hulme and J. Roth, (New York: Collier, 1961) 124–125.

79. Boudin, et al.; and "National War Council."

80. Miller 261.

81. Baumann 34. See also Holt 232; and Begin 36.

82. Nechayev 84.

83. Stern 275. She also reports that the theme of violence included a fascination with and admiration of the Manson murders, even to the point of inventing the "fork sign," made like the peace sign except with three fingers instead of two (204).

84. "Weathermen Underground Statement," *Good Times* 18 Sep. 1970: 24.

85. As quoted in Laqueur 206. See also Begin 121, 373; and Holt 148–149.

86. As quoted in "Weathermen Underground Statement," *Good Times* 18 Sep. 1970: 24. See also Begin 358.

87. Vallieres 64.

88. See Nancy Harstock, "Masculinity, Citizenship and the Making of War," *Politcal Science* 17 (1984): 198-204; and Waldo Braden, "The Rhetoric of a Closed Society," *Southern Speech Communication Journal* 45 (1980): 345.

89. Stern 239.

90. MacDonald 77.

91. As quoted in "Stormy Weather," *Good Times* 8 Jan. 1970: 4.

92. Vallieres 20.

93. Many scholars have noted that violence can be used symbolically to indicate one's moral commitment. Walter Laqueur, for example, writes that "The SS too held to a perverse idealism, a belief that only they took values seriously." *Terrorism* (Boston: Little, Brown, 1977) 75. See also Jacques Ellul, *Propaganda: The Formation of Men's Attitudes* (New York: Vintage, 1965) 29; David C. Rapoport, "Fear and Trembling: Terrorism in Three Religious Traditions," *American Political Science Review* 78 (1984): 658-677; and Braden 341.

94. *The Confederate Leader*, Feb. 1985: 5. Emphasis mine.

95. Nechayev 83.

96. Vallieres 142. Emphasis and upper case his. See also "Everyone Talks about the Weather . . . ," Jacobs 447.

97. Patrick Buchanan, *Face The Nation* CBS, 30 Dec. 1984; and Habash, as quoted in Fallaci 33, 34. Emphasis mine. See also Begin 59–60.

98. Miller 347, 270, and 354.

99. Black 143, 144.

100. Roderick P. Hart, "The Rhetoric of the True Believer," *Communication Monographs* 38 (1971): 257.

101. "Communique #9," *The Angry Brigade* 9.

102. Habash, as quoted in Fallaci 33.

103. Rote Armee Fraktion, "Sur la Conception de la Guerilla Urbaine," *The German Guerilla: Terror, Reaction and Resistance* 101.

104. Hans-Joachim Klein, "Postscript: political violence and liberty," *The German Guerilla: Terror, Reaction and Resistance* 63.

105. "Honky Tonk Women," Jacobs 314.

106. "Communique #7," *The Angry Brigade* 7.
107. Habash, as quoted in Fallaci 34.
108. *New York Times* 18 Jan. 1985: A12. See also Begin 48, 378.
109. Edelman 134.
110. Black 143.
111. "Weatherground" (Communique #2), *Berkeley Tribe* 31 July 1970: 4. Ellipses in the original.
112. "Communique #7," *The Angry Brigade* 6; and "Communique #10," *The Angry Brigade* 8.
113. Stern 322.
114. Ashley, et al.
115. Habash, as quoted in Fallaci 34.
116. "Weathermen Underground Statement," *Good Times* 18 Sep. 1970: 24.
117. MacDonald 6.
118. MacDonald 166. The dilemma here is reminiscent of that which Hitler faced in *Mein Kampf*: how to simultaneously claim that the Aryan race is superior but also victimized by Versailles, the Communists and the Jews. The rhetorical gymnastics are similar, also.
119. Stern 212.
120. Stern 273.
121. Ashley, et al.; and Ono.
122. Miller 10. Similarly, Waldo Braden finds a tension present in the rhetoric of the white supremacists, a conflict between espousing violence but holding to standards of non-violence as well (346).
123. Nechayev 83.
124. MacDonald 203.
125. Miller 368, 225.

Part III
In the Mirror of the Past

[7]

Cultural Narrative and the Motivation of the Terrorist

Khachig Tololyan

Political science seems all too eager for a model, or at best a few models, that will enable generalizations suitable to its empirical discourse and instrumental aims. Understanding terrorism primarily as a form of opposition to the State and to the rule of Law,[1] political science aspires to a schematic and exhaustive typology of terrorism. However, terrorism is in fact such a complex conjunction of socio-cultural, psychological and political factors that a conceptually satisfying schema of terrorism is likely to remain elusive, at least for the time being. One way to begin is to address questions of the terrorist's self-image and motivation, because the difficulties that confront us as we grapple with these elements of the phenomenon are instructive: they reveal the persistence and inadequacy of the ethnocentric Western will to generalize from notions of ego-psychology implicit in current analyses. For example, Joseph Margolin's dismissal of crude beliefs that 'the terrorist is a psychotic' or a 'highly irrational individual' rejects some common pitfalls, only to revert to the search for a generalizing behaviorist model: 'It must be assumed that the terrorist is human. Whether rational or irrational, he is governed as we all are by the same laws of behavior.'[2] I would not dispute that terrorists are human. They are; they are socially produced, out of a specific cultural context; consequently, their behavior can not be understood by the crude – or even by the careful – application of pseudo-scientific laws of general behavior. We need to examine the specific mediating factors that lead some societies under pressure, among many, to produce the kinds of violent acts that we call terrorist. A universalizing model may in fact be applicable to the factors that belong in the explicitly political realm, but I shall be dealing with culturally specific factors which resist such generalization.[3]

Whereas the imperative of a cultural analysis is frequently acknowledged, the acknowledgment too often takes the form of lip-service. Walter Laqueur speaks eloquently against 'generalizations about the terrorist personality', which he deems of 'little validity', and insists on the importance of 'the historical and cultural context'[4] of terrorism. He then proceeds to do two things: he lists dozens of different organizations and instances of terrorism, and then, the gesture towards heterogeneity completed, he moves on in one mighty leap to make those general statements and analyses of terrorism for which his work is best known. This pattern is very widespread. Elsewhere, an analyst of wholly different background and attitudes, H.H. Cooper, remarks that 'terrorism is not a discrete topic that might be conveniently examined apart from the political, social and economic context in which it takes place .... Terrorism is a creature of its own time and place.'[5] That is exactly right, and leads immediately to considerable difficulties all too easily evaded by most students of the topic, including Cooper. The *time* relevant to a particular terrorist act or group might be the day, the month, the decade or the century previous to the event. What is more, it can be the time that is embedded in the historiography, traditional narratives, legends and myths with which a society constitutes itself as a temporal entity.

The specific forms of narrative for which I shall be making large claims are the projective narrative and the regulative biography.[6] The precise meaning of these terms will emerge as I turn my attention to an analysis of Armenian terrorism. For the present, a projective narrative is one that not only tells a story of the past, but also maps out future actions that can imbue the time of individual lives with transcendent collective values. In a sense, then, projective narratives plot out how ideal selves must live lives; they dictate biographies and autobiographies to come. They tell individuals how they would ideally have to live and die in order to contribute properly to their collectivity and its future. They prescribe not static roles but dynamic shapes of the time of our lives.

Similarly, the 'place' of terrorism that is, in Cooper's terms, a 'creature of time and place', is no simple geographical locale. It is not simply the 'rabbit warrens' that Casper Weinberger sees in Shi'ite Beirut, or the mist-shrouded pastures of Ireland. It can be the Promised Land of Zion and of all covenantal theology – the American Puritans, the South African Boers. It can be the revanchist's vision of a land that he has never seen or the aspiration of the alienated ecologist seeking a land unmarked by society. Not only the time and place that are, but absent times and places, as well as projected times and places, provide that context which is the domain in which a cultural vision can produce terrorists.

I take as my point of departure Professor Paul Wilkinson's brief survey, 'Armenian Terrorism', which begins by contrasting the Baader–Meinhof gang, among others, with Armenian terrorists, among others. He is especially concerned with terrorists who 'claim to be authentic champions of a whole ethnic community'. Wilkinson cites the Irish, Croatians and Armenians as having produced such terrorists, who are said to secure 'a broader and more loyal base of political sympathy and support'[7] than groups like the Baader–Meinhof. The way in which Wilkinson establishes authenticity is directly relevant to my argument: he cites historical precedents. Whereas there are no roots of valid grievance and reactive terrorism reaching down into the German past, he points out, the Armenians have a history of both: oppression, pogrom, genocide and then terrorism as a response to them are said to be 'part of a very long tradition' of Armenian history; as a result, the 'well-springs of ... terrorist violence' lie 'deep in national psyches and traditions'.[8] Committed as I am to notions of the social construction of individual motivation through narrative, I find a great deal that is appealing in this respect for history and tradition. It is therefore all the more disappointing to find Professor Wilkinson writing, two pages later, that 'the roots of modern Armenian terrorism lie in ... tragic events of sixty-eight years ago', namely in the genocide, and in the examples provided by earlier terrorism. 'Young Armenians are ready to go on suicide missions', he writes, because they have both a grievance and an exemplar of terrorism as a proper response to that grievance.[9]

What seems striking about both Professor Wilkinson's otherwise very good analysis and several less creditable discussions of the same topic is the disciplinary rush to the politicization of terrorism. By 'politicization' I mean that the profession of political science seems powerfully impelled to turn enormously complex events into mere, or only, or just *political* facts that can then be seen as motivating other political acts, including terrorism. This reduction happens despite frequent genuflection in the direction of the complexity of social phenomena. The history of certain nations is seen as a series of basically political events which, as though moving through a vacuum of social life, become links in a chain of other politico-diplomatic events, and eventually stretch across the decades to cause yet more political events. Whether the causes be genocide, loss of sovereignty or loss of land, when they result in terrorism the model is the same at its core: one set of events, described as political, functions as a 'cause', creating among its victims a set of agents who are motivated either by politics or by pathology to commit another set of acts described as terrorist.

What is crucially lacking in such a model is the concept of *mediation*, or a serious consideration of the possibility that past events, including the rare purely political events, are perpetuated, disseminated and experienced in a particular culture not as political events but as narratives that transcribe historical facts into moral or immoral acts, vehicles of social values. Such acts sometimes become symbols, models or paradigms of behavior, especially when they are internalized, when the narratives no longer exist 'out there' in the culture, to be sampled occasionally, but in the minds of individuals, as part of the mental equipment with which they are raised to perceive the meaning of events, to interpret them, and to launch new ones. Whether we are speaking of the tale of the 47 masterless samurai made so popular in inter-war Japan, or of the Armenian projective narratives I shall be discussing shortly, we can venture one relatively safe generalization: *terrorism with an authentically popular base is never a purely political phenomenon*. A few other commentators have said this in general terms. Moshe Amon, significantly a professor of religion writing as an outsider for an audience of political scientists, suggests that 'the legitimacy of terrorist movements may stem from a mythological model adopted by the terrorists and endorsed by large segments of society'.[10] All too often in writings on terrorism, the word 'mythology' lacks the complex meaning implied in Amon's sentence; rather, it comes to refer to that set of mystifying beliefs which happens to provide the underpinnings of national liberation movements that employ terrorism. To one reading through the professional literature with the outsider's eye, it sometimes seems that the entire question of cultural difference or specificity is handled by the ritual invocation of the tired truism that 'one man's terrorist is another man's freedom fighter'. Under the aegis of this cliché, the whole set of questions that I want to consider is then overlooked, shunted aside.

One explanation for the inability of commentators to carry through with the insight that they need to evaluate culturally specific accounts of terrorism is the potency of the analytic model which was developed in the study of, and found its early illustrations in, groups close to home, like the Baader–Meinhof gang. The vocabulary and categories with which such terrorists are described in the literature are remarkably consistent. The pivotal terms are ideology, alienation and pathology. Such terrorists are correctly said to be better educated than the average Western citizen, with greater access to abstract theory and ideology. They are said to suffer from 'biographical deficits'[11] and psychopathologies ranging from sadism to 'a desire to express hate and revenge, to smash, to kill and to disrupt – or simply to feel big'.[12] Finally, they are seen as estranged from the mainstream of their society, forced to find shelter, for a time, among relatively alienated populations of student radicals, and in time to lose even that base of passive support. It is not my intention to dispute this characterization, which may be adequate in many contexts. But it too often persists even when the analysis moves on to consider groups like the Irish or Armenian terrorists. Endowing these movements with more authentic, perhaps even legitimate, grievances is something that the more thoughtful analysts, like Professor Wilkinson, are willing to do. But the model of personality, of relations with the rest of society, and therefore of motivation, which is grafted on to the descriptions of terrorists in these movements, remains unchanged. The persistence of the model of the individual terrorist as an alienated Western youth is remarkable, and not without serious consequence. It disables any effort to give a culturally specific description of the way in which different societies maintain their vision of their collective selves with different projective narratives, and so produce different terrorisms and different terrorists. The act of terrorism may well continue to have identical legal status in the courts of Western governments (although even this can be disputed to some degree). Yet if our aim as scholars is not merely to dismiss the complexity of an act by reference to its legal classification, but rather to understand it, we must acknowledge the ways in which cultural meanings and culturally inscribed motives are relatively autonomous of legal codes.

At this point, I must invoke Clifford Geertz's well-known phrase, 'thick description', and move from my more general theoretical critique to a case study that will illustrate what I see as the promise of an alternative mode of inquiry. I will take my examples from the terrorist group whose writings are in the native language I know best, and who are products of Middle-Eastern Armenian society. I mean to lay equal stress on both elements, writings and society. It is not enough to know the dates of pogroms and genocide, or to scan the English-language communiqués of the rather prolific terrorist groups, especially the ASALA, the Armenian Secret Army for the Liberation of Armenia. Their vehement, error-laden English and French, or Arabic and occasionally even Turkish broadsides allow an observer to develop a fairly clear sense of their programs and activities, and of the extent to which the PLO, say, or Kurdish guerrillas and oddly interpreted traditions of Marxism-Leninism have influenced them. But their Armenian writings do not merely recapitulate this material. They also reveal minds steeped in a recognizable Armenian idiom that has roots, not in a 68-year old genocide, but in 15 centuries of both learned and popular discourse, in ecclesiastical ritual and popular narrative, and, perhaps most importantly, in living song. Alone among the commentators I have read, Professor Wilkinson acknowledges, in one sentence, the importance of literature and religion to the tradition of Armenian resistance;[13] I want not only to confirm that, but also to enlarge greatly the claims that may be made about their significance.

The traditions and texts that constitute Armenian social discourse cannot simply be mutely juxtaposed against the ideological pamphlets of terrorists; nor can the terrorists simply be seen as being in opposition to Armenian society, as alienated, fringe elements of their culture. The Armenian writings of terrorists' pamphlets are thoroughly intertextual, in the sense of being explicitly allusive to and continuous with mainstream Armenian social discourse. This stands in sharp contrast to the texts and situations which have thus far provided the models for the study of terrorists' self-image and motivation. It is easy to mock and dismiss the turgid theoretical pronouncements of groups like the Baader–Meinhof gang by pointing to the chasm that separates them from the discourse of ordinary life and ordinary Germans. Reinhard Rupprecht, for example, has observed that German terrorists often 'retreat from family and the ordinary way of life' as a prelude to coming under the influence of ideologies.[14] The Armenian situation very nearly requires that we reverse this observation. Armenian youth in the post-genocide diaspora, when they retreat from family, tend to do so in the direction of assimilation; they do not become terrorists. Those who *do*, speak in the accents of parents and grandparents, in the language of sermons and of the dominant political party, even when furiously rejecting the latter's more cautious platforms. The 'biographical deficits' of Armenian terrorists are usually the slaughter of most of their grandparents' generation, an event conveyed to them vividly through detailed narrative. Yet such memory is never by itself enough to cause terrorism. There are always more grievances than guerrillas, revolutionaries or terrorists. The catalyst here is the coupling of the vivid collective memory of injustice with traditional and valued paradigms for action, paradigms embodied in projective narratives. To be an Armenian in an 'ordinary' way in many Middle Eastern communities means, first, that one understands the present experience of injustice in terms of familial stories and national narratives that are deeply intertwined. Second, one anticipates any confrontation with such injustice in terms of narratives of earlier resistance. These are projected upon both the present and the future as morally privileged patterns for action and for interpretation of that action; hence the term 'projective narrative'.

Before I give an account of the ways in which diaspora culture is shaped by the master-narratives involved, and of their effect on Armenian terrorism, I must further qualify certain of my terms. In an Armenian diaspora that numbers nearly 1.5 million people in some 30 countries, a typical Armenian is a fiction, not unlike that of the typical international terrorist. Not all diaspora Armenians are relevant to a discussion of terrorism. Only one Armenian terrorist captured or otherwise identified is American-born; another is French-born; the remainder were all born in Lebanon, Iran, Syria or Turkey. Both the ordinary Armenian and the terrorist of my analysis come from a certain stratum of Middle-Eastern Armenian communities, a stratum that makes up a minority of the Armenian population of Iran, possibly a plurality in Syria and probably a majority in Lebanon. In most of these cases, the terrorist and the relevant stratum both live in a common cultural reality. The foundations of this cultural reality are not just endogamy or cuisine; they are religious, linguistic, rhetorical and mythic. This primarily verbal and narrative reality is maintained through a network of churches, schools, athletic unions, youth and student groups. Obviously, none of these institutions have the production of terrorism as their aim: their purpose is to reproduce and perpetuate a certain culture in a diaspora under the pressure of assimilation. Of the elements which give that Armenian cultural tradition its cohesion and shape, perhaps the most central is a ubiquitous cluster of stories. Among those I shall turn now to, two are part of the cultural experience of every Armenian in the diaspora; others are specific to the strata mentioned above.

The first of these is the story of the genocide, which is always articulated at two levels, the national and the familial. On each level one encounters both a story of traumatizing events and an invocation of place. The first story is of the planned slaughter of a Nation and the appropriation of a Fatherland; the other is the tale of how family members died and a reminiscence of the ancestral village or town. Those familiar with older Armenians anywhere in the diaspora and with Armenian life in the relevant Middle Eastern communities will know the importance of compatriotic associations and of the frequent question 'where are you from?', which always has a double import: where in the diaspora are you from, and where in the lost Fatherland were your grandparents from? This concern is reinforced by a resurgent practice of naming children after lost places and landmarks: Ani and Ararat, Van and Masis, Daron and Nareg.

The second ubiquitous narrative dates from the second half of the fifth century AD, and is the story of Vartan and the martyrs, whose memory is commemorated by a Saints' Day in the calendar of the Armenian Apostolic Church. Armenian children encounter their story at Church, in Sunday school, in kindergarten and elementary school. More advanced students in the parochial school systems of the Middle East encounter it in extended narrative form, usually in contemporary Armenian but sometimes even in the classical Armenian in which it was written down by the cleric Yeghishe. This narrative has been ably translated and controversially edited by the Harvard scholar, Robert Thomson,[15] who believes that the historically accurate residue in the narrative is small, and that the model for the heroic resistance and martyrdom of Vartan and his men derives more from the Biblical books of the Maccabees than from reality. However, the debate about the historical accuracy of the work is beside the point here. The invocation of the model of the Maccabees only serves to underscore the ways in which the Vartan story enables and sanctions certain kinds of resistance, endowing it with a mantle of traditional and religious authority. While this religious dimension was vital in the period extending from the fifth to the nineteenth centuries, it has steadily become less so since. In the nineteenth century, the increase of literacy, the revival of Armenian literature and the accessibility of secular education combined to spawn a dozen versions of the tale. The first important Armenian romantic poet composed one of his most important poems about the battlefield where Vartan and his followers fell in battle against the Sassanid Persians. Two of the most important early romantic historical novels authored by Raffi, the Armenian equivalent of Victor Hugo, invoke Vartan as model, while a third takes related figures from the same era for its heroes and villains. In the process of secularization of the tale and proliferation of its versions, two words have remained in play: *martyros*, from the Greek martyr, and *nahadag*, its Armenian synonym. In many recountings of the tale, in speeches, sermons, laments and funeral orations, the formulaic line most frequently invoked is *mah imatzyal anmahootyun e*, that is, 'death knowingly grasped is immortality'. The line is pivotal to Yeghishe's text, and refers to the willingness of Vartan and his followers to risk all in defense of Armenian Christianity, conceived then (as now) as a crucial component of national identity.

The crisis which provoked the remark was brought on by the Persian Empire's insistence, in AD450/1, on converting the Armenians, who had been Christian since AD301, to militant Zoroastrianism. Defiant Armenian princes and clergy were summoned to Ctesiphon, the capital of the Sassanid empire, submitted to coerced conversion, and upon their return to Armenia vacillated about imposing a similar conversion on the mass of their subjects until events took matters out of their hands. Proselytizing Persian priests forcibly converted altars to fire-altars. They were attacked by enraged Armenians led by a priest, and the conflagration spread. The Persian army invaded; Vartan (the hereditary commander of the Armenian armies) and his troops met it in unequal battle. He and 1,036 of his followers fell, and 30 years of passive resistance punctuated by minor uprisings followed until AD484, when Vartan's nephew obtained a favorable treaty of peace and autonomy from an otherwise embattled Persian empire. Such are the bare bones of the story. What matters to my analysis is the way in which what was originally a struggle for religious tolerance, local autonomy and feudal privilege became an exemplary narrative of virtuous action, in defense of national identity and personal honor, simultaneously. Today, it retains the most potent aspects of martyrology without any longer being a tale that inspires religious piety as such; it has been reinterpreted, through its many nineteenth-century retellings, as primarily a struggle for national identity. Its exemplary status can be made clearer by comparison with a medieval parallel. As Christ's life, narated in sermons and pictured on cathedral windows, constituted an invitation to *imitatio Christi*, an exemplar revealing the way by which to live one's life so that it conformed to the highest ideals of the community as embodied in the New Testament narratives, so also Vartan's life and death are endlessly narrated with a passion that establishes them as models of exemplary courage and virtue. Today, even in Sunday schools in the USA, the grandchildren of pacific third-generation Armenian-Americans still learn to recite a rhyme that declares: *Hye em yes, hye em yes/Kach Vartanin torn em yes*, namely, 'I am Armenian, I am Armenian/ the grandchild of valiant Vartan'. The first and second statements are equal, and they imply a regulative autobiography: to be Armenian is to acknowledge Vartan as ancestor. To acknowledge as ancestor one who is not a blood relative is to acknowledge his moral and symbolic authority. In an ethnically pluralist America, the lines and the tradition may have no further import. In the Middle East, where Armenians are less assimilated and much beset, the statement and the Vartan stories as a whole come into play as projective narratives.

The omnipresent narratives of the genocide and of Vartan provide a frame for a series of more specific narratives of Armenian heroism and sacrifice. The most popular form in which these are embodied is song, learned in early childhood in schools and clubs, and in formal and informal public occasions where they are spontaneously sung. In the US, where the music of Elvis Presley is sometimes relegated to 'oldies' radio programs, it is difficult to imagine the musical practice of a culture in which disco music coexists with songs composed mostly in the period 1890–1920 in honor of executed revolutionaries and guerrillas fallen in combat. In the US, of course, only a very small portion of Armenian-Americans retain this musical and narrative culture; Western records, cassettes, television and video dominate both musical and non-musical narrative, for Armenians as for other ethnic groups. But in the Middle East, in the countries whence most Armenian terrorists have come, at least a plurality of the people retained this traditional culture until very recently. In Lebanon, confessional warfare is temporarily reviving its fading vitality. Armenian bookstores still sell songbooks containing such songs. Of these, one has the status of a national anthem. The quatrain inevitably included in all versions ends with the lines: *Amenayn degh mahe me e/Mart me ankam bid merni/Paytz yerani oom ir azki/Azadootyan ge zohvi* – 'Death is the same everywhere/and a man dies only once/ Lucky is he/ who dies for the freedom of his nation'. Another, composed in 1896, honors the revolutionaries who occupied the Franco-Turkish Banque Ottomane in

Istanbul. They held hostages and demanded access to the European powers and press in the hope of publicizing the plight of the Armenians during a moment of persecution and pogrom particularly vicious even by the Sultan Abdul Hamid's high standards. Nearly a century later, the song is still sung spontaneously, with something of the ease with which an American might put a golden oldie on the turntable as a party winds down. Of course, this and other songs do not explicitly affirm the legitimacy of terrorism. Their sentimental melodies and depictions of suffering, daring, rare partial success and heroic death constitute projective narratives which serve to establish the willingness to act against very high odds, and to accept violent death, as essential elements of the character of those who would honorably live out lives that are socially approved precisely because their paradigm is represented in projective narratives. Literally dozens of other songs from this period celebrate small victories and large, heroic defeats that testify to Armenian endurance in what Wilkinson calls their 'very long tradition of resistance'.[16] This tradition is alive in the web of culture, not just a matter for the learned, the books, the museums. It is inscribed into the minds of a certain proportion of diaspora Armenians as they grow up; it partially but importantly constitutes their Armenianness.

The final cluster of traditional narratives that should be mentioned consists of stories of the Armenian assassins who, in 1921–23, after the genocide, struck down several members of the Young Turk junta responsible for its organization, chief among them Talaat Pasha. Other stories concern the killing of Armenian traitors, or even particularly oppressive Tzarist officials in Eastern Armenia. These stories have been restricted to a more narrow audience, because they are not enshrined in song. Still, they are familiar to many. They were invoked in countless discussions and articles in the first few years of the revival of Armenian terrorism, which began with Kourken Yanikian's revenge-killing of two Turkish officials in Santa Barbara, California, in 1973. Of course, to a detached observer, there is a clear sense in which the earlier assassinations do not provide appropriate models for thinking about terrorism directed against officials whose guilt could only be established after extended moral and philosophical argument, if at all. Direct participation in a genocide is a different order of crime from working for the civil service of the contemporary Turkish state, however much that state continues to benefit from the crimes of the Young Turks while distorting the historical record. The fact that phrases like 'the avenging arm of Talaat's assassins can strike again' were used to discuss such complex issues provides one measure of the saturation of Armenian culture by this narrative idiom of persecution and revenge. The persecution has been very real, of course, and revenge is not to be easily dismissed as a value or motive; what must be underscored is that they are not political facts that are politically institutionalized in Armenian life, but complex cultural and psychological phenomena woven as narratives into the matrix of what passes for ordinary life in certain Middle Eastern societies.

Since my aim has been to depoliticize the discussion of terrorism, that is, to counter the tendency of political science to reduce terrorist acts to mere disturbances of the political order caused by political motives, I have so far avoided the exposition of Armenian political realities. By no means all, but certainly much, of the maintenance of the narrative traditions has been the work of intellectuals, teachers, artists, organizers and activists who are or were, at one time or another, under the influence of the *Hye Heghapokhaganneri Dashnagtzootyun*, the Federation of Armenian Revolutionaries, founded in 1890, in the Tzarist Empire, as a confederation of existing student radical groups heavily influenced by the Narodniki. In the diaspora, since the Sovietization of the short-lived independent Armenian Republic, this party, known in English by the acronym ARF, has struggled for dominance, which it achieved in Lebanon, Syria and Iran to a considerable degree in the 1920s and then again between 1948 and 1967. There are very few card-carrying 'Dashnags' in the diaspora; there are tens of thousands of sympathizers and many ex-Dashnags. As with members of the Roman Catholic Church, so with Dashnags the imprint of its political culture is not easily removed, even from those in rebellion against its dogma. That dogma has been a rhetorically potent but politically ineffective declaration of the rights of the Armenian people to a restored homeland, not accompanied by action. It has been difficult, for Armenians scattered in a diaspora, to conceive of a course of action likely to result in the recognition of genocide, let alone the restoration of their lost homeland.

The gap between rhetoric and action has been all the more underscored by the nature and origins of ARF culture. Since it was the dominant party in the resistance against Turkish persecution from 1890 on, a very large proportion of the songs, tales, memoirs and formal literary narratives from this period are about its cadres and heroes. It is not an exaggeration to say that the political entity called the Dashnag party in the diaspora has been, above all else, a cultural institution, even as it has exercised a serious measure of political power in the Armenian quarters of Beirut. Almost everywhere, its prestige and capital have been its past achievements and defeats, as commemorated in the narratives discussed. From Papken Suny at the Banque Ottomane to Kevork Chavoush, Aghpyoor Serop and his wife Soseh, and to Antranig Pasha, the larger-than-life heroes of Armenian projective narratives, men and women both, have been predominantly members or former members of the ARF. Until 1973, its cultural institutions were the chief custodians of the projective narratives I have described. Ironically, the first generation of terrorists spoke insistently of the bankruptcy of ARF rhetoric and of its failure to live up to its own narrative traditions as a motive for the formation of their own units. Many of these terrorists had broken away from ARF-dominated youth groups after being saturated by their unacted projective narratives. The frequency of indignant or ironic citation of these heroic models in the early pamphlets of the ASALA is readily apparent to anyone familiar with the relevant strata of Armenian culture.

My argument rests, of course, on several interdependent claims. One is that it is reductive and finally inadequate to think of terrorist acts as only a political response to political facts, past or present. Neither political nor psychological explanations can compensate for a lack of analysis of the cultural milieu that provides the medium in which political facts are interpreted and engender new acts. Discussions of motivation and self-image that depend primarily on the manipulation of psychological and behavioristic categories inevitably trivialize the cultural matrix. Second, I have made narrative the major conceptual category of my analysis, suggesting that in cultures like the Armenian, terrorism is not the product of a particular individual's alienation, but the manifestation of a desire to give one's individual life an iconic centrality in the eyes of the community, which professes to value certain forms of behavior articulated in narratives. I say 'professes' because, of course, only a very tiny proportion of people sentimentally moved by either popular or high-cultural fictions are actually tempted to enact them. Life imitates art and other fictions only rarely; but imitate it does.

I have given a detailed account of the dominant narratives and the socio-political structures that mutually sustain each other in the Armenian diaspora because these narratives animate 'the example[s] set by predecessors' which Martha Crenshaw sees, in another context, as 'contribut[ing] to make the terrorists' purpose salient'.[17] It remains to demonstrate that a direct link exists between the narratives, on the one hand, and the terrorists and their diaspora audience, on the other.

Such a demonstration requires textual analysis of Armenian writings by the terrorists, by the sympathetic interpreters of their words and deeds, and even by their critics. Over the past five years, I have read some 4,000 pages of such texts. Clear evidence of the links we seek is abundant in them. Limitations of space require that I limit myself to only a few examples. These were obtained by my *random* scanning of five issues of the ASALA periodical, *Hayasdan*, and of one not-randomly selected ARF publication.

The genocide is massively present everywhere. It is constantly referred to as the double crime of mass murder and dispossession that can justify any terrorist act, which is inevitably seen as minor in comparison with this crime. The genocide is denounced as the reason why the diaspora exists and why assimilation can ravage most Armenian communities. Known as 'white massacre', assimilation is portrayed as inevitable in the diaspora, and as the completion of the genocide, which is invoked by photographs that stud many texts whose actual content is not the genocide. Thus, a communiqué about a terrrorist operation, or a theoretical piece on Third World Marxism, can be 'illustrated' by reduced and poorly reproduced photographs of Armenian dead from the genocide. Typically, no more direct relation need be established, because internalized social discourse can be counted upon to do that work. The cover of one issue of ASALA's periodical features a photograph of a pile of skulls and a caption (in French) that translates as: 'that the 24th of April may become a day of struggle'.[18] That date, in 1915, marks the day when mass arrests of

Armenian intellectuals in Istanbul 'officially' launched a genocide already begun in late March in the plains of Anatolia. The thought is elaborated in a longer Arabic caption and embroidered upon elsewhere in this as in all issues. Killings of Kurdish civilians and guerrillas in south-eastern Turkey are viewed as a continuation of the Armenian genocide and as part of the age-old dream of Turkification; this is perhaps true, but hardly argued carefully by means of ordinary evidence. All is told as part of the narrative of an ongoing genocide: first the Armenians, then the assimilative cultural genocide of the diaspora, then Kurdicide. The implication is that we know this story, and we know its awful outcome, and we also know what must be done in response to it. All this does not remain at the level of the generalized story; there are practical details which reinforce it. Whereas an American military operation might be named Rolling Thunder, the ASALA often names its attacks after lost comrades and also after lost territories. The attack on Ankara Airport was named Garin, the Armenian name of the city of Erzerum; other 'commando groups' bear the names of the old and new heroes of projective narratives: 'Antranig Pasha', say, or 'Yanikian'. It is as if the terrorists' actions are responses to the double question I alluded to earlier: whom did you lose and what place did you lose?

The Vartan narrative is not as ubiquitous, but is present in ways direct and indirect in the periodicals examined. The ASALA publications are illustrated with the photographs of fallen terrorists; the captions include an incongruous coupling of the Christian and the Marxist: all the dead are *nahadag-ungers*, that is, martyr-comrades. One issue[19] has a paragraph describing the death of a terrorist that reads, in part (in my own translation): '*Fedayee* Megerdich Madurian completed his mission before he exploded a grenade he carried attached to his waist, thus showing that the Secret Army is determined to continue in the path of "death knowingly grasped" – of "*imatzyal mah*"' – cited in the original classical Armenian from Yeghishe's Vartan narrative. Such an explicit identification of ASALA cadres in 1983 with the Vartan of AD451 constitutes a rejection of the simplifying Western notion of a suicide mission. Vartan and his men did not commit suicide; they went to do battle against large odds that in fact proved deadly to some of them, but their act was not suicidal in motive, their defeat did not lead to extermination, and the word suicide is not associated with their action. This is the narrative logic applied even to acts that are, in fact, inevitably fatal to the perpetrators when carried out in Turkey proper. Yet they are represented as standing and fighting to the death for Armenia.

Even opponents and critics of the terrorists, who (whatever the impression given by the popular press) are legion in the Armenian community, invoke the Vartan narrative. Khachig Pilikian, an artist living in London, recently privately published his own critique of terrorism in which he attacks terrorists who refuse the challenge of enduring creatively as a diaspora and instead resort to violence. In doing so, he refers to ASALA cadres as 'new *fedayeen*, little lefties of brave Vartan'.[20] The clause is incoherent but significant. The ASALA terrorists are dismissed, but precisely in the terms they proudly claim for themselves: as leftists, as heirs of the Armenian *fedayees* of the pre-genocide resistance, as descendants of Vartan, as youthful and therefore daring (and therefore unwise, according to Pilikian).

The terrorists of the Secret Army see themselves as the heirs of the 'abandoned' and even 'betrayed' traditions of the early ARF; they neglect the historical context in which the ARF organized resistance against Turkish oppression of Anatolian Armenians who then were living on their ancestral territories, not scattered in a diaspora. Thanks to the very narratives they have inherited from ARF-dominated culture, they find it possible to shoulder the goals of ARF rhetoric without examining too closely why those goals remained unfulfilled. The logic of ASALA analysis in the end owes more to the logic of the dominant narratives of Armenian culture, to the employment of sacrifice on the altar of national identity, than to Marighella or Lenin or George Habash. Despite the radical changes in that historical context over the centuries, the projective narrative that dictates the logic of action and projects that action and its agents into the future retains its stubborn structure, inherited from textualizations of history that begin in the Vartan narratives and have continued since. Thus, the blinding by an accidental bomb explosion of ASALA leader Yenikomshian is compared to the death, under similar circumstances but a full 75 years earlier, of Krisdapor Mikayelian, a member of the founding trinity of the ARF.[21] This comparison recurs throughout the early 1980s publications of the ASALA, even in some of the most vituperative essays attacking the contemporary ARF. The deep structure of such discourse has its own pre-analytic logic. It resembles most what scholars of literature and religion call typological-prefigurative narrative, in which historical and contextual changes intervening between two events do not necessarily create a discontinuity of meaning-making, of interpretative procedure. Just as Abraham sacrificing his son Isaac prefigures God sacrificing his son Christ, so also the whole of the Old Testament prefigures the New, and the book of Apocalypse the end of the world in nuclear holocaust, all proclaimed by persons who think with the same narrative 'logic' as the ASALA.

Regulative biographies are retrospective manifestations of a similar logic. Kourken Yanikian's killing of two Turkish diplomats in 1973 was the isolated act of a solitary individual, a classic example of the work of the lone assassin. ASALA became active in early 1975, and from the beginning it appropriated Yanikian's action as something it was not, and has reinscribed it within the narratives of continuity and repetition as an instance of 'rebirth'. That this can be done to an action that has no relation to organized terrorism either early or late is testimony to the belief that the master-narratives have on collective thought. Thus, the April 1981 issue of *Hayasdan*[22] features a photograph of Yanikian. The caption reads: '*verkerov li jan fedayee*' – a nearly untranslatable address to the *fedayee* bleeding, like Christ or Saint Sebastian, from many wounds, but more importantly a quotation from the first line of a famous song of the early 1900s. Although he was neither wounded nor a *fedayee*, Yanikian is nevertheless not understood in the context of his life, of his real biography, or even in the context of the brief autobiography we can glean from his utterances. He is assigned a regulative biography, and understood through it.

What the ASALA does in this instance with Yanikian, it often does with its own cadres. After the fact of the terrorist act, cadres are depicted in regulative biographies that interpret their actions in terms of past narratives and of the values the living tradition assigns to actions in those narratives. Even in more general essays about their own actions, they represent the design of their political project in terms of these narratives. Thus, an article occasioned by Shahan Natali's death, in the August 1983 issue of *Hayasdan*,[23] eulogizes this long-ago expelled member of the ARF as 'the first Armenian Nemesis' along with other famed avengers from the same organization – Tehlirian, Torlakian, Yerganian – who assassinated Talaat Pasha, Behaeddin Shakir and Jemal Azmi, three architects of the genocide. These names are intoned together with Yanikian's and to them is added the phrase 'the martyrs and imprisoned warriors of the ASALA', all enlisted in a resonating roll-call that blurs history, context and nuance. All become actors of the same master-narrative. The device of the roll-call that erases individual motives and historical detail is not, of course, unique to the Armenian situation. To glance for a moment outside my purview, at a context where my approach might be relevant in the hands of a seasoned observer of Irish culture, let me cite what seems to me the most Armenian of Willian Butler Yeats's poems, 'Easter 1916'. He ends that famed poem with a similar short list:

> And what if excess of love
> burdened them til they died?
> I write it out in a verse-
> MacDonough and MacBride
> and Connolly and Pearce,
> Now and in time to be
> wherever green is worn
> are changed, changed utterly:
> a terrible beauty is born.

We might endlessly debate the terrible beauty of the events referred to, but the potency of the intoned list is indisputable. The list enlists; it tells us little about the different individuals and their different motives, but rather inscribes them in a past and future narrative, valid wherever green is worn, wherever, the poem implies, the sacrifice and resurrection of Christ which we celebrate at Easter are known as narratives of salvation. This is what it is to be a martyr or a *martyros* or a *nahadag-unger*, a martyr-comrade whose death is always represented as a choice of enlistment in the narrative of national salvation, which requires the individual's death as the price of the national collectivity's resurrection.

To cap this brief sampling of the intertextuality that obtains between terrorist discourse and the master-narratives of the culture in question, let me glance at the ways in which other Armenians have interpreted Armenian terrorism. One of the best-known acts of recent years was the seizure of the Turkish embassy in Lisbon by Armenian Revolutionary Army, or ARA, terrorists. It ended when an explosion killed all five terrorists. Some believe an accident caused the detonation of explosives brought in by the ARA cadres; others believe it was a group suicide committed when the terrorists realized they were about to be captured by Portuguese commandos reputed to be well-trained by Britain's SAS. While the facts are in dispute, the interpretation of it by a segment of ARF-dominated Armenian society is not. Throughout that part of the community, the reach of regulative narrative is unchallenged. What is more impressive, even to a scholar accustomed to its power, is a poem composed in Soviet Armenia, by a poet who was born and recently died there, in the USSR, and who most probably knew of the terrorism only through Voice of America broadcasts and tourists' stories. He wrote a celebration of the heroism of the Lisbon Five, as they are generally known, in which the refrain is:

Hishek, Hyer, inchbess Tizbon
Yereg Tizbon, aysor Lisbon ...

and continues with:

Yeg, vor Vartann Avarayri
Anedzk tarna Turkin vayri.

In Armenian, Tizbon is the pronunciation of Ctesiphon, the capital of the Sassanid Empire where Vartan and others were forced into a conversion they later renounced. The rhyme with Lisbon ushers in the whole Vartan-narrative in the lines which mean, translated loosely (as they must be): 'Come, Armenians, [and recall] how it was in Tizbon/Yesterday Tizbon, today Lisbon'. To make his point even more unmistakable, the poet writes in the latter lines: 'Come, let the Vartan of Avarayr/Become the curse of the savage Turk'. This poem is found reprinted in an Armenian-language weekly published in Canada,[24] read entirely by recent immigrants from the Middle East, who can be counted upon to see the logic of narrative: the Sassanid empire is dead, Ctesiphon is a heap of ruins that some tourists to Baghdad may visit, but the struggle is the same. The narrative of 451 still applies in 1985.

At a certain level of analytical abstraction, there is a sense to the logic. Armenians continue to struggle for cultural identity, which is perceived by them, and by so many other ethnics, as a self-evident value in its own right. That culture was produced by centuries of resistance in unequal struggle. Given the presence of some 'political' factors beyond the range of this analysis, such a culture, I have been trying to suggest, is able to produce and sustain a certain level of terrorist activity, even in diaspora conditions, perhaps especially in diaspora conditions. For the Armenians in the diaspora, there is no state that can conduct their political life for them, that can challenge, for example, Turkish misrepresentations of Armenian history, or claim the legitimate use of force. The absence of a state and a country means that there is no possibility in the diaspora for enacting a classical narrative of social revolution on either the Marxist or another model: neither Angolan revolution nor Afghan guerrilla war is possible. Under such circumstances and in the conditions that have prevailed in the Middle East since 1967, the dominant cultural narratives overdetermine conditions that help to produce terrorism and are in turn reanimated by it. Such terrorism produces new heroes for old stories. It would be a mistake for analysts to delude themselves into believing, as the terrorists themselves have, that the true audience and target of Armenian terrorism is Turkey and its NATO allies. Neither of those is likely to be moved; at most, a few nations might express a desire to set the record straight on the genocide. But the true audience of Armenian terrorism remains the Armenian diaspora, whose fraying culture is constituted to a remarkable degree by old stories, and who see in contemporary terrorists Vartan's refusal to abandon cultural identity and national rights.

NOTES

I am grateful to Professors Martha Crenshaw of Wesleyan University and David C. Rapoport of UCLA for inviting me, a humanist, to contribute to the deliberations of an APSA panel where the first version of this article was given, and for providing me with references to relevant work. My thanks also to Professor Ellen Rooney of Brown University for her careful reading of earlier drafts.

1. For example, Richard Clutterbuck, *Guerrillas and Terrorists* (London: Faber, 1977), p.11.
2. Joseph Margolin, 'Psychological Perspectives in Terrorism', in Y. Alexander and S. Finger (eds.), *Terrorism: Interdisciplinary Perspectives* (New York: John Jay Press, 1977), p.271.
3. To resist such universalization is not, of course, to devalue the political realm, which remains indispensable to the study of terrorism. However, as I argue in the body of this article (which is part of a book on Armenian terrorism in progress), certain terrorist movements cannot be understood by political analysis alone, or even *primarily* by standard methods of such analysis, no matter how nuanced. It is necessary to distinguish between – and for purposes of analysis, temporarily to separate – the political ideology and behavior of terrorist movements from the larger and more innocuous political culture of the ethnic group from which the terrorists originate. Finally, political ideology and political culture both must in turn be situated in the larger culture. The core assumption of my argument is that Armenian terrorism in particular (along with some other terrorisms emanating from ethnic populations), can never be fully understood simply by reference to the objectives it announces and the antagonists it identifies. One must always take into account its embeddedness in the political culture from which it emanates and which it seeks to renew or transform by action.
4. Walter Laqueur, *Terrorism* (Boston: Little, Brown, 1977), p.120.
5. H.H.A. Cooper, 'Voices from Troy: What Are We Hearing?' *Outthinking the Terrorist: An International Challenge*, Proceedings of the Tenth Annual Symposium

on the Role of Behavioral Science in Physical Security, Defense Nuclear Agency, Washington, DC, 1985, p.95.

6. I derive the latter term from 'regulative psycho-biography', a locution I encountered in Professor G.C. Spivak's 'The Political Economy of Women as Seen by a Literary Critic', unpublished. It has a somewhat different meaning in her work than that given to it here.
7. Paul Wilkinson, 'Armenian Terrorism', *The World Today* (Sept., 1983), p.344.
8. Ibid.
9. Wilkinson, p.346.
10. Moshe Amon, 'Religion and Terrorism: A Romantic Model of Secular Gnosticism', in D.C. Rapoport and Y. Alexander (eds.), *The Rationalization of Terrorism* (Frederick, MD: University Publications of America), p.82.
11. Reinhard Rupprecht, 'Terrorism and Counterterrorism in the Federal Republic of Germany', *Outthinking the Terrorist*, op. cit., p.73.
12. Clutterbuck, op. cit., p.94.
13. Wilkinson, op. cit., p.344.
14. Rupprecht, op. cit., p.73.
15. Robert Thomson, tr. and comm. Yeghishe, *History of Vartan and the Armenian War* (Cambridge, MA: Harvard University Press, 1982).
16. Wilkinson, op. cit., p.344.
17. Martha Crenshaw, 'Incentives for Terrorism', *Outthinking the Terrorist*, op. cit., p.18.
18. *Hayasdan* (*Armenia*, in Armenian), 24 April 1981 (Special Issue).
19. *Hayasdan*, 16 June 1983, p.47.
20. Khachig Pilikian, *Refuting Terrorism: Seven Epistles from the Diaspora* (London: Heritage of Armenian Culture Publications, 1984), p.21.
21. *Hayasdan*, Dec. 1980, p.16.
22. *Hayasdan*, April 1981.
23. *Hayasdan*, Aug. 1983, p.14.
24. Hovhanness Shiraz, 'Lisboni Voghchageznerin' (poem in Armenian), *Horizon* (Montreal, Canada), 29 July 1984, p.6.

[8]

Striking with Hunger: Cultural Meanings of Political Violence in Northern Ireland

BEGOÑA ARETXAGA

This entire book is a novel in the form of variations. The individual parts follow each other like individual stretches of a journey leading towards a theme, a thought, a single situation, the sense of which fades into the distance.

—Milan Kundera, *The Book of Laughter and Forgetting*

In 1981 ten Republican men fasted to their deaths in the Long Kesh prison of Belfast while attempting to achieve Special Category (political) status denied them by the British government. For the prisoners, political status amounted to five concrete demands: use of their own clothes instead of prison uniforms; no prison work; free association inside the jail; a parcel, a letter, and a visit per week; and restoration of lost remission of sentence. The strike was the culmination of a long fight in which dirt and nakedness were the prisoners' weapons. During this fight the refusal of the prison uniform became an encompassing and emotionally loaded symbol of a transforming political culture. At first, the fact that four hundred men would be willing to live for years naked, surrounded by their own excreta, and to face death by starvation before putting on a prison uniform may seem perhaps a bizarre show of stubbornness. After all, the Nationalist community (the main IRA audience) did not accept British standards on Irish affairs and did not consider IRA prisoners to be regular criminals.[1] The British administration on the other hand implicitly acknowledged the prisoners' special character by de facto applying special legislation to them. Why, then, engage in a long and torturous battle to settle an identity—political versus criminal—that seemed obvious from the start? The struggle over political identity was a struggle over the power to define the terms of the conflict in Northern Ireland. But this is clearly insufficient to understand the powerful motivations and symbolic constructions that enabled the prisoners to create and endure horrific living conditions and to orchestrate their own deaths. It also does not explain why the British administration did not accede to the prisoners' demands when their refusal was strangling political relations with Ireland and increasing the already high level of political tension in Northern Ireland.

This chapter is an exploration into the cultural construction of political violence, both as a form of colonial domination and of resistance to that domination, through an interpretation of the 1981 Irish hunger strike. I consider this hunger strike a complex political event and a rich multilayered cultural text in which different political, historical, and personal strands converge—overdetermining and deconstructing each other—to create a situation generative of cultural meaning and social change. I do not present here, however, a full history of the multiple political and social relations that resulted in the hunger strike. Nor do I assess its political implications for the different parties involved (Nationalists, Loyalists, the British administration, the Irish administration). My attempt, rather, is to apprehend the "bizarre" reality of a group of men who forced their way out of prison in a line of coffins.

I suggest that the hunger strike is best understood when placed into the larger context of the Anglo-Irish colonial relationship and the set of meanings and cultural identities that relationship created. In this light I interpret Nationalist narratives of history and personal memories of dispossession. I also examine key categories used by colonial England in defining its political and economic relations with Ireland and their bearing on the British view of the current Northern Ireland conflict.

The meaning of the prisoners' identity is a central question in understanding the experience of political relations in the Northern Ireland Nationalist communities. This experience is condensed in the 1981 hunger strike, a historical event that renewed old scars and added new ones to the heavily burdened political consciousness of Northern Ireland.

THE "TROUBLES": HISTORICAL NOTES AND THEORETICAL CONSIDERATIONS

The current conflict in Northern Ireland—or, as the locals call it, the "troubles"—began in 1968 with the campaign for Catholic civil rights. Its roots, however, are grounded in the formation of the Northern Ireland statelet[2] and extend back to the seventeenth century when the native Ulster population was dispossessed and displaced by Protestant Scottish and English settlers.[3] In the eighteenth century, the ill-fated rebellion of the Jacobin United Irishmen against the British colonial government gave rise to the Republican tradition in Ireland. The nineteenth century saw the growth of the

Industrial Revolution in what is now called Northern Ireland, the beginning of communal riots between Protestants and Catholics, and the organization of Protestant Ulster in favor of the union with England and against self-government for Ireland.

The identification of the Conservative party in England with Ulster Unionists fostered the growth of the latter and set the political conditions leading to the partition of Ireland in 1921. The partition was a product of British imperialist contradictions, which—having fed Ulster unionism with its opposition to Irish autonomy—devised no better form of reconciling the conflicting interests of Ireland's Nationalist majority and Ulster's Unionist minority than to create a new statelet in which Protestant Unionists would constitute a permanent majority over Catholic Nationalists. To this end, the boundaries of Northern Ireland were explicitly drawn to include six of the traditional nine counties of Ulster, ensuring a religious cleavage of 820,000 Protestants (most of whom supported the British connection) and 430,000 Catholics (most of whom were against it) (Darby 1983). The result was an inherently unstable state, riddled with discrimination and political violence.

Northern Ireland was born amid bloodshed and social disturbance. The formal opening of its parliament in June 1921 was preceded and followed by riots and attacks on Catholic districts. Between July 1920 and July 1922, 453 people were killed in Belfast: 37 members of the Crown forces, 257 Catholics, 157 Protestants, and 2 of unknown religion. Of the 93,000 Catholics in Belfast, 11,000 were fired or intimidated into leaving their jobs, and 23,000 were driven out of their homes by police forces and Protestant mobs (Farrell 1976).

Soon after the formation of Northern Ireland, the Unionist government established the bases for the political and economic discrimination of the Catholic minority. In 1922 the existing electoral system of proportional representation, which hitherto had given Nationalists certain control in local government, was abolished. Simultaneously, electoral boundaries were redrawn to ensure a Unionist majority, even in the councils of Nationalist enclaves such as the city of Derry. The government of Northern Ireland also restricted franchise by excluding nonratepayers from voting.[4] Because the Unionist councils actively discriminated against Catholics in housing allocations and public employment, also encouraging discrimination in the private sector, Catholics were twice as likely to be poor as were Protestants and therefore much more likely to be left out of electoral politics. As a result, a quarter of the adult population was disenfranchised, the majority of whom were Catholics (Cameron Report 1969).

The structure of Northern Ireland was underpinned by a heavy security apparatus (Flackes and Elliott 1989). The regular police force, the Royal Ulster Constabulary (RUC), was overwhelmingly Protestant; and the parttime voluntary police known as B-specials were exclusively Protestant and were known for their anti-Catholic practices (Farrell 1976). Repressive legislation gave the police wide-ranging powers. The Civil Authorities (Special Powers) Act of 1922, used most often against the Catholic population, provided extensively for actions that represented a practical abrogation of civil and legal rights in the rest of Britain (Hillyard 1983). Such actions included arrests and internment without trial, house searches without a warrant, and censorship. This piece of legislation also introduced the death penalty for possession of explosives and gave the minister of home affairs power to examine the bank accounts of citizens and to seize money if he suspected terrorism (Rowthorn and Wayne 1988).

The judiciary also gave Catholics little confidence. The majority of judges who have been appointed since 1922 in Northern Ireland have been associated with the Unionist party and therefore have been openly anti-Nationalist. The formation of Northern Ireland exacerbated tensions between Catholics and Protestants, deepening existing resentments and creating new fears and suspicions. Rioting and violence occurred during the economic depression of the 1930s and again during the 1950s.[5]

In 1967 the Northern Ireland Civil Rights Association (NICRA) was formed to campaign for housing, an end to job discrimination, and universal franchise. The government failed to make the minimal reforms necessary to appease Catholic discontent, and the campaign intensified. Political tension reached a breaking point in August 1969 when Protestant mobs and local police attacked and burned houses in the Catholic Bogside district of Derry and the Catholic Lower Falls area of Belfast. On August 14, the day after the attack on Lower Falls and two days after that on Derry, the British government sent its army into Northern Ireland. The scene was set for the rebirth of the IRA and the longest violent conflict in Irish history.

Since 1969 a range of social scientists has contributed to the rapidly growing literature about the conflict in Northern Ireland.[6] Most researchers have used the categories from political economy to explain the crisis. They locate the knot of the problem in clashing economic interests and market relations, thus seeing political violence as the result of British or Unionist capitalism in its different shapes and contradictions (Collins 1984; Farrell 1976; O'Dowd et al. 1980). The assumption here is that colonialism is first and foremost an economic phenomenon masked as religious sectarianism in Northern Ireland. There is no question about the economic motivations of colonialism; yet as interpretative sociology has suggested since Weber, economics is not devoid of cultural meaning. Colonialism not only exploits and despoils, it also creates meanings and shapes feelings. As with other political categories (e.g., class) that appear to be "natural," colonialism is also a historically made cultural phenomenon.[7] The political conflict in Northern Ireland, I argue, is shaped by and interpreted through cultural models and symbols deeply rooted in the history of the Anglo-Irish colonial relationship. Anthropologists (Burton 1978; Feldman 1991; Sluka 1989) working in Belfast have been more concerned than other social scientists about the cultural conceptions permeating the structures of inequality in Northern Ireland.

The importance of cultural narratives has been also addressed by historians (Foster 1988; Lyons 1979; Steward 1986) and cultural critics (Deane 1983, 1984; Kearney 1988). Yet these cultural critiques have frequently ignored the webs of power through which cultural narratives are spun. There is still a need to develop a view of political behavior that is capable of apprehending historical actors as they move through cultural space interpreting, manipulating, and changing power relationships. The notion of culture as multidimensional space through which people move in purposive action has been elaborated by James W. Fernandez (1986). In this chapter I attempt to endow this space with those relations of power and dominance that so strongly delineate the contours of people's experience in Northern Ireland. This chapter has a twofold aim: first, to show the weaknesses of simplistic political causalism by showing political relations as culturally constructed through time and second, to critique a view of culture as decontextualized structural systems.

The 1981 Irish hunger strike provides a frame in which it is possible to meaningfully explore the interweaving of historical, political, and cultural processes. When Bobby Sands decided to fast to death against Britain, he was following an international political legacy that had gained moral legitimacy since the time of Gandhi. At the same time, he was reinterpreting and enacting the cultural model of the Christian sacrifice. Furthermore, he was introducing a cultural change because in the process of reinterpretation and enactment, he gave this model new meanings by infusing it with mythological images of Gaelic warriors and modern ideas of national liberation.[8]

But Sands was also simultaneously fighting a concrete political battle in a way that influenced, at least temporarily, the balance of power between Britain and the Republican movement in Northern Ireland. For the people in Northern Ireland, history took a new, unexpected turn. By history I do not mean simply a chronology of events or a determining cultural narrative or the interplay of both, as Marshall Sahlins (1981, 1985) has suggested. The Irish writer Colm Toibin (1987) has compared narratives of Irish history to poetry in the sense that both enable similar emotional moves. I take this emotional quality seriously because I think it is what empowers people in political action. In Northern Ireland, history is understood primarily in existential terms—as a predicament that gives meaning to people's lives, legitimizing their politics and charging their actions with emotional power. This history is condensed in key events that, taken from Irish historical chronology, have become part of the cultural consciousness of people. To miss the existential quality in the "making" of history, both as event and narrative, is to disown history of agency and leave the creative force of human emotion unaccounted for or reduced to structural determinism. In this chapter I see history as a continuous attempt to resolve existential paradoxes, on both the individual and collective levels, in a cultural field inscribed with the changing meanings of the colonial relationship. Bobby Sands and nine other men died, and the horror of these deaths created a new space of meaning.[9] It is to the exploration of that space that I now turn.

FASTING AGAINST BRITAIN

The 1981 Irish hunger strike became an international event, so much so that representatives of different foreign countries attended the funeral of or sent their official respects to Bobby Sands, the first hunger striker to die.[10] The British political establishment termed the hunger strike suicide and reasserted its resolve not to give in to criminals. Although eager to negotiate a way out, the Catholic church also condemned the strike as suicide and warned the prisoners that they were committing a mortal sin. The prisoners and their supporters—that diverse community of relatives, friends, neighbors, acquaintances, and fellow Republicans of the Catholic ghettos—believed the prisoners, far from being suicidal, were fighting for their dignity with the last weapon left to them: their bodies—their lives.

When conversing about the social impact of these deaths with Republican people, I was surprised to hear a local cultural argument. Hunger striking has become part of modern political culture since the time of Gandhi and has been widely used by political movements in different parts of the world. Yet the lack of allusion to this internationally shared political weapon is striking. Instead, the prisoners and their supporters drew on a past native tradition for the meaning of the fast. The hunger strike, I was told, had a deep cultural resonance because it was an ancient Gaelic practice that if one were unjustly wronged and the wrong was not recognized and remedied, one was entitled to fast at the door of the wrongdoer until justice was done. If one died, moral and social responsibility for that death fell onto the person against whom the fast had been carried out.[11]

There is evidence of fasting as a juridical mechanism for arbitration of certain disputes in Gaelic Brehon law (Foster 1988; Kelly 1988). Yet there is probably little resemblance between the cultural milieus of Gaelic Ireland and industrial Belfast. The link between ancient Gaelic practices and contemporary political ones is an imagined (in the sense of culturally constructed), although a powerful, one. For the Republican people I talked to, however, the linkage was not a cultural construction but an "objective fact"; it made up a clear historical continuity. It is interesting that the existence of this Gaelic practice was being used in the 1980s to confer meaning and legitimacy to a controversial political action and to fashion it—not in terms of an international political culture but in terms of Irish history. In Northern Ireland, where national identity is perennially questioned, Republicans were reconstructing their Irish identity by establishing a lineal historical continuity between them and their preconquest ancestors.

The reinterpretation of Irish mythology and folklore for political purposes was not novel. It had its precedent in the literary renaissance that characterized the cultural and political turmoil in turn-of-the-century Ireland. W. B. Yeats elaborated on the theme of the hunger strike in his play *The King's Threshold*, in which a poet fasts against the king who abolished the customary right of the poets to sit at the king's council.[12]

By the 1970s, hunger strikes in Ireland were if not a survival of ancient custom at least a well-known practice in political culture. Ironically, political fasting owes its popularity in Ireland not to Republican men but to suffragist women, who were the first to resort to hunger striking as a means of political pressure in 1911–1913.[13] The tactic proved quite successful and was soon adopted by Republican Nationalists. In 1917 Tomas Ashe, president of the Irish Republican Brotherhood (a forerunner of the IRA), died on a hunger strike for refusing to wear the prison uniform and do prison work. Terence MacSwiney, Lord Mayor of Cork and officer commanding the local IRA, died similarly in 1920.[14] There were hunger strikes in 1923, 1940, and 1946. But by the 1960s, all this history was fairly distant for Nationalists in the north.

It would appear that the young Republicans of the late 1970s, many of whom grew up in the urban ghettos of the northern working class during the relative calm of the 1950s, shared little with the Irish heroes of the first part of the century, many of whom belonged to a cultural or social elite and who for the most part had not directly experienced sectarian or class oppression. Furthermore, that Republicans have resorted to hunger strikes in different historical moments does not necessarily imply they endowed it with the same meanings. We must ask, therefore: What was the meaning of the fasting that resulted in ten dead men in 1981? A Republican woman recalled that time in these terms:

> It was so bad during the hunger strike that people actually turned to praying; 'cause if they [the British army] killed children [in the streets], what wouldn't they do? We thought we all were going to die.[15]

Republicans talk about the hunger strike with a deferential respect, almost awe. Voices are lowered, and their gaze gets lost in distant space. In many houses, portraits of the hunger strikers or memorials of Bobby Sands can be seen hanging on the wall under the rubric "our martyrs" beside a picture of the Sacred Heart or the Virgin Mary, and the Victorian landscape of Catholic West Belfast still shows the vestiges of that time. For Republicans it was a point of no return. As with Easter 1916,[16] for them May 1981 was "the beginning of the end." The end of what beginning?

OUT OF THE ASHES AROSE THE IRA[17]

In 1934 Lord Craigavon, the first minister of Northern Ireland, declared in a memorable discourse, "All I boast is that we have a Protestant parliament and a Protestant state."[18] In 1968, when the Northern Ireland Civil Rights Association increased the pressure to change the sectarian character of Northern Ireland and win civil rights for Catholics, the inner contradictions of the state had become so entrenched that it proved irreformable. Repression was unleashed, riots broke out, and the conflict came to a head with the burning of Catholic houses in Belfast and Derry by Loyalist mobs and B-specials in August 1969. It was after what one participant called "this nightmare" that the Provisional IRA was formed in January 1970.

In 1969 the IRA had practically disappeared, leaving the Catholic districts without the community defense force the IRA had become during the riots of the 1920s and 1930s. People expressed their mounting helplessness and frustration on the walls, where graffiti bitterly screamed: "IRA = *I Run Away*." The IRA, which had remained practically inactive after the violence of the 1920s, launched a campaign in the late 1950s. Operation Harvest, as it was called, consisted of a series of attacks on police stations along the border with the Irish Republic. This was conceived to stir up nationalist feeling and create an insurrectionary mood. The Catholic population, however, was unreceptive to an armed campaign. The result was a political failure reflected in the 1959 Westminster elections, with the vote for Sinn Fein (the political wing of the IRA) declining drastically (Farrell 1976: 216). Following this, the IRA leadership—embittered by the lack of popular support and divided over future tactics—called off the campaign.

The 1962 IRA convention marked the beginning of a turn toward a more socialist republicanism that was increasingly concerned with socioeconomic issues. The shift from military struggle to agitational politics left the IRA ill prepared for the upsurge of sectarian violence in 1969. The Catholic Lower Falls area, which suffered the brunt of intimidation and house burning, had only a handful of IRA volunteers and a few rusty weapons. The lack of infrastructure made the IRA deeply reluctant to intervene because it feared the use of arms would justify harsh repression from local police (RUC) and B-specials, to which the IRA would be unable to respond logistically. In addition, the leadership—which at the time was located in Dublin, fairly far from the unfolding reality of the north—feared armed intervention would further polarize the Protestant and Catholic working class and preclude their alliance along common class interests.

From the vantage point of the community, however, the situation was quite different because people were being intimidated, threatened, and burned out of their homes by voluntary police and hostile Protestant mobs. In their view, if the IRA had a role it was as a defense force—as in the 1920s and 1930s—and in August 1969 they expected the IRA to take on that role. One citizen told me a story that illustrates the mood of the community in those early days:

> I think everybody was involved then, everybody. But there were no arms. I was driving with Tony one night and we had a flat tire, and Tony suddenly pulls out a gun and gets out of the car and says to me to change the tire, and we went around the corner because the Loyalist mobs were getting closer and closer. I had not a clue he had a gun, but thank God he had it. And he fired a few shots to scare them [the Loyalists], and then our people [were] shouting for him to fire more and becoming angry [that] he was not shooting enough. And I remember a man shouting at him, "Give it [the gun] to me if you are not going to shoot." But he couldn't because he didn't have enough bullets, and the Loyalists had [ammunition] and they were many.

There was increased community pressure for the IRA to use whatever weapons it had. Its reluctance and inadequate preparation resulted in resentment and discomfort on the part of many people in the Catholic ghettos. Some IRA volunteers disagreed with the organization's leadership and its policy of subordinating armed struggle to other political tactics. Under these circumstances the IRA was split at its annual convention in January 1970, and a new organization—the Provisional Irish Republican Army (PIRA)[19]—was established. PIRA immediately attracted hundreds of young men, especially in Belfast and Derry where the violence of 1969 and the ensuing presence of the British army had left them eager to take some "real" action.

In April 1971 PIRA launched a major bombing campaign against commercial targets. Four months later internment without trial was introduced by the government of Northern Ireland upon consent of the British government, and thousands of people in the Catholic ghettos were arrested (Farrell 1976: 281). After increasing pressure from the internees, Secretary of State for Northern Ireland William Whitelaw conceded political status to Republican prisoners in June 1972. In March 1976, however, under the so-called Policy of Normalization, the British government put an end to internment and abolished Special Category status for political prisoners. From then on, Republican prisoners were to be considered and treated as ordinary criminals and be forced to wear prison uniforms and do prison work.

Republican prisoners rejected the criminal label. Ciaran Nuget—the first political prisoner to experience the new policy—could wear only a blanket when he spurned the prison uniform, thus inaugurating what became known as "the blanket protest," which lasted four and a half years. Protesting Republican prisoners were confined to isolation without reading materials or other sorts of stimulation, locked up in their cells twenty-four hours a day—naked except for a blanket—and routinely sentenced to the punishment cells. The only time the prisoners—three-quarters of whom were between seventeen and twenty-one years of age—left their cells was for their monthly visit, weekly shower, and daily slop out.

In March 1977 the prison authorities decided that the prisoners would not be allowed to wear a blanket while outside the cells. This meant they had to leave their cells naked, exposing themselves to the warders' jeering at their bodies—especially their genitals—as well as to frequent beatings.[20] After eighteen months of this treatment, the prisoners responded with the "no-wash protest." They refused to leave their cells either to wash or to slop out. At first, chamber pots were emptied through the spy holes in the cell doors and the windows. When these were blocked by the warders, the prisoners began to smear their excreta on the walls of their cells (Fairweather et al. 1984). The indefinite continuation of this stalemate led in 1980 to the first hunger strike[21] and in March 1981 to the second hunger strike and ten men dead.

For Margaret Thatcher, the prisoners' suffering was self-inflicted because it would end at once if they conformed with the law and put on the prison uniform. For the Republican prisoners, however, to do so was to renounce their very identity. The meaning of this identity, as soldiers of an army of liberation fighting a war with Britain, transcends the individual self to constitute the defining terms of a power struggle. The philosopher Albert Memmi (1965: 128) noted the political significance of the military identity in the colonial context when he talked about the use of khaki uniforms by Tunisian rebels: "Obviously they hoped to be considered soldiers and [be] treated in accordance with the rules of war. There is profound meaning in this emphatic desire as it was by this tactic that they laid claim to and wore the dress of history."

For the IRA prisoners, to wear a prison uniform meant to assume Britain's definition of reality and accept the judgment that Ireland's history was no more than a concatenation of criminal acts. That attitude contradicted not only their symbolic construction of nationality but, as we see later, their very existential experience. Furthermore, the prison uniform meant downgrading to the level of criminals not only themselves but also their families and the community to which they belonged. Ultimately, wearing the uniform was to admit that moral and ethical distinctions lay only in the weight of the dominant force.

Only an arbitrary date marked the distinction between a political prisoner and a criminal. Those Republicans sentenced before March 1976 were considered prisoners of war and enjoyed the privileges accorded this status. Those sentenced after that date were regarded as criminals. For members of the same organization—sharing principles, goals, and gaol—nothing but a "decree" differentiated them, a decree that, cast as "the Law,"[22] exempted the British establishment from political responsibility for the prison crisis while forcing Republicans to the last line of subversion. For Republicans, to reject the moral value of the law that classified them into opposed categories was to defy the arbitrariness of a superior power, to reassert their dignity and humanity. Paradoxically, to achieve that aim, Republicans sentenced after March 1976 lived in the most degrading and inhuman conditions and ultimately died.

The criminal–political dichotomy that converted the prison uniform into such a charged symbol is ultimately about ethical distinctions and political legitimation. Most people I talked to emphasized the low level of criminality in Northern Ireland. With internment, the jails—filled with Catholics—and prisons took a central place in people's lives. This was a difficult adjustment that was made only because of the shared knowledge of the political reasons for imprisonment. The pretense of criminality was not only unbelievable for people but was unpalatable, especially for Republicans for whom the new policy represented a criminalization of Irish history. A popular song of the time expressed this sentiment clearly:

> But I wear no convict's uniform
> Nor meekly serve my time
> That Britain's might call Ireland's fight
> Eight hundred years of crime.

The importance of the word *dignity* was soon evident in my fieldwork. It epitomized the accumulated feelings of the experience of being a Catholic in Northern Ireland: "Some outsiders think they understand what is going on here, but they don't. They don't know what it means to be observed, humiliated, made to feel inferior, day by day in your own country." That the Republican prisoners saw the prison uniform as a denial of their identity and therefore of their human dignity was clearly expressed by Bobby Sands (1982: 93):

> That's a word: "Dignity." They can't take that from me either. Naked as I am, treated worse than an animal, I am what I am. They can't and won't change that. . . . Of course I can be murdered, but while I remain alive, I remain what I am, a political prisoner of war, and no one can change that.

Bobby Sands legitimized his politics on a plane surpassing contingent law. The premises guiding his actions rest on an ethically superior order. It is this transcendental conviction, along with a deep emotional bond among them, that allowed the prisoners to create moral value out of the most degrading conditions. The first day of his hunger strike, Bobby Sands (1982: 153) wrote, no doubt as testament for the future:

> I am a political prisoner because I am a casualty of a perennial war that is being fought between the oppressed Irish people and an alien, oppressive, unwanted regime that refuses to withdraw from our land. I believe and stand by the God-given right of the Irish nation to sovereign independence, and the right of any Irishman or woman to assert this right in armed revolution. That is why I am incarcerated, naked and tortured.

I agree with Michael Taussig (1987) when he says that it is not in conscious ideology, as customarily defined, but in a dialectics of images and story-like creations that people delineate their world, including their politics. How did those young men and women prisoners of the late 1970s arrive there? What supported them during those years in which they survived practically naked and surrounded by their own excreta? What was the meaning of such apparently stubborn and irrational conduct? As an anthropologist I am interested in the cultural formations of meaning and their articulation through personal experience because it is at the intersection at which cultural constructions blend together with unique personal (or collective) experience that modes of feeling are shaped and new meanings created.

The protesting prisoners in the late 1970s were the children caught in the riots of a decade before. Mairead, twenty-nine years old when I met her, was sentenced to twenty years imprisonment in March 1981. She was nine years old when the "troubles" started and twelve when she and her family moved—as a consequence of intimidation—from their predominantly Protestant district to Twinbrook, a new Catholic housing estate at the outskirts of West Belfast. Mairead's grandparents lived in Falls Road—the heart of Catholic West Belfast—at the center of the intimidation, burnings, and killings in the early stage of the present conflict. When the "troubles" began, Mairead and her sister stayed with their grandparents on the weekends and witnessed some of what was going on:

> At eleven years of age we had to be actually escorted to and from the school buses by our teachers because the local Protestant youths living near our school would gather and throw bottles and stones at us. One day I can remember witnessing them trailing three young Catholic boys from the bus—a crowd of about twenty of them did it—and they gave them really bad beatings with sticks, and the rest of us were terrified and turned to get help from the other people standing by, but whether because of fear or whatever, none of them would interfere. The young boys in question had to be taken to hospital, they were that badly beaten.

As with many other refugees fleeing from other parts of Belfast, Mairead's family went back to the ghetto they had left in 1966 and began to live in unfinished houses without doors, windows, electricity, water, or anything else:

> I'm not kidding you; in fact the BBC made a Panorama film about the slum conditions the people in Twinbrook had to live in, and in the film they interviewed my mother and filmed us sitting eating on the floor by candlelight. I can remember hearing of a young boy of seventeen from the Twinbrook state being shot dead by Loyalist gunmen at the garage where he was apprenticed at the Lisburn Road—that happened the night we moved to the [housing] estate.

Mairead later came to know the sisters of this boy, and they told her the details of his killing. Mairead's world was changing dramatically; and this change was becoming meaningful through whispers, memories, and stories:

> My granny would take us around the Falls and explain who had been killed. They'd recall the Belfast riots of the 1920s and 1930s, the execution of Tom Williams and other such things.

When she tells me about why she became involved in the armed struggle, it is not a conventional ideology or a set of doctrinal ideas about socialism or national liberation that is described. That came later during the obligatory reflection imprisonment imposes on so many people. When she recalls her early motivations, what comes to her is experience encapsulated and conveyed—as it always is—in images and stories: "Witnessing RUC/British army brutality left a profound image on most of the young teenagers then." Witnessing violence is mentioned again and again in the reminiscences of the people I talk to. "I learned my politics in the street, by witnessing what was going on," said Anne, another protesting prisoner.

A friend, Pauline, evoked the smell of the houses burning in the Lower Falls where she was living and the terror of abandoning the house with only a trash bag full of clothes, not knowing where to go or what was happening. The world shaped by those early impressions created a mode of feeling that led those young teenagers to get involved in a war they came to interpret as theirs. That world was also rendered meaningful by earlier memories, those of parents and grandparents who were marked by the riots of the 1920s and 1930s. Individual experience was embedded in collective memory as a frame of interpretation.

Bobby Sands was no exception in the formation of those early modes of feeling. He was fifteen when the "troubles" began. He was living in Rathcoole, a predominantly Protestant area. There were only six Catholic families on his street. One day the Ulster Defense Association (UDA), a paramilitary group that became notorious for assassinating Catholics, staged a march down his street. The Sands family kept the lights out while Bobby waited on the stairs clutching a carving knife. On another occasion he was coming home when two men stopped him. One produced a knife and cut him. Groups of youths began to gather outside the house shouting "taigs out!"[23] The intimidation increased until the Sands fled Rathcoole for Twinbrook in 1972. Shortly afterwards Bobby Sands joined the IRA (Beresford 1987: 58–59).

THE CREATION OF THE WILD IRISH

The Irish intellectual Seamus Deane (1983: 11) has said that

> the language of politics in Ireland and England, especially when the subject is Northern Ireland, is still dominated by the putative division between barbarism and civilization. Civilization still defines itself as a system of law; and it defines barbarism (which by the nature of the distinction cannot be capable of defining itself) as a chaos of arbitrary wills, an Hobbesian state of nature.

The use of the barbarism-civilization dichotomy to convey colonial relationships between Ireland and Britain has a long history that goes back to the sixteenth century. In 1600 Elizabethan England undertook a massive colonizing effort in Ireland, which until then had been very much under the control of Gaelic chiefs and their native Brehon laws with the exception of "the Pale," as the area around Dublin was known. Prior to 1600, during the years 1565–1576, there were a number of privately sponsored colonizing efforts in Ireland. These campaigns were accompanied by an outpouring of rhetorical justifications underlying the uncivil and savage nature of the Irish (Canny 1973). Queen Elizabeth I, who wanted her Irish subjects to be "well used" during the colonizing campaign, was later willing to condone the massacres of colonizers such as Essex in Ulster and Gilbert in Munster on the grounds that the Irish were a "rude and barbarious nation . . . whom reason and duty cannot bridle" (Canny 1973: 581). This posture was not unusual; it had previously been adopted by the Spaniards to justify the massacres of Indians in the New World.

In the sixteenth century, the newly "discovered" people were still very much perceived through a medieval prism deformed with the fantasies of the marvelous and the monstrous. Despite evidence to the contrary, voyagers and explorers presented the natives of Africa and America to the European public as "half-human, hairy wild men, degraded by daily tumults, fears, doubts, and barbarous cruelties" (Hodgen 1964: 362). The Renaissance "savage" (with its profound pejorative connotations) replaced the medieval human monster, becoming a central category in European thought. Not only was savagery projected onto people of distant lands, but the Irish neighbors fell into this category as well. Edmund Spenser's *A View of the Present State of Ireland,* written in 1596, summarized the then-current arguments for the wildness and barbarity of the Irish and advocated harsh military policy as the only path by which to civilize them.

The Elizabethan colonizers not only were familiar with travel writings and Spanish literature on the conquest of the New World and their images of barbarism; they were also well versed on available "knowledge" of the Irish. Two popular sources dealing with the Irish were Sebastian Muenster's *Cosmographiae Universalis* written in 1544 and *Theatrum Orbis Terrarum* written by the geographer Abraham Ortelius in 1570. Both describe the Irish as wild, uncivil, and cruel. Sixteenth-century colonizers in Ireland were also strict Protestants to whom the Catholicism of Gaelic Ireland (which did not fully conform with Roman liturgy) was simply paganism. The Irish, said historian William Camden in 1610, were "in some places wilde and very uncivill," among whom there was "neither divine service; nor any form of chapella . . . no Altars at all . . . the Missal or Masse booke all torne" (quoted in Hodgen 1964: 365).

The social structure was similarly interpreted according to medieval models of barbarism. Although Gaelic society was structured in a complex and hierarchical form, the positions of political authority as well as land tenure were not fixed by right of inheritance but had a contractual character and could be redefined in every generation. This coupled with the Gaelic practice of transhumance accounted for a great deal of fluidity in Gaelic society, which the English interpreted as barbaric chaos (Foster 1988). Once the barbarous and pagan character of the native Irish was established, Elizabethan England concluded that "it was England's duty to educate the Irish brutes" (Smyth as quoted in Canny 1973: 588). Many English colonizers cited Spanish sources to justify their harsh measures in dealing with barbarous people.[24] By the beginning of the seventeenth century, 85 percent of the land in Ireland had been expropriated and given to Protestant planters and Cromwellian soldiers.

The sixteenth-century English held a dualistic conception of barbarian societies. Against all evidence, there were—for Smyth as well as for Spenser—two kinds of people in Ireland: the tyrannical and cruel lords governing the docile and simple tenants. It was part of the civilizing mission to liberate the latter from the tyranny of the former (Canny 1973). The official English view in the 1600s argued that it was not a war of conquest that was being waged in Ireland but the "rooting out" of a few "unnatural and barbarous rebels" (Foster 1988: 35). In a similar vein, it has been characteristic of British officials since the early 1970s to portray the Catholic community in Northern Ireland as composed of ordinary peace-loving people who are sick of the wicked terrorists who dominate them. The British army has been portrayed as a neutral third party whose duty it is to defend the common people from the tyranny of terrorists cast as brutal gangsters.

As with the English of four centuries ago, during the last twenty years in Northern Ireland the British government has combined the imagery of a murderous and hated group of terrorists with generalized intimidation against the Catholic minority. The incongruity of this policy has not deterred British governments, who seem systematically reluctant to learn from their own history.[25] When the military occupation and the policy of criminalization failed to "normalize" the political climate in Northern Ireland, the British establishment—instead of reassessing its policies—went back to its deep-rooted anti-Irish prejudices and concluded that the Irish were irrational and untractable. From the standpoint of British dominant ideology, the 1981 hunger strike was the ultimate proof of Irish irrationality because it was perceived as a totally arbitrary and self-inflicted action (O'Malley 1990). The situation was blamed on prisoners' depravity in the same way seventeenth-century colonizers such as Moryson blamed Irish ills on Gaelic perversity (Foster 1988). That they still think of the Irish—at least those in Northern Ireland—as basically barbarian is expressed by many comments: Two suffice as examples.

The BBC broadcast a series of interviews on the "Tonight" program in the spring of 1977, with Bernard O'Connor—a school teacher—and Michael Lavelle—a production controller at a factory—in which the two made allegations about the use of torture by the interrogators at Castlereagh interrogation center. After the program, conservatives in England and Northern Ireland protested strongly, accusing the BBC of aiding terrorism and demanding tougher security measures. The respected *Sunday Times* added to the controversy by stating that "the notorious problem is how a civilized country can overpower uncivilized people without becoming less civilized in the process" (quoted in Curtis 1984: 55). If the Tories saw the allegations of torture as a sign of the strength of terrorist propaganda in the media, the liberal English were concerned about degeneration. The dilemma is an old one. The problem is not the legitimacy of overpowering others—that is granted by the others' inferiority—but how to avoid degradation while in contact with them. Far from being "naturally" superior, civilized morality seems easily corruptible.

A more recent instance of the resilience of British anti-Irish prejudice is the reply of the former lord chancellor Lord Hailsham to the suggestion made by the Irish government in September 1989 that the Diplock courts—trials without jury presided over by only one judge—in Northern Ireland should be replaced by a more suitable alternative such as a three-judge court. Lord Hailsham dismissed the suggestion as silly and ignorant. When a journalist challenged him, saying the Diplock courts were a cause of deep grievance for the Nationalist community, Lord Hailsham answered, "That is because they don't think. It's as simple as that, they just don't think and on certain subjects they are incapable of thought."[26] Nationalists responded to this statement with sarcasm. For them it was nothing new; they had heard it many times and felt it many more.

Perhaps nothing embodies the image of the wild Irish people more clearly than the image of the terrorist. They are the "other" par excellence, criminals depicted with apelike features maintaining an armed tyranny over the Nationalist community.[27] This image legitimizes the permanent deployment of the British army and local police, who—according to the British master narrative—are in Northern Ireland to defend "ordinary people" from the tyranny of the terrorists. That this idea is challenged by the everyday contempt of these "ordinary people" for the security forces in the Catholic districts has not changed British officials' perceptions of the problem.

In a 1989 TV program about British troops in Northern Ireland, soldiers openly expressed their anxiety at moving in a terrain that was perceived as impenetrable, unknown, and filled with danger.[28] It is interesting that British soldiers perceived Belfast ghettos as exotic and untamed much as the sixteenth-century Elizabethan soldiers perceived the Irish landscape—whose dense woods, bogs, lakes, and mountains concealed and sustained resistance (Foster 1988). Yet little in West Belfast distinguishes it from the working-class neighborhoods of Liverpool, Newcastle, or Glasgow—the hometowns of the British soldiers. Little differentiates their styles of life, customs, or language—except, of course, the multiple army posts and police barracks dotting the area as landmarks competing with the chimneys of the now-abandoned linen mills for historical hegemony and the murals and political graffiti endlessly painted over by the army and repainted by the natives.

The impoverished landscape of West Belfast is familiar; yet, like the remote Irish woods, it still conceals resistance. For the British soldiers it remains impenetrable, even when every household is surveilled; by virtue of this perceived impenetrability, the landscape becomes defamiliarized and the people who inhabit it become strangers. The soldiers' perception, however, is far from innocent or spontaneous estrangement. They are trained in special sessions to see the population and the environment as things to be wary of and to tame. When they get to Belfast, they see what they are conditioned to see: potential criminals on every corner rather than people too similar to themselves to be aliens. Some soldiers admitted seeing every person as a potential terrorist who could slay them at any moment. Others spoke of being seduced in the vertigo of the game, of having fun by beating someone now and then. The cultural dynamic reinforces itself. Their patrolling, arbitrary searches, and continual harassment anger the population, which views them with obvious disdain; this in turn reinforces the soldiers' perception of the Irish as hostile strangers. The contradiction is clear: Although the problem of Northern Ireland is defined by the British government as one provoked by an organized bunch of criminals, the British policy criminalizes—de facto—the entire Catholic population.

In 1976 the British government defined IRA members as criminals, yet the treatment of these criminals was insidiously different from standard procedure. Torture was used to extract confessions, and special courts without juries were created to try IRA members. Yet for Britain, the prisoners' refusal to accept this disparity was a new example of their barbarism. The horrific imagery of degradation the "no-wash" protest provided could not to the British mind be anything but proof of a bizarre nature.[29]

When Bobby Sands began to fast, all attempts at mediation by Irish politicians, human rights organizations, and the Catholic church were in vain. When, in the middle of his fast, Bobby Sands was elected to Westminster Parliament by 30,492 votes, people in the Catholic ghettos thought the British government would be obliged to recognize the political character of the prisoners. Their hopes were frustrated. Margaret Thatcher's response was her now-famous phrase: "A crime is a crime is a crime. It is not political, it is a crime" (Beresford 1987: 115). This answer further alienated the Nationalist community and convinced many people that the only language Britain would understand was the language of force.[30] If Thatcher's intransigence was aimed at breaking the Republican movement and undermining its popular support, it achieved the opposite: The IRA and Sinn Fein rose in popularity. After the success of Sands's electoral campaign, Sinn Fein initiated a process of reorganization to lead a more comprehensive political strategy known as "the armalite and the ballot box" (a combination of political organizing, electoral campaigning, and armed struggle), which has consistently secured it representatives in the local and Westminster elections. Most important, perhaps, the British strategy during the hunger strike left a deep scar in the consciousness of many Nationalists:

> Nobody who went through that experience can say that it didn't profoundly affect their lives. No matter what happens we cannot give up the struggle now.

THE SYMBOLISM OF THE HUNGER STRIKE

You gather strength when you think of the people in the outside and your comrades, from their deaths, because you know they have died for you.

—Republican prisoner

Some commentators on Irish Republicanism have emphasized the ideology of martyrdom that impinges on this movement. It has frequently been claimed that the mythology of sacrifice determines IRA violence and the support the IRA receives in the Catholic ghettos (Kearney 1988). This explanation assumes that myths have a force of their own and are capable by themselves of inducing people's behavior. It implies a vision of human conduct devoid of consciousness and choice. This view also presupposes both a powerful IRA leadership skillfully using its militants' suffering to draw people's support and a blind following of the rank and file. These interpretations fail to explain why people have responded to that symbolism at certain moments but not at others. It is important to remember that Nationalists have not always supported the IRA to the degree that they do now. As mentioned previously, the IRA campaign of the late 1950s had to be abandoned for lack of popular support, and the IRA was bitter about this. Little attention was paid to the IRA prior to 1969. People from the Catholic ghettos of Belfast voted mainly for the conservative and parliamentarist Nationalist party and the moderate Labor party.

The mythology of sacrifice as the alleged cause of the current political violence in Northern Ireland seems to me to be a new origin myth that conveniently allows one to ignore the field of power relations at play in the use of political violence, both by the state and by the IRA, and its ramifications. Further, this mythology reinforces the too common view of Irish people as irrational myth followers. This is not to deny the existence of a mythology of sacrifice in the Nationalist community, especially in the Republican section; rather, it is to deny that the sacrificial narrative constitutes the etiology of the IRA violence. Such violence belongs more to the history of British colonization in Ireland and, in its contemporary fashion, to the peculiarly sectarian form that colonization took in the North. I thus wish to explore how the symbolism of sacrifice embedded in Catholic mythology becomes at certain political conjunctures, such as that of the 1981 hunger strike, a meaningful frame for political action.

The heroic symbolism of Republican culture has its origins in the Irish cultural revival of the turn of the century. W. B. Yeats perhaps did the most to create the image of the sacrificial hero that became so important to the imagination of the 1916 uprising.[31] And if Yeats reinvented a glorious mythological past populated with Gaelic warriors, Patrick Pearse infused it with Christian imagery and revolutionary action. One of the artificers of the 1916 uprising, Pearse conceived heroic sacrifice as an act of renewal, firmly believing that the sacrifice of a selected few would stir the dormant spirit of the nation and lead it to statehood. Not coincidentally, the day chosen for the revolt was Easter Monday.[32] The rebellion, which lacked popular support and was badly organized, was crushed rapidly; the participants were arrested and their leaders executed. Yet Pearse was right in a sense because the intended exemplary executions provoked generalized social disturbances in Ireland, leading ultimately to the war of independence and the Anglo-Irish treaty of 1922 that severed the northeastern corner of Ireland from the rest of the country. Easter 1916 became a glorified, crucial event—not only in Republican mythology but also in the official historical narrative of the new Irish state.

Myths as meaningful frames of interpretation require a social context in order to become more than interesting stories. By the 1950s, the political significance of the symbolism of sacrifice was eclipsed for Nationalists in Northern Ireland. It was after the violence of 1969 that this symbolism was endowed with a new life and meaning in terms of political behavior. The imagery of sacrificial heroism then took on a new "force," in Renato Rosaldo's sense of the term—that is, it became not only a cognitive structure but also an emotional experience defined by the subjects' position within the field of social relations (Rosaldo 1989). During the "blanket protest," a profusion of religious imagery emphasized the Christ-like sacrifice of the Republican prisoners. Yet it was not the leadership of the IRA or of Sinn Fein who created this imagery. In fact, Sinn Fein paid little attention to the prisoners in the early stages of the protest, and the IRA was opposed to the hunger strike.[33] It was the prisoners themselves and their relatives who increasingly saw in their existential predicament a parallel with the Christian narrative.

When I asked Pauline, a Republican supporter who had been in jail herself, what the era of the hunger strike was like, she said: "It was a dramatic time for all of us but specially for the families. They say about Jesus, well, Bobby Sands died for us all." There is virtually no house in Catholic West Belfast that does not have an image of the Sacred Heart and one of the Virgin Mary, just as there is no house that has not experienced military searches, police harassment, or the loss of a loved one. Religion is as deeply anchored in the Catholic experience of the world in Northern Ireland as is dispossession. Starting with the Penal Laws introduced by Britain in 1695, to be a Catholic became progressively synonymous with being Irish.[34] After Ireland was partitioned in 1922, religion in Northern Ireland became—more clearly than ever before—a parameter of one's position in the web of social relations. Being Catholic in the new statelet signified being disadvantaged and discriminated against. Religion continued to be another word for national identity. Eamonn McCann (1980: 9) begins his story of growing up in a Catholic ghetto by saying, "One learned quite literally at one's mother's knee that Christ died for the human race and Patrick Pearse for the Irish section of it."

The Catholic church was not eager to propagate revolutionary values, however. The church was careful to keep on good terms with the political establishment, systematically condemning the IRA and any serious attempt to challenge the status quo by political or military means. The emergence of the IRA in 1970 seriously threatened the tight control priests had maintained over the Catholic community. This is how Siobhan (a Nationalist woman) recalls it:

> They [the priests] had complete control of people then; if there was trouble in a family or in the street, the priest would come with a stick and beat up the troublemakers or sort out the family problem. Because, even in those days [before the "troubles"] Catholics did not call the police. There were the priests who had the social control and knew everything about everybody.

The generalized violence that accompanied the beginning of the "troubles" upset these traditional relations of authority just as it upset social relations in general.

People did not mechanically apply religious models to the political arena; these were re-created and infused with new meanings. Thus, if the Christian ideal of sacrifice and endurance had served the church in preaching resignation to the suffering of this world, Republicans transformed it into a model of resistance. Suffering and endurance were now understood as active ways of changing this world. The statement of Terence MacSwiney (the Republican mayor of Cork who died in a hunger strike in 1920) was revived: "It is not he who inflicts the most but he who suffers the most that will conquer." The church condemnation of IRA violence and the prisoners' protest alienated many people who found too great a disjuncture among religious convictions, priests' political opinions, and their own experience:

> My cutting point was when "so and so" was killed and the priest would not allow his coffin into the church for his funeral. I thought that was terrible, because let's put things straight, if somebody steals you something, that's stealing

> isn't it? Well, that's what England has done: steal a part of this country. And I thought, this priest has been in the war and what is the difference? People go to war and kill hundreds of other people for no other reason than to steal somebody else's land, and they get a proper funeral. And what is the IRA doing? Fighting a war against Britain who stole this land! And they are Catholic men, and they cannot get a proper Catholic funeral? I told this to the priest and he had no answers, so I said this is it, and I didn't go back to church.

Forced out of the institutional frame, people discovered new meanings for their religiosity and new expression in the readily available political field. A Republican prisoner put it this way: "I am not an atheist, I don't think I could ever be, but I don't believe in the church. It is difficult to be critical of the church because it is so much a part of your upbringing, and we had never heard before of a feminist Christian or a socialist Christian. But people [are] looking now for other models, like the theology of liberation for instance."

During the years of the "blanket protest" and the hunger strike, a proliferation of leaflets and murals in support of the prisoners portrayed them as Christ-like figures. The physical appearance of the prisoners (with long hair and beards, their bodies covered only with blankets) strengthened this identification. As conditions worsened in the jail and solutions to the stalemate seemed far away, the parallel with the religious model of Christ became even stronger. For the relatives and prisoners, this model contained the moral legitimation for their struggle in the face of widespread condemnation from the church, the media, and the political establishment. The Yugoslavian philosopher Elias Canetti observed that praying is a rehearsal of wishes. During the "blanket protest," the prisoners went to mass and prayed the rosary daily. When the hunger strike began, they started praying the rosary twice a day while relatives and supporters prayed it on the street at the same time. "Praying was a form of drawing strength," said the former prisoner Eileen. "Even I who am not very much of a believer prayed when I was arrested." Many of the prisoners were believers, and so were their supporters on the outside. Bobby Sands was a strong believer, and he defended his political position in religious terms when the chaplain of the jail, Father Faul, tried to dissuade him from his strike on moral grounds: "What greater love hath a man than to lay down his life for the life of his friends?" And that is how much of the Nationalist community felt as well.[35]

Sands's writings are filled with religious imagery. Metaphors of sacrifice and also of hell transpire from his imagination. Sacrifice and hell are intimately woven together to capture an experience bordering on the surreal. "The Crime of Castlereagh" is a poem of 145 stanzas in which Sands talks about interrogation and jail.[36] Sands (1982: 44) imagines the space of Castlereagh interrogation center—with its cells and its corridors—as hell with its devils torturing him, trying to eat his mind and rip his soul apart, tricking him into evil deals, and offering comforts in exchange for his secrets:

> This Citadel, this house of hell
> Is worshipped by the law.
>
> Some bear the stain of cruel Cain,
> These are the men of doom.
> The torture-men who go no end
> To fix you in that room.
> To brutalize they utilize
> Contrivances of hell,
> For great duress can mean success
> When tortured start to tell.

In a space that is neither life nor death, Bobby Sands (1982: 50) perceives other prisoners as nightmare phantoms carrying the burden of a fate heavier than themselves: "Each looked like a loss, each bore a cross / Upon his bended back."[37]

In the interrogation center the parameters of reality blur. Space is distorted; unmastered; changing; pregnant with fear, threats, and promised comfort. Nor is there control of time; permanent lights make day and night indistinguishable. Creating uncertainty and confusion in the detainee is a big part of the interrogation game. There one is left to one's most inner solitude to confront the ultimate dilemma of confession, that crucial operation of power producing truth through "the body of the condemned" (Foucault 1979). The production of truth was, in Northern Ireland as in any society founded on the degradation of a human group, vital to its justification and survival. In extracting confessions, the point is not the congruity of fact and evidence but the fabrication of social truths. "The truth-power relation remains at the heart of all mechanisms of punishment," Michel Foucault (1979: 55) has said. An important component of this relation is, of course, the humiliation of the confessant. Obliged sometimes to confess nonexistent realities incriminating oneself and others, the confessant is deprived of individuality and of the last ground from which to resist normalization. Yet confession also represents a tempting relief from the agony of interrogation. Hence the dilemma, the distorted reality, the displacement of meanings that frequently produce a hallucinatory quality. Sands's devils turn into serpents, and he sees himself surrounded by the inferno's beasts (1982: 56):

A demon came his eyes aflame
And round him was the law.
They danced like in Hades and rats in plagues
And Christ I froze in awe.
They spun a cord this gruesome horde
On loom of doom and sin,
To make a noose that would induce
A tortured soul within.

His is a journey between life and death. Despite its nightmarish quality, there is a literalness in this space of death because Sands does not know if he is going to come out of it alive or (like detainee Brian Maguire) die on the path. This literalness becomes chillingly real during the hunger strike. As Michael Taussig (1987) has shown, the meaning of this experience cannot be conveyed in rational discourse because reality loses its cleavages and appears as a bad dream, leaving an indelible print. Sean, a blanket prisoner, expressed it one night: "For some people prison time is like a nightmare from where they never come out again even if the sentence is served and they can go home." As one woman said, "How do you explain a nightmare?" Only deep-rooted metaphors and images can convey the inexpressible. For Sands, religious imagery and poetic language provided the semantic and emotional space to interpret and transmit his experience.[38]

In the horror of incarceration, amid deprivation and dirt, there is always the temptation of giving in, of ending the torture by conforming with prison rules. But salvation—that is, victory over the evil wrongs of Britain—demands endurance. Sands (1982: 64) saw in his predicament a Christ-like Calvary:

The time had come to be,
To walk the lonely road
Like that of Calvary.
And take up the cross of Irishmen
Who've carried liberty.

If Bobby Sands saw himself walking to Calvary, the last step would be the ultimate sacrifice. Sands's decision to go on a hunger strike against Britain was a coldly weighted one. It was made, contrary to the media interpretations of the time, against the wishes of the IRA leadership.[39] Sands and the other prisoners saw it as a political last resort; but once the crisis escalated and the decision to fast to death was taken, it was the Christian myth of sacrifice—deeply rooted in his upbringing—that he seized.

If the Christian myth provided Bobby Sands with a "model for action" (Geertz 1973), it also constituted an interpretative frame for Nationalist supporters. The "force" of the sacrifice metaphor can thus be seen not only in the graffiti and murals of the urban landscape but also in how it moved people in the political arena. I agree with James Fernandez (1986: 6) that metaphoric assertions people make about themselves or about others "provide images in relation to which the organization of behavior can take place." In the Catholic ghettos, demonstrations and riots escalated. If the Nationalist community moved in the direction of revolt, the Loyalist community was affected in the opposite direction. Among Protestants, the hunger strike stirred deep fears and anxieties about the Catholics. As Padraig O'Malley (1990) has pointed out, the "no-wash" protest reaffirmed their belief in the inherent dirtiness and inadequacy of Catholics: "If cleanliness is next to godliness," asked Peter Robinson, MP, leader of the Democratic Unionist party, "then to whom are these men close?" (quoted in O'Malley 1990: 163). The prisoners' deprivation was, from the viewpoint of Protestants, as self-imposed as their second-class status and only deserved disdain. If Catholic walls cried, "Don't let Sands die," Protestant wards demanded, "The time is now for Sands to die" (Rolston 1987). Tension rose as the countdown went on. Assassinations of Catholics by paramilitary Loyalists increased,[40] as did the number of people killed by British troops in nonriot situations. Among the latter were seven children.

Sean MacBride (1983: 5), winner of the Nobel Peace Prize in 1974 and the Lenin Prize for Peace in 1977 and founding member of Amnesty International, concluded: "The hunger strike must be understood in terms of the historical memory of British colonial misrule."[41] This historical memory is a contested subject in Ireland. But whatever the different constructions, historical memory plays a deep role in political legitimacy. Historic actors do not play in an atemporal space or in a symbolic vacuum. The prisoners protesting in Long Kesh, especially the hunger strikers, saw themselves as the perpetuators of a long tradition of resistance that went back eight centuries. The force and immediacy of this history transpire in Bobby Sands's writings when he juxtaposes men from different generations and sociopolitical contexts to create a single, identical tradition: "I remember, and I shall never forget, how this monster took the lives of Tom Ashe, Terence MacSwiney, Michael Gaughan, Frank Stagg, and Hugh Coney" (1982: 91).

History for Republicans is not merely an intellectual legacy. If religious symbolism gives meaning to the incomprehensible—people willing to die of starvation—history makes meaningful the present as it unfolds in existential experience, directing action in the world. As Siobhan commented, "Some people say we have to forget history, but we have to remember it because history repeats itself, and we have to be prepared." And Mary: "The troubles in 1969 caught us completely unprepared, but that shouldn't have happened. We should have known better with the history we got."

History for the Republican prisoners was not a detached knowledge learned at school but was the crystallization of a mode of feeling: "History was forced on me," said Anne. It conveyed for Republicans the kind of inevitability contained in tragedy because tragedy is ultimately about facing paradoxical dilemmas. For the hunger strikers the choice was to accept the criminal definition, in which case they were psychologically if not politically defeated, or to die, in which case they were also damned. Feeling deprived of everything else—their country, their history, and their self-definitions—death became the only act to preserve their humanity. Yet the nature of the tragedy appears strongest in the experience of the women, mainly mothers, who had to decide between saving the lives of their sons by betraying them or being loyal to them by losing them:

> It was traumatic for the mothers because it's a reversal of all [that] it means to be a mother, a reversal of all [that] you have done for your son. You've struggled all your life to put food in their bellies, sometimes at the expense of yourself, and to watch them die of starvation.

* * *

The scars of the past are slow to disappear
the cries of the dead are always in our ears
Only the very safe
Can talk about right and wrong . . .

—Paul Doran

The hunger strike was a watershed in Irish history, the social and political consequences of which are still being assessed. My concern here has been to reflect on a kind of experience that appeared to me as inexpressible. I have tried to show meaning in what seemed bizarre, meaningless, and futile. In the process, what seemed rational and civilized has became irrational and strange. Is it not the task of the anthropologist to show how porous, vulnerable, and context-bound our categorizations of reality are? The leading question of this chapter was how the ten Irish men—terrorists, criminals, martyrs: that for us matters little—who died voluntarily in 1981 came to make that decision. In answering this question, I have tried to decipher the interlocking contexts encompassing their actions with meaning and the new cultural meanings created through their own interpretation and the interpretation of others. It is not for me to decide whether the hunger strikers were right or wrong or if what they achieved was worse than what they were trying to overcome. In her superb novel *Beloved*, Toni Morrison tackles this dilemma. When it is suggested to Sethe that killing her baby to save her from slavery might be worse than slavery itself, she answers, "It ain't my job to know what's worse. It is my job to know what is and to keep them away from what I know is terrible. I did that" (Morrison 1987: 165). And that, too, is what the hunger strikers did. Just as Sethe's killing her baby cannot be understood without the unforgettable scar of slavery, so the starved bodies of the Irish hunger strikers are meaningless outside the ongoing imprint of British colonization.

NOTES

Many people contributed to the final version of this chapter. I am especially grateful to Kay Warren who first encouraged me to write it and who tirelessly commented on the subsequent drafts. I must also thank the participants in the Culture and Conflict seminar at Princeton University, particularly Davida Wood and Michael Hanchard with whom I have had many challenging discussions. I have benefited greatly from the critiques and suggestions of James Boon, Barbara Corbett, James Fernandez, Ernestine Friedl, John Kelly, Michael Jimenez, Michael Merrill, Gananath Obeyesekere, and Darini Rajasingham. The responsibility for possible mistakes and misinterpretations is, of course, only mine. Thanks also to Pauline Caulk who typed an early draft and helped with numerous queries about word processing. This chapter is based on fieldwork research conducted in Belfast from October 1988 to December 1989 and September to October 1990. My major debt is to the people in Belfast who shared their lives and concerns with me and made my work possible. I respect their wishes to remain anonymous. The research was funded by a Social Science Research Council Doctoral Dissertation fellowship and a MacArthur Foundation grant, administered through the Center of International Studies of Princeton, directed by Henry Bienen.

1. People in Northern Ireland use the terms Catholic or Nationalist community to signal an ethnic-political identity vis-à-vis Protestant-Loyalist or British. Thus, "the Nationalist community" is in this sense a homogeneous "imagined community"— to use Benedict Anderson's celebrated notion—of shared history, cultural forms, and ethos. Far from being homogeneous, however, the Nationalist community is characterized by dissenting social and political positions that at times have accounted for acute intracommunal conflict. With this in mind, it is possible, however, to talk about a Nationalist community to refer to that shared culture and ethnic identity in which

Nationalists of different persuasions partake. It is in this sense that the notion of Nationalist community is used in this chapter.

2. Although not completely independent, from the start Northern Ireland enjoyed a high degree of autonomy with its own parliament, government, judiciary, and police bodies. The term statelet is generally used to refer to the small size as well as the quasi-independent character of Northern Ireland.

3. In regard to the Ulster Plantation, see Canny (1987) and Foster (1988).

4. Ratepayers refers to people who own houses or who rent them from the local council. An adult person without a tenancy did not pay rates (nonratepayer) and according to the Northern Ireland legislation, was not entitled to vote in local elections.

5. The 1930s also witnessed a short-lived alliance between the Catholic and Protestant working class in response to the terrible economic conditions of life. The brief coalescence, however, was dismantled by selective repression against Catholics and the stirring up of the Protestant supremacist ideology by the Unionist leaders and members of the government, who constituted the landowners and financial class of Northern Ireland. For more information, see Farrell (1976).

6. For a guide to and a recent appraisal of this literature, see Darby (1983) and Whyte (1990).

7. For an excellent and now-classic account of the cultural construction of a political phenomenon, see Thompson (1963).

8. The polyvalent significations of the sacrifice model can be seen in the Republican funerary memorials as well as in murals seen throughout the Catholic districts. The use of these mythical models, such as the Gaelic warrior Cuchulain and Jesus Christ, in the political arena has its main antecedent in Patrick Pearse, leader of the 1916 uprising.

9. Michael Taussig (1987) has insisted on the need to examine the cultural meanings created in contexts in which political terror and violence are endemic. In these contexts torture and death become a privileged space in the creation of meaning.

10. The U.S. government expressed deep regret. The president of the Italian senate sent his condolences to the Sands family. Thousands marched in Paris. The town of Le Mans named a street after him. In India the *Hindustan Times* accused Britain of allowing a member of the Parliament to die of starvation, and the opposition of the Upper House stood for a minute of silence. Iran sent an ambassador to the funeral. The Soviet Union condemned Britain for its policies in Northern Ireland. Poland paid tribute to Sands. Bombs exploded near British premises in France, Milan, and Lisbon; and there were demonstrations in several countries (Beresford 1987: 132).

11. The interpretation of Irish political hunger strikes in the light of the ancient Gaelic practice of fasting is not idiosyncratic of Republican nationalists. Researchers have often referred to it in their analysis; see, for example, Beresford (1987), Fallon (1987), and O'Malley (1990).

12. W. B. Yeats wrote *The King's Threshold* in 1904. The first version of the play ended with the poet still alive. In 1924, after the death of Terence McSwiney, he rewrote the play. In his second version, the poet dies and so do his followers.

13. These women must have been influenced by the history of political fasting in other parts of the British empire, especially in India and overseas (Morris 1978). For discussion of the Irish suffragists, see Fallon (1987) and Owens (1984).

14. MacSwiney was a poet, playwright, and philosopher. The symbolism of the single, ultimate sacrifice is transparent in his writings. Like Pearse, he believed a symbolic act would awaken the consciousness of Ireland.

15. Unless otherwise indicated, unidentified quotes come from discussions I had with Republican people during fieldwork in Belfast. To preserve anonymity, I have left the quotes unidentified in some cases and used pseudonyms for the sake of the narrative in others.

16. The Easter 1916 rebellion, with its subsequent executions, was the prelude to the war of independence and the Anglo-Irish treaty that gave rise to the Irish Free State and Northern Ireland.

17. Graffiti in Catholic West Belfast.

18. Northern Ireland Parliamentary Debates, House of Commons, vol. 16, cols. 1,091–1,095, cited in Farrell (1976). Lord Craigavon was a company director and a landowner; he also held various positions at Westminster Parliament.

19. The other part of the split, the Official IRA, laid down its arms in 1972. I use the general IRA or the Provisionals to refer to the PIRA. For a comprehensive history of the IRA, see Bell (1980) and Coogan (1980).

20. The Long Kesh medical officer recorded 114 cases of injury to H Block prisoners in 1978. Minister of State Don Concannon denied the abuse of prisoners, stating that no punishment had ever been imposed on warders for that reason.

21. The first hunger strike, led by Brendan Hughes, began in 1980. It was called off after fifty-three days when the British administration produced a document that seemed to concede implicitly to the prisoners' five demands. Once the hunger strike was abandoned, the British government claimed the demands were not contained in the document, a position that prompted the second hunger strike.

22. Corrigan and Sayer (1985) have shown the centrality of the ideology of "the Law" in the development of the British state and the role it played in different historical moments in advancing upper-class and imperialist interests.

23. "Taig" is a derogatory word for Catholic, something like "nigger" in the United States.

24. The most extended Spanish influence was Peter Martyr Anglerius's *De Orbe Novo* (1555). According to Margaret T. Hodgen (1964), Peter Martyr was an "inveterate gossip" whose account of the discovery of America departed greatly from Columbus's descriptions, employing the fabulous invention of the medieval travel genre more than any kind of realist description.

25. The British introduced internment despite its having been proven disastrous in the past. The same applies to the criminalization policy.

26. "Hailsham in Bitter Attack on Irish," *Irish News*, September 19, 1989, 1.

27. This is not only reserved for Nationalists. When it comes to British mainstream perceptions of Ireland, Catholic and Protestants alike are frequently portrayed as brutish and irrational.

28. In her chapter in this volume, Kay B. Warren calls attention to the cultural construction of space as a symbolic map of interethnic power relationships. In Guatemala, the army manipulates Mayan cultural meanings to infuse the local geography with new symbolic marks of violence and institutionalized terror. See also Warren (1989: 40–44).

29. I refer here to that dominant ideology that creates and shapes public opinion. This dominant ideology was contested in Britain, if only by small groups who campaigned in favor of the Irish prisoners.

30. Despite the general perception that Thatcher was the main obstacle to a political resolution, the leaders of the main political parties, including the Liberal party and the Labor party, shared her position on the issue.

31. For the imagery of the 1916 uprising, see Thompson (1982). For an account of the 1916 rebellion in Ireland in the broader context of the British empire, see Morris (1978).

32. For an excellent biography of Patrick Pearse, see Edwards (1977).

33. The Relatives Action Committee was formed in 1976 by relatives of Republican prisoners (mainly women) to campaign in support of the prisoners' demands. The organization was a response to the apparent indifference of political parties, including Sinn Fein, to the prisoners' predicament.

34. The Penal Laws disenfranchised Catholic and Presbyterian religious practice. They denied Catholics and dissenting Protestants access to education, the right to vote, and access to government jobs. In the case of Catholics, they drastically curtailed land rights so that in 1775, Catholics held only 5 percent of the land. The Penal Laws must be understood in relation to the role of Protestantism in the formation of the English state. To Corrigan and Sayer (1985), it was the establishment of a state church in the 1530s that laid the ground for a potent fusion of Protestantism and English nationalism. Catholics in England and Ireland became the immediate "Papist" enemy that reinforced English national unity.

35. There were other feelings as well—a sense of powerlessness produced as much by the British attitude as by the inability to disengage from the hunger strikes. The situation was so polarized that not to support the hunger strikers was to support the British. There was also anger at the IRA, even among supporters of the hunger strikers, because many people believed the IRA had the power to order an end to the fast.

36. It falls outside the margins of this chapter to explore the larger cultural tradition of the Irish ballad wherein much of Sands's poetry is embedded. Suffice it to mention the interesting resemblance between "The Crime of Castlereagh" and "The Ballad of Reading Gaol"—the celebrated work of that other great Irish poet, Oscar Wilde, who was also condemned to jail for being an outcast (if of a different type) by a British court.

37. For an account of the uncertainty and surrealism of the experience of interrogation, see Timerman (1981). For an excellent interpretation of this experience, see

Taussig (1987). The experience of living in a space between life and death, where the line between the real and the imagined blurs, has been exceptionally captured by Mexican writer Juan Rulfo in his novel *Pedro Paramo* (1987).

38. As Lila Abu-Lughod (1986) has suggested, poetry can provide an alternative cultural discourse that allows people not only to express deep experiential feelings but also to persuade others to action, especially in situations of intense personal suffering. By using a stylized cultural form, poetry can resort to images and metaphors that may differ greatly from everyday discourse. Thus, the religious imagery and emotional vulnerability contained in Bobby Sands's poetry contrast strongly with the hardened, uncompromising attitude of Sands, the military strategist and officer commander of the IRA, in Long Kesh prison. Both the poetic and politico-military discourses were inextricably linked cultural devices through which collective and personal meanings were constructed, articulated, and enacted by Bobby Sands during the prison protest.

39. For the IRA leadership, priority had to be given to the military effort. A hunger strike was seen as divesting its resources because of the need to give attention to campaigns and propaganda and due to the political risk of the unsure outcome.

40. Bernardette Devlin, elected member of Parliament in 1971 and forefront campaigner for the prisoners, was badly wounded; and several outspoken supporters were killed by Loyalist paramilitary organizations.

41. A key event in this sense is the Irish Famine of 1854 when English economic policies in Ireland allowed one million people to die of hunger. No doubt the 1981 fast had deep historical resonances; many people in Ireland, although disagreeing with the hunger strikers, thought the English were again starving Irish people.

BIBLIOGRAPHY

Abu-Lughod, Lila. *Veiled Sentiments: Honor and Poetry in a Bedouin Society.* Berkeley: University of California Press, 1986.

Anderson, Benedict. *Imagined Communities: Reflections on the Origin and Spread of Nationalism.* London: Verso, 1983.

Anglerius, Peter Martyr. *De Orbe Novo.* (The Decades of the Newe Worlde or West India), translated by Richard Eden. 1555.

Bell, J. Bowyer. *The Secret Army: The IRA 1916–1979.* Cambridge, Mass.: MIT Press, 1980.

Beresford, David. *Ten Men Dead: The Story of the 1981 Irish Hunger Strike.* London: Grafton Books, 1987.

Burton, Frank. *The Politics of Legitimacy: Struggles in a Belfast Community.* London: Routledge and Kegan Paul, 1978.

Cameron Report. *Disturbances in Northern Ireland: Report of the Cameron Commission.* London: Her Majesty's Stationary Office, Command 532, 1969.

Canetti, Elias. *The Human Province: Notes 1942–1972.* New York: Seabury Press, 1978.

Canny, Nicholas P. "The Ideology of English Colonization: From Ireland to America." *William and Mary Quarterly* 30 (1973): 575–598.

______ . *From Reformation to Restoration: Ireland 1534–1660.* Dublin: Helicon, 1987.

Collins, T. *The Centre Cannot Hold.* Dublin: Bookworks, 1984.

Coogan, Tim Pat. *The IRA.* London: Fontana Books, 1980.

Corrigan, Phillip, and Derek Sayer. *The Great Arch: English State Formation as Cultural Revolution.* New York: Basil Blackwell, 1985.

Curtis, Liz. *Ireland: The Propaganda War: The British Media and the "Battle for Hearts and Minds."* London: Pluto Press, 1984.

Darby, John, ed. *Northern Ireland: The Background to the Conflict.* Belfast: Appletree Press, 1983.

Deane, Seamus. *Civilians and Barbarians.* Derry: Field Day Theatre Company, 1983.

______ . *Heroic Styles: The Tradition of an Idea.* Derry: Field Day Theatre Company, 1984.

Edwards, Ruth Dudley. *Patrick Pearse: The Triumph of Failure.* London: Gollancz, 1977.

Fairweather, Eileen, Roisin McDonough, and Melanie McFadyean. *Only the Rivers Run Free: Northern Ireland: The Women's War.* London: Pluto Press, 1984.

Fallon, Charlotte. "Civil War Hungerstrikes: Women and Men." *Eire-Ireland* 22 (1987): 3.

Farrell, Michael. *Northern Ireland: The Orange State.* London: Pluto Press, 1976.

Feldman, Allen. *Formations of Violence: The Narrative of the Body and Political Terror in Northern Ireland.* Chicago: University of Chicago Press, 1991.

Fernandez, James W. *Persuasions and Performances: The Play of Tropes in Culture.* Bloomington: Indiana University Press, 1986.

Flackes, W. D., and S. Elliott. *Northern Ireland: A Political Directory, 1968–1988.* Dublin: Gill and Macmillan, 1989.

Foster, R. F. *Modern Ireland 1600–1972.* London: Penguin, 1988.

Foucault, Michel. *Discipline and Punish: The Birth of the Prison,* translated by Alan Sheridan. New York: Vintage Books, 1979.

Geertz, Clifford. "Religion as a Cultural System." In Clifford Geertz, ed., *The Interpretation of Cultures.* New York: Basic Books, 1973, 87–126.

Hillyard, Paddy. "Law and Order." In John Darby, ed., *Northern Ireland: The Background to the Conflict.* Belfast: Appletree Press, 1983, 32–61.

Hodgen, Margaret T. *Early Anthropology in the Sixteenth and Seventeenth Centuries.* Philadelphia: University of Pennsylvania Press, 1964.

Kearney, Richard. *Transitions: Narratives in Modern Irish Culture.* Manchester: Manchester University Press, 1988.

Kelly, Fergus. *A Guide to Early Irish Law.* Dublin: Dublin Institute for Advanced Studies, 1988.

Kundera, Milan. *The Book of Laughter and Forgetting.* New York: Alfred A. Knopf, 1980.

Lyons, F.S.L. *Culture and Anarchy in Ireland 1890–1939.* Oxford and New York: Oxford University Press, 1979.

MacBride, Sean. "Introduction." In Bobby Sands, *One Day in My Life.* London: Pluto Press, 1983.

McCann, Eamonn. *War and an Irish Town.* London: Pluto Press, 1980.

Memmi, Albert. *The Colonizer and the Colonized.* Boston: Beacon Press, 1965.

Morris, James. *Farewell the Trumpets: An Imperial Retreat.* New York: Harvest/HBJ, 1978.

Morrison, Toni. *Beloved: A Novel.* New York: Alfred A. Knopf, 1987.

Muenster, Sebastian. *Cosmographiae Universalis.* Basilea: Henrichum Petri, 1554.

O'Dowd, Liam, Bill Rolston, and Mike Tomlinson. *Northern Ireland: Between Civil Rights and Civil War.* London: CSE Books, 1980.

O'Malley, Padraig. *Biting at the Grave: The Irish Hunger Strikes and the Politics of Despair.* Boston: Beacon Press, 1990.

Ortelius, Abraham. *Theatrum Orbis Terrarum.* Antuerdiae: A. R. Sandensen, 1570.

Owens, Rosemary Cullen. *Smashing Times: A History of the Irish Women's Suffrage Movement 1889–1922.* Dublin: Attic Press, 1984.

Rolston, Bill. "Politics, Painting and Popular Culture: The Political Wall Murals of Northern Ireland." *Media, Culture and Society* 9 (1987): 5–28.

Rosaldo, Renato. *Culture and Truth: The Remaking of Social Analysis.* Boston: Beacon Press, 1989.

Rowthorn, Bob, and Naomi Wayne. *Northern Ireland: The Political Economy of the Conflict.* Cambridge: Polity Press, 1988.

Rulfo, Juan. "Pedro Paramo." In *Obras.* Mexico: Fondo de Cultura Economica, 1987.

Sahlins, Marshall. *Historical Metaphors and Mythical Realities: Structure in the Early History of the Sandwich Islands Kingdom.* Ann Arbor: University of Michigan Press, 1981.

______ . *Islands of History.* Chicago: University of Chicago Press, 1985.

Sands, Bobby. *Skylark Sing Your Lonely Song: An Anthology of the Writings of Bobby Sands.* Cork and Dublin: Mercier Press, 1982.

______ . *One Day in My Life.* London: Pluto Press, 1983.

Sluka, Jeffrey A. *Hearts and Minds, Water and Fish: Support for the IRA and INLA in a Northern Ireland Ghetto.* Greenwich, Conn.: JAI Press, 1989.

Spenser, Edmund. *A View of the Present State of Ireland.* 1st ed. Dublin: Sir James Ware, 1633. Oxford: Clarendon Press, 1970.

Steward, A.T.Q. *The Narrow Ground: Patterns of Ulster History.* Belfast: Pretani Press, 1986.

Taussig, Michael. *Shamanism, Colonialism, and the Wild Man: A Study in Terror and Healing.* Chicago: University of Chicago Press, 1987.

Thompson, E. P. *The Making of the English Working Class.* London: Penguin, 1963.

Thompson, William Irwin. *The Imagination of an Insurrection, Dublin, Easter 1916: A Study of an Ideological Movement.* West Stockbridge, Mass.: Lindisfarne Press, 1982.

Timerman, Jacobo. *Prisoner Without a Name, Cell Without a Number.* New York: Alfred A. Knopf, 1981.

Toibin, Colm. *Martyrs and Metaphors.* Letters from the New Island Series. Dublin: Raven Art Press, 1987.

Warren, Kay B. *The Symbolism of Subordination: Indian Identity in a Guatemalan Town.* 2d ed. Austin: University of Texas Press, 1989.

Whyte, John. *Interpreting Northern Ireland.* Oxford: Clarendon Press, 1990.

Yeats, W. B. *The King's Threshold.* 1st ed. London: A. H. Bullen, 1904. London: Macmillan, 1937.

[9]

Martyrdom and Witnessing: Violence, Terror and Recollection in Cyprus

PAUL SANT CASSIA

This paper examines the relationship between history, memory and experience in Cyprus by reference to the 1955–59 EOKA armed nationalist struggle, and its subsequent interpretation by Greek Cypriot villagers. While ethnic remembering as sponsored by political authorities was unambiguous, personal villager accounts of the past are constructed differently, according to notions of witnessing, experience, suspicion, attribution of motives, etc. Villagers evoke memory and witnessing of the past, and of themselves, to make statements about morality, responsibility and merit. The tension between official accounts of the past ('history') and experience ('witnessing') suggests that the nation state in Cyprus has been an imagined community, but in a completely different sense to that outlined by Anderson. It has always been an imagined community in the past, or in the future – never in the divisive present.

Introduction: Between History and Memory

This paper examines the relationship between history, memory and experience in Cyprus by reference to the 1955–59 EOKA armed nationalist struggle, and its subsequent interpretation by Greek Cypriot villagers. I examine how individuals make sense of events that have a direct bearing on the present years after they occurred. In such contexts history is neither dead, nor dispassionate, nor uncontested. It can be both reinforced and subverted by experiences that individuals had, which they recount in various ways. This paper is therefore about social memory, but it is grounded in the anthropology of experience – the means by which direct personal experiences of the past and events are interpreted and offered as morally compelling and authentic narratives to either re-enforce or subvert official (ethnic) histories. The notion of 'experience' of events, of having witnessed (and hence participated in) them, is particularly significant because in evoking the past in a manner that authenticates the narrators' claims, individuals are trying to (re)interpret their own and others' actions, or contest statist histories. Edward Bruner has suggested that experiences are expressed in narratives which can be seen as constitutive performances: 'narratives are not only structures of meaning, but structures of power as well'.[1] That the telling of stories, which by their very nature links past, present and future, does things needs little demonstration. On the one hand as the telling of stories is so variable, we need to examine how shifting meanings, attributions and readings can themselves influence social action. On the other we ought to critically examine whether Jerome Bruner's suggestion that texts about lives inflect the past towards those versions is dangerously solipsistic.[2]

My particular concern is with the armed liberation struggles. Once struggles are 'over', shifting alignments of power render contentious the significance and recounting of the past. Condensed pasts, such as uprisings, as inscribed with human agency, seem condemned to continual reinterpretation (or even re-imagining). This is not just a matter of memories changing across time (and therefore becoming less 'true'), as if memories are mainly merely 'personal' and 'individual'. These they certainly are by definition. Rather, it is how memories are collectivised and/or socialised, in and through narratives, how and where these narratives are embedded (e.g. in space, material artefacts, imaginary landscapes, monuments, or even the body, etc), and how these narratives historicise memories.

Paul Veyne has suggested that 'the historian explains plots ... human plots',[3] and that 'history is an art, like engraving or photography ... history is a work of art by its efforts towards objectivity in the same way that an excellent drawing by one who draws ... is a work of art to some degree and supposes some talent on the part of its author'.[4] This classicist view resembles Lucian who used the metaphor of Phidias to present history as a 'mirror of human life' (*speculum vitae humanae*). It needs to be supplemented by an understanding of the role of memory. Here some of the views of Peter Burke are useful. He suggests that historians should be concerned with memory from two points of view: memory as a historical source, to produce 'a critique of the reliability of reminiscence' (oral history), and memory as 'a historical phenomenon' *per se*. In a passage worthwhile quoting because it goes to the heart of the tense relationship between history and memory he concludes that he prefers to see 'historians as the guardians of the awkward facts, the skeletons in the cupboards of social memory'.[5] The metaphor of 'skeletons in cupboards' takes on a particularly messy ring when we have to deal with areas of ethnic conflict such as Cyprus, Yugoslavia, and other parts of the Balkans and Middle East where 'ethnic cleansing' has long been practised. Burke concludes with his vision of history: 'there used to be an official called the "Remembrancer" – a euphemism for the debt collector ... One of the most important functions of the historian is to be a remembrancer'.[6] The metaphor is powerful and evocative. History as memory of this sort may well be existentially and ethically unproblematic in many contexts but for an anthropologist working with the recent past the 'debts' are real, often conceived of in terms of blood, not transcribed in a centrally located register but in different ones, some official, others unofficial, and many historical debt collectors are employed by powerful vested interests. Who keeps the records, who calls the debts, who remembers or forgets them, and how 'payment' is to be made are all contested. There are different ways of registering and valorising memories as 'debts': bodies of dead fighters, houses, the lost and disappeared, etc. Narratives about the past are historically performative both for the present as unfolding in the future, and for the past as seemingly immutable. They inevitably raise notions of responsibility and power, distributing these on the local and the global. Elocutors identify themselves by attempting to explain why events evolved within the imaginable possibilities available to them as actors then, which with hindsight, they may have exploited differently, or even why they were 'powerless' to act in any other way. In parallel work on moral responsibility in Zimbabwe, Werbner has suggested that 'historical narratives are unfinished moral narratives, in which traces of past faults impinge on the present and compel people to act'.[7] What are the implications for the relationship between the past as memory, and the nation-state's project of the manipulability of history?

Nationalism, Civil Society and the State

Cyprus is a predominantly Greek speaking island with a substantial Turkish minority (18 per cent), the descendants of the Ottoman settlers during the period of Ottoman domination (1571–1878). Greek Cypriots point out with some justification that the dominant culture with the greatest continuity since at least the fourth century BCE has been Greeko-Hellenistic, and subsequently Christian. In 1878 Turkey ceded the island to Britain against the protests of the Greek Cypriots who desired *enosis* (Union with Greece). Modern Cypriot history can be divided into three main phases: 1955–63, 1963–74 and 1974 to the present. In the 1950s the secret organisation EOKA, initiated an armed struggle in favour of *enosis*, under the military guidance of George Grivas, a Cyprus-born Greek army officer who had been involved in murky right-wing groups in Greece in the late 1940s. The populist movement for *enosis* was politically led by the ethnarch, Archbishop Makarios, subsequently President of the Republic of Cyprus. Differences soon emerged between Archbishop Makarios and General Grivas. Instead of union with Greece the island was given independence with power sharing between the Greek and Turkish communities under the Zurich agreements, with Britain, Greece and Turkey as Guarantor Powers.

Relations between Greek Cypriots and Turkish Cypriots, generally peaceful for decades, had plummeted when, during the 1955–59 'Emergency', colonial authorities began recruiting Turkish Cypriot auxiliary policemen in place of Greek Cypriots to suppress civilian demonstrations in favour of *enosis*. Turkish Cypriots, alarmed at the prospect of becoming a minority in a potentially Greek state, insisted that if Greek Cypriots were given their *enosis*, they too should be allowed to form part of Turkey in a *taksim* (division) or double-*enosis*. A Turkish Cypriot underground armed organisation (Volkan, later TMT – the Turkish Cypriot Resistance Organization) was established in 1955, but was not formally banned until July 1958.[8] Communal fighting broke out in summer 1958, and both EOKA and TMT soon attacked not just members of opposing ethnic groups, but also members of their own group. EOKA assassinated left-wing Greeks as 'traitors', and TMT murdered left-wing Turks because they were in alliance with left-wing Greeks who were far from keen on union with a 'monarcho-fascist Greece'. Deteriorating relations with Greece and Greece's threats to have recourse to the UN prompted Britain to involve Turkey with important long-term consequences.[9]

In the second period (1963–74) relations between the two communities worsened over interpretations of the constitution which gave the Turkish Cypriots a blocking position far in excess of their numerical strength. Greek Cypriot irregulars attacked Turkish Cypriot villages, and violence flared in 1963–67. Turkish Cypriots withdrew to armed enclaves where they were also blockaded by the Greek Cypriots. In effect Turkish Cypriots withdrew from the Republic of Cyprus, set up their own administration and refused to pay taxes.

By the late 1960s, among the Greek Cypriots internal discontent by those largely excluded from power and government employment was skilfully exploited by mainland Greek army officers stationed to train the Greek Cypriot National Guard. With CIA funds they armed a new secret organisation called EOKA B to destabilise the Republic of Cyprus, remove Makarios, and install a figure more beholden to the Greek colonels and the US.[10] Grivas returned secretly to Cyprus in 1971 to train and organise a destabilising campaign against the Republic.

EOKA B should be considered as distinct from EOKA A, but ideologically it presented itself as its heir. It was linked to the same individual (General Grivas) who considered the first EOKA struggle of 1955–59 cut short with independence. It claimed to be directing its actions towards achieving the historical destiny of Cyprus (Unification with Greece) 'betrayed' by Makarios and his entourage, and it exploited a model of social mobility established through the EOKA struggle based upon the patriotic taking up of the gun. Some individuals who had played a prominent part in the 1955–59 struggle were active in it. The society split vertically between *Makariaki* and *Griviki*. Violence and bombings were common and there was an attempt on Makarios' life. The state was obliged to rely on its own special forces of small groups of armed men linked to national politicians loyal to Makarios, some of whom were ex-EOKA fighters.[11] On 3 July 1974 Makarios openly requested of the Greek Junta to withdraw its army officers in Cyprus, accusing them of directing the activities of EOKA B. On 15 July the mainland Greek-commanded National Guard together with EOKA B staged a coup, but Makarios escaped abroad. Widespread fighting broke out between coupists and Makarios supporters. A puppet regime was established. Turkey interpreted that its role as one of the Guarantor Powers allowed it the right to military intervention. Turkey's aim was to protect Turkish Cypriots, but whereas it had the right to restore the *status quo ante*, it did not have the right to effectively partition the island, occupy one half, expel its (Greek) inhabitants, and install a puppet regime.

The invasion provoked some killings of unarmed Turkish Cypriots by irregular Greek forces. Britain, the other Guarantor Power, stood by. During the 'peace operation', some 1600 Greek Cypriots went 'missing', presumed killed by the Turks. Although the Republic of Cyprus was re-established with the return of Makarios, the Turkish army has not left. In 1976 Greek Cypriots in the north fearful for their own safety, moved south to the areas under the control of the Republic of Cyprus. Turkish Cypriots, similarly fearful, but also under threat from the Turkish authorities, moved north under Turkish army control. In 1983 Turkish Cypriots proclaimed the Turkish Republic of Northern Cyprus (TRNC), only recognised by Turkey. The two communities are now separated and there have been ineffectual attempts at unification within a new constitutional federal framework.

EOKA differed from many other national liberation groups in important ways. It conducted a guerrilla war not for independence but for union with another country. Its members consisted exclusively of one ethnic group in a multi-ethnic society, and it did not gain the support of the other ethnic group who increasingly viewed it as deeply antithetical to its interests. It established a dangerous precedent for accession to political power which delegitimised normal parliamentary political processes. It was rapidly overtaken by events and it manifestly failed to achieve its goals. Indeed, an organisation presenting itself as its successor (EOKA B) set in motion a disastrous series of events (the coup and the Turkish invasion, occupation of half of the island, extensive loss of life, dislocation and destruction). If EOKA were to be judged on purely formal criteria it failed dismally on all accounts. Yet the power and potency of the myth of the significance of EOKA has not diminished. Its heroes are still glorified and commemorated in national parades and festivities, and the glory of those days has now entered Greek Cypriot political folklore.

History, Memories and Myths

Any historical analysis of the EOKA struggle cannot be pursued solely through official records, useful as they are. It has also to be studied in terms of (i) how the participants themselves conceptualised the historical significance of their actions, (ii) how, and by reference to what, they rationalised their actions, and (iii) how events were narrated by themselves, and, later, by others. Clearly these three areas overlap, but have to be kept distinct. In this section I show how the nature of the struggle legitimised violence as sacrifice by reference to significant episodes in Greek history which held an almost mythic value. These, in turn, informed accounts on those involved in the struggle, the *agonistes* (fighters), and contributed to the emergence of 'mythbiographies'. These individuals were keen to maintain oral accounts of their roles in the struggle, rather than historical accounts of the struggle, which may have encouraged a more critical interpretation of the events.

When the young EOKA militants took to the hills they had been taught at school that the island was Greek and its historical destiny was to be united with Greece. Anti-colonial struggles dominated world news. The EOKA struggle was not just a military struggle. It was political, pursued in international fora and the media. Despite colonial control of the media and repressive press laws, the public was kept informed through the cyclostyled sheets (*filladia*) of Grivas, EOKA, its political wing PEKA, and the religious organisation ANE. Yet *agonistes* (guerrilla fighters) could not then offer their personal accounts. Most were on the run. In addition, individuals may have been involved in activities they did not wish to talk about. The same occurred with the British. As Ian Martin, then a British army interpreter in Cyprus, points out, savage reprisals, beatings, torture and perjury were commonly practised by British soldiers and officers.[12] Thus individuals were aware that they were 'making history', but there were also serious limitations on what could be talked about.

If the actions that were historical, and the unfolding of individual agency as narrated, were interpenetrated by myth, the subsequent historical recounting of the EOKA struggle, its historicising, took place within an oral context in a small scale society. After 1959 many military activists (including Grivas) were not involved in political decisions and were bypassed. With few exceptions *agonistes* did not become politicians, although many came to wield political power. Most *agonistes* did not write much about their roles as historical actors in the drama of ethnic recovery of the past that the EOKA struggle represented. Indeed many felt betrayed, and there are accounts that the population felt 'confused and disappointed' with the Zurich agreements. As compensation and reward many were given governmental positions, land, and other resources.[13] In face of the more polished literate, skilled, urbane politicians, *agonistes* emphasised agency, sacrifice and performance. The society was primarily oral – everyone knew who was involved. Although many could and did claim that they had fought for *enosis*, it was the photographs of wanted men in particular – reproduced in books, newspapers and *kaffenia* – that demonstrated to everyone that they (in contrast to the vainglorious boasts of others) had risked life and limb for 'history', for the 'ethnos' which was a metaphor of unity, wholeness and greatness in the past, and that therefore they deserved the positions of privilege that they so easily captured in the post-1960 period.

Oral accounts and the circulation of stories about *agonistes*, usually whispered or confided, reinforced their local power. Many came from humble backgrounds and had few qualifications to take part in the running of a modern state.[14] Yet they dominated informal political life, and some entered the murky interface between the police and the criminal underworld.[15] Apart from the more readily discernible reasons why they did not commit their memoirs to writing (youth, lack of literary skills) *agonistes* had an interest in the production of history as living memory, rather than the consumption of history as document. They were interested in maintaining the circulation of stories about them in an oral form, in being known and remembered, and in being talked about, rather than in potentially more contextualising written texts. Stories reinforced their power. They performed their stories. They historicised themselves through mythbiographies whispered by others. Writing was much more associated with slander through newspapers or night-time anonymous leaflets.

The privileging of the oral, and hence of memory, was encouraged by the fact that in the early post-1960 period most people agreed on the significance of the events, or seemed obliged to agree. The EOKA struggle was so traumatic, and the justness of the cause so self-evident, so historically justifiable and unquestionable, that few alternative accounts were entertained. So successfully had people been convinced, and convinced themselves, that on the institutional level no alternative accounts were given currency. Certainly it was unpatriotic to give any other account. AKEL, the (large) Communist Party, was silent on this matter, and while communists had their individual memories of events, these were rarely given official expression by the party, eager to rehabilitate itself through the process of new parliamentary politics. Anyone who openly suggested that EOKA *agonistes* were anything but heroes risked a beating, or worse. There was therefore little available space for contestation, and attention soon shifted to the thorny problem of relations with the Turkish Cypriots, which reinforced the belief that the EOKA struggle was unproblematical, not requiring re-evaluation.

By the early 1960s two paradigms of historical self-evidency had been established for the Greek Cypriots. First, the EOKA struggle was a glorious event, even if it had not resulted in union with Greece. Second, Greek Cypriots were concerned that the Turkish Cypriots as a minority in a predominantly Greek island should not impede the majority Greek Cypriot population from realising their 'self determination', from holding the proper and efficient workings of the state hostage to their demands, or from threatening the unitary sovereignty and integrity of the state. Far less envisionable was the future. *Enosis* was not officially dead. 'Self-determination', the new slogan, was suitably ambiguous to be initially appealed to by both the nationalist right and a more independist left. Turkish Cypriot fears were thus not assuaged. To Greek Cypriots, Greece was 'Mother Greece', Athens the 'National Centre', and a guarantor that the island would be protected from Turkish designs. This was society initially quite sure what it wanted to remember. This was an ethnic rather than a national remembering: the island was Greek, the Turks were a minority who settled much later than the Greeks, they were almost interlopers, some were even 'apostasised Christians', Cyprus was 'our island' *(nisi mas)*, and the Turkish Cypriots should not stand in the way of Greek 'self determination'. Such commemorative rather than memorial memories were kept alive through the EOKA museum in Nicosia, and through the various statues gracing public places.[16]

While ethnic remembering was unambiguous, personal accounts were constructed differently, according to notions of witnessing, experience, suspicion, attribution of motives, etc. In the next sections I examine the relationship between official histories and personal memories. I show how, after the coup and the invasion, which dealt a serious blow to Greek nationalism in Cyprus, various political parties have re-interpreted the past in order to strategically allocate blame and responsibility for the coup. I then examine how villagers evoke memory and witnessing of the past, and of themselves, to make statements about morality, responsibility and merit.

Official Rememberings and Personal Recollections

Distrust and Empowerment

Individual memories can reinforce and contest official memories, or more precisely remembrances. For the purposes of this article I take memory to be 'plastic', but not in the sense that it can be shaped as either 'true' or 'false'. I suggest the Mannheimian notion that 'memory', or more precisely what is remembered, is shaped by, and expressed through, dominant climates of interpretation and recollection. In Cyprus, especially in the aftermath of the EOKA struggle, there was a dominant general interpretation of the recent past that was confident and unambiguous in what it wanted to remember (as well as forget). As I show these very areas are now less surrounded by confidence. The notion parallels Bellah *et al.*'s notion of 'communities of memory'.[17]

Here we are faced with a more complex situation than the obvious belief that 'he who controls the past controls who we are'.[18] Apart from the fact that no-one can be said to control the past, such a perspective begs some important questions. First, it is not so much individuals in the modern world but complex institutions that manufacture the past. Second, the 'past' is not a limited or finite, nor self-evident resource but one that is constantly reworked. The 'past' can be seen as 'capital', and like capital put to new uses. Third, the past is often embedded in relations between men and things, artefacts, places, etc. Finally, such a perspective merely suggests a conscious repression of memory as 'truth' that needs to be brought to light. What is consciously repressed can also be consciously recalled. Particularly interesting for the anthropologist is not so much what is officially remembered and forgotten in institutions, museums, artefacts, etc., although this is certainly important. Rather, it is the complicity in remembering and forgetting that inevitably helps constitute a community. This complicity can be both active and passive. In this paper, I am particularly interested in passive complicity: the silences and disapprovals that surround alternative accounts and recollections, even though individuals may themselves have had different experiences. We do not just witness the past through our experiences. We also witness the past when we accompany others in their narratives of remembering.

Individual recollections and memories based upon experiences can both reinforce or contest official rememberings. Although the relationship between individual memories and collective remembering is complex and lies at the intersection of psychology and anthropology beyond the scope of this paper, we need to retain some notion of the individual as a social actor, as an active creative participant in society, i.e., not just with how societies remember, or with social memory, but also with how individuals can contest or reinforce these dominant climates of interpretation. 'Social change' is not merely a matter of changes across time, but also of changes in the understanding of the past.

When examining how perceptions of the EOKA struggle have changed in Cyprus over the past 30 years several questions are raised. First, how are events recounted many years later? A personal account of a series of events, a recollection, may be given different glosses as it is recounted. How do we make sense of these shifts? Relations between individual recollections and official remembrances are critical here.

Second, if as is commonly maintained, the 'history' of Cyprus has not been definitively 'written' and is so ambiguous, how do villagers make sense of their lives within changing national political alignments? Many Cypriots believe in the 'unwrittenness' of their post-1960 history. A sense of structural incompleteness or openness marks their perception of this period. Nor is there just one official history, but various competing ones. Political parties sponsor different accounts of the past. This has two implications: a collective disempowerment is accompanied paradoxically by personal empowerment. On a collective level, if the past has yet to be written and to be known, the present is also uncertain and potentially unknowable. Yet while collective history is 'unknown', 'hidden' or even distrusted, individuals empower themselves by referring to their own personal experiences. Experiences and personal accounts are thus privileged and achieve a compelling force precisely because official histories are distrusted or not trustworthy. Experience can thus generate 'truth' (and empower) through personal omniscience. This can be rhetorically contrasted to the falsity of official mendacious history. Men often say *ego to ezisa* (lit. I lived through this – i.e., I know/have direct experience) to mean: don't listen to official history. The term used here: *istories polles* (many rumours/histories) collapses and reduces official history to rumour. Here, a brief digression on truth and lying may be useful.

History, 'Truth' and Witnessing

Greek Cypriots passionately believe that there are 'truths of history' that are self evident, unambiguous, even concealed. They also acknowledge that some truths may have to be concealed, and that this may apply to both villager accounts of local social relations and official accounts. Generally, they profoundly distrust official histories that give primacy to records, disembedded from their social contexts.

Individuals see themselves as *martyres*, as witnesses of events, as guardians of the past, from the struggles with the British to the loss of 'half the island to the Turks', and as witnesses of the actions of individuals in these events. In some cases individuals are not talking to the ethnographer as just interested (or prying) individuals, but as members of ethnic groups, aware of the (sometimes overrated) power of writing and the role of foreigners in determining the history of the island. One must exercise due caution in interpreting what is recounted, not as either true or false, but as far more complex, enmeshed in complex agendas which individuals are in the process of scripting.

The struggle for the truths of the past is rendered even more acute because while most Cypriots believe that their history has yet to be written, i.e., disclosed, many often maintain that certain aspects of inter-ethnic relations (such as killings) should be 'forgotten' and not written, while others should be 'remembered'. This is not merely a matter of structural amnesia, it is also a matter of power relations. To many villagers 'history' is also full of hidden secrets, about the participants, about secret plans and about grand designs. Some of these they claim to perceive; for others they proclaim their existence, which, because of their very nature they can never know anything about. In short, in places like Cyprus; and possibly in the Lebanon, the Middle East and the former Yugoslavia, we need to develop a history of histories, both written/official and oral/unofficial – about how they interact in complex ways, about how some histories can only remain oral whereas others should be written, in spite of the fact that few believe them from their own experiences and yet recount them while also subverting them. And we need to investigate the implications.

Political Parties and Contested Pasts

Nation-states have their own myths and symbols. Cyprus presents an almost unique case of a society that subscribes to a symbolism of statehood, conscious that it contains some very serious and basic flaws. Its heroes lost their lives in pursuit of an ideal that was never achieved, and indeed provided a model for subsequent politics that led to disaster (*Katastrophe*, a word used to describe the Asia Minor debacle of 1922). Its two founder heroes (Makarios and Grivas) soon split. Commemoration ceremonies to honour them are ambiguous and antithetical. Those honouring Makarios present him as a previous ethnarch rather than an ex-President, thus reinforcing the attribution of saintliness as a victim of worldly acts of evil men. Commemoration memorials in honour of Grivas were until recently deeply embarrassing to the government. Rightists claim that Grivas' idealism led him into a trap set by unscrupulous 'outsiders'. Leftists assert that Grivas 'knew' (*iksere*, which could also mean predicted) that Turkey would invade, but he and the extreme right preferred 'double *enosis*' anyway. Taken together, then, the messages and meta-language of the two memorial services can hardly be said to constitute a coherent and integrated nationalist ideology.

Dominant narrative paradigms of Greek Cypriot identity have changed across time. In the first period of the *enosis* ideal (1955–63) the past was viewed as ethnic oppression, the present as a glorious resistance and the future as ethnic realisation. By contrast, in the post-invasion period the past is seen as an ethnic betrayal, the present as ethnic oppression and the future as a dangerous ethnic limbo. Whereas national public functions previously commemorated a Hellenism that was not achieved or was unachievable, they now commemorate a Hellenism that is lost forever while a discourse of 'betrayal' by Mother Greece permeates popular belief. The question therefore is why have there not been radical official reinterpretations of the past, including the role of the EOKA struggle.

A major reason is an institutional one. For a long time after the coup and the invasion no political party dared reinterpret Greek Cypriot political history along lines that were too divisive partly because of the perceived need for ethnic unity in dealing with the problem of the Turkish occupation and the establishment of the Turkish Republic of North Cyprus (TRNC) in 1983. The critical area of contention has been the allocation of responsibility for the coup and the invasion, rather than a radical reinterpretation of the progress of Greek nationalism in Cyprus. Shifting party alliances played their part. In the late 1970s and 1980s the alliance between the Centre Right Democratic Party (DIKO – *Dimokratikon Komma*) of the ex-president Spiros Kyprianou, and the Communist Party (AKEL), accused the more right wing Democratic Rally Party (DISY – *Dimokraticos Synayermos*) of Glavkos Clerides of harbouring coupists. Such alignments were influenced by attitudes towards intercommunal talks. Nowadays an alliance between the DIKO and DISY has led to a downplaying of the coup, and Grivas has been rehabilitated.

AKEL, the Communist Party, the party most likely to have benefited from such an excavation of the past, has an ambiguous political history. It had originally denounced EOKA as an Anglo-American organisation of agents provocateurs.[19] Although it supported Makarios and his policies, it had also been constrained to accept the *enosis* ideal, which makes its claim to support ethnic alliances across class lines suspect to the Turkish Cypriots. In line with its Marxist perspectives AKEL labels the EOKA struggle an anti-colonial struggle *(antiapikiakos agonas)*, while the right calls it a freedom struggle *(apelerofthiki agona)*. Leftists were largely excluded from the struggle. Ironically colonial authorities, more worried about communist influence, declared AKEL illegal in 1955, while the greatest threat to colonial rule came from the right.[20] The latter was deeply suspicious of the left either as potential traitors or as atheistic 'non-Greeks'. AKEL has trodden a fine line: it insists that it favoured a 'mass based peaceful political struggle' *(mazikou eirinikou politikou agona)*, a class struggle involving the Turkish Cypriots, a position soon rendered difficult to pursue realistically by the turn of events and by nationalists on both sides of the ethnic divide. On the other hand it is keen not to be seen to be questioning the EOKA struggle because men lost their lives in pursuing freedom from British rule.

By contrast in the post-1974 period the right wing was embarrassed by two major facts. First, many Grivas supporters and the *enosis*-now movement labelled *praksikopimaties* (coupists, an offensive term) gravitated to the Clerides' DISY (Democratic Rally) party. *Praksikopimaties* were believed to have 'eaten' (*efaghan*), i.e., received money from 'outsiders' (*kseni*) to destabilise the Makarios regime. Second, Clerides was believed to have angled to take Makarios' place as President. As the Greek

Cypriot intercommunal negotiator he sanctioned the population swap-over, interpreted as proof that he favoured a de facto double *enosis* or partition. With his election to the Presidency the right was rehabilitated. This has implications for accounts not just about the (Greek) past, but also of the EOKA struggle, and of relations between Greek and Turkish Cypriots.

Morality Plays: Silences, Complicities and Responsibilities

Villagers often engage visitors in accounts of modern Cypriot history. This is more than an attempt to inform the visitor. It is an attempt to go over the same ground, almost obsessively, to tell stories to discover themselves and who they are. And the central subject of most accounts is: how did we come to be as we are? How did our country and society finish up divided? Clearly, they know the 'answers', but in so recounting them they are recapturing the past and anticipating the future. They confirm White's suggestion that 'every historical narrative has as its latent or manifest purpose the desire to moralise the events of which it treats'.[21] These stories also bring out the dialectical relationship between fate and narrativity. 'Fate is recounted',[22] and it is through the process of narrativising that fate is brought forth: 'narrative time is, from the outset, time of being-with-others'.[23]

Coffee-shop accounts of recent Cypriot history can be divided into those that deal with national events, and those that deal with local ones embedded in a national context. The two cannot easily be separated. I first discuss national history, and then local history. The former is important to contextualise how individuals talk about local events. Villager accounts of recent Cypriot history are influenced by official statements, but cannot be reduced to them. Villagers elaborate them upon in significant ways. Villagers sometimes strategically utilise official rhetoric against the state. This is not merely for public consumption and therefore 'untrue' or lacking in significance. Context and the ontological status of the past are critical. Thus killings of Turks by Greeks, something passed over in silence by the Cypriot government, are divulged although often accompanied by the statement 'don't write this down', further replicating and reinforcing the state-imposed taxonomisation of time, memory, writing and 'forgetfulness'. In other cases they are admitted in an off-hand manner, or positively displayed.

Villager accounts of the past have a number of common features. First, most are asserted in discourse in a series of discrete elliptical statements. In being recounted they create a sense of community. The narratives also often move from, or involve, many non-sequitors. For example, it is widely believed that plans were in existence from the 1960s purporting to show Turkish zone of influence and corresponding to the present Turkish zone of occupation. These are cited to demonstrate that the Turks had long planned to occupy half the island. The 'use of history to repress historicity' is found in other societies characterised by ethnic conflict, such as Ireland.[24] Cause and consequence are collapsed in recursive history. These are morals about the power of writing. Writing has a magical power which conjures reality and makes things happen. Writing is the inscribing of state history and state power on to the lives of individuals. It is therefore imperative to witness it, to expose it through the autonomy of speech, for writing can easily 'erase itself' and thus conceal the intentions of power. In villager cultural categories such plans prove that the Turks always wanted to take over half the island, and the responsibilities of the other participants (including themselves) therefore diminish.

Another implication is an apologetic revisionism. Greek Cypriots recount their past history as a lack of foresight: we, the Greeks, providing the Turks with an opportunity to occupy half the island. Such a rhetorical position is a coded form of ethnic self-criticism. It unites both Greek Cypriots and mainland Greeks because it glosses over the attribution of responsibility. The implication is not that *enosis* was wrong, but rather that the way it was pursued was stupid. It also counterpoises a cultural stereotype of the Turks against a Greek self-image: the cunning, mentally agile, but sometimes rash Greek against the plodding, but long-sighted Turk. The Turks are often presented as having been politically unsophisticated in the period before 1960 when they are described as having been 'asleep'. After the British involved them in policing duties in 1958, and thus divided the population according to the Greek Cypriots, the Turks 'awoke'. Villagers often say: *I turki chimounde vathya; emeis tous eksipnisame.* (The Turks were in a deep sleep; we Greeks woke them up) (*eksipnisan*, awaking, is cognate with *eksipnada*, becoming aware and intelligent.) This shows a grudging admiration for the Turks as long term planners, as strategists rather tacticians.

Recently a vocabulary of justification and counter-justification has evolved to explain the coup and the invasion. This links 1974 with 1955. The argument goes as follows: 'we should never have taken on the British Empire, we should have pursued our struggle peacefully rather than through military means. How could we have had the temerity to take on the British? We thought we were *pallikaria* (brave but rash youths), and look what we have got in return. The British have long memories and when they got the opportunity they paid us back.' Such explanations provide a useful vocabulary of justification ('we thought we were *pallikaria*'), of debt, and a vocabulary of counter-justification ('when the Brits had the chance they paid us back') to explain how things are as they are. These accounts provide insights to the elocutors' political views. Leftists emphasise the foolhardiness of the armed struggle, and the futility of taking on the 'Anglo-Americans' who control, *elehoun*, the region. Rightists emphasise filiation: '*Dhen boreis na kseries ton anglo*. You can never know the British (lit. the Englishman). You may think they are your best friends and you then discover they are your worst enemies.' Such discourses derive from a long history of historical complaints about betrayal by Britain.

The significance of these accounts is twofold. First they can be seen as akin to morality plays. They suggest the notion of ineluctable fate, of *moira*, where individuals who have received some warnings of their fate if they follow a course of action nevertheless blindly go ahead. This account is pushed by the leftists who claim that they had warned against the armed struggle being pursued without the support of the Turks. The connection of fate with the division of the island is pursued both through what is said and through the language itself: 'we thought we were *pallikaria*, and look what happened: *mas mirazan tin Kyprou*: they divided up the island (this could even mean that unspecified outsiders separated Greek and Turkish Cypriots).' *Moira*, fate, is also related to division. The connection is reinforced through the evocation of rash young men (*pallikaria*) who do not heed the advice of those wiser than them.

A second reading is that it is also is a coded way of saying that the EOKA struggle was wrong or misjudged despite still receiving official approval. It does so through the themes of filiation and responsibility. By recasting official rhetoric which glorifies the young men who took part in the struggle as idealists, and as pure and manly, they capitalise on the double meaning of *pallikari* which can also mean unthinking, touchy in responding to offence, and lacking the gravitas and *logiki* of mature, responsible married men. This image is similar to that of the Homeric hero. Such narratives nevertheless implicate Britain and Cyprus in a type of morality play where the actors are personalised, just as Greece was previously turned into *Mitera Ellada* (Mother Greece). A Great Power, Britain (villagers use the words *Meghali Vretania*) is presented as lacking the maturity to respond in a measured way to the provocations of a few *pedhia* (children), *pallikaria* (representing the Cypriots). Indeed while the argument seems to be self-critical, which in a way it is, it also ironically deflates Britain's claim to have behaved in a fair, high minded and impartial manner as befits a Great Power, and which legitimated its politics to a colony by reference to its mission to civilise. Instead Britain acted in a mean, petty and vindictive manner by repaying us, not in the manner one would respond to a child's obstinacy but to an enemy. For *I Meghali Vrettania*, in the language of the family, did not act so *meghali* (i.e. adult) after all. Nor did it intervene in 1974 when it should have done so as a Guarantor Power. Small wonder that villagers express a great deal of disenchantment with the roles assumed by the major powers, such as Britain and Greece, who were supposed to have held the ring. If, as is often claimed by these powers, 'the Greek and Turkish Cypriots cannot get on well together', villagers ironically invert this to lay bare the pretence that the 'adults' (i.e. the major, Guarantor Powers) were not as responsible as they presented themselves to be.

Fighters and Butchers: *Agonistes che khapsyes*

Villager accounts of violence and nationalism enable them to make statements about themselves, local individuals, morality, right and wrong, and entitlements to social recognition. They often link EOKA A with EOKA B. It thus makes little sense to separate the two because villagers use one to talk about the other, and because they inevitably draw morals about fate, merit, culpability and destiny – all profoundly historical issues. They talk about EOKA in its A or B forms as a means to talk about violence. Rightists talk about EOKA A as a vehicle to talk about EOKA B, whereas leftists use EOKA B to talk about EOKA A. They thus move in different directions in time in order to arrive at the same destination: a moral account on the present with all its divisions. They are witnesses (*martyres*) to the past in the double sense of *martyria* – as witnesses to the past, and as martyrs of (from) the past. Inevitably they also construct a moral of the deterioration of violence.

Case example: the Hero, the Butcher, and the Butter Boys (voutiro pedhia, i.e., soft young men)

The following account by a man who was involved in EOKA A groups a number of themes: the *katastasi*, the tension between young and old, the glorification of the past, the actions of EOKA B, the spiritual godchild of the *enosis*-now movement, and village culture. Present were the elocutors' son-in-law, an elderly leftist friend of the family who disagreed with *enosis*, and myself. I give the whole account and then proceed with the analysis. 'Christos' begins by talking about two EOKA colleagues who were wanted by the British. Some aspects have been exaggerated. That does not necessarily devalue his narrative, because as anthropologists we should also be interested in those aspects of the past that people consciously emphasise or conceal, themselves aware that their listeners, members of the same culture, will be highly attuned to the rhetoric that they evoke. Fortunately, I subsequently discovered a published account of the incident he describes.

'Yiannis' and 'Hambis' didn't fear anyone. But there was a difference between them and the others who were younger. Some young men who were 17 years old or thereabouts wanted to go into the *agona* and I told them: '*Re pedhia,* don't go. You don't know what you are going in for'. They went along just the same and got killed that evening. In a struggle you need young men of above 20 years who know what they are going in for. The young ones went in without knowing what the risks were. In a war you have to know what the risks are. If you are aware that you can cop it, you are much more careful. I remember once [and here he seems to contradict the essence of what he just said] when Yiannis and I ambushed a convoy of British trucks close to the Chiftlik. Yiannis was wearing a white shirt and could be seen like the stars on a dark night. He just stood there and started shooting, *takka, takka, takka*. Bullets passed by. He didn't care at all about being hit. He was lucky and they didn't get him; I don't know how. We got (*epiasame*) 3 English soldiers that day [clearly an exaggeration] and you should have heard the soldiers crying like children: 'mummy, mummy'.

At this point one of his audience, the elderly leftist friend, interjected probably to question the veracity of his statement in a coded way, but also because leftists condemn the role of EOKA : 'You (plural) (*essies*) were therefore murderers (*foniades*)'. Christos did not reply, stopped a minute, then addressed his *gambros* (son-in-law):

The young men nowadays do not know how to fight, nor do they want to. Do you think that if the Turks were to come now that they would fight? They'd raise six flags each with half a crescent. Nationalism has ended now and it is mainly felt by youths below the age of 30. Killing wasn't a problem. It was just like hunting. When you've got a bird in your sights, *re koumbare, na ton pekseis*, you just shoot it. That's all there is to it. It's just like hunting game – *opos ta poullia*. It was fear that kept the *agona* going – fear most of all. There were no courts, no lawyers. If you were suspected of betraying or of saying anything you could well have prepared your own *mnimeo*. You couldn't take any risks. That is what happened to the Mukhtar of Chili. In the morning he said something, and words travel from mouth to mouth. In the afternoon he was called and he understood that something was wrong. He was in the *agona*. When he entered the room they got him through the window. I never told my wife anything. We were well organised. I'd go out at 9pm and plan to return at 10pm at the coffee-shops. I'd go to a coffee-shop at 9pm, say something – a joke or a story so that others would hear and could swear that I was there and then slip quietly away. I'd return on the dot at 10 and make my presence felt. So that if the English rounded up the men and beat them up, they could only swear that I was there. There was no way they could say anything else.

Yiannis and Hambis were like lions. They didn't fear anyone – not even their mother and father. They were the type of men who would have eaten others as *souvlakia*. I would take any means of transport to get to Psilo Ambeli – on foot, often on tractors, anything would do. Nobody knew the members of other omadhes. We were 9–10 in the Vrisi (a pseudonym) *omadha* (team). I knew a few more because I am from Psilo Ambeli (a pseudonym). I didn't even tell my wife that I was in the *omadha*.

Yiannis was a *pallikari*. Once, when I was discussing the new *Mukhtari* (Headmanship) at the kafeneion where my shop is now, I was discussing with Phylaktou, the leftist, about the *Mukhtari*. Phylaktou was saying that he objected to Yiannis becoming the *Mukhtar*. I told him that he would become *Mukhtar* whatever he said. Yiannis was passing by and he heard the conversation. He stood outside and then came in. He gave Phylaktou four *pazzous* (slaps) like this and left him on the ground and told him: 'I'm going to be the *Mukhtar* of this place'. He was a tough one – forget that he is now getting older. Then nobody could tell him anything. Once he found a Turk in the Paphos Marketplace who had sent him to jail, where his nose was broken. He hit him, gave him *pazzous* like this and told him: 'Go and tell your boss that I did this to you'.

But Dighenis and Makarios were right about how the situation changed. It was those anarchists from Paphos, 'Pashis', and the others. I know them all. They went berserk and just shot up the Turks [in 1963 and 1974]. 'Pashis' lined up 7 Turks in Moutallos and just shot them down in cold blood. But do you know what this means, *re koumbare*? It's a bit like going to the butcher and cutting up a pig – just meat. Pashis said that he would eat the Turks like *souvlakia*. I say that for what he did I could put a skewer through him from his ass (*Kolos*) to his mouth, and roast him like a *souvla*. They should never have done that. Do you know what that means *re koumbare*?

Nowadays when I go into the Post Office and the clerk gets annoyed because I do not have the right change I get angry. Once I threw the letter in his face and said 'You're going to serve me properly. You're a young man and you're in your job because I put you there. *Mesa stin katastasi* you were nothing and I put you there. So don't give me any of your shit.'
(Fieldwork, Summer 1988)

Clearly there is much bravado here, but this is part of the performance that requires analysis. When I first heard this account I did not know how to deal with it, in terms of what was true or 'false'. I just tried to remember it and write it down. Nor am I sure now whether some of the details I wrote were correct transcriptions – for example, the number of casualties, which made me sceptical about the validity (which in a naive empiricist perspective, I defined in terms of 'truth') of the account. Subsequently, some details which I wrote down without understanding their import became clearer, and authenticated it even if some of the details I discovered were clearly wrong. I learnt later that mortally wounded men often cry out for their mothers.[25] This was a detail that could not reasonably have been fabricated.[26]

To understand Christos' account we have to appreciate the context. This is an account for intimate consumption. Indeed most accounts of the events of 1955–59 (the *katastasi*) and, especially, 1974 are rarely talked about openly in Cyprus, because they are recent, because passions are still high and because it may be dangerous for the narrator. Another reason is that in contrast to, for example, Gilsenan's accounts of narratives and violence in the Lebanon, most violent events were not enacted out in full view of the villagers, working out their complex interpersonal and group dynamics.[27] Most violence in Cyprus in the 1955–59 period took place off-stage as concealed guerrilla activity with few observers. Significantly, violence that was displayed and enacted in full view of the media was stage-managed by the British when they captured *agonistes* and often went wrong, such as when the fighter G. Afxentiou was burned alive in his hide-out, and became a Greek martyr. By contrast, in the intense short 1974 period violence was forced through, rather than displayed or enacted, precipitative rather than condensed, in a situation of extreme social tension. The urgency of the 1974 events left individuals with little time to enact their social dramas, to plan out their responses, or to play to an 'audience'. Indeed many attempted to justify their hasty, violent actions by claiming 'this was war', which at the same time socially de-legitimated their actions.

The very exclusion of an audience for the enactment of the 1955–59 events privileges the person claiming the narrative role as a participant. This operates on two levels. First, the 'truth value' of the account cannot be contradicted directly and can only be questioned parabolically as it were, by seeming to accept it at face value, but then recasting the intentional stance of the narrator transforming it, in the felicitous phrase of Gilsenan, from gallous act to dirty deed. 'You were therefore murderers' interjects the leftist, to which Christos does not reply. Second, the authorial claims of the narrator to guide his audience back to the past in order to lead us forward to the present requires the complicit silence of the subject, Yiannis. It is almost essential that Yiannis' claims to authority in the village as a *pallikari*, subsequent *Mukhtar* and finally successful hotelier, be accompanied not by any of his accounts of his actions, which would turn him into a vainglorious boaster, but by what others say. Christos builds Yiannis' reputation to elliptically claim kudos for himself. Christos had been less successful than other *agonistes*, and felt that his deservingness had not been socially recognised: *'Mesa stin katastasi* you were nothing and I put you there. So don't give me any of your shit.' As the dominant man in the household he was about to be eclipsed by his son-in-law. Thus one of his aims is to claim authority over both the young (represented by his son-in-law, a government office employee, and myself), and the leftist. He exploits both the official heroisation of the *agonistes* and the gaps in official accounts to establish his authority by talking of first hand experience. Christos shifts easily from the 1950s to the 1970s. There is no explicit reference to nationalist ideals. Yet to him nationalist ideals are an important differentiating mark between the past and the present, the older men like himself and the young. There is little idealism of the institutional aspects of EOKA. Yet there were occasions when young men assumed heroic proportions, although a fine line separates heroism and foolhardiness. Christos differentiates between the young men of his time, but he also contrasts them collectively to the youth nowadays.

Christos then groups together the two national leaders, Makarios and Grivas, by-passing the latter's role in subsequent Cypriot history. As an ex-EOKA man he still looked up to him, and he refers to him by his mythological name (*Dighenis*). He blames the invasion on those 'outsiders' from Paphos, whom he labels 'anarchists'. This is an effective way of distancing himself from those men whose formal ideology did not differ substantially from his. He does not label them 'ultra rightists' (*akra dekshii*), a word normally used by the left, nor does he call them 'traitors' (*prodotes*), for this would logically involve the contradiction that the ideal of *enosis* could be betrayed by actually trying to bring it about. Rather, by being labelled anarchists their actions become uncontrollable, unpredictable and profoundly anti-Hellenic. In doing so he does not engage in the anti-mainland Greek sentiments favoured by the left, and he neatly sidesteps the whole issue of the role of Greece. He presents them as mindless, a theme reinforced by reference to their gratuitous and cold-blooded killing of Turks. Finally he returns to a sore point felt by many ex- EOKA fighters – that while they had fought for ethnic and national rights by risking their lives, the young lack ideals and benefit. The young are personified by the pen-pushing supercilious clerk at the Post Office, a symbol of government power, literacy, contact with the outside world, and a job which in villager categories is the essence of being paid to do nothing. Villagers send few letters, and receive mainly official pieces of paper from government, usually a source of anger and resentment.

The narrative is also a moral about violence and about the movement from socially acceptable to socially unacceptable violence through the images of the *pallikari-agonistis* of EOKA A to the *khasapis-prodotis* (butcher-traitor) of EOKA B. The *agonistis* is a young man, modelled on the kleftic hero, whose enthusiasm and purity is nevertheless vulnerable.[28]

Youth is an advantage but it can also be a disadvantage if combined with foolhardiness. *Agonistes* had to be pure. They replicated in their lives and deaths the supreme almost Christ-like notion of sacrifice, a sacrifice made through violence and their being killed. EOKA A was a fanatically puritan organisation. British products were boycotted and Grivas expected *agonistes* (especially from villages) to keep away from the polluting world of women.[29] Catechism lessons were an important means for the recruitment of young men and women. Many of the biographies of killed *agonistes* written later emphasised the notion of a *kalo pedhi* , (lit. a good boy), religious, respectful of authority. The young man is often presented as a virtuoso: as a child he is more knowledgeable than other older boys in religious matters, and he excels in most activities.[30] Purity and pollution were areas over which EOKA and the colonial authorities fought symbolically. The Colonial government gave 'information handouts' to the foreign press declaring that girls of school age had been 'required to prostitute themselves with fellow members of EOKA. Details were left to the imagination, with the suggestion that some sort of oath-taking orgy was prescribed.'[31]

It was through his body, alive or dead, that the *agonistis* became a hero. Yiannis is said to have taken on two armed soldiers with his shepherd's stick and driven them out of his village. He has dominated village life for 30 years. The *agonistis* displays his identity, in contrast to informers who, Judas-like, betray the identity of others, and arrive hooded with soldiers.[32] He does so with little destructive technology because power resides in him and his body, which is transformed when dead into a sacrificial offering. He is different from the later EOKA B men who hide in tanks, protected by their cold metallic technology of fear, attacking the archbishop's palace. They indulge in overkill, and gut buildings. The *agonistis* displays himself, enforcing his views by his presence, if necessary by his fists. He is even visible at night. His body bears the mark of previous oppressions, personal vendettas against him pursued under the cover of the colonial state. His performance individualises him; he aims to be remembered, just as he remembers past wrongs. By contrast, EOKA B men are masked. It is through the combination of their Kalashnikovs and the mask as a symbol of their non-accountability that they terrorise and swagger across the village square imposing curfews just like the British. Like their masters, the *Anglo-Amerikani*, they are a series of masks behind further masks, the *ksenos daktilos* (the foreign finger). In contrast to the EOKA A *agonistis*, they do not signify themselves as performing individuals. Rather they represent violence, and leave bodies and death in their wake.

The emphasis of Christos' account is that whilst the *agonistis'* body is the greatest sign of his integrity as an ethnic hero (alive through his performance, or even as dead through his sacrificial body), the EOKA B gunmen leave their mark as political fanatics by their dissolution of bodies. Christos uses different words for killing in the two contexts. For the ambush he uses the word *epyase* – caught or took, a word used for hunting or fishing. There is a linkage between the hunter and the hunted; the soldiers are humanised through their suffering, sentient beings with speech, boys with mothers. By contrast for the EOKA B character, Pashis, he used the word *esfakse* – slaughtered, used also for animals, an imagery reinforced by reference to skewers, *souvlas*, etc. The account of the murder of the Turks is emptied of all feeling except anger at the inhumanity of the perpetrator by his dehumanisation of his victims. Feldman, who has analysed narratives of violence in Northern Ireland, identifies an analogous structuration of two models of violence: that of the 'hardman' and that of the paramilitary. 'In the cultural shift from hardman to gunman the relations of visibility and invisibility that govern the relation of the agent of force to the object of force are inverted. The hardman attained visibility through the objectivification of his own body. The paramilitary achieves political visibility by objectifying the bodies of others.'[33] He continues: 'In the hardman tradition the opponent is defined performatively. In the sectarian murder. the victim is defined taxonomically.'[34] The two models of violence can be compared:

Agonistis/Pallikari	*Khasapis/Prodotis*
(Fighter/Brave Young Man)	Butcher/Traitor
EOKA A	EOKA B
Depoliticised violence	Politicized/narrow violence
Nationalist	Traitor
Face (identity) displayed	Face (identity) masked
Individualised performance	Depersonalising performance
Body displayed	Body concealed in tanks or hidden
Voluntary action/offered	Paid, i.e. Bought
Against enemies of *ethnos*	For enemies of *ethnos*
Ready to sacrifice his life	Ready to sacrifice others
Masked informants led to their betrayal	Masked performers
Use of hand and physical force	Displayed guns
Territorialisation of violence	Violence Deterritorialised
(located in and protecting their areas)	(not in their areas – easier to kill victim, chosen precisely because he is not known by killer)
Model: kleftic hero	Model: hired killer

The transformation of the *agonistis* into a martyr culminated through his being killed in action. Here the symbolism of the Christ-like notion of sacrifice emerged. When the first *agonistis* was killed, Foley observed: 'along the route at every village, hundreds knelt in the road, while flowers were heaped on his coffin to shouts of 'Well done!' and 'Long live EOKA!'.[35]

The heaping of flowers on the coffin recalls the *epitafios* – the decoration of Christ's empty tomb with flowers at Easter, symbolising his triumph over death. Forewarned, colonial authorities secretly buried the bodies of *agonistes* killed in action in the central prisons. In response, the places of their killing became places of pilgrimage, and *agonistes* killed in battle were symbolically buried in the village square by the church rather than in the village cemetery. Authorities discovered that posters of the Wanted, especially of *agonistes*, killed by the security forces, moved from being signs of state repression to becoming commemorations of heroes, adorned with flowers and laurel leaves in coffee shops and offices. Candles were lit in churches for captured fighters. Finally, the authorities buried the 16 men executed in the central prisons, rather than returning their bodies to their kin. There was no burial service. In response, memorial services were held in the churches.

The polar images of the *agonistis* and the EOKA B gunman are models from two different periods about action and performance to construct moral discourses about acceptable violence, responsibility, and morality. They are of course almost 'ideal types'. In practice there was a more ambiguous figure in the 1955–59 period – that of the *agonistis* who gets dangerously close to becoming a hired killer, and at the same time fabricating information, or even staging a killing in order to fabricate information. This figure was also an EOKA member and some were involved in dubious activities. Here we enter the murky world of protection rackets, criminality, and informers. And we are dealing with often unattributable killings (which leave 'unwitnessed actions') rather than unambiguous ambushes of the army in the countryside, disclosed through witnessed performances. A notorious example was Nikos Sampson, who shot British soldiers in Nicosia, disposed of his weapon through an accomplice, photographed the bodies and the scene, and sold the photographs to the newspapers as a reporter. Sampson led attacks on Turkish Cypriots in the 1963–64 disturbances, and was installed as Junta Presidential puppet in the 1974 coup.[36] It is this type of shadowy figure that both the Greek Cypriot elite and the Turkish Cypriots condemn. The urban educated elite look(ed) down on *agonistes*. They deny that the fight was mainly carried out by fighters in the countryside, claiming most of the work was done by demonstrations in towns, which focussed world media attention. *Agonistes*, they claim, were 'mercenaries whose families were paid'. This difference reflects resentment at their spectacular political and social mobility following Independence. Indeed, following Independence, some fighter cliques were involved in vendettas and alliances with underworld figures.[37] Their descent into womanizers (*gynekas*) heralded the loss of their public esteem. Another reason may be that in the towns the struggle was pursued more in the morally uncertain and unattributable world of informing, manufacturing evidence and spreading rumour, i.e., it demanded more moral compromises.[38]

Christos' statement ('fear kept the *agona* going') conceals as much as it discloses. It attributes fear with agency and effectivity, and suggests that participants used it with conscious instrumentality. But for people not directly involved there was much greater ambiguity, which may well have reinforced EOKA's programmes, but not in the sense that a simple mechanical reading of 'fear kept the agona going' would suggest. The problem for EOKA was that a killing had to be 'signed' such that its motive and authentification was unambiguous to the public, and that it was authorised. In other words, that the person was killed because he had betrayed the organisation. Certain categories such as communists or village headmen were perceived as lukewarm towards EOKA and more likely to become informants. Cover was available to individuals, either within or outside EOKA, to pursue their own private vendettas, and to combine their 'professional' and 'private' interests. The cellular structure of EOKA made such vendettas more possible. Grivas soon realised this danger and sent out a 'general order' 'saying that unauthorized letters were being sent out by some of his people, threatening death. In future he would personally approve every such letter, and "executions" carried out without his approval would be regarded as murder'.[39] Counter-insurgent groups could also commit killings to discredit EOKA, or plant 'evidence' disguising their agency. EOKA leaflets were illegal, but the authorities soon found it useful to connive in giving them veracity. Authorities presented renegades from EOKA with fake Grivas leaflets. In one particular case a renegade who had betrayed his two companions, was claimed by the authorities to have given them 'a list of one hundred traitors who were due for execution by EOKA. In another week the list had grown to two hundred names from all over the island, said the officials, including many EOKA members and sympathizers who had fallen under suspicion.'[40] This was implausible. The authorities then tried to situate the murder of a *mukhtar* by claiming that he was first on the list, etc. Warnings were sent out to wanted men that their executions had been ordered by Grivas. Some left-wingers were also killed by masked men and, in an attempt to generate a split between AKEL and EOKA, the government claimed that all victims were AKEL members.[41]

The situation became infinitely more complex with the emergence of inter-ethnic mass violence. The upshot is that ambiguity is a critical part of terror. Indeed, perhaps it is the most critical component. All participants had interlocking agendas which encouraged the generation of violence and the fabrication of complex patterns of concealed attribution of violent acts. What made the situation distinctive was that a mass-based movement was involved, and the terror did not have one centre, as in dirty-war Argentina, but multicentres. Paradoxically, conflicting accounts may well reinforce the belief that there are single transcendent truths that can be discovered. Pitt Rivers commented that in Andalusia where lies have much currency, and are expected to be told, individuals develop particular skills to extract what they would consider to be the truth from beneath the tissue of lies. He uses the metaphor of the money changer: it takes a money changer to recognise false currency. We can therefore more fully appreciate the significance of Christos' statement that fear kept the *agona* going. It was not a single mono-causal fear, but fears refracted through prisms of simulation and dissimulation.

In a perceptive review of a leftist critique of the EOKA struggle, Panayiotou has suggested that 'if EOKA had to resort to so much violence against the local population, it must have faced a serious problem of legitimacy'.[42] This is an important assertion, but it circumvents the issue. It was legitimacy *per se* that was being struggled over, not the legitimacy of particular organisations, or particular tactics, despite the fact that we can easily slip into perceiving it in the latter's terms. Terror was a critical feature of the struggle, yet agency was often unsigned, but infinitely attributable. In other words, people were in fear of their lives, but one could never know for certain why a person was killed, and who did so. The stories and interpretations were not incidental to the killings, beatings or warnings, but central to the unfolding of events. They *made* the event historically – i.e. they gave it a historical explanation, and located it causally. A publicly expressed (rather than privately confided) interpretation, nevertheless, entailed a risk for the elocutor. In such highly polarised, violence-prone contexts, it exposed him to criticism and potentially to retribution, because it could lead to subsequent betrayals, threats to life, capture, etc. Interpretations were not value free but politically committing, and potentially life endangering, both for the elocutor and for others.

Here the notion of witnessing is important. By witnessing I mean not merely that one has seen an event, but rather than one makes a socially expressed commitment to a particular interpretation of events. A witness is not a mere observer, but a participant in the shaping of events through their interpretation. This implies risks. It is not just factual accuracy that is at issue, but taking a stand for the truths of which one is convinced. A witness is socially and personally accountable for the truthfulness of his testimony and this testimony has social repercussions. Witnessing is thus a political act. In highly charged contexts where violence was enacted (viewed as crimes by the state and necessary patriotic actions by EOKA), a statement of having witnessed an event was not disinterested, but politically and personally committing for the witness. It is not a statement of fact that emerges out of uncontested observation, but a will to 'truth' that has to be asserted personally against opposition and at personal risk. Witnessing can raise profound moral issues, quite apart from any 'incidental' personal risks (violent retribution, etc.) involved. It also legitimates. One witnesses to whom one holds up as a supreme authority. In the *enosis* struggle one could either witness to the state (by providing information), or witness to EOKA as nationalist struggle (by keeping silent). Witnessing through silence was also witnessing, and could subsequently (and perhaps perversely) be claimed as a positive act of support. In such a highly polarised context both the volunteering or withholding of information, through the interpretation of events, can be considered to be witnessing as the political legitimation of authority. Nor was it necessarily the case that witnessing to the state (upholding 'law'), was the expression of a citizen's duty, whilst witnessing for EOKA (by keeping silent) was a response to intimidation. State law did not have much legitimacy. Both the state and EOKA applied violence and intimidation on ordinary members of the public. Indeed, indiscriminate violence was more likely to be applied by the army, whilst more targeted intimidation practised by EOKA. It was not a matter of upholding 'law' against 'terrorist violence', even though this is how the colonial state presented it, because the state was also involved in the application of violence on the public, directly or indirectly.

The struggle was thus not so much over the control and pacification of violence and the upholding of the rule of law (a scenario preferred by the colonial authorities), but rather over the management of violence, repression and intimidation for the legitimisation of authority. At issue was *whose* authority was upheld (and thus legitimated), through the witnessing of terror (i.e. the giving or withholding of critical information): the state's or EOKA's? Both involved major risks to the individual, and to others. If anti-colonial uprisings are seen merely in terms of the legitimisation of violence, one bypasses how authority is legitimated. It assumes that legitimacy is transcendentally separable from violence, while implicitly maintaining that violence is not separable from legitimacy. To see the issue in terms of the legitimisation of violence is to reproduce the authority of the state in a double Hegelian sense: the state is not seen just as the highest expression of reason/violence, but also the state is the ultimate producer of reason/violence. And this 'reason' takes two forms: it links up the power of the state with violence in almost instrumental, 'reasonable' terms (the state as the ultimate guarantor of the rule of law, as having a 'monopoly of violence' which can ultimately be deployed if it is threatened by illegitimate means), to therefore ensure the 'rule of reason'. Second, it is interiorised such that 'reason' supports this construction. If we accept, following Evans Pritchard, that there is reason in magic, and that there is order outside the state, then we should also be attuned to the possibility that the structuration of violence in the modern state is an aspect of a specific form of reason.[43]

There were thus two critical domains of contestation between the colonial state and EOKA: first, over the legitimisation of violence as a means to an end; and second, over the production, signification and guarding of secrets, in an infinite regression of masks. In setting itself up as a secret organisation, EOKA did not just plumb the depths of a deep seated and historically embedded suspicion of the colonial state. It incised itself as subversive by the very act of displaying itself to the state as a domain of secrecy, surrounded by sacred oaths, to be protected by life and sacrifice, to which the state had no ingress. Killings of 'traitors' were not just 'functional' attempts to ensure compliance, and to guard identities, nor were they just paranoid fears (which they may well have been). In such a climate of fear and secrecy, killings 'created' 'traitors', a belief both EOKA and the colonial state inadvertently conspired to give currency to (although of course they disagreed in its interpretation). It is not so much that 'betrayals' led to retribution (killings); it is rather that killings helped generate the dominant climate of fear of betrayal, and thus provided a ready-made rationale for such violence. Killings were thus signs, signifiers of secrets as secrets with no signifieds, which gave currency to the notions of betrayal, commitment and accountability. Killings dislodged reason and replaced it with fear that searches desperately for other 'proofs' to render such killings 'explicable' – 'reasons' which include betrayal, etc. Violence is as much expressive as instrumental. While EOKA was anti-left, the anonymous and infinitely attributable authorship of killings makes it difficult to prove that there was a systematic policy to do so.[44] Rather than perceiving the establishment of EOKA as a 'counter-revolutionary secret organization' bent on killing them as leftists seem to believe, EOKA violence had the effect of making them think so.

On a more mundane level, it was not so much that EOKA had a serious problem of legitimacy, it was rather that the nationalist struggle in its general outlines did not, and EOKA managed to monopolise spectacular resistance in military and symbolic domains to the massive oppression by the colonial state. By being provoked into hanging young men for just carrying arms the state catapulted itself into an assault on reason. The nationalist struggle effectively uncoupled the power of the state inherent in the equation: reason/violence. The colonial state seemed to be using violence unreasonably such that it 'lost legitimation' in the eyes of the population. Furthermore, it was difficult for individuals to differentiate between opposition to EOKA's violent tactics, and more peaceful means, especially because the Colonial authorities suppressed political agitation and exiled the major political figure, Makarios. Sacrifice of life was an important means whereby EOKA apotheiosised the population through its children. Its claim to fighting for liberation, and fear of retribution guaranteed its effective operation.

The colonial state had a greater problem of 'legitimacy'. Electoral politics had been banned since 1931. By the end of the emergency the colonial administration had lost any shred of local support. Charles Foley, editor of the *Times of Cyprus*, provided a first-hand account of events (1962). Massive repression by colonial authorities contributed to focus collective overt hostility towards the colonial government. The dynamics of massive crushing repression can generate support for such organisations. Repression can itself turn passive complicity into active complicity in support for an organisation. A search in a village for EOKA men that yields nothing (*dhen tous eipame* – 'we didn't tell them'), becomes active complicity in the very act of being recounted ('we hid them' or 'we protected them'). Fear can sometimes conspire with events to turn silence into resistance.

Conclusion

> It is one of the curiosities of Cyprus that things have always happened in the past or are going to happen in the future. The difficulty is to find the moment when they actually happen in the present.
>
> *Lord Radcliffe, Constitutional Commissioner*

This paper has been concerned with the tensions between official rememberings and personal recollections. Both state sponsored nationalist ideology and ordinary people construct narratives about the past, and they intersect and interact in complex ways. There are two conclusions. The first is that the relationship between official rememberings and personal recollections/experiences is highly complex and double-edged. Official (Greek Cypriot) state sponsored views of the past, which is peopled with actors of determinate ethnic identities (Greeks, Turks, etc.), are not only highly selective, but often questioned and subverted by its citizens' narratives of experiences of that past. Others have made this point for other parts of the Greek world.[45] Conversely, personal recollections based upon experiences can reinforce official rememberings. Often, without necessarily wanting to, individuals can help sustain structures of power and memory. The claim 'we got on well with the Turks in the past' is often echoed by personal experiences. One can call this an active complicity in supporting official views. But personal recollections are much more complex, and richer, than officially sponsored history, and individuals also remember violence by Greek Cypriots against the Turkish Cypriots. When individuals mention such inter-communal killings but say to the anthropologist 'don't write this down', they are engaging in passive complicity with officially sponsored accounts. It should be noted that the internationally recognised Republic of Cyprus has hardly attempted to bring Greek Cypriots who killed other Greek Cypriots in 1974 to justice, much less men like Pashis from Paphos who killed other citizens of the state, but of a different ethnic identity. Interestingly, whereas in the immediate post-1960 period the Greek Cypriots were confident in what they wanted to remember, they are now more confident in what they want to forget – mainly the bloodshed in the immediate post-coup period.[46]

Cypriot villagers are divided in how they view the past, the significance of events and the allocation of responsibility. Such differences stem from their political positions. How does one allocate responsibility to others and to oneself? Is this to be on an individual, political, collective or ethnic level? How does a man explain the actions of a co-villager who may have been involved in violent activity or even in some cold-blooded killings? How does that man talk about his own actions? One way they do so is to move from one level to another involving different narratives, often appealing to nationalist ideology. In discussing violence in Cyprus, Peter Loizos points out that 'contexts are essential for understanding even acts like murder'.[47] Certainly, but I would add that these contexts are only made evident, transparent and opaque at the same time, by the stories that men tell. In recounting them they create performances. Such performances are often constrained by the perceived necessity to construct their present and their future in a collective way, certainly in contrast to the Turks. The mythical narratives sponsored by the State about the past paradoxically provide this commonality in the present. Inevitably it is cast in ethnic terms. Greek and Turkish Cypriots thus nominally subscribe to such official myths to create a common present and a common future, well aware that the past is divided and contentious. In contrast to what is normally asserted that nationalism requires the construction of a common past, the example from Cyprus suggests that it needs such myths only to create a common future.

The contrast between the stories villagers told about the *agonistes* and their conscious dissimulation of ever having been an *agonistis*, merits reflection. Yiannis never volunteered information on himself and discouraged questions. Hambis (who was pro-EOKA B) always acted out the role of an irritating ironic fool in public to such an extent that everybody knows that the only way they can deal with him is to humour this persona. This makes the narratives of violence somewhat different to those discussed by Gilsenan for the Lebanon. In contrast to Gilsenan's villagers, men did not talk much about how they talked, partly because such actions were off stage, and were intended to be kept so in order to sustain their power. By expecting people to know and yet not to recount except in intimate contexts, the power of such men was sustained. When such actions slipped into the public domain, as with the case of Pashis and EOKA B, men lost esteem partly because in using such powerful and dangerous resources in forcing through situations at the behest of outsiders, they delegitimated themselves.

Following Michelet and Renan, Anderson has suggested that the modern nation-state needs not just common rememberings, nor just common forgettings, but rather a complicity in remembering to forget.[48] In contrast to tribal societies where there is a complicity in forgetting to remember, the nation-state needs to remind itself constantly and paradoxically of its complicity – first in remembering, and only secondly in forgetting. In other words it is an active process rather than a passive result. To pun on etymology – the nation-state needs to amnesty the past in order to amnesia the present, i.e., forget differences in the present. Tribal society, by contrast, needs to amnesia the past in order to amnesty the present, i.e. forgive differences in the present. The modern nation-state therefore needs not just a common history, nor just to invent it where it is not there, as Gellner suggested, but rather presupposes a specifically novel way of constructing history. The nation-state does not just emerge historically in the evolution of society and polity, but also when the conceptualisation of history (and hence of time) has itself been changed (clearly a by-product of changes in social organisation, industrialisation, literacy, etc.). It is the manipulability of history rather than its falsifiability (as in the classical world) that the nation-state requires, and brings into being as its ultimate ruse of conscious conviviality.

Inspired by one of Michelet's gnomic statements, Anderson calls this process paradoxically 'The Reassurance of Fratricide'.[49] The case of Cyprus is certainly distinct. The fratricide between Greek Cypriots in the pre- and immediate post-coup period is forgotten by the state, whilst the ethnicide by the Greek Cypriots such as Pashis on Turkish Cypriots is recalled officially by both the people and the state as a fraternal conviviality: 'we got on well with the Turks like brothers' (*san adelphia*), while the ethnicide by the Turks on the Greek Cypriots is remembered – indeed not forgotten. Ethnic fratricide is forgotten, while ethnicide is remembered as fratriphilia masquerading as ethnophilia. It is surely ironic that the Greek Cypriots are obliged to remember and imagine the basis of the state as a fratriphilia ('we got on well....') before the pernicious malignant effects of ethno-nationalism ('The Turks were asleep we woke them up') destroyed that very state. But the 'lesson' of nationalist historiography is that the horror and terror of fratricide must be remembered to create an imaginable fraternity in terms of a common ethnicity. The nation-state in Cyprus has been an imagined community, but in a completely different sense to that outlined by Anderson. It has always been an imagined community in the past, or in the future – never in the divisive present. One can perhaps therefore more fully appreciate the frustrations of the British Constitutional Commissioner that things in Cyprus always seemed to happen in the past, or the future and rarely in the present.

NOTES

Various versions and sections of this paper were delivered at seminars at the Universities of Cambridge, Oxford, Durham, and King's College, London. I should like to thank the participants and in particular Roderick Beaton, John Davis, Stuart Holland, David Holton, Robert Layton, Peter Loizos and Yiannis Papadakis for their comments. Persisting errors for interpretation and fact are mine alone.

1. Edward Bruner, 'Experience and Its Expressions', in V. Victor Turner and Edward Bruner (eds), *The Anthropology of Experience* (Chicago: University of Illinois Press 1986) p.144.
2. Jerome Bruner and Susan Weisser, 'The Invention of Self: Autobiography and its Forms', in David Olsen and Nancy Torrance (eds), *Literacy and Orality* (Cambridge: University Press 1991).
3. Paul Veyne, *Writing History. Essay on Epistemology* (Manchester: Manchester University Press) p.88.
4. Ibid., p.229.
5. P. Burke, 'History as Social Memory', in T. Butler (ed.), *Memory* (Oxford: Blackwell 1989) p.100.
6. Ibid., p.111.
7. R. Werbner, 'Human Rights and Moral Knowledge. Arguments of accountability in Zimbabwe', in M. Strathern (ed.), *Shifting Contexts* (London: Routledge 1997) p.13.
8. Anderson suggests that 'the British consciously permitted TMT to operate as a counterfoil to EOKA'. David M. Anderson, 'Policing and Communal Conflict: The Cyprus Emergency, 1954–60', *Journal of Imperial and Commonwealth History* 21/3 (Sept. 1993) pp.177–207.
9. Holland has noted that 'ever since the Lausanne treaty of 1923 the colonial government in Nicosia had been very careful to avoid giving the slightest hint to Turkey that there might be a chance for it to put a foot back in the Cypriot door' (p.164). 'Hotting up the Turks' he notes 'became a feature of British tactics after 1954 as the prospect of Greek recourse to the UN became real' (p.164). Robert Holland, 'Never, Never Land: British Colonial Policy and the Roots of Violence in Cyprus, 1950-54', *Journal of Imperial and Commonwealth History* 21/3 (Sept. 1993) pp.148–176.
10. S. Panteli, *A New History of Cyprus* (London: East-West Publications 1984) p.392.
11. P. Sant Cassia, 'Patterns of Covert Politics in Cyprus', *European Journal of Sociology* 24 (1983) pp.115–35.
12. Ian Martin, 'The "Cyprus Troubles" 1955–1960', *Kampos. Cambridge Papers in Modern Greek* 1 (1991) pp.65–84.
13. Peter Loizos, *The Greek Gift* (Oxford: Basil Blackwell 1975). Paul Sant Cassia, 'Patterns of Politics and Kinship in a Greek Cypriot Community, 1920–1980', Unpublished PhD Dissertation, Cambridge, 1981.
14. Loizos, *Greek Gift* (note 13).
15. M. Drousiotis, *EOKA. I Skoteini Opsi* (Athens: Staxy 1988).
16. P. Connerton, *How Societies Remember* (Cambridge: CUP 1989). Y. Papadakis, 'The Politics

of Remembering and Forgetting', *Journal of Mediterranean Studies* 3/1 (1993).

17. R.N. Bellah, R. Madsen, W.M. Sullivan, A. Swidler and S.M. Tipton, *Habits of the Heart: Individualism and Commitment in American Life* (Berkeley: University of California Press 1985).
18. D. Middleton and D. Edwards, *Collective Remembering* (London: Sage 1990) p.10.
19. Charles Foley, *Island in Revolt* (London: Longmans 1962).
20. Cf. Holland (note 9) pp.158–9.
21. H. White, 'The Value of Narrativity in the Representation of Reality', in W.J.T. Mitchell (ed.), *On Narrative* (Chicago: University of Chicago Press 1981) p.14.
22. P. Ricoeur, 'Narrative Time', in Mitchell (note 21) p.184.
23. Ricoeur, ibid. Freud called a 'screen memory' – 'a "memory" of unity, plenitude manufactured and mapped out onto the past in order to disguise a present anxiety'.
24. A. Feldman, *Formations of Violence* (Chicago: University of Chicago Press 1991) p.18.
25. Peter Loizos (personal communication) has pointed out to me that this is a Greek trope.
26. Foley (note 19) p.210. The independent minded editor of the *Times of Cyprus* gave an account of this incident and the response by the soldiers to the ambush.
27. M. Gilsenan, *Lords of the Lebanese Marches* (London: I.B. Tauris 1996).
28. J.K. Campbell, 'The Greek Hero', in J.G. Peristiany and Julian Pitt-Rivers (eds), *Honour and Grace in Anthropology* (Cambridge: CUP 1992).
29. Women members were not allowed to wear lipstick, and had their heads shaved if it was believed they had done wrong.
30. Cf. G. Hadjikostis, *Evagoras Pallikaridhes. O Iroas kai o Poiitis* (Nicosia: Kostas Epiphaniou 3rd ed., 1984).
31. Foley (note 19) p.163.
32. Foley (note 19) p.186.
33. Feldman (note 24) p.54.
34. Ibid.
35. Foley (note 19) p.50.
36. The causality of the shootings being staged for images thus predates the Gulf and Bosnian wars, with the difference that whereas the staged killings are photographed after the event and can thus capture the horror on the faces of the spectators, the video bombs anaesthetise the viewer who views the target as object before the carnage.
37. Cf. Drousiotis (note 15).
38. Many people could play a double game: one EOKA informer framed both recommendations given him by the Governor and Grivas.
39. Foley (note 19) p.56.
40. Ibid., pp.159–60.
41. Ibid., p.177. Interestingly, extreme right wing supporters of EOKA appear to believe that AKEL and the communists did betray the struggle. In this they paradoxically appear to substantiate AKEL members' claims that EOKA had a conscious policy to exterminate leftists, or at least that killings of leftists were justified.
42. A. Panayiotou, 'History without Taboos', *The Cyprus Review* 6/1 (1994) pp. 89–98, esp. p.94.
43. See M. Taussig, *The Nervous System* (London: Routledge 1992) p.115.
44. One would therefore have expected more examples of these unambiguous killings. At the same time because there are sufficient examples of the killings of leftists, it is easier to maintain this belief, especially because leftists expect there to be little evidence, or more precisely for that evidence to be concealed, and thus validate their initial belief. My own view is that communists were both predisposed to be lukewarm towards the struggle, and pre-scripted by EOKA leaders to be traitorous and hence infinitely more suspect. Thus while for EOKA the killing of leftists may have been even paranoid responses to 'fear of betrayal', to the public they provided the causology of death as traitorhood, while for leftists they provided a victimology. Furthermore, leftist accounts of EOKA bypass the fact that some leftists joined EOKA and the populist goal of *enosis* had the support of the majority of the population, including officially AKEL.
45. M. Herzfeld, *The Poetics of Manhood* (Princeton: Princeton University Press 1985).

46. Indeed, so pressing has this need become that recently there has been an attempt to group together 'the fallen' from both 1955–59 and 1974 (those who gave their lives resisting the Turkish invasion). This offers ambiguous glory to both the extreme right and left. To the extreme right, an overly enthusiastic hagification for those who died in 1974 can seem like a coded form of criticism, because (i) they can be imputed to have brought about their deaths through having provoked the Turkish invasion, and (ii) some of the fallen may have in fact been killed by the coupists, not the Turks. The monuments thus can in certain contexts appear as profoundly anti-EOKA and profoundly anti-Greek nationalist, partly because EOKA B drew some legitimisation from EOKA A. This seems to have happened recently in the left-wing mining village of Mitsero where a monument to the six men who died in 1974 was strongly objected to by the right wing. Monuments derive their meaning as much from contexts of interpretation, as from what they actually depict. For the left this grouping together can appear offensive because it commemorates the deaths of those who were sacrificed by the right wing and turns them into heroes together with the first EOKA people, who they view as anti-left.
47. P. Loizos, 'An Intercommunal Killing in Cyprus', *Man* 23 (1988) p.650.
48. Benedict Anderson, *Imagined Communities*, 2nd ed. (London: Verso 1991).
49. Ibid., p.199.

[10]

Terrorist Tales

Gerald Cromer

Context

A Verbal Strategy

Modern terrorists have tended to minimize the effect of words. Peter Kropotkin (1978: 93–5), for instance, contended that they get lost in the air, like the empty chiming of bells. Actions, on the other hand, awaken the spirit of revolt. He therefore sang the praises of those men of courage who are not satisfied with words and are ever searching for the means to transform ideas into actions. Just one daring deed of theirs, Kropotkin insisted, may in a few days make more propaganda than one thousand pamphlets.

Notwithstanding their glorification of the deed, Kropotkin and other terrorists by no means abandoned the use of words to further their cause. In fact Johannes Most (1978: 106) insisted that, once an action was carried out, the most important thing is that the world learn about it from the revolutionaries. He therefore urged his colleagues to put up posters setting out the reasons for their actions in order to make them palatable to the people. It is this, above all, Most concluded, which puts the reactionaries in a rage.

Scholars of terrorism have been deeply influenced by the anarchist concept of the propaganda of the deed. Hence their emphasis on terrorism as theatre and the fact that it is aimed at the people watching rather than at the actual victims (Schmid and de Graaf, 1982; Weimann, 1994). Researchers have paid much less attention, however, to the terrorist's 'love–hate relationship with language' (Miller, 1983: 346) and the fact that their violent strategy is invariably backed up by a verbal one.[1] In contrast to the plethora of research on the media coverage of terrorism, very few studies have been carried out on terrorist propaganda. Despite the fact that the latter is widely regarded as the hallmark of political terrorism (Watson, 1975: 1) it has been almost completely neglected.

Propaganda campaigns, like the actions they are meant to explain, are aimed at a variety of audiences. Even though the desired end is different in each case, terrorist propaganda has an overall objective, the progressive movement to increasing levels of commitment to the aims of the group (Wright, 1990: 166). The ultimate goal is therefore to create a cadre of activists who are characterized by total and unquestioning loyalty to the terrorists' cause. These true believers have to justify their resort to violence, both in their own eyes and in the eyes of others. They are engaged in propaganda and autopropaganda at one and the same time (Cordes, 1988: 151). And as Jacques Ellul (1971: 29–30) has pointed out, the latter sets in motion a continuous interaction or, to be more precise, an upward spiral, between words and deeds. 'He who acts in obedience to propaganda can never go back. He is now obliged to *believe* in that propaganda ... to continue to advance in the direction indicated by propaganda, for action demands more action ... and he gets more deeply involved by repeating the act in order to prove that it was just.'[2]

Joanne Wright (1990) and others have tried to differentiate between propaganda themes according to the kind of audience involved. However, there does not seem to be a clearcut distinction between them. Most of the material is of a multipurpose nature, and even those publications that are geared to a particular audience – either the uncommitted, sympathetic or active ones – are not really distinctive. The kind of terrorist group disseminating the information is, it seems, a much more important variable in this regard.

Ideological terrorists are widely regarded as being more radical than their nationalist/separatist counterparts. Ehud Sprinzak (1991a: 52), for instance, has argued that they are characterized by transformational and extensional delegitimation, respectively. The former process is both more sudden and more far-reaching. It involves a complete break with society and a total personal metamorphosis. In order to understand why this is the case it is necessary to look at the terrorists' relationship to their parents' generation.

> There would seem to be a profound difference between terrorists bent on destroying their own society, the 'world of their fathers', and those whose terrorist activities carry on the mission of their fathers. To put it in other words, for some, becoming terrorists is an act of retaliation for real and imagined hurts *against the society of their parents*; for others, it is an act of retaliation against society *for the hurt done to their parents*. For some, it is *an act of dissent against parents loyal to the regime*; for others, *an act of loyalty to parents damaged by the regime*. (Post: 1984: 243)

This contrast finds clear expression in the propaganda of the two kinds of terrorist groups. Thus, in her comparative analysis of the Red Army Faction and the Provisional IRA, Joanne Wright (1990: 21) drew attention to the fact that ideological movements are forward-looking and make few historical references. Nationalist and separatist groups, on the other hand, are backward-looking. They tend to idealize past generations and revere ancient heroes. Whilst the present study suggests that this dichotomy is, in fact, less clearcut, it does provide a suitable framework for reviewing the research on terrorist propaganda.

Accounts

Previous studies have presented a rather haphazard picture of terrorist propaganda and autopropaganda. Bandura's (1990) analysis of mechanisms of moral disengagement is the only one that provides some kind of order by placing them at different points in the self-regulatory process. For the purposes of the present study, however, it is more instructive to consider the kinds of arguments used under two broad headings: images of self and images of others. As Richard Leeman (1991: 46) has pointed out, terrorist propaganda 'constructs a bipolar world which clearly divides between good and evil'. Consequently, it is best conceived of as a kind of morality play in which the forces of light are pitted against the forces of darkness.

Terrorists occasionally resort to the language of non-responsibility (Bandura, 1990: 170). In particular, they use the agentless passive form in order to portray their violent actions as the work of impersonal forces rather than as the result of human choice. However, this kind of response is the exception rather than the rule. Terrorists invariably use justifications rather than excuses; they accept responsibility for their actions but deny the pejorative quality associated with them (Scott and Lyman, 1968: 47).[3] Hence the war of labels, in which terrorists refer to themselves as an army, guerillas or freedom fighters, is not just a matter of semantics. It is indicative of the fact that terrorists feel that right, if not might, is on their side.

Moral justifications tend to take the form of what Sykes and Matza (1957: 669) referred to in a somewhat different context as an appeal to higher loyalties. Engaging in violence, although illegal, is legitimate. Breaking the law, terrorists insist, is permissible, even admirable, because it is in accordance with a more important norm. Invariably terrorists reinforce this moral argument with the pragmatic one that it is impossible to defeat the enemy by peaceful means. Engaging in terror is the only way to achieve the movement's goal. It is the strategy of last resort (Cordes, 1988: 156).

Terrorists also exploit the contrast principle in order to influence moral judgment of their actions. Thus in certain instances they compare themselves with leaders of democracies born of violence against aggressive rule (Bandura, 1990: 171) or with other illustrious revolutionaries of the past such as Karl Marx and Che Guevara (Cordes, 1988: 160–61). More frequently, however, these advantageous comparisons are of a negative nature.

4 *Narratives of Violence*

Terrorists devote more of their propaganda to provocation stories and other unfavorable depictions of the enemy than they do to favorable portrayals of themselves (Miller, 1987: 392; Picard, 1991: 94–7). Attacks of this kind divert attention from their own violent actions and, more pertinently, blame them on the state (Tugwell, 1982: 275–6). Their resort to violence, the terrorists argue, is a justifiable reaction against particular actions of the government or/and the structural violence of the system as a whole (Leeman, 1991: 46–51).

This condemnation of condemners (Sykes and Matza, 1957: 668) finds its clearest expression in the war of labels between terrorists and the state. In many instances this battle is not limited to the renaming or recharacterization of the enemy. Rather than simply depicting the state and its representatives in negative terms, terrorist propaganda refers to them in exactly the same way as they themselves are labeled – as terrorists, criminals and even subhumans.[4]

Dehumanization of the enemy is, in fact, a central theme in terrorist propaganda and autopropaganda alike (Bandura, 1990: 180–82). Divesting their adversaries of human qualities and referring to them as barbarians or beasts of one kind or another can, of course, be an account (Scott and Lyman, 1968) and a technique of neutralization (Sykes and Matza, 1957) at one and the same time. It would seem, however, that terrorists resort to this particular kind of rhetoric in order to justify their actions in their own eyes rather than in the eyes of others. Portraying the enemy as a whole or the direct victim of violence as less than human can be a particularly effective mechanism of moral disengagement. Terrorists are led to believe that they are simply giving the pigs what they deserve.

Terrorist propaganda, like any other morality play, does not simply pit the forces of light against the forces of darkness; it also relates to the outcome of the conflict between them. With good on their side, the terrorists will surely defeat the enemy who is, after all, the incarnation of evil. The battle may, of course, be a long and bitter one, but success is assured. It is just a matter of time. Despite the seemingly insurmountable odds, victory is inevitable (Tugwell, 1986: 6; Wright, 1990: 144–6, 158–61).

Projective Narratives

Studies of the propaganda of nationalist and separatist movements draw attention to the widespread tendency amongst academics to politicize terrorism.[5] Whilst this approach may be suitable for the analysis of ideologically oriented groups it is thought to be totally inappropriate for the study of nationalist ones. Political reductionism, Tololyan (1988) and others have argued, fails to take account of the extent to which nationalist groups are an integral part of the wider cultural context. Terrorist propaganda is intertextual, and it is therefore imperative to consider the different ways in which it is in dialogue with mainstream national discourse and the master narratives of the culture in question.

The cultural specificity of each movement makes it difficult to generalize about this kind of terrorist propaganda. Nevertheless, a review of the few studies that have been carried out suggests that it is possible to delineate certain similarities in the way in which different nationalist/separatist movements try to justify their resort to violence. For the purposes of analysis they are best considered under two broad headings, the construction of histories and life histories, and the appropriation of religion.

The propaganda of all nationalist and separatist movements is replete with historical references. The terrorists and their enemies, both external and internal, are compared to famous and infamous figures from bygone days. Consequently, the analogies always take the form of narratives about earlier examples of resistance to oppression (Barnur, 1998: 64–70). Telling these stories constitutes what Tololyan (1988: 219) has referred to in his groundbreaking study of the ASALA (Armenian Secret Liberation Army) as a process of mediation. Particular events are not conceived of as mere political facts. They are rather perpetuated and disseminated as narratives that help to clarify the present situation. Aretxaga's (1993: 244–5) conclusions regarding the IRA (Irish Republican Army) are therefore of more general significance: 'Individual experience is embedded in collective memory as a frame of interpretation … History makes meaningful the present as it unfolds in existential experience, directing action in the world.'

Clearly, the resort to history is not simply meant to help understand old feats of heroism but also to engender new ones. Terrorist propaganda hails past acts of bravery and resistance in order to encourage similar actions in the present. It therefore consists of a series of projective narratives that are descriptive and prescriptive at one and the same time.

> They not only tell a story of the past but also map out future actions that can imbue the time of individual lives with collective values … dictate biographies and autobiographies to come … tell individuals how they would ideally have to live and die in order to contribute properly to their collectivity and its future. (Tololyan, 1988: 218)

Projective narratives of the ideal life and death are backed up by a martyrology (Zameret, 1974: 85–8) or regulative biographies (Tololyan, 1988: 230) of those who personified them. Thus the life histories of those who fell in the struggle for independence are constructed in such a way that they can be portrayed as examples of the national ideal. Those who are engaged in violence are depicted not as outcasts from society but as paradigmatic figures of its deepest values. They are to be praised rather than punished for their actions.

This particular reading of history and life histories is, of course, very different from earlier ones, especially that of the religious authorities. Their concentration on divine intervention, for instance, is replaced by an emphasis on human action or what Schatzberger (1985: 57) referred to as the motif of the active deed. Notwithstanding this and other disagreements, the terrorists find it difficult to attack the defenders of the faith head on. If and when they do so, their criticism is often couched in religious terms. Nationalist and separatist propaganda is replete with symbols made effective by centuries of ecclesiastic rhetoric and practice.[6]

As a result of this tendency to appropriate religious language and rituals, traditional models are rarely discarded. They are rather transformed and infused with new meanings (Aretxaga, 1993: 240; Arthur, 1996: 272). Thus the Haganah, Etzel and Lehi – the three movements that fought against the British mandate in Palestine – reinterpreted and/or adapted a wide variety of religious precepts, texts and rituals in their attempt to undermine the traditional understanding of them (Schatzberger, 1985: 38–46).[7] Although the concepts of sacrifice and martyrdom are as central to the propaganda of both the ASALA and the IRA as they are to church sermons and other forms of religious discourse, the message conveyed is exactly the opposite. Sacrifice is redefined as heroic death and hailed as the harbinger of national renewal. Consequently, resignation to suffering in this world is derided. Active resistance to oppression and the creation of a better world is the order of the day (Aretxaga, 1993: 244; Tololyan, 1987: 100).

By attacking traditional religion in this way, nationalist and separatist groups clearly damage the authority of the church and synagogue. However, this is only half the story. Paradoxically perhaps, the terrorists' offensive against the spiritual authorities endows their violent actions with a religious aura of their own. By using the vocabulary and imagery of the church they secularize religious myths and sanctify their own cause at one and the same time (Tololyan, 1987: 95; Arthur, 1996: 276–7).

Previous studies (Schatzberger, 1985; Zameret, 1974) indicate that the propaganda of the three movements that fought against the British mandate in Palestine was essentially similar to that of other nationalist movements. They do suggest, however, that their appeal to both history and tradition was more intricate and more varied than that of the ASALA and IRA. To discover the extent to which this was in fact the case, it was decided to conduct a comprehensive analysis of the propaganda of Lehi (Lohamei Herut Yisrael/ Fighters for the Freedom of Israel) – the most extreme of the three groups – with regard to both its ends and the means it used to achieve them.

The core of this chapter takes the form of an analysis of the contemporary, historical/metahistorical and biographical narratives told to justify Lehi's resort to violence, and the movement's continuing dialogue with the traditional religious discourse. These thick descriptions provide the basis for the development of models of the internal structure of terrorist tales, the interaction between them and the different ways in which they relate to opposing narratives. However, before presenting the results of the study it is necessary to provide a short description of Lehi's two fronts, 'the front of fire and blood against the external British enemy' and 'the front of persuasion and propaganda against opponents and the apathetic at home'. A brief introduction of this nature is an essential prerequisite for understanding everything that follows.

Fire and Blood

With the outbreak of the Second World War in September 1939 the leaders of the yishuv (the pre-state Jewish settlement in Palestine) found themselves in a serious dilemma. They were caught between 'the hammer of the White Paper and the anvil of the war' (Lev-Ami, 1979: 130). The British government which earlier in the year had placed rigid restrictions on Jewish immigration, land purchase and settlement, was now in the forefront of the struggle against Nazi Germany. The official policy of the Jewish Agency was 'to fight Hitler as if there was no White Paper and to fight the White Paper as if there was no war'. In practice, however, the leaders of the yishuv only adhered to the first part of this declaration. They supported the war effort against Germany and the other Axis powers and called a halt to the struggle against the mandatory authorities.

Etzel (Irgun Zva Leumi/National Military Organization) which was associated with the right-wing Revisionist movement also announced a cessation of hostilities. Within a short time, though, this conciliatory stance toward the British led to a rift within the Irgun. Avraham/Yair Stern,[8] the movement's emissary to the Jewish community in Poland, insisted that the armed struggle against the mandatory authorities continue unabated. After a period of intensive infighting, he formed a rival group, the National Military Organization in the Land of Israel. After fierce competition over conscripts and arms supplies, Yair found himself at the head of a tiny and poorly equipped group of fighters who were determined to be the vanguard of the struggle against the British mandate in Palestine.

Drawing attention to the traditional British policy of divide and rule, Yair argued that Whitehall, and not the local Arab leaders, constituted the major obstacle to the establishment of a Jewish state. There was, he insisted, an irreconcilable clash of interests between the British Empire and those of the yishuv. There was no possibility, therefore, of any form of cooperation or even compromise between the two sides. The yishuv had to continue the armed struggle until the British were forced to relinquish the League of Nations mandate and leave the Promised Land to its rightful owners.

Yair and his followers did not only adopt a more militant stance towards the mandatory authorities. They also cited different reasons for taking up arms against them. It was the British presence in Palestine rather than the way they behaved there that made it imperative to join 'the front for sovereignty in the Land of Israel'.

> What and where is the war front of the Hebrew people? Who is the enemy and what is the aim? ... The problem is one of domination here in the land. Not only because British rule is bad, but because it is foreign. We are not fighting the White Paper but the situation that makes it possible. We are not fighting the decrees but those who make them ... The truth about liberation throughout the generations is: sovereignty is a means to implement an idea. Whilst the power is in foreign hands, there is no value to the enterprise. (Fighters for the Freedom of Israel (1982), 1: 121–2)

This emphasis on the very existence of the mandate reflected Yair's stance on the raison d'être of the Zionist movement. Referring to 'the natural striving of every nation to a free homeland', he took exception to the rationale of other strands of Zionism.

> Why are the Polish, French and Greeks fighting? To solve the Polish, Greek or French problem? No! They are fighting to free their homeland and to achieve independence in it as a cultural goal in its own right, and not in order to solve a problem ... Not a solution to the problem of the people but a solution to the problem of the land. (Fighters for the Freedom of Israel (1982), 1: 137)

Stern and his followers were therefore unwilling to accept any form of partition or even to settle for the whole of mandatory Palestine. The boundaries of the Jewish state were to be in accordance with the divine promise to Abraham – from the river of Egypt to the great river, the river Euphrates: 'The land that was ours will be ours. All of it.'

Setting out to achieve these ends, the National Military Organization in Israel first carried out a number of bank robberies in order to gain the funds needed to finance its operations against British personnel and installations. These attacks led to constant harassment by the mandatory authorities and the eventual imprisonment and/or killing of most members of the fledgling movement. Stern and his followers were also ostracized by the yishuv because of their insistence on continuing the armed struggle against the British, and the fact that two of their operations led to the inadvertent killing of Jews. With the murder of Yair by CID officers in February 1942, the organization ceased to function. It was 'almost the end of the road' (Ivianski, 1991: 158).

Seven months later, a number of prominent members of the movement escaped from the British detention camp, Mizra, and began to rebuild it. Renamed Lohamei Herut Yisrael/Fighters for the Freedom of Israel, the movement was now run by a triumvirate. Yitzhak Shamir was responsible for the day-to-day organization and operation of the movement, Natan Yellin-Mor took charge of external relations and Yisrael Eldad headed the propaganda effort. Under their leadership Lehi entered its period of maturity (Ginosar, 1985: 8). The new leadership followed in Yair's footsteps with regard to both the ends of the movement and the means used to achieve them. However, they were not placed beyond the pale in the same way. The times were changing.

The lessening threat and eventual demise of Nazi Germany gave the leaders of the yishuv more room for maneuver. The growing awareness of Britain's responsibility for the death of thousands of Jews as a result of its restrictive policy and the subsequent disillusionment with the anti-Zionist policies of the new post-war Labour administration prompted a revival of the armed struggle against the British government. Etzel and Lehi began to cooperate with each other in July 1945, and four months later they formed the Hebrew Resistance Movement with the mainstream Haganah. Although Lehi remained by far the smallest and the most extreme of the three groups, it had a radicalizing effect on its larger and more moderate counterparts. They too went onto the attack against the British mandate in Palestine.

These forms of cooperation were short-lived and often fraught with tension. The more extreme cases of individual terror such as the assassination of Lord Moyne, the British resident minister in the Middle East, were vehemently condemned by the leaders of the yishuv. Even in these instances, though, the response to Lehi's actions was by no means unequivocal. In fact the defiant court appearances of the two assassins and other movement activists engendered a certain amount of respect for their total commitment to the cause.

Sometimes together, sometimes separately, and sometimes even at loggerheads with each other, the three movements forced the British government to relinquish its mandate over Palestine. Two weeks after the establishment of the State of Israel, Lehi joined the Israeli Defence Forces as a separate unit. A small group continued to operate in Jerusalem but they were forced to disband after the assassination of Count Bernadotte, the United Nations mediator. With that operation, Lehi exploits and the movement as a whole came to an end.[9]

10 *Narratives of Violence*

Propaganda and Persuasion

In order to show that its actions were rooted in 'deep ideological concepts and cold political logic', Lehi's violent strategy was accompanied by a verbal one. The 'language of firearms' went hand-in-hand with 'a verbal attack'. Each was regarded as an indispensable ingredient in the struggle for independence. Thus the lead article in the first issue of *Hamaas* (The Deed) declared:

> The Fighters for the Freedom of Israel teach the doctrine of deeds. This paper will undertake one part of the work of instruction. The deeds themselves, written in blood in the war for the homeland, will carry out the other part. The blood and the war will be an example and a model. The writing on paper will accompany the armed struggle. They will flourish together. Both of them will awaken and demand: Join, because the time has arrived – *for action*! (Fighters for the Freedom of Israel (1982), 1:326)

Lehi leaders praised the movement's propaganda campaign in the same way as they did the actions it was meant to explain. Thus they hailed potential recruits who endangered themselves putting up posters against the orders of the mandatory authorities and thereby demonstrated their suitability for carrying out even more dangerous tasks as fully-fledged members of the movement. Lehi publications also included tributes to those who continued working in the propaganda campaign. They drew attention to both the increase in circulation of the movement's publications and their growing influence on public opinion. British attempts to thwart Lehi's propaganda efforts were frequently cited as the clearest indication of the vital role they played in the struggle against the mandatory authorities.

Event-related communiqués (Miller, 1987: 390) were published after most terrorist actions. Although often embellished in one way or another, they always included three items: a claim of responsibility, followed by an explanation of the rationale for the action and a warning that similar ones would be carried out in the future if the movement's demands were not met.

Much of Lehi's propaganda effort was directed to the publication of a series of newspapers for the yishuv in general and the younger generation in particular.[10] These were devoted to the coverage of, and commentary on, current events. Other printed material published on a less regular basis was of three kinds: pamphlets in memory of Yair and others killed or executed by the British, protocols of the trials of Lehi members and doctrinal texts explaining the movement's stance on a wide range of ideological and political issues.

'The Voice of Fighting Israel, Voice for Liberating Israel' went on the air every Monday and Tuesday evening for between 15 and 20 minutes. The broadcasts included the movement's response to current events and its stance on more long-term issues. In this case, however, the medium was more important than the message. Listeners were thought to be influenced by the mystery of a secret radio station in general, and the oratory of the announcers in particular. Natan Yellin-Mor (1974: 292), who wrote the script for the broadcasts, felt that they represented the two sides of Lehi.

> Ilana (Geula Cohen) – the fervent enthusiasm, the exhilaration that can prime fighters for any action, the emotions that can determine life and death, the element that is beyond reason and reckoning. Gad (Natan Marpish) – the masculine element, the unwavering belief in final victory, the convincing argument, the resoluteness to move towards the danger and victory with open eyes.[11]

Both the different kinds of written material and the radio broadcasts were conceived of as propaganda, 'an answer to the waverers', and autopropaganda, 'a conceptual basis for armed actions and the instincts and feelings that precipitate them'.[12] The campaign as a whole, in common with that of other terrorist groups, was meant to encourage a gradual increase in commitment to the movement's cause. The aim was 'to inculcate the idea of a war of liberation amongst the masses by transforming their unconscious support into conscious awareness, and turning this awareness into a commitment to action'.

With the exception of a number of pamphlets on internal matters such as methods for ensuring secrecy and educational curricula, Lehi publications were not designed with a specific audience in mind. They were almost all directed at the yishuv in general, and even those that were earmarked for a particular group (such as 'for the rank and file' or 'an answer to the skeptics') were in no way distinctive. For the purposes of this study, therefore, Lehi propaganda can be treated as a single unit of analysis. There is no need to differentiate between one source and another.

Fortunately, almost all the material published by Lehi has been collected in two volumes under the title, *Fighters for the Freedom of Israel (1982), Collected Works*. They constitute the subject matter of this study. As naturally occurring rather than provoked material,[13] these writings provide a non-distorted view of Lehi's credo. Written in situ, they afford what is undoubtedly the most authentic picture of the movement.

12 *Narratives of Violence*

Text

The Supreme Command

Time and again Lehi propaganda pointed to the failure of both political and practical Zionism. Neither of them had succeeded in bringing the British mandate to an end. It was necessary, and therefore justifiable, to use force against the 'foreign ruler'. That was the only way to achieve freedom and independence.

> Those for whom the future of the homeland and the nation are dearer than anything else in the world decided not to be deterred by the power of the enemy, and to go to war over the right to a life of freedom and independence. A real war. A war of victims and blood, because all other means failed. The hopes of achieving the end by peaceful means, by negotiation and pleading have been dashed. There is only one solution. Liberating force. (Fighters for the Freedom of Israel (1982), 1: 941)

But Lehi's use of violence was not only defended as a strategy of last resort. Movement leaders and rank-and-file members alike tended to vindicate themselves on moral rather than pragmatic grounds. In order to do so they had to justify the fact that they both violated the laws of the British mandatory authorities and rejected the authority of the organized yishuv.

The British laws regarding Palestine were invariably portrayed as being violent and therefore illegitimate. According to Lehi, they were contrary to the stipulations of the mandate and, even more importantly, they were unjust and immoral.[14] Movement activists who were brought to trial therefore rejected the jurisdiction of the courts. They neither denied their actions nor offered excuses for having committed them. Without exception they insisted on being recognized as a belligerent party and being tried as prisoners of war, or they totally rejected the right of the British to sit in judgment.

> The issue is not whether or not a Jew is hung. It is not a question as to whether a Jew is sentenced to five or fifteen years' imprisonment. The issue is much deeper and more painful – deeper than the gallows and more painful than prison. Who is the judge, and who is the hangman here? (Fighters for the Freedom of Israel (1982), 1: 742)

This rejection of the ephemeral British laws went hand-in-hand with an appeal to 'the sphere of eternal ideas such as freedom, liberty and equality'. Thus Lehi members swore allegiance to 'the law of the movement of Hebrew freedom fighters' and adhered to 'the supreme command, the command of life for our people'. Its authority, they argued, derived from the natural law concerning 'the right of each nation to freedom in its homeland, and to fight against the oppressor and the exploiter'.[15] This supreme law took precedence over all others.[16]

Lehi leaders were convinced that they 'gave expression to the unconscious desire of the entire nation'. The fact that the movement was supported by only a very small minority of the yishuv was attributable to everybody else's 'lack of courage to say openly what is hidden in their heart'. Lehi therefore had to help them express their feelings and thereby come to the realization that they did, in fact, support the movement's actions.[17] There was, however, no need to wait for the process to reach fruition. Lehi could, indeed should, continue to act in accordance with 'the law of the Hebrew Underground' because 'those who fight must not expect the support of the majority or seek the love of the masses'.[18]

Despite their belief in the need to assume the role of the vanguard, Lehi leaders were sensitive to the widespread criticism of their unauthorized actions. Hence the frequent reference to the danger of 'obedience for the sake of obedience'. They contended that compliance with the majority is just a means to an end. As 'a principle independent of content' it can easily deteriorate into a kind of idol worship or fascism, and must therefore be avoided at all costs. Disobedience is in certain situations both necessary and commendable.[19]

Lehi propaganda related to doctrinal dissension as an indispensable feature of 'fighting movements'. It enables them to move from 'conceptual chaos' to ideological clarity and, in turn, to create the appropriate framework for the struggle for national independence. In an article suitably subtitled 'an answer to the waverers', Lehi described this process of 'ideological differentiation' and explained its positive functions:

> Every fighting movement goes through many transformations until it achieves its goal. If it has not reached perfection, if its leaders deviate from the correct path, the thousands have to separate from the tens of thousands. If they disappoint, the hundreds will undoubtedly leave the thousands and seek a new way and a separate framework. This is not a disaster. On the contrary, it is a historical necessity that cannot be escaped and should not be prevented. The separate groups, that are split and disunited, do not delay realization [of the fighting movement's goals]. In accordance with the law of the survival of the fittest, those which do not have a right of existence will wither away. One framework will weather all the storms and fulfill its role by engaging in a consistent and uninterrupted war. (Fighters for the Freedom of Israel (1982), 1: 224)

The inevitability of this process did not prevent Lehi propoganda singing the praises of those who helped bring it to fruition.[20] Time and again both the leaders and rank-and-file members of the movement were portrayed as positive deviants (Dodge, 1985: 18) because they surpassed the conventional expectations regarding the extent to which people should devote themselves to 'the life of the nation'.

> Those concerned about the situation ask themselves every day, 'How can I endure to see the evil that shall come unto my people and how can I endure to see the destruction of my homeland?' And because they cannot bear to see either of these things, they listen to the voice of their conscience and choose the only path that can save their homeland and their people. They do not relinquish the yoke of duties. On the contrary, they take extra duties upon themselves ... Because they left the fold in order to be stricter rather than more lenient with themselves they can fearlessly face the trial of the people. (Fighters for the Freedom of Israel (1982), 1: 582)

Having accepted 'a fighter's morality – a strict morality that demands the sacrifice of all personal pleasure for the sake of the goal', Lehi members can face the verdict of history with equanimity.

Accusing the Accusers

Lehi propaganda, in common with that of other terrorist movements, devoted more space to negative portrayals of internal and external enemies than it did to positive self-depictions. Thus local Arab notables were frequently criticized for being stooges of the British, and Jewish leaders were fiercely attacked for not taking appropriate action against 'the foreign ruler'. Guided by self-interest rather than the national one, Labour Zionists preferred to come to terms, and even work together, with the mandatory authorities. Whilst this response or, to be more precise, lack of response, may have first been 'a mistake arising out of a certain naïveté', it soon became the premeditated policy of those at the helm of the yishuv. There was, therefore, no excuse for their inaction.

Arabs and Jews alike were mainly criticized for the nature of their relationship with the British. It was they, after all, who were 'the number one enemy'. Pointing to the sins of commission and omission of Whitehall, Lehi attacked the mandatory authorities for being criminal, terrorist and even subhuman. In doing so the movement leaders resorted to exactly the same terms as the British government used against them. Invariably, however, they drew attention to the fact that Whitehall was prepared to countenance certain kinds of violence such as the killing of women and children, unarmed prisoners and combatants who had already surrendered, which Lehi rejected outright. 'We are different,' they insisted, 'because we are fighters, not wild pigs or the scum of the earth.'

But the 'accusation of the accusers' was by no means limited to British actions against the yishuv. Lehi propaganda often emphasized the fact that the movement was fighting against the very existence of a foreign ruler: 'not against a bad commissioner but against the commission, not against the implementation of the mandate but against the fact that it was not given to the Hebrew people'. It was the mere presence of the British in the Promised Land rather than the way they behaved there that constituted the core of the problem. That is what made the mandatory authorities an 'a priori enemy' and, in turn, a justifiable target of the Freedom Fighters of Israel.

Lehi's resort to violence was also justified by denying its actual victims (Sykes and Matza, 1957: 668). 'Not everyone who kills is a murderer, and not everyone who obeys the law is holy. Anyone who kills a murderer is holy, and anyone who obeys the law of a murderer is a killer.' Notwithstanding this kind of generalization, Lehi propaganda often pointed out why particular individuals had been singled out for assassination. Thus a front-page article in *Hehazit* (The Front) related to 'the twofold significance' of the unsuccessful attempt on the life of the British High Commissioner in Palestine.

> MacMichael is liable to death for his crimes. His hands are soaked in Hebrew blood. He killed more than 200 blockade runners on the Patria and more than 700 on the Struma. MacMichael is also responsible for the death of tens of thousands who never boarded the boats and were killed in the gas chambers because he closed the escape routes to the homeland. MacMichael is a mass murderer but he is also guilty of the murder of individuals. We will avenge the blood of Yair, the leader and commander of the freedom fighters. He is responsible for the murder of Avraham Amper and Zelig. He has to pay with his blood for the blood of his victims … But MacMichael the criminal was not the sole target of the attack. The freedom fighters were not only concerned with punishment of the individual. The fire was directed at the High Commissioner of the occupying power and the regime that he symbolized and represented. (Fighters for the Freedom of Israel (1982), 1: 645)

This slide from the macro-target to micro ones (Miller, 1987: 400) was by no means limited to those at the top of the power pyramid. All army and police personnel were either 'direct or indirect' murderers and therefore they all 'deserved death'. Nobody could excuse himself on the grounds that he was carrying out the orders of his superiors. After all, it is always possible to refuse orders, or to return to England. Each person's willingness to stay and enforce British policy was therefore regarded as clear proof of his 'wicked intentions'.

> Everyone is responsible. Every soldier, every policeman. Every clerk, from the least to the most important. From the post office clerk to the Prime Minister.

> That is the law of the enemy. Their responsibility is collective because their interests are collective, because their decisions are collective and because the execution of them is collective. The enemy – Britain ... That is not easy? That is difficult? Right, but it is the truth. So see, recognize, and draw the right conclusions – the first prerequisite for victory. (Fighters for the Freedom of Israel (1982), 2: 134)

Notwithstanding this highly negative portrayal of the British government and its local representatives in Lehi propaganda, movement leaders were well aware of the danger of their followers humanizing the enemy and the consequent difficulty in taking violent action against them. They therefore warned their followers to concentrate on the task at hand, and not be distracted by any positive feelings toward those chosen to be the target of their actions.

> Sometimes the victim, the target of the bullet, appears, and he is flesh and blood like you and me. A son, a husband, a father. Is it not the destruction of life, love and hope? ... It is the enemy! He is guilty of the murder of hundreds of thousands. Because of him mothers became bereaved of their offspring, children became orphans, and entire families were destroyed. He is the devil at the gate of the homeland. He is a murderer ... Death to the enemy – freedom to the homeland. (Fighters for the Freedom of Israel (1982), 2: 448)

And if the propaganda or, to be more precise, the autopropoganda has worked, 'the finger presses the trigger'.

Members of the Underground were enjoined to retaliate measure for measure: 'pillage for pillage, destruction for destruction, blood for blood'. Extending the biblical concept. Lehi leaders took the argument a step further and instructed their followers to give 'two eyes for an eye, two teeth for a tooth' and so on. They justified this response in terms of the relative worth of the protagonists. 'Our blood is more precious than your blood, and our flesh is more holy than your flesh. Our life is better than your lives because we are fighting for a life of freedom and you are fighting for the right to a life of exploitation.'

We Will Succeed

Lehi leaders tried to convince their followers not to be overinfluenced by short-term ups and downs in the fortunes of the movement. 'A success is not a victory', they warned, and 'a failure is not a debacle.' Despite temporary setbacks on both the external and internal fronts, the Freedom Fighters of Israel would eventually win the day. Neither the physical oppression by the gentiles nor 'the spiritual oppression due to the denunciation by Jews' would deter them from continuing their armed struggle until the British left the Promised Land.

At each stage of the campaign Lehi propaganda drew attention to local and global events that were thought to have confirmed the movement's reading of the situation. Only those who were 'blind or foolish' did not see what was happening. Otherwise 'the truth was clear to all'. Not surprisingly, however, this argument was made most forcefully after the British relinquished their mandatory powers and handed them over to the League of Nations. Lehi leaders insisted that it was they who had made the price of governing so high that it was no longer worthwhile for Whitehall to hold on to the reins of power.

But the belief in ultimate victory was not based only on an analysis of unfolding events and the reaction they engendered in the yishuv. It was also derived from an understanding of 'the logic of the process'. Lehi was fighting for the most basic right and the most pressing need – that of national independence. The British, however, were just trying 'to cling on to another chunk of land in the empire'. Fired by greed alone, they did not have the will or dedication of freedom fighters. Their attempt to hold on to the reins of power was therefore doomed to failure from the outset.

> There is hope because brute physical force, the force of violence and malice cannot stand up against the force of those who fight with firearms and for an ideal. There is hope because the force of evil is unable to suffer losses. It is ready for easy victories and to kill defenseless people, but its nerves will fray when faced day after day with the danger of falling into the hands of the Hebrew fighter. (Fighters for the Freedom of Israel (1982), 2: 59–60)

According to this view of the situation, the ratio of forces was deceiving. Lehi was not, in fact, fighting against insurmountable odds. The movement's spiritual strength gave it 'an extra weapon that cannot be measured in material terms'. When taken into account, though, it was clear that Lehi had a distinct advantage over the physically superior empire. Thus, just six months after Lehi took up arms against the British, *Bamahteret* (In the Underground) raised the question whether it was possible that 'we who are the bearers of a great ideal' would fail, and answered as follows:

> Anyone, who out of defeatism, says that it is not worth fighting for a cause that has so few supporters, is just a materialist. He does not have the right to be amongst us, and it is better that he leave. One does not decide to fight for a cause on the basis of how many people are doing so, but from an understanding of its rightness. We believe because we are right, and not because we have a chance to succeed. We will succeed because we believe. (Fighters for the Freedom of Israel (1982), 1: 68)

It was, therefore, just a matter of time until victory was achieved.

In the Mirror of the Past

This ultimately optimistic reading of the continuing struggle against the British mandate was backed up by 'the lessons of history'. Lehi propaganda was replete with comparisons between contemporary events and those of yesteryear. Of course, this interpretive process was not conceived of as an intellectual exercise. It was meant to be both a guide and a goad to action: 'The past demands. History is binding.'[21]

Each and every protagonist was compared to figures from bygone days. Heroes and villains alike were portrayed as being essentially similar, or even as better and worse than those that preceded them. Thus the British were compared to all the arch enemies of the Jewish people, from Pharaoh to the tyrants of modern times. Frequent reference was made, for instance, to the Greeks and Romans who destroyed the First and Second Temples, respectively. To take just one example of each of these regimes:

> Antiochus Epiphanes was no worse than the British king and ministers ... To impose heavy taxes, eject Jews from the Western Wall, close the gates of the country, kill Jews, torture women, and force Jewish clerks to work on the Sabbath. What else is necessary to merit the name Antiochus Epiphanes? (Fighters for the Freedom of Israel (1982), 1: 253)

> The British now like the Romans then ... are stealing our homeland, subjugating us with their armed legions, desecrating everything that is holy to us and degrading us into the dust ... Evil Britain is just like evil Rome. However, the War of the Jews will not be an illustrious page in the annals of Britain. She will not inscribe the caption 'Judea is captured' on her coins. Judea will not fall a third time. (Fighters for the Freedom of Israel (1982), 2: 56)

Significantly, the British were most frequently compared to Amalek, the apogee of evil in tradition and the only nation that the Jews were commanded to completely destroy. In this particular case, allusions were often made to the biblical text in order to draw attention to the similarity between the two enemies. The British, like Amalek in its time, 'attack the stragglers and block the road leading to the Hebrew kingdom in Zion'.[22]

Lehi propaganda also included comparisons between the British mandate and Nazi Germany. The latter was not regarded as an ahistorical phenomenon or even as sui generis. Hitler was essentially the same as other enemies of the Jewish people, 'the Hitlers of yesterday, the Hitlers of today and the Hitlers of tomorrow'. In fact some, including the British, were worse. Not only did they fail to prevent German atrocities and commit many of their own; they also occupied the Hebrew homeland. And that, according to Lehi, is the most hideous crime of all, 'the absolute evil that everything else stems from'.[23]

The Arabs were regarded as being less of a threat than the British. They were therefore referred to as a rival (yariv) rather than as an enemy (oyev). Nevertheless, they too were placed within the framework of Jewish history. On the basis of a traditional rabbinic interpretation of the meeting between Esau and Jacob after a separation of 20 years,[24] the Arabs could be dealt with in one of three ways – gifts, prayer or war. The military approach was to be resorted to only if the other approaches proved ineffective.

> We tried to persuade the Arabs, in words of prayer and explanation. We also tried to influence them with gifts. After all, there is not one country in which Arabs have achieved a comparable standard of living to the one they have here … But to no avail. Consequently, only one option remains – that of war and conquest. If the Arabs do not listen to our prayers or respond to our gifts, they will have a war on their hands. (Fighters for the Freedom of Israel (1982), 2: 852)

Interestingly, Lehi resorted to the same historical events to attack their enemies within the yishuv. The leaders of the Jewish settlement in Palestine were likened to the Judenrat in the lands occupied by Nazi Germany and to the Hellenists at the time of the destruction of the First Temple. Once again the comparisons were often of an invidious nature. The contemporary situation was thought to be even worse than it had been in the past. Thus Lehi recalled the presence of the mixed multitude of non-Jews who joined the slaves that Moses took out of Egypt, and argued that

> now at the end of two thousand years of exile a mixed multitude is arising amongst the leaders of the nation … In Egypt the mixed multitude did not decide the fate of the people … The leaders fought against them and they were disposed of in the wilderness. But alas for the nation in which the mixed multitude is at the helm. The people believe in their leaders and are tricked into following them. For many generations the entire nation has to suffer because of the sins of the mixed multitude. (Fighters for the Freedom of Israel (1982), 2: 906)

The resort to Jewish history extended, of course, to Lehi itself. The writings included a myriad of references to a long list of heroes who had fought for national liberation from biblical times (for example, Gideon and David)[25] until the period of the yishuv (for example, Joseph Trumpeldor). Lehi leaders and members portrayed themselves as the latest link in 'the chain of heroes of the Jewish people, a people who had fought for its freedom with more force, more strength, more sacrifice and more determination than any other nation in the world'. The Maccabees, though, were their role model par excellence.[26]

Throughout the year and particularly during Kislev (the month in which Hanukkah, the Festival of Lights commemorating the Maccabean triumph over the Greek Seleucid Empire, occurs) all the Lehi publications drew attention to the implications of the Hasmonean victory over seemingly insurmountable odds. Despite their small numbers, it was argued, the members of Lehi must also perform 'a Maccabean act'. In order to avoid the 'wretched life of a third-class citizen' they have to conduct 'a war of national liberation, a war against the Hellenists and traitors, a war of terror, and a war on the battlefield, against the alien ruler in the land'.

Timeless Truths

The story of Lehi's struggle against the British presence in Palestine and the historical analogies used to encourage it were incorporated in a broader metahistorical narrative. Jewish history, it was argued time and again, is characterized by a certain continuity. 'Whilst times change and enemies change, the overall pattern remains the same, because it is based on timeless truths' regarding both the Gentile determination to destroy the Jews and their failure to do so.

> The world does not want the Jews to exist. The popes did not want, Napoleon did not want, Hitler does not want, Stalin does not want, Roosevelt does not want. Only the means used to destroy the Jews have changed over time. The Inquisition, the Sanhedrin in Paris, liberalism, the concentration camps. (Fighters for the Freedom of Israel (1982), 1: 158)

But, despite the variety of methods used, the Jewish people will never be destroyed. Other empires rise and fall but it is invincible.

> We are sons of a nation that has been witness to the rise and fall of people and kingdoms, but we continue and will continue to exist. We are sitting on the land that has seen many rulers and many conquerors: the Babylonians, Persians, Egyptians, Greeks, Romans, crusaders and Turks. All of them thought that they would rule here for ever. Where are their governments? What mark did they leave in this land? ... There is no power in the world that will suppress the Jewish longing for freedom. There is no ruler that will seize the land that is designated for us. (Fighters for the Freedom of Israel (1982), 1: 811–12)

In order to transform this dream into reality, Jews have to take their future into their own hands. After more than 2000 years of exile they have to transform themselves from being the object of history into its subject.

Suffering may continue for a long time, but at least it will be the active suffering of war rather than the passive suffering of persecution. It will therefore serve a purpose instead of being to no avail.

Lehi propaganda always emphasized the determination of Jewish freedom fighters rather than the extent to which they were successful. The fact that they fought, not that they won, was regarded as the crucial factor. However, this dichotomy is somewhat misleading because all those engaged in the struggle for Jewish independence are victorious in the end. Even if they lose a battle, they transmit the love of freedom to their contemporaries and to future generations. Following in the footsteps of Nachshon, who jumped into the Red Sea before God split it in two,[27] Jewish freedom fighters always gain 'a victory in defeat'.

> The nachshonim [bold ones] ... jump into the water before it is divided. Some of them struggle with the waves and are eventually victorious. Others fail and drown. Even though they sink, however, their cause is by no means a lost one. By jumping into the sea they awaken the hope in the hearts of those standing on the shore, and in the end they jump in as well. (Fighters for the Freedom of Israel (1982), 1: 574)

The struggle for independence continues unabated and will eventually be crowned with success. Victory is assured.

The Power of Parallelism

The 'Jewish liberation struggle', like that of other nations, is in certain ways unique. Each one depends on 'the people, geography and historical circumstances' concerned. However, these differences are of relatively minor importance. They relate to form and not to content. Consequently, it is important to understand and explain, not only the lesson of Jewish history, but also those of other nations who fought or are still fighting for their freedom.[28] Hence the widespread use of analogies and comparisons. They were thought to 'substantiate and emphasize the essence of all struggles for national independence'.

Lehi writings were replete with references to the evils of British imperialism. They had, of course, assumed different guises at different times, but the basic aim was always the same: the perpetuation of oppression. 'Missionaries with the cross, merchants with gold, and soldiers with arms' were all enlisted to further the political and economic interests of the British Empire around the world. By recounting the stories of nations who had freed themselves from British tyranny, such as the United States of America and South Africa, and those still in the process of doing so (for example, India and

Ireland), Lehi reiterated the lesson learnt from Jewish history. Only armed resistance would lead to the expulsion of 'the foreign ruler' and the establishment of an independent Jewish state in the Promised Land.

Lehi propaganda invariably portrayed British imperialism as more despotic than any other kind of foreign rule, and even as 'the most perfect regime of oppression'. Nevertheless, frequent reference was also made to the fate of other colonial powers. Thus the collapse of the Austro-Hungarian and Ottoman empires was often cited as proof of the fact that the mightiest rulers could be brought down by determined action on the part of subjugated nations. Leaders of the yishuv should therefore follow the example of foreign heroes as well as those of the Jewish people. Garibaldi, de Gaulle and others were also appropriate models for the struggle against the British presence in Palestine.

Clearly, the history of other nations like that of the Jewish people took the form of a projective narrative. They were not just meant to be recalled, but also to be reactualized.[29] In order to drive this message home, Lehi took the argument a step further. The fact that the stories were taken from 'throughout the ages and from all around the world' suggested that they were not just examples of a longstanding and worldwide phenomenon, but proof of a universal law regarding the fate of national liberation movements. Lehi's call to arms against the British was not based only on a host of precedents. It was rooted in the very nature of the relationship between the oppressor and the oppressed.

The Iron Law of Liberation

The 'longstanding law of the conqueror' asserts that oppressors never give up control voluntarily. They do everything within their power to safeguard or, to be more precise, to further their political and economic interests. Consequently, nations hoping to gain independence cannot rely on either the conscience or the mercy of their oppressors. They have to fight for their rights because 'a motherland is only extricated from the claws of the rapacious conqueror with blood; the blood of the enemy and the blood of those fighting for the national home'.

This struggle for independence always assumes the same form. It is started by a small minority which arrives at a correct reading of the situation and draws the appropriate conclusions as to how to change it. Their initial resistance leads to further and even more cruel oppression. However, this is to no avail. In fact the attempt to suppress the revolt both deepens and widens the resistance to oppression. Besides 'fanning the flames of hatred, strengthening the will to make war, and intensifying the aspirations for freedom' of those already involved in the struggle for independence, it also transforms them into 'an exemplary model' for others. More and more of their compatriots accept the need to take up arms and actually do so. There are, of course, further losses and defeats, but the struggle for freedom continues to gain momentum and, in accordance with 'the iron law of liberation', is eventually crowned with success: 'Any subjugated nation that is not contaminated by a spirit of degeneration and has a desire to live will fight for its freedom. Any nation that fights for its freedom will in the end be victorious.'

This law is explained, in part at least, by the fact that national liberation movements do not need to achieve an outright military victory in order to gain independence. It is enough to create 'a permanent state of war that demands constant preparedness of large forces and causes a continuing feeling of unrest'. This forces the oppressor to ask the question whether 'the gains are not outweighed by the losses' and, in turn, to decide that it is in his best interest to concede defeat and grant independence to the fledgling nation.[30]

Even this limited victory cannot be explained in terms of the physical power of the liberation movement. Its 'spiritual superiority' over the oppressor also has to be taken into account. This advantage derives from the righteousness of the movement's cause:

> The oppressor has greater numbers and more physical power, but these are not the only factors that determine the outcome of a war. There is also the force of justice that guides the hand holding the weapon. The spiritual superiority that accompanies the physical force is the determining factor. It bestows courage on the freedom fighters, enabling them to advance and attack under lethal gunfire. The lack of spiritual strength and awareness of justice cause consternation and panic in the hearts of the persecutors and reveal the full extent of their fear. (Fighters for the Freedom of Israel (1982), 2: 45–6)

This difference between the oppressor and the oppressed was also attributed to their contrasting fortunes. Pointing to the willingness of freedom fighters 'to fight until the last bullet and to their last breath' and the tendency of persecutors 'to retreat when the situation becomes dangerous in order to save their lives', an article in *Hehazit* (The Front) concluded that the oppressed

> are always prepared to suffer more and to sacrifice more because they do not have anything to lose besides the chains of servitude. As far as they are concerned, retreat means subjugation and losing the image of God. For the occupant, however, defeat does not mean being vanquished. It only entails the loss of certain luxuries. (Fighters for the Freedom of Israel (1982), 1: 879)

24 *Narratives of Violence*

Military strength is therefore deceptive. Previous liberation struggles indicate that 'not everything that appears weak is in fact weak, and not everything that gives the impression of being strong is, in fact, strong'. Other factors, both spiritual and material, have to be included in the balance of forces. When they are taken into account the final result is clear. In the end, right always overcomes might.[31]

The Complete Picture

Even though Lehi's projective narratives were replete with references to those who throughout the ages had fought and died in the struggle for national independence, the movement understandably took special pride in the feats of its own members. Regulative biographies of Lehi heroes hailed the physical bravery and spiritual courage of those who met their death in combat or on the scaffold. However, this was by no means the whole story. Portrayals of the fallen were not limited to the period during which they fought in the underground. Lehi propaganda also related to their formative years and posthumous influence. Life histories of Yair and those who followed in his footsteps included detailed descriptions of how they first learnt, then lived, and finally became part of the movement's projective narrative.[32]

Time and again Lehi drew attention to the heterogeneity of the members of the underground. The idea was to show how people of different backgrounds and with different personalities had come together to further their common cause of liberating the homeland. Not surprisingly, therefore, this motif was particularly prominent in the portrayals of those who carried out a mission together. Thus obituaries for the two assassins of Lord Moyne – Eliahu Beit Zuri[33] and Eliahu Hakim – emphasized the fact that they grew up in totally different socioeconomic circumstances and had completely different temperaments. Nevertheless, they joined forces in Cairo and stood steadfastly together in life and death.

> Two Jewish soldiers. Two worlds. One from a house of poverty and suffering who worked to keep himself and his family. The other from an affluent home who gave up all the luxuries for the suffering and hunger of the underground. One an intellectual who loved philosophy and poetry. A logical and thinking man. The other a man of action and healthy, simple emotions. Two worlds with regard to education, living standards and character. And they met. Fired by one love. The love of freedom for the homeland and the people. Joined together in action. Joined together in death. One body, one idea, one war, one scaffold. (Fighters for the Freedom of Israel (1982), 2: 438)

When recounting the biographies of individual members, Lehi propaganda often drew attention to events or attributes that were regarded as early signs of their suitability for, and interest in, the movement. Thus Eliahu Hakim's tendency to stand up for himself in children's games was cited as the first indication of his courage. His subsequent lack of success in school was attributed, not to a lack of ability, but to the distractions of 'an agitated body, and a heart that yearns for action'. Clearly, therefore, it was only a matter of time before Hakim went underground and took up arms against the British.

Notwithstanding this rite of consistency (Lofland, 1969: 124–7), Lehi propaganda also drew attention to critical events in the lives of these and other heroes that led them to the realization that they had to join the movement. For Eliahu Hakim the sight of Arab rioters was 'the first spark'. In the case of Beit Zuri, it was the evidence or, to be more precise, the mere presence, of British police in the Hebrew homeland. Explaining the reasons for his actions to the Cairo court he recalled:

> I was sitting in the balcony of our house in Tel Aviv and saw a crowd of people marching in the street shouting slogans and carrying flags. I asked the adults standing next to me to explain what was happening and they told me it was a demonstration. Suddenly a group of British policemen appeared and began to disperse the demonstrators with their clubs. A strange question entered my mind: why could these English policemen hit one of my brothers and why couldn't the demonstrators hit back? I was unable to find an answer to this question and to many others of a similar nature. Only after a number of years did I reach the conclusion that the Englishman can come to my country, be a policeman, and do whatever takes his fancy because it is under foreign rule ... I understand that the only way to fight the British rule that is based on violence is to use force ... and to attack their representatives who are responsible for all our troubles. (Fighters for the Freedom of Israel (1982), 1: 925–30)

Witnessing violence prompted the nascent heroes to take a deeper look at things. They placed their own personal experiences in a historical perspective and began to see 'the complete picture'.[34] This, in turn, convinced them of the need to become one of the Freedom Fighters of Israel. Hence the oft-made claim that they, and they alone, understood the contemporary situation and were prepared to draw the appropriate conclusions. The decision to join the underground brought many of the young recruits into conflict with their parents. For ideological and/or personal reasons they objected to their children's decision to take up arms against the British. But, to no avail. Having internalized Lehi's projective narrative, the new generation of Jewish heroes were determined to act it out at all costs.

Body and Soul

Those who took up arms against the British portrayed themselves and were portrayed by others as the continuation or renewal of 'the tradition of bravery in Israel'. As Anshel Shpilman explained to the British judges during the course of his trial for carrying an illegal weapon:

> You, who are acquainted with the Bible, should know that the story told in the Book of Samuel is not just a historical record for us. The name of David is more than history. For us it is life ... A new generation has arisen, a new kind of Jew who feels the blood of David and the Hasmoneans in his blood. A connection has been made between our live bodies and the souls that roam around in these mountains. A connection has been made between our souls that aspire to freedom and the dry bones buried in this land. This connection leads to thunder and lightning. (Fighters for the Freedom of Israel (1982), 1: 752–3).[35]

The need to ensure complete secrecy prevented Lehi from describing the exploits of its members in any detail. Attention was concentrated instead on how they met their death in the underground. The movement's propaganda was replete with references to the physical bravery of those killed and injured by the British. Stories were told about how they fought against insurmountable odds and to the bitter end. Frequent mention was also made of the fighters' willingness to endanger themselves to save their colleagues and their refusal to reveal the secrets of the underground even when subjected to the infamous British methods of torture. Despite undergoing 'superhuman pain', Lehi's members went to their death with 'the purity of the silent'.

These and other feats of bravery were rooted in the deep historical consciousness of those who took up arms against the British. They had internalized Lehi's projective narrative and therefore understood the need to follow in the footsteps of earlier heroes. It was, however, the underground members' enormous spiritual strength that enabled them actually to do so. This was particularly the case with regard to those who were killed on the gallows. Numerous articles and even special publications provided detailed descriptions of how they went to their death 'standing upright and with complete equanimity'. Beit Zuri, Hakim and others were not simply 'noble men of action'. They were, first and foremost, 'spiritual heroes'.

Those who fell at the hands of the British were portrayed as a combination of two seemingly antithetic components – body and soul, book and sword, dream and action. However, these attributes were always regarded as being complementary rather than in conflict with each other. There was a synthesis, not a contradiction between them. 'The two elements, spirit and matter, complement each other. They blend together into a mixture of supreme spirit. The mission gives direction to the weapons, and the sword paves the way for the mission' (Fighters for the Freedom of Israel (1982), 1: 381).

A profile of Yair published shortly after he was killed by the British hailed him as the supreme embodiment of all these positive attributes, and concluded that he was 'the acme of perfection':

> He combined all the talents and traits of the Jewish race in his personality. The blood of earlier heroes flowed in his veins. He loved the nation like them. He loved freedom like them. He loved the motherland like them. In common with earlier heroes he was jealous about his beliefs. Like them he hated the oppressor, the destroyer of the motherland. Like them he mobilized his brothers to a war of liberation. He stood at their head and fell like one of them. Like a Maccabee. Like a zealot. Like an asteroid. He was perfect.

Henceforth Yair was portrayed in superhuman terms, as 'a figure from another world'. Those who thought that his demise would be the death-knell of the Freedom Fighters of Israel were proved wrong. They mistakenly measured Yair according to the standards of ordinary mortals, but he was different from those who live and die. His supporters continued to be spell-bound by his 'penetrating insight, logical mind and will of iron'. Yair had lit a fire in their hearts, and thereby became the burning bush that is never consumed.

Those who followed in Yair's footsteps were invariably portrayed in exactly the opposite way. Thus one of the fallen was referred to as 'a simple and innocent youngster without any pretensions whatsoever', and Lehi members in general were depicted as being essentially similar to everybody else in the yishuv. 'They emerged from amongst you. They are your flesh and blood.' The message was clear: 'If a typical youngster, an unknown soldier of the nation can die in this way, surely there are thousands and even tens of thousands like him who are prepared to risk their lives. Happy is the nation whose sons are like this.' Two kinds of heroes were therefore held up as an example and model for the younger generation: the superhuman and the human, the perfect and those 'striving for perfection'.[36]

Smiling to the Generations to Come

The British killed the bodies but not the souls or the spirit of the Fighters for the Freedom of Israel. The martyrs sacrificed their ephemeral life, but in doing so they gained an eternal one 'in the memory of the free nation in an independent homeland'. Obituaries for those who died at the hands of the British declared that 'the blood of earlier heroes flowed in their veins and now their blood flows in ours', or in more traditional Jewish terms that 'their souls are bound in the bond of our lives, and our lives are bound in the bond of their magnanimous deep souls'.

Having lived and died in accordance with Lehi's projective narrative, the movement's fallen became an integral part of it. Time and again, therefore, Lehi propaganda emphasized the fact that they did not die in vain. Their martyrdom was made meaningful by the life it gave to the cause.[37] 'The war continues, so there is significance to their death.' Or, in the words of an Irish poem that appeared on the masthead of *Hamaas* (The Deed):

> They say
> We did everything we could,
> But if the task is not completed
> It will be as if we did nothing.
> They say
> Our deaths do not belong to us,
> But to you.
> Whatever you do with them
> That will be their meaning. (Fighters for the Freedom of Israel (1982), 2: 434)

The relationship between the fallen and those who followed in their footsteps was often portrayed as a reciprocal one. According to this view of things, each side helped the other. Those killed by the British provided a role model for future generations. However, it was the knowledge that their sacrifice would be emulated by others that enabled them to take up arms and risk being killed in the first place. Thus Yair 'went to the end because he did not see his death as the end, but as the beginning of a new tradition in Israel'. Those who continued it tried to follow their leaders' example. Thus when recruits swore allegiance to the movement they promised:

> If I am captured, I will not recognize the right of the enemy to put me on trial. If the court, which is one of the instruments of repression of the foreign power, sentences me to death, I will go to the gallows with pride and peace of mind in the belief that my death will educate thousands of other fighters who will continue to struggle and ensure the victory of our mission. (Fighters for the Freedom of Israel (1982), 2: frontispiece)[38]

In accordance with this oath, Eliahu Beit Zuri put on the red execution garb and declared that it was 'the most beautiful suit I have ever worn'. His fellow assassin, Eliahu Hakim, even grinned on his way to the gallows. He was, he said to the hangman, 'smiling to the generations to come'. In contrast to their peace of mind, Winston Churchill, the ruler of a mighty empire, was 'enraged, angry and agitated'.[39] This was no coincidence because

> despite temporary victories the British Prime Minister felt that his cause is lost. Immunity is not forever and the evil power will be crushed. The two who were hung felt, knew, and believed that the goal which they devoted their lives to would be achieved. Their land will be liberated and the Hebrew people will go from slavery to freedom. (Fighters for the Freedom of Israel (1982), 1: 944)

Clearly therefore, the scaffold was an ideal stage for the morality play between the forces of good and evil.[40] The gallows provided the most effective way of revealing both the true nature of the protagonists and the final outcome of the confrontation between them.[41] The Freedom Fighters of Israel and the British mandatory authorities 'stood barefaced, one against the other', and their contrasting expressions were indicative of the fact that light would eventually conquer darkness. 'The end was clear from the very beginning.'

Do Not Rely on Miracles

All the terrorist tales described so far were directed against the narratives of the British government and the leaders of the Jewish yishuv. Lehi's major external and internal enemies were criticized, for their presence in the Promised Land and for their failure to take the appropriate actions against it, respectively. However, in addition to these two targets, the movement's propaganda was also directed against traditional Judaism and those who lived according to its dictates. Time and again religious Jews were lambasted for believing in divine help rather than human action, and their consequent failure to take part in the struggle for national liberation.[42]

Significantly, Lehi's attack on 'the official representatives of the Torah' was invariably couched in religious terms. Movement leaders tried to justify the resort to violence by giving pre- or post-traditional interpretations of privileged texts (Kirk, 1979: 96; Ophir, 1994: 206). They also appropriated religious language and rituals in an attempt to invest their actions with an aura of sanctity. Paradoxically, therefore, terror was seen as being anchored in tradition and an alternative to it at one and the same time.

Lehi propaganda was replete with citations of those religious commandments which were thought to be an endorsement of the movement's resort to violence. They included both biblical precepts (an eye for an eye, a tooth for a tooth, and so on,[43]) and Talmudic injunctions (for example, if anyone comes to kill you, kill him first[44]). Not surprisingly, frequent reference was made to the twin concepts of obligatory and voluntary war. One of the former – to completely wipe out the memory of Amalek – was equated with the commandment, 'Thou shalt not kill', and another obligation – to conquer the Land of Israel – was regarded as more important than all 613 biblical precepts.

> We were also present at the giving of the Torah on Mount Sinai. We heard the commandment, Thou shalt not kill ... but He also said you shall completely wipe out the memory of Amalek ... We also heard the commandment to Moses to conquer the land with blood and fire ... Why did Maimonides not include it amongst the 613 commandments? According to Rav Kook, he did not count the declaration of the unity of God and conquering the land as separate commandments because they are more important than all the others. They are all dependent on them. (Fighters for the Freedom of Israel (1982), 2: 483–4)

The teachings of the prophets were frequently invoked. The references were all of a particular rather than a universalistic nature. Thus the masthead of the monthly newspaper *Hamaas* (The Deed) was often adorned with prophecies of divine retribution upon those who did not revere the Lord. It was argued that the precepts of forgiveness, love and justice are initially directed toward fellow-Jews. Love of other nations is reserved for the messianic era when those nations would have learnt the law of the Lord and would 'come to bow down at Mount Zion'. Until then, the Gentiles would be the object of divine revenge, and 'the Hebrew fighter entrusted with implementing the prophecy'.

There are, according to a series of articles on Jewish messianic movements, two schools of thought regarding the final redemption: a romantic passive one which holds that, even though the Messiah tarries, the Jewish people should wait patiently until he comes, and a pragmatic active one which insists that they do everything within their power to hasten his coming. Lehi, of course, opted for the latter. Quoting a rabbinic dictum to the effect that it is forbidden to rely on miracles, movement leaders stressed the need to 'galvanize the nation into taking real actions in order to cast off the yoke of the Gentiles'.

Lehi's understanding of biblical and rabbinic texts was often different and sometimes even diametrically opposed to the traditional interpretations. For instance, the law of retaliation – an eye for an eye, a tooth for a tooth, and so on – was only applied in the case of personal damages and has long been abandoned in favor of monetary compensation for the injured party. This departure from tradition was even more marked with regard to a number of religious rituals. However, despite or maybe because of their criticism of these aspects of the Jewish heritage, Lehi leaders felt the need to appropriate them in support of their resort to violence.

Traditional mourning customs were always regarded as an empty and meaningless ritual. Everything goes exactly to plan 'in accordance with programs of prayer services and public meetings, rising in memory of the dead, cantorial trills and public speeches'. Rather than hallowing the memory of the fallen, these ceremonies lead to their desecration. Even more importantly, this kind of mourning acts as a catharsis and therefore precludes the possibility of transforming dolor into deeds. Sorrow should, however, be 'a source of rage and a goad to action'. Thus, after 11 members of Lehi were killed in an attack on the Palestine Railroad workshops in Haifa, the readers of *Hehazit* (The Front) were urged to respond by taking up arms against the British:

> In remembrance of the 11 for whom the war of liberation was the entire purpose of their existence, who fell in battle holding their weapons, we fly our flag at half-mast. We will not express our pain in tears, our grief in eulogies, or our sorrow in words. We will forge the weapons of war from the blood of the fallen. Our pent up anger will be transformed into a fighting rage. We will vent our anger in cruel and redemptive action. And when the victory chant is heard, it will awaken the fallen of the nation to everlasting life. (Fighters for the Freedom of Israel (1982), 2: 127–8)

Lehi adopted a similar stance towards the Jewish festivals. They also portrayed them as an impediment to action.[45] Significantly, this tendency was particularly marked with regard to Passover and Hanukkah, the festivals which commemorate the liberation of the Jewish people from Egyptian bondage and Greek dominion, respectively.

A rabbinic dictum recited during the Passover Haggadah service states that 'in each generation every person must look upon himself as if he actually came out of Egypt'. However, Lehi leaders believed that even this injunction was not forceful enough.

> No more vague yearnings without obligation. No more pious hopes of freedom. No more empty phrases. We are writing a new Haggadah with our blood. Every Jewish body is like a letter inscribed in the book of redemption. Many generations will envy us because we have the chance to act; because we are privileged to keep the Festival of Freedom with our bodies. (Fighters for the Freedom of Israel (1982), 2: 1009)

In contrast to the traditional idea that the lights of the menorah are holy, and must therefore only be used for the purpose of 'publicizing the miracle' of the rededication of the Temple, those fighting against the British were sanctified.

> We will burn our bodies. Let our bodies be transformed into wicks. Let our hatred become oil and let our faith be the flame ... Let our bodies turn into burning candles. Let our blood be the holy blood of Hanukkah. This blood and these candles are sacred and it is a religious obligation to use them. (Fighters for the Freedom of Israel (1982), 1: 841–2)

Only 'redemptive actions' of this kind, Lehi argued, fulfill the ultimate aim of the Jewish festivals – 'not just a recollection of a past event but its transformation into a living Torah in the present and the future'.

Praying with a Rifle

For Lehi the struggle for national liberation was 'the holiest idea' of the Jewish people. In fact it was frequently referred to as the Torah and portrayed in exactly the same way – as unchangeable and all-inclusive:

> Our Torah is the liberation of the motherland for the people. The return of the people to its national home and the establishment of the Kingdom of Israel is the expression of the creative Hebrew spirit. It is forbidden to either add or detract from this Torah. Study it again and again, because everything is included therein. (Fighters for the Freedom of Israel (1982), 2: 837)

Adherence to the 'commandments of history' or the 'commandments of the heroes of Israel throughout the generations' was therefore expected to be as strict as that of religious Jews to the divine laws.[46] Lehi members also had to be 'as heedful of a lighter precept as of a weighty one'.[47] Alluding to the Shema, a prayer that traditional Jews recite three times a day, and on their deathbed, those who had taken up arms against the British were called upon to carry out each mission 'with all your heart, with all your soul, and with all your might'.[48] Freedom, like God, was holy. It also demanded unlimited and endless love.

The sacred nature of Lehi's ends led to a sanctification of all the means used to achieve them: 'Nothing is improper in a holy war.' Quoting the revisionist poet Uri Zvi Greenberg, the movement's propaganda extolled 'the Jewish soldier who prays with his rifle'.[49] Yair extended this idea in the following poem that he dedicated to his late father:

> Like my father who carried his bag with a prayer shawl to synagogue on the Sabbath
> So will I carry holy rifles in my bag to the prayer service of iron with a quorum of renascent men.
> Like my mother who lit candles on the festive eve
> So will I light a torch for those revered in praise.
> Like my rabbi who taught me to read in the Torah
> I will teach my pupils: stand to arms, kneel and shoot.
> Because there is a religion of redemption – a religion of
> the war of liberation
> Whoever accepts it – blessed be he; whoever denies it – cursed be he.
> (Fighters for the Freedom of Israel (1982), 1: 207–8)

Religious terms were also used to describe those who fought against the British. In an allusion to God's deliverance of the Children of Israel from Egypt, they were hailed as 'the outstretched arm of the Hebrew people'.

Those who were killed in the struggle for independence were lauded for having 'sacrificed their life on the altar of the motherland'. An announcement of the death of one of Lehi's members concluded with the opening words of the Kaddish, the traditional prayer in memory of the dead. However, the emphasis was completely different. The fallen hero rather than the eternal God was being sanctified.

> We stood to attention in his memory. Arieh! Listen to the memorial prayer of your brothers and the oath of allegiance to our cause. As long as we live, we will fight for the freedom of Jerusalem and pray, *like you*, for the peace of Israel: with a rifle and a mine. Blessed and praised be the memory of anonymous soldiers, the fighters for the Kingdom of Israel. Magnified and sanctified be his great name. (Fighters for the Freedom of Israel (1982), 1: 76)

This kind of reverence was not reserved only for those who were killed while actually fighting the British troops. All members of Lehi who met their deaths at the hands of the mandatory authorities were accorded the same treatment. Thus Sarah Bilski, an 18-year-old girl who died as a result of British gunfire, was eulogized in the following way:

> Quietly, seriously and lovingly, she carried out every task that was imposed on her. There is nothing profane in the work of the underground. Everything is holy. She was still wearing her white apron and peeling potatoes for her trainees, when a round of ammunition … (Fighters for the Freedom of Israel (1982), 2: 78)

The nature of the argument is clear. Lehi's aim of liberating the Hebrew homeland was holy. So too, therefore, were all those who fought for it, and any means by which they did so.[50]

Put Not Your Trust in Princes

The Lehi attack on traditional Judaism focused on its belief in divine intervention and consequent lack of human initiative. Paradoxically, however, this argument was often an important ingredient in the movement's critique of its secular opponents. Labour Zionism, Lehi recalled, had begun as a revolt against an outmoded religious tradition. With the passage of time, though, it had also been rendered obsolete and become 'a belief of yesteryear'. In a special youth edition of *Hehazit* (The Front), the younger generation was therefore urged to repudiate 'the defunct ideas and superstitions' of their parents.[51] They, in common with the religious faith that preceded them, were based on a belief in the power or willingness of external agents to help liberate the Jewish homeland. Unfortunately, however, human princes were as impotent or unresponsive as the divine king. The younger generation must therefore

> shake off the yoke of the tradition of superstitions according to which someone is listening to our protests and speeches. [The previous generation] revolted against the prayer book claiming that our prayers are not heard in heaven. The younger generation must say the same thing with regard to the political arena. Gentlemen! Nobody is listening to your 'prayers' from your new 'prayer book', from your newspapers and conventions. There are no 'good Englishmen'. There is no 'conscience', no 'sense of justice'. Even your strikes don't make them tremble, in the same way as you claimed that God is not shocked by fasts. (Fighters for the Freedom of Israel (1982), 1: 246)

This argument was often taken a step further. Not only was the inaction of Labour Zionism equated with that of traditional Judaism; it was regarded as being even worse. After all, Jewish passivity is much more deplorable in the homeland than in exile. And, in the case of secular Zionists at least, it is also 'morally indefensible'. Throughout the centuries of exile, religious Jews did not adopt an active stance because they believed in divine providence. All they had to do was obey God's commandments and wait for the Messiah. However, the leaders of the yishuv had no faith in God. Nevertheless, they failed to draw the necessary conclusion that they, and they alone, can liberate the Jewish homeland.

Once again Lehi resorted to the Maccabean analogy to drive this message home. Whilst religious Jews have always celebrated the Festival of Hanukkah as a commemoration of a divine miracle, the secular Zionists reinterpreted it and emphasized the bravery of those who took up arms against, and eventually defeated, the Greek Seleucid Empire. Their aim, of course, was to encourage similar acts of valor in the contemporary struggle for a Jewish state. However, even the leaders of the yishuv had failed to follow in the footsteps of the Maccabees. They were therefore much more blameworthy than their religious predecessors.

> There is something even more shameful than the passivity of the Jews in exile. Our forefathers regarded themselves as Jews who had to bear the punishment of exile until God had mercy and redeemed them by means of a miracle ... They celebrated Hanukkah accordingly. Our forefathers believed that the events of Hanukkah were a miracle. Not as allegory or a parable, but a real miracle. They turned a blind eye to the war itself and the bravery of the Maccabees. They lit candles, recited the song of praise and waited for another miracle. ... However, the holy people were destroyed. Those who replaced them are full of words and rhetoric. They always bear the names of the Maccabees on their lips, but they are not prepared to follow their example – to wage a war of national liberation

> against the Hellenists and the foreign ruler in our land. This is the simple truth and only criminals and hypocrites can distort or disregard it. (Fighters for the Freedom of Israel (1982), 1: 251–4)

Nothing, Lehi insisted, had really changed. The leaders of the yishuv were no longer physically in exile, but they had failed to rid themselves of its spiritual legacy. 'They are in the East, but their hearts remain in the depths of the West.'

Master Text

Narrative Structure

Previous studies have suggested that the propaganda of nationalist and separatist groups differ from that of ideological ones in two ways: in form and in content. It is based on narratives rather than accounts,[52] and presents the situation as a repetition of the past rather than as an entity in its own right. Thus the ASALA, IRA and other national terrorists tell projective narratives in an attempt to convince themselves that they are the real patriots, and to persuade their fellow-countrymen to follow in their footsteps. The Fighters for the Freedom of Israel also told stories, and they too looked at the present through the prism of the past. In fact, this study suggests that Lehi narratives were both more detailed and more varied than those of other nationalist movements. Before concluding, an attempt will therefore be made to delineate the major characteristics of these terrorist tales by developing models of their internal structure, the interaction between them, and the different ways in which they are in dialogue with opposing narratives.

All the terrorist tales meet the essential requirement for a narrative – an evaluative framework in which good or bad character help to produce happy or unfortunate outcomes (MacIntyre, 1981: 456). They all pitted the forces of light against the forces of darkness and foretold that the former would ultimately prevail. The different elements of the story are, of course, intertwined. For the purposes of analysis, however, they are best considered under three separate headings: casting, altercasting (Weinstein and Deutschberger, 1963) and forecasting.[53] They refer to the image of self, the image of others and the result of the conflict between the protagonists, respectively.

The positive casting of self was based on two different but interrelated factors, the rightness of the terrorists' cause and their willingness to devote and even sacrifice their lives to help ensure its success. Invariably, this selflessness was portrayed not just, or even mainly, as an inherent characteristic of those concerned. Altruism was attributed instead to the worthiness of the struggle for national liberation. The cause brings out the best in people and encourages them to sacrifice their self-interest 'on the altar of the motherland'.

Lehi leaders engaged in altercasting out of an awareness of the fact that their image was inversely correlated with that of their foes. However, this was by no means the only reason why they did so. Lehi's negative portrayal of the British was thought to provide justification for their resort to violence. It was, after all, a reaction to the prior actions or the mere presence of the foreign ruler in the motherland. By condemning the condemners (Sykes and Matza, 1957: 668) in this way, terrorism became permissible and even commendable in the eyes of its perpetrators and, it was hoped, in the eyes of their fellow-countrymen.

Forecasting that Lehi will eventually win the day was based on what Yehoshafat Harkabi (1971: 30) has aptly referred to as the romanticization of the human factor. The few were confronting the many, but their numerical inferiority was more than compensated by enormous spiritual strength and a firm belief in the rightness of their cause. These virtues would enable Lehi to expel the foreign ruler and achieve national independence. According to conventional wisdom, might is right, but in fact exactly the opposite is the case. Right is might, and it will therefore ultimately prevail.

These three themes – casting, altercasting and forecasting – were most clearly apparent in the contemporary narrative. They appeared and can be discerned, however, in both the historical and metahistorical tales and also in the biographical one. Each and every narrative took the form of a morality play between the forces of good and evil at the end of which the former emerge victorious. The protagonists did, of course, differ from one terrorist tale to the other, but the story and the conclusion were always the same.

Nested Narratives

The present study began as an attempt to analyze the different regulative biographies and projective narratives that Lehi leaders told in order to justify the use of violence both in their own eyes and in the eyes of their fellow-countrymen. It soon became apparent however, that these individual and collective stories of the past persecution of Jews and their resistance to it were just two of the many stories that appeared in the movement's propaganda. Together they formed an intricate network of nested narratives (Gergen and Gergen, 1983: 263).[54]

Lehi propaganda provides a classic example of the way in which life histories are embedded in the story of the group within which those concerned find their identity (Connerton, 1989:21). In this particular case, though, individual lives were not only transcribed as examples of the collective. Hailing their physical bravery and spiritual strength in the struggle against the British was only one of the ways in which life history and history were interrelated. The biographies invariably included references to how Lehi's heroes first learnt, then lived and finally became part of the movement's projective narrative.

Determined to avoid the pitfalls of political reductionism, Tololyan (1988), Aretxaga (1997) and others tried to place national terrorist organizations in their broader cultural context. They drew attention, in particular, to the way in which each movement understands and explains the current situation in the mirror of the past. In doing so, however, these scholars have overreacted to the politicization of terrorism. Clearly, Lehi leaders did not always conceive of their struggle against the British in terms of previous oppression and resistance. Current events were often referred to as 'mere political facts' (Tololyan, 1988: 219). In such instances the narrative was oblivious to the past. It concentrated instead on the here and now.

It is arguable that the mere attribution of Whitehall's policies to the traditional antisemitism of the British establishment and/or to its longstanding desire to safeguard the political and commercial interests of the British Empire suggested that the contemporary struggle was, in certain ways at least, a repetition of earlier instances of oppression and resistance. However, the belief that the present is best understood in terms of the past found its clearest expression in the analogies that Lehi leaders and rank-and-file members made between their struggle and earlier ones for national independence. Sometimes the propaganda effort revolved around past Jewish campaigns. On other occasions it focused on those of other national liberation movements. In both cases, though, the message was the same: the present is merely a mirror of the past and it is therefore imperative to learn the lessons of history so as not to become or, to be more precise, to remain its victims.

The current campaign against the British and past struggles for Jewish independence were all regarded as the enactment of two broader metahistorical narratives. One related to the eternal Gentile hatred of the Jews and the eventual victory of the Chosen People. The other was based on the natural law that all nations will in time take up the struggle for independence and ultimately achieve their goal. Once again the message was the same in both cases. Whether Lehi was the latest manifestation of the Jewish or the universal struggle for national liberation, it would eventually achieve its end: expelling the foreign ruler and creating an independent state in the Promised Land.[55]

As Gergen and Gergen (1983: 264) have pointed out, macronarratives lay the foundations within which micronarratives are constructed. Thus the metahistory provides the framework for understanding both past struggles and the contemporary one against the British.[56] This is, however, only one aspect of the interaction between the different levels of terrorist tales. After all, if either the Jewish or the universal metanarrative was not confirmed by actual events it would soon become obsolete. Micronarratives fill in the details. In doing so, they make the metanarratives real and keep them alive.[57] Narrative fidelity (Fisher, 1987: 105–23) is a two-way process: it works in both directions.

Dialogic Narration

In their intriguing analysis of dialogic narration, Bruner and Gorfain (1984: 60) argued that 'any given telling takes account of previous and anticipated tellings, and responds to alternative and to challenging stories'. Even if this is not explicitly stated, it constitutes a response to the unacknowledged dialogic force of alternative accounts. They compel attention from those entering the field of discourse.

Lehi leaders were forced to engage in a dialogue with three other stories, those of the British, traditional Judaism and Labour Zionism. The present study has only analyzed the continuing war of words with 'the official representatives of the Torah'. This polemic is of particular interest because of its intricate intertextuality. However, it is important to look at the form and content of all three dialogues (see Table 1.1). Although they were neither autarkic nor monolithic entities, this kind of breakdown helps to understand the major thrust of each dispute.

Table 1.1 Dialogic narration

Opponents	Narrative	Content	Form
Britain	Foreign	Victimizer/Victim	Inversion
Orthodox Judaism	Prior	Martyr/Hero	Appropriation
Labour Zionism	Dominant	Egoist/Altruist	Contrast

Lehi countered the foreign narrative by claiming that its actions were, in fact, reactive. The Freedom Fighters of Israel had not started the cycle of violence. They had simply responded to the presence of the mandatory authorities in the Promised Land. Consequently, members of Lehi, together with the rest of the yishuv, were the objects of violence and not its instigators. The British were the victimizers and the Jews, as usual, were the victims.

This guilt transfer (Tugwell, 1982) found linguistic expression in Lehi's penchant for inverting labels. They deviantized the British in exactly the same ways as they themselves were delegitimated by the foreign ruler. Thus the mandatory authorities were frequently referred to as criminals (for example, murderers, robbers and pirates), terrorists (as in references to terrorist laws and terrorist government) and even subhuman (for example, barbarians and Nazis[58]). They, not Lehi, were the scum of the earth.

Lehi leaders never attacked orthodox Jews for being ritually observant. Their criticism was limited to the religious reading of history. It focused on their belief in divine intervention and their reliance on the coming of the Messiah. Confident of his coming and willing to wait until he did so, religious Jews did not feel the need to take the initiative in changing the course of Jewish history. Some even felt that it was forbidden to do so. Lehi, in contrast, believed in both the need and the efficacy of human action. Its members therefore mustered all their physical and spiritual strength to expel the foreign ruler and establish a Jewish state in the Promised Land.

Lehi portrayed the heroism of its members as being diametrically opposed to the passivity and martyrdom of their religious predecessors. Time and again, however, they claimed that all aspects of the struggle against the British – its ends, the means used to achieve them and those who took part in it – were holy. Hence Lehi's widespread appropriation of religious language, texts and rituals to justify their resort to violence. Whilst the content of the movement's rhetoric emphasized discontinuity, its style pointed to a certain continuity with the religious past. Together they were meant to show how terror was anchored in Jewish tradition and constituted an alternative to it at one and the same time.

Labour Zionism accepted the need for, and even advocated taking, concerted action against the mandatory authorities. However, Lehi propaganda criticized its leaders for not doing so. Their failure to practice what they preached was attributed to the selfishness, shortsightedness or sheer wickedness of those concerned.[59] In contrast, both the leaders of Lehi and its rank-and-file members were depicted as being blessed with foresight and being highly altruistic. They were the only people in the yishuv who both understood the situation and took the necessary steps to change it.

The claim to uniqueness found linguistic expression in a wide variety of dichotomies between the leaders of the movement and their Labour Zionist counterparts. One set of images, for instance, was of a religious nature: spirit v. matter, sacred v. profane, pure v. impure and human v. immortal. Another focused around the dimension of time: death v. life, past v. future, men of yesterday v. men of tomorrow and blind v. prophetic. Clearly, however, the aim of all these images and, for that matter, all the others that were used, was the same. They were meant to emphasize the difference between those who collaborated in one way or another with the mandatory authorities and those who fought steadfastly against them. The former told an unacted projective narrative (Tololyan, 1988: 226); the latter lived it to the full.

The Zionist Counternarrative

These models of the internal structure of terrorist tales, the interaction between them and the different ways they enter into a dialogue with opposing stories draw attention to certain similarities between Lehi narratives and those of other secular Zionists. A detailed analysis of this is, of course, beyond the confines of this study. Before concluding, however, it is important to look, albeit briefly, at this broader cultural context and consider its effect on Lehi's propaganda effort.

Studies of the social myths and collective memory of the Zionist movement have drawn attention to the centrality of the mythical plot structure about the successful stand of the few/forces of light against the many/forces of darkness (Gertz, 1986: 622; Zerubavel, 1995: 216–21).[60] This particular construction of the past was based on two narratological strategies – curtailing and expanding the end (Zerubavel, 1995: 221–5). The former involves concluding the story at a high point during the struggle, thereby portraying it as a success rather than a failure. The latter is based on continuing the story to a later point in history. Failure is presented as heroic death, and heroic death as victory in the eyes of posterity.

The Zionist reconstruction of the past was by no means limited to the recounting of particular events. It also related to the major turning points or periodization of Jewish history (ibid.: 15–17). Since the major yardstick for evaluating the past was the bond between the people and the land, it was divided into two major periods – antiquity and exile. With the advent of the modern Zionist movements, Jewish history entered into a third phase of national revival. The binary model, however, remained intact. After all, the re-establishment of an independent Jewish state in the Promised Land was not regarded as something new, but as a return to the grandeur of the period before the dispersion.

This dichotomous view of the past led to a complete negation of the Diaspora. Criticism of traditional Judaism, and even more of those who lived in accordance with its dictates, became a central feature of the Zionist ethos. Not only were orthodox Jews taken to task for their passive and unproductive lifestyle; they also provided the contraconception (Gusfield, 1963: 27) for the nascent secular state. In almost every field of endeavor the sabra was portrayed as a symbolic inversion of the stereotyped image of the Jew in exile (Almog, 1997: 127–37).

The similarity between these themes and those of the Lehi narratives is by no means coincidental. It reflects the underlying agreement between secular Zionists of all persuasions on two central issues: the primacy of the national as opposed to the religious aspect of Jewish peoplehood, and the reliance on human action rather than divine intervention in determining the course of Jewish history. This broad consensus on the aims of the Zionist movement and the way to achieve them was both mirrored and influenced by its newly created collective memory.

Clearly, however, Lehi's reading of the Jewish past was also meant to validate its own diagnosis of the contemporary situation and justify the kind of violence used to change it. Time and again, therefore, the historical and metahistorical narratives tried to 'appropriate the national myth and convert it into a party possession' (Gertz, 1986: 625). In doing so, these terrorist tales both incorporated and opposed the Zionist counternarrative. They adopted its major themes and adapted them to the needs of the Freedom Fighters of Israel at one and the same time.

Notes

1 These terms were first used together by Bonnie Cordes (1988: 151). However, more than a decade earlier, Weisband and Roguly (1976: 280) divided the operational strategy of terrorism into three parts: the ideology of the movement, the actions it carries out, and the verbal strategy used to justify them.

2 Maurice Tugwell (1981: 22) made the same point ten years later with specific reference to terrorist propaganda.

3 In many instances terrorists even use acclaiming tactics (Schlenker, 1980: 162–4) and war stories (Toch, 1993: 200–203) in order to maximize their responsibility for the action and/or its desirability.

4 See Leeman (1991) for a more detailed analysis of the reflective dialogue between terrorists and the state. He drew attention to the different ways in which counterterrorist rhetoric mirrors that of the terrorists, and to the advantages of a non-reflective strategy. Barnur (1998: 33–44, 76–82) has shown how both the Israeli government and the PLO (Palestinian Liberation Organization) tried to dehumanize each other by comparing their opponent's actions to those of Nazi Germany.

5 Tololyan (1988: 219–20) also referred to the tendency to pathologize terrorism and explained why it is equally inappropriate for the study of nationalist and separatist movements.

6 This pattern is by no means restricted to nationalist movements. Thus Rapoport (1991: 123) has drawn attention to the extent to which the vocabulary of Russian secular terrorists was saturated with Christian symbol and metaphors, especially those relating to the crucifixion, resurrection and Second Coming. 'Can one find more appropriate images for revolution,' he asked, 'than those showing how destruction can lead to rebirth?'

7 Schatzberger (1985: 42–3) referred to this practice as pseudo-religious because of the

movements' selective use of traditional texts and their tendency to quote them out of context.

8 Avraham Stern adopted the name of Eleazar Ben Yair, the leader of the Jewish revolt against the Roman Empire on Massada in 72AD.

9 Lehi ran as the Fighter's Party in the first parliamentary elections, but only managed to gain one seat in the Knesset.

10 For a more detailed description of the different newspapers, see Zameret (1974: 76–7).

11 Recalling her experience as a broadcaster 20 years earlier, Geula Cohen (1966: 92) wrote as follows: 'I was never a born announcer. If nonetheless I managed to do an effective job for twenty-minute periods twice a week, it was only by virtue of the voice clamoring within me, the voice I stifled for several thousands of minutes during the rest of the week, and which I had been stifling for thousands of years. If I performed well, it was not because I was in any way a professional; it was simply because I believed in that voice and abandoned my body to it, letting it rend me, burn me, char me to ashes if necessary. After every broadcast, the smell of cinders was in my nose. Something in me was being offered up on an altar.'

12 According to Zameret (1974: 77), reading and discussing the regular newspapers and the more sporadic material constituted Lehi's major educational activity. It took place two or three times a week, and on each occasion cell leaders had to report the response of their members to the appropriate authorities.

13 This dichotomy is taken from George Steinmetz's (1992: 490) study of the role of social narratives in working-class formation.

14 Lehi tried to drive this message home by showing how the British government supported those national liberation movements that did not endanger their own political and economic interests.

15 The resort to violence was also portrayed as a normal phenomenon that arose out of 'a natural tendency to hate foreign rulers' and 'the healthy striving for a war of liberation'.

16 The appeal to higher loyalties (Sykes and Matza, 1957: 669) sometimes took the form of an assertion that everybody should act in accordance with their inner convictions rather than obey laws that are against their conscience.

17 In a similar vein, Lehi propaganda attributed a number of disturbances in Tel Aviv to 'the frustration of the masses', and argued that their 'instinctive desire for action should be channeled into the war of liberation against the British'.

18 See Ivianski (1991: 158–61) for further details of Lehi leaders' constant concern with 'the issue of majority and minority'. The movement's propaganda is therefore replete with examples of what Richard Leeman (1991: 60–62) has referred to as the rhetorical tension between elitism and populism.

19 Lehi leaders were often at pains to point out that the Zionist movement began as a revolt against the Jewish establishment in Central and Eastern Europe.

20 On one occasion, however, Lehi propaganda used the agentless passive form (Bandura, 1990: 170) in an attempt to evade responsibility for the nonconformist behavior: 'Breaking the fence is not necessarily a sign of pig-headedness ... Perhaps it was already completely broken and unable to stand up to the storm of the times. Perhaps the fence simply disintegrated, and there was no need to breach it' (Fighters for the Freedom of Israel (1982), 1: 885).

21 Lehi leaders commended those academics who used their knowledge in the service of the struggle for independence and called upon all historians to write about the past in a way that would encourage their contemporaries to fight for a better future.

22 Compare Deuteronomy 25: 17–19. The British were also referred to as Amalek because they shot and killed Yair from behind.

23 Lehi propaganda also drew attention to the hypocrisy of the British. In contrast to the Nazis, they always talked about justice while acting cruelly and inhumanely.

24 See Koheleth Rabbah 9: 18.

25 Three biblical heroes, Moses, Ehud and Yael, were actually referred to as terrorists, for their killing of an Egyptian, the King of Moab and Sisra, respectively.

26 The Maccabean revolt has, it seems, been incorporated into one of the major projective narratives of the ASALA. For further details, see Tololyan (1988: 223).

27 This rabbinical interpretation of the biblical story can be found in the Babylonian Talmud Tractate Sotah 36b–37a.

28 Paradoxically, a series of articles entitled 'How Nations Fight For Their Freedom' was preceded by a statement to the effect that the example of the Maccabees was sufficient, and that there was therefore no need to read the 'breathtaking stories' of other liberation movements.

29 This term is borrowed from the historian Yosef Hayim Yerushalmi (1982: 44–5), even though he uses it in a rather different way.

30 This point is reminiscent of Maurice Tugwell's (1981: 17–18) theory of the asset-to-liability shift.

31 Lehi propaganda also drew attention to the fact that terrorist groups always gain post-facto legitimation from both their internal and external enemies after the achievement of national independence. 'That is the power of facts.'

32 These three stages of the life histories correspond to Fine's (1995: 135–6) narrative types: horror stories, war stories and happy endings.

33 Beit-Zuri was named after a Hasmonean fortress in the Judean Hills.

34 Writing about the IRA hunger strike of 1981, Aretxaga (1997: 89) concluded that 'witnessing had for these prisoners the force of self-evidence, the power of knowledge that cannot be contested and needs no further elaboration; a kind of knowledge that defies linguistic containment to infuse instead a form of political transcendence'.

35 Lehi propaganda often drew attention to the fact that many of those who went to their death on the gallows did so with a Bible in their hands.

36 Katriel and Shenhar (1990: 368) have pointed out that 'Only great deeds are worthy of mythologization, but the greater their grandeur the more difficult they are to emulate … This message simultaneously engenders a sense of possibility and impossibility, an uneasy balance of empowerment and self-doubt.' However, for some unknown reason this kind of ambivalence was not apparent in Lehi portrayals of the human, and even the superhuman, heroes.

37 Linenthal (1982: 56–9, 78–80, 102–5), writing about the image of the warrior in America, referred to this phenomenon as regenerative sacrifice.

38 This quotation is taken from the second version of the oath of allegiance to the movement. The first one appears in Fighters for the Freedom of Israel (1982), 1: 29.

39 Winston Churchill was referred to as 'the real hangman' who 'pulled the rope' in London.

40 Lehi also regarded the courts of law as an ideal site for 'removing the mask of hypocrisy from the face of the foreign ruler' and providing 'an example and model of the hidden spiritual strength of the Hebrew freedom fighter'.

41 The scaffold was also used as a metaphor for British policy vis-à-vis the yishuv. Reference was made, for instance, to 'the execution rope that is placed on the neck of the Jewish people in its homeland'.

42 Lehi also attacked traditional Judaism's emphasis on the religious rather than the national aspect of the Jewish people. However, this particular criticism was made less frequently and is less relevant to the present study.

43 Exodus 21: 23–5.
44 Babylonian Talmud Tractate Sanhedrin 74b.
45 Lehi propaganda included revised versions of some of the most important prayers (for example, Kol Nidrei and the confession of the Day of Atonement). All the changes made, and particularly the omission of God's name, were designed to emphasize the movement's reliance on human action rather than divine intervention in the struggle for independence.
46 History rather than God would also be the ultimate judge of man's actions. 'One thing is clear. A proper course of action that ends in failure is wrong; an improper course of action that ends in victory is strictly kosher.'
47 Ethics of the Fathers 2: 1.
48 Deuteronomy 6: 5. Lehi members were also instructed to hate the British with 'all your heart and all your might'.
49 In a similar vein, Matityahu Shmuelevitz referred to his being hanged by the British as a 'final prayer'.
50 This argument was sometimes turned on its head. Those who fought and died in the struggle for national liberation were thought to have sanctified the homeland with their blood.
51 Elsewhere they were referred to as 'idols, the work of their hands'.
52 John Thompson's (1984: 198–200) observations concerning the narrative form of ideology suggest that this dichotomy may be less clearcut. Further research is needed to see whether this is, in fact, the case.
53 Having decided to use this term, I came across it in an analysis of Greek Resistance narratives. 'Classical themes,' Janet Hart (1992: 64) argued, 'are privileged over those of class. Patriotism and the nation are stressed, either as parental or Titan figures, and generally the resistance qua nation is cast in a morality play in which good is forecast to prevail over evil.'
54 Apter and Saich (1994: 14) also used this term in their analysis of the way in which the short, intermediate and long stories of Chinese revolutionary discourse 'were made to fit inside each other like nesting boxes'.
55 The particular/Jewish and general/universal narratives correspond to what Michael Walzer (1994: xi) has aptly referred to as thick and thin moral arguments. Contrary to his major argument, though, they were not addressed to audiences at home and abroad, respectively. Both sets of narratives were used to justify Lehi's resort to violence within the confines of the yishuv.
56 This principle can be applied, albeit to a lesser extent, to the interaction between the general/universal and particular/Jewish metanarratives.
57 This is particularly the case because Zionist narratives are characterized by what Margaret Somers (1992: 605) has referred to as 'denarrativization'; that is, they are built on concepts and explanatory schemes that are in themselves abstractions.
58 These labels correspond to the three levels of recognition discussed by Wagner-Pacifici (1986: 136–61) in her intriguing study of the Italian response to the abduction of Aldo Moro.
59 Lehi leaders never attributed the inaction of their Labour Zionist counterparts to legitimate differences of opinion regarding the appropriate response to the mandatory authorities. In fact, they always enclosed the word 'ideological' in inverted commas so as to emphasize that the real reasons lay elsewhere.
60 Gertz (1986: 626) also drew attention to the centrality of this particular mythical plot structure in Zionist narratives about the struggle against internal enemies.

References

English

Aretxaga, Begona (1993), 'Striking With Hunger: Cultural Meanings of Political Violence in Northern Ireland', in Kay Warren (ed.), *The Violence Within: Cultural and Political Opposition in Divided Nations*, Boulder: Westview Press, 219–53.

Aretxaga, Begona (1997), *Shattering Silence: Women, Nationalism and Political Subjectivity in Northern Ireland*, Princeton: Princeton University Press.

Arthur, Paul (1996), 'Reading Violence: Ireland', in David E. Apter (ed.), *The Legitimization of Violence*, New York: New York University Press, 234–91.

Bandura, Albert (1990), 'Mechanisms of Moral Disengagement', in Walter Reich (ed.), *Origins of Terrorism: Psychologies, Ideologies, Theologies, State of Mind*, Cambridge: Cambridge University Press, 161–91.

Bruner, Edward M. and Phyllis Gorfain (1984), 'Dialogic Narration and the Paradoxes of Massada', in Edward M. Bruner (ed.), *Text, Play and Story: The Construction and Reconstruction of Self and Society*, Washington, DC: American Ethnological Society, 56–79.

Connerton, Paul (1989), *How Societies Remember*, Cambridge: Cambridge University Press.

Cordes, Bonnie (1988), 'When Terrorists Do the Talking: Reflections on Terrorist Literature', in David C. Rapoport (ed.), *Inside Terrorist Organizations*, London: Frank Cass, 150–71.

Dodge, David L. (1985), 'The Over-Negativized Conceptualization of Deviance: A Programmatic Exploration', *Deviant Behavior*, 6(1), 17–37.

Ellul, Jacques (1971), *Propaganda: The Formation of Men's Attitudes*, New York: Alfred A. Knopf.

Fisher, Walter R. (1987), *Human Communication as Narration: Toward A Philosophy of Reason, Value and Action*, Columbia: University of South Carolina Press.

Gergen, Kenneth J. and Mary M. Gergen (1983), 'Narratives of the Self', in Theodore R. Sarbin and Karl E. Scheibe (eds), *Studies in Social Identity*, New York: Praeger, 254–73.

Gertz, Nurith (1986), 'Social Myths in Literary and Political Texts', *Poetics Today*, 7(4), 621–39.

Gusfield, Joseph R. (1963), *Symbolic Crusade: Status Politics and the American Temperance Movement*, Urbana: University of Illinois Press.

Kirk, J. Andrew (1979), *Liberation Theology*, Atlanta: John Knox Press.

44b *Narratives of Violence*

Kropotkin, Peter (1978), 'The Spirit of Revolt', in Walter Laquer (ed.), *The Terrorism Reader: A Historical Anthology*, New York: New American Library, 90–96.

Leeman, Richard W. (1991), *The Rhetoric of Terrorism and Counterterrorism*, New York: Greenwood Press.

Lofland, John (1969), *Deviance and Identity*, Englewood Cliffs, NJ: Prentice-Hall.

MacIntyre, Alasdair (1981), *After Virtue: A Study in Moral Theory*, Notre Dame: University of Notre Dame Press.

Miller, Bowman H. (1983), 'The Language Component of Terrorist Strategy', unpublished PhD thesis, Georgetown University, Washington, DC.

Miller, Bowman H. (1987), 'Terrorism and Language: A Text-Based Analysis of the German Case', *Terrorism*, 9(4), 373–407.

Most, Johannes (1978), 'Advice for Terrorists', in Walter Laquer (ed.), *The Terrorism Reader: An Historical Anthology*, New York: New American Library, 100–108.

Ophir, Adi (1994), 'From Pharaoh to Saddam Hussein: The Reproduction of the Other in the Passover Haggadah', in Laurence J. Silberstein and Robert L. Cohn (eds), *The Other in Jewish Thought and History: Constructions of Jewish Culture and Identity*, New York: New York University Press, 205–35.

Picard, Robert G. (1991), 'How Violence is Justified: Sinn Fein's *An Phoblacht*', *Journal of Communication*, 41(4), 90–103.

Post, Jerrold M. (1984), 'Notes on a Psychodynamic Theory of Terrorist Behavior', *Terrorism*, 7(3), 241–56.

Schmid, Alex P. and Jenny de Graaf (1982), *Violence as Communication: Insurgent Terrorism and the Western News Media*, Beverley Hills: Sage Publications.

Scott, Marvin B. and Stanford M. Lyman (1968), 'Accounts', *American Sociological Review*, 33(1), 48–62.

Sprinzak, Ehud (1991a), 'The Process of Delegitimation: Towards a Link-age Theory of Political Terrorism', *Terrorism and Political Violence*, 3(1), 50–68.

Sykes, Gresham M. and David Matza (1957), 'Techniques of Neutralization: A Theory of Delinquency', *American Sociological Review*, 22(6), 664–70.

Tololyan, Khachig (1987), 'Martyrdom as Legitimacy: Terrorism, Religion and Symbolic Appropriation in the Armenian Diaspora', in Paul Wilkinson and Alasdair M. Stewart (eds), *Contemporary Research on Terrorism*, Aberdeen: Aberdeen University Press, 89–103.

Tololyan, Khachig (1988), 'Cultural Narrative and the Motivation of the Terrorist', in David C. Rapoport (ed.), *Inside Terrorist Organizations*, London: Frank Cass, 217–33.

Tugwell, Maurice (1982), 'Guilt Transfer', in David C. Rapoport and Yonah Alexander (eds), *The Morality of Terrorism: Religious and Secular Justifications*, New York: Pergamon Press, 275–89.

Tugwell, Maurice (1986), 'Terrorism and Propaganda: Problem and Response', *Conflict Quarterly*, 6(2), 5–15.

Watson, Francis M. (1975), *Terrorist Propaganda,* Gaithersburg, MD: International Association of Chiefs of Police.

Weimann, Gabriel (1994), *The Theater of Terror: Mass Media and International Terrorism,* New York: Longman.

Weinstein, Eugene A. and Paul Deutschberger (1963), 'Some Dimensions of Altercasting', *Sociometry,* 26(4), 454–66.

Wright, Joanne (1990), *Terrorist Propaganda: The Red Army and the Provisional IRA 1968–1986*, New York: St Martin's Press.

Zerubavel, Yael (1995), *Recovered Roots: Collective Memory and the Israeli National Tradition,* Chicago: University of Chicago Press.

Hebrew

Almog, Oz (1997), *The Sabra–A Profile,* Tel Aviv: Am Oved.

Barnur, Coresh (1998), 'Rhetoric in the Cycle of Terror: The Coverage of the Coastal Road Incident and the Litani Operation in the Israeli and Palestinian Press', unpublished MA Thesis, Bar-Ilan University: Ramat Gan.

Ginosar, Pinhas (1985), *Lehi Revealed: Minutes of the Conferences of the Fighters for the Freedom of Israel*, Ramat Gan: Bar-Ilan University Press.

Harkabi, Yehoshofat (1971), *On Guerilla,* Tel Aviv: Ma' arachot.

Ivianski, Zeev (1991), *Studies in Resistance and Revolt,* Tel Aviv: Yair Publications.

Lev-Ami, Shlomo (1979), *By Struggle and Revolt: Haganah, Irgun and Lehi,* Tel Aviv: Ministry of Defence.

Schatzberger, Hilda (1985), *Resistance and Tradition in Mandatory Palestine,* Ramat Gan: Bar-Ilan University Press.

Yellin-Mor, Natan (1974), *The Fighters for the Freedom of Israel,* Jerusalem: Shikmuna.

Zameret, Zvi (1974), 'The Educational Activities of Lehi', unpublished MA thesis, Hebrew University of Jerusalem, Jerusalem.

Part IV
In the Name of God

[11]

The Logic of Religious Violence

Mark Juergensmeyer

> 'When the struggle reaches the decisive phase may I die fighting in its midst.' – Jarnail Singh Bhindranwale

In the mid-1970s, when militant young Sikhs first began to attack the Nirankaris – members of a small religious community perceived as being anti-Sikh – few observers could have predicted that that violence would escalate into the savagery that seized the Punjab in the 1980s. The Sikhs as a community were too well off economically, too well educated, it seemed, to be a party to random acts of terror. Yet it is true that militant encounters have often played a part in Sikh history, and in the mid-1960s a radical movement very much like that of the 1980s stormed through the Punjab. The charismatic leader at that time was Sant Fateh Singh, who went on a well-publicized fast and threatened to immolate himself on the roof of the Golden Temple's Akali Takht unless the government made concessions that would lead to the establishment of a Sikh-majority state. The Indian government, captained by Prime Minister Indira Gandhi, conceded, and the old Punjab state was carved in two to produce a Hindu-majority Haryana and a new Punjab. It was smaller than the previous one, and contained enough Sikh-dominated areas to give it a slim Sikh majority.

The violence of this decade, however, seems very different from what one saw in the 1960s.[1] For one thing, the attacks themselves have been more vicious. Often they have involved Sikhs and Hindus indiscriminately, and many innocent bystanders have been targeted along with politically active persons. The new Sikh leader, Jarnail Singh Bhindranwale, was stranger – more intense and more strident – than Fateh Singh was, and the goals of Bhindranwale and his allies were more diffuse. Government officials who were trying to negotiate a settlement were never quite certain what their demands were. In fact there was no clear consensus among the activists themselves as to what they wanted, and the items on their lists of demands would shift from time to time. In 1984, shortly before she gave the command for the Indian Army to invade the Golden Temple, an exasperated Indira Gandhi itemized everything she had done to meet the Sikh demands and asked, 'What more can any government do?'[2]

It was a question that frustrated many observers outside the government as well, a good many moderate Sikhs among them. But frustration led to action, and those actions made things worse. The Indian army's brutal assault on the Golden Temple in June 1984, and the heartless massacre of Sikhs by Hindus in Delhi and elsewhere after the assassination of Mrs Gandhi in November of that year caused the violence to escalate.

Still, it is fair to say that quite a bit of bloodshed originated on the Sikh side of the ledger, and within the Sikh community anti-government violence achieved a religious respectability that begs to be explained.

The Rational Explanations

The explanations one hears most frequently place the blame for Sikh violence on political, economic and social factors, and each of these approaches is compelling. The political explanation, for instance, focuses on the weakness of the Sikh political party, the Akali Dal, and its inability to secure a consistent plurality in the Punjab legislature. This is no wonder, since the Sikhs command a bare 51 per cent majority of the post-1966 Punjab. Moreover, the Muslims, who comprised the Punjab's other non-Hindu religious community before 1948, were awarded a nation of their own at the time of India's independence, so it is understandable that many Sikhs would continue to long for greater political power, and even yearn for their own Pakistan.[3]

The economic explanation for Sikh unrest is largely a matter of seeing the achievements of the Sikhs in relation to what they feel their efforts should warrant, rather than to what others in India have received. Compared with almost every other region of India, the Punjab is fairly well-to-do. Yet Sikhs complain, with some justification, that for that very reason they have been deprived of their fair share: resources from the Punjab have been siphoned off to other parts of the nation.[4] Agricultural prices, for example, are held stable in India in part because the government maintains a ceiling on the prices that farmers in rich agricultural areas like the Punjab are permitted to exact. In addition some Sikhs claim that industrial growth has been hampered in the Punjab as the government has encouraged growth in other parts of India, and that the Punjab's agricultural lifeblood – water for irrigation from Punjabi rivers – has been diverted to farming areas in other states.

The social explanation for Sikh discontent is just as straightforward: the Sikhs are a minority community in India, and their separate identity within the Indian family is in danger. Since the religious ideas on which Sikhism is based grew out of the nexus of medieval Hinduism, Sikhs fear they could be reabsorbed into the amorphous cultural mass that is Hinduism and dissappear as a distinct religious community.[5] The possibility is real: Sikhism almost vanished in the latter part of the nineteenth century. But in this century secularism is as much a threat as Hinduism, and like fundamentalist movements in many other parts of the world, Sikh traditionalists have seen the secular government as the perpetrator of a dangerous anti-religious ideology that threatens the existence of such traditional religious communities as their own. In the perception of some Sikhs, these two threats – the religious and the secular – have recently combined forces as the Hindu right has exercised increasing political power and Mrs Gandhi's Congress Party has allegedly pandered to its interests.[6]

There is nothing wrong with these political, economic and social explanations of Sikh unrest. Each is persuasive in its own sphere, and together they help us understand why the Sikhs as a community have been unhappy. But they do not help us understand the piety with which a few Sikhs have justified their bloody acts or the passion with which so many of them have condoned them – even the random acts of destruction associated with terrorism. Nor are they the sort of explanations one hears from Sikhs who are most closely involved in the struggle. The socio-economic and political explanations usually come from observers outside the Sikh community or from those inside it who are least sympathetic to the militant protesters. The point of view of the activists is different. Their frame of reference is more grand: their explanations of the conflict and its causes achieve almost mythical dimensions. To understand this point of view we have to turn to their own words and see what they reveal about the radicals' perception of the world about them.

The Religious Rhetoric of Sikh Violence

To understand the militant Sikh position, I have chosen to focus on the speeches of Jarnail Singh Bhindranwale, the man who was without dispute the most visible and charismatic of this generation's militant leaders.[7] He was also the most revered – or despised, depending on one's point of view. During his lifetime he was called a *sant*, a holy man, and a few Sikhs have been bold enough to proclaim him the eleventh *guru*, and thus challenge the traditional Sikh belief that the line of ten gurus ended with Gobind Singh in the early eighteenth century.

Jarnail Singh was born in 1947 at the village Rodey near the town of Moga. He was the youngest son in a poor family of farmers from the Jat caste, and when he was 18 years old his father handed him over for religious training to the head of a Sikh center known as the Damdani Taksal. The leader came from the village Bhindran and was therefore known as Bhindranwale, and after his death, when the mantle of leadership fell on young Jarnail Singh, he assumed his mentor's name. The young leader took his duties seriously and gained a certain amount of fame as a preacher. He was a stern one at that: Jarnail became famous for castigating the easy-living, easy-drinking customs of Sikh villagers, especially those who clipped their beards and adopted modern ways. He carried weapons, and on 13 April 1978, in a bloody confrontation in Amritsar with members of the renegade Nirankari religious movement, he showed that he was not afraid to use them. This episode was followed by an attack from Nirankaris that killed a number of Bhindranwale's followers, and further counter-attacks ensued.[8] Thus began the bloody career of a man who was trained to live a calm and spiritual life of religious devotion.

Although he was intitally at the fringes of Sikh leadership, during the late 1970s Bhindranwale began to be taken seriously within Akali circles because of his growing popularity among the masses.[9] He seemed to have been fixated on the Nirankaris: his fiery sermons condemned them as evil. He regarded them as a demonic force that endangered the very basis of the Sikh community, especially its commitment to the authority of the Sikh gurus. And in time he expanded his characterization of their demonic power to include those who protected them, including the secular government of Indira Gandhi.

Much of what Bhindranwale has to say in sermons of this period, however, might be heard in the sermons of Methodist pastors in Iowa or in the homilies of clergies belonging to any religious tradition, anywhere on the globe. He calls for faith – faith in a time of trial – and for the spiritual discipline that accompanies it. In one sermon he rebukes the press and others who call him an extremist, and explains what sort of an extremist he is:

> One who takes the vows of faith and helps others take it; who reads the scriptures and helps others to do the same; who avoids liquor and drugs and helps others do likewise; who urges unity and cooperation; who preaches Hindu-Sikh unity and coexistence ... who says: 'respect your scriptures, unite under the flag, stoutly support the community, and be attached to your Lord's throne and home'.[10]

Like many Protestant ministers, Bhindranwale prescribes piety as the answer to every need. 'You can't have courage without reading [the Sikh scriptures]', he admonishes his followers: 'Only the [scripture]-readers can suffer torture and be capable of feats of strength'.[11] He is especially harsh on backsliders in the faith. Those who cut their beards are targets of his wrath: 'Do you think you resemble the image of Guru Gobind Singh?' he asks them.[12] But then he reassures the bulk of his followers. Because of their persistence in the faith, he tells them, 'the Guru will give you strength', adding that 'righteousness is with you'.[13] They will need all the strength and courage they can get, Bhindranwale explains, because their faith is under attack.[14]

Lying only slightly beneath the surface of this language is the notion of a great struggle that Bhindranwale thinks is taking place. On the personal level it is the tension between faith and the lack of faith; on the cosmic level it is the battle between truth and evil. Often his rhetoric is vague about who the enemy really is. 'In order to destroy religion', Bhindranwale informs his congregation, 'on all sides and in many forms mean tactics have been initiated'.[15] But rather than wasting effort in explaining who these forces are and why they would want to destroy religion, Bhindranwale dwells instead on what should be the response: a willingness to fight and defend the faith – if necessary, to the end.

> Unless you are prepared to die, sacrificing your own life, you cannot be a free people .... If you start thinking in terms of service to your community then you will be on the right path and you will readily sacrifice yourself. If you have faith in the Guru no power on earth can enslave you. The Sikh faith is to pray to God, take one's vows before the Guru Granth Sahib [scriptures] and then act careless of consequences to oneself.[16]

At other times Bhindranwale cites what appear to be specific attacks on Sikhism, but again the perpetrators are not sharply defined; they remain a vague, shadowy force of evil. 'The Guru Granth [scripture] has been buried in cowdung and thrown on the roadside', Bhindranwale informs his followers. 'That is your Father, your Guru, that they treat so.'[17] On another occasion he urges his followers to 'seek justice against those who have dishonored our sisters, drunk the blood of innocent persons, and insulted Satguru Granth Sahib'.[18] But the 'they' and the 'those' are not identified.

Occasionally, however, the enemy is more clearly specified: they are 'Hindus', 'the government', 'the press', the Prime Minister – whom he calls that 'lady born to a house of Brahmins'[19] – and perhaps most frequently Sikhs themselves who have fallen from the path. This somewhat rambling passage indicates these diverse enemies and the passionate hatred that Bhindranwale feels towards them:

> I cannot really understand how it is that, in the presence of Sikhs, Hindus are able to insult the [scriptures]. I don't know how these Sikhs were born to mothers and why they were not born to animals: to cats and to bitches .... Whoever insults the Guru Granth Sahib should be killed then and there .... Some youths complain that if they do such deeds then nobody harbours them. Well, no place is holier than this one [the Golden Temple] .... I will take care of the man who comes to me after lynching the murderer of the Guru Granth Sahib; I'll fight for his case. What else do you want? That things have come to such a pass is in any event all your own weakness .... The man whose sister is molested and does nothing about it, whose Guru is insulted and who keeps on talking and doing nothing, has he got any right to be known as the son of the Guru? Just think for yourselves![20]

And in a similar vein:

> Talk is not enough against injustice. We have to act. Here you raise your swords but tomorrow you may wipe the dust from the sandals of sister Indira .... We have the right to be Sikhs .... The dearest thing to any Sikh should be the honor of the Guru .... Those foes – the government and Hindus – are not dangerous. Rather one has to be wary of those who profess Sikhism yet do not behave as Sikhs.[21]

As important as Bhindranwale feels the immediate struggle is, he reminds his followers that the Sikh tradition has always been filled with conflict, and that the current battles are simply the most recent chapters in a long ongoing war with the enemies of the faith. The foes of today are connected with those from the legendary past. Indira Gandhi, for instance, is implicitly compared with the Moghul emperors: 'The rulers [the Congress party leaders] should keep in mind that in the past many like them did try in vain to annihilate the Gurus.'[22] In other speeches, Bhindranwale frequently looks to the past for guidance in dealing with current situations. When Sikhs who had sided with government policies come to him for forgiveness, for instance, he refuses. 'I asked that man', explains Bhindranwale, 'had he ever read a page of our history? Was the man who tortured Guru Arjūn pardoned?'[23]

Occasionally Bhindranwale refers to some of the specific political, economic and social demands made by more moderate Sikh leaders. He supports these demands, but they are not his primary concern. In fact, the targets of these demands are often characterized simply as 'injustices', illustrations of the fact that the Sikh community is abused and under attack.[24] Since the larger struggle is the more important matter, these specific difficulties are of no great concern to Bhindranwale; they change from time to time. And it is of no use to win on one or two points and fail on others. Compromise is impossible; only complete victory will signal that the tide has turned. For that reason Bhindranwale scolds the Akali leaders for seeking a compromise settlement of the political demands made by Sikh leaders at Anandpur Sahib in 1973. 'Either full implementation of the Anandpur Sahib resolution', Bhindranwale demands, 'or their heads'.[25]

In a sense, then, Bhindranwale feels that individual Sikh demands can never really be met, because the ultimate struggle of which they are a part is much greater than the contestation between political parties and factional points of view. It is a vast cosmic struggle, and only such an awesome encounter is capable of giving profound meaning to the motivations of those who fight for Sikh causes. Such people are not just fighting for water rights and political boundaries, they are fighting for truth itself.

Clearly the religious language of Sikh militants like Bhindranwale is the language of ulitmate struggle. But two related matters are not so obvious: why is this language attached to the more mundane issues of human politics and economics? and why is it linked with violent acts?

A Pause for Definitions: Violence and Religion

Before we turn to these questions,, however, it might be useful to pause for a moment for definitions. Since I want to look at issues having to do with the general relation between violence and religion, not merely those that affect the Sikhs, it might be useful if I describe what I mean by these terms.

I will restrict my use of the word violence to actions that are aimed at taking human life – that intend to, and do, kill. Moreover, I mean especially abnormal, illegal, shocking acts of destruction. All acts of killing are violent, of course, but warfare and capital punishment have an aura of normalcy and do not violate our sensibilities in the same way as actions that seem deliberately designed to elicit feelings of revulsion and anger from those who witness them.[26] By speaking of violence in this restricted way, I mean to highlight the characteristics that we usually associate with terrorist acts.

The term religion is more difficult to define. I have been impressed with the recent attempts of several sociologists to find a definition that is not specific to any cultural region or historical period, and is appropriate for thinking about the phenomenon in modern as well as traditional societies. Clifford Geertz, for instance, sees religion as the effort to integrate everyday reality into a pattern of coherence that takes shape on a deeper level.[27] Robert Bellah also thinks of religion as the attempt to reach beyond ordinary reality in the 'risk of faith' that allows people to act 'in the face of uncertainty and unpredictability'.[28] Peter Berger specifies that such faith is an affirmation of the sacred, which acts as a doorway to a different kind of reality.[29] Louis Dupré' prefers to avoid the term 'sacred', but integrates elements of both Berger's and Bellah's definition in his description of religion as 'a commitment to the transcendent as to *another* reality'.[30]

What all of these definitions have in common is their emphasis on a certain kind of experience that people share with others in particular communities. It is an experience of another reality, or of a deeper stratum of the reality that we know in everyday life. As Durkheim, whose thought is fundamental to each of these thinkers, was adamant in observing, religion has a more encompassing force than can be suggested by any dichotomization of the sacred and the profane. To Durkheim, the religious point of view includes both the notion that there is such a dichotomy, and that the sacred aspects of it will always, ultimately, reign supreme.[31] Summarizing Durkheim's and the others' definitions of religion, I think it might be described as the perception that there is a tension between reality as it appears and as it really is (or has been, or will be).

This definition helps us think of religion as the subjective experience of those who use religious language, and in fact it is easier with this definition to speak of religious language, or a religious way of looking at the world, than to speak of religion in a more reified sense.[32] When we talk of the various 'religions', then, we mean the communities that have a tradition of sharing a particular religious point of view, a world view in which there is an essential conflict between appearance and a deeper reality. There is the hint, in this definition, that the deeper reality holds a degree of permanence and order quite unobtainable by ordinary means, as religious people affirm. The conflict between the two is what religion is about: religious language contains images both of grave disorder and tranquil order, and often holds out the hope that despite appearances to the contrary, order eventually will triumph, and disorder will be contained.

Why Does Religion Need Violence?

There is nothing in this definition that requires religion to be violent, but it does lead one to expect religious language to make sense of violence and to incorporate it in some way into the world view it expresses. Violence, after all, shocks one's sense of order and has the potential for causing the ultimate disorder in any person's life: physical destruction and death. Since religious language is about the tension between order and disorder, it is frequently about violence.

The symbols and mythology of Sikhism, for instance, are full of violence. The most common visual symbol of Sikhism is the two-edged sword (*khanda*), supported by two scabbards and surrounded by a circle. Sikhs often interpret the two edges of this sword as symbolizing spiritual and worldly foes,[33] and they say that a battle sword (*kirpan*) is included among the five objects that Sikhs are supposed to wear at all times to symbolize an awareness of these same enemies.[34] Unlike the Bible, the sacred scriptures of the Sikhs – known collectively as the *Guru Granth Sahib* – do not contain accounts of wars and savage acts, but the stories of the Sikhs' historical past are bloody indeed. In fact, these stories have taken on a canonical character within Sikhism, and they more vividly capture the imagination than the devotional and theological sentiments of the scriptures themselves. The calendar art so prominent in most Sikh homes portrays a mystical Guru Nanak, of course, but alongside him there are pictures of Sikh military heroes and scenes from great battles. Bloody images also leap from brightly-colored oil paintings in the Sikh Museum housed in the Golden Temple. There are as many depictions of martyrs in their wretched final moments as of victors radiant in conquest.

Because the violence is so prominent in Sikh art and legend, and because many symbols of the faith are martial, one might think that Sikhs as a people are more violent than their counterparts in other areas of India. But if one leaves aside the unrest of the past several years, I do not think this can be demonstrated. It would be convenient to say that the prestige of violent symbols in the Sikh religion has increased Sikhs' propensity for violent action, or that the Sikh religion is violent because Sikhs as a people are violent, but I do not think either of these arguments can be made very convincingly.

The fact is that the symbols and mythology of most religious traditions are filled with violent images, and their histories leave trails of blood. One wonders that familiarity can prevent Christians from being repulsed by the violent images portrayed by hymns such as 'Onward Christian Soldiers', 'The Old Rugged Cross', 'Washed in the Blood of the Lamb', and 'There is a Fountain Flowing with Blood'. Or perhaps familiarity is not the issue at all. The central symbol of Christianity is an execution device – a cross – from which, at least in the Roman tradition, the dying body still hangs. From a non-Christian point of view, the most sacred of Christian rituals, the eucharist, looks like ritual cannabalism, where the devout eat the flesh and drink the blood of their departed leader. At a certain level, in fact, this interpretation is accurate; yet few would argue that the violent acts perpetrated by Christians over the centuries are the result of their being subjected to such messages.

The ubiquity of violent images in religion and the fact that some of the most ancient religious practices involve the sacrificial slaughter of animals have led to speculation about why religion and violence are so intimately bound together. Some of these speculators are among the best known modern theorists. Karl Marx, for instance, saw religious symbols as the expression of real social oppression, and religious wars as the result of tension among economic classes.[35] Sigmund Freud saw in religious rituals vestiges of a primal oedipal act that when ritually reenacted provide a symbolic resolution of feelings of sexual and physical aggression.[36] More recently, Rene Girard has revived the Freudian thesis but given it a social rather than psychological coloration. Girard sees the violent images of religion as a symbolic displacement of violence from one's own communal fellowship to a scapegoat foe.[37]

What these thinkers have in common is that they see religious violence as a symptom of and symbol for something else: social hostility, in the case of Marx; sexual and physical aggression, in the case of Freud; social competition, in the case of Girard. They may be right: religion and other cultural forms may have been generated out of basic personal and social needs. Yet it seems to me that even without these explanations the internal logic of religion requires that religious symbols and myths express violent meanings.

Religion deals with the ultimate tension between order and disorder, and disorder is inherently violent, so it is understandable that the chaotic, dangerous character of life is represented in religious images. Of course, the religious promise is that order conquers chaos; so it is also understandable that the violence religion portrays is in some way limited or tamed. In Christianity, for example, the very normalcy with which the blood-filled hymns are sung and the eucharist is eaten indicates their domestication. In ritual, violence is symbolically transferred. The blood of the eucharistic wine is ingested by the supplicant and becomes part of living tissue; it brings new life. In song a similarly calming transformation occurs. For, as Christian theology explains, in Christ violence has been corralled. Christ died in order for death to be defeated, and his blood is that of the sacrifical lamb who atones for our sins so that we will not have to undergo a punishment as gruesome as his.

In the Sikh tradition violent images are also domesticated. The symbol of the two-edged sword has become an emblem to be worn on lockets and proudly emblazened on shops and garden gates. It is at the forefront of the worship center in Sikh *gurudwaras* where it is treated as reverently as Christians treat their own emblem of destruction, the cross. And the gory wounds of the martyrs bleed on in calendar art. As I have suggested, Sikh theologians and writers are no more hesitant to allegorize the meaning of such symbols and stories than their Christian counterparts. They point toward the war between good and evil that rages in each person's soul.

The symbols of violence in religion, therefore, are symbols of a violence conquered, or at least put in place, by the larger framework of order that religious language provides. But one must ask how these symbolic presentations of violence are related to real violence. One might think that they should prevent violent acts by allowing violent feelings to be channelled into the harmless dramas of ritual, yet we know that the opposite is sometimes the case. The violence of religion can be savagely real.

Why Does Violence Need Religion?

A reason often given to explain why religious symbols are associated with acts of real violence is that religion is exploited by violent people. This explanation, making religion the pure and innocent victim of the darker forces of human nature, is undoubtedly too easy; yet it contains some truth. Religion in fact is sometimes exploited, and it is important to understand why people who are engaged in potentially violent struggles do at times turn to the language of religion. In the case of the Sikhs, this means asking why the sort of people who were exercised over the economic, political and social issues explored at the beginning of this article turned to preachers like Bhindranwale for leadership.

One answer is that by sacralizing these concerns the political activists gave them an aura of legitimacy that they did not previously possess. The problem with this answer is that most of the concerns we mentioned – the inadequacy of Sikh political representation, for instance, and the inequity of agricultural prices – were perfectly legitimate, and did not need the additional moral weight of religion to give them respectability. And in fact, the people who were primarily occupied with these issues – Sikh businessmen and political leaders – were not early supporters of Bhindranwale. Even when they became drawn into his campaign, their relation with him remained ambivalent at best.

There was one political demand, however, that desperately needed all the legitimization that it could get. This was the demand for Khalistan, a separate Sikh nation. Separatist leaders such as Jagjit Singh Chauhan were greatly buoyed by such words of Bhindranwale as these:

> We are religiously separate. But why do we have to emphasize this? It is only because we are losing our identity. Out of selfish interests our Sikh leaders who have only the success of their farms and their industries at heart have started saying that there is no difference between Sikh and Hindu. Hence the danger of assimilation has increased.[38]

> When they say the Sikhs are not separate we'll demand separate identity – even if it demands sacrifice.[39]

Bhindranwale himself, interestingly, never came out in support of Khalistan. 'We are not in favor of Khalistan nor are we against it', he said, adding that 'we wish to live in India', but would settle for a separate state if the Sikhs did not receive what he regarded as their just respect.[40] Whatever his own reservations about the Khalistan issue, however, his appeal to sacrifice made his rhetoric attractive to the separatists. It also raised another, potentially more powerful aspect of the sacralization of political demands: the prospect that religion could give moral sanction to violence.

By indentifying a temporal social struggle with the cosmic struggle of order and disorder, truth and evil, political actors are able to avail themselves of a way of thinking that justifies the use of violent means. Ordinarily only the state has the moral right to take life – for purposes either of military defense, police protection or punishment – and the codes of ethics established by religious traditions support this position. Virtually every religious tradition, including the Sikhs', applauds non-violence and proscribes the taking of human life.[41] The only exception to this rule is the one we have given: most ethical codes allow the state to kill for reasons of punishment and protection.[42]

Those who want moral sanction for their use of violence, and who do not have the approval of an officially recognized government, find it helpful to have access to a higher source: the meta-morality that religion provides. By elevating a temporal struggle to the level of the cosmic, they can bypass the usual moral restrictions on killing. If a battle of the spirit is thought to exist, then it is not ordinary morality but the rules of war that apply. It is interesting that the best-known incidents of religious violence throughout the contemporary world have occurred in places where there is difficulty in defining the character of a nation state. Palestine and Ireland are the most obvious examples, but the revolution in Iran also concerned itself with what the state should be like, and what elements of society should lead it. Religion provided the basis for a new national consensus and a new kind of leadership.

There are some aspects of social revolution in the Punjab situation as well. It is not the established leaders of the Akali party who have resorted to violence, but a second level of leadership – a younger, more marginal group for whom the use of violence is enormously empowering. The power that comes from the barrel of a gun, as Mao is said to have remarked, has a very direct effect. But there is a psychological dimension to this power that may be even more effective. As Frantz Fanon argued in the context of the Algerian revolution some years ago even a small display of violence can have immense symbolic power: the power to jolt the masses into an awareness of their potency.[43]

It can be debated whether or not the masses in the Punjab have been jolted into an awareness of their own capabilities, but the violent actions of the militants among them have certainly made the masses more aware of the militants' powers. They have attained a status of authority rivalling what police and other government officials possess. One of the problems in the Punjab today is the unwillingness of many villagers in the so-called terrorist zones around Batala and Taran Tarn to report terrorist activities to the authorities. The radical youth are even said to have established an alternative government.

By being dangerous the young Sikh radicals have gained a certain notoriety, and by clothing their actions in the moral garb of religion they have given their actions legitimacy. Because their actions are morally sanctioned by religion, they are fundamentally political actions: they break the state's monopoly on morally-sanctioned killing. By putting the right to kill in their own hands, the perpetrators of religious violence are also making a daring claim of political independence.

Even though Bhindranwale was not an outspoken supporter of Khalistan, he often spoke of the Sikhs' separate identity as that of a religious community with national characterisics. The term he used for religious community, *quam*, is an Urdu term that has overtones of nationhood. It is the term the Muslims used earlier in this century in defending their right to have a separate nation, and it is the term that Untouchables used in the Punjab in the 1920s when they attempted to be recognized as a separate social and political entity.[44] Another term that is important to Bhindranwale is *miri-piri*, the notion that spiritual and temporal power are linked.[45] It is this concept that is symbolically represented by the two-edged sword and that justified Sikh support for an independent political party. Young Sikh activists are buttressed in their own aspirations to leadership by the belief that acts that they conceive as being heroic and sacrificial – even those that involve taking the lives of others – have both spiritual and political significance. They are risking their lives for God and the Sikh community.

Not all of the Sikh community appreciates their efforts, however, and the speeches of Bhindranwale make clear that disagreements and rivalries within the community were one of his major concerns. Some of Bhindranwale's harshest words were reserved for Sikhs who he felt showed weakness and a tendency to make easy compromises. In one speech, after quoting a great martyr in Sikh history as having said, 'even if I have to give my head, may I never lose my love for the Sikh Faith', Bhindranwale railed against Sikh bureaucrats and modernized youth who could not make that sacrifice, and ended with a little joke:

> I am sorry to note that many people who hanker after a government position say instead, 'even if I lose my Faith, may I never lose my position'. And our younger generation has started saying this: 'even if I lose my Faith, may a beard never grow on my face'. ... If you find the beard too heavy, pray to God saying ... 'we do not like this Sikhism and manhood. Have mercy on us. Make us into women ....'[46]

But most Sikhs in Bhindranwale's audience, including the youth, were not the sort who would be tempted to cut their hair; and few, especially in the villages where Bhindranwale had been popular, were in a position to 'hanker after a governmental position'. People, such as the Akali leaders whom Bhindranwale castigated for making compromises for the sake of personal gain, were no doubt objects of contempt in the villages long before Bhindranwale came along, and by singling them out, Bhindranwale identified familiar objects of derision – scapegoats – that humbled those who had succeeded in worldly affairs and heightened the sense of unity among those who had not.

Bhindranwale made a great plea for unity. 'Our misfortune is disunity', he told his audiences. 'We try to throw mud at each other. Why don't we give up thinking of mud and in close embrace with each other work with determination to attain our goals.'[47] Those who eventually opposed him, including the more moderate Akali leader, Sant Harchand Singh Longowal, regarded Bhindranwale as a prime obstacle to the very unity he preached. During the dark days immediately preceding Operation Bluestar in June 1984, the two set up rival camps in the Golden Temple and allegedly killed each other's lieutenants. It is no wonder that many of Bhindranwale's followers, convinced the Indian army had a collaborator inside the Golden Temple, were suspicious when Bhindranwale was murdered in the raid and Longowal was led off safely under arrest. No wonder also that many regarded Longowal's assassination a year later as revenge for Bhindranwale's.

While he was alive, Bhindranwale continued to preach unity, but it was clear that what he wanted was for everyone else to unite around him. He and his supporters wished to give the impression that they were at the center, following the norm of Sikh belief and behavior, and that the community should therefore group around them. This message had a particular appeal to those who were socially marginal to the Sikh community, including lower-caste people and Sikhs who had taken up residence abroad. Some of the most fanatical of Bhindranwale's followers, including Beant Singh, the assassin of Indira Gandhi, came from the Untouchable castes (Beant Singh was from the lowest caste of Untouchables, the Sweepers), and a considerable amount of money and moral support for the Punjab militants came from Sikhs living in such far-away places as London, Houston, and Yuba City, California.

These groups gained from their indentification with Bhindranwale a sense of belonging, and the large Sikh communities in England, Canada and America were especially sensitive to his message that the Sikhs needed to be strong, united and defensive of their tradition. Many of Bhindranwale's supporters in the Punjab, however, received a more tangible benefit from associating with his cause: politically active village youth and small-time clergy were able to gain support from many who were not politically mobilized before. In that sense Bhindranwale was fomenting something of a political revolution, and the constituency was not unlike the one the Ayatollah Khomeini was able to gather in Iran. In so far as Bhindranwale's message was taken as an endorsement of the killings that some of these fundamentalist youth committed, the instrument of religious violence gave power to those who had little power before.

When Does Cosmic Struggle Lead to Real Violence?

The pattern of religious violence of the Sikhs could be that of Irish Catholics, or Shi'ite Muslims in Palestine, or fundamentalist Christian bombers of abortion clinics in the United States. There are a great many communities in which the language of cosmic struggle justifies acts of violence. But those who are engaged in them, including the Sikhs, would be offended if we concluded from the above discussion that their actions were purely for social or political gain. They argue that they act out of religious conviction, and surely they are to some degree right. Destruction is a part of the logic of religion, and virtually every religious tradition carries with it images of chaos and terror. But symbolic violence does not lead in every instance to real bloodshed, and even the eagerness of political actors to exploit religious symbols is not in all cases sufficient to turn religion towards a violent end. Yet some forms of religion do seem to propel the faithful rather easily into militant confrontation: which ones, and why?

The current resurgence of religious violence around the world has given an urgency to attempts to answer these questions, and to identify which characteristics of religion are conducive to violence. The efforts of social scientists have been directed primarily to the social and political aspects of the problem, but at least a few of them have tried to trace the patterns in religion's own logic. David C. Rapoport, for instance, has identified several features of messianic movements that he believes lead to violence, most of which are characterized by a desire for an antinomian liberation from oppression.[48]

My own list of characteristics comes directly from our discussion of the religious language of cosmic struggle. It is informed by my understanding of what has happened in the Sikh tradition, but it seems to me that the following tenets of religious commitment are found whenever acts of religious violence occur.

1. The Cosmic Struggle is Played Out in History

To begin with, it seems to me that if religion is to lead to violence it is essential for the devout to believe that the cosmic struggle is realizable in human terms. If the war between good and evil, order and chaos, is conceived as taking place in historical time, in a real geographical location, and among actual social contestants, it is more likely that those who are prone to violent acts will associate religion with their struggles. This may seem to be an obvious point, yet we have some evidence that it is not always true.

In the Hindu tradition, for instance, the mythical battles in the Mahabharata and Ramayana epics are as frequently used as metaphors for present-day struggles as are the actual battles in Sikh and Islamic history and in biblical Judaism and Christianity. Like members of these traditions, Hindus characterize their worldly foes by associating them with the enemies of the good in their legendary battles. The main difference between the Hindus and the others is that their enemies are mythical – that is, they seem mythical to us. To many pious Hindus, however, the stories in the epics are no less real than those recorded in the Bible or in the Sikh legends. A believing Hindu will be able to show you where the great war of the Mahabharata was actually fought, and where the gods actually lived. Moreover, the Hindu cycles of time allow for a cosmic destruction to take place in this world, at the end of the present dark age. So the Hindu tradition is not as devoid of images of divine intervention in worldly struggles as outsiders sometimes assume.[49]

The major tradition that appears to lack the notion that the cosmic struggle is played out on a social plane is Buddhism. But this is an exception that proves the rule, for it is a tradition that is characteristically devoid of religiously sanctioned violence. There are instances in Thai history that provide Buddhist justifications for warfare, but these are rare for the tradition as a whole. In general, Buddhism has no need for actual battles in which the pious can prove their mettle.

2. *Believers Identify Personally with the Struggle*

The Buddhist tradition does affirm that there is a spiritual conflict, however: it is the clash between the perception that this imperfect and illusory world is real and a higher consciousness that surmounts worldly perception altogether. And in a sense, the struggle takes place in this world, in that it takes place in the minds of worldly persons. This kind of internalization of the cosmic struggle does not in itself lead to violence, and Buddhists are not ordinarily prone to violent deeds. Nor are Sufis, the Islamic mystics who have reconceived the Muslim notion of *jihad*. To many Sufis, the greater *jihad* is not the one involving worldly warfare, but the one within: the conflict between good and evil within one's own soul.[50]

This talk about the cosmic struggle as something inside the self would seem to be easily distinguishable from external violence, but in Sikh theology, including the rhetoric of Bhindranwale, they go hand in hand. 'The weakness is in us', Bhindranwale was fond of telling his followers. 'We are the sinners of this house of our Guru.'[51] Militant Shi'ite Muslims are similarly racked with a sense of personal responsibility for the moral decadence of the world, and once again their tendency toward internalization does not necessarily shield them from acts of external violence. The key to the connection, it seems to me, is that at the same time that the cosmic struggle is understood to impinge about the inner recesses of an individual person, it must be understood as occurring on a worldy, social plane. Neither of these notions is by itself sufficient to motivate a person to religious violence. If one believes that the cosmic struggle is largely a matter of large continuing social forces, one is not likely to become personally identified with the struggle; and if one is convinced that the struggle is solely interior there is no reason to look for it outside. But when the two ideas coexist, they are a volatile concoction.

Thus when Bhindranwale spoke about the warfare in the soul his listeners knew that however burdensome that conflict is, they need not bear it alone. They may band together with their comrades and continue the struggle in the external arena, where the foes are more vulnerable, and victories more tangible. And their own internal struggles impel them to become involved in the worldly conflict: their identification with the overall struggle makes them morally responsible, in part, for its outcome. 'We ourselves are ruining Sikhism', Bhindranwale once told his congregation.[52] On another occasion he told the story of how, when Guru Gobind Singh asked an army of 80,000 to sacrifice their heads for the faith, only five assented. Bhindranwale implied that the opportunity was still at hand to make the choice of whether they were to be one of the five or the 79,995.[53] He reminded them that even though the cosmic war was still being waged, and that the evil within them and outside them had not yet been purged, their choice could still make a difference.

Sikhism is not the only tradition in which this link is forged between the external and internal arenas of the cosmic struggle. Shi'ite Muslims bear a great weight of communal guilt for not having defended one of the founders of their tradition, Husain, when he was attacked and martyred by the vicious Yazid. During the Iranian revolution some of them relived that conflict by identifying specific foes – the Shah and President Jimmy Carter – as Yazids returned. There was no doubt that such people should be attacked. Radical Shi'ites in Iran were not about to compound their guilt and miss an historical opportunity of righting an ancient wrong.

The same sort of logic has propelled many Christians into a vicious anti-Semitism. It is a mark of good Christian piety for individuals to bear the responsibility for the crucifiction of Jesus: the theme of Christians taking part in the denial and betrayal of Jesus is the stuff of many a hymn and sermon. Some Christians believe that the foes to whom they allowed Jesus to be delivered were the Jews. Attacks on the present-day Jewish community, therefore, help to lighten their sense of culpability.

3. The Cosmic Struggle Continues in the Present

What makes these actions of Sikhs, Shi'ites and anti-Semitic Christians spritually defensible is the conviction that the sacred struggle has not ended in some earlier period, but that it continues in some form today. It is a conviction that also excites the members of the Gush Emunim, a militant movement in present-day Israel, who have taken Israel's victory in the Six Day War as a sign that the age of messianic redemption has finally begun.[54]

Not all Israelis respond to this sign with the same enthusiasm, however, just as not all Christians or Shi'ite Muslims are convinced that the apocalyptic conflict prophesied by their tradition is really at hand. Many of the faithful assent to the notion that the struggle exists within, for what person of faith has not felt the internal tension between belief and disbelief, affirmation and denial, order and chaos? But they often have to be persuaded that the conflict currently rages on a social plane, especially if the social world seems orderly and benign.

Bhindranwale took this challenge as one of the primary tasks of his ministry. He said that one of his main missions was to alert his people that they were oppressed, even if they did not know it. He ended one of his sermons with this fervent plea: 'I implore all of you in this congregation. Go to the villages and make every child, every mother, every Singh realise we are slaves and we have to shake off this slavery in order to survive.'[55]

In Bhindranwale's mind the appearances of normal social order simply illustrated how successful the forces of evil had become in hiding their demonic agenda. His logic compelled him to believe that Punjabi society was racked in a great struggle, even if it showed no indication of it. Long before the Punjab was torn apart by its most recent round of violence, Bhindranwale claimed that an even fiercer form of violence reigned: the appearance of normal order was merely a demonic deception. Bhindranwale hated the veil of calm that seemed to cover his community and recognized that his own followers were often perplexed about what he said: 'Many of our brothers, fresh from the villages, ask, "Sant Ji, we don't know about enslavement." For that reason, I have to tell you why you are slaves.'[56]

The evidence that Bhindranwale gave for the oppression of Sikhs was largely limited to examples of police hostility that arose after the spiral of violence in the Punjab began to grow. Some of his allegations, such as the account he gave of the treatment meted out to followers who hijacked Indian airplanes, have a peculiar ring:

> If a Sikh protests in behalf of his Guru by hijacking a plane, he is put to death .... None of the Sikhs in these three hijackings attacked any passenger nor did they damage the planes. But the rule is that for a fellow with a turban, there is the bullet ... . For a person who says 'Hare Krishna, Hare Krishna, Hare Rama', there is a government appointment. Sikh brothers, this is a sign of slavery.[57]

Those who attempted to combat Bhindranwale could not win against such logic. If they responded to Sikh violence they would be seen as oppressors. If they did not respond, the violence would escalate. And even if there was neither violence nor repression, the absence of the overt signs of conflict would be an indication to Bhindranwale of a demonical calm.

4. The Struggle is at a Point of Crisis

On a number of occasions, in referring to the immediacy of the struggle, Bhindranwale seemed to indicate that the outcome was in doubt. His perception of the enormity of the evil he faced and of the torpor of the Sikh response made his prognosis a dismal one. Sometimes he felt that the best efforts of a few faithful Sikhs were doomed: 'today', he darkly proclaimed, 'the Sikh community is under threat'.[58] But on other occasions he seemed to hold out a measure of hope. Things were coming to a head, he implied, and the struggle was about to enter 'the decisive phase'.[59]

What is interesting about this apocalyptic rhetoric is its uncertainty. If the outcome were less in doubt there would be little reason for violent action. If one knew that the foe would win, there would be no reason to want to fight back. Weston LaBarre describes the terrible circumstances surrounding the advent of the Ghost Dance religion of the Plains Indians: knowing that they faced overwhelming odds and almost certain defeat, the tribe diverted their concerns from worldly conflict to spiritual conflict, and entertained the notion that a ritual dance would conjure up sufficient spiritual force to destroy the alien cavalry.[60]

LaBarre concludes that sheer desperation caused them to turn to religion and away from efforts to defend themselves. But by the same token, if they knew that the battle could be won without a struggle, there also would be little reason for engagement. The passive pacifism of what William James calles 'healthy-souled religion' – mainstream Protestant churches, for example, that regard social progess as inevitable – comes from just such optimism.[61] Other pacifist movements, however, have been directly engaged in conflict. Menno Simons, the Anabaptist for whom the Mennonite church is named, and Mohandas Gandhi are examples of pacifist leaders who at times narrowly skirted the edges of violence, propelled by a conviction that without human effort the outcome they desired could not be won. In that sense Gandhi and Bhindranwale were more alike than one might suspect. Both saw the world in terms of cosmic struggle, both regarded their cause as being poised on a delicate balance between oppression and opportunity, and both believed that human action could tip the scales. The issue that divided them, of course, was violence.

5. *Acts of Violence Have a Cosmic Meaning*

The human action in the Sikh case is certainly not pacifist, for Bhindranwale held that there would be 'no deliverance without weapons.'[62] He was careful, however, to let the world know that these weapons were not to be used indiscriminately: 'It is a sin for a Sikh to keep weapons to hurt an innocent person, to rob anyone's home, to dishonor anyone or to oppress anyone. But there is no greater sin for a Sikh than keeping weapons and not using them to protect his faith.'[63] Contrariwise, there is no greater valor for a Sikh than to use weapons in defense of the faith. Bhindranwale himself was armed to the teeth, and although he never publically admitted to any of the killings that were pinned on him personally, Bhindranwale expressed his desire to 'die fighting', a wish that was fulfilled within months of being uttered.[64]

According to Bhindranwale, those who committed acts of religiously sanctioned violence were to be regarded as heroes and more. Although he usually referred to himself as a 'humble servant, and an 'uneducated fallible person',[65] Bhindranwale would occasionally identify himself with one of the legendary Sikh saints, Baba Deep Singh, who continued to battle with Moghul foes even after his head had been severed from his body. He carried it manfully under his arm.[66] In Bhindranwale's mind, he too seemed destined for martyrdom.

To many Sikhs today, that is precisely what Bhindranwale achieved. Whatever excesses he may have committed during his lifetime are excused, as one would excuse a lethal but heroic soldier in a glorious war. Even Beant Singh, the bodyguard of Indira Gandhi who turned on her, is held to be a saintly hero. Perhaps this has to be: if Indira was such a demonic foe, her assassin must be similarly exalted.

Even those who value the sense of order that religion provides sometimes cheer those who throw themselves into the arena of religious violence. Such people are, after all, struggling for good, and for that reason their actions are seen as ultimately producing order. But until such recognition of their mission can be achieved among the more conservative rank and file, such activists are forced, as prophets and agents of a higher order of truth, to engage in deeds that necessarily startle. Their purpose is to awaken good folk, mobilize their community, insult the evil forces, and perhaps even to demonstrate dramatically to God himself that there are those who are willing to fight and die on his side, and to deliver his judgement of death. The great promise of cosmic struggle is that order will prevail over chaos; the great irony is that many must die in order for certain visions of that victory to prevail and their awful dramas be brought to an end.

NOTES

Support for this project has come from the Woodrow Wilson International Center for Scholars. I greatly appreciate the kindness of the staff of the Center, the collegiality of the Fellows, the diligence of my research assistant, Jonathan Hornstein, and the critical judgment of my collegues, Sucheng Chan and Jack Hawley, who have read this paper in draft form and helped me to improve its flow of thought. I have also benefited from discussions of some of these ideas in a Dupont Circle sub-group of the World Affairs Council in Washington, DC, a discussion group at the World Bank, and a faculty and student gathering at Amherst College.

1. For general background on the Punjab crisis in the 1980s and a chronicle of events leading up to it, see Mark Tully and Satish Jacob, *Amritsar: Mrs Gandhi's Last Battle* (London: Cape, 1985), Amarjit Kaur, *et al., The Punjab Story* (New Delhi: Roli Books International, 1984), and Kuldip Nayar and Khushwant Singh, *Tragedy of Punjab: Operation Bluestar and After* (New Delhi: Vision Books, 1984).
2. Indira Gandhi, 'Don't Shed Blood, Shed Hatred', All India Radio, 2 June 1984, reprinted in V.D. Chopra, R.K. Mishra and Nirmal Singh, *Agony of Punjab* (New Delhi: Patriot Publishers, 1984), p.189. Indian government officials seemed to be genuinely caught off-guard by the Sikh militancy. I remember once in the summer of 1984 when the Indian Consul General in San Francisco turned to me after we had been on a radio talk show and said, 'I haven't a clue; can you tell me why in the devil the Sikhs are behaving like this?'
3. The demand for a Khalistan – a Sikh state similar to Pakistan – was raised by a small number of Sikh militants, including a former cabinet minister of the Punjab, Jagjit Singh Chauhan, who set up a movement in exile in London. It was not, however, a significant or strongly supported demand among Sikhs in the Punjab until after Operation Bluestar in June 1984. The Indian government's account of Chauhan's movement is detailed in a report prepared by the Home Ministry, 'Sikh Agitation for Khalistan', reprinted in Nayar and Singh, *Tragedy of Punjab*, pp.142–55.
4. The Anandpur Resolution supported by leaders of the Akali Dal focused primarily on economic issues. For an analysis of the Punjab crisis from an economic perspective, see Chopra, Mishra and Singh, *Agony of Punjab*.

5. The fear of the absorption of Sikhism into Hinduism is the frequent refrain of Khushwant Singh; see, for instance, the final chapter of his *History of the Sikhs*, Vol.2 (Princeton, NJ: Princeton University Press, 1966). He attributes the cause of many of the problems in the Punjab in the mid-1980s to this fear as well; see his *Tragedy of Punjab*, pp.19–21.
6. For an interesting analysis of the general pattern of religious fundamentalism in South Asia of which the Hindu and Sikh movements are a part, see Robert Eric Frykenberg, 'Revivalism and Fundamentalism: Some Critical Observations with Special Reference to Politics in South Asia', in James W. Bjorkman (ed.), *Fundamentalism, Revivalists and Violence in South Asia* (Riverdale, MD: Riverdale, 1986).
7. I am grateful to Professor Ranbir Singh Sandhu, Department of Civil Engineering, Ohio State University, for providing me with several hours of tape-recorded speeches of Sant Jarnail Singh Bhindranwale. Professor Sandhu has translated some of these speeches, and I appreciate his sharing these translations with me. For this article I am relying primarily on the words of Bhindranwale. They are found in the following sources: 'Sant Jarnail Bhindranwale's Address to the Sikh Congregation', a transcript of a sermon given in the Golden Temple in November 1983, translated by Ranbir Singh Sandhu, April 1985, and distributed by the Sikh Religious and Educational Trust, Columbus, Ohio; excerpts of Bhindranwale's speeches, translated into English, that appear in Joyce Pettigrew, 'In Search of a New Kingdom of Lahore', *Pacific Affairs*, Vol. 60, No. 1 (Spring 1987) (forthcoming), and interviews with Bhindranwale found in various issues of *India Today* and other publications.
8. The spiritual leader of the Nirankaris, Baba Gurbachan Singh, was assassinated at his home in Delhi on 24 May 1980. Bhindranwale was implicated in the murder, but was never brought to trial. Kuldip Nayar claims that Zail Singh, who became President of India, came to Bhindranwale's defense at that time (Nayar and Singh, *Tragedy of Punjab*, p.37).
9. It is said that Bhindranwale was first brought into the political arena in 1977 by Mrs Gandhi's son, Sanjay, who hoped that Bhindranwale's popularity would undercut the political support of the Akali party (Nayar and Singh, *Tragedy of Punjab*, p.31, and Tully, *Amritsar*, p.57–61).
10. Bhindranwale, 'Address to the Sikh Congregation', pp.10–11.
11. Bhindranwale, excerpt from a speech, in Pettigrew.
12. Ibid., p.15.
13. Ibid.
14. Bhindranwale, 'Address to the Sikh Congregation', p.1.
15. Ibid.
16. Bhindranwale, excerpt from a speech, in Pettigrew.
17. Ibid.
18. Bhindranwale, 'Address to the Sikh Congregation', p.10.
19. Ibid., p.2.
20. Bhindranwale, excerpt from a speech, in Pettigrew.
21. Ibid.
22. Ibid.
23. Ibid.
24. Bhindranwale, 'Address to the Sikh Congregation', pp.1–5, and ibid., p.14.
25. Bhindranwale, excerpt from a speech, in Pettigrew.
26. For an interesting discussion of the definition of violence and terror in political contexts see Thomas Perry Thornton, 'Terrorism as a Weapon of Political Agitation', in Harry Eckstein (ed.), *Internal War: Problems and Approaches* (New York: The Free Press, 1964); and David C. Rapoport, 'The Politics of Atrocity', in Y. Alexander and S. Finger (eds.), *Terrorism: Interdisciplinary Perspectives* (New York: John Jay, 1977).
27. Clifford Geertz defines religion as 'a system of symbols which acts to establish powerful, pervasive and long-lasting moods and motivations in men by formulating conceptions of a general order of existence and clothing these conceptions with such an aura of factuality that the moods and motivations seem uniquely realistic' ('Religion as a Cultural System', reprinted in William A. Lessa and Evon Z. Vogt, (eds.), *Reader in*

Comparative Religion: An Anthropological Approach (New York: Harper & Row, 3rd ed., 1972), p.168).

28. Robert Bellah, 'Transcendence in Contemporary Piety', in Donald R. Cutler, *The Religious Situation: 1969* (Boston: Beacon Press, 1969), p.907.
29. Peter Berger, *The Heretical Imperative* (New York: Doubleday, 1980), p.38. See also his *Sacred Canopy: Elements of a Sociological Theory of Religion* (Garden City, NY: Doubleday, 1967).
30. Louis Dupré, *Transcendent Selfhood: The Loss and Re-discovery of the Inner Life* (New York: Seabury Press, 1976), p.26. For a discussion of Berger and Dupré's definitions, see Mary Douglas, 'The Effects of Modernization on Religious Change', *Daedalus*, Vol.III, No.1 (Winter 1982), pp.1–19.
31. Durkheim describes the dichotomy of sacred and profane in religion in the following way: 'In all the history of human thought there exists no other example of two categories of things so profoundly differentiated or so radically opposed to one another .... The sacred and the profane have always and everywhere been conceived by the human mind as two distinct classes, as two worlds between which there is nothing in common .... In different religions, this opposition has been conceived in different ways'. Emile Durkheim, *The Elementary Forms of the Religious Life*, trans. by Joseph Ward Swain (London: George Allen & Unwin, 1976) (originally published in 1915), pp.38–9. Durkheim goes on to talk about the sacred things that religions encompass; but the first thing he says about the religious view is the perception that there is this dichotomy. From a theological perspective it seems to me that Paul Tillich is saying something of the same thing in arguing for the necessary connection between faith and doubt (see, for example, the first chapter of his *Dynamics of Faith*).
32. On this point I am in agreement with Wilfred Cantwell Smith who suggested some years ago that the noun 'religion' might well be banished from our vocabulary, and that we restrict ourselves to using the adjective 'religious' (*The Meaning and End of Religion: A New Approach to the Religious Traditions of Mankind* (New York: Macmillan, 1962), pp.119–53).
33. For the significance of the two-edged sword symbol and its links with the Devi cult revered by people, such as Jats, who have traditionally inhabited the foothills of the Himalayas adjacent to the Punjab, see W.H. McLeod, *The Evolution of the Sikh Community* (Oxford: Clarendon Press, 1976), p.13.
34. Ibid, pp.15–17, 51–2. These five objects are known as the five K's, since the name for each of them in Punjabi begins with the letter 'k'. The other four are uncut hair, a wooden comb, a metal bangle and cotton breeches. See also W. Owen Cole and Piara Singh Sambhi, *The Sikhs: Their Religious Beliefs and Practices* (London: Routledge & Kegan Paul, 1978), p.36.
35. Karl Marx, 'Contribution to the Critique of Hegel's Philosophy of Right', reprinted in Karl Marx and Friedrich Engels, *On Religion* (New York: Schocken Books), p.42; see also Engels' class analysis of a religious revolt, 'The Peasant War in Germany' in the same volume, pp.97–118.
36. Sigmund Freud, *Totem and Taboo*, trans. by James Strachey (New York: W.W. Norton, 1950).
37. Rene Girard, *Violence and the Sacred*, trans. by Patrick Gregory (Baltimore and London: Johns Hopkins University Press, 1977); see especially Chapters 7 and 8. What is not clear in this book is how symbolic violence leads to real acts of violence; this link is made in a subsequent study of Girard's, *Scapegoat*, trans. by Patrick Gregory (Baltimore and London: Johns Hopkins University Press, 1986).
38. Bhindranwale, excerpt from a speech, in Pettigrew.
39. Ibid.
40. Bhindranwale, 'Address to the Sikh Congregation', p.9.
41. See my article, 'Nonviolence', in Mircea Eliade (ed.), *The Encyclopedia of Religion* (New York: Macmillan, 1987). For the ethic of non-violence in Sikhism see Cole and Sambhi, *The Sikhs*, p.138. For Sikh ethical attitudes in general see Avtar Singh, *Ethics of the Sikhs* (Patiala, India: Punjabi University Press); and S.S. Kohli, *Sikh Ethics* (New Delhi: Munshiram Manoharlal, 1975).

42. An excellent anthology of statements of Christian theologians on the ethical justification for war is Albert Marrin (ed.), *War and the Christian Conscience: From Augustine to Martin Luther King, Jr.* (Chicago: Henry Regnery, 1971). On the development of the just war doctrine in Christianity, with its secular parallels, see James Turner Johnson, *Ideology, Reason, and the Limitation of War: Religious and Secular Concepts, 1200–1740* (Princeton: Princeton University Press, 1975).
43. Frantz Fanon, *The Wretched of the Earth* (New York: Grove Press, 1963).
44. For a discussion of the term *qaum* in the Untouchable movements, see my *Religion as Social Vision* (Berkeley and London: University of California Press, 1982), p.45.
45. Joyce Pettigrew argues that the *miri-piri* concept 'gave legitimacy to the political action organized from within the Golden Temple' (Pettigrew, op. cit.). This 'political action' was the establishment of an armed camp of which Bhindranwale was the commander; it was to rout this camp that the Indian army entered the Golden Temple on 5 June 1984, in Operation Bluestar.
46. Bhindranwale, 'Address to the Sikh Congregation', p.13.
47. Ibid., p.8.
48. David C. Rapoport, 'Why does Messianism Produce Terror?' paper delivered at the 81st Annual Meeting of the American Political Science Association, New Orleans, 27 August – 1 September 1985. Although I find Rapoport's conclusions helpful, and in many ways compatible with my own, his emphasis on messianic movements seems unnecessary. The notion of messianism is largely alien to the Asian religious traditions, and much of what he says about it could be said of religion in general. See also his 'Fear and Trembling: Terrorism in Three Religious Traditions', *American Political Science Review* 78:3 (Sept. 1984), pp.658–77, which includes case studies of the Thugs, Assassins and Zealots and the essays in David C. Rapoport and Y. Alexander (eds.), *The Morality of Terrorism: Religious and Secular Justifications* (New York: Pergamon, 1982).
49. There are also examples in other cultures where mythic battles are thought to have had a historical effect. At a recent presentation at the Wilson Center, for instance, Professor Billie Jean Isbell described the influence of the notion of cosmic cycles of order and chaos in traditional Andean cosmology on the propensity for violence of the Sendero Luminoso tribal people of Peru ('The Faces and Voices of Terrorism', Politics and Religion Seminar, Wilson Center, 8 May 1986).
50. The term *jihad* is derived from the word for striving for something, and implies 'the struggle against one's bad inclinations' as well as what it has come to mean in the popular Western mind, holy war (Rudolph Peters, *Islam and Colonialism: The Doctrine of Jihad in Modern History*, The Hague: Mouton Publishers, 1979, p.118).
51. Bhindranwale, 'Address to the Sikh Congregation', p.7.
52. Bhindranwale, excerpt from a speech, in Pettigrew.
53. Bhindranwale, 'Address to the Sikh Congregation', p.13.
54. For an interesting analysis of the Gush Emunim, see Ehud Sprinzak's essay in this volume.
55. Bhindranwale, 'Address to the Sikh Congregation', p.8.
56. Ibid., p.2.
57. Ibid., p.3.
58. Bhindranwale, excerpt from a speech, in Pettigrew.
59. Ibid.
60. Weston LaBarre, *The Ghost Dance: Origins of Religion* (London: Allen & Unwin, 1972).
61. William James, *The Varieties of Religious Experience* (Cambridge, MA: Harvard University Press, 1985) (originally published in 1902), pp.71–108.
62. Bhindranwale, 'Address to the Sikh Congregation', p.10.
63. Ibid., p.10.
64. Bhindranwale, excerpt from a speech, in Pettigrew.
65. Bhindranwale, 'Address to the Sikh Congregation', p.14.
66. Bhindranwale, excerpt from a speech, in Pettigrew.

[12]

Messianic Sanctions for Terror

David C. Rapoport

A most striking development in recent years has been the use of theological concepts to justify terrorist activity, a phenomenon which I have called "holy terror."[1] The most notorious instance has occurred among the Shia, where the attempt to revive *jihad* (holy war) doctrines has produced some remarkable incidents in Lebanon and elsewhere. A major feature of the Shia episodes has been a striking willingness, even eagerness, to die, a disposition sustained by the belief that one who is killed while fighting in a *jihad* is guaranteed a place in paradise. This promise of an extraordinary personal benefit for assailants who die (a perversion, incidentally, of the traditional doctrine) gives Shia terror an awesome dimension in the eyes of potential victims.[2]

In the United States abortion clinic bombers regularly cite scripture to justify their deeds, and several scripture-based, messianic, right-wing terrorist groups have emerged in the last few years, the most prominent being "The Covenant, the Sword and the Arm of the Lord" and "The Order."[3]

Another and most interesting case came to light in Israel in 1984 when the government convicted Jewish terrorists who had organized the "Temple Mount Plot," a conspiracy to destroy Muslim sacred shrines built on Judaism's holiest site, that of the second temple. If the shrines were obliterated, the construction of a third temple would be possible at last, a circumstance which some visualize to be a precondition of the coming of the Messiah.[4] It has been alleged, too, that American Christian messianic groups (who may be interested in creating conditions for Armageddon) have furnished funds for third temple enterprises, a project which has certainly been very dear to some Christian elements for more than a century.[5] I do not know whether the Messiah will come if the third temple is built, but I do know that if the Muslim holy sites are blown up catastrophic results could ensue which may indeed put us one step closer to an Armageddon. But will it be the one scripture describes?

Holy terror seems new to us, but prior to the French Revolution it was the dominant, perhaps only form of terror. And holy terror, whenever it appears, is usually linked to messianism. Two well-known historical examples are the Assassins (*Nizaris*) or *Fidayeen* of Islam[6] and the Jewish Zealots and *Sicarii*. The Assassins emerged in the eleventh century, persisted for two hundred years, and are the first known example of an international conspiracy organized by a state, a conspiracy which threatened the governments of several Islamic realms.[7] The Zealots, who lived earlier in the first century, survived for a shorter period, some sixty years, but they had enormous significance. They successfully provoked a massive rebellion against Rome, one which ended in catastrophe, for the second temple, the ritual center of Judaism, was destroyed. The final act in the rebellion was a gruesome mass suicide at Masada. Subsequently, the revolt inspired two more massive uprisings in successive generations. As a result Judea was depopulated, large Jewish centers in Roman-controlled Cyprus and Egypt were decimated, and the final tragedy of the second

Comparative Politics January 1988

exile or Diaspora occurred, whose traumatic impact on Jewish consciousness became the central Jewish experience for the next two thousand years and altered virtually every institution of Jewish life.

No single messianic terror group has occupied such a prominent place in Christianity. Christian messianic movements have been numerous and episodic and have had comparatively less effect. Still, the Christian examples are much better documented than those in Islam and Judaism, and they are important and instructive, too, because Christian terror is not so intimately connected to underground organizations. The Crusades, for example, had an essential messianic component which produced some grotesque forms of violence, especially among the poor who launched what some historians have called Peoples' Crusades.[8] And for brief moments in the late medieval period the Taborites and the Anabaptists created public arrangements which could be called systems of state terror.

It is, of course, a commonplace among the historians and sociologists of messianic movements that they often produce terror. But two key issues have been ignored which I want to address. Most messianic groups have not engaged in terror, and indeed they are often committed to pacifism, especially those in the Christian tradition. One wants to know therefore why a group behaves in one way rather than the other and what the relationship is between such seemingly different matters as pacifism and terrorism.

Bryan Wilson's admirable *Magic and the Millennium* comes closest to discussing these issues, but he is concerned mainly with external circumstances—the impact of colonialism upon indigenous peoples—and rarely focuses on those elements of beliefs which predispose some messianists to terror.[9] Furthermore, he makes no distinction between violence and terror, a difficulty he shares with many students of messianism.[10]

The principal question I want to discuss, then, is why messianism produces terror sometimes, or, better still, what the logical and psychological links are between specific messianic motifs and terror. The problem of external circumstances will *not* be treated; my concern is with the internal dynamics. Although I will use a few examples from Islam and from primitive societies, I will focus on traditional Jewish and Christian experiences which have always provided the basic paradigms for the rest of the world.

Let us begin by making clear how I shall be using the two key terms, terror and messianism. Most academics see the terrorist as one who uses violence unlawfully for political purposes, and there is a strong tendency to describe terrorists as members of small underground rebel groups that employ hit and disappear (that is, guerrilla-like) tactics.[11] I prefer the more traditional conception, which, as we shall see, is especially appropriate for messianic experiences. In this view, terror is understood as extranormal or extramoral violence, a type which goes beyond the conventions or boundaries particular societies establish to regulate coercion. These conventions identify justifications and establish limits and immunities which enable one to distinguish between the appropriate and inappropriate social responses to criminal as opposed to belligerent activities.

Rebels sometimes accept the same restraints that governments do. It would be very difficult, for example, to distinguish the methods of the major protagonists in our own revolutionary and civil wars. But other times they do not. The distinguishing characteristic of the terrorist, therefore, is a deliberate decision to abandon these restraints or to refuse to accept as binding the prevailing moral distinctions between belligerents and neutrals, combatants and noncombatants, appropriate and inappropriate targets, legitimate and illegitimate methods. The terrorist *knows* that others will regard his actions as shocking or as atrocities, and this is one reason why he acts as he does, for his object in using terror for messianic ends is to create a "new consciousness" by methods which provoke extreme emotional reactions—panic, horror, revulsion, outrage, and sympathy. In this respect, any person or group may commit terrorist acts; certainly rebels may do so, but so can large armies and established authorities, as the cases of the Crusades and the Zealot-*Sicarii* revolt illustrate. The nature of the act, not the status of the persons who commit it, is the critical feature.

What will be meant by messianism? One who believes in messianism is one who has faith that there will be a day in which history or life on *this* earth will be transformed totally and irreversibly from the condition of perpetual strife which we have all experienced to one of perfect harmony that many dream about. In some messianic visions it is imagined that there will be no sickness and no tears, that we will all be wholly *liberated* from government, a condition of perfect freedom. History ends in all messianic visions *because* God has promised us that it would. At His appointed time He will intervene in our affairs, saving a "righteous remnant," all those who deserve to be saved.[12]

If I may be permitted a brief digression, one should note that, while messianic movements are worth studying in their own right, understanding them also has value for the light they may throw on related phenomena. Certain terrorist groups, like those which came out of the student movements in the 1960s, are often called messianic for good reason, though they have no religious underpinning. Stripped of its theological dimension, the messianic aspiration, moreover, bears an extraordinary similarity to those of the "great" revolutions of France, Russia, and China, and a kinship between messianism and revolution has been recognized by persons as different as Burke and Engels, Talmon and Hobsbawm. It was the French Revolution, too, which gave terror its first secular justification, and terror was an essential part of the Russian and Chinese experiences.

Hobsbawm makes the *minimum* case for linking messianism to revolution and to revolutionary terror. Messianism is a necessary social illusion for generating the "superhuman efforts" revolutions require. "Would the Bolsheviks have [made the revolution] to exchange the Russia of Tchekov for that of Khrushchev?" For a moment within the small group of revolutionaries, messianism produces an ideal society, and, "when normal modes of behavior creep in again," the disappointed revolutionaries use terror, for they want to believe the ideal is betrayed, not that it is flawed.[13]

I will provide some more material concerning these parallels as we go along, mostly in the footnotes, but I must return to our basic concern, the subject of religious messianism. Each messianic vision or paradigm contains its own particular details, which pertain to matters like timing, agents, process, and signs. Some of these details, and hence, some of the visions, seem peculiarly conducive to terror. But no matter what the particular content of a belief may be, its significance depends initially on two conditions. Believers must think that the day of deliverance is near or imminent, and they must also think that their actions can or must consummate the process. When these conditions are fulfilled, then and only then will six substantive details of a messianic vision influence the recourse to terror. They are (1) the nature of the desired action, (2) the cause or character of the messianic aspiration, (3) the proof that believers think may be necessary to demonstrate sufficient faith, (4) the moral qualities ascribed to participants in the messianic struggle, (5) the "signs" or "portents" of

Comparative Politics January 1988

a messianic intervention, and (6) the character of the deity's involvement. Messianic beliefs, it should be stressed, rarely form a coherent whole and are usually sufficiently ambiguous to allow participants to choose between alternatives or abandon one course for another when this appears more productive. Finally, a particular religious culture often has a variety of paradigms to choose from.

Imminence and Human Agency: The Necessary Conditions

Clearly, one can believe both that a messianic era is predestined and that the day of deliverance is neither near nor predictable. But it does seem unreasonable to think that in all times in all circumstances those who believe that a day of reckoning must occur will also remain content with a doctrine that says that this day is always very far off and/or unknowable. The histories of religions with messianic components seem to confirm both propositions. While a sense of imminence is not present usually, it does appear intermittently and sometimes after very long periods of absence. Eight centuries after the messianic vision became firmly rooted in Jewish consciousness through the prophet Isaiah, a sense of imminence finally was aroused in the generation before the Zealot-*Sicarii* revolt and shortly before the development of Christianity. The first five centuries of Christianity exhibited numerous Christian and Jewish messianic episodes, which then ceased until the Crusades in the eleventh century when they began again. A third period occurred in the sixteenth and seventeenth centuries, a fourth during the French Revolution, and another one is apparently developing today.

The hope which a messianic vision supplies is obviously important for the orthodox revealed religions, because without it the rest of the religious tradition may seem onerous or meaningless, and it is quite conceivable that a messianic vision is necessary for the survival of some revealed religions. Judaism had good reason, therefore, to retain its faith that a messiah would come,[14] and the conception was passed on to Christianity and to a lesser extent Islam, where it is known as Mahdism and is especially significant among the Shia. For the Sunni the line between the *Mahdi* and a *mujaddid* is often blurred, the latter being a "renewer of the faith" who revitalizes the community Mohammed established and in effect becomes a state-builder.

While the value of a messianic belief may be self-evident, when a sense of imminence takes over, when some believe that the world will end tomorrow or within a foreseeable future, a variety of dangerous reactions may occur just because so much anxiety will be generated concerning who will be saved and how. Hugh Schonfield's description of the Jews in the first century is not farfetched. "The whole condition of the Jewish people was psychologically abnormal. The strangest tales and imaginings could find ready credence. . . . Almost every event was seized upon to discover how and in what ways it represented a Sign of the Times and threw light on the approach of the End of the Days."[15]

Such anxieties can uproot the orthodox religion itself. Certainly the first targets, and most of the time the *only* targets, of messianists are coreligionists whom they believe are corrupted or contaminated. Since the traditional religion, moreover, is the initial source of the messianic belief, disappointment may induce an exodus from the parent religion altogether. In a messianic episode in Crete (476), many, believing that the sea would part for them as it did for Moses, threw themselves in and drowned. "Many of the Jews of Crete," an eyewitness observed, "subsequently embraced Christianity."[16]

Orthodox religious leaders attempt to forestall messianic anxieties and explosions in a variety of ways. The most direct way is to deny some of the central tenets of messianism. The Council of Ephesus (431) went right to the root of the matter: it denounced the doctrine of collective salvation on earth as heretical error and fantasy, asserting that the messianic promise pertains only to individuals and to their life after death, an event in the spiritual world. Normally, most Christians have accepted this view, but the relevant Biblical passages can be interpreted differently, and no council could prevent Christians from occasionally believing different interpretations.

Never being able to deny that messianism was a collective phenomena pertaining to the "righteous remnant" who were to continue inhabiting this world, the Jewish tradition was in a weaker position. The rabbis did try to defuse potential tensions by making the Jew's primary responsibility to attend to ordinary living even in the face of clear evidence of a messianic presence. "If you have a sapling in your hand," Rabbi Yochanan Ben Zakkai taught, "and they tell you that the Messiah has come, first plant the sapling and then welcome the Messiah." Sound advice, but not advice always followed.

Spokesmen for the orthodox religions always find it necessary to deny that one could ever know the time for a messianic epoch, and they sometimes even make strenuous efforts to prevent individuals from publicizing contrary views. In England during the Restoration it was a criminal offense to speculate on the date of the Second Coming.[17] Shia authorities in the ninth century denounced the "time determiners" as "liars" who spread "disillusionment and despair."[18] And an early medieval rabbi wrote, "May the curse of heaven fall upon those who calculate the advent of the Messiah and thus create political and social unrest among the people."[19] Each of these cases provides evidence that, as soon as the speculation about the date of the great event becomes a popular activity, there is an inevitable tendency (based I suppose on wishful thinking) to believe that it will happen sooner and sooner or become more and more imminent.[20]

In England speculation was an integral part of seventeenth-century upheavals, just as it was an essential element in the three disastrous rebellions which Jews waged against the Romans much earlier. When a date has been fixed by an existing messianic tradition, one can expect anxieties to intensify as centuries pass and the imminence of the date becomes more apparent.

> Many misfortunes would have been prevented. Many blood stained pages of our history would have been left unwritten, if the rabbinic injunction against calculating the date of the Messiah's appearance had been heeded. As it was, the arrival of *every* date suggested by one or the other of the rabbis caused general excitement among the people. At such times there was never wanting an imposter or a self-deluded dreamer to come forward and take advantage of the opportunity, and thereby bring misery and horror upon thousands.[21]

In Islam the *hadith*, or traditions of Mohammed and his companions, is "a framework for defining what the community is, a framework which is the basis of education and learning as much as practical life."[22] One of these traditions is that the *Mahdi* will emerge at the beginning of a new century according to the Islamic calendar. The startling attack in 1979 on the Grand Mosque of Mecca, Islam's holiest shrine, which staggered the Saudi dynasty, occurred in the first hour of the first day of the Islamic year 1400. The assailants, who came from twelve countries including the U.S., named one of their number the *Mahdi*, and nearly every detail in the assault seemed contrived to follow a well-known Islamic tradition.[23] This same tradition has produced other examples. A century ago Chinese Gordon's army was massacred in Khartoum by the Sudanese *Mahdi* who had staked his claim to be the *Mahdi* on the first day of the Islamic year 1300. In the same period several *Mahdi* movements emerged elsewhere, the most conspicuous being the Sanusi movement in Libya, utilizing the same general expectation that that century was *the* century. In Egypt today three messianic groups (one of which assassinated Sadat) have appealed to this dating tradition.[24] It is conceivable that the Iranian revolution may be linked to it too.

Dating traditions in the past created a sense of imminence, and they will continue to do so in the future. I suspect, for instance, that as we approach the year 2000, which is an important date for Christian speculators, messianic expectations will spread rapidly. Does one need to be reminded that messianic expectations at the end of the millenium following Christ were an essential part of the passions which created the Crusades?

There are, in addition to dating traditions, other elements of beliefs relevant to the question of imminence which can be illustrated by looking at the contemporary situation. A most conspicuous characteristic of our world since the 1950s is a general revival of religious enthusiasms,[25] and this revival, like earlier ones, necessarily draws attention to the messianic component in the revealed religions, a component which is usually ignored. Clearly, religious enthusiasm is not messianism, but each religious revival probably stimulates dormant sentiments that a messianic delivery could be imminent.[26]

Messianism is always associated with the presence of "signs," and in our day it is easy for the believer to see two of the most prominent signs in messianic eschatology. In most Jewish, Christian, and Islamic messianic visions, the "Last Days" emerge in the context of world catastrophe, and the spectre of such a possibility has haunted everybody's imagination ever since World War II, most of all in the form of nuclear holocaust but also as ecological, technological, and demographic disasters. Indeed, "end of the world" thinking has become so striking in secular circles that the apocalyptic theme in religious thought has gained some intellectual respectability, as Carl Jung's fascinating *Answer to Job* demonstrates. Never before has the end of the world seemed so feasible, and, since messianism often functions as a device to explain catastrophe, one would expect it to emerge naturally whenever catastrophe is either experienced or anticipated.[27]

A second sign is the restoration of the state of Israel, a common theme in apocalyptic prophecies. The reestablishment of Israel, especially after the Six Days War when the holy places were regained, has had an enormous impact on various American Christian messianic groups loosely lumped together as "fundamentalists." Their interest goes back to the early nineteenth century, when the extraordinary and humiliating failures of millenarians in using Biblical dating schemes to predict the Second Coming compelled them instead to emphasize more the significance of signs or portents, the most important being the restoration of Israel to its ancient homeland.[28] Indeed, in America Zionist activity may have developed among Christians before it did among Jews.[29]

The return to the Land has excited Jewish messianic expectations, as one should have anticipated, and the Six Days War produced the first important genuine Jewish messianic movement since the seventeenth century, the Gush Emunim (Bloc of the Faithful). Indeed, anticipated possession of the Land is a *sine qua non* of Jewish messianic movements, and in the past its actual repossession after an exile has had enormous consequences. In the First and Second Commonwealths messianic sentiments were stirred too, as they have been today, and it is conceivable that every restoration of Israel will tend in time to generate messianic movements.[30]

Parenthetically, one should note that Islamic messianic expectations are linked to Christian and Judaic ones too. At least in some traditions the *Mahdi* is supposed to appear soon after Christ returns, though it is a moot point just what effects Second Coming anticipations among Christians have had on messianic activity in Islam.

A messianic belief becomes imminent, one might conclude, either because one of its components (such as dating traditions) leads a believer directly to that position regardless of events in the real world or when one of its components can be used as a sign to interpret events of the world as indicators of imminence. But even if the obstacles to making imminence credible are overcome, no action will ensue until the believer also thinks that he can influence messianic events, which means he must deny directly the teachings of the religious establishments on this issue. Among the Jews, for example, a rabbinic tradition persists that the Messiah's advent was fixed in the creation of the world, and even God therefore cannot hasten or retard the process.[31] The problem, however, is that messianism makes sense or is attractive largely *because* we believe that the righteous and the wicked must have different fates. Consequently some believers will conclude, despite what the authorities want us to think, that what we do must count after all. When a sense of imminence takes root, some believers must find it psychologically impossible to regard their actions as irrelevant, because the consequences of being mistaken are so immediate and momentous. *At the very least,* they will act to secure their own salvation. And once the initial barrier to action has been overcome, it will only be a matter of time before different kinds of action make sense too. Soon they may think they can shape the speed or timing of the process.

Range of Conceivable Actions

Clearly, there is no one prescribed way to accomplish these purposes. Messianic speculators have suggested various possibilities, not all consistent with each other, and in the past different movements have tried different courses. One can speak of a range of plausible actions. Believers may make choices, swinging radically sometimes from one alternative to another.

Some activities are patently nonviolent. Proselytizing is common. One may give property away to discharge debts, finance missionary work, and show one's love for humanity as did the Millerites, an American messianic movement (predecessor of the Seventh Day Adventists) in upstate New York in the 1840s. Messianic groups sometimes travel great distances to a sacred site where redemption is supposed to begin. After the Jews were dispersed in the wake of the second temple's destruction, messianic episodes for the next nineteen centuries normally induced a collective exodus to the Holy Land. Groups of Indians in Brazil periodically would peacefully migrate to find "The Land of No Evil." Numerous

Melanesian cargo cults in the twentieth century awaited deliverance in designated spots. In Jamaica not long ago the Ras Tafari, a black group, organized several times to go to Ethiopia, which they believed the Bible had identified as the site for the Messiah to appear.[32] The Doukhobors, a Russian pacifist sect that was established in the eighteenth century and moved to Canada a century later, began a trek in late autumn 1902 to find a "land of ever-lasting sunshine."[33] Those who have seen the film *Close Encounters of the Third Kind* may recall that the migration to the site of messianic deliverance was a central theme there too.

Action to signify a change of identity or the purification of community often accompanies migration: crops, livestock, and all means of gaining livelihood may be destroyed in a holocaust. Because these objects are mechanisms we use to discharge normal or daily obligations, their destruction symbolizes or represents the emergence of the "new" form of humanity and a faith that one has taken an irreversible step into the new world. In nineteenth-century Russia, the Skoptsi (who numbered tens of thousands, including nobles, officials, rich merchants, and peasants) believed that the messianic period would be populated by sexless beings; therefore, to prove that one really believed, the condition for joining the movement was castration for the men and the cutting of the breasts for the women.

The purification and migration process are more familiar as part of the western experiences in another form. When believers think that an advent is not immediate, they often create a sacred community which tries to separate itself completely from the profane world. These groups initially are characterized by hypernomian behavior, that is, asceticism, excessive self-discipline, and a stringent observation of rules which comprehend every aspect of the individual's life. Sometimes they distinguish themselves from the existing society further by violating conventions sanctified by intense emotional sentiments. The Adamites and Doukhobors were nudists, and many groups attacked sexual and marital conventions by becoming celibate or instituting plural marriages. The ethos of this hypernomian community—and the persecution which may ensue—gives messianists cause to identify themselves as the "righteous remnant."

In Islam the term *Mahdi* (the "right-guided one") connotes "rising from concealment" and/or "rebellion against constituted authority."[34] A group which withdraws has as another purpose the intention to find a better and more secure base in order to organize a violent return. For this reason, perhaps, it might be better to call an Islamic group a hypernomian "counter-society," for the term counter-society seems to have, in the academic literature, the connotation that a violent confrontation is intended.[35] The pattern is reflected in Mohammed's own career which probably provides the archetype or model. When he failed to convert his own people in Mecca, he fled to Medina (*Yathrib*), from which he returned later in triumph.

The significance of that event is indicated by the fact that Islam's calendar begins with it and that Muslims are obliged to set themselves apart or migrate (*hajara*) if they cannot practice their religion suitably. This tradition of creating counter-societies is a way of recapitulating the circumstances of Islam's birth—a pattern which is observable in very different kinds of communities as well.[36] The Assassins (1090–1275) organized Islam's most notorious counter-society, but they were not the first to do so, and the formula is repeated over and over again through to our own century, as indicated by the examples of the major Egyptian terrorist organizations in the 1970s, one of which assassinated Sadat.

So expected is the messianic recourse to violence in the Islamic world that even Jewish messianism there is often violent too. It is interesting to note, by way of contrast, that in the diaspora circumstances of the Christian world, Jewish messianism rarely has been violent.

The fate of hypernomian groups which withdraw seems more complicated in the Christian world than in Islam. Christian groups usually withdraw not so much to fight as to wait. If society does not leave them alone or compels them to participate, they may resist initially by pacifist methods, even accepting martyrdom, perhaps to remind God of the price being paid for His tardiness! Sometimes, after a difficult period, the groups change their course and actively engage the larger society, moving in the process directly from pacifism to terror. The Anabaptists and Taborites of medieval Europe come to mind as examples,[37] and they were apparently preceded by the Jewish Essenes in the first century. A more recent instance is the case of the Doukhobors' "Sons of Freedom" element which broke the pacifist traditions of the main body in Canada to engage in terror intermittently for several decades after World War II.[38]

The striking change appears puzzling, so much so that one eminent authority has described the process as a "mutation," a term which seems inappropriate for it means a "new species" not able, or at least not likely, to resume its earlier character.[39] But earlier ways are resumed, and therefore there is a "doctrinal logic" to these changes. Whether one chooses pacifism or terror, one still is rejecting the existing conventions governing coercion, and thus there is some consistency in the dynamic. Also because messianism is doomed to failure in its own terms, its life has to be episodic, and it would be quite surprising for the hope to persist and reappear again and again unless there were alternative ways to strive for it. In the messianic visions of the revealed religions, there are several possible courses of action suggested. Believers, thus, can choose to do different things or different things at different phases of the process. The two dominant images in these paradigms are that of the "suffering servant" and that of the "avenging angel," the latter most often representing the final days or the days of destruction.

Pacifism, then, can be understood as activity appropriate only while waiting for messianic activity to begin, behavior which in the case of Christian offshoots also seems to embody the spirit of original religion. To usher in the new age another kind of behavior is necessary. It should be remembered that Christianity, which originally was probably a messianic offshoot of Judaism, developed its own pacifist tradition in the wake of the terror in the Zealot-*Sicarii* revolt, and many of these early pacifists believed that in His Second Coming Christ would have a sword. It is not surprising, therefore, to find that, when messianists who abandon pacifism become convinced that they were mistaken about the timing of the process, they often revert to pacifist traditions. Anabaptist history reflects this rationale: the group returned to pacifism after a gruesome experience with terror during the Reformation.

The pattern occurs infrequently in Islam, though the sword is supposed to be used as a last resort and for defensive purposes only. Nonetheless, Islam has a few striking examples to parallel the Christian practice. Some observers have interpreted the dynamics of Shia life in a similar way. Although pacifism and terror may not be appropriate terms, "Shi'ism can . . . accord legitimacy both to passive submissiveness and explosive activism . . . at times [it] has been understood . . . to justify submission to oppression and injustice, since the

Comparative Politics January 1988

prevalence of injustice might be interpreted as a sign of the imminent return of the Twelfth Imam (and the messianic era). On the other hand, certain clerics have argued that active opposition to corrupt sovereign power and a positive emphasis on restoring justice will hasten the return of the Twelfth Imam."[40] In nineteenth-century Iran the Babi messianic movement began in a terror campaign but upon defeat transformed itself into the Bahai, a pacifist group. And there seem to be examples of primitive peoples in North America and Africa doing the same thing in the wake of the decisive failure of their insurrections to extricate themselves from western domination.[41]

Bryan Wilson's study of the Christadelphians, a contemporary British messianic movement, emphasizes something else which is relevant as well, namely, that pacifism sometimes can be nourished by a profound hatred and not simply by love.

> Christadelphianism is basically a revolutionary organization, vigorously opposed to the social order. . . . But this attitude is not translated into social action, although at the appointed time there would be disposition to do so. . . . The Christadelphian is in conflict with the prevailing social order but powerless to organize its overthrow. . . . Reform [is] useless . . . he [does] not want the world to get better; he [is] opposed to peace, and he want[s] war. Misery was the world's lot and his pronouncement of the fact [falls] little short of active rejoicing. He was emotionally involved in his predictions for disaster out of which he alone would emerge triumphant.[42]

A study of the sequence of events in the Zealot-*Sicarii* uprisings, which were preceded by an extensive passive resistance campaign, reveals another reason, based on what I would call psychological circumstances and not belief. Angry unarmed demonstrations will tax superbly disciplined troops, the Romans learned. When this discipline breaks down, the atrocities which result, especially when women and children participate, may so disturb a community that virtually any countermeasure seems justified. There are comparable instances in the modern world (such as Northern Ireland and Cyprus) which suggest that there is a connection between passive resistance and terror which is independent of the messianic ethos.

The Cause

If a messianic believer thinks that he must participate in a struggle to "force the end," the nature of the messianic aspiration itself or the cause will become a factor conducive to terror. This is our second element of belief. It would seem rather obvious that, when the stakes of any struggle are perceived as being great, the conventional restraints on violence diminish accordingly. For example, wars which threaten the very existence of the belligerent parties are normally more savage than those for territory or trade, and it is common knowledge that the appearance of revolutionary states in an existing international order introduces a new level of ruthlessness in world politics. If nothing else were involved, the extraordinary image messianists often sketch of the future—the transformation of human existence itself—can induce one to waive limits. While the details of the messianic existence may differ, since the outcome is always a perfected society, the effect on the scope of violence would seem to be uniform in all cases.

One reason why restraints on conflict are sometimes accepted by belligerents is that they anticipate that there will be more wars in the future and that therefore it would be advantageous for all parties to accept limits. The messianic struggle, on the other hand, will end all wars. To accept restraints for humane or prudential reasons might only delay the outcome.

Unreal expectations necessarily create bitter disappointments and savage responses. Perhaps the most common one is the hunt for the "traitors" responsible. The Zealots-*Sicarii* and the Anabaptists had their reigns of terror which resemble those which came later in the great revolutions of France, Russia, and China. Another natural response may be a group decision that the messianic date is not imminent as the group had thought initially. Accordingly, it adopts a less aggressive attitude toward the world, and this attitude sometimes incites a dissenting element to engage in desperate actions against the larger society hoping that the latter's response might compel the messianic group to resume its initial stance. This *may* have been the motive behind the frenzied mutilation murders of whites in San Francisco (1973–1974) by the Fruit of Islam, an element which broke away from the Black Muslim movement when this movement began moderating its extraordinary militancy. There are secular parallels too. The origin of the Italian Red Brigades has usually been understood as an attempt to make the Communist Party believe in revolution again.

The belief that a purge will be beneficial can take other forms. In Israel when the Camp David Accords were struck, it seemed to a few members of the Gush Emunim that a process of relinquishing the Land had begun, that God was allowing the messianic opportunity to slip from Israel's grasp because the people had sinned in allowing Muslims to retain sacred shrines on Israel's holy sites.

> It [Camp David] was a direct signal from Heaven that a major national offense was committed, a sin that was responsible for the political disaster and its spiritual consequences. Only one prominent act of desecration could match the magnitude of the setback: the presence of the Muslims and their shrine on Temple Mount, the holiest Jewish site, the sacred place of the first, second and third (future) Temples.[43]

Proof

A third element, which contains a range of variable details, would be the "evidence" needed to demonstrate faith. If hypernomian behavior or traditional tests seem ineffective, new tests to prove moral worthiness might be contrived. In the first century some believed the condition of God's intervention to be His conviction that the believer's faith was unshakeable, and perhaps the most striking single action in this regard occurred when the Zealots decided to burn their own food supplies after Jerusalem was taken, signifying that they had indeed placed all their trust in Him. In being bound by His promise to rescue the righteous remnant, He had to act. While the Zealots thought that there was no better way to demonstrate commitment, most rabbis subsequently interpreted this as an effort to blackmail God which could not possibly succeed.

A similar process has been observed in some nineteenth-century rebellions in Algeria. "The apocalyptic could interpret concern for practical organizational considerations as a sign of doubt about the ultimate arrival of divine assistance. Strategic planning, military training and the building up of supplies appeared as distractions from the true task of the apocalyptic, namely the preaching of hope, deliverance, . . . the realm of justice, [and] the superiority of faith over common sense."[44]

The most striking quality of the religious terrorist in Islam, especially among the ancient Assassins, whose ritual and method effectively prevented escape, seems to be an eagerness to seek martyrdom.[45] The reward in paradise is the most common explanation, but to be a martyr, as the term itself indicates, is "to bear *witness* for the truth," and martyrdom, hence, is a mechanism to demonstrate fidelity, an act which also dispels the doubts of believers and aids proselytizing efforts. Among the Jews in the period preceding the Zealot uprisings a similar kind of martyrdom developed for the first time.

The line between martyrdom and suicide obviously is not always clear, as the gruesome spectacle at Masada indicates. In Christian messianic sects suicides of this sort occurred especially in Russia during the seventeenth century. The most recent example occurred at Jonestown, which has been called a case of revolutionary "suicide," a testament to the belief that the act would have consequences in both the natural and supernatural worlds.[46]

Josephus, who is our only source, suggests that, as the course of the Zealot revolt developed, a rather extraordinary process unfolded. The rebels began to act in ways directly antithetical to the spirit of hypernomianism, as though they thought that true fidelity was not measured by unswerving commitment to religious norms as much as it was by willingness to violate religious taboos, by one's ability to deny limits. When the *Sicarii*, for example, mounted their assassination campaign against Jewish priests who they charged had succumbed to Hellenistic influences, the attacks normally occurred on the most holy days. The message was clear; even the most sacred occasion or circumstance could not provide immunity.[47] Josephus' description of the deplorable fate of a Roman garrison illustrates this point again. After receiving a safe passage agreement secured by a covenant, the most inviolable pledge Jews could make, the troops surrendered.

> When they had laid down their arms, the rebels massacred them; the Romans neither resisting nor suing for mercy but merely appealing to the Covenant!. . .The whole city was a scene of dejection, and among the moderates everyone was racked with the thought that he should personally have to suffer for the rebels' crime. For to add to its heinousness, the massacre took place on the sabbath, a day on which from religious scruples Jews abstain from the most innocent acts.[48]

As the assailants in such situations obviously understand, the aggrieved will perceive violence of this sort as atrocities and are likely to respond in kind, providing the original assailant with a fresh justification for new atrocities. Thus, when the news of the massacre reached the Greeks of Caesarea, the Roman capital of Judea and a major source of military recruitment, they massacred the entire Jewish population there. The Jews elsewhere took revenge by indiscriminate attacks on Greeks wherever they could find them, and the Greeks responded in kind. By such means the conflict involved more and more participants who were pulled into an ever-escalating struggle by atrocities which manipulated their fear, outrage, sympathy, and guilt.

The antinomian ethos implied by these acts is a strikingly common feature of messianic movements.[49] Gershom Sholem's analysis of the Sabbatian movement which inflamed seventeenth-century Jewry demonstrates that its participants believed that the condition of liberation was the systematic violation of every sacred precept.

> When fulfilling each commandment the pious Jews says a blessing. But according to the new messianic formulation introduced by Sabbatai Zevi himself, he says: "Praised be He who permits the forbidden," a formula which the defenders of the Jewish tradition rightly regarded as the epitome of this revolutionary heresy.[50]

> Through a revolution of values what was formerly sacred became profane and what was formerly profane [became] sacred. . . . More than anything else . . . the "radicals" insisted on the potential holiness of sin. . . . The Gordian knot of the exilic Jew had been cut and a vertigo that ultimately was to be his undoing seized the newly liberated individual: genuine desires for a reconsecration of life mingled indiscriminately with all kinds of destructive and libidinal forces tossed up from the depths by an inexpressible ground swell that undulated wildly between the earthly and the divine.[51]

An Islamic parallel may be the attack described above on the Grand Mosque in Mecca in 1979. The shrine is the holiest in Islam. The assault occurred during a uniquely holy period, the beginning of the year when Mohammed's *hijra* occurred, and also during a holy moment, a time of prayer. Fighting in that place or during those times has always been prohibited.[52]

The process at work in these examples reminds one of the term coined by the French theologian Jacques Ellul to describe the more bizarre activities of student radicals in the 1960s, "desacralization," the pressing need for those who see themselves involved in the creation of a new world to profane all the sacred symbols and norms of the old.[53] Nineteenth-century Russian anarchists were engaged in an identical effort, and those familiar with Isaac Bashevis Singer's *Satan in Goray* will remember that the desacralization process among the Sabbatians is its major theme.

The Sabbatians did not employ or teach terror; their antinomianism was a secret affair. But a doctrine of this sort must in time create an interest in terror, and the Frankists, a Sabbatian offshoot, though they did not practice it, did preach that terror was holy, and their language strikingly resembles that of the Russian anarchist Nechaev, usually considered the creator of modern revolutionary terror.[54]

Medieval Christian antinomianism was practiced more publicly. The Brethren of the Free Spirits and the Adamites, who moved from a phase of hypernomianism during which they were known as Flagellants, believed that they had entered into a state of grace or had literally become gods incapable of sin. "A man who has a conscience is himself Devil and hell and purgatory." The Adamites declared that "blood must flood the world to the height of a horse's head. . . . From their island stronghold" they "waged what they called a Holy War. . . . They set villages on fire and cut down or burnt alive every man, woman, and child they could find," justifying their acts "with a quotation from Scripture: 'And at midnight there was a cry made. Behold, the bridegroom cometh.' "[55] In the first crusade the

Tafurs who "represented" the poor, and as such "exalted as a Holy People worth far more than the knights," normally massacred all the inhabitants of places captured. One incident bears a striking resemblance to Josephus' description of the fate of the Roman garrison which surrendered to the *Sicarii,* and perhaps it was no accident that it took place on the same spot in Jerusalem. Among the Tafur atrocities reported by Christian sources were instances of cannibalism to signify superior commitment or to prove themselves free of sin.[56]

Signs or Portents

The fourth element consists of the various "signs" or visible proof that a deliverance is in process. Most messianic visions associate the destruction of the old order and the birth pangs of the new with a series of cataclysms so profound and so unique that they appear to dissolve both the laws of nature and of mortality. The world appears to be in the grip of uncontrollable forces: earthquakes, floods, volcanic eruptions, falling stars, widespread famines, raging epidemics, revolutionary wars, gruesome massacres, the dissolution of the most elementary social units, and, above all, the unprecedented persecution of the righteous. The terror and horror described is meant to distinguish this struggle from those which have always engaged men. When we believe that a sign of deliverance is a period of inconceivable woe and that the period has not yet occurred, there will be some eager to do their part, and both the commission and provocation of atrocities seem to be means admirably designed for that end. If the road to Paradise runs through Hell, if the fulfillment of the Promise depends upon life becoming as unbearable as possible, violence can have no limits because it cannot be associated with a principle that tells us when to stop because we have either succeeded or we have failed. When disasters do not bring redemption, the obvious remedy is to make the suffering even more profound, but in principle there is no way to demonstrate that our situation is as horrible as it can be.

The Participants

The fifth element is the description provided of the participants' moral nature, for our picture of the enemy always shapes our view of the kind of struggle we must wage. In the language of Dead Sea scrolls, the struggle is seen as a war against the Sons of Darkness, or in other messianic contexts against Amalek,[57] Satan, and the Anti-Christ. The enemy is wholly evil, always dangerous, in short, something other than human. Binding agreements are impossible to make because the restraints which the enemy accepts or proposes are designed for the sole purpose of lulling us into complacency. Against such an antagonist the temptation becomes overwhelming to argue that everything is permissible, that he must be mercilessly destroyed.

In Islam the Holy War or *jihad* which normally is waged against people who are not Moslems has always been governed by rules protecting the rights of noncombatants and prisoners. But in the eyes of Islamic terrorists, those who profess Islam but are essentially hypocrites or apostates have always been the epitome of evil and as such have forfeited all rights, as an influential contemporary terrorist theorist has made clear.

> Governments in the Islamic world today are in a state of apostacy. . . .Of Islam they preserve nothing but its sheer name, although they pray, fast and pretend to be Muslims. Our *sunna* has determined that the apostate be punished more severely than he who has always been an infidel. *The apostate must be killed even if he is in no position to fight while an infidel does not merit death in such a case.*[58]

Justifications for unlimited violence are strengthened when we see *ourselves,* and not simply our cause, as wholly righteous, an essential feature of antinomianism, indeed part of its very definition. The medieval Christian Free Spirits and Adamites literally believed themselves to be gods and hence able to commit acts which were grotesque by conventional moral standards. Similar phenomena are central issues of Dostoevski's novels *Crime and Punishment* and *The Possessed* which treat the nineteenth-century anarchists who are the architects of modern secular terror. The picture of the participants in the cases of both the Christians and Dostoevski reminds one of claims often made by contemporary secular terrorists that the enemy is a symbol or beast, not a person, and that the freedom fighter cannot be a terrorist regardless of the methods employed.

God's Role

The sixth and final element is the character of divine intervention. Will God participate in the struggle? In ancient Israel the wars in which God participates are always different from those between human forces only. Whether we are talking about messianic activities or of the earlier wars to gain the Promised Land, which seem to be a model for the messianic conflict, these differences are sustained.

The simple fact of divine participation produces a paralyzing terror or dread which dissolves the enemy's resolution and negates his advantage of superior numbers and equipment. God fights by means of famine, pestilence, and other natural disasters which spread devastation indiscriminately. At its worst, a violent conflict between humans gives the victor a choice concerning the lives and fortunes of the defeated, and normally conquerors preserve in order to possess. At their best, such wars may be subject to conventions concerning the disposition of populations and properties never engaged or no longer involved in the conflict. But in sharp contrast to this practice, the enemy and its properties had to be exterminated completely in Israel's early holy wars, lest its continued existence corrupt Israel. In the later messianic wars terror seems to be violence without restraint or violence that transcends those limits which ordinary concerns for utility and morality dictate.

Jung's description of John's vision of the apocalyptic wars in *Revelation,* a book which is essential to a variety of Christian messianic movements, is worth citing.

> [It] is a terrifying picture that blatantly contradicts all ideas of Christian humility, tolerance, love of your neighbor and your enemies, and makes nonsense of a loving father in heaven and rescuer

> of mankind. A veritable orgy of hatred, wrath, vindictiveness and blind destructive fury that revels in fantastic images of terror and fire overwhelms a world which Christ had just endeavoured to restore to the original state of innocence and loving communion with God. . . . In all my experience I have never observed anything like it, except in cases of severe psychoses and criminal insanity.[59]

Let me conclude quickly. Once a messianic advent appears imminent, preexisting paradigms guide the expectations and, therefore, the actions of believers, paradigms which, for the most part, are the creation of the dominant or orthodox religious cultures, such as Judaism, Christianity, and Islam. When the paradigms are vague and conflicting, believers must make choices and may abandon some for others more promising and equally legitimate. This also means that there will be differences between single movements and distinct phases which seem contradictory within a single movement. Yet in every case powerful impulses towards terror are inherent in the beliefs of a world about to be destroyed, the gains imagined, the character of the participants, and God's methods. Beyond all this, and I cannot emphasize the point enough, terror is attractive in itself to messianists just *because* it is outside the normal range of violence and for this reason represents a break with the past, epitomizing the antinomianism or complete liberation which is the essence of the messianic expectation.

NOTES

1. David C. Rapoport, "Fear and Trembling: Terrorism in Three Religious Traditions," *American Political Science Review*, 78 (September 1984), 658–77.

2. The somewhat panicky concern to protect government buildings in Washington after Shia suicide attacks in Lebanon is indicative. In December 1983 the *Los Angeles Times* reported that a four minute bomb warning in Coast Guard headquarters provoked a mass exodus of officers leaving the enlisted men behind. In several television interviews after the U.S. embassy in Kuwait was destroyed in 1984, all my interviewers seemed convinced that there was no defense against suicide attacks and that the supply of martyrs must be inexhaustible. For an interesting study of suicidal terrorism which explodes some myths associated with it, see Ariel Merrari, "The Readiness to Kill and Die: Suicidal Terrorism and Indiscriminate Violence in the Middle East," unpublished paper, Psychology of Terrorism Conference, Woodrow Wilson International Center for Scholars, Washingtoin, D.C., March 16–18, 1987. I describe the Shia tactic in Lebanon as a perversion because it entails suicide, which the Islamic tradition prohibits. For an interesting parallel perversion, see Rapoport, "Fear and Trembling."

3. Bruce Hoffman, "Right Wing Terror in the U.S.," *Violence, Aggression and Terror*, 1 (January 1987), 1–25.

4. A very thorough account of the plot is contained in Ehud Sprinzak, "Fundamentalism, Terrorism and Democracy," colloquium paper, Woodrow Wilson International Center for Scholars, September 15, 1986. A later version of this paper entitled "From Messianic Pioneering to Vigilante Terrorism: The Case of the Gush Emunim Underground" will be published in *The Journal of Strategic Studies*, 10 (September 1987).

5. The allegations are made by Barbara and Michael Ledeen, "The Temple Mount Plot," *The New Republic* (June 18, 1984), 20–23, but the parties identified have denied all these allegations. Cf. Eti Ronel, "The Battle over the Temple Mount," *New Outlook*, 27 (February 1984), 11–14, and Janet Aviad, "Israel: New Fanatics and Old," *Dissent*, 31 (Summer 1984), 11–14. Neither Aviad nor Ronel discusses this issue, but they do refer to the moral support by some diaspora Jews.

6. The Assassins called themselves Nizari and were an offshoot of the Ismaili who came out of the Shia. Nizari assailants were known as *fidayeen*, dedicated or consecrated ones. See Rapoport, "Fear and Trembling," pp. 664ff.

7. Assassin communities were located in remote mountain fortresses, which M. G. S. Hodgson describes as a "league of city states." *The Order of Assassins* (The Hague: Mouton, 1955), p. 99.

8. See Norman Cohn, *The Pursuit of the Millennium*, rev. ed. (New York: Oxford University Press, 1970), pp. 61–71, 98–108. Particularly interesting is the discussion of the Tafurs (vagabonds?) in the first crusade who sometimes seem to have roasted and eaten the corpses of their enemies.

9. Bryan Wilson, *Magic and the Millennium* (London: Heinemann, 1973), chap. 8.

10. Kenelm Burridge and Michael Barkun do distinguish violence and terror, and their suggestions are interesting though confined to terror as an element in the antinomian ethos. See Kenelm Burridge, *New Heaven, New Earth: A Study of Millenarian Activities* (Oxford: Blackwell, 1969); Michael Barkun, *Disaster and the Millennium* (New Haven: Yale University Press, 1984).

11. The earliest contemporary discussion of terrorism emphasized the extranormal character of the violence as its distinguishing feature. See Thomas P. Thornton, "Terror as a Weapon of Political Agitation," in Harry Eckstein, ed., *Internal War* (New York: Free Press, 1964); E. V. Walter, *Terror and Resistance: A Study of Political Violence* (New York: Oxford University Press, 1969); David C. Rapoport, "The Politics of Atrocity," in Yonah Alexander and Seymore Finger, eds., *Terrorism: Interdisciplinary Perspectives* (New York: John Jay, 1977); and H. Price, Jr., "The Strategy and Tactics of Revolutionary Terrorism," *Comparative Studies in Society and History*, 19 (1977), 52–65. The more common recent definitions do not distinguish between violence and terror. See, for example, Charles A. Russell, L. J. Banker, and Bowman Miller, "Out Inventing the Terrorist," in Yonah Alexander, David Carlton, and Paul Wilkinson, eds., *Terrorism, Theory and Practice* (Boulder: Westview, 1979).

12. We have excluded two other messianic forms, one which posits salvation as an event in the spiritual or unseen world, the orthodox Christian doctrine, and another which is wholly secular, such as Marxism. My characterization corresponds roughly to Yonina Talmon's description of millenarism. But she speaks of movements, not beliefs, and therefore specifies imminence as a necessary feature. See "Millenarism," *Encyclopedia of the Social Sciences* (New York: Macmillan, 1968). While the notion of a personal savior was once essential to the definition, the term presently is virtually interchangeable with millenarism and chiliasm. The apocalyptic group is a particular kind of messianic group. In this paper I have not distinguished between "premillenarian" and "postmillenarian" doctrines. The first visualizes a single, sudden, dramatic destructive advent, while the second sees an initial advent which is spiritual and/or gradual, which is displayed in the unfolding of history and may or may not be followed by a violent occurrence. The postmillenarian view, which is the source of the secular doctrine of progress, was characteristic of nineteenth-century messianic groups like the Mormons. See Stow Persons, *American Minds* (New York: Henry Holt, 1958), pp. 176–77. The Gush Emunim, an Israeli messianic group which has a fundamental concern to settle the West Bank, has a postmillenarian view which reserves an essential role for violence.

13. Eric J. Hobsbawm, *Primitive Rebels* (Manchester: University Press, 1959), pp. 60ff. Hobsbawm uses the term millenarianism instead. Wilhelm Muhlman calls such situations "charismatic," a context of collective excitement, belief in miracles and wonders, and extreme sensitivity to signs. Wilhelm Muhlman, *Messianismes révolutionnaires du tiers monde* (Paris: Gallimard, 1968), pp. 186–87. Hobsbawm notes a similar phenomenon among nineteenth and twentieth century Andalusian anarchists. An uprising broke out every ten years for some eighty years "when something in the local situation made action imperative or when some impetus from outside fanned the glow of latent revolutionism into a flame. Some piece of news, some portent or comet, proving that the time had come would penetrate into the village. It might be the original arrival of the Bakunist apostles in the early 1870s, the garbled news of the Russian Revolution, the news that a Republic has been proclaimed or that an Agrarian Reform Law was under discussion." Hobsbawm, *Primitive Rebels*, pp. 86–8. It seems that in the general analysis of revolution, too, the notion of imminence is a necessary but rarely appreciated concept.

14. The place of the messianic hope in Jewish liturgy is discussed in Julius Greenstone, *The Messiah Idea in Jewish History* (Philadelphia: Jewish Publication Society, 1906), appendix.

15. Hugh J. Schonfield, *The Passover Plot* (New York: Geis, 1965), p. 19.

16. Greenstone, *The Messiah Idea*, p. 111.

17. Christopher Hill, "Till the Conversion of the Jews," UCLA Clark Library Lecture, October 30, 1981, in Richard Popkin, *Millenarianism* (Los Angeles: University of California Press, forthcoming).

18. Wilson D. Wallis, *Messiahs: Their Role in Civilization* (Washington, D.C.: American Council on Public Affairs, 1943), pp. 85–86.

19. *Babylonian Talmud, Sanhedrin* 97a.

20. A leader's description of how the Millerites, an American messianic movement in the 1840s, were impelled by the demands of their followers to fix a date for the Second Coming is interesting in this regard. "At first a definite time was generally opposed; but there seemed to be an irresistible power attending its proclamation, which prostrated all before it. It swept over the land with the velocity of a tornado, and it reached hearts in different and distinct places almost simultaneously, and in a manner which can be accounted for only on the supposition that God was [in] it. The lecturers among the Adventists were the last to embrace the views of the time . . . [but ultimately they] could but exclaim, 'What were we, that we should resist God. It seemed to us to have been so independent of human agency that we could but regard it as a fulfillment of the midnight cry.' " Quoted in Leon Festinger et al., *When Prophecy Fails* (Minneapolis: University of Minnesota Press, 1958) p. 20. Note how Raphael Patai explains the hostility towards the time speculator: "The results of all these efforts in widely different periods to discover a method of calculating the date of the advent had a common conclusion—that the Messiah would come soon, not in a distant and indefinite future but in their own (the calculators') lifetime." *The Messiah Texts* (New York: Avon, 1979), p. XXXVIII.

21. Greenstone, *The Messiah Idea*, p. 108.

22. Ayman Al-Yassini, *Religion and State in Saudi Arabia* (Boulder: Westview, 1985), pp. 124–9. The tradition is

discussed in detail in Abdulaziz Abdulhussein Sachedina, *Islamic Messianism: The Idea of the Mahdi in Twelve Shiism* (Albany: S.U.N.Y. Press, 1981), pp. 150–180.

23. Michael Gilsenan, *Recognizing Islam* (London: Croom Helm, 1982), p. 17.

24. Edward Mortimer, *Faith and Power: The Politics of Islam* (New York: Vintage, 1982), pp. 75–9, 181–2.

25. Gottfried Osterwal writes, "Contemporaneous history is to a large extent the history and growth of new religions and cults. There is hardly a region in the world that in the last two or three [decades] has not given birth to a new religious movement or that has not seen the sudden revival of some old messianic belief. And hardly a week passes . . . somewhere where another prophet arises whose message of a soon coming 'messiah' and the imminent destruction of the 'present world' becomes the basis of a new messianic movement or religious awakening. Over 6000 of such new religious movements have been reported from Africa. Since the Second World War hundreds of new religions arose in Japan and a similar number has been reported from the Philippines. The thousands of cargo cults and prophetic movements in New Guinea and Oceania are well-known, Southeast Asia . . . Latin America . . . North America and Europe [show] that the expectation of the soon coming Messiah . . . is a universal phenomenon." *Modern Messianic Movements as a Theological and Missionary Challenge* (Elkhart: Institute of Mennonite Studies, 1973), p. 7.

26. "Millenarian enthusiasm [has] always flourished when men thought and cared deeply about religion and when political convulsions tempted them to deduce that the Time of the End was approaching." P. G. Roger, *The Fifth Monarchy Men* (London: Oxford University Press, 1966), p. 132. One also could argue the reverse position, that catastrophe breeds messianism which then produces an interest in religion.

27. Michael Barkun, "Divided Apocalypse: Thinking about the End in Contemporary America," *Soundings: An Interdisciplinary Journal*, 66 (Fall 1983), 257–280. Barkun's perceptive essay is the source for the themes in this paragraph. In the eyes of those who experienced it, the fall of Rome probably provided an early parallel to our sense that the world can be destroyed.

28. Timothy P. Weber, *Living in the Shadow of the Second Coming: American Premillenialism 1875–1982*, enl. ed. (Grand Rapids: Zonderwan, 1983), ch. 6. The restoration of Israel has, of course, been interpreted in different ways at various times. In the Crusades it was understood to be the conquest of the holy places. In the late medieval period, groups like the Taborites and Anabaptists imagined themselves to be the new Israel, and seventeenth-century English Protestants agitated to send the Jews back to Zion. See note 32 for an African version.

29. W. E. Blackstone in 1891 got 413 of the most prominent Americans, headed by the Chief Justice, J. P. Morgan, and John D. Rockefeller, to sign a "memorial" on behalf of the Russian Jews urging President Harrison to pressure the Turks to give Palestine back to the Jews. This was five years before Herzl's *Der Judenstaat* and six before the first international Zionist conference! See Weber, pp. 138ff.

30. Sprinzak, "Fundamentalism."

31. *Babylonian Talmud, Sanhedrin* 97b.

32. "Ethiopia shall soon stretch her hands unto God." *Psalms*, 68:31. Some African messianic sects have called themselves Ethiopian. See George Shepperson, "Ethiopianism and African Nationalism" *Phylon*, 14 (1953), 9–18.

33. George Woodcock and Ivan Avakumovic, *The Doukhobors* (London: Faber and Faber, 1968), pp. 173–82.

34. D. S. Margoliouth, "On Mahdis and Mahdism," *Proceedings of the British Academy* (London: Oxford University Press, n.d.), p. 213.

35. Emmanuel Sivan suggests using the term counter-society, which was originally employed by Kriegel to describe the French Communist Party and then by students of Islam. " 'A counter-society is a mirosociety which constitutes a closed society while maintaining some ties with society as a whole. The counter-society must be capable of being self-enclosed in order to avoid fragmentation or abdication. It must prevent alien influences from penetrating it yet must remain sufficiently open and aggressive to draw from the outside whatever it cannot itself produce. It must pursue the dream of ultimately becoming a majority. It struggles to demolish the old society while at the same time hoping to become heir to that society: radical destruction on the one hand, preservation for the sake of the new order on the other.' Joined to these two major functions is a third one, the counter-society as a model for the future." Emmanuel Sivan, *Radical Islam* (New Haven: Yale University Press, 1985), p. 85. Sivan notes further that Dannawi describes Muhammed's original group of followers as an exemplary " 'countersociety.' . . . operating in the heart of the *jahili* (corrupt?) society . . . and engaged in battle against the latter, 'for the barbaric society tends to react harshly using all the means at its disposal: murder and banishment, torture and pressures, ridicule and seduction.' "

36. Examples of archetype imitations in different periods are discussed by Hodgson, *The Order of Assassins*, pp. 77–80; Rapoport, "Fear and Trembling;" T. Hodgkin, "Mahdism, Messianism and Marxism in the African Setting," in P. Gutkind and P. Waterman, eds., *African Social Studies: A Radical Reader* (New York: 1977); Sivan, *Radical Islam*, chap. 4; Gilsenan, *Recognizing Islam*, chap. 7; Peter Von Sivers, "The Realm of Justice: Apocalyptic Revolts in Algeria (1849–1879)," *Humaniora Islamica*, 1 (1973), 47–60; and Marilyn Robinson Waldman, "The Popular Appeal of the Prophetic Paradigm in West Africa," *Contributions to Asian Studies*, 17 (1983), 110–14.

37. Cohn, *The Pursuit of the Millenium*, pp. 198–281.

38. See Simma Holt, *Terror in the Name of God: The Story of the Sons of Freedom Doukhobors* (Toronto: McClelland and Stewart, 1964), and Woodcock and Avakumovic, *The Doukhobors*, chap. 13.

39. Wilson, pp. 36–37.

40. Marvin Zonis and Daniel Brumberg. "Shiism as Interpreted by T. Khomeini: An Ideology of Revolutionary Violence," in Martin Kramer, ed., *Shiism, Resistance and Revolution* (Boulder: Westview, 1987), p. 49.
41. Ibid., chaps. 8 and 9. Wilson suggests that the normal course of revolutionary messianism is *from* "military" to "pacific" values, but I cannot tell whether his evidence would support the terms terrorism and pacifism as substitutes. Von Sivers, "The Realm of Justice," p. 50, speaks of the "oscillation" between "revolutionary activity" and a retreat into "quietist brotherhoods" which he has informed me is widespread in Islam. He also told me that the "brotherhoods" have pacifist elements but did not believe there was evidence that the different activities referred to different phases visualized for the messianic process; the brotherhoods are models for life in the transformed society. This picture does not seem fundamentally different from my own.
42. Bryan Wilson, *Sects and Society* (Berkeley: University of California Press, 1961), p. 351.
43. Sprinzak, "Fundamentalism," p. 8.
44. Von Sivers, "The Realm of Justice," p. 56.
45. See Rapoport, "Fear and Trembling."
46. John R. Hall, "The Apocalypse at Jonestown," in Ken Levi, *Violence and Religious Commitment* (University Park: Pennsylvania State University Press, 1982), pp. 36–54.
47. Josephus, *Antiquities of the Jews*, H. St. Thackeray, transl., *Loeb Classical Library*, (London: Heinemann, 1962), XVII, p. 23.
48. Josephus, *The Jewish War*, ibid., II, p. 457.
49. The Oxford English Dictionary defines an antinomian as "one who maintains that the moral law is not binding upon Christians under the law of grace," and the word generally refers to persons who do not believe themselves bound by social rules or standards.
50. Gersom Scholem, *The Messianic Idea in Judaism* (New York: Schocken, 1971), p. 75.
51. Ibid., p. 112.
52. I am grateful to Ibrahim Karawan who suggested the parallel.
53. Jacques Ellul, *The New Demons* (London: Mowbray, 1975), pp. 48–87. Nineteenth-century anarchists often "desanctified" themselves by committing acts that they regarded as personally obscene, the object being to break the hold of society's moral conventions over their feelings. For a similar process among the Weathermen and the Japanese Red Army, see Rapoport, "Politics of Atrocity."
54. Scholem, *The Messianic Idea*, pp. 126–34. "The annihilation of every religion and positive system of belief—this was the 'true way' the 'believers' were expected to follow. Concerning the redemptive powers of havoc, Frank's imagination knew no limits: 'Wherever Adam trod a city was built but wherever I set foot all will be destroyed for I came into the world only to destroy and annihilate.' " Ibid., p. 130. Compare this with Nechaev: "The revolutionary . . . knows only one science: the science of destruction. . . . He enters the world . . . only because he has faith in its speedy and total destruction. . . . He must not hesitate to destroy any position, any place, or any man in this world—all must be equally detested. . . . If he has parents, friends, and loved ones, he is no longer a revolutionary if they can stay his hand." "Revolutionary Catechism" in David C. Rapaport, *Assassination and Terrorism* (Toronto: CBC, 1971), pp. 79–81.
55. Cohn, pp. 148–63.
56. Ibid., pp. 65–7.
57. The Amalekites who attacked a weak and exhausted Israel in a particularly cruel fashion personify a boundless evil which God has obliged Israel to exterminate. For the use of Amalek by the Gush Emunin, see Uriel Tal, "Foundations of a Polilical Messianic Trend in Israel," *Jerusalem Quarterly*, 35 (Spring 1985), 43ff.
58. My emphasis. The quotation is from Faraj's *The Absent Precept*, quoted by Sivan, who says that Sadat's assassins "meditated" on the work. Sivan, *Radical Islam*, pp. 128, 103. See my discussion of a similar theme among early Muslim terrorists in Rapoport, "Fear and Trembling."
59. Carl Jung, *Answer to Job* (Princeton: Princeton University Press, 1973), pp. 76, 95.

[illegible]

[illegible] decided that [illegible] no longer [illegible] of the name and the [illegible] and the persecution of the people that was named after Him, so He ordered the State of Israel to be, which is a total contradiction to the Diaspora.

If the Diaspora with its humiliations, defeats, persecutions, second-class status of a minority etc. means hillul hashem, then a sovereign Jewish State which provides the Jew home, majority status, land of his own, a military of his own and a victory over

[13]

Violence and Catastrophe in the Theology of Rabbi Meir Kahane: The Ideologization of Mimetic Desire

EHUD SPRINZAK

In 1976, following a brutal terrorist attack on a school in the Israeli border town of Kiriyat Shmone, an attack that took the lives of many children, the late Rabbi Meir Kahane, leader of the extremist movement Kach (Thus!) wrote a short essay, *hillul hashem* (the desecration of the name of God). In the essay, which was never published and was only available for Kach members in a mimeograph form, Kahane presented his answer to the Kookist theology of Gush Emunim (the Block of the Faithful) regarding the process of heavenly redemption and the origins of the State of Israel. It was also the first time that he fully developed his revenge theory and elaborated upon the kind of violence he has been engaged in since 1969.

> The debate about the religious legitimacy of the State of Israel and its place in our history has already been conducted within religious circles for a long time. It has focused on the penetrating and real question: How can a religious Jew see the hand of God in a state that was established by Jews who not only do not follow the paths of God, but reject Him openly or, at best, are passive to His blessed existence? . . .
>
> The State of Israel was established not because the Jew deserved it, for the Jew is as he has been before, rejecting God, deviating from his paths and ignoring His Torah, but all this is immaterial to the case. God created this state not for the Jew and not as a reward for his justice and good deeds. It is because He, be blessed, decided that He could no longer take the desecration of his name and the laughter, the disgrace and the persecution of the people that was named after him, so He ordered the State of Israel to be, which is a total contradiction to the Diaspora.
>
> If the Diaspora, with its humiliations, defeats, persecutions, second class status of a minority . . . means hillul hashem, then a sovereign Jewish State which provides the Jew home, majority status, land of his own, a military of his own and a victory over

> the defeated Gentile in the battlefield – *is exactly the opposite*, Kidush Hashem (the sanctification of the name of God). It is the reassertion, the proof, the testimony for the existence of God and his government.[1]

Kahane's short essay was a major attack on the prevailing Zionist ideo-theology of the time, the Kookist philosophy of Gush Emunim. According to Rav Kook Sr., the founder of the Kookist school, the State of Israel was created by the Zionists as part of a heavenly plan to redeem the people of Israel. The founding fathers of Zionism who established the secular movement in a clear defiance of most orthodox authorities were not sinful heretics who acted against God and abrogated his orders. Although secular and unobserving they were, unknowingly, God's holy emissaries. God Himself acted to revive the nation and in His mysterious way chose to do it through the secular Zionists. The secular State of Israel, according to the Kookist school is therefore not a sin but a reward, a graceful indication that God has finally decided to forgive *all* his people, not just the orthodox faithful. It is holy for its intrinsic value, for what it is and does for the Jews.[2]

In total contrast to Gush Emunim, Rabbi Meir Kahane believed that 'not the Jews, are responsible for the establishment of the State of Israel but, paradoxically, the Gentiles'. The State of Israel was established not because the Zionists, 'who did not repent(!)', deserved it, but as a result of the actions of the Gentiles. The perennial humiliation of the Jew by the Gentile world was, according to this strange theory, also a humiliation of God since his chosen people were being repeatedly persecuted. Following the Holocaust, God could no longer stand this humiliation and had the State of Israel established as his revenge against the Gentiles. Thus, the Jewish State is virtuous not because of what it does to the Jews but for what it inflicts upon the Gentiles. It is not an expression of reward but of punishment. Not the Jews deserve it but the Gentiles![3] The specific Gentile may not be the same, but he is always there, the Nazis, the Blacks, the Christian Church, the Russians, and, of course, the Arabs.

Kahane's intense radicalism, immense passion, and irrevocable commitment to his political struggle seemed to be exclusively rooted in this one element, the insatiable urge to beat the *Goy* (Gentile), to respond in kind for the two-milleniums old vilification of the Jews. Many Jews have expressed since time immemorial the Jewish antagonism towards the cruel Gentile nations which have repeatedly harassed and persecuted them and were responsible for their mass murder. A review of Kahane's writings leaves no doubt that he was by far the most extreme representative of this school in modern times. Kahane's hostility to the Gentiles may not be the cardinal presupposition of his political theology, but it is certainly its most dominant emotional and psychological theme. And what was unique about Kahane was that he openly sought revenge. So strong was the rabbi's rejection of the Gentile world and his urge for revenge that it may not be erroneous to sum up the Kahane assertive psychology by the phrase 'I take revenge therefore I am'. And since the rabbi believed he expressed the opinion of the Halakha (Jewish Law) and the voice of God, it is not surprising that the vengeance the Jews are expected to take is according to him not simply a personal act, but God's very revenge for the humiliation He Himself suffered through the desecration of his people.

> Do you want to know how the Name of God is desecrated in the eyes of the mocking and sneering nations? It is when the *Jew*, His people, His chosen, is desecrated! When the *Jew* is beaten, God is profaned! When the *Jew* is humiliated God is shamed! When the *Jew* is attacked it is an assault upon the Name of God! . . .
>
> Every pogrom is a desecration of the Name. Every Auschwitz and expulsion and murder and rape of a Jew is the humiliation of God. Every time a Jew is beaten by a Gentile because he is a Jew, this is the essence of hillul hashem! . . .
>
> An end to Exile – that is Kidush Hashem (the sanctification of the name of God). An end to the shame and beatings and the monuments to our murdered and our martyrized. An end to Kaddish and prayers for the dead . . . An end to the Gentile fist upon a Jewish face. . . .
>
> A Jewish fist in the face of an astonished Gentile world that had not seen it for two millennia, this is Kidush Hashem. Jewish dominion over the Christian holy places while the Church that sucked our blood vomits its rage and frustration. This is Kidush Hashem. A Jewish Air Force that is better than any other and that forces a Lebanese airliner down so that we can imprison murderers of Jews rather than having to repeat the centuries old pattern of begging the Gentile to do it for us. This is Kidush Hashem . . . Reading angry editorials about Jewish 'aggression' and 'violations' rather than flowery eulogies over dead Jewish victims. That is Kidush Hashem.[4]

Kahane's use of the formal Halakhic terminology of hillul hashem (the desecration of the name of God), and kiddush hashem (the sanctification of the name of God), should not mislead the reader to believe that this is a conventional Jewish discourse. What really comes out of these emotional statements is Kahane's idiosyncratic conviction that the very definition of Jewish freedom implies the ability to humiliate the Gentile. The stronger the Jew is, the more violent and aggressive, the freer he becomes. Kahane may not have gone as far as George Sorel and Franz Fanon in claiming that violence is a moral force in history or that violence sets one free, but he shared many similarities with both, especially Fanon.[5] For in a sense he proposed that Jewish independence and a Jewish State are not enough. Jewish sovereignty does not provide a full and satisfactory solution for the Jewish problem, for it only solves the misery of exile.

There is, however, another wound which has to be healed, the pain of humiliation, the misery of thousands of years of discrimination and victimization, the bleeding memories of generations of vilified Jews, killed for their religion. Kahane, it is important to stress, did not concentrate solely on the Holocaust, though his profound reaction to the Nazi genocide of the Jews during World War II had been a dominant theme in his actions and writings since the days of the American Jewish Defence League (JDL): The Holocaust was a natural product of anti-Semitism which could develop in any 'normal' nation and is still a historical possibility.[6] According to Kahane, the Holocaust, and the countless pogroms that preceded it, left in the nation's collective psyche an almost irreparable damage. Jewish independence alone cannot redress the damage, only a concrete revenge, a physical humiliation of the Gentiles. Therefore, Kahane, just as Franz Fanon, was not satisfied with a peaceful liberation. A military force that astonishes the world is needed, 'a fist in the face of the Gentile'.[7]

Catastrophic Messianism

An examination of the style of Kahane's writings and public speeches reveals that his revenge theory and legitimation of Jewish violence are consistently intermingled with a sense of disaster and tragedy. Jewish history since the destruction of the Second Temple is according to him nothing but a series of horrendous holocausts, the last of which has finally moved God to establish the State of Israel and avenge His desecrated honor. It is therefore not surprising that the other side of Kahane's 'logical' theology of violence was his emotional sense of catastrophe, a deep conviction that before the Jewish condition will get better things will become a much worse. Long before the evolution of Kahane's pessimistic prophesies regarding the future of the present State of Israel he made himself the prophet of doom and gloom of American Jewry. An essential part of his personal decision to move to Israel was his growing 'catastrophic Zionism', a fully-fledged ideology which predicted the inevitable coming of a new holocaust and called upon the Jews of Diaspora to move to Israel before it became too late. Nineteenth-century Zionism, it should be recalled, had a very strong catastrophic component. Its most influential theoreticians, Leo Pinsker and Theodor Herzl, came to their conclusion that Zionism was inevitable as result of the physical insecurity of the Jews in eastern Europe at the turn of the century. They convinced themselves as well as many generations of young Zionists that the anti-Semitism of their time was so severe that it was just a matter of time before the entire nation was eliminated by either physical destruction or spiritual assimilation.[8] The doctrine of *Shlilat Hagalut* (the Negation of Diaspora) was a direct product of this catastrophic Zionism.

Catastrophic Zionism started to decline following the evolution of the Zionist enterprise in Palestine and the success of the post-1917 political Zionism. With the exception of Vladimir Jabotinsky's 1930s warnings of growing European anti-Semitism it greatly declined. The 1948 establishment of the State of Israel, the emergence of the powerful American Jewry and the respectable presence of Jewish communities all over the democratic West have left the thesis of catastrophic Zionism with little explanatory power. But Kahane did not care less. In 1968 he began to talk about the gathering storm and the incipient disaster. It was just a question time before the enemies of the Jews overcame their guilt feelings about the destruction of European Jewry and started to plan the new holocaust. America of the melting pot, the dream country of millions of Jewish immigrants, Kahane told his audience, had started to undergo in the 1960s an economic recession, as well as severe moral and social crisis. It was just a question of time before the classical scapegoat, the Jew, was discovered and acted upon.[9]

Kahane's 'catastrophic Zionism' was the rationale behind his 'program for Jewish survival', the subtitle of his 1972 book *Never Again* and his comprehensive call for a series of steps in order to save American Jewry from extinction. While most of the suggestions had to do with an internal reform of Jewish life in America, the ultimate step called for was immigration to Israel. As much as Jews could help themselves in Diaspora by returning to full Judaism and by defending their rights and dignity, the Diaspora was doomed. The deterministic logic of anti-Semitism which was rediscovered by the vociferous rabbi left no chance for a long range Jewish survival outside of the State of Israel.[10] And while America of the 1960s was portrayed by Kahane as a troubled land, a modern version of Sodom and Gomorrah, Israel, the modern reincarnation of the land of the prophets and great conquerors was all good. It was the true answer to all the Jewish miseries of the time. The young state which managed to free itself by force from British colonialism and to build a military machine capable of defeating all the Arab anti-Semites was the manifestation of all of Kahane's early dreams. It had provided the only conditions for the breeding of the new Jew, a healthy and complete Hebrew national.[11]

Kahane's 1971 immigration to Israel and his increasing disappointment with its secular culture (and with the refusal of its leaders to listen to him) had made him reformulate his catastrophic theory. In 1973 and 1974 the leader of the JDL wrote two long essays: *Israel's Eternity and Victory* and *Numbers 23:9*, in which he first developed his catastrophic Messianism.[12] The entire theory was based on a verse from Isaiah 'In its time, I will hurry it (the redemption)' (Isaiah 60), and on its Rabbinical interpretation 'If they, the Jews, merit it I will hurry it. If they do not merit it, it will come "in its time"' (Sanhedrin 93). Redemption, according to this theory, is inevitable. It is part of God's plan and does not depend on what the people of Israel do or do not do. What is, however, left to the Jews is *the choice*, the determination of how and when does redemption take place. If they repent then, according to Kahane's interpretation of the sources, 'I will hurry it' meaning that redemption will come quickly and without pain. But if they do not, then redemption will come 'in its time', that is, following great troubles, wars and immense disasters. The establishment of the State of Israel in 1948 and 1967 victory of the Six Day War were unmistakable signs for God's desire to 'hurry it' provided the right attitude of the nation and its readiness to repent. Following the ordeal of the Yom Kippur War (1973), which indicated the existence of a serious problem on the road to salvation, Kahane saw fit to warn the people of Israel about the awaiting disasters should they not respond to God's gesture and return to orthodox Judaism.

In 1980 Kahane had plenty of time to reconsider his grand ideo-theology. He was placed on 'administrative arrest' of nine months in the Ramla maximum security prison for planning to blow up the Muslim Dome of the Rock on the Temple Mount. The months were one of his most productive periods, for he completed two major books, *Thorns in Your Eyes* and *On Redemption and Faith*. However, the most original essay he wrote in jail was *Forty Years*. The book's novelty was Kahane's daring conclusion that in 1948, the year Israel obtained its independence, the nation was given a grace period of forty years in order to repent and to prepare for God's hurried redemption. But there was an implied warning in the deal. If no repentance took place, an inevitable redemption ('in its time') was to occur, not out of God's grace but out of His fury and through a tremendous disaster. The miraculous victory in 1967 indicated that God had been keeping His promise and that it was now time for the people to fulfill its part. But by 1980, just eight years before the final deadline, no repentance had yet taken place and the nation's time was running out.

> Consider, Jew. If it is indeed true what I say, then the refusal to heed is more than mere luxury. It is destruction. And then consider a second thing. *If it is true that the forty years began with the rise of the State – how many years are left*?
>
> Too few. So little time to make the great decision that will either bring us the great and glorious redemption, swiftly, majestically, spared the terrible sufferings and needless agonies, or G-d forbid, the madness of choosing the path of unnecessary, needless holocaust, more horrible than anything we have yet endured. As we stand on the crossroads, with one direction that of glorious life and redemption, and the other the path of prior tragedy and holocaust, the choice is ours. We are the masters of our destiny if we will only choose the path that the Al-Mighty pleads us to walk upon.
>
> My people; my dear and foolish people! We speak of your life and those of your seed, your children and grand children. Choose wisely! The Magnificence is yours for the asking. The horror will be yours for the blindness. Choose life, but quickly; there is little time left. *The forty years tick away*.[13]

From 1980 Kahane became Israel's prophet of doom and gloom. Apart from his political programs that called for the expulsion of the Arabs from Israel and for the Judaization of the country, his books were full of warnings regarding the coming catastrophe. It is very hard to tell how deeply the leader of Kach believed in his own predictions, and whether we had here an article of faith of a prophet in the tradition of Jeremiah, or an expression of a troubled person who knew no one took his theories seriously. But Kahane did discuss the issue of catastrophe in private interviews, and said that even if he was the prime minister a catastrophe would still take place if the nation did not repent willingly.[14]

Creating a Violent Order

One of the most characteristic elements of Kahane's career was that unlike many high priests of violence and catastrophe, his teachings never remained in the books. In fact, many of Kahane's theories, had been written *after the fact*, after the JDL's or Kach's violent operations had already been conducted. Had the extremist rabbi been entrusted with power he might just as well have created the catastrophe he had been warning against all along. Thus an essential part of the Kahane phenomenon is the conscious attempt on his behalf to create a violent order, to shape a Kahane-inspired *weltanschauung* in which anti-Gentile violence and terror are part of the rules of the game. Already in the days of the American JDL, Kahane emphasized the importance of physical force. One of the pillars of the JDL's operative ideology was the notion of 'Jewish iron'. Kahane, it is true, did not invent either the idea or the metaphor: he adopted it from the ideology of Vladimir Jabotinsky, the ideologue of Revisionist Zionism. The expression *Barzel Yisrael* (Iron Israel), according to Jabotinsky, meant that in the Diaspora or under foreign rule, Jews were no longer to bow to their oppressors but were called upon respond to them in kind and with physical force, if necessary. It also meant that the sovereign Jewish State should have a strong army, capable of defending it against all threats. Kahane was so impressed with the notion of 'iron' and the application of physical force for self-defense, that he divided the JDL in America into two groups: the *Chaya* groups and the Scholar groups. Chaya in Hebrew means animal, and Chaya squads were in charge of the use of violence against the League's rivals.[15] Teaching his young followers to act and feel like animals, Kahane wanted them to believe that the JDL was the core group of a new breed, free of the traditional Jewish 'ghetto mentality'. and that they themselves were like 'the Jews of old'.

> Once upon a time, the Jew was not a member of the ADL [the American liberal Anti-Defamation League, an organization highly critical of the JDL's violence] – neither in form nor in spirit. It was not in the role of Mahatma Gandhi that the Jews fought at Massada; the men of Bar-Kochba and Judah Macabee never went to a Quaker meeting. The Jews of old – when Jews were knowledgeable about their religion, when they turned the page of the Jewish Bible instead of turning the Christian cheek – understood the concept of the Book and the Sword. It was only in the horror of the ghetto with its fears, neuroses, and insecurities that the Jew began to react in fright rather than with self-respect. That is what the ghetto does to a Jew.[16]

When he was brought to trial in New York in 1971, one of the main charges against Kahane was illegal possession of guns, ammunition and explosives. The leader of the JDL, who did not hesitate to ally himself with the Mafia boss Joseph Colombo – who established in New York the fake Italian-American Civil Rights Association[17] - had no problem translating the idea of 'Iron Israel' into the actual use of firearms against the enemies of the Jews. Some of his followers, members of the JDL and probably of a Chaya squad, planted a bomb in the offices of Sol Hurok, the Jewish producer who used to bring Russian artists to America. The bomb that set the place ablaze killed a young Jewish secretary who worked for Hurok.[18] It was the beginning of a series of terrorist acts which identified the behavior of the JDL and its splinter groups long after Kahane left the US. Since the mid-1970s, the American League has been consistently referred to by the FBI as a terrorist organization.

Kahane never denied his penchant for concrete violence and in his own account of the story of the Jewish Defense League, devoted a whole chapter to the justification and rationalization of JDL's violence. While making the usual argument that 'violence against *evil* is not the same as violence against *good*', and that violence for self-defense is fully legitimate, Kahane reached his famous conclusion that since Jews have been victimized for so long, 'Jewish violence in defense of Jewish interest is *never* bad'.[19] According to this theory Jewish violence is nothing but an extension of *Ahavat Isroel* (Jewish love), the natural brotherly sentiment that requires Jews to care for and help each other regardless of the conditions involved.[20]

In Israel, there was no place for further expression of 'Jewish iron', since from 1948 the country has been sovereign and Jabotinsky's notion has been realized in the Israel Defence Forces (IDF). But unlike Jabotinsky's recognized successors, Kahane apparently had not been satisfied. Though he did not establish Chaya teams in Israel, he maintained that if the state was incapable or unready to react in kind against those who spill 'so much as one drop of Jewish blood', then it was the duty of individual Israelis to do so. Slowly and without admitting that he was an ideologue of terrorism, Kahane took to legitimizing anti-Arab terror, a message fully absorbed and acted upon by his followers. One of Kahane's great historical heroes was David Raziel, the first commander of the Etzel underground in Palestine during the second half of the 1930s. It was Raziel who in 1937 introduced Jewish massive counter-terrorism against the Arabs, in opposition to the official Zionist policy of *Havlaga* (restraint). Raziel's idea, that uninvolved Arab civilians should pay for what was happening to Jewish civilians, was especially attractive to Kahane.[21] And he never cared to recognize the fact that Raziel's successors, including the admired Menachem Begin, had renounced indiscriminate terrorism already in the 1940s and became, after the establishment of the State of Israel, respectful of the law and fully confident in the Israeli Army.

In 1974 Kahane first came up with the idea of TNT (Hebrew acronym for *Terror Neged Terror* – Jewish terrorism against Arab terrorism). In

The Jewish Idea, he suggested that a 'world-wide Jewish anti-terror group' be established and that this group must be organized and aided in exactly the same way as the terrorists are aided by the Arab governments. With a totally serious face, the government of Israel must deny any connection with the group, even while allowing the same training bases on its soil as the Arab states allow the terrorists.[22] Kahane even recommended at the time the application of indiscriminate terrorism against the population of those Arab countries which provide the PLO with financial, political and military support.[23]

Kahane's idea to apply brutal Jewish counter-terrorism did not change much over the years, and in his latest book he vowed to establish, upon assuming the leadership of Israel, special Jewish anti-terror groups that would operate all over the world and help Jews wherever there is trouble, disregarding the local authorities and their laws.[24] Since the government of Israel was not receptive to his notions, Kahane's followers and other individuals inspired by his idea, soon started to act on their own. Out of fear of the Israeli police and secret services, they did not try to establish a permanent terror organization, but rather engaged in occasional anti-Arab atrocities, using the symbol of TNT.[25] Kahane's devotees were actively involved in the intensification of the conflict between Jews and Arabs in the West Bank in the 1970s. Yossi Dayan, for example, a student of Kahane and later the Secretary General of Kach, has been caught and arrested several times for provoking the Arabs in the Tomb of the Patriarchs in Hebron. In an interview he once boasted,' I had more trials than the number of stars on the American flag'.[26] Before the recent Arab uprising which has changed all the rules of public conduct in the West Bank, it was Kahane's followers who usually acted in response to Arab attacks, although by the middle of the 1980s such pretexts as acting only in reaction to Arab violence were decreasingly needed. Craig Leitner, a Kahane student, described a typical mid-1980s operation:

> One day towards the end of July 1984, I agreed with Mike Gozovsky and Yehuda Richter to operate against the Arabs. We left Kiriyat Arba in a hired car, headed towards Jerusalem . . . That night around 23.00, we went to the Neve Yaacov area. Yehuda was driving. Around midnight, we saw an Arab in his twenties walking along the road. I said 'let's stop the car'. I went out and hit the Arab with my fist on the shoulder. I also kicked him. He escaped into the night. We continued to Hebron and it was decided – I don't remember by whom – to burn Arab cars. We had in our car two plastic bottles containing four and a half litres of gasoline. In Hebron Yehuda stopped the car. Mike took the

> gasoline and poured it under several cars, maybe three. Following the burning of the cars by Yehuda, we moved, not waiting to see what would happen. Dogs were around and I was afraid that they would wake up the neighbors, or perhaps bite us and we would get rabies.[27]

When asked for his reaction to the activities of Leitner and his friends, who later fired on an Arab bus wounding several innocent passengers, Kahane expressed total approval. He said that he was sorry that they would have to spend years in prison and added that, in his eyes, they were Maccabees. Later, Kahane placed Yehuda Richter, the main suspect in the operation, as number two on his list for the Knesset. Had Kach won two seats in 1984, Richter would have been released due to the immunity of Israel's Knesset members. When asked once by a journalist whether he would be willing to instruct his followers not to hit innocent Arabs who happened to be nearby the location of a terror incident, Kahane responded bluntly by saying, 'No, I would not. As long as they are here we are lost. I have no way of knowing if this Arab or another is innocent. The real danger is the demographics [the danger that the Arabs will outnumber the Jews in Israel]'.[28]

Kach was intensely violent long before the recent Palestinian uprising. Its entire posture, the yellow shirts with the black clenched fists, the attacks on Arab families from within the green line (the pre-1967 Israeli border) that move into Jewish neighborhoods, the chasing of innocent Arab workers for the fun of it, the anti-Arab 'victory parades', the attempts to break leftist meetings in a style reminiscent of the 1920s Italian and German Fascists, have all spelled out hooliganism and violence. Especially violent has been Kach's most aggressive local stronghold, the Kiriyat Arba branch in the West Bank. Kahane's devoted followers there have initiated since the mid-1970s countless violent operations against the local Arabs. Unlike several Gush Emunim activists who usually resorted to anti-Arab violence in response to previous Arab attacks, and who said all along that they were ready to tolerate peaceful Arab presence in the area, Kach people have never concealed their hope for a massive emigration. The only reason for their relative restraint has been their fear of the security forces. In 1986, and following the intensification of Arab-Jewish violence, they established the 'Committee for the Preservation of Security' which was to patrol the roads in the area. But the committee that was established as a defensive instrument against Arab rock-throwing became during the *Intifada* (the Palestinian uprising in the West Bank and Gaza) a most aggressive vigilante group. Its notorious commander, Shmuel Ben-Yishai, publicly declared that any incident involving a harassment of Jewish traffic would make him shoot to kill without warning.

> I do not shoot in the air, I shoot to kill. It is stupid to fire the entire magazine in the air! Only the Jews speak about the 'purity of the arms'. Just a minute! Listen who is talking about morality: Shamir, the biggest terrorist [Itzhak Shamir, Israel's prime minister, was the commander of the Lehi terrorist underground during the 1940s]? Rabin who killed Jews on *Altalena* [a 1948 arms ship brought to Israel without official permission by the Irgun underground and destroyed by an army unit under the command of young Itzhak Rabin, Israel's 1980s minister of defence]? The Americans who murdered the Indians?[29]

In 1988 Ben-Yishai's statement was no longer an exception among the settlers of Judea and Samaria and the larger non-Kach radical right. Palestinian violence in the occupied territories has 'confirmed' what Kahane had been saying about the Arabs (and the Gentiles in general) all along. It was another attempt to 'humiliate' the Jews and to 'kill' them if possible. For most of these people it has been an indication that the decisive battle for Eretz Yisrael has already started. For a few devoted Kahane supporters it was a sign for a huge gathering storm and a possible beginning of the 'pre-redemption' catastrophe that in 1980 was predicted by Kahane to take place within about eight years.

Kahane's Sacred Violence in an Historical and Comparative Perspective

It is important to stress that Rabbi Kahane did not claim to be either a Jewish revolutionary or a religious innovator. Kahane maintained he was 'totally bound by the Halakha' and believed that in every respect, he was a genuine representative of legitimate Judaism which started with Abraham, the first Jew.[30] Whenever confronted with orthodox critics or opponents he argued that they misinterpret the authoritative texts and that he was fully ready to debate them on Halakhic grounds. But was he right? Is Kahane's revenge theology simply a reformulation of earlier Jewish theories of violence? Is it possible to explain the Kahane phenomenon by ancient or modern Jewish traditions? A careful examination of the case shows that though the leader of Kach drew upon a long line of Jewish activists, his theory of revenge is unprecedented and new. This inquiry shows further that a much stronger clue to the Kahane enigma is provided by non-Jewish expressions of his time but that even these sources do not fully explain the entire phenomenon.

The question of what should the powerless Jews do about the exile and the persecutions of the Gentiles has occasionally emerged in rabbinical deliberations since the destruction of the Second Temple (AD 70) and the Bar Kochba revolt (AD 132–135), which ended all Jewish independence in Eretz Yisrael. It was especially pressing in times of great misery when the anti-Semitic operations involved the massacre of many thousands of Jews. The major rabbinical position, which had many variations, viewed the exile as a punishment for sins committed by the nation. The creation of the Diaspora, according to these interpretations, was no chance turn of events. God's hand was directly involved in Jewish catastrophe and the Jews were expected to pay in full for their sins. The Jews were, furthermore, sworn not 'to rebel' against the Gentile nations and to wait patiently for their heavenly redemption. A prominent variation of this interpretation saw the exile as an 'ennobling punishment' and 'as proof of God's continued election of the Jews'.[31] However, there always existed a minority position which saw no holiness in passivity. While not denying God's overall responsibility for the humiliating reality of Diaspora, some medieval scholars, for example, called upon Jews to cherish historical acts of revolt and resistance such the Hasmonean rebellion, and recommended that 'When it is within our grasp, kill them'.[32]

The rise of modern Zionism involved a very dramatic challenge to the tradition of Jewish inaction, for it called upon the Jews to liberate their nation from the curse of Diaspora passivity and reassert themselves as a free people. The most radical proponent of this approach was the writer and essayist Micha Yosef Berdichevsky (1865–1921). Extremely critical of the rabbinical tradition which identified virtuous Judaism with scholarly study of the Torah and Talmudic hair splitting, Berdichevsky called for the revival of the 'Judaism of the sword'. Generations of young Zionists who were first faced with the massive anti-Jewish pogroms in eastern Europe and later with the growing violence of the Arabs in Palestine, were deeply moved by his earthly message.

> Excessive thinking drained most of our vitality, the very substance of our life. It made us too much the people of the book, too knowledgeable a nation . . . We have too much thinking, give us feeling and life, life as it really is . . .
>
> The best sons of the nation recognized the importance of the land for the people and fought for it gallantly. They had a living and feeling spirit . . .
>
> Samson who said 'let me die with the Philistines' is greater than Samson the blind, who had to escape.[33]

As early as 1907, a small Jewish organization which named itself

'Bar Giora' organized in Palestine for self defense. Originating in earlier Jewish self-defense groups which operated in Russia against the pogroms, its founders swore never to bow to Gentile aggression. In 1909 Bar Giora expanded itself into 'Hashomer' (the Watchman) which assumed the task of countering Arab violence in Palestine and securing Jewish farms and communes. This legendary organization, which remained a source of inspiration for thousands of young Zionists a long time after it was gone, adopted the motto 'Judea fell in blood and fire; in blood and fire shall Judea rise'.[34] In 1920 Hashomer transformed itself into the 'Hagana' (Defense), and became the foundation for the future Israeli Army.

While the founders of the Hagana saw their organization as the opposite quintessence of the powerless and passive ghetto Jew, their military thinking never went beyond the concept of self-defense. This was even true of Vladimir Jabotinsky, the most radical critic of the organization, who was later to become the political head of the more extreme semi-military 'Etzel' (National Military Organization in Israel). Jabotinsky, to be precise, did not like the idea of self-defense, but the reason for that had nothing to do with a theory of holy revenge. Jabotinsky was a great advocate of the legal creation of a Jewish army as a political step towards the establishment of a Jewish State in Palestine. His entire thinking about the military was legal and political.[35] Etzel's commanders in Palestine, who were not as legal and formal as their political head, were very unhappy with the concept of restrained self-defense of the Hagana, which in the second half of the 1930s provided – so they thought – an inadequate response to the growing Arab terrorism. Consequently during 1937–39 they engaged in a massive counter-terrorist campaign against the rebellious Arabs in Palestine. But in their eyes there was nothing ideological or holy about this struggle. It was a temporary, bloody, and ugly fight, the sole purpose of which was to prove that terrorism does not pay and that the Arabs were more vulnerable than the Jews.[36]

The termination of Arab terrorism in 1939 (and the beginning of the Second World War) brought an end to Etzel's terror campaign, and when the organization resumed its violent operations against the British in 1944, the logic of the fight and its practise had nothing to do with revenge or holy violence. It was perceived as a struggle for national liberation, a fight against oppression and foreign rule. Menachem Begin, the commander of Etzel and a future prime minister of Israel, explained that his decision to take up arms was not taken before all other efforts to convince the British to grant independence to the Jews failed miserably:

What use is there in writing memoranda? What value in speeches? If you are attacked by a wolf in the forest do you try to persuade him that it is not fair to tear you to pieces, or that he is not a wolf at all but an innocent lamb? Do you send him a 'memorandum'? No, there was no other way. If we did not fight we should be destroyed. To fight was the only way to salvation.

When Descartes said: 'I think, therefore I am,' he uttered a very profound thought. But there are times in the history of peoples when thought alone does not prove existence. A people may 'think' and yet its sons, with their thoughts and in spite of them, may be turned into a herd of slaves – or into soap. There are times when everything in you cries out: your very self-respect as a human being lies in your resistance to evil.

We fight, therefore we are![37]

The small 'Lehi' (Israel's Freedom Fighters), an extremist underground which in 1940 split from Etzel and immediately started to fight the British, was more radical than its parent organization. Unlike Etzel, it practised individual terrorism against the British and was determined and ruthless. It was also more traditional in its approach and on occasions referred to the Torah as its source of inspiration. But none of Lehi's ideologues had glorified revenge for the sake of revenge or saw himself as the holy avenger of Jewish blood spilled by the Gentiles for over two millenniums. Lehi's people tried, on the contrary, to ignore the existence of the Diaspora. They projected themselves as Jewish revolutionaries fighting a colonial regime in order to revive their pre-occupation commonwealth. Their concept of violence was political and was profoundly influenced by the revolutionary traditions of the Russian Narodnaya Yolia, the Italian Risorgimento, the Irish Sinn Fein, and Polish revolutionary nationalism.[38] There was certainly a revolutionary splendor in the struggle but in no way did it project a heavenly sanctified revenge. In 1943, at the height of the anti-British struggle, Itzhak Shamir, one of Lehi's head commanders and the present Israeli prime minister, explained and justified Lehi's anti-British struggle in these words:

Neither Jewish ethics nor Jewish tradition can disqualify terrorism as a means of combat. We are very far from having any moral qualms as far as our national war goes. We have before us the command of the Torah, whose morality surpasses that of any other laws in the world: Ye shall blot them out to the last man. We are particularly far from having any qualms with regard to the enemy, whose moral degradation is universally admitted here.

> *But first and foremost, terrorism is for us a part of the political battle* being conducted under the present circumstances, and *it has a great part to play: speaking in a clear voice to the whole world, as well as to our wretched brethren outside this land, it proclaims our war against the occupier*.[39]

There is, thus, no question that Rabbi Kahane's expressions of violence were not isolated and that in Jewish history, especially modern, an activist strand emerged which advocated Jewish aggression and violence as part of the reassertion of the nation and its struggle for independence. But the similarity between the ideas of the major spokespersons of this school and the idiosyncratic theology of violence of the leader of Kach ends very early. While Kahane glorified in his writings the thought of Vladimir Jabotinsky, and spoke very highly of the Etzel and Lehi commanders Raziel, Stern and Begin,[40] he went far beyond their conception of legitimate violence. Not only did Kahane sanctify any anti-Gentile violence by calling it kiddush hashem, a term reserved in traditional Judaism to martyrdom, but he also made no distinction between the desired pre- and post-independence Jewish violence. Kahane intentionally ignored the fact that all his militant heroes who lived to see the establishment of the State of Israel, looked at Jewish violence as an instrument to win independence and became after 1948 non-violent Israeli citizens. And he played down the point that none of them was ever ready to disregard completely local or international law in the name of 'Jewish love'. There is clearly a cosmic element in Kahane's theology of violence, an insatiable drive for revenge which goes beyond time and space and becomes metahistorical.[41] Not a single Jew before Rabbi Meir Kahane had systematically resorted to this language and imagery.

While the review of modern Jewish activism is helpful in portraying the historical Jewish context within which the Kahane militant imagination had developed, an inquiry of the formative years of Meir Kahane in Christian America provides an additional clue to its concrete evolution. This examination shows that much of Kahane's provocative style was developed during the 1960s and was the rabbi's personal response to violent black organizations such as the SNCC (Student National Coordination Committee) and the Black Panthers. There are, in fact, many indications that as much as Kahane was outraged by the anti-Jewish and pro-Arab sentiment of the ideologues of these organizations, he was impressed by their aggressive posture and offensive language.[42] If blacks in America could challenge the white majority in the way they did, why shouldn't Jews adopt the same style towards these blacks and the 'anti-Semitic Gentiles' in general? There was a lesson to be learned from the aggressive speeches of Stokely Carmichael and Eldridge Cleaver:

> We are talking about survival. We are talking about a people whose entire culture, whose entire history, whose entire way of life have been destroyed. We are talking about a people who have produced in *this* year a generation of warriors who are going to restore to our people the humanity and the love that we have for each other. That's what we are talking about *today* . . . We are talking about becoming the executioners of our executioners.[43]

The turbulent reality of the 1960s, in which radical students and minority groups in America took to the streets and spoke freely about 'offing the pigs', or 'bringing down white *Amerika*', had attracted the young rabbi and sensitized all his memories of Jewish heroism in ancient and modern times. The ambitious young man, who had apparently been dreaming about a great historical role in the life of his people, and was always enchanted by aggressive behavior, had identified a golden opportunity to make a difference.[44] Not only could he take upon the new enemies of the Jews in a highly visible way but he could do it, just as they did, with a large dose of aggression and violence. The application of media-attracting violence as well as symbols like 'Jewish Power' (vs. Black Power) which worked for the black revolutionaries was so skillfully imitated by Kahane that he outdid in fact, all his rivals. Between 1969 and 1971 Kahane's small JDL became one of America's most recognized minority action groups. It was just a question of time before its jubilant leader transformed his brand of Jewish vigilantism into a comprehensive anti-Gentile violence and was ready to apply it against the Russians, the Libyans, the Syrians, and potentially against the rest of mankind.

While there is no indication that Rabbi Meir Kahane actually read the most influential 1960s theory of violence, Franz Fanon's *The Wretched of the Earth*, the similarity between the two ideologies is striking. The idea that the brutal violence of the oppressed may heal their psychological wounds, caused by years of humiliation and persecutions, was not Kahane's. It was developed by Franz Fanon in a very elaborate way. Although Fanon has never pronounced this violence holy, he came very close to its glorification.

> Colonialism and imperialism have not paid their score when they withdraw their flags and their police forces from our territories. For centuries the capitalists have behaved in the underdeveloped world like nothing more than war criminals. Deportations, massacres,

> forced labor, and slavery have been the main methods used by capitalism to increase its wealth, its gold or diamond reserves, and to establish its power.[45]
>
> But it so happens that for the colonized people this violence, because it constitutes their only work, invests their characters with positive and creative qualities. The practice of violence binds them together as a whole, since each individual forms a violent link in the great chain, a part of the great organism of violence which has surged upward in reaction to the settler's violence in the beginning. The groups recognize each other and the future nation is already indivisible . . .
>
> At the level of the individual violence is a cleansing force. It frees the native from his inferiority complex and from his despair and inaction; it makes him fearless and restores his self respect . . . Illuminated by violence, the consciousness of the people rebels against any pacification. From now on the demagogues, the opportunists and the magicians have a difficult task.[46]

But as appealing as a 'Fanonian' interpretation of Kahane may be, there is nevertheless a huge difference between the two, an ontological dissimilarity which far exceeds the obvious theoretical gap between the orthodox Jewish rabbi and the devoted black Marxist. Unlike Kahane's, Fanon's theory of violence is not implying cosmic struggle and does not stretch beyond time and space. It is limited to the struggle against colonialism which is expected to be over by the time all Third World nations reach independence. While Fanon's revenge sentiment is very strong, it is nevertheless political and therefore controlled. This is not the case with Rabbi Kahane. As was shown above, Kahane may have used political arguments to communicate his message, but his theology of violence was not political. Those Jews who think that the establishment of the State of Israel marks the end of holy Jewish violence, for the Israeli Army can defend the interest of the Jews routinely and legally, are wrong. It is an illusion to believe that anti-Semitism will come to an end just because the State of Israel exists. The perennial state of affairs in which the Gentiles wish to desecrate the Name of God through the humiliation and persecution of His people, is not about to change until the arrival of the Messiah and the complete redemption of the world. Consequently, Jews should constantly fight the Gentiles wherever they are. And since no Jewish violence can be wrong there is no reason to worry about legality or restraints. A Kahane-like kiddush hashem is needed now as it ever was. It is, thus, possible to conclude that neither Kahane's violent Jewish predecessors nor Franz Fanon and his followers can fully account for the Kahane phenomenon.

In Search of Meaning: The Kahane Phenomenon as the Ideologization of the Mimetic Desire

Because no Jewish or non-Jewish precedent of the past or the present seem to account for the Kahane phenomenon and since Kahane has never let anyone study his psychology or motivation from a close range, it appears that a useful way of making a general sense of the case is by applying to it some relevant psycho-literary and psycho-historical studies. René Girard's *Violence and the Sacred* provides in this respect perhaps the best intellectual tool to deal with Kahane.[47] What is useful about the Girardian methodology is not its empirical basis or wide social applicability. Girard's way of illuminating the essence of human violence does not deal with the average man or the crowd in the street. It studies instead the great mythological individuals who set in ancient times the lower and higher parameters of the human experience. The lack of direct sources drives Girard to look for them in areas social scientists rarely scan, Greek mythology and classical tragedy. Girard deals with what Max Weber would have called ideal types, pure cases and people who do not usually exist in real life but who define through their personal traits and behavior the very essence of the human condition. Many observers of Meir Kahane may not like to think of him as an historic hero and an exceptional cultural phenomenon but his personality, ideas and behavior seemed to contain the stuff of a mythological and demonic figure. His hatred of the Gentiles is greater than life and so was the intensity of his revenge theory and the extremity of his political solutions. Kahane's complete dedication to his destructive cause, despite his repeated failures and ordeals could have easily made him a literary hero of a classic Jewish tragedy were one ever written for Girard to analyze. While he would probably never had admitted that, there are many indications that the leader of Kach saw himself on occasions as the *avenging angel* of the Jewish people.

Girard's analysis of human violence, which seems particularly applicable to the Kahane case, is the theory of the mimetic desire. Violence according to Girard is a most fundamental feature of the human nature which is created and perpetuated by two basic mechanisms: *desire* and *mimesis*. Man is born with a bundle of desires, a very basic one of which is the drive to imitate the other and to obtain the same objects the other wants. Consequently, a very rudimentary conflict is created which is the root cause of all violence. The colliding desires for the same objects are bound to produce physical conflict and that violence is likely to be reproduced by the mimetic desire, the human wish to imitate the violence of the other and to destroy him by a greater dose of the same thing.

> Violent opposition, then, is the signifier of the ultimate desire, or divine self sufficiency, of that beautiful totality whose beauty depends on its being inaccessible and impenetrable. The victim of this violence both adores and detests it. He strives to master it by means of a mimetic counterviolence and measures his own stature in proportion to his failure. If by chance, however, he actually succeeds in asserting his mastery over the model, the later's prestige vanishes. He must, then, turn to an ever greater violence and seeks out an obstacle that promises to be truly insurmountable.[48]

The very origins of primitive religion are, according to Girard, the social need to reduce violence between members of the same community, who are driven by the mimetic desire to destroy each other, by providing them with surrogate victims: either sacrificial animals or humans of external societies against which their natural and reproductive violence can be directed. Only religion can control the potency of the mimetic desire, and prevent the self-destruction of the community. Religion produces myths, rituals, and taboos around the 'sacrificial crisis' that people respect and obey.

> Mimetic desire is simply a term more comprehensive than violence for religious pollution. As the catalyst for the sacrificial crisis it would eventually destroy the entire community if the surrogate victims were not at hand to halt the process and the ritualistic mimesis were not at hand to keep the conflictual mimesis from beginning afresh.[49]

An examination of Rabbi Meir Kahane in view of Girard's theory is very illuminating for it provides a conceptual context which fits both the person and the phenomenon. Kahane, the person, is the epitome of the mimetic desire. His greatest wish was to out-violate the violators of the Jews. Despite the political context of the argument there is no political thinking about this vengeance, for such thinking always implies some restraining considerations as well as some distinction between strategy and tactics. But in Kahane there is only one passion, an insatiable desire to avenge the perennial vilification of the Jews, to humiliate the Gentile, to be stronger than the other, and to demonstrate the strength by physical force. Kahane may have spoken in the name of religion but he was definitely out of its Girardian boundaries. Instead of imposing checks and controls on the violence of the community, as does Girard's primitive religion, Kahane's religion releases all safety valves. It strives to liberate the mimetic desire of the Jew, long held in judicious check by generations of Halakhic sages, and set it free. Portraying the Gentile as the epitome of anti-Jewish violence, it propagates the 'Gentilization' of the Jew so that a real revenge can take place. It calls for an eye for eye policy and preaches response in kind for thousands of years of Gentile brutality and violence.

But if Meir Kahane, the individual Jew who is determined to take revenge, fits the Girardian prototype of the mimetic desire by practising it, Rabbi Kahane, the political leader, goes beyond Girard and ideologizes the mimetic desire. Thus, what was unique about Kahane, which sets him apart from all Jewish avengers, is the elevation of the mimetic desire into a politico-religious norm. To the 'political Kahane' the 'fist in the face of the Gentile' was not simply an act of revenge, an eye for eye. It is also not a suggestion for the application of massive retaliation in kind. It is kiddush hashem, a sacred obligation all the believers, and Jews in general, are told to respect and follow. Kiddush hashem, it is important to remember, has been traditionally associated in Judaism with martyrdom, the greatest sacrifice a believer can commit, bringing about his own death in the Name of God. By ideologizing and sanctifying anti-Gentile violence, Kahane reversed Girard's primitive religion and in fact, all religion. While the function of primitive religion is to reduce tensions and to control violence, the function of Kahane's operational Judaism creates tensions and produces violence on a massive scale. The problem with this approach is that unlike all Girard's examples which are either taken from Greek tragedy or tribal anthropology, Kahane's theology is real and is practised in Israel in the last years of the twentieth century.

NOTES

1. Rabbi Meir Kahane, 'hillul hashem', (A Kach mimeographed article, n.d.-Hebrew). Kahane was assassinated in New York City on 5 Nov. 1990.
2. On Gush Emunim, see Gideon Aran, 'From Religious Zionism to Zionist Religion: The Roots of Gush Emunim and Its Culture' (Unpublished Doctoral Dissertation, Hebrew University of Jerusalem, 1987-Hebrew); David Newman, ed., *The Impact of Gush Emunim* (London: Croom Helm, 1985); Zvi Raanan, *Gush Emunim* (Tel Aviv: Sifriyat Poalim, 1980-Hebrew); Danny Rubinstein, *On the Lord's Side: Gush Emunim* (Tel Aviv: Hakibbutz Hameuchad, 1982-Hebrew); Ehud Sprinzak, 'Gush Emunim: The Iceberg Model of Political Extremism', *Medina Mimshal Yeyehasim Beinleumiim*, No. 17, (Fall 1981-Hebrew); 'Gush Emunim: The Politics of Zionist fundamentalism in Israel', (New York, NY: The American Jewish Committee, 1986); for a recent review of the Gush Emunim literature, see Eliezer Don-Yehiya, 'Jewish

Messianism, Religious Zionism and Israeli Politics: The Impact and Origins of Gush Emunim', *Middle Eastern Studies*, Vol. 23, No. 2, (April 1987), pp.215–34.

3. On the strong anti-Gentile motive in Kahane's thinking, see Aviezer Ravitzky, 'The Roots of Kahanism: Consciousness and Political Reality', *The Jerusalem Quarterly* No. 39, 1986.
4. Kahane, *Listen World, Listen Jew* (Tucson, AZ: The Institute of Jewish Idea, 1975), pp.121–22.
5. Cf. George Sorel, *Reflections on Violence* (New York, NY: Collier, 1961); Franz Fanon, *The Wretched of the Earth* (New York, NY: Grove Press, 1968).
6. Cf. Gerald Cromer, 'The Debate About Kahanism In Israeli Society 1984–1988', *Occasional Papers* (New York, NY: The Harry Frank Guggenheim Foundation, 1988), p.35.
7. In his *The Story of the Jewish Defense League* (Radnor, PA: Chilton Book Company, 1975), Kahane has a special chapter titled: 'Violence: Is This Any Way For a Nice Jewish Boy To Behave?', in which he provides the rationale for the violence of the American Jewish Defense League. The reader is told that among its other purposes, 'Jewish violence is meant to . . . Destroy the Jewish neuroses and fears that contribute so much encouragement to the anti-Semite as well as Jewish belief in his own worthlessness. We want to instill self-respect and self-pride in a Jew who is ashamed of himself for running away', p.142.
8. Cf. Howard M. Sachar, *A History of Israel* (Jerusalem: Steimatzky, 1976), pp.14–15, 38–41.
9. Kahane, *Never Again: A Program for Jewish Survival* (New York, NY: Pyramid Books, 1972), pp.74–101.
10. Ibid., 'The Anti-Semites', pp.72–104.
11. Ibid., 'Zionism', pp.151–74.
12. Cf. Kahane, *Israel's Eternity and Victory* (Jerusalem: The Institute of Jewish Idea, 1973-Hebrew); *Numbers 23:9* (Jerusalem: The Institute of Jewish Idea, 1984-Hebrew).
13. Kahane, *Forty Years* (Miami, FL: Institute of the Jewish Idea, 1983), pp.6–7.
14. According to Kahane's deterministic logic, the only condition for complete salvation is a full repentance of the entire nation. His expected takeover of political power may have been a big step in the right direction, but since he did not plan to impose a forced repentance on the entire people, it would 'probably not satisfy God'. He would have tried to tell the people about the disaster that awaited them but if they chose not to listen then even he would be unable to save them. Author's interview with Kahane, 12 June 1988.
15. Kahane, *The Story of the Jewish Defense League*, pp.278–79. Janet L. Dolgin, *Jewish Identity and the JDL*, (Princeton, NJ: Princeton University Press, 1977), Ch.3.
16. Kahane, *The Story of the Jewish Defense League*, pp.99–100.
17. For Kahane's own account of this strange association see, Rabbi Meir Kahane, ibid. pp.185–91.
18. Cf. Yair Kotler, *Heil Kahane* (Tel Aviv: Modan, 1985-Hebrew), pp.103–8. Kahane never bothered to apologize for the killing of the innocent secretary. Instead he complains in his book on the JDL about the refusal of the Jewish establishment to bail out the three JDL youngsters accused of 'Jewish political crime'. Kahane, *The Story of the Jewish Defense League*, p.191.
19. Ibid., pp.141–42.
20. Ibid., pp.75–80.
21. Cf. Kahane, 'hillul hashem', p.3; *Listen World, Listen Jew*, pp.88–89; *From the Knesset Stand: The Speeches of Rabbi Kahane in the Knesset* (Jerusalem: Kach Movement, n.d.-Hebrew), p.11.
22. Kahane, *The Jewish Idea*, p.14.
23. Kahane, '*hillul hashem*', p.3.
24. Cf. Kahane, *Uncomfortable Questions For Comfortable Jews*, (Secaucus, NJ: Lyle Stuart, 1987), p.269.

25. Since May 1975 the initials TNT have occasionally surfaced following mysterious attacks on Arab institutions in Jerusalem. A small group that called itself TNT was arrested in 1975 after setting two Arab buses on fire. Cf. *Yediot Achronot* 18 June 1975. Threat letters sent to Arab leaders were also signed by TNT. In Dec. 1983 there was another series of sabotage acts in Jerusalem associated with TNT. Cf. Yakir Tzur, 'Military Background, Expertise in Sabotage and Extremist Ideology', *Kol Hair*, 16 Dec. 1983.
26. Quoted in Kotler, *Heil Kahane*, p.257.
27. Quoted in Nadav Shragai, 'Going for the Action', *Ha'aretz*, 27 Nov. 1984.
28. Quoted in Haim Shibi, 'Wherever There is Blood Spilled You Find Kahane', *Yediot Achronot*, 2 Aug. 1985.
29. Yair Avituv, 'All is Well in the Kasba', *Kol Hair*, 12 Aug. 1988.
30. This is based on numerous talks and interviews I have personally conducted with Kahane.
31. David Biale, *Power and Powerlessness in Jewish History* (New York, NY: Schocken Books, 1987), pp.37–38.
32. Quoted by Biale, ibid, p.38.
33. Cf. Micha Yosef Ben-Gurion (Berdichevsky), *Collected Essays* (Tel Aviv: Dvir, 1951), p.47.
34. Quoted in Ian Lustick, 'Solipsistic Terrorism in the Arab-Israeli Conflict' (Draft paper presented at the Ford Foundation Conference on Terrorism, Wesleyan University, May 1989), p.5.
35. On Jabotinsky's ideas about the need for a Jewish army as well as about revolt and violence, see Yaacov Shavit, *The Mythologies of the Right* (Beit Berl: the Sharett Institute, 1985-Hebrew), Ch.3.
36. Cf. David Niv, *The Battle for Freedom; The Etzel* (Tel Aviv: The Klausner Institute, 1975-Hebrew), Part II, pp.40–42.
37. Menachem Begin, *The Revolt* (Tel Aviv: Steimatzky, 1951), p.46.
38. Cf. Joseph Heller, *Lehi: Ideology and Politics, 1940–1949* (Jerusalem: Keter, 1989-Hebrew), pp.151–57.
39. Itzhak Shamir quoted in Ian Lustick, 'Solipsistic Terrorism in the Arab-Israeli Conflict', pp.10–11.
40. Kahane's admiration for the commanders of Etzel and Lehi has been expressed in many books of his, see, for example, Kahane, *Never Again*, pp. 163–74.
41. On the element of cosmic struggle in religious violence, see Mark Juergensmeyer, 'The Logic of Religious Violence' in David Rapoport (ed.), *Inside Terrorist Organizations* (London: Frank Cass, 1988), pp.185–90, and his essay in this volume.
42. Cf. Kahane's obsession with the Black extremists of the 1960s has been expressed in many of his articles and books. See, for example, references to Stokely Carmichael and Eldridge Clever in Kahane, *The Story of the Jewish Defense League*, pp.64–69; 199–203; and also Ch.6 (Jewish Power).
43. Stokely Carmichael, 'A Declaration of War', in Massimo Teodori (ed.), *The New Left: A Documentary History*, (Indianapolis, Bobbs Merill, 1969), pp. 281–82.
44. Cf. Michael T. Kaufman, 'The Complex Past of Meir Kahane', *The New York Times*, 24 Jan. 1971, pp.1, 51.
45. Franz Fanon, *The Wretched of the Earth*, p.101.
46. Ibid, pp.93–95.
47. René Girard, *Violence and the Sacred*, (Baltimore, MD: The Johns Hopkins University Press, 1977).
48. Ibid, p.148.
49. Ibid.

[14]

Absolute Rescue: Absolutism, Defensive Action and the Resort to Force

JEFFREY KAPLAN

The murder of Dr David Gunn in 1993 by Michael Griffin made a decisive break with the pro-life rescue movement's 20-year history of non-violent protest against abortion in America. That act opened the floodgates to other violent attacks on doctors, and brought to public notice a violent splinter sect of the larger millenarian subculture dedicated to the 'rescue' of the unborn. This essay seeks to detail the stages through which the radical fringe of the rescue movement passed before they came to embrace the necessity of 'Defensive Action'. By allowing the rescuers to speak in their own voices, it is hoped that the study will contribute to a greater understanding of the process by which a millenarian movement turns from non-violent witness to violent activism.

Rescue those being led away to death;
hold back those staggering toward slaughter. Proverbs 24:11

> *Imagine 50 Christians, totally committed to God, who lose everything because of their obedience to Him, and no longer have any ties or obligations in the world, who can easily risk all...They [the abortion industry] are just hanging themselves by making us stronger.* Shelley Shannon, June 1993[1]

The rescue movement is dead. Such was the view of rescuers interviewed for this research. The select few willing to pay the increasingly draconian price of true rescue – in rescue terminology the interposition of the body of the rescuer between the killer and his intended victim – have dwindled to a paltry few. And many of these are paying the price of that faithful witness in the jails and prisons of America. Of the groups profiled in these pages in my Autumn 1993 review article, 'America's Last Prophetic Witness: The Literature of the Rescue Movement',[2] Operation Rescue National is a shadow of its former self, functioning more as a traveling tent revival than a rescue organization, the Missionaries to the Preborn have suffered a leadership schism and the missionaries themselves are enmeshed in the court system, while for reasons that may not at this time be made public, the Lambs of Christ have ceased their rescue activities.[3]

What is more, the rescue community, already estranged from its mainstream pro-life parent, has been torn asunder by an increasingly divisive debate over the utility of the resort to violence in defense of the unborn. This debate, conducted as are all internal debates within the rescue movement in the pages of key rescue journals and among adherents themselves, has served both to polarize the once cohesive world of rescue and to create an increasingly bitter chasm between rescuers and the larger pro-life constituency.[4]

This study seeks to illustrate the complex of factors which have led to this state of affairs. More, this work will attempt to present these events as they are seen through the eyes of the adherents of the faction of the rescue community which has accepted the necessity of the use of force. In so doing, it is hoped that it will be possible to translate for a secular, scholarly audience an apocalyptic millenarian *Zeitgeist* which is at this writing still very much in the process of formation. Much of what follows thus relies heavily on the assistance and the writings of the rescuers themselves. A great deal of internal material, letters, prison diaries and extensive correspondence has been made available to this research. Interviews and personal letters too have played a considerable role in what follows. Yet of equal import are the rescue journals, magazines and newsletters in which the theology of rescue is even now evolving.

In the attempt to introduce the scholarly community to the *Zeitgeist* of the rescue world, this article allows the rescuers to speak in their own voices. For this reason, the terminology employed throughout the article reflects the accepted pattern of discourse within rescue's most determinedly millenarian adherents, those who have accepted at least the theoretical possibility of the efficacy of the resort to deadly force. Thus, the terms 'baby' rather than fetus, 'deathscorts' rather than clinic escorts, 'death culture' or 'abortion culture' for American culture, 'murder' or 'child killing' for abortion, 'abortuary', 'killing center' or 'child killing industry' for for-profit abortion clinics, 'Prisoner of Christ' for jail or prison inmate, and, on occasion, 'killer' or 'mass murderer' for abortionist, are not only intrinsic to the discourse of the movement, but are necessary if the movement's worldview and its recent actions are to be made comprehensible to a scholarly audience. In this context, the term 'abortionist' is itself controversial. Yet the term remains in the text as it is not only the most accurate description of the profession, but because the various readers of earlier drafts of this work could suggest no alternative which was not either linguistically clumsy or utterly artificial. In the final analysis, this contribution seeks to present the rescue movement on its own terms and in its own words without the distraction of an intrusive scholarly voice. The rescue movement today is a little studied, poorly understood oppositional millennial movement which, in taking its challenge to the prevailing attitudes of the America of the 1990s, has struck a raw nerve in the dominant culture. The social critique which rescue offers centers on the most delicate and deeply personal issues of our time: the relative values placed on individual freedom and reproductive rights versus our society's traditional reverence for babies and children, for families, and, at the deepest level, for life itself.

Thus the powerful emotions unleashed on both sides of the 'abortion wars', and thus the decision to allow the scholarly community to see and hear for themselves the rescue movement's powerful indictment of the contemporary world. It is hoped that through this work, it will be possible not only to better understand rescue as a social movement, but of equal import to the task of this volume, to follow the evolution of an oppositional millenarian appeal from its optimistic beginnings through an increasingly apocalyptic and despairing phase and, ultimately, to the adoption of a seemingly hopeless course of revolutionary violence.

The study will be divided into two sections: worldview and the resort to force. The voices in which it is written are those of such imprisoned rescuers as Shelley Shannon (convicted of shooting Wichita abortionist George Tiller), convicted clinic bomber John Brockhoeft and Paul Hill, sentenced to death for killing the abortionist John Britton. Other voices will be heard as well – those counseling an adherence to rescue's twenty year old ethos of pacifism and non-violence. It is hoped that together, this chorus of 'prophetic witnesses' will serve to illuminate this American pariah movement.[5]

I. Worldview

The Conversion Experience

You know, every pro-lifer has a story... Joe Scheidler[6]

Virtually every rescuer can point to a moment in which a general feeling of uneasiness with abortion was catalyzed into a sudden, intense realization that abortion was indeed murder and that some concrete action had to be taken to save the babies from imminent death. For some, this moment was the culmination of feelings of remorse over some personal involvement with the abortion culture. Perhaps a woman had an abortion, or a man urged or financed such a procedure. More often, however, that moment of enlightenment came as a result of having seen the graphic evidence of the reality of abortion.

For John Brockhoeft, that moment came on Saturday, 28 December

1985. On that bitterly cold day, while taking part in a peaceful pro-life demonstration outside a Planned Parenthood clinic in Cincinnati, activist Melody Green displayed the bodies of seven aborted babies respectfully laid out in seven tiny caskets. The effect on Brockhoeft was immediate, but what to him was immeasurably more shocking was the indifference of the public and of the ever-present pro-choice demonstrators to this indisputable evidence of the evils of abortion. Brockhoeft's life had changed forever, for suddenly:

> ...My heart was overwhelmed with grief and love for the babies, fury and rage toward the criminals...and...deep shame and embarrassment before God. I was ashamed of being an American and, *especially*, an American *man*; ashamed of being part of a lukewarm church...I was ashamed of myself for having done nothing during the first years, and so little thereafter, and for having put off the doing of what I felt was my duty to my God and my country, namely, the exertion of actual force to preempt the slaughter of my people, to protect the lives of American babies.[7]

'The Silent Scream', a graphic film of an abortion narrated by former abortionist Bernard Nathanson, was Shelley Shannon's introduction to the movement:

> I've always known abortion was wrong. In 1987 or thereabouts, I read a short article by Melody Green describing Dr. Nathanson's film, 'The Silent Scream'. She described the baby trying to get away from the abortionist, but it couldn't. And when he killed it, its mouth went open like it was screaming. Until then, I never thought about the babies being killed. It was like suddenly waking up, and finding that there were other people who were also awake, but most weren't.[8]

This film too is alleged by Michael Griffin to have triggered his resolve to kill abortionist David Gunn: an act which opened the floodgates to the resort to the 'justifiable homicide' of abortionists to save the lives of their victims.[9]

So intense was the impact of the visual image of an aborted baby on individual rescuers that it was little wonder that signs depicting horrific images of the results of burned bodies resulting from saline abortions or the dismembered corpses left by suction abortions became ubiquitous at non-violent rescues throughout the nation. As John Brockhoeft's narrative illustrates, it was felt that if the American public could but see the awesome truth of abortion, they would rise as one to put a stop to the practice. More, this realization of the slaughter of the innocent would be the catalyst for the awakening of the Church whose silence is perceived by rescuers as the greatest crime of the abortion culture. That both the church and the populace would remain unmoved may be safely posited to be the genesis of the apocalyptic view of American culture which characterizes the millenarian ethos of the rescue movement.[10]

The Awakening

> *The wrath of God burns furiously against the USA, and we are poised for destruction. Why? It is not only for the rare satanic zeal which kills babies. It is because of the pervasive lukewarmness which kills babies.* John Brockhoeft[11]

By their own testimony, rescuers before their conversion to the truth of the abortion culture were an unremarkable group. Primarily white, largely middle and working class, deeply religious members of independent fundamentalist or evangelical Protestant churches or devout Catholics, rescuers are products of an idealized America in which truth, justice and basic goodness are sure to triumph in the end.[12] Theirs was, in John Brockhoeft's words, an America whose colonial Golden Age myth is one of a Christian nation in which 'Everybody was a Christian, unashamed of the gospel.'

> That's how it was in the beginning, and that's the way it was all along in America for hundreds of years – even until within a relatively few years ago – even within my short lifetime.[13]

That the American public was hostile to the simple truth offered by the rescue community, and worse that the Church itself was indifferent to rescue's plea for the lives of 'Christ's least brothers' to use the terminology of the Lambs of the Christ, was the first step on the road to rescue's current demonization of American culture. But it was only the first step, for despite the hostility displayed to the rescue message, the rescue community for almost two decades held true to its original commitment to nonviolence. It took much more than this to bring about the current climate. For if indifference was the first step in the disillusionment of rescuers with American society, the experience of violence at the hands of those that the civics texts of the 1950s and 1960s held to be the guardians of order was the next great shock.

Police, Prisons and the 'Deathscorts'

> *Do not be afraid of what you are about to suffer. I tell you, the devil will put some of you in prison to test you, and you will suffer persecution for ten days. Be faithful, even to the point of death, and I will give you the crown of life.* [Rev. 2:10]

In the 'Siege of Atlanta' in 1988, the staunchly pacifist Operation Rescue lost its innocence. Rescue would never again be the same. Randall Terry's *Accessory to Murder* offers an instructive portrait of this time of trial.[14] Atlanta split Operation Rescue and gave birth to the Missionaries to the Preborn, but it was an experience which was to have an even more profound impact on the rank and file rescuers. John Brockhoeft had been taken into custody by BATF agents on 7 May 1988, two months before the events in Atlanta, but Shelley Shannon was there. So were hundreds of others. Atlanta's police and prisons apprised rescuers of the grim truth that their non-violent witness would not soon awaken America to repentance or the Church to renewal.

It was in Atlanta that police systematically adopted the use of 'pain compliance' tactics designed to force rescuers to walk under their own volition to waiting police vans, and it was in Atlanta too that rescuers were introduced to the terrible conditions to which prisoners are subjected in much of urban America. Given the social backgrounds of the rescue community – men and women who had never before considered even the possibility of violating the lawful orders of police and courts – this was a revelation in itself.[15]

Atlanta was in fact a mere taste of what was to come. In the wake of the Siege of Atlanta, violence at the clinics – violence in which rescuers often found themselves to be the victims – escalated rapidly. Rescuers assert that the primary sources of clinic level violence centered on the volunteer clinic escorts (or in rescue parlance, deathscorts), and on some local police departments. Jail conditions under which rescuers were held deteriorated rapidly as well.

In the formation of the currently prevalent apocalyptic worldview of the rescue community, the volunteer clinic defense teams – the so-called deathscorts – deserve more than a passing mention. Clinic volunteers are a diverse group. Escorts come from many walks of life; men and women, feminists, liberal activists, and perhaps most notably for the rescuers, members of such homosexual activist groups as Act Up and Queer Nation.[16] It is clear from this research that, in the view of the rescuers, much if not most of the violence around clinics which occurred during rescue's pacifist heyday came from the highly emotional, too often vituperative, and occasionally physically abusive behavior of the 'deathscorts'. That the rescuers' outrage at the behavior of the clinic guards was fully reciprocated by the escorts' disgust for the actions of the rescuers is clear as well from the literature.[17]

A central irony of the rescue movement lies in the fact that rescue, intended as a non-violent action with the dual intent of preventing the death of a baby in the immediate sense and of awakening American society and the American Church to the devaluation of the value and quality of human life which has taken place in recent years, has in practice unleashed the most negative emotions on both sides of the barricades. Consistently, the anger generated between the groups encamped outside the clinic door has brought about verbal confrontations intended to attack that which each side holds most dear. Thus began a process of dehumanization on both sides which served to lower the threshold to the resort to violence. On the rescue side, terms such as 'deathscorts' and the Nazi era metaphor in which the term is often couched, as well as the characterization of the abortionist as 'killer' or 'murderer' has served this purpose. On the part of the escorts – particularly those from homosexual organizations – the terminology of abuse has been explicitly anti-Christian and often sexual and scatological as well. For rescuers hearing such epithets, it took little imagination to interpret these imprecations as explicitly and unambiguously satanic. Thus the confirmation of the view that the abortion clinics of America are literal altars to Satan, and that those involved in the abortion industry – particularly the clinic volunteers – are literal witches and satanists.[18] Indeed, Shelley Shannon notes that her own decision to resort to force was influenced by listening to a taped sermon comparing the abortion clinics of America to satanic altars.[19] John Brockhoeft is equally explicit:

> It is a well known fact that some people who deliberately and knowingly worship Satan take jobs in abortion chambers....How could a real satanist resist an opportunity to participate in human sacrifice with immunity from prosecution? And we have discovered that to be accepted in some satanic covens a young woman must submit to the initiation of getting pregnant and aborting the baby.[20]

Taking the lessons learned in Atlanta, some local police departments began to respond to Operation Rescue's mass events with an increasing violence. Pain compliance holds served to force rescuers to abandon their positions 'voluntarily', and thus increased both police efficiency and reduced the chance of police injuries incurred in the process of carrying sometimes hefty rescuers determined to remain limp. Yet the line between 'pain compliance' and outright brutality is exceedingly thin, and some departments went far beyond the call of duty. The litany of such events serves as a résumé for veteran rescuers. Atlanta, Pittsburgh, West Hartford, and Los Angeles are particularly memorable.[21] Pain compliance holds became more severe, including the use of nunchukas, a Philippines martial arts weapon, by Los Angeles police. Shelley Shannon's description of such police techniques in Portland in a 13 January 1990 rescue are typical of this turn to greater police force.

> Police & pro-aborts worked arm in arm. They were nice to pro-death but extra brutal to us. I had my eyes closed praying...Whenever I opened them, I saw people getting tortured. They messed up Linda's wrist [Linda Wolfe, her wrist was broken], also kicks. They did get one guy by the jaws (I should have told him to put his chin down *Before* they get to you). Pro-aborts were laughing, having fun. 'Woe unto you who laugh now'....One violent officer [name deleted] grabbed a handful of Derek's hair and yanked him up & away by it saying 'Get off those officers!' That was weird, I thought, because there were no officers...Then he grabbed a handful of my hair and pulled me up by it, telling me to get off the imaginary officers...I saw the big officer with grayish hair and mustache, who always threatens to break our arms, club Derek and say 'get up!' Poor Derek. He's only 19 yrs. old. It made a sick sound...[22]

With the rise in police brutality came an increasingly severe prison regime, culminating in the events in the Pittsburgh jail in 1989.[23] In Pittsburgh, the casual violence and degradation which is the norm in America's urban jails was replaced with the alleged sexual abuse of female rescuers by male officers in full view of male prisoners. For rescuers, little emphasis is placed on individual suffering. Beatings are shrugged off, and the violence of some local police departments have come to be accepted as the price of admission to the rescue culture. Sexual abuse, threats of rape or other forms of implied or actual sexual violence intended to degrade or humiliate female rescuers however, is something else. Rescue is an intensely religious form of Christian witness whose primary emphasis centers after all on procreation and the dignity of human life. In such a culture, sexuality is a central concern. Thus the reaction to events in Pittsburgh. There, rescuers assert that after having covered their badges, Pittsburgh police roamed through the bus where female rescuers were manacled, beating them with nightsticks. Worse was to come:

> They took the women to the men's jail. Cops and guards dragged them up five flights of stairs, pulling out clumps of hair, ripping the clothes off them. These men strip searched the women, fondled and molested them, shouted obscenities, paraded them naked up and down in front of the men's cells. They ripped rosary beads apart, threw Bibles into trash cans.
>
> No one cared. The newspapers and churches were not interested. [24]

As important to the formation of an apocalyptic world view as were events such as those in the Pittsburgh jail, it must be kept in mind that a municipal jail is primarily a holding cell. Stays are of relatively short duration, and mass rescues of the Operation Rescue variety tend to quickly overwhelm these facilities. The prison system itself can be far worse. Here, rescuers come in contact with the most violent of criminals, and here too rescuers encounter the most hardened of prison guards. Remarkably, this research indicates that for rescuers, the prisoners are seen in a considerably more positive light than are guards or prison officials. The explanation for this anomaly may lie in part in the rescuers' view of prisoners as a potential mission field as much in need of hearing the Gospel's message of hope as are the unborn themselves (Heb. 10:33 and 13:3, 1 Peter 3:19, and Rev. 2:10). Prisoners for their part appear to have been, by and large, protective of incarcerated rescuers. Not so prison guards and prison officials.

A number of rescuers, following the example of Joan Andrews, have made it a point not to cooperate in any way with prison authorities. Some, such as the Lambs of Christ, even refuse to give their names, to leave voluntarily unless all of their number are released, or to pay fines or court costs. Such defiance is hardly conducive to the maintenance of order in penal institutions, and defiance is dealt with harshly in America's prisons. In such an atmosphere, it is only natural that the treatment of rescuers – hardly career criminals and brought up with a naïve view of American justice – would be less than gentle. Conversely, it is hardly a revelation that rescuers would see a pattern to their individual experiences of mistreatment which would indicate to many the existence of a pervasive evil underlying the visible pattern of events. Such suspicions in the prison diaries and internal communications of rescuers clearly begin to reflect these suspicions as early as 1989. Remarkably, for many rescuers, these observations are often broached with a humor belying their deadly seriousness.

To give an early flavor of this evolution, the following text compresses a diary written by Shelley Shannon from 21 October 1989 to 2 November 1989 as a guest of the Fulton County Jail in Atlanta for a stay of '10 days, 6 hours, 17 minutes'.[25]

> All along its seemed like a spiritual battle: God giving us tickets on sale so we could fly ... and leading me and [name deleted] to come instead of paying a fine ...There's a feeling something great is going to happen in Atlanta...
>
> We are now in a filthy holding cell waiting to check into Fulton Co. Jail...One lady in here told us when she finally got a blanket, it had b. m. on it, and even later she got another but she said it smelled like man's stuff. Everyone is telling us about the conditions in the jail...worse than any prison any of them have been in...
>
> ... There are some in here who aren't saved (Help us, please God; to help them) ... [name deleted] is pregnant and doesn't want to tell

> them because another lady ... was given pills and started bleeding. She quit taking them and I'll try to get some out. She did have a miscarriage though. They say it was thyrozine (?) [sic] in the kool-aid to take away your sex drive. If so, it doesn't work on the lesbians...
>
> [A] lady told us how [Oregon rescuer] Linda Wolfe saved her twin babies ... A guy was going to set her up in prostitution and pay her bail and for her abortion. She said she was going to kill her child just to get out ... Linda came over to her and they talked a long time. And she decided not to get an abortion and has been sitting here in jail paying the price for choosing to do the right thing. She's getting back with her husband and he's really happy about the twins. She also told us a lot of inmates came in pregnant and end up with miscarriages after receiving 'medication'. [name deleted] has been doing good – she has delivered witches and prostitutes crying out to Jesus to deliver them! P. T. L. [Praise the Lord]!..
>
> ... I wrote for my prayer request that 'God will revive America and His people who are called by His name will turn from their wicked ways in repentance'....

Shelley Shannon's notes are not atypical of the rescue literature at the time of the 'Siege of Atlanta'. There was in the published literature, as in private correspondence, the same call to save an America seen as contaminated by the vile sins of child murder, sexual vice and selfish materialism. Yet the rescuers' America of 1988–89 was still God's 'city on a hill'. The experiences of Atlanta, however, began to cast the shadow of doubt about America's salvation among the rescue community, and by late 1989 or early 1990, rescue literature began to take an increasingly despairing tone. That God would soon act to cleanse the land from the stain of abortion remained an article of faith. But how? It rapidly became clear that salvation would not take place by means of the courts and the political system. With this realization came the decisive break between rescue and the larger pro-life movement.[26]

The Political Process and the Legal System

> *Beginning officially with the passage of the Freedom of Choice Act – we, the remnant of God-fearing men and women of the United States of Amerika [sic], do officially* ***declare war*** *on the entire child killing industry.* [*The Army of God Manual*, 1994][27]

The 1973 Supreme Court decision legalizing abortion on demand in the now famous *Roe v. Wade* case, like the 1962 ruling against prayer in the public schools, served as a wake-up call to segments of the religious community that something in America was seriously amiss. The confirmation of the decision in 1973's *Doe v. Bolton* which found three proposed restrictions to full abortion access in a Georgia statute unconstitutional served primarily to confirm to the rescue community that justice for the unborn would not soon be forthcoming from the courts of a fallen America.[28] More relevant restrictions on the public witness of rescuers, however, have sounded the death knell of rescue which opened this essay, and it is these restrictions – some ironically gaining overwhelming majorities for passage in response to some act of rescue violence – which were key ingredients in the turn to violence by some in the rescue movement. What follows examines only a few of these developments: the use of civil litigation and the RICO statute to deter rescuers, the rescuers' furor over the proposed Freedom of Choice Act (FOCA), and the criminal penalties of the Freedom of Clinic Entrances Bill (FACE).

There is something faceless yet inexorable about the workings of the legal system. In rescue parlance, the free standing abortion clinics of America offer an obvious address for the rescuers' war against Satan. The abortionist and the ubiquitous 'deathscorts' give the devil's timeless evil a human face, while at their worst, the police give this evil a cadre of enforcers. Yet what effective rejoinder could be offered to a missive such as the following?

> Dear Ms Shannon,
>
> I represent the Lovejoy Surgicenter, Inc. [a Portland abortion clinic]. This letter is written to advise you that you have until 12:00 noon on July 21, 1992 to pay ... $504,486.43 plus attorney fees and costs...by the above stated deadline.
>
> If you fail to meet this deadline, I have been instructed to immediately initiate a legal action for collection...THIS IS THE FINAL DEMAND ON THIS ACCOUNT BEFORE LEGAL ACTION IS INITIATED.
>
> Very Truly Yours,
> [Name Withheld][29]

The Lovejoy suit which resulted in this demand was a 1991 civil action alleging simple trespass against the Advocates for Life Ministries and several individuals associated with the Oregon rescue community. On 2 May 1994 the United States Supreme Court refused to hear an appeal of the case, effectively letting the judgment stand. It was only one of a blizzard of similar suits. The failure of rescuers either to make restitution or to cease their activities provoked the application of the RICO (Racketeer Influenced and Corrupt Organizations Act) statute against members of the rescue community. An early RICO suit was filed by the National Organization of

Women against the father of organized rescue in America, Joseph Scheidler of the Pro-Life Action League in Chicago.[30] The suit, dismissed by both the Federal District Court and the Seventh Circuit Court of Appeals was, to the surprise of many legal observers, upheld by the Supreme Court in 1994. Conversely, the rescue community evinced no surprise whatever.[31] The barrage of civil litigation for them was merely of a piece with the criminal legislation which was designed at first to marginalize and later to crush the rescue movement.

The Freedom of Choice Act (FOCA) debate in 1989 and the draconian Freedom of Clinic Entrances (FACE) bill of 1994 together served to sever whatever lingering faith the rescue community might have had in the institutions of the US government. It was not always so. The administration of Ronald Reagan gave considerable hope to both the pro-life constituency and the rescuers that somehow the answer to overturning *Roe v. Wade* lay in the political process; an optimism that was perhaps unwarranted, but did serve to link the rescue community with its pro-life parent.[32] In retrospect, this illusion of official sanction seems to have served as a brake on the drift toward direct action. The clinic burnings of the early 1980s demonstrate that the use of force was already a potential court of last resort for the movement. Similarly, the administration of George Bush, less charismatic by far and less sincerely committed to the pro-life cause, at least gave the appearance of fighting a holding action in defense of the unborn.[33]

The 1992 election of Bill Clinton dashed this tenuous faith in the efficacy of the political system. In Bill and Hillary Clinton, rescuers were faced with a new political equation. The Clintons were unabashed advocates of maintaining the *Roe v. Wade* status quo and were backed by a liberal coalition which prominently featured the nemesis of the rescue message: feminists and gay advocacy groups. More, President Clinton was fully prepared to translate that commitment into policy terms, making FACE inevitable.

For their part, some rescuers expressed their horror at the specter of the Clinton presidency less in political than in theological terms. As the political aspirations of the rescue community faded, a rapid evolution took place which has considerable precedent in the history of the Christian West. That is, the current troubles were translated into theological terms and placed as part of the End Times' scenario of the Book of Revelations. One prominent feature of this apocalyptic scenario led to ongoing speculation as to whether President Clinton was in fact the literal Antichrist.[34] Indeed, the presence of the Antichrist on earth would do much to explain the failure of the Church to awaken and rally to the defense of the babies. Another more secular feature of this rapid loss of hope in American democracy was the demise of the touchstone of the political faith upon which the rescue movement was founded: that one day the movement would emerge from its pariah status to be recognized as the successor to the Civil Rights movement of the 1960s.[35]

The Freedom of Choice Act was introduced in the House of Representatives in 1989. FOCA, a bill yet to be passed, would have guaranteed a woman the right to abortion at any time and for any reason up to the point of 'viability', that is, until the point of fetal development whereby the baby could live outside the womb. While FOCA was not in itself written to terminate the activities of the rescue community, it did have the effect of demonstrating to rescuers the hostility of the American political system to the moderate pro-life message and thus confirmed the rescuers' manichaean perceptions of American culture. The declaration of war against America's death culture offered at the top of this section from the *Army of God Manual* is indicative of the impact of FOCA on the rescue community. With the controversy surrounding FOCA, the growing rift between the moderate pro-lifers and rescue grew deeper and at this writing widens by the day.

The despair evinced by that *Army of God Manual* quote is, however, most probably a product of hindsight rather than an authentic reaction to FOCA in 1992. For the rescue community as a whole, it was not until the 1994 passage of the Freedom of Clinic Entrances Act that it became unambiguously clear that the American government under the Clinton presidency had moved from general hostility to the pro-life message to a determination to destroy the rescue movement itself. That the full implications of the FACE bill only belatedly dawned on much of the rescue community may be in part due to the offer which the US Senate extended to rescue leaders to testify about their own experiences of violence and abuse at the hands of both local police departments and the deathscorts guarding the clinics.[36] Congress, however, was less concerned with violence against rescuers than that which was aimed at abortionists, in particular the killing of Dr David Gunn in Florida and the wounding of Dr George Tiller in Wichita, both in 1993.

FACE was constructed to create a so-called 'bubble zone' separating rescuers from the entrances to abortion clinics. In this, FACE was hardly innovative. For some years, municipal authorities in various locations around the country had experimented with such 'bubble' or 'no speech' zones in response to rescue activities. These local legislative and administrative efforts were in turn essentially political actions modeled on the court injunctions which clinic operators had obtained to restrain the activities of rescuers at their establishments. FACE, then, merely took this welter of local injunctions and ordinances and created from them a law which makes it a federal offense to interfere with any person seeking an abortion and setting stiff sentencing guidelines which are crafted to deter all but the most faithful rescuers.[37] This makes it a relatively simple matter to isolate and incarcerate this remnant. As of this writing, FACE does appear to have successfully accomplished this objective.

As criminal penalties became more draconian, the number of rescuers inevitably declined. Of the faithful remnant who chose to persevere, there was an inevitable radicalization which served to divide the heretofore highly cohesive rescue community. The following section will therefore concentrate exclusively on that portion of the rescue faithful which finds no alternative to the resort to force in defense of the unborn.

II. The Resort to Force

In the atmosphere of December 1994, a John Salvi III was inevitable. His actions – random shots fired into abortion clinics that resulted in the deaths of two employees and the wounding of several others – broke the one inviolable rule of the rescue movement: do nothing which would endanger the unborn child. Salvi's written statement, put out on 4 January 1995 over the AP wires and relayed to this researcher via the Internet, reveals a young man obsessed with fears of anti-Catholic conspiracies, but it has nothing to say of abortion.[38] Yet the sudden escalation of clinic violence could not help but draw in such marginal personalities as John Salvi. There had been for some years a gradual erosion of the barriers against the resort to deadly force among some of the most radical voices in the rescue movement. More, as the apocalyptic world view of the rescue community solidified in the cauldron of the 1980s, and as the courts and the Clinton administration succeeded in criminalizing rescue and driving much of the pacifist majority to the sidelines or into the prisons, the isolated voices which had been arguing for a resort to force were brought to the fore. This section will attempt to trace that evolution.

The clinic bombers of the 1980s, people such as John Brockhoeft and Marjorie Reed, were scrupulous in their determination that the destruction of, in rescue terminology, the killing centers would be accomplished with absolutely no loss of human life. For them, the destruction of the property would be sufficient to, at least for a time, halt the slaughter of the unborn.[39] This tactic did sometimes succeed in halting abortions for a brief time. Yet in urban areas, pregnant women determined to go ahead with their decision to abort had but to make an appointment at another clinic, while even in more rural areas, it is highly unlikely that any woman was forced to carry to term against her will. Clearly, a far greater commitment to the use of force would be needed if abortion was to be stopped through violent means.

Before such a commitment could be made however, the most determined members of the rescue community had one more psychological bridge to cross. This was the realization that not only was the American death culture beyond redemption, but that it would be necessary actively to confront the killers on their own terms. With FACE, war had been declared on the most faithful of God's people, just as since the 1973 advent of *Roe v. Wade*, a war had been declared on the unborn. If, then, it was to be war, and if the babies were to be rescued, then no legitimate option other than to take up arms in defense of the unborn remained. This realization was, however, far from immediate and remains to this day the province of a minority of the rescue community.

The internal debate that began in the late 1980s to seriously consider the resort to deadly force was conducted primarily among imprisoned rescuers – Prisoners of Christ in rescue parlance – and between these incarcerated rescuers and a handful of activists on the outside. It continued and deepened in the pages of certain rescue journals, and in book form courtesy of Michael Bray.[40] At the core of this discourse are several key themes, each of which had long been present in the literature and the internal debates of rescue. The necessary innovation in this reformulation is merely one of emphasis rather than originality. Thus, the 1960s American Civil Rights movement metaphor was supplanted by an almost exclusive focus on the holocaust, on Nazi Germany and on the resistance to that prototype of the modern culture of death.

The Third Reich and the American Holocaust

From its inception, the rescue movement was not loathe to publicize the marked parallel which they perceived between the Nazi policy of genocide against the Jews and others in Europe and the slaughter of millions of babies yet in the womb.[41] Indeed, Randall Terry's optimistic first book, *Operation Rescue*, has the slogan '*You* can stop the abortion holocaust in America!' emblazoned on its back cover. In this early pacifist period, the rescue movement reached back into this period of history for its two great heroes: Corrie Ten Boom and Dietrich Bonhoeffer. Both resisted the Nazi government's genocidal policies on religious grounds, and both suffered greatly for their actions. Yet as the movement's mood darkened, it was increasingly to the example of Bonhoeffer that the rescuers turned. Rescue's interpretation of both of these heroes is instructive in tracing the movement's turn from pacifism to violence.

Corrie Ten Boom's stature derives from her efforts to protect Jews from Nazi occupation forces in wartime Holland. Her witness was solidly based on biblical grounds and utterly non-violent. Her eventual arrest and incarceration in the Ravensbruck concentration camp is posited by rescuers as analogous to their suffering in the jails and prisons of America; an opportunity to share God's Word of ultimate hope with fellow inmates and guards alike. Yet concomitant with the drift of the faction of rescue which would opt for or support direct action, the example of Corrie Ten Boom's non-violent attempt to rescue the Jews would be devalued in comparison with Dietrich Bonhoeffer's resort to direct action against Adolf Hitler.[42]

Dietrich Bonhoeffer (1906–45), the distinguished German bishop and theologian whose resolute opposition to Hitler and the barbarism of the Nazi state would lead to his execution for his involvement in the wartime plot to assassinate the Fuehrer, is today the undisputed model for emulation of the Defensive Action wing of the rescue movement. Indeed, so intense is this lionization that a distinct form of hagiography is beginning to appear in the rescue literature which appears to elevate Bonhoeffer almost to Christ-like stature:

> The Lord Our God has always been ultimately in control! Bonhoeffer was executed before you were born. The Lord could have kept him from it. Bonhoeffer was willing to die defending others. He volunteered to die! He became more powerful in death than in life! Had he survived the war, Christianity and the world may have forgotten him. Do not rob him of his voluntary and glorious sacrifice! Do not rob us of the legacy he handed down to us![43]

Bonhoeffer's actions, however, were not undertaken on a whim, nor were they permissible in any but the most dire situations. Indeed, in one of Bonhoeffer's earliest essays, political action by the Church is specifically prohibited in all but the most dire historical circumstances:

> [the church] recognizes the absolute necessity of the use of force in this world, and also the moral injustice of certain concrete acts of the state which are necessarily bound up with the use of force. The church cannot in the first place exert absolute direct political action, for the church does not pretend to have any knowledge of the necessary courses of history. Thus, even today, in the Jewish question, it cannot address the state directly and demand of it some definite action of a different nature.[44]

Given the grim social and political climate facing rescuers today, it is little wonder that many of this community would identify their own travails with Bonhoeffer's gradual drift from a Romans 13 style subordination to state authority to a suicidal attempt to excise from the world the radical evil of Adolf Hitler's regime through the use of deadly force. Thus the current hagiographic treatment of Bonhoeffer in the rescue literature, and thus too the demand for Bonhoeffer's original writings by many in the rescue community. Shelley Shannon, for example, recalls reading several of

Bonhoeffer's books during her evolution toward Defensive Action.[45] In essence, many rescuers have come to see the world around them as precisely analogous to that of Dietrich Bonhoeffer: society has become literally satanic, sanctioning the mass extermination of helpless human beings and the only just response of God's church is to recognize that in contemporary America a state of war exists between good and evil, between the servants and collaborators of the abortion culture and the people of God, and to act accordingly.

The Imagery of War

The road leading from the rescue movement's 20 years of fruitless non-violent witness to the *Army of God Manual*'s declaration of war against 'the child killing industry of Amerika' is not so long as it would appear on first glance. Like the remarkably similar declaration of war against ZOG [Zionist Occupation Government] issued by Robert Mathews and the Order, the manichaean imagery of a beleaguered remnant under siege by the forces of a decayed and utterly irredeemable culture were present in the discourse of rescue virtually from its inception.[46] Once again, the mark of the rescuers who would adopt or condone the resort to force is merely one of degree rather than innovation. More, it would not be long before the state of war between the 'Defensive Action' wing of rescue and the dominant culture would engulf the rescue movement itself. Thus, the disavowal of rescue violence by such rescue leaders as Randall Terry or the current Operation Rescue leader Flip Benham would be posited as weak, cowardly and effeminate at best, treasonous at worst.[47] This is the state of the rescue movement today.

John Brockhoeft states this proposition simply and eloquently: 'abortion is a war crime which means that our nation has been in a state of war since 1973'.[48] In a 26 November 1994 interview published in the rescue literature, Paul Hill, currently under a sentence of death for killing a Florida abortionist and his volunteer bodyguard, sees no need to expound on the state of war between rescue and the death culture. It is a given fact of life: 'In every war, men have been willing to go out and risk death, or separation from their families, to defend their country and their neighbors... I've done the same thing.'[49] And in times of war, such primary Christian values as love and charity – values which are at the heart of the rescue movement – are too often allowed to fall by the wayside:

> There are very few (that I know of) who are my enemies on a strictly personal basis (perhaps no more than one or two). In accordance with Jesus' mandate, I do love those enemies and pray for them. But during this time of war, this time of grave national crisis, I do not love any

> member of this reprobate anti-Christ nation within our borders which wages war against my people.[50]

With the certainty that the contemporary United States is but a mannered reincarnation of Nazi Germany, that the abortion holocaust is merely a continuation of the Nazi Holocaust, and that the death culture would stop at nothing in its unceasing war against the faithful remnant of God's people, the transformation of a faction of the rescue movement from a pacifist witness with a deep and abiding faith in the efficacy of the American system and the transforming power of God's Church into a movement willing to take up arms was complete. Even so, the resort to lethal force was slow in coming. Rather, there was first a gradual escalation from rhetoric to the destruction of property, and this was followed by an increasing personalization of the struggle as the rescue message, driven from the abortuary door, would increasingly come to encamp on the sidewalk of the abortionist's home. Prayer too began to change, as the Missionaries to the Preborn in Milwaukee pioneered the use of imprecatory prayer to call down the wrath of God onto the head of the abortionist, beseeching God either to change his heart or to take his life.[51] At last, despairing of the efficacy of non-violent witness, convinced of their persecution by the courts and of their victimization through extraordinary violence from police and clinic guards, and facing an administration in Washington determined to protect abortion access by the criminalization of rescue activities, the rescue movement faced an intractable dilemma. Nevertheless, it took Michael Griffin, a peripheral figure in the world of rescue, to force the movement to make such a decision. That evolution is the focus of the remainder of this study.

Toward Lethal Force

> *The more the authorities take our legal redress away the more compelling to do more drastic measures. It is going to get a whole lot worse. Blood will be shed [and] not just the babies' blood either.* [letter from imprisoned female clinic arsonist][52]

Despite the violence at clinics, despite the taunts of the ubiquitous deathscorts and the all too frequent violence of the police and the prisons, and in the face of an increasingly hostile public climate, the rescue message until the late 1980s remained one of reverence for all human life – born and unborn. Beneath the surface, however, there were other stirrings. While angry words on both sides of the clinic door were slowly dehumanizing the dreaded 'other' for all concerned, there was even among the most pacific of rescuers a marked ambivalence toward the use of force at levels below that which would physically harm even the most culpable of human beings.

First, there was the destruction of property. In this, there was a rapid escalation which would be typical of all aspects of the rescue movement in the 1980s. It began innocuously enough with, of all people, that most pacifist of rescuers, Joan Andrews. Her crime was to unplug a suction machine in the course of a rescue. The legal penalties she would pay for this futile if deeply symbolic act confirmed to her and others both the manichaean nature of the present day culture of the United States and, on a purely pragmatic level, that the penalties for doing far greater damage to the property of the child killing industry could be no more harsh than that for merely pulling a plug. So why not take a hammer or a tube of glue next time and destroy the hated killing device all together? At least the clinic would have to obtain a replacement at some considerable expense, and perhaps the brief down time faced by the clinic would result in the saving of a child's life. From the destruction of equipment, it was but a small step to entering a clinic in the dead of night intent on wreaking the greatest possible damage on equipment, furnishings and patient records. In the world of rescue in those pre-Clinton days, it was thought that no price would be too high to pay for the life of a single child. Thus, even during the clinic's working hours, it was not unusual for rescuers, having got past the clinic door, to find various ways of disabling equipment. From the destruction of equipment, it was only a short step to the next innovation of the rescuer's craft: butyric acid and the attempt to make clinics uninhabitable by the introduction of noxious odors.[53]

As the clinic confrontations sharpened and the perceptions of the rescuers grew ever darker, there was a rapid increase in the sophistication of the tactics employed on both sides. What had begun as low level, non-violent localized skirmishes soon became more coordinated actions taking place on an increasingly national scale as both sides began to form networks to share information, intelligence and experiences. Thus for example, at roughly the same time that local police departments began the routine use of pain compliance techniques, rescuers adopted the crawl – a slow, inexorable procession of rescuers on their hands and knees seeking to crawl under police barricades and, if need be, between the legs of policemen in an effort to get to the clinic door while imitating as closely as possible the helplessness of the baby. It was at this time of tactical experimentation that Joseph Scheidler published his remarkable *Closed: 99 Ways to Stop Abortion* which, until the appearance of the *Army of God Manual*, served as the primary source of rescue tactics.[54]

So important is this increasing identification of the rescuers with the babies in the resort to force that it is deserving of some attention. In the early stages of this research, it became clear that some imprisoned rescuers were convinced that they had heard the cries of unborn babies from within the walls of the abortion clinic. Shelley Shannon certainly did, although she is somewhat reticent about saying so publicly, and the notes and letters of other rescuers bear this out as well. This intensely mystical sense of unity with the unborn explains much of the turn to increasing levels of violence among some of the most committed rescuers, for to hear the cry of a single, helpless child about to lose his or her life acts as a powerful goad to action.[55] The kind of political and public relations calculations so dear to the hearts of the pro-life movement pale in comparison to the distress of that one, single child so in need of help. Thus the often frantic nature of some rescues. Thus, too the often extravagant means employed by rescuers to merely delay the business of a targeted clinic – Kryptonite bicycle locks giving way to incredibly complex devices into which a rescuer will lock himself until the fire department or other emergency service is able to cut him loose for example.[56]

It was this intense identification with the babies which at last goaded John Brockhoeft to abandon peaceful protest and to become one of the early clinic bombers. In order to overcome his fear of being caught and imprisoned, indeed, as a necessary prerequisite to for the first time in his life stepping outside the law, Brockhoeft concentrated on his total identification with the babies:

> I put myself in the baby's place, reminding myself that I had to love that baby as myself. 'My arms will be torn away from my torso tomorrow! My skull will be crushed until fragments cave inward and cut into my brain!' I imagined how terrible the physical pain would be! I thought of my right arm being dismembered, and as I thought of it, I bore in mind that my arm would not be taken off cleanly with a sharp surgical instrument while under anesthesia. No, it would be brutally torn out of the shoulder socket and twisted off! It would hurt so bad! But I did not think only of the terrible physical pain. I imagined the terrible mental horror and terror of looking at my right shoulder, and my right arm is gone! And blood is gushing out of where it had been!... If I, like the baby, was going to suffer so much and then die tomorrow morning, and I knew I was being killed unjustly, I would not be too afraid to go to the death chamber with gasoline and destroy it tonight.[57]

The mid-1980s marked the high point of the clinic bombings.[58] There was a natural progression from the destruction of instruments to the incineration of buildings. It was simply a matter of the economy of scale. If the destruction of equipment would cripple a clinic for a day or two, and if butyric acid would be good for a week or so, how much more effective would be the total destruction of a facility? And if caught, how much harsher the penalty? Certainly, the rescue community was loath to speak ill of the clinic arsonists, given the demonstrable effectiveness of their actions and their extraordinary care that no person be harmed by the clinic fires.[59]

Every first time prisoner receives an education behind bars for which no college could have prepared him or her. For rescuers, these lessons were largely spiritual – the jails and prisons of America were of primary importance in the formation of the apocalyptic millenarian *Zeitgeist* of the rescue movement today. These lessons could be of more worldly import as well. One imprisoned rescuer for example writes:

> We also learn a lot in jail, and are able to teach a lot. For instance, since I have been here I've learned the one last piece of info I needed to have a complete knowledge of pipe bombs (not that I will ever need or use that info). I've taught a very lot of people much about abortion and/or bombs. I wasn't sure that was wise, but it gets boring. I've become friends with gang members and others. I make it a point to be sure that robbers find out that most killing centers charge 'cash only' and *lots* of it, and the fact that abortionists tend to carry large amounts of 'cash only' home with them at night. It's true that we learn a lot of things we never wanted to know while in jail. But also learned in jail was: destroying fingerprints with WD40, knocking out plexiglas with a mallet or how to cut through it, 'bullet proof' isn't really, lots of other stuff. I fully intend to get a great deal out of all jail or prison time that I serve, as far as stopping abortion.[60]

The clinic arsons did have some local effect on the availability of abortions. The cost, however, was high. The bombers turned out to be amateurs and were rather easily rounded up and incarcerated. Even a Vietnam veteran such as John Brockhoeft found that military training was poor preparation for the world of the urban guerrilla. The prison experience, however, had a powerful radicalizing effect on the bombers, and it took little time for the lessons learned in the prisons to be communicated to the rescue community as a whole. These lessons were communicated among rescuers through letters and personal visits – indeed, Shelley Shannon made pilgrimages to visit such incarcerated clinic bombers as John Brockhoeft – and were facilitated through the regular publication of prisoner lists through such ministries as the Milwaukee-based Prisoners of Christ.[61]

As the apocalyptic mindset of the rescuers became increasingly fixed in the early 1990s, incarcerated clinic arsonists were already debating the heretofore unthinkable: a turn to lethal violence. One such Prisoner of Christ, in a remarkable series of letters written in this period to a fellow rescuer, offers a microcosmic view of this rapid evolution. It may be safely posited that this prisoner – in another life a midwestern housewife – reflects much of her prison experience in her various stratagems (or in her own terms, 'fiendish plots'). Some of the earliest of these are at best rudimentary. Such a non-starter was a plan to free pro-life prisoners: 'Wherever there is a prison that is holding pro-lifers ... the town nearest to the prison that has an abortion mill, hammer it until they close down [then] picket the Bureau of Prisons headquarters demanding release of our hostages.'[62] Within a year, this Prisoner's ideas would become increasingly sophisticated, culminating in a 16-page manifesto in which the resort to deadly force is seriously broached.

Despite the ominous mood of the rescue community, however, it would not be until Michael Griffin's 1993 killing of David Gunn that the resort to lethal force would move from internal debate to actuality.

Ten Boom or Bonhoeffer?

When Michael Griffin, at best a peripheral member of the rescue community, shot and killed Florida abortionist David Gunn, his act was portrayed in the public arena as if a dam had burst and a torrent of pent up rage was unleashed by the pro-life movement. In short order, Shelley Shannon shot and wounded a Milwaukee doctor whose late term abortion practice and combative stance toward the rescue movement had made him for many rescuers the caricature of the predatory abortionist, George Tiller. Then Paul Hill shot and killed another Florida abortionist, John Britton, and his volunteer bodyguard. All within the space of two years. Lesser known was Alabama abortionist George Patterson, shot to death in an apparent robbery attempt as he was leaving a pornographic movie house in Mobile, Alabama, in 1994. Lesser known still is the shooting of a Canadian abortionist, Garson Romalis, in his home while his wife and daughters were present. While no suspect has been apprehended, the Canadian government is proceeding on the assumption that a member of the rescue community is responsible, and is acting accordingly.[63]

Yet for the shooters themselves, and indeed for the rescue community as a whole, the underlying motivations for the resort to lethal force had little to do with anger. In fact, the passages in 'America's Last Prophetic Witness' which came in for the most criticism among rescuers dealt with the unquestioned acceptance by this researcher of the proposition that Michael Griffin acted from some sense of inarticulate rage. Rather, Shelley Shannon gently suggested:

> Now you have me curious. Do you think that I was angry, hateful, or in a rage when I shot Tiller? There were witnesses, also when M. G. [Michael Griffin] shot & killed the FL mass murderer. From what I read, mainly in Life Advocate, he (Michael) seemed peaceful &

> calmly turned himself in. Now he doesn't remember shooting him, unfortunately. I promise you, Michael is an extremely godly person.[64]

Shelley Shannon was quite correct in her criticism. Rage had little to do with the turn to violence against human beings among a few rescuers. Rather, there was as we have seen a rapid intensification among even the most determinedly pacifist of rescuers of an apocalyptic millenarian mindset which diagnosed the current epidemic of child killing as of a piece with the timeless war of Satan against the people of God, save that now that age old battle was reaching its apogee and thus its inevitable conclusion. With such a *Zeitgeist*, it was no great leap to accept that America was at war – and that the most helpless victims of this war are the unborn. Schooled in the brutality of the streets and the jails, identifying ever more intensely with the babies in the womb, finding ever more convincing parallels between the German National Socialist state of the 1930s and the America of the 1990s, and at last with true interposition legislated virtually out of existence, it was little wonder that there were voices in the rescue movement calling for more resolute action to halt the holocaust. The signs of this change were there for all to see. A theology of violence was already evolving. More, the rescue community as a whole was, almost imperceptibly, edging ever closer to an acceptance of the proposition that there could be found a solid, biblical basis for the resort to deadly force. The death of David Gunn was in this sense less an epochal event in the history of rescue than the culmination of a process already too far advanced for anyone to stop.

In small ways, the deep reverence for all human life had begun to fray among some members of the rescue community. Imprecatory prayer, highly controversial in rescue circles, was one such step. While calling upon God to act against a human being could in one sense absolve the faithful of responsibility for the resulting actions, in a deeper sense this imprecation may be said to constitute a call to blood vengeance which seems far from the spirit of contemporary Christianity. More tangible was the widespread adoption by rescuers of Joseph Scheidler's call to 'adopt an abortionist'. This program brought the nonviolent rescue witness from the doors of the clinic to the homes of the abortionists themselves. The goal was to apprise the families and neighbors of the favored abortion provider of the manner in which the doctor made his living. The tactic was occasionally successful in persuading the abortionist to find other employment, but again on another level, the program both personalized the confrontation and diminished the private space needed by both sides to decompress from the constant pressure of the abortion conflict.[65] In these and other small ways, the seeds of violence were present in the rescue world for some time. FACE, however, may have been the defining moments.

A primary factor in assuring almost 20 years of non-violent rescue was the intense identification of the rescuer with the babies. The Lambs of Christ, for example, identify themselves when arrested as Baby Doe, while Father Norman Weslin was called Father Doe. The actions of these and other rescuers were, to the greatest degree possible, modeled on an imitation of the helplessness of the baby in the womb. A practical aspect of this identification is the belief in rescue circles that to save a baby – even one baby – is a miracle and thus the confirmation of God's blessing on the rescue endeavor. To save that one baby was in fact worth almost any price which could be paid by the rescuer, and it was this intense identification with each unborn child which allowed the rescuer to live with the guilt of not having been able to prevent, in rescue parlance, the murder of the rest of the almost 4,400 babies which rescuers hold to be the average daily casualty rate of the American abortion holocaust. Ironically, as long as true rescue through interposition was possible, the rescue community was largely deaf to those among its number who called for more resolute action. To save one baby was of such great importance that to risk long-term incarceration was seen as counterproductive. Who then would be left to save the baby whose life would be terminated tomorrow? Or the day after?

FACE changed these calculations. Interposition would with the stroke of a pen be legislated out of existence. If a second or third arrest for non-violent rescue had the same price as, say, manslaughter, well... To a determined minority of rescuers, the choice was both stark and, given all that had gone before, remarkably easy to make. If Corrie Ten Boom's non-violent witness would not be tolerated by the death culture, what was left other than the example of Dietrich Bonhoeffer? This realization brought to the fore of the internal rescue debate the 'absolutism' of John Brockhoeft and the Defensive Action theory of Paul Hill.

Absolutism, like Paul Hill's Defensive Action theory, rests on a strongly biblical foundation and reflects a deeply held apocalyptic millenarian worldview. For both however, the resort to deadly force against abortionists has a pragmatic surface which complements its millenarian core. On a purely pragmatic level, the killing of one abortionist has the anticipated effect both of saving every baby scheduled to die that day and of persuading abortionists everywhere to find another means of livelihood. Medical students tempted to enter the profession too are expected to think twice before accepting employment in an abortion clinic. In this respect, the absolutist wing of the movement has opted for true terrorism, although this choice is most often cloaked in the mantle of justifiable homicide intended solely for self defense and the defense of family members or neighbors from imminent, deadly peril.

On a tactical level, this strategy has an undeniable efficacy. Abortionists have been frightened into closing their practices, and young doctors willing to take up the mantle are increasingly few and far between.[66] Despite this short term utility however, the resort to deadly force has not yet found the favor of the majority of rescuers and it horrifies the broad pro-life constituency. Aside from moral considerations, these opponents point to the undeniable fact that the turn to violence has brought disaster on the movement in the form of punitive legislation. More, after the highly publicized killings of abortion doctors, the political climate has become increasingly hostile, making the dream of overturning *Roe v. Wade* more distant than ever. This argument too has undeniable efficacy, but it is at this point that the movement's core millenarianism becomes most evident. What care millenarians, after all, for the long term political implications of their actions? As John Brockhoeft so eloquently points out: 'if we do not act now to halt the slaughter, God will act for us! When He returns, sword of vengeance in hand, what profit will be the most prescient of political stratagems?'

Absolutism and Defensive Action

> *The only possible way future historians will fail to see 1993–1994 as a turning point in the Abortion War is if we do not have any more history, due to having been swept away by the cup of God's wrath. And if this divine judgment falls on our nation, it will be not only because of a few hundred wicked people shedding the innocent blood of babies. It will be because of the 150,000,000 Americans going around proclaiming the name of Jesus Christ and being LUKEWARM AT THE SAME TIME!* [John Brockhoeft][67]

Michael Griffin's killing of David Gunn was an epiphany for John Brockhoeft. His 'Brockhoeft Report' was intended as a book which was hand written a chapter at a time from his prison cell. Griffin's act fit perfectly with 'The Brockhoeft Report's' apocalyptic millenarian interpretation of abortion and what abortion portends for contemporary American culture.[68] Taken together, Brockhoeft calls his view absolutism, and absolutism brooks absolutely no compromise with the American death culture. Absolutism springs from a total identification with the babies, and every person, every act, is judged with reference to the abortion issue.

For Brockhoeft, America is undeniably at war with the faithful remnant of Christians who would dare to stand against its killing industry. Satan is unambiguously involved in this war, and any action which deals a blow to Satan's murderous henchmen, the abortionists of America, is a laudable act in and of itself. For Brockhoeft, history is approaching its denouement where it is preordained that the people of God will be assured of power – either through their own actions, or as a consequence of the return of the Lord.

When that day comes, there will be a reckoning. All who were culpable, either by active participation in the abortion holocaust or by passive acquiescence to it, are in some measure guilty of a war crime, and a Nuremberg-like tribunal will be instituted to try these miscreants and to mete out punishments commensurate with the gravity of their crimes against the unborn:

> Believe now! Repent now! And know this: that if the brave among those who proclaim His name are too few to assume authority through their own (blessed by God) exertions, then the Lord Jesus Christ will soon return and install the few in office through almighty, irresistible power. Either way, unless you repent, there is no hope for you to escape. When the Lord came 2,000 years ago it was as a lamb, gentle, to show mercy. This time it will be to show justice.[69]

Thus, every woman who has had an abortion, every man who knowingly facilitated an abortion, will face capital charges and, if guilty, will pay the ultimate price.

Paul Hill's Defensive Action theories, no less Bible-centered than John Brockhoeft's absolutism, eschews grandiose millenarian proclamations in favor of a more pragmatic formulation of the problem. In the wake of Michael Griffin's resort to force, Hill's writings reflected the same sense of excitement as did those of John Brockhoeft. Unlike Brockhoeft, however, Hill was free to take decisive action, and, indeed, it was Griffin's act which ultimately convinced Hill to move from rhetoric to action. Indeed, once Griffin had shown the way, no careful reader of the rescue literature could have mistaken Hill's intent, nor could there have been any doubt as to the identity of the intended target. As early as September 1993, the *Life Advocate* ran a detailed story of the covert operation by which Paul Hill, John Burt, Don Gratton and Floyd Murray identified John Britton as David Gunn's replacement. According to John Burt, 'As suspected, the new killer in Pensacola is another of those bottom-feeders on the food chain... He is a circuit riding abortionist named John Bayard Britton of Fernandina Beach'.[70]

Paul Hill's Defensive Action statement, issued in the wake of the killing of David Gunn, today serves as a primary source of suspects for the current Portland Grand Jury's conspiracy inquiry.[71] The statement itself is deceptively simple. Issued concurrently with the Defensive Action declaration however, were a series of detailed scriptural studies which serve as the biblical foundation for Hill's resort to force. The original statement reads:

> We, the undersigned, declare the justice of taking all godly action necessary to defend innocent human life including the use of force. We proclaim that whatever force is legitimate to defend the life of the born child is legitimate to defend the life of an unborn child.
>
> We assert that if Michael Griffin did in fact kill David Gunn, his use of lethal force was justified provided it was carried out for the purpose of defending the lives of unborn children. Therefore, he ought to be acquitted of the charges against him.[72]

While the press and public concentrated on the implications of Hill's statement of support for Michael Griffin, movement literature gave considerably more attention to the more detailed expositions issued by Hill through the Defenders of the Defenders of Life Ministry in Bowie, Maryland. These are carefully reasoned treatises utilizing biblical proof texts (Exodus, Acts and Numbers are particularly cited) to support each point. Of this material, perhaps the most accessible is his 1994 essay, 'Should We Defend Born and Unborn Children With Force?'[73]

This essay systematically examines every facet of the Defensive Action argument; that is, for the resort to force in defense of the unborn. Hill opens his case by maintaining that there is an essential distinction between the wisdom of using deadly force to save babies and the justice of the action. Perhaps in his view, the pro-lifers are correct that in the current climate, it is not politically wise to use force, given the costs of taking the action both to the individual rescuer and to the wider pro-life cause. But in the eyes of God and by the laws of man, it is just to rescue those unjustly condemned to a violent and terrible death, and justice must outweigh the wisdom of political expediency when a precious human life hangs in the balance.

Reverend Hill then makes a biblical case for Defensive Action. Based on numerous proof texts, he concludes:

> *There is no question that deadly force should be used to protect innocent human life...* If you dispute this clear teaching of the Bible you will have assumed the unbearable burden of having to prove the justice of using force to protect the born, but not the unborn. *You can no more deny your responsibility to defend the unborn with force than you can deny the good Samaritan's responsibility to aid the wounded and the dying traveler.*[74]

Hill's ethical basis for Defensive Action is strongly millenarian. Citing the example of Phineas, he asserts that the individual has an over-riding ethical responsibility to do all in his power to turn God's just wrath from the American people:

> *Though sin has fanned God's righteous anger to a searing blaze, the*

shedding of guilty blood has cooled the flame and saved the people from destruction.[75]

What follows is a learned disputation answering ten objections to Defensive Action theory. Then, with odes to Dietrich Bonhoeffer and Phineas, Hill argues for the duty of waging a just war, for taking up arms in a just cause, and concludes with a call to action which is strongly reminiscent of the Posse Comitatus theory of the radical right wing:

> As we put our convictions into concrete actions, millions who are indifferent to abortion or accepting it as expedient will be forced to reconsider... When this occurs, the time will have arrived for the lower civil magistrate and those in positions of power to call the multitudes to unified action.[76]

Reverend Hill concludes with the prophesy that Defensive Action will ultimately succeed in stopping the abortion holocaust. This felicitous outcome rests on the twin foundations of an unbounded faith in the basic goodness of the American people and faith in the certainty of divine intervention on the side of the faithful remnant:

> There is an ultimate shock and horror that comes from considering that the death of Dr Gunn may have been justified. Once this shock has passed, the truth and duties involved will have an abiding effect. *These truths will grip men's minds and not release them from their duties.* Men will be forced to admit their horrendous neglect and will respond with zealous repentant hearts... *If we will but act in true repentance and faith God will bless our zealous but feeble efforts with abundant success.* Therefore, we must act in a decisive and timely manner.[77]

The Rescue Movement Today

> *Paul Hill and I have been writing. He's doing great. Thank the Lord! Some Christians are publicly saying he sinned in what he did, that he's a murderer, and even that he 'acted as Satan's agent'. That's blasphemous since he more accurately could be described as acting as God's agent. I'm totally convinced that God called Paul to do what he did, and he obeyed, while Christ went before, opened doors, prepared the way, and worked everything out. Whether or not we are willing to accept the truth of it, God himself kills people, so it can't always be wrong [Gen. 38:7, 10; Ex. 12:29; Acts 12:21–23]. God has people kill people [Ex. 32:26–28], and He has approved of some killing [Numbers 25; 1 Sam. 2:25]. To say that killing is always sinful is to call God sinful. God, however, does not approve of the shedding of innocent blood (murder), including the slaughter of defenseless*

little babies. Protecting babies, stopping the murders of the innocent, is right and just, even if it takes the use of force to do so. I certainly won't condemn Paul Hill. Shelley Shannon[78]

FIGURE 1
CARTOON BY SHELLEY SHANNON, 1994

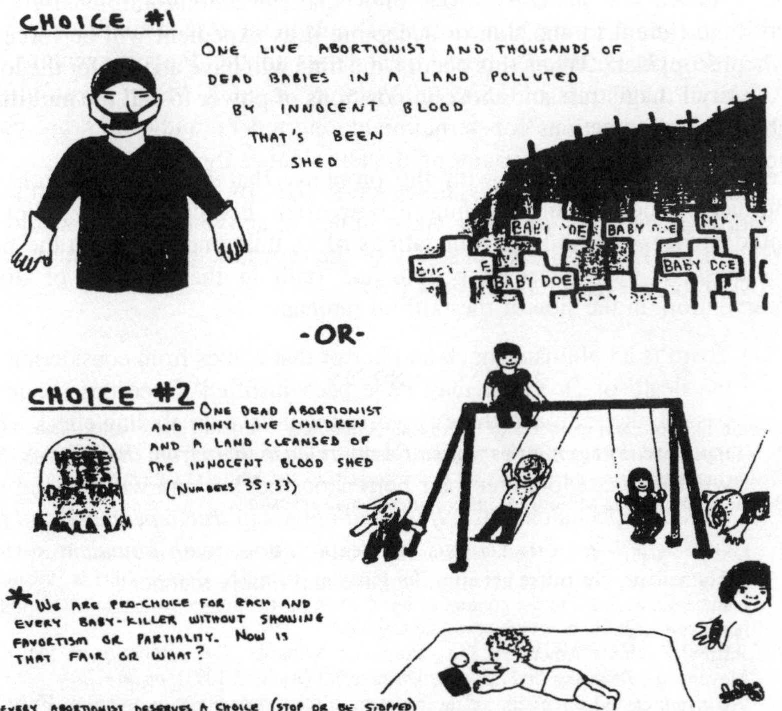

Note: Numbers 35:33 reads:
Do not pollute the land where you are. Bloodshed pollutes the land, and atonement cannot be made for the land on which blood has been shed, except by the blood of the one who shed it.

The resort to lethal force has split the rescue community, it has further distanced that community and its prophetic witness from the mainstream pro-life coalition, and it has allowed the courts and the Clinton administration to move against the rescue movement with such force as to make true rescue an all but suicidal enterprise. In response, the rescuers who have opted for Defensive Action, or who have lent public support to it, are increasingly isolated within the rescue community and estranged from the dominant culture. Symptomatic of this isolation is the intense bonding which links rescuers imprisoned for acts of violence. Shelley Shannon, John

Brockhoeft and Paul Hill, for example, lionize each other in their public writings and pronouncements. For Shelley Shannon in particular, this intense cult of devotion has been problematic. Shelley Shannon's public and private writing reveals a woman of great sincerity, piety, and most striking, humility. Her occasional remonstrations against these public affirmations of adoration have led to some highly emotional reactions – in particular from John Brockhoeft.[79]

At the same time, the threat of violence has had some deterrent effect on individual abortionists. This atmosphere of fear has had some short term utility to even the most non-violent of souls in the rescue community. Thus, when Joseph Foreman's post-Missionaries to the Preborn venture, The American Coalition of Life Activists, released a 'dirty dozen' list of abortionists, there was consternation among federal authorities, pro-choice activists, and presumably, among the abortionists themselves.[80]

This minor success pales, however, in light of the fact that such public relations maneuvers are being taken in lieu of active rescues. It would be a tragic irony if the primary casualty of the turn to Defensive Action would prove to be the rescue movement itself.

NOTES

I would like to thank members of the rescue community – in particular Shelley Shannon – for their support and assistance in this project. Thanks are due as well to Prof. David C. Rapoport for his encouragement at the genesis of this research, to the editorial patience of Prof. Michael Barkun, and to Doug Milford for his comments and suggestions.

1. Letter to author from Shelley Shannon, written from her home in Grants Pass, Oregon, almost two months before her arrest for shooting abortionist George Tiller in Wichita. The comment was made in the context of her disdain for the numerous lawsuits resulting from her involvement in non-violent rescue activities.
2. Jeffrey Kaplan, 'America's Last Prophetic Witness: The Literature of the Rescue Movement', *Terrorism and Political Violence* 5/3 (Autumn 1993), pp.58–77.
3. For a rare candid discussion of the problem in the rescue literature, see Rev. Bruce Evan Murch, 'Is Rescue Dead ... And If So, What Do We Do Now?' *Life Advocate* (Sept. 1994), pp.33, 40. Cf. David J. Garrow, 'Clinic Violence a Sure Sign Anti-Abortion Movement is Dying', *Anchorage Daily News*, 15 Jan. 1995, J4.
4. For the purposes of this research, the mainstream pro-life movement is treated as distinct from the rescue movement. The mainstream pro-life movement is composed of local and national organizations, with the National Right to Life perhaps playing the most prominent role. The pro-life movement functions as an umbrella for a broad spectrum of viewpoints, but is distinguished by its commitment to pursuing its goals through established legal and political channels. Rescue conversely was founded in conscious imitation of the Civil Rights Movement of the 1960s in which peaceful albeit extra-legal civil disobedience would be the primary avenue of protest.
5. The term 'pariah' was first applied to the rescue movement in 1989 by the only civil libertarian to have taken note of the unusually harsh treatment of rescuers and the remarkable silence of such champions of the right to protest as the American Civil Liberties Union. Nat Hentoff, '"Pain Compliance" Amounts to Torture', *The Advocate* 5/5 (Dec. 1989), p.15, repr. from undated issue of the *State Journal*, Lansing, Michigan.

6. Interview with Joe Scheidler, 2 Feb. 1993.
7. John Brockhoeft, 'The Brockhoeft Report 12', *Prayer + Action Weekly News* (Dec. 1993), pp.5–7. The reference to a 'lukewam church' is drawn from Revelation 3:15–16, 'I know your deeds, that you are neither cold nor hot. I wish you were either one or the other! So, because you are lukewarm – neither hot nor cold – I am about to spit you out of my mouth.'
8. Letter to author from Shelley Shannon, 24 Sept. 1994. Cf. 'Did She Aim for His Arms?' *Prayer + Action Weekly News* (March 1994), p.44; and Spencer Heinz, 'Praying With Fire: The Genesis of Shelley Shannon', *The Sunday Oregonian*, 14 Nov. 1993.
9. Cathy Ramey, 'Shots Fired: Griffin's Trial in Pensacola', *Life Advocate* (April 1994), pp.12–16. Paul Hill cites Griffin's act as the key event in convincing him of the necessity of, in his terms, Defensive Action to prevent the abortionist from carrying out his purpose. See 'Paul Hill Interview: November 26, 1994', *Prayer + Action Weekly News* (Nov. 1994), p.43. For a diverse collection of conversion stories, Paul deParrie, *The Rescuers* (Brentwood, TN: Wolgemuth & Hyatt, 1989).
10. The best exposition of this thesis is Joseph Foreman, *Shattering the Darkness: The Crisis of the Cross in the Church Today* (Montreat, NC: Cooling Spring Press, 1992). Cf. Randall Terry, *Accessory to Murder: The Enemies, Allies and Accomplices to the Death of Our Culture* (Brentwood, TN: Wolgemuth & Hyatt, 1990) and Randy Alcorn, *Is Rescuing Right: Breaking the Law to Save the Unborn* (Downers Grove, IL: InterVarsity Press, 1990).
11. John Brockhoeft, 'The Brockhoeft Report 12', *Prayer + Action Weekly News* (Sept. 1994), p.11.
12. This sociological generalization is drawn from my own research among imprisoned rescuers, and is confirmed by observations of the rescue community in Chicago and elsewhere. Cf. deParrie, *Rescuers* (note 9).
13. John Brockhoeft, 'The Brockhoeft Report 10', *Prayer + Action Weekly News* (June 1994), p.5. The source for this view is credited to a public school history textbook; Henry W. Bragdon and Samuel McCutchen, *History of a Free People*.
14. The genesis of *Accessory to Murder* may be found in Terry's incendiary Letter from Fulton County Jail, 10 Oct. 1989. See 'Randy Terry Writes From Jail', *The Advocate* (Nov. 1989), pp.8–10. Cf. Kaplan (note 2), p.67.
15. A good, published source of these reminiscences is Josephine County Right to Life, 'Testimonies from Jailed Rescuers: Operation Rescue Siege of Atlanta – July–Oct '88'. Cf. Tom Watson, 'Abortion Opponents Charge Police Brutality, Declare 'War'', *USA Today*, 5 Oct. 1988; or 'Police Get Tough at Protest', *Atlanta Daily News*, 5 Oct. 1988.
16. The participation of homosexual activists in clinic confrontations with rescuers was noted in Kaplan (note 2), p.72 n.9. The presence of these activists as escorts was confirmed in my interview with Coleen Connell, the head of the ACLU's Reproductive Rights Project in Chicago, 14 Feb. 1993.
17. For a view from the perspective of the escorts, see Judith A. Dilrorio and Michael R. Nusbaumer, 'Securing Our Sanity: Anger Management Among Abortion Escorts', *Jnl of Contemporary Ethnography* 21/4 (Jan. 1993), pp.411–38. For a less enlightening polemic, see Faye Ginsburg, *Contested Lives: The Abortion Debate in an American Community* (Berkeley, CA: California UP, 1989).
18. For just such an explicit statement from the perspective of the Lambs of Christ, see Kaplan (note 2), p.63. 'Pro-abortion satanists' are noted as attending Shelley Shannon's trial. See Shelley Shannon, 'Shelley Shannon Trial From the Perspective of Shelley Shannon', *Prayer + Action Weekly News* (April 1994), p.4.
19. Shelley Shannon, 'Toward the Use of Force', *Prayer + Action Weekly News* (May 1994), p.55.
20. 'The Brockhoeft Report 1', *Prayer + Action Weekly News* (Dec. 1993), p.10. For a discussion of the social construction of Satanism in contemporary America, see Jeffrey Kaplan, 'Multigenerational Satanism: The Eternal Conspiracy', *American Studies* (forthcoming).
21. Rescuer Tom Herlihy ranks these cities according to the scale of police brutality and gives not overly fond reminiscences of each in an undated *New York Post* article reprinted in the Drexel Hill, Pennsylvania, newsletter, *The Rescuer*. Ray Kerrison, 'Police Brutality', *The Rescuer* 5/6 (May–June 1991), p.10. Randall Terry concurs with this list. For considerable

detail, see Terry (note 10), pp.137–68.

22. Shelley Shannon, unpub. notes, 13 Jan. 1990.
23. The events described herein have become a matter of established orthodoxy among rescuers. Prof. Michael Barkun notes that a Pittsburgh clinic escort of 'unimpeachable integrity' finds the following account to be not credible based on her own experiences in Pittsburgh, and on her knowledge of the city. This source recalls as well that Pittsburgh's heavily Catholic police force seemed in her view rather more sympathetic to the rescuers than to the escorts. She notes as well that after a break-in to the clinic in question, the clinic suffered over $20,000 in damage due to tar which was poured over the equipment and furniture. While it is the norm rather than the exception that rescuers and clinic escorts see the same events in diametrically opposite ways, and while it is impossible to find independent confirmation of these events, it is of paramount importance that rescuers believe the version of events published in the rescue and the religious literature without reservation, and react accordingly.
24. Ray Kerrison (note 21). Events in Pittsburgh are described in brief in a full page advertisement in the mainstream Catholic newspaper, *The Wanderer*. 'Sexually Molested Pro-Life Women Seek Justice: Offenders May Get Off Free', *The Wanderer*, 3 Jan. 1991, p.10. For sources in the rescue literature, see 'Pittsburgh Police Abuse Rescuers', *The Advocate* (May 1989), p.4; and 'Pittsburgh Nightmare: 'I Wish They'd Broken My Arms", *The Advocate* (Nov. 1990), p.24.
25. Shelley Shannon, unpub. prison notes. Several testimonies from Atlanta are available to this research, but few are as reflective – and occasionally quite humorous – as those of Shelley Shannon. It is instructive of conditions in Atlanta that Shelley Shannon's notes contain an account of her arrest at her Grants Pass home almost immediately upon her return to Oregon. This incarceration is described as a pleasant holiday weekend in comparison to Atlanta's hospitality.
26. A good source for the philosophical dimensions of this split is the anti-violence consensus of pro-lifers and pacifist rescue leaders in 'Killing Abortionists: A Symposium', *First Things* 48 (Dec. 1994), pp.24–31.
27. This latest revision of the *Army of God Manual* was repr. in *The Prayer + Action Weekly News* (Dec. 1994), p.11. It is notable that the spelling of 'Amerika' strongly recalls the practice of 1960s left wing radicals at a similar stage of despair that the nation could be reformed by legal means.
28. The three proposed restrictions were: (1) The abortion must be performed in a state-accredited hospital; (2) The abortion must be approved by the hospital's abortion committee; and (3) The attending physician's medical judgement must be confirmed by independent examinations of the patient by at least two other physicians [410 US 179 or 93 S. Ct. 739]. An excellent scholarly source for the legal and political implications of the abortion controversy is Barbara Hinkson Craig and David M. O'Brien, *Abortion and American Politics* (Chatham, NJ: Chatham House, 1993). For an explicitly pro-life point of view, see Marvin Olasky, *Abortion Rites: A Social History of Abortion in America* (Wheaton, IL: Crossway Books, 1992).
29. Letter from Portland, OR, legal firm to Shelley Shannon, 10 July 1992.
30. For a brief synopsis of RICO and the *Now v. Scheidler* suit, see Kaplan (note 2), pp.75–6, n.40. An earlier suit was filed in Portland, interview with Kathy Rumey, 16 Oct. 1995.
31. See 'High Court Upholds RICO', and 'Supreme Court Issues Narrow; Harmful Decision in NOW's RICO Suit', *Life Advocate* (March 1994), p.20. It is highly significant that so important a decision – a decision which made it unlikely that any rescuer could hope to have a RICO judgment overturned in the courts of America – was relegated to p.20 and was reported in brief, almost terse terms. For an earlier, somewhat more optimistic report on the occasion of the Supreme Court's agreeing to hear the suit, see 'Clinton Administration Urges Overturning NOW v. Scheidler Acquittal', *Life Advocate* (July 1993), pp.37–8.
32. Ronald Reagan, *Abortion and the Conscience of the Nation* (Nashville, TN: Nelson, 1984).
33. Barbara Hinkson Craig and David M. O'Brien (note 28).
34. Interview with Fr. Norman Weslin, 5 Aug. 1993. Wonderfully illustrative photographs making the rounds in rescue circles feature Bill Clinton with a large 666 written on his forehead. A theologically dubious example has a leatherclad Bill Clinton, replete with saxophone, and

a nattily dressed Hillary against a backdrop of memorial posters for aborted babies, with both Clintons sporting 666 on their foreheads. 'Clinton Display at Picket draws Federal Attention', *Life Advocate* (Dec. 1993/ Jan. 1994), p.8. An excellent source for the political contexts into which the Antichrist has been projected through the ages is Bernard McGinn, *Antichrist* (NY: Harper San Francisco, 1994).

35. For a good capsule summary of the tactical models of early rescue from the abolitionists to the Civil Rights movement, see Phillip F. Lawler, *Operation Rescue: A Challenge to the Nation's Conscience* (Huntington, IN: Our Sunday Visitor, 1992), pp.136–41. For a brilliant analysis, see Foreman (note 10), pp.25–36.
36. 'Congress Hears Truth on Pro-Abort Violence', *Life Advocate* (July 1993), p.15.
37. 'FACE Bill Passed, Signed by Clinton', *Life Advocate* (July 1994), pp.8–9. Sentencing provisions include six months incarceration and a $10,000 fine for a first 'exclusively non-violent' offense and 18 months and a $25,000 for each additional offense thereafter.
38. After some puzzlement in rescue ranks, Salvi's statement was characterized as delusional and psychotic and Salvi himself treated as a curiosity with no connection to the rescue movement. 'Year Ends With Shootings at East Coast Abortuaries', *Life Advocate* (Feb. 1995), pp.20–22.
39. The ongoing Brockhoeft Report discusses the fires he set in abortion clinics in Ohio and Florida in considerable detail. See 'The Brockhoeft Report 1–4', *Prayer + Action Weekly News* (Dec. 1993), and 'The Brockhoeft Report 5–6', *Prayer + Action Weekly News* (Feb. 1994). Letter from Marjorie Reed, 25 Jan. 1993. Marjorie Reed, currently serving a 12-year sentence for 'aiding and abetting' a clinic arson, is considerably less well known outside rescue circles than John Brockhoeft. For a rare public appearance, see Marjorie Reed, 'Oh Please Spare Me (Or a Day Before the Grand Jury)', *Life Advocate* (Aug. 1994), p.38.
40. Michael Bray, *A Time to Kill* (Portland, OR: AFL, 1994).
41. The Nazi metaphor is common to the larger pro-life constituency as well. See C. Everett Koop, 'The Slide to Auschwitz', in Reagan (note 32), pp.41–73.
42. Corrie Ten Boom is something of a cult icon to rescuers and to other members of the evangelical subculture. She is the stuff of sermons, articles, and even comic books to inspire children. A good example of this praxis in the context of rescue is 'Kenny Sacht: A Pastor Continues to Rescue despite upheaval in His Church', *The Advocate* (Feb. 1990), p.3. For an early source positing Ten Boom and Dietrich Bonhoeffer as equivalent models for emulation, see Randall Terry, *Operation Rescue* (Springdale: Pai Whitaker House, 1988).
43. Joe Bartlett, 'Dietrich and George and the Time Machine', *Prayer + Action Weekly News* (May 1994), p.15. This Christian 'science fiction' includes a paean to Shelley Shannon as a 'Bonhoeffer-like figure'.
44. Klaus Scholder, *The Churches and the Third Reich, Volume One: 1918–1934* (Philadelphia, PA: Fortress Press, 1988), p.276. Scholder's two volume history is the best introduction to Bonhoeffer's theology in its historical context. For a good example of how this challenging material is distilled and disseminated to rescuers of a non-scholarly bent, see Alcorn (note 10), pp.111–16. So vital is Bonhoeffer's theology beyond the narrow worlds of rescue and evangelical Christianity that the American Academy of Religion plans to hold a panel discussion on Bonhoeffer's legacy at its 1995 meeting in Philadelphia.
45. Shelley Shannon, 'Toward the Use of Force', *Prayer + Action Weekly News* (May 1994), p.55; 'Did She Aim for His Arms: Report on the Trial of Rachelle Shannon', *Prayer + Action Weekly News* (March 1994), p.47. She recalls two of these titles as: *Life Together* (note 51) and *Letters and Papers From Prison*.
46. The preamble of the Order's declaration states: 'We, the following, being of sound mind and under no duress, do hereby sign this document of our own free will, stating forthrightly and without fear that we declare ourselves to be in full and unrelenting state of war with those forces seeking and consciously promoting the destruction of our faith and our race'. See Kevin Flynn and Gary Gerhardt, *The Silent Brotherhood* (NY: Free Press, 1989), pp.357–8. Good sources for the war imagery of the early rescue movement are Randall Terry's first two books, *Operation Rescue* (note 42) and *Accessory to Murder* (note 10).
47. 'The Brockhoeft Report 15', *Prayer + Action Weekly News* (Jan. 1995), p.11.
48. 'The Brockhoeft Report 14', ibid. (Nov. 1994), p.54.

49. 'Paul Hill Interview' (note 9), p.42.
50. 'The Brockhoeft Report 12', *Prayer + Action Weekly News* (Sept. 1994), p.15. John Brockhoeft would not take this (or any other) public position without biblical warrant. In this case, his formulation is based on Ecclesiastes 3:8 'A time to love, and a time to hate; a time of war, and a time of peace'.
51. Imprecatory prayer was introduced in these pages in Kaplan (note 2), p.77, n.49. While it would be impossible to document the efficacy of this spiritual weapon, the Missionaries and other rescuers believe in its power without question. More, it should be noted that as of 1991, Milwaukee abortionists have had unusually high incidences of strokes (Drs Tarver and Woo) and sudden death (Dr Leon Gillman), all within the space of a year, and all after having been the subjects of imprecation. 'Craft Quits!: Sixth Abortionist to Stop Killing in 10 Months', *The Advocate* (May 1991), p.6. The Missionaries did not however pioneer the use of the imprecatory psalms as a weapon of war. No less a figure than Dietrich Bonhoeffer counseled:

    > Can we, then, pray the imprecatory psalms? In so far as we are sinners and express evil thoughts in a prayer of vengeance, we dare not do so. But in so far as Christ is in us, the Christ who took all the vengeance of God upon himself, who met God's vengeance in our stead, who thus – stricken by the wrath of God – and in no other way, could forgive his enemies, who himself suffered the wrath that his enemies might go free – we, too, as members of this Jesus Christ, can pray these psalms, through Jesus Christ, from the heart of Jesus Christ.

    Dietrich Bonhoeffer, *Life Together*, John W. Doberstein, trans. (San Francisco, Harper & Row, 1954), p.34.
52. This letter was written to a rescuer closely identified with the resort to force. The names of both the author and recipient will be withheld.
53. Joan Andrews tells her story in Joan Andrews with John Cavanaugh O'Keefe, *I Will Never Forget You* (San Francisco: Ignatius Press, 1989). Butyric acid became something of a fad among rescuers determined to close a clinic but unwilling or unable to take sterner measures. Shelley Shannon appears to have been among these *aficionados*. 'Shannon Hints at Butyric Acid Involvements', *Life Advocate* (April 1994), p.6. That the tactic remains in use today, see 'Clinic Acid Dosing Raises Fear', *Life Advocate* (Oct. 1993), p.16.
54. Joseph M. Scheidler, *Closed: 99 Ways to Stop Abortion* (Westchester, IL: Crossway, 1985). Joseph Scheidler's role in the movement is controversial. The father of the rescue movement, Scheidler felt it necessary to update his book in 1992, stressing his commitment to non-violence against persons. At the same time, Scheidler never met a rescuer or pro-lifer he did not like. Thus, he gives unqualified support and counsel to all who ask, whether they be committed pacifists, clinic bombers or those who would resort to lethal force. Thus too the interest shown in Scheidler by the current Portland Grand Jury inquiry into the possibility of a national conspiracy against the abortion industry, and so too the decision of NOW to file the flagship RICO suit against Scheidler and his Pro-Life Action League. On the conspiracy inquiry, see 'FBI Undertakes Conspiracy Inquiry Into Clinic Violence', *New York Times*, 4 Aug. 1994; and 'Abortion: Who's Behind the Violence?' *US News and World Report*, 14 Nov. 1994.
55. This intensely mystical experience of unity with the unborn appears to be evocative of the voices heard by Joan of Arc and by a long line of medieval female saints engaged in intensely emotional devotions.
56. An excellent example of the lengths to which this can go can be seen in the pretzel-like contraption employed by two rescuers in Fargo, ND. These rescuers chained themselves with Kryptonite locks into a clothes dryer, and in turn had these dryers fixed into the body of an old car with an array of chains and metal. The car was then pushed in front of the clinic door. One of the rescuers, Tim Lindgren, commented that his predicament, helplessly encased in total darkness, unable to know what was happening outside of his steel tomb, reminded him of the unborn baby in the womb. 'Rescuers Go Far in Fargo to Save Babies', *Life Advocate* (Jan. 1995), p.19.
57. 'The Brockhoeft Report 3', *Prayer + Action Weekly News* (Dec. 1993), p.31.

58. Movement figures have clinic bombings peaking in 1984 when 18 clinics were bombed and 11 others suffered damage from arson. These numbers sharply declined from 1985, although the numbers are in some dispute in movement literature. Kaplan (note 2), p.60. For its part, the National Abortion Federation generally agrees with these numbers, finding 1984 to be the most active year with 18 clinics bombed and 6 damaged by arson. NAF figures from 1977–91 count 34 bombings and 60 arsons. Dallas A. Blanchard, *The Anti-Abortion Movement and the Rise of the Religious Right: From Polite to Fiery Protest* (NY: Twayne Publishers, 1994), pp.56–7.
59. For a riveting step by step account of the destruction of an abortion clinic, see 'The Brockhoeft Report 5 and 6', *Prayer + Action Weekly News* (Feb. 1994). For an intensely negative scholarly polemic against clinic bombers, rescuers and conservative Christians in general, see Dallas A. Blanchard and Jerry J. Prewitt, *Religious Violence and Abortion* (Gainesville, FL: Florida UP, 1993). Blanchard's vendetta is reprised in Blanchard, *The Anti-Abortion Movement* (note 58). Cf. Julie Ingersoll's review of the Blanchard and Prewitt volume in *Terrorism and Political Violence* 6/1 (Spring 1994), pp.98–100.
60. Letter to author from imprisoned rescuer, name withheld, Feb. 1994.
61. The Prisoners of Christ ministry was a function of the Missionaries to the Preborn in Milwaukee. In the wake of the split between Pastor Matt Trewellah and the Rev. Joseph Foreman, the POC newsletter has relocated with Rev. Foreman to California.
62. Name of author and recipient withheld, 1991.
63. For details of these lesser known cases, see 'Bottom of the Barrel: Abortionists – The Dregs of Society', *Life Advocate* (Nov. 1994), pp.10–14; 'Canadian Abortionist Shot', ibid. (Dec. 1994), pp.28–9; and 'Canada Targets Pro-Lifers: Media and Government Forces Seek to Destroy Pro-Life Movement', ibid. (Jan. 1995), pp.10–15.
64. Letter from Shelley Shannon, 10 June 1994. She is reacting to Jeffrey Kaplan, 'America's Last Prophetic Witness' (note 2), p.59.
65. Joseph M. Scheidler (note 54), pp.154–6. Cf. 'Taking the Battle Home: Tactics Get Tough With Abortionists', *Life Advocate* (Feb. 1994), pp.10–13. For an example of the occasional success story, see 'After Home Picket, Abortionist Quits', ibid. (July 1993), pp.18–19.
66. There is no dearth of reporting on abortionists who seek other means of livelihood out of fear of violence in the rescue literature. Typical are 'Abortionist Shooting Spurs Another to Quit', and 'Women's Center Discontinues Abortions', *Life Advocate* (Nov. 1994), pp.28, 31. For an example of the justifiable homicide argument, see Cathy Ramey, 'Strategy for the Future: The Pro-Life Exception or "By Any Means Necessary"', *Life Advocate* (July 1993), pp.66–7. On the dearth of candidates to become abortionists, see 'Abortion Clinics Search for Doctors in Scarcity', *New York Times*, 31 March 1993; and 'Planned Parenthood Starting to Train Doctors in Abortion', ibid., 19 June 1993.
67. 'The Brockhoeft Report 4', *Prayer + Action News* (Dec. 1993), p.48.
68. The ongoing 'Brockhoeft Report' is serialized in *Prayer + Action Weekly News*, where the first installment appeared in Dec. 1993. Shelley Shannon was until her arrest the original editor. Fortuitously, Dave Leach in Iowa, editor of the various *Prayer + Action Weekly News* editions, stepped forward to continue the work. Perhaps the best summaries of absolutism are contained in the Dec. 1993 edition containing 'The Brockhoeft Report 1–4', and 'The Brockhoeft Report 7', *Prayer + Action Weekly News* (March 1994).
69. 'The Brockhoeft Report 7', ibid., p.19.
70. 'Florida Pro-Lifers ID Replacement for Gunn', *Life Advocate* (Sept. 1993), p.19. The term 'bottom feeder' is taken from a comic book issued by a Texas ministry portraying abortionists as the catfish-like bottom feeders of the medical profession. The comic book was mailed to students in medical schools across the country. See '"Bottom Feeder" Humor Upsets Abortionists', ibid., p.21.
71. 'FBI and BATF Start Reno-Inspired "Witchhunt"', *Life Advocate* (Oct. 1994), p.8.
72. 'Pro-Life Pastors and Leaders Declare Justice of the Use of Force', *Life Advocate* (October 1993), 18. The statement can be found as well in the *Prayer + Action Weekly News* (Nov. 1994), pp.17, 19.
73. Paul J. Hill, 'Should We Defend Born and Unborn Children With Force?' *Prayer + Action Weekly News* (Sept. 1994), pp.25–38. This essay was written to further clarify points made

by Rev. Hill on the occasion of his appearance on the Phil Donahue television program. A transcript of that interview can be found in 'Phil & Hill', *Prayer + Action Weekly News* (Aug. 1994), pp.45–8. For other useful material on Paul Hill, see: 'Paul Hill Interview (note 9), pp.42–6; Paul J. Hill, 'Who Killed the Innocent – Michael Griffin or Dr. David Gunn?' *Life Advocate* (Aug. 1993), pp.40–3; and 'An Interview With Paul Hill', ibid. (Jan. 1995), pp.26–9. On Hill's killing of John Britton and James Barrett, as well as the strong condemnation of the act from pro-life and rescue quarters, 'Hill Says, "Now is the Time...".', *Life Advocate* (Sept. 1994), pp.10–15.

74. Hill (note 73), p.27.
75. Ibid., p.28. The example of Phineas and his resort to deadly force in a successful effort to shield his people from the wrath of a justly angry God is of considerable importance to a number of contemporary American millenarian appeals. In the world of Christian Identity for example, Richard Kelly Hoskins draws on this source to posit a phantom order of avengers from the dawn of time, the Phineas Priesthood. See Richard Kelly Hoskins, *Vigilantes of Christendom* (Lynchburg, VA: Publishing Co., 1990). Cf. my review essay on the influence of this text in *Syzygy: Jnl of Alternative Religion and Culture* 1/2–3, pp.271–3.
76. Ibid., pp.36–7. The Posse Comitatus was a (very) loosely organized movement in the American heartland which rejected the legitimacy of all civil authority above the level of county sheriff. For an introduction through the perspective of the late Posse founder William Potter Gale, see Cheri Seymour, *Committee of the States: Inside the Radical Right* (Mariposa, CA: Camden Place Communications, 1991).
77. Hill (note 73), p.37.
78. Letter from Shelley Shannon, 9 Sept. 1994.
79. The intensity of this emotion can be glimpsed in 'An Open Letter From Joe Bartlett to Shelley', *Prayer + Action Weekly News* (Oct. 1994), pp.43–7. This letter, most notable for comparing Shelley Shannon to Dietrich Bonhoeffer, canonizing her and Paul Hill as movement martyrs, and excommunicating Michael Griffin from their number due to his having 'flip-flopped, compromised, betrayed his friends, and threw away his honor for nothing', was written in lieu of an installment of 'The Brockhoeft Report' due to Brockhoeft's despair at having been asked by Shelley Shannon to leave her out of his writings lest she be further glorified for her actions.
80. Those named on the list are:

Joseph Booker (Jackson, MS)
David Allred (Los Angeles, CA)
James and Elizabeth Newhall (Portland, OR)
Thomas Greysinger (Fort Washington, MD)
Douglas Karpen (Houston, TX)
Paul Seamers (Oconomowok, WI)
George Tiller (Andover, KS)
Warren Hern (Boulder, CO)
Steven Kaali (Dobbs Ferry, NY)
George Kabacy (Canby, OR)
Howard Silverman (Boston, MA)
Ulrich Klopfer (Fort Wayne, IN)

Of these, recent television news reports have singled out Joseph Booker as at greatest risk, and Mississippi rescuer and signer of Paul Hill's original Direct Action statement, Roy McMillan, as the most likely to act. On the warmth of the McMillan/Booker relationship, see 'Abortionist Accused of Pointing Gun at Crowd of Anti-Abortion Protesters', *Life Advocate* (June 1994), p.32. On the history of the ACLA and its actions in Mississippi, see 'ACLA: New National Activist Coalition Begins in Mississippi', *Life Advocate* (Oct. 1994), pp.15–18.

[15]

A Manual of Islamic Fundamentalist Terrorism

RAPHAEL ISRAELI

The current wave of so-called 'suicide-bombings' perpetrated by Muslims has been part of Shi'ite Islamic idealization of suffering and death, meant for the Believer to identify with the ordeal of Imam Hussein in the seventh century CE. It was revived by the Shi'ite Hizballah in Lebanon against the Americans and the Israelis, and then expanded by Sunnite Palestinian Islamists, such as Hamas and Islamic Jihad, and even by avowedly 'secular' Palestinian groups such as the Fatah's al-Aqsa Brigades and Tanzim. But the justifications for all those groups are, nevertheless, curiously Islamic. This article presents the text written by a prominent cleric and diffused in the Palestinian media, rationalizing suicide-bombing as the ultimate mode of struggle against Muslim enemies.

Apologia

In June 1988, at the height of the first *intifada* declared by the Palestinians against 'Israeli occupation and repression', a text was published as an appendix to an issue of the Muslim fundamentalist organ *al-Islam wa-Filastin* (Islam and Palestine), which carried a very detailed and intriguing analysis of what it took to become an 'Islamikaze'.[1] This term was coined by the present author in 1997, when he described the making of the new brand of Muslim terrorists in Afghanistan. It was a fallacy to dub these people 'suicide-bombers', because their primary concern was to kill their enemies, not themselves, though they were ready to sacrifice themselves in the process.

Typologically, they came closest to the Japanese *kamikaze* of the Pacific War in World War II, and therefore it was suggested to combine that term with Islam and create a new word.[2] When that Arabic text came to the attention of this author, after the 'Islamikaze' term had been coined and diffused, *post factum* justification was added to warrant the present article which establishes a linkage between the outer-objective definition of 'Islamikaze', and the inner-subjective terminology suggested by the Arab-Muslim writer of that text.

Introduction

A.J. Wensinck has demonstrated the resemblance between the Christian and Muslim doctrines of martyrology, down to small details and to the parallel development of the two. He has also shown that the ancient roots of both go back to the Jewish monotheistic concepts of death and martyrdom for the sake of God (*kiddush Hashem*), and also included philosophical and ascetic elements from Hellenic tradition.[3] Incidentally, even the etymological transition from the Qur'anic *shahid* as a 'witness' into the self-sacrificing martyr of later times[4] can be traced in Christian tradition as well, inasmuch as the 'witness' to the deeds of God in the New Testament, developed into martyrs.[5] Also in the domain of the rewards of the martyr, both traditions maintain he is promised an eternal life of bliss in the highest position in Paradise, close to God Himself and above the righteous and regular pious Believers. The martyr is assured of exoneration for his sins and from the torments of the Day of Judgment, and in both the martyr is the mediator who intercedes before God on behalf of Believers in order to alleviate the burden of their sins.

Understandably, during the lifetime of the Prophet and the expansion of Islam, the martyrs who perished in the battle acquired precedence over all other Believers. But when the Islamic Empire settled down and the fighting zeal receded, the expansion of Islam was pursued more by Sufi mystics and the question of martyrdom through other avenues came to the fore. If the mystic missionary put himself in the service of Islam at great risk, by traveling distances and penetrating uncharted territory, then why was his brand of martyrdom less than the classic fighter who died in combat? Interpretations of martyrdom as the supreme spiritual state of the Believer, who knows how to control his worldly desires and rein in his ambitions advanced to the forefront. Ghazali, the eminent medieval mystic (d. 1111), said that 'Anyone submitting (*Islam* = submission to the Will of Allah) totally to Allah in his battle against desires, is himself a martyr…'.[6]

Roots of the 'Islamikaze'

In the contemporary Middle East, due to the vicious conflict opposing the Arab-Muslims to Israel, and in consequence of the sustaining support the United States of America, and to a lesser extent the rest of the West, are perceived as extending to Israel, there has been a revival of the old notions of martyrdom. It is true that all Arab casualties of the half-dozen wars between Israel and its neighbors in the twentieth century were considered martyrs. But the Hizballah in Lebanon gave it the greatest impetus in the last two decades of the century. A new model of martyrdom was introduced, one where the Believer died in the process of destroying the enemy. The Hizballah derives from Shi'ite Islam, dominant in Iran, and one has to look at the trunk in order to comprehend the branches.

The re-living of the legendary suffering of Hussein in Karbalah in AD 680, before he was annihilated with his followers by Yazid – the son of the Umayyad founder – Mu'awiyya, is central in Shi'ite communities. The *ta'zia,* a kind of passion play, displayed on 'Ashura Day by processions of the pious who beat themselves, is the apex of identification with the suffering of Hussein.

Suffering as a theme unto itself, including self-inflicted bleeding and death, has become a way of life for the devout Shi'ite, a fashion of expressing selfless sacrifice in honor of the assassinated son of Ali, the first true Imam and successor of the Prophet, who had been skipped over by three 'imposter' Caliphs who took over power before him. The bitterness of the Shi'ia, the downtrodden and persecuted branch of Islam (a branch in Lebanon called itself the 'Downtrodden on Earth', as a sign of honor), is best expressed in the anger and rush for self-sacrifice on the one hand, and the posthumous glorification of the martyrs after their death.

When young Iranians were encouraged to clear minefields during the first Gulf War (1980–88), with 'keys to Paradise' hanging on their innocent necks, their parents were congratulated by family friends for the martyrdom of their children. All those horrendous sacrifices were immortalized in the memorial for the martyrs in Teheran, a water fountain colored blood-red, symbolizing the endless flow of suffering and blood.

'The skies are shrouded in black, rivers of tears are flowing, Hussein arrives in Karbalah to sacrifice himself for Allah. This is the 'Ashura story, tend your ears to listen to its sadness, let your tears flow for the King of the Martyrs, because he will bring you to Paradise'.[7] These are lyrics to a song of those mourning 'musical-passions' re-enacted in Iran and elsewhere to commemorate the martyrdom of Hussein. These reenactments, and the generally militant demands by the Shi'ites for their rights, adopted a low profile for centuries (a state of *intidhar* – namely waiting and expectation), associated with the principle of *Taqiyya* (dissimulation), adopted after the mysterious disappearance (not death) of the Twelveth Imam for self-preservation in a hostile environment. That state of expectation for the return of the absent Imam provided the driving power behind Twelver Shi'ism, inasmuch as it encouraged the Believers to suffer and wait. The more they waited and suffered, the closer was his return (like the 'pangs of the Messiah' in Judaism). If anyone claimed to be the re-appearing Imam, he was immediately condemned as an imposter, and treated accordingly.

The last decades of the twentieth century, however, saw an ideological and political quantum jump under Ayatullah Khomeini, which has taken the

Shi'a from passivity and expectation to activity and aggression, namely making the human will predominate over fate or over the 'natural course of events'. This is possible in Shi'ite theology which recognizes the head of the clerical hierarchy as the *marja' taqlid*, the supreme reference who commands the emulation of the Believers.

In fact this major figure, who gains his superior status through his scholarship and religious authority, is the supreme *mujtahid*, the 'striver' to interpret the will of the Hidden Imam who is the actual ruler of the world. The *mujtahid* thus acquires in the Shi'a the power of legislator, and his rulings are the law. This is the reason why Khomeini spoke about *wilayat faqih* (the rule of the jurist), for only such Heaven- and Imam-inspired jurists, who are the upper echelon of the mullahs, could be *clairvoyant* enough to detect the Truth and pass it on to others. Khomeini himself wrote that 'only the mullahs are able to take people to the streets and motivate them to die for Islam, and bring them to beg that they be allowed to spill their blood for Islam'.[8]

The new activism brought about by the Islamic Revolution in Iran has taken up the tragic death of Hussein, which used to be viewed as a murderous and cowardly act. Hussein becomes not someone to be mourned, but a heroic leader in battle and a model worthy of emulation on the way to Paradise. He, the paradigm of martyrdom, will ensure the admission to heaven of the new generations of martyrs. Hence we learned of the flocking of millions of adults and children to the mosques in Tehran when the war with Iraq broke out (October 1980) and a call for volunteers to the front was sounded by the government.

The demand for martyrdom by far exceeded the needs of the military. Children were urged to go to the front without their parents' permission, and were used to clear minefields. They expressed their happiness at 'rushing to Paradise in unison with their friends', under the promise that in Paradise they would be able to unite and pursue their worldly worry-free life.

The eagerness for death through martyrdom often prompts young Iranian demonstrators to join processions, covered by their death shrouds, to signify that not only they defy death, but that they are also ready for it. They were swept under the magic rhetoric of their leader, whom some saw an incarnation of the Hidden one, when he said that life was illusory and merely a corridor to the real life in Paradise, and therefore not worth living. The activation of the martyrdom of Hussein, which in Iran has involved a real change in the *ta'zia* ceremonies on 'Ashura Day, has also transcended Iran's boundaries and been made a model for other Shi'ites, as in Lebanon where Hizballah and the Amal Shi'ites have adopted the same style.

Moreover, Hizballah, the active long arm of Iran in its quest to internationalize the Iranian Islamic Revolution, has been adopting a militant and aggressive stance in its pursuance. It not only routinely uses violence on the Israeli–Lebanese borders, but is known to aid terrorism across the world against Israeli and Jewish interests, such as blowing up the Jewish Community Center and the Israeli Embassy in Buenos Aires in the 1990s. It also cooperates with the Palestinian *intifada*, both in coordinating joint operations against Israel and in supplying arms and instruction in terrorist warfare. The Karine A affair, which exploded into the open when a ship loaded with Hizballah weapons was seized by Israel in the Red Sea on its way to Gaza (2002), illustrates this connection.

Above all, the doctrine of the 'Islamikaze', that is, active death in martyrdom, was revived by the Hizballah. The first acts were performed in the early 1980s against the American and Israeli presence in Lebanon, but as the Israeli presence in the southern part of that country wore on, those operations were intensified until they became routine. It took another decade or so before that mode of action was emulated by other Muslim terrorist groups, most notoriously the Sunnite Hamas and Jihad.

The transition occurred when fundamentalist Sunnite scholars, such as Sheikh Qardawi, provided the missing link between the 'natural' vying for suffering of fundamentalist Shi'ism, which pushed martyrdom to emulate the slain Imam Hussein; and the general Islamic hallowed idea of martyrdom and its rewards, now to inflict damage on the enemy, even at the cost of one's life. The long succession of *fatwas* (religious verdicts) delivered to fill this gap provided rationalization to the now mostly Palestinian Sunnite 'Islamikaze' groups to launch their deadly attacks.

Palestinian 'Islamikaze'

The Sunnite fundamentalist groups adopted the Shi'ite ways, not only by embracing the Iranian and Hizballah mode of operation, but also by creating their own version of the supreme sacrifice and suffering inherent in the Shi'ite *ta'zia* ceremony. In the field of battle and terrorism for the sake of Allah, we have seen 19 members of al-Qaeda committing collective 'Islamikaze' acts on American soil on 11 September 2001. Al-Qaeda fighters in Afghanistan defied death in the face of American air power, as do Hamas and Islamic Jihad in the Palestinian Authority, the Gama'at in Egypt, the Abu Sayyaf group in the Philippines, or the Muslim terrorists in Kashmir and India. In Algeria they kill their own compatriots as they attack foreigners.

This Sunni terrorism becomes more daring in the operations, to the extent that it becomes more common and banal. Not only the massive 'Islamikaze' attack on 11 September, with probably more to come, but especially the almost daily attacks in Israel against civilians by Hamas and Islamic Jihad, have rendered these harrowing acts routine, to the point that they risk becoming accepted as 'part of life', as if they were God-ordained and impervious to human preventive initiative.

The Sunni fundamentalist groups are able to draw other Sunnis into the circle of self-sacrificing terrorist groups, like the *Tanzim*, the *Aqsa* or the Popular Front among the Palestinians, who are not avowedly fundamentalists or Muslim zealots. It is quite extraordinary to watch members of the Marxist-oriented Popular Front talking of *jihad* and *istishhad (*martyrdom) when they set out for their operations. They realize the high status of the 'Islamikaze' in their society, and since they act against the same enemy, they have no compunction gaining popularity through using fundamentalist vocabulary and discourse. The Sunni 'Islamikaze' are edging towards their Iranian model not only ideologically, but even in the mores and patterns of behavior. For example, the headgear of the Hamas people parading in the streets of the Palestinian Authority, under the permissive eyes of its security forces, the video cassettes they leave behind for their loved ones are often used by their operators as a 'patrimony', as an 'educational' tool to recruit others; the slogans, citations from the Holy Scriptures, and words of praise about martyrdom, are all ominous imitations of the Shi'ite model.

Most intriguing, however, is the example of the Sunnite *ta'zia*-in-reverse, widely and repeatedly practiced by Hamas and perhaps others. We have seen that the Shi'ite martyrdom was closely associated with suffering and bitterness, first out of passive identification with the supreme martyr, Imam Hussein, and then the Islamic Revolution, which pushed the protest into the domain of action, remained essentially a 'within-the-family' sort of affair. Hamas and Islamic Jihad have developed a new pattern to re-play, re-emphasize, boast about and delight in the suffering they inflict on their victims.

Indeed, every now and then, especially when the Palestinian Authority fails to intervene following major acts of terrorism which leave dozens of Israelis dead or maimed, local chapters of Hamas set up processions to mark the event. With their headgear of the *shahid*, slogans of martyrdom shouted, Israeli and American flags burned and puppets representing Israeli and American leaders stabbed by a frantic crowd, they arrive at the end of the procession, during which, invariably, they shoot abundantly in the air with illegal weapons – and then the harrowing orgy of 'celebrations' begins.

We have become 'accustomed' to the sights of Palestinians and other Muslims deliriously and ecstatically exhibiting jubilation after a 'successful' terrorist attack against America has been carried out –

exemplified in the Twin Towers and Pentagon attacks – or against Israel or Jews at large, with no one to rein them in. On these occasions they distribute sweets, dance in the streets, and cry slogans of 'Allah Akbar' – the war-cry of Muslims in general – as if to attribute to Him those great deeds against their sworn enemies.

What the demonstrators in person are unable to deal their enemies they perform symbolically, praising Allah for His intercession on their behalf. Often, the latest target destroyed, for example an Israeli bus with dozens of passengers, is meticulously reconstructed in paper, cardboard and cloth, painted so as to imitate the original, and then set ablaze to cries of delight of watching crowds. All the while, the perpetrators of the actual horror against the actual Israeli bus or its successors run around the stage shooting long bursts in the air, shouting blood-freezing war cries, invoking the Power of Allah, smashing the burned bus carcass, and stabbing with their bayonets the 'remnants' of the slain 'passengers'.

In Nablus, an 'exhibition' of this kind was presented to the general public in the city public square, which showed in detail the replicas of blown-up limbs and body pieces of Israelis that had perished in a restaurant attack by Hamas 'Islamikaze'. The reports of the deeply disgusted foreign correspondents, and the protests of the Israelis, convinced the Palestinian Authority to move the exhibition indoors – but not to close it down and arrest its promoters. It is understood that by widening the scope of the viewers of those scenes among the Muslims, who are not fundamentalists, to the point of rendering them a sort of popular street theater, the organizers came to elicit respect and esteem for the deceased heroes to encourage the *shahids* of tomorrow.

Unlike the inward-turning stories of suffering reenacted by the Shi'ites for the sake of commemoration, identification and self-hardening to stand the excruciating things to come, Hamas hardens its crowds and cultivates audiences by boasting about gruesome suffering inflicted upon the enemies. This change of focus, or a *ta'zia* in reverse, emanates from the difference between the Shi'ite universal doctrine of *istishhad* as the ultimate way to identify spiritually with Hussein, and Hamas whose most urgent goal is to bring down its enemy.

In Palestinian thinking, the most atrocious injustice was done to them by Israel by its very birth and continued existence. Not only is its occupation of their territory resented, but its very presence in their midst and vicinity exposes their own helplessness. Both had begun from the same departure point half a century ago, but while their sworn enemy had progressed, settled down its refugees, prospered and advanced, they are still rotting in refugee camps for the third generation with the gap between them and Israel growing. Their refugees have remained dependent upon UN flour supplies and foreign aid (which is, ironically, American and Western, which they detest, rather than Arab and Islamic).

Nothing is more humiliating to the Palestinians than that. They hate Israel, which shows them what they had failed to achieve, and they spurn America, to whom they must turn as beggars. Rather than striving to equal Israel, to eliminate their dependence on America, they would rather attack them both and wipe out the constructive model which constantly exposes them to shame. This is why when the Oslo process was at its hopeful beginnings, it was the fundamentalist Hamas which rejected it for fear that it might reinforce and eternalize the superior stature of Israel, which they could neither bear nor tolerate. The ensuing demonizing of Jews, Zionists and Israel, and the legitimization of ruthless attacks, aimed at intimidating the Israelis and wrecking their economy, are part of the mechanism of this externalized *ta'zia* in reverse, which focuses on the suffering inflicted on the enemies, instead of extolling their own suffering and sacrifice. The Twin Towers horror, also inflicted by Sunnite 'Islamikaze' (al-Qaeda is one of their organizations), can be interpreted in the same vein. Bin Laden and other Muslims throughout the world delighted in the humiliation of America.

In Shi'ite Islam after the end of the Gulf War (1988), acts of 'Islamikaze' were restrained after they peaked in the 1980s. In Lebanon, where it all started, the Hizballah leadership concluded that the exaggerated use of over-zealous youth for those acts often ended in the death of the perpetrator without inflicting enough casualties on the enemy to justify that sacrifice. Sheikh Fadlallah issued a *fatwa*, allowing acts of 'Islamikaze' only on special occasions.[9] Sheikh Na'im Qassem, the Deputy Secretary of Hizballah, translated the guideline of his spiritual leader into specific directives, which he issued to the organization and released to the public in a press interview:

> First, one must obtain the authorization of an accredited Mufti. Anyone seeking to sacrifice himself, especially by car-bomb or blowing himself up, must first consult with a cleric of the Holy Law, because the soul is dear and can be expended only for the sake of the Islamic Umma.
>
> Secondly, after the religious authority delivers its verdict, the political leadership of the movement must deliberate on the political and military merits thereof. For when the same goals can be obtained without self-sacrifice, we do not send any martyr to his death. The Islamikaze act is efficient only when other means are not deemed [by the leadership] to attain the same results.[10]

When the 'Islamikaze' martyrdom was adopted by the Palestinians in the 1990s there were tremendous debates among Palestinian scholars of the

Holy Law whether or not they should be sanctioned. Dr Hamza Mustafa, Head of the Shari'a College at al-Quds University, and himself a member of the Jerusalem-based Supreme Islamic Council, was emphatic in a press interview:

> Allah has determined that whoever commits suicide will end up in Hell. It is clear that suicide is unreservedly prohibited, because his soul is not his private property but belongs to Allah. There are those who believe that when suicide is committed as part of an act of war against the enemy, it is not forbidden, but most believe that suicide is prohibited in any case.[11]

A perception had crystallized in those days that while the tiny Islamic Jihad group opted for 'Islamikaze' bombings, as part of its world of self-sacrifice,[12] the larger and more popular Hamas did not encourage its membership to engage in this operation. For example, Sheikh Jamil Tamimi, one of the leaders of the Muslim Movement in the West Bank, was often quoted as totally opposing these acts, not only due to the loss of life involved, but mainly because of the categorical prohibition against self-immolation in Islam. He recognized that some Muslim scholars did permit this operation in the context of war, but he emphasized that he personally was opposed to this interpretation.[13]

At the same time, however, Izz a-Din al-Qassam,[14] a hallowed name and symbol for both the Hamas and the Islamic Jihad, was cited as urging his followers to martyrdom, because 'martyrdom is only the beginning of the road … *jihad* is either victory or martyrdom …'.[15] 'Victory or martyrdom' as a slogan and battle-cry naturally encouraged people to sacrifice themselves. After the first 'Islamikaze' act against Israelis in Beit Lid in 1994, perpetrated by Islamic Jihad, one of the Gaza mosques' loud speakers proclaimed: 'Islamic Jihad has announced long ago that we have hundreds of volunteers for martyrdom, ready at any minute to hurt the Zionist enemy and burn the land under his feet'.[16]

The Manual of Martyrology

So while no authority in Islam permits suicide *per se*, those who allow, indeed urge, the martyr to sacrifice his life, use the commonly held view that the soul belongs to Allah to facilitate its return to Him. An accidental or incidental death incurred during battle, which is commonly dubbed *istishhad*, even when the martyr did not willingly and by choice embrace it, is not a *'amalyya istishhadiyya* (an *act* of martyrdom), which would mean that the individual has taken the conscious decision to sacrifice his life for the Islamic cause. In this case, where the martyr has considered his act as imperative to achieve his goal, he has 'purposely thrown himself to his death, confident that he is rushing to Paradise'.[17] And since he neither wished nor prepared any way of retreat, he must perish together with his targeted, or incidental, victims. Martyrdom is, however, limited by the prohibition against killing innocent people, and the essence of the matter then becomes the definition of who is innocent and who is not.

The author of the *Readings in Islamic Martyrology*[18] indeed addresses himself to these basic dilemmas. He cites *shari'ah* sources which negate suicide, from the Qur'an and the authoritative collections of Hadith. It is unlawful for any Muslim to commit suicide by poison, jumping from a high place, self-stabbing, or suffocation, under the threat of Hell punishment. Islam prohibits suicide out of despair from life, with a view of avoiding suffering due to illness, injury, poverty, fear, disaster, imprisonment and torture.

Killing others can only be undertaken 'justly', based on a Qur'anic injunction, namely for adultery, murder, apostasy and those who deserted the company of the Believers.[19] By avoiding generalizations and overarching and abstract principles, and keeping strictly faithful to the detailed cases of prohibition mentioned in the sources, the writer thus prepares his readers to conclude that everything not expressly forbidden is allowed.

The most fascinating aspect of these prohibitions is that they rest on the requirement in the Qur'an[20] regarding the sanctity of human life, and the superior role of humans in Allah's creation. It is fascinating because it stands in stark contradiction to the seemingly unbearable facility with which the 'Islamikaze' kill themselves. The resolution of this contradiction is the whole innovative import of the new convoluted interpretations undertaken by fundamentalist Muslim scholars, as in the text under discussion. Man was created, according to the *Qira'a*, with the belief in Allah imprinted in his heart, and all his strength and spirit are devoted to the straightening up of the created world. In order to guide man to follow the right path, Allah sent prophets, apostles and His Messenger Muhammad, together with the Qur'an and the *sunna* (tradition of the Prophet). Hence, the purpose of man on earth is to worship Allah (*'ibadat Allah)*, which is more important even than human life. However, this treatise claims, these two themes of the sanctity of human life and the worship of Allah are not contradictory.

This world is the scene of the struggle between good and evil, between the worship of God and the worship of Satan, the choice between a life of belief and the option of disbelief. The right choice will bring one to eternal life in Paradise. Namely, if one devotes his life in this world to worship Allah, he will achieve eternal life. Thus, the laws of *jihad* do not contradict the prohibitions of self-immolation and of killing others unjustifiably, but are complementary to them.

And this is precisely what makes Islam a perfect religion in terms of its regard for human life: namely, the preservation of human life on the one hand, but also self-sacrifice for the sake of Allah on the other. For contrary to other doctrines, which permit killing in the pursuit of material benefit, Islam values human life. But Islam values the worship of Allah more. Setting human life as the supreme value, it permits injustice to persist without opposition, thus violating human dignity. Conversely, the worship of Allah which applies the tenets of making justice and upholding right (*iqamat al-'adl wa-ihqaq al-haqq*), in itself constitutes the delicate balance between these two values. This balance exists only in Islam, making it as the supreme human and cultural model.

Naturally, when the author of this dissertation posits the worship of Allah as supreme, and the way of *jihad* as the superior apex of worship, he inescapably comes to the conclusion that any Believer who follows divine guidance with regard to *jihad* and emulates the Prophet in this respect, must evince his willingness to die for Allah.[21]

To support his conclusion, the author relates to a famous Hadith, where the Prophet undertook to die for Allah, to come back to life and then die once again.[22] This means that there was no bigger goal in the Prophet's own existence than to die for Allah, and repeatedly so. Therefore, this tenet constitutes, in the author's mind, a divine guideline that applies everywhere at all times. Hence the necessity for believers to embrace the road of self-sacrifice (*tad'hia)* and spiritual devotion *(badhl a-nafs)*, which thereby become central motifs in the author's concept of *jihad*. He recounts many episodes from the life of the Prophet where the latter proved his devotion to these themes in his *jihad* battles against his enemies.[23] This ought to be the standard behavior of all Muslims who seek battle at the highest level of risk. For this purpose, the author recognizes three kinds of battles, graded in accordance with the level of risk involved:

1. Where the chances to die or to emerge alive are even. In this case, the surviving fighter would deserve honor (*karama)*, and if he should perish, his death would be considered martyrdom (*shahada)*. An illustrious Muslim fighter, Khalid ibn al-Walid, was quoted as wondering every day during his battles whether he was escaping from the day of *karama* or that of *shahada*. That meant that dying in this fashion was a winning proposition in either case.[24]
2. Where the balance of power is against the Muslims, the Muslim fighter needs to display much more audacity. Once again in many such battles, in which the Companions of the Prophet (*sahaba)* participated, the

Messenger of Allah provided a personal example by fighting very close to the eye of the storm, in defiance of the dangers the enemy posed to him. Such harsh battles, where some of the *sahaba* made the ultimate sacrifice after they sustained so many wounds that their corpses became unrecognizable,[25] become the high standards of combat to be followed by other Believers.

3. A third category of battle is when self-sacrifice becomes imperative. This is where the act of *jihad*, itself highly regarded and lavishly rewarded in Heaven, transcends into an act of martyrdom (*istishhad*). The difference between standard self-sacrifice and spiritual devotion on the one hand, and deliberate act of martyrdom on the other, is that here a special strategy is adopted by a group of Muslims to rescue the entire Muslim army or Muslim *umma* with a view to disrupting the enemy's war plans or sow disarray in its ranks; or is geared to hurt the enemy's morale and boost the Muslims', or is likely to bring such a disaster upon the enemy as to increase his losses and decrease those of the Muslims.

The latter mode of combat is the highest in the eyes of the author and conforms typologically to the 'Islamikaze' *modus operandi*. The author regards the 'Islamikaze' not as a current, normal and routine strategy to fight the enemy in the battlefield, but as a tactical device to be used when regular conventional battles are about to be lost, and no other avenues available. In this context, we may digress to find grounds to interpret the Twin Towers disaster, or the daily attacks by Hamas and Islamic Jihad against Israel, once the Palestinian *intifada* had failed to bring Israel to its knees. It is also noteworthy that when Yasser Arafat realized that his declared campaign against Israel was falling flat on its face, out of despair he joined the fray by stating before delirious and equally dispirited crowds that he was ready to be a *shahid* for the sake of 'liberating' Jerusalem – and urged his followers to launch the *jihad* to realize the evasive dreams of the Palestinians.[26]

In this ultimate model of self-sacrifice, it is the Prophet himself or his *sahaba* who makes daring self-sacrificing moves to save the entire Muslim strategy on the battlefield. From cases of this sort, drawn from the personal histories at the time of the Prophet, the author deduces implicit permission to Muslim sacrifice for the public interest.[27] The author says that, today, the 'Islamikaze' carries explosives on his body in order to carry out his mission; in the times of the Prophet the audacious fighter threw himself on the swords of the enemy, but both modes of action are essentially the same.

Similarly, valiant Muslim fighters had to dismount their horses which were no match for the elephants of the enemy, and attacked those immense and frightening animals with their swords, even though they were trampled upon and slaughtered. So today, an 'Islamikaze' can defy with his body the enemy's planes and tanks, and perish under their weight, or blow himself up in a minefield, in order to facilitate the passage of his fellow fighters into enemy territory, or their retreat into safety. In both cases, the gates of Paradise are open to receive the new martyrs.[28]

Thus, the author builds his argument tier after tier: first, he designates the value of the worship of Allah over the value of human life; then the *jihad* as the supreme form of worship. Since the *jihad* involves self-sacrifice, three levels thereof are identified, the highest and most commendable is the *act of martyrdom*. All stages are soundly grounded on the precedents set by the Prophet himself or his Companions.

This piece, which has been considered as having the power of a *fatwa*, confronts the contradiction between its sanctification of death and the Qur'anic injunction to preserve life and escape peril. Once again precedents from the time of the Prophet and his Companions are cited, for example of the fighter who threw himself literally to his death when he attacked single-handedly an entire Byzantine column, whereupon a discussion ensued about whether that hero did not unnecessarily throw himself into certain death. The real peril is not death in battle, but in turning one's attention to material life and neglecting *jihad* activity.[29]

The same goes for the explicit Qur'anic prohibition to commit suicide,[30] and the author has to perform an intellectual somersault in order to circumvent the issue and prove his point. He says that while both suicide and acts of martyrdom require the express act of will of the perpetrator, what matters is not the act, but the intention (*nia*) of the martyr. A case in point was of a martyr who appeared on the Day of Judgment and claimed that he fought for Allah, but Allah reminded him that his courage was displayed only so that it could be said of him that he was courageous, whereupon he was dragged on his face and consumed by the fire of Hell.[31]

This turn of the argument is extremely important, for it leaves the final judgment to Heaven, inasmuch as even when a man is considered by his peers, eye-witnesses and contemporaries as a well-deserved martyr, Allah may scrutinize his intention and decide otherwise. Conversely, a man may be considered by humans to have committed a despicable suicide, but when Allah examines his intentions, He might reward him with the highest degree of martyrdom and in Paradise. And this is precisely what sets suicide, a flight from the vagaries of life, apart from an act of martyrdom, which is a human response to the call of Allah to sacrifice oneself for the sake of Islam, and to inflict loss on the enemies of Allah.

The remaining question is whether martyrdom is the domain of the elected few who can cultivate the requisite pious intention, or is given to the choice of every willing individual Muslim. An analogy is suggested in laws of conversion. Muslims are allowed to renege on their faith outwardly, under duress or threat on their lives, as long as in their hearts they did not budge from their creed.[32]

However, as against that permission *(rukhsa)*, there exists also personal resolve (*'azima*), which is admittedly more difficult to pursue and to experience, and refusing to abandon the faith even in the face of certain death. But those who choose this course out of their own resolve, in spite of the allowance made by the Shari'a in cases of imminent peril, of course attain the highest levels of martyrdom and reward.[33] And since in every operation against the enemy there is a danger of death, the only issue is one of the degree of the threat. Any act of martyrdom of the 'Islamikaze' kind carries with it certain death, though everything is ultimately in Allah's hand, and this is what places it at the apex of martyrdom.

Summary

The problem remains to discern the circumstances under which this weapon is to be used, and to detect the enemy to be targeted. First of all, the act of martyrdom is an expression of *jihad*, and is often pursued as an act of self-defense against an enemy who has invaded Muslims in their own homes and territory, when it becomes incumbent upon individual Muslims to use force. Therefore, unlike state-led *jihad*, the duty of the entire Islamic polity, in this case an individual duty (*fard 'ayn*) is to be performed by the Muslims closest to the enemy.

In Palestine, the arena discussed specifically by the author, he focuses on the duty of *jihad* against the combined 'Judeo-Western onslaught'. There, attacks and oppressive acts against Muslims are physical and concrete: expulsion, killing, wounding and imprisoning. They concern the take-over of Muslim Holy Places to replace them by Jewish ones, Judaization of Muslim land and violation of the honor of Muslim women. The expansion of Israel especially serves as a launching pad to conquer more Muslim countries and form a Western base to 'diffuse Jewish corruption, Westernization, humiliation, enslavement and exploitation'.[34]

These combined actions by the enemy amount to a war of annihilation against Islam, something that impels any Muslim to take up *jihad* without waiting for permission from Muslim authorities. 'The Zionist enemy must be attacked by all means permitted by the Shari'a, not only by the Palestinians but by the entire Muslim Umma. Zionism is not a local enemy, it is a universal one, it is the sword that tears apart this blessed land'.[35] This analysis leads the author to conclude that the actual battle is of the third category which makes acts of martyrdom imperative and entails an individual commitment by every Muslim to engage the enemy.

The current danger to the Muslim *umma* is great both due to the rifts and splits within Muslims, and the combined power of the Zionist enemy and his allies. The situation of the Muslims today is worse than in Crusader times, therefore *jihad* in Palestine acquires its own imperative and urgent character, and requires acts of martyrdom to take precedence over all other modes of warfare. All the pre-required conditions to launch such acts exist in Palestine with regard to the Zionist enemy, particularly when all other conventional military avenues have proved insufficient or ineffective, in view of the military superiority of enemy tactics, equipment and technology. Even laying explosives in enemy targets and then seeking refuge would not help, due to his vigilance or due to the random effect on victims – who may turn out to be women and children.[36]

On the other hand, in an act of martyrdom, the explosive is focused on precise targets. Moreover, due to the interception of weapons and explosives by Israel before they could be activated, it becomes imperative to use the little there is in the most focused and infallible manner, through the 'Islamikaze'. Many consequences flow from this conclusion:

1. The precise targets chosen for these acts of martyrdom, which are supposed to spare children and women, seem to be ignored by the perpetrators, who seek soft spots, and most of the victims have been women, children and aged people;
2. the more counter-terrorist attacks succeed in paralyzing the terrorists, such as Hamas and Islamic Jihad, the more their members will be pushed to resort to acts of 'Islamikaze'; and
3. the more frequent the acts of 'Islamikaze', the more evident is the failure of the Islamist organizations in the overall campaign.

Another advantage that the author seems to ascribe to the acts of 'Islamikaze', is their effect on morale, inasmuch as 'by Allah's grace, one or two fighters succeed in breaking into the lines of the enemy, then attack a group of the enemy's forces by an act of martyrdom, thereby inflicting on him heavy damage and tottering his morale in the face of the indestructible fighting spirit of the martyrs'. By this kind of operation, the entire Islamic *umma* is rescued, as it minimizes its own casualties, maximizes the enemy's and weakens the latter's ability to retaliate. All this is certainly worth the sacrifice of a few fighters. It is imperative, however, that those who embrace this road should do it with *nia*, namely not as an escape from life and its vagaries, but with the intention of *jihad* for Allah, in order to kill the enemies. This is, in fact, the best and most economical possible way to engage in *jihad* in Palestine under the prevailing circumstances.[37]

To sum up the doctrine, which first pays lip service to the value of human life, but then posits the value of worship of Allah above it, and then *jihad* as the highest degree of worship, it may be said that it actually overlooks, dismisses and makes banal the entire humanistic concept of sanctity of life as it is understood in Western tradition. Even though the injunction to self-sacrifice in *jihad* is graduated into three levels of necessity: unnecessary if there is an equilibrium of forces with the enemy, desirable when the rapport of forces is in the Muslims' disfavor, and imperative when perilous danger threatens the community, one cannot escape the impression that this edifice of rationalizations is geared to dwarf human life in the final analysis and make it subservient to religious fanaticism.

The author seems to say that death for Allah, as long as the intention is there, has a special significance and is considered the highest form of martyrdom. In fact he is indeed speaking about the sanctity of death, which in a very round-about and paradoxical way stems from the basic assumption of the sanctity of life. Noteworthy is, however, his reluctance to bind the Muslims in general with such a harrowing and demanding injunction, and he limits it to the few who have attained such a degree of self-sacrifice as to commit it without hesitation, and who would be rewarded in the higher reaches of Paradise.

Characteristic of this treatise is that it almost disregards the 13 centuries of Shari'a developments since the era of the Prophet. For had he surveyed the entire span of Muslim Law, it is doubtful whether he would have come to the ultimate conclusion that every 'true Muslim' must be ready, eager and willing to sacrifice his life in the course of *jihad*. He himself complains in his essay, on more than one occasion, against the attempts made throughout history to 'hide the true meanings of *jihad* and martyrdom', therefore it was only natural for him to connect directly to the sources to extract his fundamentalist interpretations. For him the 'true Muslims' are those who follow the early interpretations, in contrast to those who have been spoiled and diluted by Western and modern outside accretions.

Even so, the Hadith stories cited by the author are not always accurate and sometimes are turned around as to illustrate his point. It is interesting to draw some comparisons with other versions that appear in books of other scholars such as Ibn al-Athir, but that is beyond the scope of this article. At any rate, it is clear that because some radical Muslim movements who have sanctified self-sacrifice are accused of adopting Shi'ite theology, the author is clearly making an effort to stay within the bounds of the Sunna, even if it is the most puritanical and strict interpretation thereof.

In the context of a universal Muslim combat for survival, when 'Islamikaze' acts are imperative, one is led to believe that without the supreme act of martyrdom, there is no other way to rescue Islam. Paradoxically, it is precisely the perceived impending peril to Islam which forces the martyrs to their fanatic act of self-immolation, and it is their desperate act of self-sacrifice which signals that they failed to transmit their message in some more acceptable and less horrific way.

NOTES

1. Raphael Israeli, 'Islamikaze and their Significance', *Journal of Terrorism and Political Violence* 9/3 (Autumn 1997) pp.96–112.
2. Ibid.
3. A.J. Wensinck, 'The Oriental Doctrine of the Martyrs', in *Med, Akad* (Amsterdam: 1921) Series A, No.6, pp.1–28.
4. Ignaz Goldziher, *Muhammedanische Studien* (Halle, 1989) p.387.
5. Wensinck (note 3) p.9.
6. Cited by ibid. pp.5–6.
7. Amir Taheri (a former pre-revolutionary editor of the daily *Kaihan*), *The Spirit of Allah* (Tel Aviv: Am Oved 1986) p.148 (in Hebrew). See also Emanuel Sivan, *Muslim Radicals* (Tel Aviv: Am Oved 1985) pp.192–5 (in Hebrew).
8. Tahiri (note 7) p.55. See also Hamid Algar, *Islam and Revolution* (Berkeley, CA: University of California Press 1981) pp.329–43; and Martin Kramer (ed.), *Protest and* Revolution *in Shi'ite Islam* (Tel Aviv: Tel Aviv University 1985) p.29 (in Hebrew).
9. Report by Guy Bechor, Arab Affairs commentator, *Ha'aretz*, 6 Dec. 1995, p.b2.
10. Ibid.
11. *Ha'aretz*, 23 Jan. 1995, p.6a.
12. Meir Hatina, *Palestinian Radicalism: The Islamic Jihad Movement* (Tel Aviv: Tel Aviv University 1994) pp.79–80 (in Hebrew).
13. *Ha'aretz*, 23 Jan. 1995.
14. Izz a-Din al Qassam was the founder and hero of the Islamic movement in Palestine in the 1930s, which engaged in battle both against the British Mandatory forces and the Jewish self-defense groups, until his death in combat in Samaria in 1935. His name was picked up by the Hamas, upon its foundation in 1988, and given to the military arm of the organization.
15. Hatina (note 12) p.82.
16. A citation from an Islamic Jihad distributed leaflet, *Ha'aretz*, 23 Jan. 1995, p.6a. The leaflet was reportedly headed by a citation from the Repentance Sura in the Qur'an which promises Paradise to those who kill and are killed in the battles of Allah.
17. *Qira'a fi Fiqh al-Shahada* (Readings in Islamic Martyrology) was published in 1988 as a special addendum to *al-Islam wa Filastin* (Islam and Palestine), which appears in Nicosia, Cyprus, but has been the ideological supporter of the Islamikaze operations against Israel. See *Al-Islam wa Filastin*, 5 June 1988, p.9.
18. Ibid.
19. *Qira'a fi Fiqh al-Shahada* (note 17) p.3.
20. The Cow Sura, verses 28–36.
21. *Qira'a fi Fiqh al-Shahada* (note 17) p.4.
22. Citing Malik ibn Anas, *Ahadith al-Jami' al'Saghir*, in *Qira'a fi Fiqh al-Shahada* (note 17) p.4.
23. Ibid. p.7.
24. Ibid. p.8.
25. Ibid pp.8–9.

26. Palestinian Authority Broadcasting, shown on Israeli television, 24 Jan. 2002, 20:00 News Bulletin.
27. *Qira'a fi Fiqh al-Shahada* (note 17) p.12.
28. Ibid.
29. Ibid. p.10.
30. *Qur'an*, Women Sura, verse 29.
31. *Qira'a fi Fiqh al-Shahada* (note 17) p.6. How that fake hero could appear before God prior to the expected Day of Judgment, the author does not explain, unless he means not the eschatological Day of Judgment, but the personal day of judgment of that imaginary individual.
32. The Bee Sura, verse 108.
33. *Qira'a fi Fiqh al-Shahada* (note 17) pp.10–11.
34. Ibid. p.7.
35. Ibid.
36. Ibid. pp.14–15.
37. Ibid.

[16]

Killing in the Name of Islam: Al-Qaeda's Justification for September 11

Quintan Wiktorowicz and John Kaltner

Dr. Wiktorowicz is an assistant professor of international studies and Dr. Kaltner is an associate professor of religious studies, both at Rhodes College in Memphis, Tennessee. The al-Qaeda document that serves as the basis for this article is available in Arabic and English at www.mepc.org.

> By means of this document we send a message to America and those behind it. We are coming, by the will of God almighty, no matter what America does. It will never be safe from the fury of Muslims. America is the one who began the war, and it will lose the battle by the permission of God almighty.
>
> –Al-Qaeda statement, April 24, 2002

In the wake of the September 11 attacks, President Bush moved quickly to dismiss al-Qaeda operatives as part of the lunatic fringe, religious usurpers bent on misrepresenting and "hijacking" Islam to serve terrorism.[1] This characterization was echoed in the Muslim world, where an assortment of government officials, religious scholars and opposition figures fervidly denounced the killing of civilians as un-Islamic.[2] Abdulaziz bin Abdullah al-Ashaykh, the mufti of Saudi Arabia, argued that "hijacking planes, terrorizing innocent people and shedding blood constitute a form of injustice that cannot be tolerated by Islam, which views them as gross crimes and sinful acts."[3] Muhammed Sayyid al-Tantawi, the rector of al-Azhar University in Cairo, issued a similar condemnation: "Attacking innocent people is not courageous, it is stupid and will be punished on the day of judgment. . . . It's not courageous to attack innocent children, women and civilians. It is courageous to protect freedom, it is courageous to defend oneself and not to attack."[4] Shaikh Yussuf al-Qaradawi, a prominent Islamic scholar and television personality from Qatar, emphasized that "Islam, the religion of tolerance, holds the human soul in high esteem, and considers the attack against innocent human beings a grave sin."[5]

Even Islamic fundamentalist groups issued sharp denunciations. Forty-six leaders representing an assortment of Islamist movements and groups signed a letter opposed to the attacks:

> The undersigned, leaders of Islamic movements, are horrified by the events of Tuesday 11 September 2001 in the United States, which resulted in massive killing, destruction and attack

> on innocent lives. We express our deepest sympathies and sorrow. We condemn, in the strongest terms, the incidents, which are against all human and Islamic norms. This is grounded in the Noble Laws of Islam, which forbid all forms of attacks on innocents. God Almighty says in the Holy Quran: "No bearer of burdens can bear the burden of another" (Surah al-Isra 17:15).[6]

Signatories included the general guide of the Muslim Brotherhood of Egypt, the amir of the Jamaat-i-Islami in Pakistan and Ahmad Yassin, the founder of Hamas.

To be sure, many of these condemnations were blunted by concomitant criticism of American foreign policy as the primary catalyst for al-Qaeda's war. Leaders throughout the Middle East, including traditional allies, cautioned the United States to reflect on the consequences of its "unbalanced" approach to the region (particularly vis-à-vis the Israeli-Palestinian conflict and Iraq), and public opinion in the Arab world indicated mounting resentment against perceived American hegemony and arrogance. Yet in the wake of September 11, U.S. allies and adversaries alike in the Muslim world joined President Bush in rejecting the radicalism of al-Qaeda.

Given this broad rejection, how could al-Qaeda defend killing thousands of innocent civilians in the name of Islam? Although pre-September 11 fatwas, interviews and statements by Bin Laden and al-Qaeda representatives clearly outlined the movement's belief that American civilians are legitimate targets, al-Qaeda had yet to articulate its religious rationale for attacks against civilian populations. In the first six months after September 11, al-Qaeda failed to issue a response to the maelstrom of criticism that denounced the attacks as un-Islamic. Then finally on April 24, 2002, al-Qaeda released an extended statement (approximately 3,700 words) outlining, for the first time, its religious justification for killing civilians in a total war against the United States, titled "A Statement from Qaidat al-Jihad Regarding the Mandates of the Heroes and the Legality of the Operations in New York and Washington."[7] Unlike previous al-Qaeda statements, the justification was not published by Arabic or Western newspapers and has largely been ignored by experts. Yet it provides essential insights into the movement's religious rationale for September 11 that could help American policy makers in the war on terrorism.

The 2002 statement is best understood as part of an ongoing debate about the use of violence in Islam. Al-Qaeda is a component of a broader "fundamentalist" community and as a result is actively engaged in debates about religious authority, the legitimacy of war and rules of engagement in combat. In the 1990s, most disputes focused on whether it was permissible to rebel against incumbent regimes in the Muslim world. Toward the late 1990s, this focus shifted to address the United States as an emerging enemy and the legitimacy of particular tactics in warfare against unbelievers. The 2002 document is part of this latest debate and should therefore be understood as an argument that seeks not only to outline al-Qaeda's justification, but also address alternative, competing religious interpretations about acceptable violence in Islam.

DEBATING VIOLENCE

Al-Qaeda is a radical tendency within a broader Islamic movement known as the Salafi movement. The term Salafi is

Middle East Policy, Vol. X, No. 2, Summer 2003

derived from the Arabic *salaf*, which means "to precede" and refers to the companions of the Prophet Muhammed. Because the salaf learned about Islam directly from the messenger of God, their example is an important illustration of piety and unadulterated religious practice. Salafis argue that centuries of syncretic cultural and popular religious rituals and interpretations distorted the purity of the message of God and that only by returning to the example of the prophet and his companions can Muslims achieve salvation. The label "Salafi" is thus used to connote "proper" religious adherence and moral legitimacy, implying that alternative understandings are corrupt deviations from the straight path of Islam.[8]

While Salafis all agree about the importance of the prophetic model and the paradigm of the companions, there are important interpretive differences that have engendered schisms within the movement, particularly over the proper method to create an Islamic society and protect the *umma* (Muslim community). Differences in interpretation tend to emphasize one of the following four basic methods for promoting Islam:

1) Propagation (*dawa*). Salafis who focus on this method emphasize personal piety, cleansing the corpus of *hadiths* (reported sayings and traditions of the Prophet Muhammed), and spreading proper Islam. For this group, the priority is for individuals to practice a pure understanding of Islam. This entails not only propagation and individual piety, but a program to eliminate any weak or false hadiths so that Muslims ensure they are truly following the prophetic model.

2) Advice. A large number of influential Salafis and their followers believe that it is the responsibility of the *ulama* (religious scholars) to advise leaders about Islamic legislation and regulations. In general, however, they believe this advice should be given in private.

3) Non-violent action. Some Salafis believe that it is the duty of Muslims (particularly the ulama) to openly speak out against un-Islamic actions, decisions and public policy. This can include the use of the *khutba* (Friday sermon), open letters, public speeches, demonstrations and rallies.

4) Violent action. A small, radical fringe in the Salafi community argues that it is an Islamic duty to use violence to remove leaders who do not properly follow or enforce Islam. Known as jihadis, these Salafis do not reject the other methods, but they do emphasize the necessity of violence. Al-Qaeda is part of this group.

These differences have produced debates about the proper methodology for promoting Islam, leading to often vitriolic conflicts. Because Salafis believe that there is only one accurate understanding of Islam – the model of the prophet and his companions – this creates a tendency to dismiss any differences of interpretation as deviations. It is quite common, for example, for one Salafi group to call scholars and followers from other clusters to "return to the straight path." This has even generated disagreements over who can be considered a Salafi. In particular, nonviolent Salafis, who make up the vast majority of the movement, often vehemently reject use of the Salafi label to describe the violent or jihadi elements.[9] The latter, however, identify themselves as Salafis and dismiss the other groups as misguided, ignorant (unknowledgeable about Islam) or corrupt.

The debate within the Salafi community over the use of violence has divided the movement more than any other issue. During the 1990s, as al-Qaeda developed, the initial debate between violent and nonviolent Salafis was over *takfir* – declaring a Muslim an apostate. Declaring a Muslim an unbeliever is a serious endeavor, since it could mean a death sentence. The central axis of divergence was over whether one could judge a ruler in the Muslim world an apostate according to his actions. Nonviolent groups argued that one can never know with certainty what is in an individual's heart and that so long as a ruler has a "mustard seed of *iman* (belief)," he is considered a Muslim, especially if he allows Muslims to pray and generally practice their religion. The jihadi Salafis, on the other hand, argued that the oneness of God (*tawhid*) demands that Muslims follow Islam in both belief and action. In other words, an un-Islamic belief is just as revealing as an un-Islamic action. As a result, the jihadis charged the Saudis and other regimes in the Muslim world with un-Islamic behavior and thus apostasy, and called for a jihad to remove them.

Defeats made it clear that the jihadi vision to unseat incumbent Arab regimes was at an end and the focus shifted to al-Qaeda's war against the United States and its allies.

In the late 1990s, although this debate continued, it became less relevant to Islamist struggles on the ground as jihadis faced defeat and marginalization throughout the Middle East. This was particularly the case in the largest Islamist insurgencies in Egypt and Algeria.[10] In Egypt, leaders from both the Islamic Group and Islamic Jihad declared cease-fires, and the violence came to a dramatic end. Elements from within the Islamic Group went so far as to issue a public apology for the violence and published a four-volume justification for the decision. In a move that epitomized the recasting of the jihadis, a number of Islamists from both groups attempted to establish political parties (the Sharia and Islah parties), though the regime rejected the requests for permits. Violent jihadi dissidents found themselves marginalized; many left for Pakistan and Afghanistan to work directly with al-Qaeda.

In Algeria, a similar process occurred. The regime's decision to cancel elections in 1992, as Islamists were poised to control parliament, sparked an insurgency that has claimed more than 150,000 lives. Early in the conflict, the jihadi Salafis united under the banner of the Armed Islamic Group (GIA) and attacked government officials and soldiers. In 1996, however, the GIA launched a series of civilian massacres that undermined the unity of the Islamist opposition; and groups such as the Islamic Salvation Army issued a unilateral cease-fire. The regime responded by using an amnesty program to reintegrate former Islamist fighters into society. Although a number of radical groups continue to operate, the violence has dropped substantially since the late 1990s. As a result, many Algerian jihadi Salafis placed their networks, resources and personnel at the service of al-Qaeda.[11]

For non-violent Salafis, these defeats made it clear that the jihadi vision to unseat incumbent Arab regimes was at an end (at least in the short term), and so the issue of takfir became less prominent in debates over violence. Instead, the focus shifted to al-Qaeda's war against the United States and its allies. In general, most Salafis agree that the United States is waging a war of aggression against Muslims through its actions in Afghanistan, Pakistan, Iraq and elsewhere. Differences emerge, however, over the proper response and course of action. Jihadis once again call for violence, while the non-violent Salafis promote other means, including public announcements of opposition to a U.S. presence in the Middle East, prayer, and advice to Arab and Muslim leaders.

This is the context in which one should understand al-Qaeda's 2002 justification for September 11 and the purposeful targeting of civilians. The document is part of a discursive contest over the proper methodology for fulfilling religious obligations. As a result, it reflects a carefully constructed case to undermine the legitimacy of non-violent solutions. In this respect, it makes three important arguments. First, proponents of a non-violent response to the United States are corrupt, ignorant and/or hypocritical, and therefore are not credible religious mediators. This is contrasted with the scientific, independent and religiously authentic interpretation of the jihadi Salafis. Second, the United States is waging a war against Islam. Therefore, violence is a *defensive* jihad that is incumbent upon all Muslims. And third, there is no unconditional prohibition against killing civilians in Islam. In fact, civilians can be purposely targeted under certain conditions, and these conditions are met in the current climate.

PERSUASION AND CREDIBILITY

For Muslims, scholars of Islam play a critical role as intermediaries between the sacred texts and everyday religious rituals and practices. They are seen as the inheritors of the prophetic message, intellectually equipped to interpret the immutable sources of Islam in light of the changing conditions of the temporal world. For Islamists, the scholars are central nodes in networks of religious meaning, responsible for providing guidance and mentoring students so that they might follow the straight path of Islam to Paradise in the hereafter. They provide religious interpretations and offer lessons, books and lectures for those seeking enlightenment. For Salafis, in particular, scholars are essential, since they are purveyors of knowledge capable of illuminating an unadulterated understanding of Islam based upon the example of the prophet and his companions.

Not all scholars are equal, however. There are differences in training, intellectual capacity, communicative skills and charisma, all of which affect the reputation and influence of individual scholars. Those with strong reputations develop extensive followings and can use fatwas and other vehicles to exert substantial influence. The term "scholar" (*alim*) itself does not reflect objective criteria of learning; it is subjectively derived recognition dependent upon the reputation of the individual. Whether an individual is recognized as a scholar in good standing determines the likelihood that his interpretation will be accepted.

The debate over the conditions for permissible violence is therefore more than merely a conflict over ideas; it is a struggle over sacred authority – the right to interpret Islam on behalf of the Muslim community.[12] As studies of persuasion and framing have noted, the impact of an argument is determined not only by its resonance with the experiences and worldview of the target audience, but by the credibility of the articulator as well.[13] Influence is contingent upon the trustworthiness and integrity of the scholar. A lack of credibility can undermine the effect of a religious interpretation or argument by leading an audience to question the intentions of the source and thus whether the message represents an honest assessment of Islam and the will of God.

The jihadi scholars who nurture al-Qaeda and provide religious cover for acts of violence suffer from a "reputation deficit." Many are self-taught, new Islamist intellectuals with little formal religious training. Others have spent their lives studying Islam, but a dearth of resources, sponsors and fora for communication limits their capacity to develop a reputation. There are a few classically trained jihadi scholars with global notoriety, such as Omar Abdul Rahman (the Azharite shaikh and former mufti of several radical Egyptian groups, now in jail in New York), but these are the exceptions. This is in contrast to the training of the non-violent Salafi scholars, many who hold PhDs from established Islamic universities in Saudi Arabia and are considered part of the ulama in the kingdom. Non-violent Salafis thus find ample opportunity to dismiss the jihadis as unknowledgeable or ignorant, a pejorative insult among Salafis, who pride themselves as students of learning.

The case of Umar Abu Qatada, one of the key religious scholars of the al-Qaeda network, highlights this reputation deficit. Abu Qatada began his religious training with Mohammed Nasir al-Din al-Bani (d. 1999), a renowned Salafi reformist who came to Jordan after fleeing Syria in the late 1970s. Abu Qatada was part of a small group of teenage students that included eventual luminaries of the non-violent Salafi community, such as Salim al-Hilali and Ali Hasan al-Halabi. He left al-Bani's study circle over the issue of violence and continued his studies elsewhere, eventually fleeing security services in Jordan and relocating to London. Abu Qatada developed an impressive reputation among small jihadi circles and became an important reference point for the radical jihadis in Algeria (both the GIA and the Salafi Group for Call and Combat, or GSPC). His centrality as a jihadi scholar is exemplified by his participation on the fatwa committee of al-Qaeda.[14] After the 9/11 attacks, Abu Qattada, who became known as al-Qaeda's European paymaster, went underground; but he was caught in the UK and imprisoned in late 2002.

Despite this considerable history, reformists quickly dismiss Abu Qatada as unknowledgeable. For example, when asked about Abu Qatada in an interview, Salim al-Hilali quickly denounced him as ignorant and claimed, "He is not a scholar."[15] Such assaults on the credibility of the jihadi scholars are common among the non-violent Salafis.

As a result, much of the 2002 document can be seen as an attempt to establish the credentials of the jihadis while demeaning the credibility of the non-violent reformists. Since formal pedigree favors the reformists, jihadis stress the issue of scholarly independence and integrity. The thrust of this line of argument is that the

MIDDLE EAST POLICY, VOL. X, NO. 2, SUMMER 2003

reformist scholars are "the rulers' shaikhs" – mouthpieces for Arab regimes, which, in turn, are puppets of the United States. This connotes an inextricable connection between reformist legal rulings about violence and the desire of authorities to protect American interests, thus implying that non-violent Islamic interpretations are corrupted by politics and therefore unreliable and deceitful. This is clearly the argument at the onset of the document:

> We pass on this initial report, without details or exposition, regarding the evidence of the legality of this kind of operation. Let it be a quick message to those who dress their political opinions in the garb of a legal ruling. Let it also be a call to those who oppose and condemn the operations to obey Allah, repent and return to the legal evidence. Cowardice in defending the warriors (*mujahidin*) is no better than being silent. Allah is our guide and the guide of all Muslims.

Elsewhere, the connection between opposition to the violence of al-Qaeda and the dubiousness of reformist legal rulings is again emphasized:

> These great events which changed the face of history on such a grand scale occurred in the *umma*, and it will be a great regret to anyone who blames those who brought about the operation of September. Those ignorant ones do not speak with legal evidence or reasonable logic. Rather, they speak in their masters' languages [i.e., Saudi Arabia] and in the concepts of the enemy of the *umma* [i.e., the USA].

The jihadis go even further and charge the reformists with apostasy because of their support for the American war on terrorism, an extreme condemnation that, if true, would eliminate the reformists' right to issue legal rulings.

> Despite the clarity of the matter and the obvious nature of the evidence, however, it is regrettable that many of the motives were destroyed in the comforting of America, the expressions of sorrow for her, and the legal rulings to assist her and to donate blood for her innocent (!!) victims. Legally incriminating the one who carried out the operations and expelling him from Islam is also regrettable, as is giving the Crusaders the green light to exact revenge on Muslims. This teaches all those who issue opinions that America may pursue the Afghans and Shaikh Usama Bin Laden, may Allah protect him. We warn them about apostasy because of their assistance to the Crusaders by word or by their legal rulings to Arab governments that cooperation against terrorism [by this they mean cooperation against the mujahidin] is lawful. This is defiant apostasy!

The document argues that the corruption of these religious scholars is clearly demonstrated by the hypocrisy of their rulings: the reformists condone the use of martyrdom (suicide) operations in Palestine against Israelis (including civilians) yet denounce similar operations against Americans, such as the September 11 attacks.[16] The jihadis categorize both the Israelis and Americans as "people of war": Israel occupies and oppresses Muslims in Palestine; the United States oppresses and attacks Muslims in Afghanistan, Iraq and elsewhere. More important, Israel is portrayed as an extension of an American policy to attack the Muslim world, thus representing the conflict in Palestine as only one of many strategic components designed to support U.S. aggression. As a result, they argue, one can use the same tactics and strategies against both. Those who think otherwise are influenced by a political agenda that ignores the sources of Islam and the evidence legitimating September 11:

> [Y]ou will truly be surprised by those who rule that the martyrdom operations in Palestine in which civilians fall victim are among the highest forms of jihad, and then rule that the martyrdom operations in America are wrong because of civilian deaths. This inconsistency is very strange! How can one permit the killing of the branch and not permit the killing of the supporting trunk? All who permit martyrdom operations against the Jews in Palestine must allow them in America. If not, the inconsistency leads to nothing but a type of game playing with the legal ruling.

The hypocrisy and treachery of the non-violent Salafi scholars is contrasted with the independence and purity of the jihadis' intentions. Whereas the reformists are seen as inspired by political ambition and the interests of the United States and its Arab allies, the jihadis are characterized as influenced only by a desire to implement divine will:

> [T]he only motive these young men had was to defend the religion of Allah, their dignity, and their honor. It was not done as a service to humanity or as an attempt to side with Eastern ideologies opposed to the West. Rather, it was a service to Islam in defense of its people, a pure act of their will, done submissively, not grudgingly.[17]

The 2002 document notes the purity of the mission with pride. And, in an interesting shift from earlier denials, al-Qaeda not only accepts its responsibility for September 11, but claims "that hiding all trace of the agents of the operation was not something we considered. Rather, some of the heroes were intent on leaving Islamic fingerprints on the operation."

The purity of the jihadis is contrasted with the corruption of their detractors in an effort to impugn the reputation, credibility and persuasive effect of alternative religious interpretations. As part of the debate over the use of violence in Islam, the document reflects the Salafi emphasis on the centrality of reputable scholars capable of interpreting Islam and providing guidance for others. Character assassination and charges of deception and ignorance are devices intended to weaken opposing arguments.

JUST WAR AND JIHAD

In Islam, there are two types of external jihad: offensive and defensive.[18] In Islamic jurisprudence, the offensive jihad functions to promote the spread of Islam, enlightenment and civility to the *dar al-harb* (domain of war). In most contemporary interpretations, the offensive jihad can only be waged under the leadership of the caliph (successor to the prophet). It is tempered by truces and various reciprocal agreements between the Islamic state and non-Muslim governments, such as guaranteed freedom of worship for Muslim minorities. Today, very few Islamists focus on this form of jihad.

Middle East Policy, Vol. X, No. 2, Summer 2003

The defensive jihad (*jihad al-dafaa*), however, is a widely accepted concept that is analogous to international norms of self-defense and Judeo-Christian just-war theory.[19] According to most Islamic scholars, when an outside force invades Muslim territory, it is incumbent upon all Muslims to wage jihad to protect the faith and the faithful. Mutual protection is seen as a religious obligation intended to ensure the survival of the global Muslim community. At the root of defensive jihad is a theological emphasis on justness, as embodied in chapter 6, verse 151 of the Quran: "Do not slay the soul sanctified by God except for just cause." Defending the faith-based community against external aggression is considered a just cause *par excellence*.

The focus on the just nature of defensive war united both mainstream Islamic scholars and al-Qaeda in opposition to the U.S. invasion of Iraq in March 2003.

In the contemporary period, this widely accepted notion of the defensive jihad was first put to the test in Afghanistan in the 1980s. After the Soviets invaded Afghanistan in 1979 to prop up a failing communist government, Islamic scholars throughout the Muslim world called for jihad. Thousands of Muslim fighters flocked to Afghanistan to fulfill their religious duty, supported by Islamic charities, wealthy individuals and governments in Muslim countries such as Saudi Arabia, Kuwait and Pakistan. State leaders and radical Islamists alike concurred that the jihad was an Islamic duty that could include fighting, financial support, humanitarian work or verbal assistance, depending on an individual's capacities and resources. This broad agreement was extended to justify support for jihad in other conflicts as well, including Bosnia and Chechnya.

In a disturbing confluence of opinion regarding jihad, the focus on the just nature of defensive war united both mainstream Islamic scholars and al-Qaeda in opposition to the U.S. invasion of Iraq in March 2003. In a tape aired by al-Jazeera television on February 11, 2003, as the U.S.-led coalition built its forces on the borders of Iraq, Bin Laden continued his call for jihad against the U.S. "crusaders" and their pending invasion.[20] Only a month later, before the invasion took place, Islamic scholars at al-Azhar University (Cairo), the oldest Islamic university in the world, echoed Bin Laden's sentiments and emphasized the need for a defensive jihad: "According to Islamic law, if the enemy steps on Muslims' land, jihad becomes a duty on every male and female Muslim."[21] Although the al-Azhar scholars may have used the term "jihad" to mean non-violent struggle, the justification shared al-Qaeda's theological understanding about the defensive nature of any such jihad.

Consistent with this understanding, the 2002 document frames September 11 and other al-Qaeda operations as defensive measures to protect the Muslim community from outside aggression. The argument repeats the framing in earlier al-Qaeda documents and includes a litany of U.S. aggressions and crimes against Islam: support for Israel against the Palestinians; support for Serbian genocide against

Bosnian Muslims; support for India against the Kashmiris; the U.S. invasion of Afghanistan; actions in East Timor; support for the Philippine aggression against Muslims in the south. The document frames these examples as indicative of a nefarious "Zionist-Crusader" plot to annihilate Muslims. Under this assault, al-Qaeda argues that violence is the only solution: "The only way to liberation from this humiliation is the sword, which is the only language the enemy understands that will deter it." September 11 is thus portrayed as a defensive response necessary to thwart U.S. aggression against the Muslim world.

The document also addresses a very particular criticism of al-Qaeda's war against the United States. A number of Salafis and Islamists have argued that, since Muslim governments made treaties and agreements with the United States and its Western allies, it is illegal in Islam to wage jihad against them. This is based, in part, upon a story narrated by Abdullah bin Amr in which the prophet said, "Whoever kills a *muahid* [a treaty partner] shall not smell the fragrance of Paradise though its fragrance can be smelt at a distance of forty years (of traveling)."[22] However, in many interpretations of Islamic law, treaties are revisited every ten years, and so revisions can be made depending upon changing conditions, needs or strategies. If the non-Muslim partner violates the treaty conditions first, the agreement is voided.

Responding to this line of argument, al-Qaeda dismisses the premise that the Muslims ever had viable treaties with the United States. To some extent, this is based upon the jihadi belief that governments in Muslim countries are controlled by apostate regimes and therefore cannot legitimately make treaties on behalf of Muslims. Such contracts are therefore null and void.

In addition to this outright rejection, al-Qaeda evaluates the argument on its own basis and poses a counterargument. Suppose a treaty really did exist? Is it still valid? The document argues that the innumerable acts of U.S. aggression constitute massive breaches of any hypothetical agreement. These violations render the "treaty" meaningless:

> Truly, America is not, nor has it ever been, a land of treaty or alliance. If we were to line up with the other side and say that it is a land of peace, we would say that it has turned into a land of war. That occurred with its violation of the treaty and its help to the Jews for more than fifty years in occupying Palestine, banishing its people and killing them. It is a land of war that violated its treaty when it attacked and blockaded Iraq, attacked and blockaded Sudan, attacked and blockaded Afghanistan. It has oppressed Muslims in every place for decades and has openly supported their enemies against them.

For al-Qaeda, there is no treaty, and the U.S. "atrocities" against Muslims provide the rationale for a just and defensive jihad. The argument is rooted in widely accepted Islamic principles about justice and the legitimacy of a defensive struggle and therefore appeals to mainstream understandings about warfare.

RULES OF ENGAGEMENT AND CIVILIAN TARGETING

Fighting and killing in the name of Islam are conditional, and there are important rules of engagement that dictate and

MIDDLE EAST POLICY, VOL. X, NO. 2, SUMMER 2003

limit targets and tactics. The Prophet Muhammed expended great energies elaborating what was and was not permissible during wartime, demonstrating the importance of restraint and caution on the battlefield. The prohibitions against killing innocent civilians, in particular, are numerous, and non-violent Salafis and others quote a number of hadiths to support their opposition to the September 11 attacks, including,

> Set out for jihad in the name of Allah and for the sake of Allah. Do not lay hands on the old verging on death, on women, children and babes. Do not steal anything from the booty and collect together all that falls to your lot in the battlefield and do good, for Allah loves the virtuous and the pious.

Many scholars also quote Abu Bakr, the first caliph or successor to the Prophet Muhammed. He gave the following instructions to a Muslim army setting out to battle against the Byzantine Empire in Syria:

> Stop, O people, that I may give you ten rules for your guidance in the battlefield. Do not commit treachery or deviate from the right path. You must not mutilate dead bodies. Neither kill a child, nor a woman, nor an aged man. Bring no harm to the trees, nor burn them with fire, especially those which are fruitful. Slay not any of the enemy's flock, save for your food. You are likely to pass by people who have devoted their lives to monastic services; leave them alone.

In his response to the September 11 attacks, the mufti of Saudi Arabia focused on the need to be fair and just, quoting an assortment of Quranic verses prohibiting oppression, such as "O My servants, indeed I have forbidden oppression upon Myself and I have also made it forbidden amongst yourselves, hence to not oppress each other," and "O you who believe. Be of those who stand up to Allah, as witnesses of justice. And let not the hatred of a people make you swerve away from justice toward them. Verily, be just, and that is closer to piety."[23] Qaradawi builds on such verses as well, highlighting Quran 5, 32: "Whosoever kills a human being for other than manslaughter or corruption in the earth, it shall be as if he has killed all mankind, and whosoever saves the life of one, it shall be as if he had saved the life of all mankind."[24]

Al-Qaeda, however, disputes the broad prohibition against killing civilians on two grounds. First, it takes issue with the notion that those killed in the September 11 attacks were "innocents" covered by the prophet's prohibitions. Second, al-Qaeda argues that the prohibition is not an absolute one and that there are conditions under which killing civilians becomes permissible. The movement thus takes on both the theological argument proffered against the September 11 attacks and reformist framings of the victims as innocent. The result is a broad set of conditions that provide religious justification for killing civilians in almost every possible circumstance. Only *one* condition need be met to legitimize an attack against civilians.

Condition One: The Norm of Reciprocity

The sources of Islam provide clear prohibitions against killing civilians, but al-Qaeda argues for reciprocal attacks. This is justified with reference to Quran 2, 194: "And one who attacks you, attack him in like manner as he attacked you." Thus, if the enemy uses tactics that are prohibited in Islam, these tactics become legal for the Muslims. Since the document makes the case that America has purposely targeted Muslim civilians, it presses readers to accept the logical conclusion that civilian targeting, as in September 11, is now legal. This point is emphasized with particular reference to the Palestinian struggle:

> There currently exists an extermination effort against the Islamic peoples that has America's blessing, not just by virtue of its effective cooperation, but by America's activity. The best witness to this is what is happening with the full knowledge of the world in the Palestinian cities of Jenin, Nablus, Ramallah and elsewhere. Every day, all can follow the atrocious slaughter going on there with American support that is aimed at children, women and the elderly. Are Muslims not permitted to respond in the same way and kill those among the Americans who are like the Muslims they are killing? Certainly! By Allah, it is truly a right for Muslims.

For al-Qaeda, the evidence points to a clear conclusion:

> It is allowed for Muslims to kill protected ones among unbelievers as an act of reciprocity. If the unbelievers have targeted Muslim women, children and elderly, it is permissible for Muslims to respond in kind and kill those similar to those whom the unbelievers killed.

Condition Two: Inability to Distinguish Civilians from Combatants

When attacking an enemy "stronghold" it may be difficult to distinguish combatants from non-combatants, particularly if enemy fighters hide among the general population. The Arabic term the document uses for "stronghold" (*hisn*) has an interesting semantic range in light of the targets of September 11. It refers to a place that is immune to attack either because it is well fortified or because great height makes it impregnable.[25] The connection with the targets is obvious – what American sites have been more clearly associated with fortification and height than the Pentagon and the World Trade Center? Al-Qaeda argues that so long as the stronghold is a legitimate target and enemy fighters are present, Muslims can attack, even if this means civilian casualties: "It is allowed for Muslims to kill protected ones among the unbelievers in the event of an attack against them in which it is not possible to differentiate the protected ones from the combatants or from the strongholds." So even if one grants the argument that there were innocent civilians in the buildings, which al-Qaeda does not accept, the buildings can still be attacked.

The document cites as evidence a story in which Muslims asked about the offspring and women of unbelievers who stayed behind with the enemy fighters and were killed. The prophet was said to reply, "They are from among them." In this story, the women and children of the enemy preferred to remain with their men rather than flee to safety. Once they made that decision, they ceased to be innocents because they had aligned themselves with the combatants and were now legitimate targets for the Muslim forces. The al-Qaeda document suggests that those in the World Trade Center and the Pentagon should be viewed in the same way. The distinction between combatants and

Middle East Policy, Vol. X, No. 2, Summer 2003

civilians is thereby erased since some of the latter chose to remain in "enemy territory."

Condition Three: Assistance of Civilians in "Deed, Word or Mind"

In Islamic law, the legitimacy of a target in the context of a war is typically determined by the capacity of that target or individual to fight against the Muslims. This includes enemy soldiers and leaders, as well as advisers to the military and the enemy leadership, including civilian advisers. The vast majority of civilians, however, are excluded from target lists because they are not actively engaged in battle, especially women, children and the elderly, whose capacity to fight is considered minimal in most cases.[26]

Al-Qaeda, however, broadens the definition of active participation to include roles that indirectly assist the enemy:

> It is allowed for Muslims to kill protected ones among unbelievers on the condition that the protected ones have assisted in combat, whether in deed, word, mind or any other form of assistance, according to the prophetic command.

This is based upon a story about Duraid Ibn al-Simma, a well-known Arab poet who strongly opposed Muhammad and the message of Islam. According to tradition, he was brought to the battlefield to advise the Hawazin troops about battle procedures in a conflict against the Muslims. As a very old man, he posed no physical threat to the Muslim forces, but the intelligence he provided to the enemy made him a target and led to his death in battle.

But al-Qaeda's use of this story creates an expanded understanding of combat assistance that includes not only direct support through physical participation or advice to war planners, but less direct support as well. From this perspective, the press and journalists are legitimate targets because they are American propaganda tools in the war against al-Qaeda. Academics and intellectuals working on Islam and/or terrorism can be killed because their studies and publications help inform government officials and provide knowledge that can be used against the Muslims. Employees working in businesses that supply the government and/or military can be targeted because they provide equipment and services that support the war or the leaders waging the campaign.

Since a democratically elected government reflects the will of the people, a war against Islam of this magnitude must have popular support.

The breadth of this category is underscored by al-Qaeda's understanding of American democracy. It reasons that since a democratically elected government reflects the will of the people, a war against Islam of this magnitude must have popular support. Using the term "public opinion" (*al-ray al-amm*) to represent the will of the people in a democracy, al-Qaeda argues that,

> It is stupidity for a Muslim to think that the Crusader-Zionist public opinion which backs its government was waiting for some action from

> Muslims in order to support the Crusader war against Islam and thereby enkindle a spirit of hostility against Islam and Muslims. The Crusader-Zionist public opinion has expended all it has in order to stand behind the nations of the cross, executing their war against Islam and Muslims from the beginning of the colonization of Islamic countries until the present day. If the successive Crusader-Zionist governments had not received support from their people, their war against Islam and Muslims would not have taken such an obvious and conspicuous form. It is something that would not attain legitimacy except by the voices of the people.

This reflects the logic of an earlier fatwa issued by Hammoud al-Uqla al-Shuaybi just after September 11, which was adopted by the jihadi Salafis. In the fatwa, al-Shuaybi argues,

> [W]e should know that whatever decision the non-Muslim state, America, takes – especially critical decisions which involve war – it is taken based on opinion polls and/or voting within the House of Representatives and Senate, which represent directly, the exact opinion of the people they represent – the people of America – through their representatives in the Parliament [Congress]. Based on this, any American who voted for war is like a fighter, or at least a supporter.[27]

Given this perspective, al-Qaeda scoffs at the notion that those killed in the September 11 attacks, including those in the World Trade Centers were "innocent civilians." These individuals could be targeted because they assisted the government in its war against Muslims by "deed, word or mind." The economic significance of the towers as sources of revenue for the government (through taxes or business, for example) further damned its occupants. This condition is so expansive as to include virtually any individual in the United States (or allied countries).

Condition Four: The Necessity of War

The document argues that it is permissible to "kill protected ones among the unbelievers in the event of a need to burn the strongholds or fields of the enemy so as to weaken its strength in order to conquer the stronghold or topple the state." Throughout, al-Qaeda defines the World Trade Centers as enemy "strongholds," in effect directly linking the centers to the government and thus to the "war" against Muslims. In such an interpretation, the use of flying suicide bombs is equivalent to "burning" the stronghold.

Condition Five: Heavy Weaponry

Al-Qaeda uses a story about the prophet in which he was asked whether the Muslim fighters could use the catapult against the village of Taif, even though the enemy fighters were mixed with a civilian population. The Arabic term for catapult (*manjaniq*) refers to any stone throwing siege engine. In the early Islamic period and later, such devices proved quite effective against targets that were well fortified and difficult to overcome, but they were inaccurate and imprecise. Taif, located southeast of Mecca, was taken by Muslim forces in 630 CE. They resorted to the use of catapults in their assault because the city was surrounded by a high brick wall. Al-Qaeda likens the catapult as a

Middle East Policy, Vol. X, No. 2, Summer 2003

heavy weapon to the planes used in the September 11 attacks. This is also the religious evidence used by jihadis to rationalize the acquisition and possible use of weapons of mass destruction.

Condition Six: Human Shields

Al-Qaeda argues that it is permissible to kill women, children and other protected groups if the enemy uses them as human shields (*turs*). Although the religious evidence for this is not outlined in the document, it seems to derive from a fatwa by the medieval Islamic jurist Ibn Taymiyya that is widely cited by jihadis:

> The Islamic scholars have unanimously agreed that when the Kafir [unbeliever] takes Muslims as human shields, and the Muslims fear defeat if they do not attack, then it becomes permissible to fire, but we aim at the Kafir. Some scholars have said that it is permissible to fire even if ceasing fire will not form any kind of danger to Muslims.[28]

This understanding is thus rooted in the consensus of the scholars rather than explicit textual evidence.

Condition Seven: Violation of a Treaty

The final condition is when the enemy violates its treaty with the Muslims. "It is allowed for Muslims to kill protected ones among unbelievers if the people of a treaty violate their treaty and the leader must kill them in order to teach them a lesson. This is just as the Prophet did among the Bani Qurayza." According to Islamic tradition, Muhammad made a treaty with the Qurayza tribe soon after the *hijra*, or migration to Medina in 622 CE. It is reported that he was later persuaded to break that alliance and tear up the treaty. The Qurayza did not engage in hostile activity against Muslims but probably negotiated with the enemy while Medina was under attack. Upon learning of their betrayal, Muhammad besieged them for 25 days. When they unconditionally surrendered, their men were killed and their women and children were sold into slavery.

The sheer breadth of these conditions leaves ample theological justification for killing civilians in almost any imaginable situation. The notion that civilians become legitimate targets because of "deed, word, mind or any other form of assistance" (condition three) is so broad that it encompasses virtually every American. This is particularly the case since the document emphasizes the connection between supportive public opinion in a democracy and the ability of the government to wage an extended war against Muslims. And since only one condition need be met to provide a religious rationale for attack, al-Qaeda justifies terrorism under an almost inexhaustible array of possible scenarios and conditions.

CONCLUSION: ECHOES OF ALGERIA

These justifications echo the rationale used by jihadi Salafis during the civil war in Algeria, which could foreshadow the future direction of al-Qaeda operations. During the conflict between the government and Islamist rebels, jihadi groups massacred civilians, assassinated public personalities (including Berber singers, feminist leaders and academics), and targeted members of the press. Between 1996 and 1998, civilians were killed en masse in a directed and purposeful strategy of total war that eventually claimed more than 150,000 lives (mostly civilians). The rationale used to justify these killings represents a chilling precursor to the 2002 al-Qaeda document.

As in the al-Qaeda justification, the jihadis in Algeria broadened the understanding of combat to include any individual or group seen as complicit in the regime's counterinsurgency efforts against the Islamists. In an interview with *al-Djamaa*, which claimed to represent the "official voice of the GIA in the West," GIA chief Abu al-Moudhir argued that civilians who fought against the jihad by "force, talk or with the pen" were legitimate targets,[29] reflecting a doctrine of total war. As a GIA communiqué put it, "There is no neutrality in the war we are waging. With the exception of those who are with us, all others are apostates and deserve to die."[30]

This Manichaean worldview condemned broad swathes of the civilian population to death. Reporters and the press were attacked as extensions of the regime used to "cover its crimes and rationalize its aggression."[31] The jihadis supported killing those "who do not pray, who drink alcohol and take drugs, homosexuals, and immodest or debauched women."[32] Seven Trappist monks were beheaded for "mixing with [the Algerian people], living with them, and blocking the way of Allah by calling people to Christianity, and these are the worst ways of fighting the religion of Allah and Muslims."[33] Even children attending government-controlled schools were not immune to violence.[34] The scope of the violence was startling, and no quarter of society was immune from attack.

Given the stark parallels between the justifications for killing civilians in Algeria and the 2002 al-Qaeda document, the Algerian conflict may portend the future direction of al-Qaeda operations. Algerian jihadis attacked civilians with machetes, burned people alive, and slit throats in a brutal violence rationalized through broad categorization of legitimate civilian targets. The murder of reporter Daniel Pearl, whose throat was slit by al-Qaeda operatives in Pakistan, mirrors the brutality of the Algerian campaign. Al-Qaeda has thus far relied mostly on bombs and planes, but it is clear from the 2002 document that the echoes of Algeria could become louder as the jihadis continue to expand their war against U.S. civilians.

[1] Address to a Joint Session of Congress and the American People, September 20, 2001. Available at http://www.whitehouse.gov/news/releases/2001/09/20010920-8.html.

[2] See www.unc.edu/~kurzman/terror.htm for a listing with sources. In the following quotes, the original sources are cited.

[3] http://saudiembassy.net/press_release/01-spa/09-15-Islam.htm.

[4] Agence France Presse, September 14, 2001.

[5] http://www.islamonline.net/English/News/2001-09/13/article25.shtml.

[6] MSANews, September 14, 2001, http://msanews.mynet.net/MSANEWS/200109/20010917.15.html; Arabic original in *al-Quds al-Arabi* (London), September 14, 2001, p. 2, http://www.alquds.co.uk/Alquds/2001/09Sep/14%20Sep%20Fri/Quds02.pdf.

[7] Although al-Qaeda's main website was shut down after September 11, it was subsequently hosted at various alternative sites, including one run by The Center for Islamic Studies and Research (*markaz al-dirasat wal-buhuth al-islamiyyah*), which posted the al-Qaeda statement. We would like to thank Paul Eedle for bringing the document to our attention.

[8] See Quintan Wiktorowicz, "The New Global Threat: Transnational Salafis and Jihad," *Middle East Policy*, Vol. 8, No. 4, December 2001, pp. 18-38, and *The Management of Islamic Activism: Salafis, the Muslim*

Brotherhood, and State Power in Jordan (Albany: State University of New York Press, 2001).
[9] Wiktorowicz's interviews with Salafis in Jordan from 1996-1997 and a phone conversation with the president of the Quran and Sunna Society of North America (a U.S.-based Salafi organization), February 18, 2002. After Michael Doran published "Somebody Else's Civil War" in *Foreign Affairs*, Vol. 81, No. 1, January/February 2002, pp. 22-42, he received an onslaught of complaints from non-violent Salafis for his characterization of al-Qaeda as part of the Salafi movement (Wiktorowicz's conversation with Doran, December 2002).
[10] See, for example, Fawaz Gerges, "The Decline of Revolutionary Islam in Algeria and Egypt," *Survival*, Vol. 41, No. 1, Spring 1999, pp. 113-125.
[11] See Quintan Wiktorowicz, "The GIA and GSPC in Algeria," *In the Service of al-Qaeda: Radical Islamic Movements*, ed. Magnus Ranstorp (New York: Hurst Publishers and New York University Press, forthcoming).
[12] Dale F. Eickelman and James Piscatori, *Muslim Politics* (Princeton, NJ: Princeton University Press, 1996).
[13] See, for example, Robert D. Benford and David A. Snow, "Framing Processes and Social Movements: An Overview and Assessment," *Annual Reviews in Sociology*, No. 26, 2000, pp. 611-639.
[14] *United States District Court vs. Usama Bin Laden et al.*, 2001.
[15] Wiktorowicz's interview with Salim al-Hilali, Amman, Jordan, April 2, 1997.
[16] Many leading Islamic figures who condemned the attacks in New York and Washington have lent their support to Hamas attacks in the Palestinian territories, including well-known scholars such as Qaradawi.
[17] This characterization was repeated by Bin Laden in a tape aired on al-Jazeera television prior to the U.S. invasion of Iraq in 2003. Perhaps addressing charges that al-Qaeda is linked to Saddam Hussein, he emphasizes that the mujahidin must fight "for the sake of the one God" and that "fighting in support of the non-Islamic banners [ethnicity, nation, etc.] is forbidden. Muslims' doctrine and banner should be clear in fighting for the sake of God. He who fights to raise the word of God will fight for God's sake." An English translation of the tape is available at http://news.bbc.co.uk/2/hi/2middle_east/2751019.stm.
[18] In addition to the external jihad, there is the inner jihad or struggle against the ego (*jihad al-nafs*). The prophet referred to the latter as the "greater jihad."
[19] See, for example, John Kelsay and James Turner Johnson, eds., *Just War and Jihad: Historical and Theoretical Perspectives on War and Peace in Western and Islamic Traditions* (New York: Greenwood Press, 1991); and James Turner Johnson, *The Holy War Idea in Western and Islamic Traditions* (University Park, PA: The Pennsylvania State University Press, 1997).
[20] http://news.bbc.co.uk/2/hi/2middle_east/2751019.stm.
[21] *The Washington Post*, March 10, 2003.
[22] *Sahih Bukhari*, Vol. 9, Book 83, No. 49.
[23] Official statement by Abdul Aziz al-Alshaykh, mufti of Saudi Arabia, posted at www.fatwa-online.com/news/0010917.htm.
[24] See www.islamonline.net/English/News/2001-09/13/article25.shtml.
[25] See Edward William Lane, *An Arabic-English Lexicon* (8 vols; London: Williams & Norgate, 1863-1893; repr., Beirut: Librairie du Liban, 1980), pp. 2, 586.
[26] There are, of course, exceptions to this. Radical Islamists often argue that Israeli women, for example, are legitimate targets because they serve in the military.
[27] An English translation of the fatwa was posted at www.azzam.com after September 11. The fatwa was dismissed by reformist Salafis in Saudi Arabia. The Council of Ulama argued that the statement was "not worth adhering to." The council also contested Shuaybi's authority to issue fatwas. See www.fatwa-online.com/news/0011017_1.htm.
[28] Ibn Taymiyya, *Majmua al Fatawa*, 28/537.
[29] AFP, August 7, 1997.
[30] AFP, January 21, 1997, in FBIS-NES-97-013.
[31] Armed Islamic Group communiqué, issued January 16, 1995.
[32] *Al-Majallah*, March 14-20, 1999, pp. 21-22, in FBIS-NES-1999-0323.
[33] Armed Islamic Group communiqué, issued April 18, 1996.
[34] See, for example, AFP, September 21, 1994, in FBIS-NES-94-184.

Part V
In Comparison

[17]

The Role of Ideology in Terrorists' Target Selection

C. J. M. DRAKE

Ideology plays a crucial role in terrorist's target selection; it supplies terrorists with an initial motive for action and provides a prism through which they view events and the actions of other people. Those people and institutions whom they deem guilty of having transgressed the tenets of the terrorists' ideologically-based moral framework are considered to be legitimate targets which the terrorists feel justified in attacking. As an extension of this, ideology also allows terrorists to justify their violence by displacing the responsibility onto either their victims or other actors, whom in ideological terms they hold responsible for the state of affairs which the terrorists claim led them to adopt violence. While it is not the only factor which determines whether a potential target is attacked, ideology provides an initial range of legitimate targets and a means by which terrorists seek to justify attacks, both to the outside world and to themselves.

Terrorist attacks are occasionally called 'indiscriminate'. The implication is that the act of violence has been committed with little thought as to who or what is harmed, the random infliction of harm – and the attendant publicity – supposedly bringing sufficient benefits for the terrorists. In practice, however, attacks by non-state terrorist groups are rarely indiscriminate. Target selection is instead determined by a number of factors, and the terrorists' ideology is central to this process, not only because it provides the initial dynamic for the terrorists' actions, but because it sets out the moral framework within which they operate.

Due to the stigma which has been attached to terrorism over the years, its purpose has been obscured by a desire on the part of some to damn political opponents by attaching this particular epithet to their activities – even where these activities are not violent in themselves.[1] In fact the term *terrorism* describes a particular use of violence for political ends, where the violence is intended to create a psychological reaction in a person or group of people – the psychological target – to make them act in a way which the attacker desires.[2] The physical attacks themselves are not necessarily aimed at the psychological target or targets – although they might be – but are intended to make it or them behave in a particular way.[3] It should also be borne in mind that some attacks may not be intended to cause a negative reaction – such as fear – in the psychological target, but may be intended to evoke a positive reaction. For example some attacks – such as the assassination of an unpopular person – may be intended primarily to invoke admiration and a reaffirmation of support amongst the terrorists' supporters, who, in this case, would constitute the main psychological target.

Terrorism is defined here as the recurrent use or threatened use of politically-motivated and clandestinely organised violence, by a group whose aim is to affect one or more psychological targets in order to make them behave in a way which the terrorists desire.

Terrorists' target selection is affected by a number of factors. Ultimately, terrorists seek to achieve their political aims by co-ordinating the group's resources, pattern of attacks, and any other actions – possibly including overt political activities – into an effective strategy. The strategy adopted has a fundamental effect upon the selection of targets in that – given a choice of targets – terrorists acting rationally will choose to attack those which confer the greatest benefits upon their cause. Thus, using the model of terrorism shown above, it is clear that, ideally, a terrorist group's strategy will involve attacks which maximise the chances of achieving the desired reaction by the psychological target. Terrorist strategy, and hence target selection, is also affected by factors such as the resources of the group, the reaction of society to the terrorists' actions, and the security environment within which the terrorists operate.[4] Thus, while the place of ideology in the selection process is crucial, there is no single cause which can adequately explain terrorists target selection.

A point to bear in mind is that, for reasons of either misjudgement or operational incompetence, the reaction that terrorists may actually provoke is not always the response they intended. This occurred in January 1979, in Genoa, when the Red Brigades (Brigate Rosse – BR) shot dead Guido Rossa, a popular communist union official, because he had denounced a fellow car-factory worker as a Brigadist. This killing alienated those very industrial workers whose support the BR wished to mobilise, as was shown by the large anti-BR demonstrations which followed the killing.[5] Alternatively, terrorists might attack the wrong target due to bad luck or incompetence. For example, in the Dutch town of Roermond in May 1990, Provisional Irish Republican Army (PIRA) members shot dead two Australian tourists whom they had mistaken for British soldiers.[6] A realisation that the results which terrorists achieve are not always those which they intended is important when trying to divine their motives from the results of their actions.

A Definition of Ideology

An ideology is the beliefs, values, principles, and objectives – however ill-defined or tenuous – by which a group defines its distinctive political identity and aims.[7] Some ideologies – particularly separatism and politicised religion, but others as well – may include elements of historical, semi-mythical, and supernatural beliefs.[8] What is important is that ideology provides a motive and framework for action.[9]

There may be a distinction between the professed ideology of a group and the actual beliefs of individual members. The leaders of political groups usually have a fairly specific ideology with clear political objectives, but for many of their followers a sufficient motive for belonging to the group is provided by adherence to the group or a visceral dislike of an 'enemy', however defined. In the case of terrorists, this can be seen with various far-right organisations in Britain during the late 1970s and early 1980s, and in letters from Italian fascist terrorists imprisoned in the 1970s and 1980s. In both cases, there was a clear difference between the fairly well-developed ideological beliefs of the leaders and the relatively crude prejudices of their followers.[10]

While in practice most groups' ideologies are fairly unique, for the purposes of convenience the following categories are used to classify ideologies: separatism, religion, liberalism, anarchism, communism, conservatism, fascism, single-issues, and organised crime. The inclusion of single-issue groups and organised criminal groups may be questioned on the grounds that such groups do not have an overarching ideology. Nevertheless, their political concerns do provide a rationale for their actions, fulfilling the role which more orthodox ideologies provide for other groups. In the case of single-issue groups, while they do not intend to change the system of government or radically alter social or economic relationships, they do try to exert influence over relatively narrow policy areas.[11] With regard to organised criminal groups, while ordinary criminal activity does not qualify as terrorism, where criminal organisations have used violence to safeguard or promote their interests by systematically intimidating politicians and public officials – as has occurred with the Mafia in Italy and with drug traffickers in Colombia – or to gain systematic immunity from the law, then these groups are subverting the policy process, an act which is ultimately political.[12]

These ideological categories are not mutually exclusive and it is perfectly possible for a group to hold to more than one political aspiration. Indeed, the beliefs of many groups form ideological hybrids. For instance, although the categories of communist and separatist are listed separately, the Basque group ETA (Euzkadi ta Askatasuna – Basque Homeland and Liberty), together with its political partner Herri Batasuna, has considered itself to be both separatist and Marxist.[13] This has caused splits in ETA.[14] Similarly the Palestinian group Hamas can be described as both a religious group and as a separatist group. It combines what it claims to be a true interpretation of Islamic tenets with the desire to set up an Islamic Palestinian state.[15] Insofar as it is an Islamic group, Hamas can be classified as a religious terrorist group, but it is also separatist because it advocates Palestinian independence.

How Ideology Influences Terrorists' Target Selection

Unless they are motivated by a pure lust for power and the benefits which it can confer, most political groups are motivated by an ideology. This is also the case with terrorist groups. The actual decision to turn to terrorism may occasionally be provided by the ideology of the group, but frequently it is determined by other strategic factors, such as the failure of non-violent methods of achieving the group's goals, or the repression of non-violent methods by state or non-state bodies.

Irrespective of how the decision to turn to terrorism has been made, when a group takes the decision to use violence, an early step is to determine who or what will be attacked. A group's ideology is extremely important in determining target selection because it defines how the group's members see the world around them. The ideology of a terrorist group identifies the 'enemies' of the group by providing a measure against which to assess the 'innocence' or 'guilt' of people and institutions. This gives rise to the idea that certain people or things are somehow 'legitimate targets'. The concept of the legitimate target should not be confused with common or legal notions of guilt and innocence. For instance, members of the Animal Liberation Front (ALF) in Britain frequently claim that although technically breaking the law, they are in fact responding to a higher law which compels them to act as they do.[16] Similarly, a member of the PIRA told Tony Parker:

> I don't expect to be judged by your rules: if Brits do that, then they'll see the IRA as a lot of ruthless maniacs which by their definition I suppose we are. Ruthless, definitely yes: and maniacs if that's what people are who're never going to see sense as you define it, well yes that'd be an appropriate word. The IRA has its own logic and oh no it's not yours.'[17]

Consequently, events and the actions of various people – both potential targets and others – are interpreted in terms of the terrorists' cause, even if the people concerned have never given the terrorists a moment's thought. For instance, according to Patricia Hearst, Emily Harris, of the Symbionese Liberation Army in 1970s California, justified the possibility of law students being killed by a bomb under a police car on the grounds that, 'Those law students are studying to be lawyers and they'll go to work for some big, piggy, corporation, and so they are pigs too.'[18]

The students' action in choosing to study law, was seen in terms of Harris' ideological mindset rather than their own perception of what they were doing. Likewise, in 1977, the PIRA carried out a short-lived campaign of assassination against prominent businessmen on the grounds that the very presence of such firms was felt to underpin the British occupation of Northern Ireland.[19] The businessmen probably did not see their actions in this light, but the PIRA did, and this meant that they became targets. The unpopularity of this campaign resulted in its swift termination. When the PIRA assassinated businessmen again, from the mid-1980s onwards, they attacked those which carried out activities deemed to be in support of the security forces, such as the maintenance of police stations, or the supply of goods or services to the security forces or their members.[20] In the meantime, the PIRA continued their bombing campaign against all forms of commercial premises in an attempt to disrupt Northern Ireland's economy, but the bulk of these attacks were not intended to kill people.

As a result of their ideological beliefs, terrorists often seek to identify their victims as being in some way deserving of the treatment meted out to them (although this does not necessarily apply where the terrorists acknowledge that they have unintentionally harmed the wrong people).[21] Furthermore, the supposed guilt of their victims absolves the terrorists – at least temporarily – of feelings of remorse for their actions, because a person who is defined as an enemy deserving punishment obviously deserves to be attacked. It also legitimises the terrorist's actions in their own minds, in those of their followers, and, they hope, in the minds of those people who are uncommitted. Thus in July 1990 the PIRA killed the Conservative MP Ian Gow with an under-car bomb because he was a close friend of the then Prime Minister, Margaret Thatcher, and was deemed to be '... central to policy decisions...'.[22] He was seen as part of the 'British war machine' responsible for the British presence in Northern Ireland, and was therefore categorised as a legitimate target. His friendship with the Prime Minister, association with her policies, and steadfast support for Ulster unionism, made him an even more tempting target – according to McKittrick almost a surrogate for Margaret Thatcher herself.[23]

The account of an Italian Red Brigadist shows how someone can be adjudged to be 'guilty' in terms of the terrorists' ideology and thus becomes a legitimate target:

> ... you carry out an enquiry on someone so there is a sort of political enquiry beforehand, but psychologically it becomes something different, you single out someone who is responsible; it is not the State as before ... with policemen, and the Flying Squad [but] real physical people, this chap does this ... and has done that and you start

> a trial ... The trial begins when you single out someone on paper, that is to say, you make a person correspond to a political need ... that chap is responsible, it is him right here and now, there is already a trial logic ... when you've already decided that he is guilty ... and what makes you different is the penalty, the penalty that you allot to that person who is guilty of those things ... he is not even a person any more, he has been emptied and you load him up with other crimes, other responsibilities.[24]

A repentant Brigadist, Massimiliano Bravi, has also noted:

> The ideals of justice turned into murderous violence directed against the men who represented the State (the human being totally crushed in his social role) and in our eyes they were the guardians and perpetrators of every possible injustice and social suffering. They were 'the unjust' and we were the 'avengers'.[25]

The notion of guilt, or indeed innocence, is thus dependent upon the subjective moral imperatives of the terrorists. For example, in March 1985, Ezio Tarantelli, a Professor of Economics at the University of Rome and an adviser to the Italian Government, was shot dead by the PCC (Partito Comunista Combattente – Fighting Communist Party; a faction of the Red Brigades) because they deemed him 'one of the most authoritative technical-political exponents in the service of large capital'.[26] The language employed shows how the use of ideological terminology drains the humanity out of people and transforms them into legitimate targets.

A good example of the difference between terrorists' perception and that of more generally accepted institutions occurred in April 1991 when a Red Army Faction (RAF) sniper shot dead Detlev Rohwedder, the Director of the Treuhandanstalt (Trusteeship Office for East German State Property – the agency responsible for overseeing the privatisation of companies formerly owned by the East German state) in his Dusseldorf home. Following the assassination, an editorial in the London-based newspaper *The Independent* condemned the RAF as, '... a tiny band of sick people representing no views beyond those concocted in their own closed minds', whilst the newspaper's obituarist called Rohwedder '... one of the good guys on the German political scene'.[27] However, the Red Army Faction communiqué following the assassination accused Rohwedder – who had previously been State Secretary in the West German Economics Ministry – of having sold arms to fascist regimes in the Third World, and of having traded nuclear know-how for uranium from the apartheid regime in South Africa. They condemned him as a 'brutal reorganizer' when manager at Hoechst Chemicals, and called him:

> One of those armchair murderers who daily go over dead bodies and who in the interest of power and profits plan the misery and death of millions of human beings.[28]

They also condemned the expansion of Germany, the imposition of 'free market economics' on East Germany and the Third World, and condemned the nature of capitalism and the price it exacted from people in the Third World.[29] By killing Rohwedder the RAF believed they were striking at the roots of the development of a racialist and capitalist 'Greater Germany' and were sending a message to people in the former East Germany.[30] For the RAF, far from being the murder of a 'good guy', the killing of Rohwedder was a moral act.

As suggested by the example of Rohwedder's killing, another important effect of ideology is that it transforms people or objects into representative symbols. A loyalist who bombed a pub in a Catholic part of Belfast in 1974 has noted how he and his colleagues 'dehumanised' Catholics, seeing them as 'animals' who gave support to the Provisional IRA.[31] This dehumanisation can be seen in the way members of the other community have been given derogatory labels. Loyalist terrorists in Northern Ireland have regarded Catholics as 'taigs' – a disparaging term for Irish Catholics. In June 1994, six Catholic men drinking in a country pub were shot dead by loyalist gunmen, one of whom called the victims 'Fenian bastards', the Fenians being a nineteenth century republican revolutionary movement.[32] On the other side of the divide, soldiers in Northern Ireland have been seen by Irish republicans as 'Brits' to be 'stiffed' [killed]. Republican terrorists have noted how they regard the soldiers as a 'uniform' representing the 'occupying force' in Ireland rather than seeing them as human beings.[33]

Such rationalisation and dehumanisation is not confined to terrorists and indeed is common in wartime. According to Glenn Gray:

> The basic aim of a nation at war in establishing an image of the enemy is to distinguish as sharply as possible the act of killing from the act of murder by making of the former an act deserving all honour and praise.[34]

Thus, during the Second World War British soldiers killed their German adversaries and vice versa, despite holding little personal animosity towards them, because they were the enemy.[35] Such rationalisations were sometimes extended to killing civilians. British aerial bombing raids against German cities were justified to the British people as revenge for similar raids by the German Luftwaffe – or indeed for the moral turpitude of the German people – as well as attacks on Germany's economic capacity.[36] Thus, on occasion, democratic states as well as terrorists have dehumanised an enemy, even when this has involved justifying the killing of civilians.

A person or institution does not have to carry out or fail to carry out some action to become a legitimate target. Just being who, what, or where one is may be enough. In May 1972, Japanese Red Army (JRA) terrorists carried out a gun and grenade attack against passengers at Lod Airport in Tel Aviv, Israel, killing 27 and injuring 70. Most of the victims were Puerto Rican pilgrims. The Popular Front for the Liberation of Palestine (PFLP) – on whose behalf the JRA were operating – justified the deaths on the grounds that by being in Israel the victims were held to have tacitly recognised the Israeli state to which the PFLP were opposed.[37] Likewise, Crenshaw makes the point that during the Algerian Rebellion of 1954 to 1962 the FLN saw bomb attacks upon any European[38] civilians in Algeria as legitimate because the Europeans' very presence made them symbols of French and settler authority in Algeria. Moreover, by virtue of being Europeans, the death and injury of these civilians had a direct influence on the conflict because it polarised the European from the Algerian population.[39] Thus, an entire racial category of people was seen by the terrorists as legitimate targets. Although the attacks were not targeted against specific individuals, it would be inaccurate to call them indiscriminate. They were intended to harm a particular – albeit very wide – category of people. This was in order to affect chosen psychological targets; the European and Algerian populations by driving them apart, and the French Government by sapping its will to rule Algeria.

This attitude on the part of terrorists explains how being a member of a particular religion or race can make someone a target for attacks without the victim or victims seeming to have done anything blameworthy. In July 1994 this was demonstrated when a building housing the Delegation of Argentine-Israeli Associations and the Argentine-Israeli Mutual Association was bombed, killing 96 people and injuring 236.[40] As the attack was thought to be in retaliation for an Israeli attack on a Hizbollah base in Lebanon the previous month, a Lebanese authority on the Hizbollah was asked why Jews were targeted in Argentina rather than in Israel. The reply was that:

> The Jews of Israel come from Poland, from Russia, from Europe or from Latin America ... What is the difference? It is the same.[41]

Thus, all Jews were seen as a legitimate target for attacks aimed at punishing the state of Israel, to which they were perceived to be affiliated.

Terrorist attacks are not always preceded by a detailed ideological inquiry. Where the target is readily identifiable, and any decisions as to the guilt of the target – whether an individual, an institution, or a group of people – have been made, target selection is quite straightforward. Bishop and Mallie point out that the initial PIRA decision in 1970–71 to kill British soldiers meant simply resuming a war against a traditional enemy.[42] The decision that British soldiers were a legitimate target had been settled a long time ago by republican ideology, which saw them as representatives of an occupying force. For instance, in November 1987 a PIRA spokesman noted that there was no need for a local unit to gain permission from a higher level to carry out a bombing attack against soldiers.[43] They were automatically seen as legitimate targets.

As well as deciding who or what may be determined as legitimate targets, ideology also allows terrorists to displace the blame for their actions onto other people. Sometimes, as in the above-mentioned RAF assassination of Detlev Rohwedder, the terrorists' victim is blamed. On other occasions the actions of others – sometimes the psychological target – are held to make the terrorists' actions inevitable. For example, according to Abu Iyad the Black September kidnapping of Israeli athletes at the Munich Olympics in September 1972, was caused by failure of the International Olympic Committee, and the international community as a whole, to accord proper recognition to the Palestinians. Likewise, he claimed that the subsequent deaths of nine of the Israelis were due to the German authorities' rescue attempt at Furstenfeldbruck Airport, rather than to the terrorists' decision to carry out the operation in the first place, and to kill the hostages once a rescue attempt was made.[44] In a similar vein, the leader of a group of Palestinian hijackers who seized a Lufthansa aeroplane in October 1977 is quoted as having said 'We don't want to shed blood … but as the imperialist fascist West German regime rejects our demands we have no choice', and at another point claimed 'What happens now is solely the fault of the fascist German government and of Helmut Schmidt.'[45] Thus, according to the terrorists the responsibility for the hijacking and its consequences lay with the psychological target rather than with the terrorists themselves. In a similar fashion, following PIRA attacks, terrorists and other republican spokesmen have claimed that all deaths in the Northern Irish conflict are ultimately the responsibility of the British for not leaving Northern Ireland.[46] Furthermore, in January 1987, the PIRA claimed that the authorities' assertion that normality had returned to Belfast forced them to bomb commercial premises in Northern Ireland to disprove the assertion.[47] Again, responsibility for the terrorists' actions was laid at the door of the psychological target.

Sometimes the overt ideological justification for an attack is supplied after the attack has occurred rather than worked out beforehand. It appears that the higher levels of the PIRA have sought to justify actions by local units after attacks which they would not have sanctioned had they received prior notice.[48] Going further, Moss records that in Turin in the late-1970s the

Red Brigades often did not issue a communique justifying an attack until after they had seen the press reaction. They then tailored it accordingly.[49] According to Willan, during this period BR targeting was often based on slipshod research and trivial considerations. On one occasion, after they had shot and wounded the wrong person, Willan claims that they rewrote the original communique so as to give the impression that the victim had been their intended target.[50]

Some terrorists have also widened the limits of what can be considered a legitimate target if such widening has made it easier for them to attack appropriate targets.[51] In the early-1970s, the PIRA – at least overtly – claimed that they primarily targeted the security forces and buildings that constituted 'economic' targets, such as shops and offices. However, as noted previously, by the mid-1980s the limits of what constituted a legitimate target was broadened to include people working with the security forces in ways which were not directly linked with security force operations. According to one PIRA member:

> Our definition of who the enemy is isn't one which follows the same line as yours either. We regard all people who support the armed forces of the British Government in any way as legitimate targets. … We'll define whether someone's helping the security forces or not: it's not for you to make the definition and criticise us for not agreeing with it. I don't know if I make that clear: probably not and if that's so then I have to say it doesn't greatly matter to me.[52]

Hence, whilst a workman involved in the construction of a police station might see himself as an innocent civilian, the PIRA would see him as a 'collaborator' liable to 'execution'.[53] The fact that he was a softer target than a member of the British Army would be a bonus in operational terms, although in symbolic terms killing a soldier would be preferable.[54] Thus, when assessing the influence of ideology upon targeting, one must also allow for operational factors such as the availability of targets and the resources of the group concerned, and also for the incompetence or idiosyncrasies of individuals or groups within the overall terrorist organisation.

Targeting Patterns of Different Ideological Groups

The influence of ideology on terrorist targeting can be seen by comparing the targets attacked by different groups. Differences between groups with different ideologies, and similarities between groups with similar ideologies, may demonstrate to a degree the extent to which ideology affects target selection.

The differences in target selection between groups holding different ideologies, but operating within the same geographical arena and with a common background of mutual communal antipathy, can be illustrated by a comparison of people killed by terrorists in Northern Ireland. The groups concerned are either republican terrorists – primarily the Provisional IRA, but also including the Official IRA (OIRA), the Irish National Liberation Army (INLA), and other smaller groups, and loyalist terrorists – primarily the Ulster Defence Association (UDA), Ulster Volunteer Force (UVF), but also other splinter groups. Although their ideologies have altered over the years, it is accurate to say that the republicans have aimed at achieving a united Ireland by excluding British rule from Northern Ireland, while the loyalists' objective has been to prevent Northern Ireland from being forced into a united Ireland. In addition, both republicans and loyalists have sought to protect the communities from which they almost exclusively derive their support – the Catholic community for republicans, the Protestant community for loyalists – from what they see as the depredations of the other side.[55]

In general, separatist terrorists – such as the Irish republican terrorist groups – tend to attack people who are members of, or co-operate with, organisations which they see as representing the 'foreign' occupier. For instance, the Basque separatist group ETA have frequently selected the Civil Guard (Guardia Civil – a national paramilitary-style police force), national police, and the military as the primary targets for their attacks in the Basque Country and elsewhere in Spain.[56] According to Clark's account, law enforcement officials and members of the armed forces (excluding alleged spies and informers against the terrorists) made up 62.4 per cent of those killed by ETA and 40.5 per cent of those wounded between 1968 and 1980.[57] Similarly Llera, Mata, and Irwin estimate that police and military officers made up 59.1 per cent of the fatalities caused by ETA operations between 1968 and 1988.[58] The heaviest casualties have occurred among the Civil Guard. This unit deploys its members outside the areas in which they were recruited. It was widely feared and seen as a symbol of Francoist repression in the Basque provinces in the 1960s and early 1970s. The Civil Guards are still seen by ETA members and their supporters as symbols of foreign – Spanish – occupation.[59] Thus, between 1968 and 1980, Civil Guard members made up 50.8 per cent of security force deaths caused by ETA attacks and 57.7 per cent of security force members wounded.[60]

On the other hand extreme right-wing terrorists – such as the Northern Irish loyalist terrorists – use terrorism to protect the existing state of affairs, sometimes claiming to protect the state from subversion. In the 1980s, the supposed function of Colombian extreme right-wing terrorist groups (often referred to as death squads), such as Death to Kidnappers (Muerte a Secuestradores – MAS) and the Association of Peasants and Ranchers of the

Magdelena Valley (Asociacion de Campesionos y Ganderos del Magdelena Medio – ACDEGAM), was to combat communist insurgents such as the April 19th Movement (Movimiento 19 de Abril – M-19), and the Revolutionary Armed Forces of Colombia (Fuerzas Armadas Revolucionarias de Colombia – FARC).[61] However, from 1985 onwards they attacked members of the Patriotic Union (Union Patriotica – UP, the FARC's legalised political party) – and members of other organisations such as peasant groups and trades unionists, which have sought to challenge the existing balance of political power.[62] By 1994 Amnesty International estimates that 1,500 UP members had been killed by extreme right-wing death squads.[63] Hundreds of trade unionists and workers have also been killed, particularly those taking strike action against their employers, as have judges and others involved in the investigation of such killings.[64] While the killings have been condemned by members of the Colombian Government, the death squads have justified them as action against subversives.[65]

The respective targeting patterns of ETA and the Colombian death squads are broadly similar to those of the republican and loyalist terrorists in Northern Ireland. For republicans, particularly the PIRA which is the largest republican terrorist group, target selection is fairly simple. Anybody who is a member of the security forces, or who aids the British presence in Ireland, is automatically considered a member of the 'British war machine', and thus a legitimate target. This includes contractors who work on military or police buildings in Northern Ireland, politicians or officials involved in the formulation of policy towards Northern Ireland, unionist politicians, informers, and anybody whom the PIRA deem to be actively collaborating with the security forces.[66]

On the other hand, while republican terrorists can identify security force members quite easily – by seeing them at work in their uniforms or identifying them entering or leaving security force premises – it is comparatively difficult for loyalists to identify and target members of republican groups. By their nature, active terrorists tend towards a degree of clandestinity. In Northern Ireland, republican terrorists also generally live in strongly Catholic areas where it would be difficult for loyalists to pick up information on individuals. By contrast, several republican political activists have been attacked by loyalist terrorists because the overt nature of their activities makes them far easier to identify as republicans.[67] However, even these targets became relatively harder to attack, as many overtly active members of Sinn Fein took protective security measures, such as reinforcing the doors to their houses. Besides, the deaths of such activists primarily affected republicans rather than the Catholic population as a whole, and the aim of loyalist terrorists has often been to intimidate the entire Catholic population.

Killing Catholics at random turned the entire Catholic population in Northern Ireland into a psychological target as all were potential targets.[68] By attacking Catholics, loyalist terrorists have hoped to force ordinary Northern Irish Catholics – particularly in strongly republican areas – to put pressure upon the PIRA to stop its terrorist campaign, and to prevent British Government moves towards a united Ireland.[69] As a result loyalist terrorists have often attacked any Catholics they can find, believing them to be sympathetic to republican terrorism or at the very least culpable for not putting pressure on the PIRA to stop their campaign, a suspicion reportedly shared by many ordinary Protestants in Northern Ireland.[70] In addition to the effect which such killings may have on the Catholic population, sectarian attacks have also provided a means for loyalist terrorists to retaliate for republican attacks. Again, such attacks have been rationalised on the grounds that those killed were somehow – even if tacitly – responsible for republican actions.[71]

The pattern of terrorist killings in Northern Ireland, as shown in Table 1, may be skewed by the gap between the terrorists' intentions and the results actually achieved. However, one can see that loyalist terrorist attacks have been mainly directed against ordinary Catholics. A number of republican terrorists or political activists have been killed by loyalist terrorists, as have a fair number of other loyalists.[72] The concentration of loyalist attacks against Catholic civilians confirms that the Catholic population as a whole has been seen as a legitimate target. The communal nature of much of the violence in Northern Ireland can be seen in the number of sectarian killings on both sides, but there is a much higher concentration of primarily sectarian killings amongst the victims of loyalist groups than those killed by the republican groups. This is what one would expect to see with loyalist terrorist groups that regards an entire community – in this case the Catholics living in Northern Ireland – as suspect or subversive.

Republican terrorists have primarily selected members of the security forces as their targets for lethal attacks. If one includes all of those people whom republicans term part of the 'British war machine' – that is members of the Army, RUC, UDR/RIR, prison officers, alleged informers, and people who work for or supply goods and services to the security forces – they represent 65 per cent of the victims of lethal republican attacks between 1969 and 1993. This accords with the republican philosophy that the forces of the Crown and their 'collaborators' are representatives of a foreign, occupying force, and can therefore be classified as legitimate targets. The decline of the proportion of British soldiers killed by republican terrorism as compared to members of the UDR/RIR and RUC is shown in Table 2. This demonstrates how – in practical terms – the PIRA and other republican terrorists have found it increasingly hard to kill British soldiers.

TABLE 1

KILLINGS IN NORTHERN IRELAND PERPETRATED BY LOYALIST AND REPUBLICAN GROUPS: 1969–1993.

	LOYALIST		REPUBLICAN	
	Number	%	Number	%
British Army[a]	1	0.1	448	26.3
UDR/RIR[a]	3	0.4	236	13.9
RUC[a]	6	0.7	297	17.4
Prison officers[a]	2	0.2	25	1.5
Alleged informers	16	1.9	65	3.8
Security force workers[b]	0	0.0	35	2.1
Internal feuds[c]	46	5.4	45	2.6
Opposing terrorists[d]	28	3.3	27	1.6
Political activists[e]	32	3.8	12	0.7
Overtly sectarian[f]	670	79.3	152	8.9
Other[g]	41	4.9	363	21.3
TOTAL	**845**	**100.0**	**1705**	**100.1**

n.b. Percentages are rounded up or down to nearest 0.1%.

a Includes former members.
b Civilian contractors and direct employees carrying out work for the security forces.
c Loyalists killed by loyalists and republicans killed by republicans.
d Republicans killed by loyalists and loyalists killed by republicans.
e Nationalists and republicans killed by loyalists and unionists and loyalists killed by republicans.
f Catholics killed by loyalists, and Protestants killed by republicans, primarily because of their religion.
g Excludes killings outside Northern Ireland. Excludes terrorists killed by their own bomb but includes other unintended deaths.

Source: M.Sutton. *Bear in mind these dead ... An Index of Deaths from the Conflict in Ireland, 1969-1993*, (Belfast: Beyond the Pale Publications, 1994), pp.196–203.

TABLE 2

SECURITY FORCE DEATHS IN NORTHERN IRELAND, 1970–1993.

YEAR	RUC[a]	UDR/RIR[b]	Army	Total
1970-1973	43	39	204	286
1974-1977	63	42	71	176
1978-1981	54	39	70	163
1982-1985	62	31	37	130
1986-1989	43	30	40	113
1990-1993	27	20	22	69
TOTAL	**293**	**201**	**444**	**938**

a Includes RUC reserves and part-time RUC
b Includes part-time UDR/RIR.

n.b. This table includes 19 security force members killed by loyalists or mistakenly killed by other security force members. The vast majority of security force deaths have been caused by republicans.

Sources: Royal Ulster Constabulary. *Chief Constable's Annual Report 1993*, 96. M.Sutton. *Bear in mind these dead*, pp.195–205.

Consequently, however desirable attacks on the British Army might be in terms of ideology, republican terrorists have tempered this with operational pragmatism and carried out a higher proportion of lethal attacks against the local security forces. Nevertheless, the continuation of attacks against the Army shows the importance which the PIRA in particular place upon such attacks.

A controversy which has arisen between Steve Bruce and Robert W. White concerns the extent to which sectarianism plays a part in PIRA's target selection. In particular, they disagree as to whether PIRA attacks upon members of the local security forces are largely inspired by sectarianism, as Bruce appears to contend, or whether they are primarily straightforward attacks upon the British state's security forces as White seems to suggest.[73] (It should be noted here that neither writer takes an extreme attitude – arguing that such PIRA attacks are wholly sectarian or wholly non-sectarian. Thus, the debate is largely concerned with the extent to which such attacks are prompted by sectarianism rather than by strategic factors.) The controversy has a degree of relevance to this article because it illustrates the extent to which the overt ideology of a group – in this case Irish republicanism – may be affected by other societal factors and thus influence the selection of targets.

The number of victims of republican sectarian attacks against civilians – including attacks by the PIRA and minor groups such as the Irish National Liberation Army (INLA) and the Irish People's Liberation Organisation (IPLO) – is indicated in Table 1. While substantial in number, such attacks make up a relatively small percentage of the overall number of fatalities caused by republican terrorists. However, as Bruce points out, in order for the PIRA to kill a Protestant it is not necessary to carry out blatantly sectarian attacks against civilians, as it is much more likely that members of the local security forces – the RUC and the UDR/RIR – are Protestants rather than Catholics. Thus an attack on a security force member is much more likely to kill a Protestant than a Catholic.[74] McKeown's statistics bear this out. He estimates that during the 20-year period up to 12 July 1989, out of 525 Northern Ireland-born security force members, prison service members, and ex-security force members killed, 486 were Protestants. This is about 93 per cent of the total security force deaths, a proportion which he notes is about the same as the proportion of the security forces which are Protestant.[75] This estimate of the religious composition of the security forces was partly confirmed by a reply to a parliamentary question in January 1993, which indicated that about 7 per cent of RUC members were Catholics – although the proportion of Catholics in the Ulster Defence Regiment by the late 1980s was much lower at less than 2 per cent.[76]

The PIRA and other republicans have claimed that their attacks on members of the RUC and the UDR/RIR have not been sectarian, but have been intended purely as attacks on the forces of the Crown.[77] Indeed Catholic members of the local security forces have been attacked.[78] Ultimately, there is a problem with ascribing this pattern of deaths to sectarianism on the part of republicans, or, alternatively, of claiming that even a totally non-sectarian targeting policy aimed at the security forces would kill this proportion of Protestants because of the religious composition of the RUC and UDR/RIR. The problem is that, despite the seeming willingness of those involved to give interviews, one cannot really get into the mind of the perpetrators of these killings, particularly their state of mind at the time of the killings. Furthermore, as with most people involved in politics, one cannot accept their subsequent public rationalisations at face-value; nor, by the same token, can one automatically dismiss them. In the final analysis, outside judgements of the motives for attacks – however well-informed – can only be based on speculation reinforced as far as possible by objective data.

Another area where it can be argued that the Provisional IRA's activities might show proof of a sectarian attitude concerns the use – and in particular the location – of bombs. While the religious details of bystanders killed by terrorist attacks are not specifically represented in Table 1 as a separate category, the large number of 'others' killed by republicans reflects their use of bombs against both property and human targets, as bombings aimed at one target frequently harm other bystanders. There is as yet no readily accessible database of the location, nature, and religion of the owners of the various buildings and other commercial and residential facilities attacked by republican terrorists during the recent troubles, and White rightly points out that there are dangers in concentrating upon accounts of specific high-profile events rather than statistics when seeking to establish a pattern of behaviour.[79] Thus one cannot definitely state that the PIRA bombing campaign in Northern Ireland has a sectarian edge. Nevertheless, as Bruce points out, through the years the PIRA do seem to have found it acceptable to detonate large bombs in predominantly Protestant areas in order to attack commercial premises or security force members and facilities.[80] High-profile examples of such attacks include the Enniskillen bombing of November 1987, which killed eleven people and injured 63, the 2,000 pound van-bomb which destroyed the Northern Ireland Forensic Laboratories in September 1992 but also damaged more than 1,000 houses in a Protestant residential area, and the Shankill Road bombing of October 1993, an attempt to wipe out the Belfast UDA leadership, but which instead killed nine Protestant civilians – including two children – and one of the bombers.[81] Overall, White's collation of the Irish Information Partnership's data shows that between 1969 and 1989 PIRA bomb attacks killed 111

Protestant civilians compared to 47 Catholic civilians.[82] While such attacks might not seem as blatantly sectarian as the deliberate assassination attempts carried out by loyalist terrorists against Catholic civilians, they do show a high degree of disdain for the importance of the lives and livelihoods of ordinary Protestants.

It can be argued that the PIRA's attitude towards such attacks is not necessarily sectarian – in the sense of being specifically aimed at Northern Irish Protestants – because the PIRA has shown the same willingness to kill and injure bystanders in its bomb attacks in England. This is often due to the nature of the bombs and the inadequate nature of the warnings given. Amongst many other incidents, these include the bombing of two Birmingham pubs on 21 November 1974, which killed 21 people and injured 162; the bomb in Warrington in March 1993, which killed two children and injured 56 other people; and the bomb in Manchester in June 1996, which destroyed part of the city centre and injured about 200 people.[83] Such attacks suggest that the PIRA's lack of concern for Protestant casualties also extends to the victims of PIRA bombs in England. One could therefore argue that this shows that the PIRA are not specifically sectarian in their attitude towards Protestants, but only if one accepts that they seem to harbour the same indifference towards the infliction of harm upon ordinary English people as they show towards Protestants.[84]

When examining overall terrorist targeting in Northern Ireland, another area which might repay further research is that of vigilante actions – or as they prefer to call it 'policing' – by both sets of paramilitary groups in Northern Ireland. Like the republican attacks on commercial premises, the figures for 'punishment' attacks on people identified by republican or loyalist terrorists as criminal or otherwise anti-social do not generally appear in the statistics on killings as most such attacks are not fatal. According to the RUC, republican groups carried out 138 punishment attacks in 1994 and 76 in 1995, while loyalist groups carried out 86 and 144 respectively.[85] Terrorists and their supporters on both sides of the Northern Ireland conflict portray these attacks as a means of preventing lawlessness within their communities, and bearing in mind that many of the terrorists live in these communities one should not dismiss their motives out of hand.[86] Nevertheless, such attacks are also a useful means by which the terrorists on both sides can, under the guise of social concern, establish control over the communities within which they operate and discourage or eliminate dissent.[87] To a degree such attacks are determined primarily by strategic rather than ideological concerns. They reflect the terrorists' desire to maintain a high degree of support in those geographical areas where they are strongest, to discourage rivals and to intimidate those who might cooperate with the security forces. However, it is notable on the republican side, that when dealing with those they deemed to be non-political criminals, the PIRA have justified their actions by referring to the need to protect the community rather than referring to their own need to maintain their support base, thus demonstrating the need for some form of moral justification for their attacks.[88]

When examining the activities of the terrorist groups in Northern Ireland, it must be realised that while statistics concerning attacks and their consequences are generally tabulated in terms of the organisations to whom responsibility for the attacks is attached, organisations as large as the Provisional IRA, the Ulster Defence Association and the Ulster Volunteer Force are not monolithic. These organisations consist of smaller groups and ultimately individuals who are, in practice, subject to greater or lesser degrees of control by the central leadership. As a result they frequently lack both the cohesion and the effective hierarchical chain of command one may expect to find in an efficient military or police organisation. Consequently operational decisions may be made by middle-ranking or junior terrorist leaders on the ground, rather than by the heads of the terrorist organisations, and thus it would be a mistake to attribute decisions about target selection to one central doctrine or mindset.[89]

The conflict in Northern Ireland shows how the different ideologies of groups operating in the same geographical and social environment develop different patterns of target selection. It is argued here that much, though not all, of the reason for this is that the ideological differences lead the terrorists to select targets of very different natures. The republicans tend to select members of the security forces or people linked to them, while the loyalists tend to select those people – primarily ordinary Catholics – whom they see as subversive of the existing order. However, as well as targeting differences between groups with different ideologies, there can also be notable differences in targeting between groups with apparently similar ideologies, such as the various European communist terrorist groups of the last thirty years.

The writings of revolutionary communist writers have been taken seriously by communist terrorists as a source of political principles and as guides to concrete action. Arrigo Cavallina of the Armed Proletarians for Communism recalls how he systematically read the complete works of Marx, Lenin, and Mao in a vain attempt to turn himself into a 'professional revolutionary'.[90] Likewise, Becker mentions the publication of Marighela's *Minimanual of the Brazilian Urban Guerrilla* in West Germany in 1970 as having provided Andreas Baader and Gudrun Ensslin – the original members of what became the Red Army Faction – with ideas such as the importance of carrying out bank robberies as a way of gaining experience.[91] Marighela also appears to have inspired the Red Brigades in Italy. The

Italian publication in 1970 of the mini-manual by Giangiacomo Feltrinelli, a publisher who set up the a forerunner to BR known as the Partisan's Action Group (Gruppo di Azione Partigiano – GAP) in 1969, provided the Red Brigades with a blueprint for organising a revolutionary communist group and running its campaign.[92] A comparison of the initial organisation of the Red Brigades in the mid-1970s with the organisation for urban guerrillas suggested by Marighela confirms this influence.[93]

Overall, communist ideology provides terrorists with a ready list of targets because, although it purports to be an objective, scientific theory of history, it also confers a strong moral sense of what is good and what is bad, and defines those people who are bad. Essentially, the capitalist ruling classes and those people and institutions who support them are bad and form the enemy. However, in most communist terrorist campaigns, ideology and strategy have been adapted to local conditions. This is in line with the thinking of communist ideologists such as Mao and Debray, who have both emphasised that the military strategy to be adopted in any given conflict is specific to that conflict.[94]

Looking specifically at the ideology of communist terrorist groups in Italy and West Germany, in particular the Red Brigades and the Red Army Faction, one finds that, although their ultimate aims were similar – to overthrow the capitalist political and economic system – there were important ideological differences which translated into differences in target selection. These ideological differences were publicised when documents captured by the Italian police in June 1988 revealed the relative failure of the RAF and the PCC faction of BR to agree a co-ordinated strategy.[95] Although the Red Brigades have specifically referred to the ultimate enemy as the Imperialist State of Multinationals (SIM) – a system characterised by the American-led domination of the Italian state by a combination of multinational corporations and NATO – in practice, Italian communist terrorists put a much higher premium upon the overthrow of the Italian state. The West German groups generally saw their objective as the destruction of international capitalism and imperialism as a whole. At a deeper level, it can be argued that the original anarchistic outlook of the original leaders of the Red Army Faction contrasted with the origins of the BR as a splinter from the Italian Communist Party whose power was largely concentrated in the factories of northern Italy.[96] This translated itself into a greater concentration on symbolic targets by the German groups, and upon industrial targets by the Italians.

The targeting pattern of communist terrorist groups in Italy and West Germany can be seen in Table 3. Again, one must allow for discrepancies between what the terrorists intended to do and the actual result. Furthermore, the relatively small number of attacks involved in the West

TABLE 3

PEOPLE KILLED, WOUNDED OR KIDNAPPED BY COMMUNIST TERRORIST GROUPS IN ITALY AND WEST GERMANY

	Italy: 1970–82		W.Germany: 1967–91[a]	
	Number	%	Number	%
Police	69	23.1	9	7.7
Judicial	13	4.3	4[b]	3.4
Penal	14	4.7	0	0.0
Political	27	9.0	5[c]	4.3
Business	85	28.4	5	4.3
Media	9	3.0	17[d]	14.5
Others	82[e]	27.4	77[f]	65.8
TOTAL	**299**	**99.9**	**117**	**100.0**

n.b. Percentages rounded up or down to nearest 0.1%.
a To 2 April 1991.
b Includes officials or politicians in judicial-related posts.
c Includes senior officials.
d Includes 16 injured in bombing of Springer Press office.
e Includes 17 targeted doctors.
f Includes 60 killed or injured in attacks on US military facilities.

Sources: D.Moss. *The Politics of Left-Wing Violence in Italy, 1969–1985* (London: Macmillan, 1989), 38. B.A.Scharlau. 'Chronology of Major Events', (Unpublished manuscript, 1992). D.Pluchinsky. 'An Organizational and Operational Analysis of Germany's Red Army Faction Terrorist Group (1972–1991)', Y.Alexander & D.Pluchinsky (eds). *European Terrorism Today & Tomorrow* (Washington DC: Brassey's (US), 1992), 57–79, 84–6.

German example leads to single attacks distorting the overall pattern. Many of the RAF's anti-American attacks were bombs intended to cause mass casualties, with the result that the attacks on US military facilities caused a high proportion – about 51 per cent – of the overall casualties. Similarly, a single bomb attack on the Springer newspaper complex in May 1972 accounted for 16 of the total of 17 media casualties. This makes the media appear to be a higher priority target than it probably was, although the same cannot necessarily be said of the proportion of casualties inflicted by attacks on US bases, given the RAF's ideological hostility to the US, which it saw as the centre of the capitalist, imperialist system.

Notwithstanding these observations, Table 3 illustrates how important differences between the ideologies of the Italian and West German groups affected their selection of targets. On the whole, the RAF attacked higher-profile targets, such as US military personnel, senior business executives, and senior government officials (US military personnel of any rank count as high-profile targets because of their high symbolic value). They tended to avoid junior officials and ordinary police officers, although police bodyguards for high-profile targets were deliberately killed in the process of attacking the primary target.

The differences between the West German and Italian communist terrorists in selecting police officers as targets illustrate the important ideological differences between them. Even if one discounts the 60 casualties caused by attacks at US bases, police officers make up 15.8 per cent of the total casualties caused by West German communist terrorists, substantially less than in the Italian case. In fact, the West German policemen killed were either incidental or secondary targets – as was the case when three bodyguards were killed during the kidnapping of Hans-Martin Schleyer in 1977, or became casualties in gun-battles which occurred when the police tried to arrest terrorists. The RAF did not deliberately select police officers as primary targets for attack.[97] On the other hand, although 27 of the Italian police officers who became casualties were killed or injured either in gun-battles where they were trying to arrest terrorists or as bodyguards to the primary target, the remaining 30 were deliberately selected as primary targets.[98] In some cases communiqués from BR sought to portray attacks on police officers as revenge for specific actions by the state. Thus, in November 1979 two carabinieri were shot dead whilst drinking coffee in a cafe in Genoa, supposedly in revenge for the suicide of an imprisoned Genoese BR member the previous month.[99] Later the same month, the Red Brigades shot dead another police officer, whom they subsequently described as an 'executioner in disguise'.[100] According to *L'Espresso*, the Red Brigades targeted ordinary police officers, in addition to anti-terrorist detectives, so as to affect police morale.[101] At the time BR justified these attacks on the grounds that whilst the capitalist state could replace its leading members, it could not operate without its lesser functionaries.[102] Thus they provided themselves with an ideological reasoning which made police officers guilty of propping up the capitalist regime in Italy. The difference in target selection concerning the police reflected the primary preoccupation of the Red Brigades and other Italian communist terrorists with targets and issues possessing a national or even local significance, as opposed to the international emphasis of the communist terrorists in West Germany.

A contrast also exists between the targeting of the business sector by Italian communist terrorists compared to the West German groups. With the exception of the bombing of the Springer publishing works, and the Schleyer kidnapping, the RAF did not target businessmen for assassination or abduction until the mid-1980s. After this point the RAF targeted high-level, prominent businessmen who represented the 'Military-Industrial Complex' (MIC) or international capitalism as a whole. When the RAF shot dead Ernst Zimmerman, the Chairman of the Federal Association of the

German Aeronautics, Space, and Armaments Industry, at his home in Munich in February 1985, they justified the killing on the grounds that Zimmerman's federation

> ... had the function to push through the interests of the MIC here in this state, on the Western European level, and thus on the international level.[103]

Likewise, in July 1986 the RAF used a bomb in a cart to kill Dr Karl-Heinz Beckurts and his driver whilst Beckurts was on his way to work. Beckurts was a director of the electronics firm Siemens and a member of the nuclear energy working group of the German National Industries Association, and as such the RAF said that he represented

> ... the course of international capital in the current phase of political, economic, and military strategy of the overall imperialist system ... Siemens – like almost no other company in the FRG [Federal Republic of Germany] – represents the concentrated power and aggression of the most reactionary factions of the bourgeoisie organized by the military-industrial complex.[104]

Subsequent business targets such as Alfred Herrhausen, Chairman of the Deutsche Bank, who was killed by a car-bomb in November 1989, and Detlev Rohwedder of the Treuhandanstalt who, as noted, was shot in April 1991, were both characterised by the RAF as men who represented the attempt of the capitalist system to dominate and subjugate the lives of ordinary workers, workers in the Third World, and of workers in Eastern Europe after the fall of the Soviet system.[105] The important point to note concerning the businessmen attacked by the Red Army Faction is that they were high-ranking, and the attacks were aimed at highlighting wide issues rather than specific industrial conflicts.

The Italian groups, on the other hand, were well-organised in some of the factories of northern Italy and, compared to the West German groups, undoubtedly gave a far higher political priority to intervening in specific domestic industrial conflicts. The Red Brigades targeted business managers whose companies were involved in conflicts with their staff, although in some cases – as with the Front Line attack on a business school – Italian communist terrorists attacked the business sector as a general category.[106] As Moss points out, those managers who were attacked tended to be those who had direct supervisory functions rather than high-level executives:

> ... foremen, security staff, workshop supervisors, technical staff responsible for production schedules, middle management from personnel offices, full-time negotiators with plant unions.[107]

In most cases the attacks took the form of maiming, with the victims being shot in the legs. Although a senior business manager had bled to death after being shot in the leg in September 1978, it was not until January 1980 that a manager was deliberately killed – Silvio Gori, a manager at the Maghera plant of Petrolchimico, died, as did two managers in Milan in November 1980.[108] The decision to kill the managers in Milan, Renato Briano of Magneti Marelli and Manfredo Mazzanti of Falck, was not taken by the BR leadership, but by a dissident, factory-based section of BR which called itself the 'Walter Alasia Column' after a Milan BR leader who had been killed in a gun-battle with the police in 1976.[109] The BR condemned this, and other actions, by the Walter Alasia column as undisciplined, although the Veneto column of BR had been responsible for the January 1980 killing of Silvio Gori, and kidnapped and later killed Giuseppe Taliercio – the personnel manager of the Montedison plant at Marghera which had made a number of workers redundant.[110] From the mid-1980s sections of the BR – which by then had fragmented – did carry out lethal attacks on high-ranking people in what might broadly be called the industrial sector. However these were generally high ranking industrial advisers or political appointees rather than businessmen.[111] After Professor Ezio Tarentelli – an economist, trade union consultant and adviser to the Italian Government – was shot dead at the University of Rome in March 1985, the subsequent BR communiqué branded him as a man who had '... learned the arts and techniques of capitalist exploitation ...', and accused him of framing policies which would lead to the imposition of lower working standards upon ordinary workers.[112]

Although both West German and Italian communist terrorists targeted politicians and officials, the nature of their targets differed somewhat. Those attacked by the Red Army Faction tended to be senior officials rather than politicians. For example Dr Gerhold von Braunmuehl, the head of the political department at the Ministry of Foreign Affairs, was shot dead in October 1986. Assassination attempts were also made in September 1988 on Dr Hans Tietmeyer, then a state secretary in the Ministry of Finance, and in July 1990 on Hans Neusel, the second-ranking official in the Ministry of the Interior and the official in charge of internal security.[113] Even this latter attack, aimed at a leading member of the German internal security apparatus, was given an international dimension when it was projected by the RAF as an attack on 'Europe as a global power' although it also referred to the RAF's demand that imprisoned RAF members be kept together.[114] No attacks have been made by the RAF on senior German politicians. However, in February 1975, Peter Lorenz, the Christian Democratic Union (Christlich-Demokratische Union – CDU) candidate for Mayor of Berlin, was abducted by the June 2nd Movement, whose ideology was more idiosyncratic than the RAF and less orientated by strict adherence to Marxist-Leninist ideology.[115]

On the other hand, despite the professed BR aim to attack the 'Heart of the State' the political targets attacked by the various communist groups in Italy primarily consisted of junior and middle-ranking members of political groups.[116] The exceptions to this were the kidnapping and subsequent killing of the former Prime Minister Aldo Moro in 1978 and the attacks on the semi-official academic advisers mentioned above. Of the 28 political targets killed, wounded, or kidnapped by Italian extreme left-wing terrorists between 1968 and 1982, 24 were members of the conservative Christian Democrats (Democrazia Cristiana – DC), who were the major partners in the various ruling coalitions in Italy between 1945 and 1993.[117] These attacks were in line with the BR 'Strategic Resolution' of November 1977 which aimed to:

> ATTACK, HIT, LIQUIDATE AND DEFINITIVELY ROUT THE CHRISTIAN DEMOCRATIC PARTY, AXIS OF THE RESTRUCTURING OF THE STATE AND OF THE IMPERIALIST COUNTER-REVOLUTION.[118]

The Red Brigadists saw the DC as having a central role in the Imperialist State of Multinationals, and attacked them accordingly.[119] Four-fifths of the attacks on the Christian Democrats occurred between 1977 and 1979, and attacks on DC property in Rome, occurred about once a fortnight during that period, putting the party in what Moss terms 'an acute sense of being under siege'.[120] Indeed, by attempting to cause chaos within the government machine, what the BR called 'disarticulating' the Italian state, the Red Brigades hoped to cause conflict within the political system and prevent it from functioning properly as a prelude to its final collapse.[121] However, despite this declaration of intent, the attack on Moro was the only successful attack upon a leading Christian Democrat politician.

Ideology was not the only reason for the differences in targeting strategy between the Italian and West German communist terrorists. Operational and strategic factors also played a part. The BR had many more members than the RAF and could carry out more actions, including actions against less prominent targets. While the RAF could have attacked low-profile human targets with much greater ease than the high-profile targets which were attacked, they chose not to.[122] Such attacks would have had far less impact upon their chosen psychological targets – international working-class opinion and workers in the Third World – than attacks on high-profile targets. In practice, their internationalist stance meant they were not as interested as the Red Brigades in trying to agitate and provoke the population within their own country, and consequently their target selection differed. Overall the RAF showed a much greater tendency to target high-profile targets than the Red Brigades, reflecting the ideological concentration on attacking international capitalism and imperialism. On the other hand, the Red Brigades, with their roots in the northern Italian factories and opposition to the Italian state, concentrated far more on attacking factory managers, ordinary police officers, and junior or middle-ranking politicians.

Having said this, one has to be aware that the Italian and West German communist terrorists did occasionally attack targets which fall outside the generalisations outlined above. Both groups carried out occasional robberies, primarily for logistical purposes, but they also attacked targets which do not fit their normal pattern. For example in December 1981 the Red Brigades abducted US General James Dozier – who was freed by the police the following month, and in February 1984 the BR shot dead Leamon Hunt, an American diplomat who was Director General of the Multinational Observer Force (MOF) operating in the Sinai peninsula following the Camp David accords between Israel and Egypt.[123] There was an Italian dimension to both attacks – Dozier was the head of NATO's land forces in southern Europe and was based in Italy, while the Multinational Observer Force in Sinai contained Italian troops. Nevertheless, these attacks were undoubtedly intended to highlight the position of the US forces in Italy – and in the Hunt case to highlight opposition to attempts to accommodate Arab governments to Israeli policy – and as such represented an awareness of events outside Italy which was not normally reflected in the activities of Italian communist groups.

The West German extreme left-wing terrorists also carried out attacks which were untypical. As mentioned above, in May 1972 the RAF bombed the administrative headquarters of the Springer newspaper company, and in May 1975 the B2J abducted Peter Lorenz. In the 1980s, in addition to attacks on traditional targets, a series of attacks occurred against targets which appeared to represent new technology or threats to the environment – a primary case being the construction of a new runway at Frankfurt Airport. These attacks do not seem to have been carried out by any of the older West German terrorist groups, but included attacks by the Revolutionary Cells. At the time, these attacks seemed to represent an attempt by the terrorists to create a link with the then growing environmental 'Green' movement in Germany, and as such differed from the typical preoccupations of the communist terrorists – particularly those of the Red Army Faction.[124]

Conclusion

In an earlier article I argued that similarities could be found among terrorists with similar ideologies – in that case conservatism – and by extension I implied that differences would be found between groups with dissimilar ideologies.[125] The targeting patterns of the terrorist groups examined here tend to bear out the contention that terrorists' targeting choices are crucially affected by their ideology and that ideological differences lead to differences in the targeting patterns of terrorist groups – even between groups which have superficially similar but distinct ideologies. Terrorists are rarely mindless or indiscriminate in their attacks, although they may appear to be so to observers who have not examined their ideological beliefs.

Of course terrorist campaigns are not static in their nature. The terrorists' ideologies may develop and alter over time, and this may be reflected in the pattern of their attacks. There are also a number of other changeable factors which need to be considered when trying to explain or understand the selection of targets by any terrorist group: such as the security environment within which they operate, the desire to maintain traditional sources of support, and the state of the group's logistics. Nevertheless, even after taking these reservations into account, it is still ideology which provides terrorists with the moral and political vision that inspires their violence, shapes the way in which they see the world, and defines how they judge the actions of people and institutions. This in turn forms their views as to who or what may be seen as a legitimate target, and to a degree it allows the terrorists to dehumanise those people whom they intend to harm – seeing them as symbols rather than as flesh and blood human beings. By establishing such parameters, the influence of ideology is crucial in determining the range of terrorists' potential targets.

NOTES

1. For example, in July 1991 David Levy, the Israeli Foreign Minister, described the Arab states' trade boycott of Israel as 'economic terrorism'. 'Israel attacks G7 linking of boycott with settlements', *The Guardian* (London), 19 July 1991. For definitions of terrorism see A. P. Schmid and A. J. Jongman. *Political Terrorism: A New Guide to Actors, Authors, Concepts, Data Bases, Theories, and Literature* (Amsterdam: North-Holland Publishing, 1988), pp.32–8.
2. M.Crenshaw Hutchinson, *Revolutionary Terrorism: The FLN in Algeria, 1954–1962* (Stanford, CA: Hoover Institution Press, 1978), p.21.
3. In this article the term *target* is assumed to refer to the physical target of a terrorist attack unless it is otherwise qualified – for instance as in the term *psychological target*.
4. For more details on such factors see C. J. M. Drake, *Terrorists' Target Selection* (London: Macmillan, 1998).

5. 'Italian Terrorists Kill a Union Aide', *Washington Post*, 25 January 1979. 'Italian Labour Protest Over Killing', *Financial Times* (London), 26 January 1979. 'Hero's Funeral for Party Victim', *Financial Times*, 29 January 1979. D. Moss, *The Politics of Left-Wing Violence in Italy, 1969-1985* (London: Macmillan, 1989), pp.105, 227. A. Jamieson, *The Heart Attacked: Terrorism and Conflict in the Italian State* (London: Marion Boyars, 1989), pp.92, 100, 123, 126, 175–6.
6. 'IRA Apologises for Mürder of Australians', *The Independent*, 29 May 1990. 'Bloody End to a Simple Day Out', *The Independent*, 29 May 1990.
7. W. A. Rosenbaum, *Political Culture* (London: Nelson, 1975), p.120.
8. M. Kramer, 'Sacrifice and Fratricide in Shiite Lebanon', *Terrorism and Political Violence* [hereafter *T&PV*], 3/3 (Autumn 1991), pp.32-3. K. Tololyan, 'Cultural Narrative and the Motivation of the Terrorist', D. C. Rapoport (ed) *Inside Terrorist Organizations* (London: Frank Cass, 1988), p.221. A. T. Q. Stewart. *The Narrow Ground: The Roots of Conflict in Ulster*, revised edition (London: Faber, 1989), pp.180–1. J. Darby, 'The Historical Background', J. Darby (ed). *Northern Ireland: The Background to the Conflict*, (Belfast: Appletree Press, 1983), p.15.
9. In some cases, particularly with communist groups, ideological writings have also provided terrorists with the outlines of a strategy. For examples see: Mao Tse-tung, *Selected Works of Mao Tse-tung*, three volumes, (Peking: Foreign Languages Press, 1965). Mao Tse-tung, *Basic Tactics*, (New York: Praeger, 1966). C. Guevara, *Guerrilla Warfare*, (New York: Praeger, 1961; Harmondsworth: Penguin, 1969). C. Marighela, *For the Liberation of Brazil*, (Harmondsworth: Penguin, 1971).
10. R. Hill and A. Bell, *The Other Face of Terror: Inside Europe's Neo-Nazi Network*, (London: Grafton, 1988), pp.95, 121–2, 125, 157, 169. Searchlight, *From Ballots to Bombs: The Inside Story of the National Front's Political Soldiers* (London: Searchlight, no date – after 1989), pp.16–19. C. di Giovanni. *Light from Behind the Bars: Letters from the Red Brigades and Other Former Italian Terrorists; True Stories of Terror, Agony and Hope* (Slough: St Paul Publications, 1990), pp.95, 99–100.
11. P.Singer, *Animal Liberation: A New Ethics For Our Treatment of Animals* (New York: Avon, 1977), pp.1–26. P. Singer, *The Animal Liberation Movement: Its Philosophy, its Achievements, and its Future* (Nottingham: Old Hammond Press), pp.5–10. F. Ginsburg, 'Saving America's Souls: Operation Rescue's Crusade against Abortion', M. E. Marty and R. S. Appleby (eds), *Fundamentalisms and the State* (Chicago: University of Chicago Press, 1993), pp.557, 573–4. D. Henshaw, *Animal Warfare: The Story of the Animal Liberation Front* (London: Fontana, 1989), pp.33–4, 92–3.
12. For the Mafia see G. Falcone and M Padovani, *Men of Honour: The Truth About the Mafia*, (Paris: Edition 1, 1991; London: Fourth Estate, 1992), pp.157–62. R.Catanzaro, *Men of Respect: A Social History of the Sicilian Mafia* (Padua: Liviana Editrice spa, 1988; New York: Free Press, 1992), pp.214–16. J.Parker. *The Walking Dead: A Woman's Brave Stand Against the Mafia* (London: Simon & Schuster, 1995; Pocket Books, 1996), and A.Stille. *Excellent Cadavers: The Mafia and the Death of the First Italian Republic*, (London: Jonathan Cape, 1995). For the Colombian drugs traffickers see J.Pearce. *Colombia: Inside the Labyrinth*, (London: Latin American Bureau, 1990), pp.1, 194–5. P. D.Scott and J. Marshall. *Cocaine Politics: Drugs, Armies, and the CIA in Central America* (Berkeley: University of California Press, 1991), pp.76, 90. S.Strong. *Whitewash: Pablo Escobar and the Cocaine Wars*, (London: Macmillan, 1995), pp.138–53. R.D.Tomasek, 'Complex Interdependency Theory: Drug Barons as Transnational Groups', W. C. Cliffs and J.R. Lee, *The Theory and Practice of International Relations* (NJ: Prentice-Hall, 1994), pp.281–2. P.Williams, 'Transnational Criminal Organisations and International Security', *Survival*, 36/1 (Spring 1994), p.111.
13. Herri Batasuna, *The 'Herri Batasuna' the Basque Country Needs*; Herri Batasuna, *The Recognition of Democratic Rigths [sic] in Basque Country*, pp.3–4, 5. R.P.Clark. *The Basque Insurgents: ETA, 1952–1980*, (Madison: University of Wisconsin Press, 1984), 275–6. F.Jiminez. 'Spain: The Terrorist Challenge and the Government's Response', *T&PV*, 4/4 (Winter 1992), p.111.
14. B. Pollack and G. Hunter, 'Dictatorship, Democracy and Terrorism in Spain', in J. Lodge

(ed.) *The Threat of Terrorism* (Brighton: Wheatsheaf, 1988), pp.127–30. F. Llera, J. M. Mata and C. L. Irwin, 'ETA: From Secret Army to Social Movement – The Post-Franco Schism of the Basque Nationalist Movement', *T&PV*, 5/3 (Autumn 1993), pp.115–16.
15. H. M. Cubert, 'The Militant Palestinian Organizations and the Arab-Israeli Peace Process', *T&PV*, 4/1 (Spring 1992), pp.32–3.
16. D. Henshaw. (note 11), pp.31, 100-1.
17. T. Parker, *May the Lord in His Mercy be Kind to Belfast* (London: Jonathon Cape, 1993), p.324.
18. P. C. Hearst and A.Moscow, *Every Secret Thing* (London: Methuen, 1982; Arrow, 1983), p.351.
19. 'Change of Tactics by the Provos', *Financial Times*, 4 February 1977. 'Can Ulster Sustain its Pepperpot Investment', *The Guardian*, 4 February 1977. 'Gunmen Fail in Bid to Assassinate Two Leading Belfast Businessmen', *The Irish Times*, 11 February 1977. 'IRA Attacks Grass Roots Imperialism', *Republican News*, 19 February 1977. 'Businessmen not Expendable, Unlike Brit Troops', *Republican News*, 26 March 1977. P. Bishop and E. Mallie, *The Provisional IRA* (London: Heinemann, 1987; Corgi, 1988), p.326. T. P. Coogan, *The IRA* (Glasgow: Fontana/Collins, 1987), pp.473, 690.
20. P. Bishop and E. Mallie (Note 19), p.421. 'Laing Bow to IRA's Threats', *The Daily Telegraph*, 2 August 1986. 'The Provo's Easiest Coup', *The Times*, 8 August 1986. 'The Gunman's Shadow Falls Across Ulster Business', *Financial Times*, 11 August 1986. 'Army Deploys 1,000 Extra Men in Ulster Repair Work', *The Daily Telegraph*, 7 September 1991. 'The Background to the Teebane Ambush', *An Phoblacht/Republican News* (henceforth AP/RN) 23 January 1992.
21. B. M. Jenkins, *International Terrorism: The Other World War* (Santa Monica, CA: RAND, 1985), p.16.
22. 'Gow Killed Because of his Influence on Thatcher, IRA Says', *The Independent*, 1 August 1990.
23. D. McKittrick, *Endgame: The Search for Peace in Northern Ireland* (Belfast: Blackstaff, 1994), pp.89–90. A. Clark. *Diaries* (London: Weidenfeld & Nicolson, 1993; Phoenix, 1994), pp.35, 121–2, 319.
24. R. Catanzaro, 'Subjective Experience and Objective Reality: An Account of Violence in the Words of its Protagonists', R. Catanzaro (ed.) *The Red Brigades and Left-Wing Terrorism in Italy* (London: Pinter, 1991), pp.190–1.
25. C.di Giovanni (Note 10), p.61.
26. Red Brigades – Fighting Communist Party, 'Communique on the Assassination of Ezio Tarantelli, a Rome University Economics Professor, in Rome on 27 March 1985', Y. Alexander and D.Pluchinsky (eds.), *Europe's Red Terrorists: The Fighting Communist Organizations* (London: Frank Cass, 1992), p.203.
27. 'Germany Tested to its Limits', *The Independent*, 3 April 1991. 'Obituary: Detlev Rohwedder', *The Independent*, 3 April 1991.
28. Red Army Faction. 'Communique on the Assassination of Detlev Rohwedder, President of Treuhandanstalt, in Dusseldorf on 1 April 1991'. Y.Alexander and D.Pluchinsky (eds.). (note 26), p.79.
29. Red Army Faction, 'Communique on the Assassination of Detlev Rohwedder', pp.79-84.
30. Ibid, p.82.
31. 'Tragedy of Ulster's Relentless Cycle of Violence', *The Independent*, 6 February 1992.
32. 'UVF Gunmen "Laughed as They Fled" Pub Massacre', *The Guardian*, 25 January 1995. S. Bruce, *The Red Hand: Protestant Paramilitaries in Northern Ireland* (Oxford: Oxford University Press [henceforth OUP], 1992), p.54. M.Dillon, *The Shankill Butchers: A Case Study of Mass Murder* (London: Hutchinson, 1989; Arrow, 1990), pp.xxiv, 24, 65, 166.
33. P. Bishop and E. Mallie (note 19), pp.182, 195. K.Toolis, *Rebel Hearts: Journeys Within the IRA's Soul*, (London: Picador, 1995), pp.126, 357–8.
34. Quoted in R. Holmes, *Firing Line* (London: Jonathan Cape, 1985; Harmondsworth: Penguin, 1987), p.360.
35. J. Ellis, *The Sharp End of War: The Fighting Man in World War II*, (Newton Abbot: David & Charles, 1980; London: Corgi, 1982), pp.319–20. R. Holmes. (note 34), pp.370, 373–5.

36. A. Calder. *The People's War: Britain 1939–1945*, (London: Jonathan Cape, 1969; Granada, 1982), pp.566–7. M. Hastings, *Bomber Command* (London: Michael Joseph, 1979; Pan, 1981), pp.125–6, 135–6. M. Walzer. *Just and Unjust Wars: A Moral Argument with Historical Illustrations*, (New York: Basic Books, 1977; Harmondsworth: Penguin, 1980), p.256. G. Best. *Humanity in Warfare: The Modern History of the International Law of Armed Conflicts*, (London: Weidenfeld & Nicolson, 1980; Methuen, 1983), pp.267–85.
37. W. R. Farrell, *Blood and Rage: The Story of the Japanese Red Army*, (Lexington, MA: Lexington Books, 1990), p.142. B. M. Jenkins. (Note 21), p.48.
38. In this context the term *European* refers to French and other European settlers in Algeria and their descendants.
39. M.Crenshaw Hutchinson, (note 2), p.19.
40. '16 killed in Bomb Attack on Jewish Groups in Argentina', *The Independent*, 19 July 1994. 'Explosion Levels Building Housing Jewish Groups', *The Guardian*, 19 July 1994. B. Hoffman and D. K. Hoffman. 'The RAND-St Andrews Chronology of International Terrorism, 1994', *T&PV*, 7/4, (Winter 1995), p.210.
41. 'Hizbollah Adopts An "Eye for an Eye" Tactic', *The Independent*, 20 July 1994.
42. P. Bishop and E. Mallie (note 19), p.171.
43. 'Bombing "Devastating" to IRA', *The Independent*, 11 November 1987.
44. A. Iyad and E.Rouleau. *My Home My Land: A Narrative of the Palestinian Struggle*, (Paris: Fayolle, 1978; New York: Times Books, 1981), pp.106, 111.
45. S. Aust, *The Baader-Meinhof Group: The Inside Story of a Phenomenon* (Hamburg: Hoffman & Campe Verlag, 1985; London: Bodley Head, 1987), p.530. Also see P. Koch and K. Hermann, *Assault at Mogadishu* (Hamburg: Stern, 1977; London: Corgi, 1977), pp.139–40.
46. 'All Killings And Tragedies Stem From British Interference', *Republican News*, 25 February 1978. D. McKittrick, *Despatches from Belfast* (Belfast: Blackstaff, 1989), p.86.
47. 'IRA warns of more bombs', *The Observer*, 1 February 1987.
48. M. Dillon and D. Lehane, *Political Murder in Northern Ireland* (Harmondsworth: Penguin, 1973), p.256. J. Bowyer Bell, *IRA Tactics and Targets: An Analysis of Tactical Aspects of the Armed Struggle, 1969-1989* (Swords: Poolbeg, 1990), pp.27, 48, 116.
49. D. Moss (note 5), p.58.
50. P. Willan, *Puppet Masters: The Political Use of Terrorism in Italy* (London: Constable, 1991), pp.201–2.
51. J. Bowyer Bell (note 48), pp.31–2.
52. T. Parker (note 17), pp.325–6.
53. 'We remain totally committed and confident in victory' -Oglaigh na hEireann', *AP/RN*, 14, (February 1991), 'The IRA Statement', *AP/RN*, 23 January 1992. P. Bishop and E. Mallie (note 19), p.421.
54. 'IRA Rings Changes To Restore Balance Of Terror', *The Guardian*, 5 May 1987. 'What's On the Agenda Now is an End to Partition', *The Irish Times*, 10 December 1986. G. Adams, *The Politics of Irish Freedom* (Dingle: Brandon, 1986), p.121.
55. For a view of republican and loyalist ideologies see: G. Adams (Note 54), K. J. Kelley, *The Longest War: Northern Ireland and the IRA* (London: Zed Books, 1988). H. Patterson. *The Politics of Illusion: Republicanism and Socialism in Modern Ireland* (London: Hutchinson Radius, 1989). L. Clarke, *Broadening the Battlefield: The H-Blocks and the Rise of Sinn Fein* (Dublin: Gill & Macmillan, 1987). T. P. Coogan (note 19). S. Bruce, *The Edge of the Union: The Ulster Loyalist Political Vision* (Oxford: OUP, 1994). S. Bruce (note 32). S. Nelson, *Ulster's Uncertain Defenders: Loyalists and the Northern Ireland Conflict* (Belfast: Appletree Press, 1984). A number of other books do not aim specifically at setting out the political vision of the paramilitaries in Northern Ireland, but are very good at describing the political and social environment within which they have developed, including: S. Bruce, *God Save Ulster: The Religion and Politics of Paisleyism* (Oxford: OUP, 1986; 1989). F.O'Connor, *In Search of a State: Catholics in Northern Ireland* (Belfast: Blackstaff, 1993).
56. R. P. Clark (note 13), p.40.
57. R. P. Clark. 'Patterns of Eta Violence: 1968-1980', P.H.Merkl (ed). *Political Violence and*

Terror: Motifs and Motivations, (Berkeley: University of California Press, 1986), p.136.
58. F. Llera, J. M. Mata and C. L. Irwin (Note 14), p.132.
59. R. P. Clark (Note 57), p.136. B. Pollack and G.Hunter (note 14), p.126. R. P. Clark, *The Basques: The Franco Years and Beyond*, (Reno: University of Nevada Press, 1979), pp.170–4.
60. R. P.Clark (Note 57), p.136.
61. 'King Coke', *The Independent*, 21 July 1990. 'In Medellin, Walls do Not a Prison Make', *The Independent*, 8 August 1992. J. Pearce. (note 12), pp.177–8, 247. Amnesty International, *Political Violence in Colombia: Myth and reality* (London: Amnesty International, 1994), p.52. C. Watson, 'Guerrilla Groups in Colombia: Reconstituting the Political Process', *T&PV*, 4/2, (Summer 1992), pp.95–6.
62. J. Pearce (Note 12), pp.1, 260-1. A. M. Bravo. 'Frontier Culture Takes to Cocaine', M.L.Smith (ed). *Why People Grow Drugs: Narcotics and Development in the Third World*, (London: Panos, 1992), p.75. C. Watson (Note 61), p.96. P. D. Scott and J. Marshall (Note 12), pp.89, 239, 262.
63. Amnesty International (Note 61), p.1.
64. J. Pearce (Note 12), pp.243, 249, 252-3, 254-5, 260-1. Amnesty International, *Getting Away With Murder: Political Killings and 'Disappearances' in the 1990s* (London: Amnesty International, 1993), pp.74, 88-9.
65. J. Pearce (Note 12), pp.196, 253, 262. Amnesty International (Note 61), pp.58, 61–2.
66. 'The Men Of War Promise Third Violent Decade', *The Independent*, 29 September 1990. 'We remain totally committed and confident in victory' – Oglaigh na hEireann', *AP/RN*, 14 February 1991. 'Freedom's Soldiers Laid to Rest in Historic Tyrone', *AP/RN*, 13 June 1991. 'UDR "Comes of Age": Loyalist Militia Renamed', *AP/RN*, 25 July 1991. 'Terrorists in and out of Uniform', *AP/RN*, 4 July 1991. 'The IRA Statement', *AP/RN*, 23 January 1992. 'Royal Salute to Murder Regiment', *AP/RN*, 4 June 1992. J. Bowyer Bell (Note 48), pp.29–32.
67. 'The Price of Survival in a Divided Land', *The Independent on Sunday*, 18 October 1992. 'Victimised', *Fortnight*, 320, (September 1993). 'Sinn Fein Death Part of Sustained Assault', *The Independent*, 10 August 1993. S. Bruce (note 32), p.277.
68. 'For Queen and Country', *The Guardian* , supplement, 19 October 1993.
69. 'Loyalist Group Threatens Catholic Massacre', *The Independent*, 8 September 1993. 'Loyalists come out shooting to defend lost cause', *The Times*, 9 September 1993. 'For Queen and Country', *The Guardian* , supplement, 19 October 1993.
70. S.Bruce (note 32), pp.58, 261, 277. S. Bruce, *The Edge of the Union*, pp.42–3. S. Nelson. (note 55), p.120. M. Dillon (Note 32), p.17. D. L. G. Hall, *The Ulster Defence Association: A Case of Change and Continuity*, MSSc, Queen's University, Belfast, 1988, pp.32–3, 81 (unpublished) 'Gritting it out on Border Farmlands', *The Irish Times*, 3 March 1983. 'Centre of Hatred Returns to Armagh', *The Irish Times*, 23 November 1983. J. Darby, *Intimidation and the Control of Conflict in Northern Ireland*, (Dublin: Gill and Macmillan, 1986), 136–7. T. Parker (Note 17), pp.293–4.
71. D. L.G. Hall (Note 70), p.256.
72. Bruce and Stevenson note that republicans have, on occasion, denied that Catholic victims of loyalist attacks were members of paramilitary groups – mainly for propaganda purposes and in order to claim government compensation for the deaths – only to honour them as members subsequently. S. Bruce, 'The Problem of "Pro-State" Terrorism: Loyalist Paramilitaries in Northern Ireland', *T&PV*, 4/4 (Spring 1992), p.79. S. Bruce. 'Northern Ireland: Reappraising Loyalist Violence', A. O'Day (ed.) *Terrorism's Laboratory: The Case of Northern Ireland*, (Aldershot: Dartmouth, 1995), 119. S. Bruce (note 32), pp.261–2. J. Stevenson, *"We Wrecked the Place": Contemplating an End to the Northern Irish Troubles* (New York: The Free Press, 1996), p.139n.
73. See: R. W. White, 'The Irish Republican Army: An Assessment of Sectarianism', *T&PV*, 9/1 (Spring 1997), pp.20–55. S. Bruce 'Victim Selection in Ethnic Conflict: Motives and Attitudes in Irish Republicanism', *T&PV*, 9/1 (Spring 1997), pp.56–71. R. W. White. 'The Irish Republican Army and Sectarianism: Moving Beyond the Anecdote', *T&PV*, 9/2 (Summer 1997), pp.120-31.

74. S. Bruce (note 73), pp.64–5.
75. M. McKeown, *Two Seven Six Three: An Analysis of Fatalities Attributable to Civil Disturbances in Northern Ireland in the Twenty Years Between July 13th 1969 and July 12th 1989* (Lucan: Murlough, 1989), p.57.
76. 'Catholics Make up 7 per cent of RUC', *The Independent*, 28 January 1993. C. Ryder, *The Ulster Defence Regiment: An Instrument of Peace?* (London: Methuen, 1991), p.196.
77. 'The Men Of War Promise Third Violent Decade', *The Independent*, 29 September 1990. R. W. White. 'The Irish Republican Army: An Assessment of Sectarianism' (note 73), p.33.
78. Ryder makes the point that early in the current troubles those Catholics who joined the UDR were especially vulnerable to intimidation, and that this – along with perceptions of anti-Catholic bias in security force activities – led to an 'exodus' of Catholics from the unit from 1971 onwards. C. Ryder (note 77), pp.45–9, 60, 196.
79. R. W. White. 'The Irish Republican Army and Sectarianism' (note 73), pp.128–9.
80. S. Bruce (Note 73), p.66.
81. 'Bombing "Devastating" to IRA', *The Independent*, 11 November 1987. 'Damage in Huge Blast Put at £20m', *The Independent*, 25 September 1992. 'Court Laboratory Bombed by IRA', *The Times*, 25 September 1992. D. McKittrick (note 23), pp.117–18. 'Loyalists Target of Sustained Campaign', *The Independent*, 25 October 1993. 'It's Going to be a Tragedy for People in the Ardoyne', *The Guardian*, 25 October 1993. 'Catholic Front line Waits in Fear for Retribution', *The Independent*, 26 October 1993. E. Mallie and D. McKittrick. *The Fight for Peace: The Secret Story Behind the Irish Peace Process* (London: Heinemann, 1996), pp.194-201.
82. R. W. White. 'The Irish Republican Army: An Assessment of Sectarianism' (note 73) pp.38-42. In particular see Table 3 on page 37.
83. C. Mullin, *Error of Judgement: The Truth about the Birmingham Bombings*, revised edition, (Swords: Poolbeg, 1990), pp.1-7, 256-66, *passim*. P. Bishop and E. Mallie (note 19), pp.257–9. 'IRA Bombers Kill Child, 4', *The Independent on Sunday*, 21 March 1993. 'Tim Parry, Victim Of IRA Bomb Blast Dies After Ventilator is Switched Off', *The Independent*, 26 March 1993. 'IRA's Message in Blood', *The Independent on Sunday*, 16 June 1996.
84. Thus in December 1978 the PIRA threatened to detonate no-warning bombs in English cities. 'IRA. Bomb England', *Republican News*, 23 December 1978. For one account of republican attitudes towards the English see: M. Dillon, *The Enemy Within* (London: Doubleday, 1994), pp.207–11.
85. Royal Ulster Constabulary, *Chief Constable's Annual Report 1995* (London: HMSO, 1996), pp.31-2.
86. For more details on paramilitary vigilantism see: 'Dispatches: Law of the Ghetto', Channel 4 (television), 26 February 1992. J. Darby. *Intimidation and the Control of Conflict in Northern Ireland* (Dublin: Gill and Macmillan, 1986), pp.159, 157–62. 'The Benefits of a Community Police Force', *Republican News* (Belfast), 27 August 1977. 'War News: IRA Action Against Drugs Trade', *AP/RN*, 10 October 1991. 'IRA Orders Shooting Victims to Quit Country', *The Independent*, 7 October 1991. 'IRA Looks Set for Victory Over Terrorist Faction', *The Independent*, 4 November 1992. 'What the IRA is Doing Now', *The Independent*, 30 September 1994. 'Rough Justice' and accompanying untitled article by Liam Kennedy, *Fortnight*, 344 (November 1995). 'Drug Wars', *Fortnight*, 347 (February 1996). 'Murky Motives for Giving Drugs Dealers Rough Justice', *The Guardian*, 3 January 1996. 'Dealing in Death', *New Statesman & Society*, 12 January 1996.
87. 'Packing a Picket' *Fortnight*, 334 (December 1994). J.Stevenson (note 72), pp.117–28.
88. 'War News: IRA Action Against Drugs Trade', *AP/RN*, 10 October 1991. 'IRA Orders Shooting Victims to Quit Country', *The Independent*, 7 October 1991. 'IRA interview: Defending the Community', *AP/RN*, 19 December 1991.
89. To see how this can affect terrorist groups in general see: J. K. Zawodny, 'Guerrilla Warfare and Subversion as a Means of Political Change'. Paper presented at the 1961 Annual Meeting of the American Political Science Association, Sheraton-Jefferson Hotel, St Louis, Missouri, 6–9 September 1961. J. K. Zawodny. 'Internal Organizational Problems and the

Sources of Tensions of Terrorist Movements as Catalysts of Violence', *Terrorism: An International Journal*, 1, nos. 3/4 (1978), pp.277–85. J. K. Zawodny. 'Infrastructures of Terrorist Organizations', L. Z. Freedman and Y. Alexander (eds). *Perspectives on Nuclear Terrorism*, , (Wilmington: Scholarly Resources Inc, 1983), pp.61–70. M. Crenshaw. 'An Organizational Approach to the Analysis of Political Terrorism', *Orbis: A Journal of World Affairs*, 29/3 (Fall 1985), pp.465–89.

90. C. di Giovanni (Note 10), p.147.
91. J. Becker, *Hitler's Children: The Story of the Baader-Meinhof Gang* (London: Granada, 1978), pp.214-15, 221, 243.
92. A. Jamieson (Note 5), p.49. A. Jamieson, 'Entry, Discipline and Exit in the Italian Red Brigades', *T&PV*, 2/1 (Spring 1990), pp.1, 3–4.
93. C. Marighela (Note 9), pp.54-6. A. Jamieson. 'Entry, Discipline and Exit in the Italian Red Brigades', ibid., p.5. A. Jamieson. (Note 5), 84–5. G. C. Caselli and D. della Porta. 'The History of the Red Brigades: Organizational Structures and Strategies of Action (1970-82)', R.Catanzaro (ed.), (Note 24), p.74.
94. Mao Tse-tung. 'Problems of Strategy in China's Revolutionary War', (December 1936), 'On Protracted War', (May 1938), *Selected Works of Mao Tse-tung* (Peking: Foreign Languages Press, 1965), Volume 1, pp.179, 181, 189, 197–8, Volume 2, p.121. R. Debray, *Revolution in the Revolution? Armed Struggle and Political Struggle in Latin America* (France: 1967; Harmondsworth: Penguin, 1968), p.21.
95. Red Brigades and Red Army Faction, 'Excerpts from Notes of a Meeting between the Red Brigades and Red Army Faction in January 1988'. Y. Alexander and D. Pluchinsky (eds.). (Note 26), pp.219-27.
96. A. Jamieson, (note 5), p.24. V. S. Pisano, *The Dynamics of Subversion and Violence in Contemporary Italy* (Stanford, California: Hoover Institution Press, 1987), p.40. S. Aust. (Note 45), pp.10–12, 63, 76–7, 146–9. J. Becker (note 91), pp.17, 62, 109, 264, 366 ff.2.
97. In 1971 Ulrike Meinhof of the RAF specifically stated that they did not target police officers who were not specifically trying to harm them. S. Aust (note 45), p.143.
98. D. Moss (note 5), p.38.
99. Associated Press, 21 November 1979. 'Gunmen Murder Italian Police', *Financial Times*, 22 November 1979. C. Schaerf, G. de Lutiis, A. Silj, F. Carlucci, F. Bellucci, S. Argentini. *Venti Anni di Violenza in Italia: 1969–1988*, volume one, (Rome: ISODARCO, 1992), p.850.
100. 'Policeman Shot Dead as Terrorists go on Trial', *Financial Times*, 27 November 1979. 'Brigades Victim', *The Guardian*, 28 November 1979. C.Schaerf et al. (note 99), p.851.
101. *L'Espresso*, 24 February 1980.
102. *L'Espresso*, 31 October 1982.
103. D. Pluchinsky. 'An Organizational and Operational Analysis of Germany's Red Army Faction Terrorist Group', Y. Alexander and D. Pluchinsky (eds.), *European Terrorism Today & Tomorrow*, (Washington DC: Brassey's (US), 1992), p.67.
104. D. Pluchinsky ibid., p.69.
105. Y. Alexander and D. Pluchinsky, (note 26), 68, 80.
106. A. Jamieson. (Note 5), 75–6, 99. D. Moss. (note 5), 81–117. V. S. Pisano (note 96), p.169. E. MacDonald. *Shoot the Women First*, (Fourth Estate, 1991; London: Arrow, 1992), pp.176–7.
107. D. Moss (note 5), p.85.
108. D. Moss (note 5), p.85. C.Schaerf et al. (note 99), p.736.
109. A.Jamieson (note 5), p.93.
110. A. Jamieson (note 5), pp.188-189. V. S. Pisano (note 96), pp.163, 165.
111. A. Jamieson (note 5), pp. 210, 212, 215–16. D. Moss (Note 5), pp.79, 80.
112. Y. Alexander and D. Pluchinsky (Note 26), pp.203–04.
113. D. Pluchinsky (note 103), pp.70, 71-72, 74-75.
114. H. Horchem. 'The Decline of the Red Army Faction', *T&PV*, 3/2 (Summer 1991), pp.71–2.
115. S. Aust (note 45), pp.286-288. J. Becker (note 91), pp.297–8.
116. A. Jamieson. (note 5), p.120.
117. D. Moss (note 5), p.120.

118. A. Jamieson (note 5), p.108.
119. D. Moss (note 5), p.122.
120. D. Moss (note 5), p.120.
121. D. Moss (note 5), p.124. A. Jamieson (note 5), p.138.
122. For more details see: D. Moss. (note 5), pp.38, 79–80, 81–117, 120, 122. A. Jamieson (Note 5), pp.75-6, 93, 99, 108, 120, 188–9, 210, 212, 215–16. V. S. Pisano (note 89), pp.163–5, 169. C. Schaerf *et al.* (note 92), p.736. E. MacDonald (note 99), pp.176–7. *L'Espresso*, 24 February 1980. *L'Espresso*, 31 October 1982. S.Aust (note 45), p.143, 286–8. J. Becker (note 84), pp.297–8. D. Pluchinsky (note 96), pp.67, 69, 70, 71–2, 74–5. Red Army Faction. 'Communique on the Assassination of Alfred Herrhausen, Chairman of Deutsche Bank, in Frankfurt on 30 November 1989', Red Army Faction. 'Communique on the Assassination of Detlev Rohwedder', Red Brigades – Fighting Communist Party, 'Communique on the Assassination of Ezio Tarantelli', Y. Alexander and D. Pluchinsky (eds.) (note 26), pp.68, 80, 203–4.
123. Red Brigades-Fighting Communist Party, 'Communique on the Assassination of Leamon Hunt, Director General of the Multinational Observer Force in the Sinai, in Rome on 15 February 1984', Y.Alexander and D.Pluchinsky (eds.) (note 26), pp.191, 197–202. A. Jamieson (note 5), pp.191, 210–11. P. Willan (Note 50), pp.335-8. D. Moss (note 5), p.273 n23.
124. H. Horchem. 'The Lost Revolution of West Germany's Terrorists', *T&PV*, 1/3 (July 1989), p.358. H. J. Horchem, *Terrorism in West Germany* (London: Institute for the Study of Conflict, 1986), pp.7, 20–1.
125. C. J. M. Drake, 'The Phenomenon of Conservative Terrorism', *T&PV*, 8/3 (Autumn 1996), pp.29–46.

[18]

Theories of Justification and Political Violence: Examples from Four Groups

GARRETT O'BOYLE

Groups that use violence also employ justifications for that violence, whether tailored for themselves, supporters or external observers. This article seeks to analyse selected examples of such justifications critically through the lens of applied ethics, specifically the justificatory theories termed deontology and consequentialism. These different approaches to justification, and the ways in which they are employed, tell us much about the self-perceptions, ideologies and psychologies of users of political violence. The paper examines whether different sorts of terrorist groups might be said to gravitate towards one particular justificatory mode rather than the other. To this end, the article presents and analyses actual and typical justificatory arguments used by the Provisional IRA, the Red Army Faction, al-Qaeda and anti-abortion militants.

Introduction

All groups that use, threaten to use, or advocate violence or force in an effort to further their political beliefs or agenda employ some form of justificatory argument to explain or support their actions. Most such forms of argument have a common core in justificatory ethical theory. This paper aims to begin an examination of the internal logic of different sorts of justificatory philosophical positions as exemplified in various groups' literature, publications and pronouncements. As such, it proceeds on two levels. First, it will introduce and briefly assess the two basic competing approaches to the justification of actions (or inactions) in ethical theory, termed *deontological* and *consequentialist*. This level might be said to involve the search for 'ideal types' or stereotypical forms of the justificatory arguments employed by different groups. The second level uses this theoretical background as a basis for the analysis of justifications actually used by violent groups. A tentative hypothesis is that the sorts of justifications used by different types of groups will tend to approximate one or other of the typical ethical positions outlined. For the purposes of this article, examples will be drawn from the literature of four different groups, each one representing a particular type. Thus, the 'revolutionary left' type will be represented by the West German Red Army Faction, active from the early 1970s until its official disbandment in 1998;

the 'national liberation movement' type will be represented by the Provisional Irish Republican Army, active in its present form since 1969; the 'religious Christian right' type will be represented by the shady and relatively leaderless network of activists who engage in campaigns of intimidation, assassination and harassment against abortion providers; and the 'Islamic extremist' type will be represented by Osama bin Laden's al-Qaeda movement.

Consequentialism and Deontology

Both consequentialism and deontology are ethical theories that seem to accord well with our commonly held moral assumptions. Yet they also often conflict with these moral intuitions and assumptions with regard to the particular courses of action that should be pursued by individuals in particular contexts. For example, deontological ethical theories tell us that the most important aspects of how we ought to live our lives are governed by moral rules that ought not to be broken. They involve the acceptance of certain specific behavioural constraints that place certain limits on the pursuit of the individual's own interests. This may be taken to mean that there are certain morally unacceptable means to a given end, even morally admirable or morally obligatory ends.[1] Certain codes or rules are intrinsically good, and should not be broken, even when breaking them might have better consequences. It is absolutist positions such as these that give rise to a sense of uneasiness and disparity with our 'common-sense moral intuitions'. A typical example would be a situation where the killing of one innocent person would save the lives of many others. Strict deontological prohibitions of murder would rule out this course of action. But, as Scheffler notes, how can it be rational to forbid the performance of a morally objectionable action that would have the effect of minimizing the total number of comparably objectionable actions that were performed, and would have no other morally relevant consequences? How can the minimization of morally objectionable conduct be morally unacceptable?[2]

In responses to paradoxes such as these, philosophical arguments such as making a distinction between positive acts and omissions (for example *killing* versus *letting die*) and concepts such as intentionality and the principle of double-effect have typically been introduced by deontologists. However, these arguments are often somewhat unconvincing. Honderich has argued persuasively that there is little or no moral difference between acts and omissions, particularly omissions that occur in the context of adequate knowledge (his argument can be succinctly expressed through the question he poses – 'how did I not turn off the radio at noon?' – and his answer: 'by *staying my hand*').[3]

Moreover, absolutist deontological positions are very hard to maintain when difficult cases arise. Deontology-based pacifism is difficult to sustain when it comes to the level of individual self-defence. If one opposes violence on deontological grounds one paints oneself into a corner, albeit a principled one. The well-worn example of a pacifist being faced with the choice of killing one individual himself, or, as a result of his refusal, ensuring that a hundred others are put to death is such a case. Strict deontology is not based on the impartial consideration of the welfare or interests of others, and thus can be said to be quite as ruthless and cold as consequentialism is often portrayed. But once it goes beyond the strict observance of prescribed rules, deontology runs into problems. Once transgression of the rule can be justified in certain circumstances for certain rules, deontology begins to break down. It begins to come down to subjective evaluation of the consequences of breaking or not breaking the rule. However, once the consideration of consequences enters the evaluative equation, we are no longer talking about deontology *per se*. Any deontological view that falls short of strict unyielding observance of the prescribed rule in effect collapses into consequentialism.

Consequentialism – the doctrine that says that the right act in any given situation is the one that will produce the best overall outcome in terms of the identified end – is often regarded by its critics as a reformulation of the crude concept of 'the end justifying the means'. From this perspective, consequentialism can also be said in certain circumstances apparently to violate our central moral intuitions. For example, it is often said that consequentialism would lead an agent to commit horrific acts as long as those acts promised (probably) to produce the best results in terms of the relevant end. Not only would it allow this, it is said, but it would also allow or encourage the general habit or attitude of contemplating or evaluating such deeds, rendering nothing unthinkable.[4]

There is a certain degree of accuracy to these accusations, as the acts prescribed by a resolutely consequentialist approach can seem to violate deeply held beliefs about how we should treat other people.[5] However, in a fundamental way, the conception of rationality that is at the core of consequentialism is the conception that people tend to use operationally in everyday decisions and interactions, and in a very wide range of contexts.[6] It is this that gives consequentialist approaches their force, even among those who do not accept them. Consequentialism can thus be seen to be the operationalization of an instrumental goal-directed rationality. This is why the dictates of deontological constraints can seem irrational: they may direct agents to act in ways that will not maximize the incidence of 'the good'.

The 'problem', if it should be called such, of the radically indeterminate nature of moral evaluation surrounds all ethical considerations. That is clear. And consequentialism has never denied that the determination of a 'good' end state of affairs involves problems of moral evaluation. Consequentialism should be seen less as a holistic theory of ethics than as a deliberative and evaluative tool. The use of a Kantian-based moralist such as Rawls to derive or determine a particular desired end state of affairs with regard to state and society should in principle pose no problem for consequentialists. But on the level of specifics, one issue is of particular importance in such an example: the relationship between ends and means. More specifically, will the use of certain means be detrimental to the value of the good one hopes to achieve? Would the achievement of a consequentialist end state based on Rawlsian principles be incompatible with infringements on peoples' rights and transgressions of considerations of justice when used as means? With regard to the justifiability of political violence used to try to attain such an end state, for how long and at what intensity will such violence be justified? One needs to recognize that societies are sets of dynamic interrelationships, rather than simple, two-stage, cause-and-effect processes. For example, in the face of political violence or civil disobedience, reforms might be granted that represent a considerable advance on the previous situation, but which fall short of the most radical interpretation of the Rawlsian principle. Assuming that the initial violence was justified, can we unequivocally say that continued violence is justified so as to attain the full effect of the radically interpreted Rawlsian principle, if such an achievement was even possible? At what point should violent means yield to reasoned political (non-violent) action? Again, the issue of 'justifiable to whom' – the perpetrators, the supporters or to some 'impartial observer' arises.[7]

Justifications for Political Violence

The relevance of these considerations to the issue of the justification of political violence lies in the definition of the good that guides the justificatory argument. First I will clarify some of the issues of the preceding section with reference to a previous example. In simple terms, deontology refers to a moral system in which states of affairs or actions are judged only, or primarily, by their accordance with a preordained set of moral rules and codes. Religiously based morality is an example. Deontological approaches to justification argue that certain acts are morally prohibited, regardless of any beneficial consequences that may be attached to them. Thus a deontologist may argue that the killing of an innocent person would be prohibited even if it could be demonstrated with certainty that such an action would save the lives of a thousand other equally innocent persons. The act in itself would simply be wrong. A consequentialist, on the other hand, judges states of affairs and actions solely or primarily by their consequences. In the above example, the consequentialist might argue that it is illogical and morally inconsistent to decline to kill one such innocent on the basis of a belief in the right to life or the illegitimacy of transgressing an individual's autonomy, when to decline so inevitably leads to other deaths that are equally to be deplored. The deontologist could then retort, even in this relatively simple example, that the intentions of the agent, the location of actual causality, and the moral status of the agent in performing or not performing the prohibited act are morally relevant issues.

The primary purpose of this sort of theoretical analysis, however, is to identify 'ideal types' of these justificatory positions, against which the sorts of justifications actually employed by groups that engage in or advocate violence can be assessed. My suggestion is that the sorts of justifications employed by different sorts of violent groups will approach one or other of the typical ethical positions outlined above, or perhaps maintain a tension between them. For example, one might expect a revolutionary left-wing group to employ a consequentialist justification. Crudely stated, it might proceed as such: 'Our use of political violence and/or terrorism is justified either (a) because we can overthrow the state and institute an egalitarian society in which all people will prosper and equally develop their distinctive human potentialities, or (b) violence will provoke the state into revealing its coercive and oppressive nature as a tool of the capitalist class, whereupon the masses will attain revolutionary consciousness.'

A group with a religiously based ideology – for example those who firebomb abortion clinics and assassinate doctors – might justify its actions deontologically in terms of divine justice: 'These abortionists are murderers, and the punishment for murder is death. We are acting in accordance with the will of God, which is to remove the stain that such abominable practices leave on his Creation.' However, they may also employ a second-order consequentialist justification, that by committing such acts they will not only remove a guilty abortion provider, but will also deter others from providing, and thus will save innocent lives in the long run.

Another issue to consider is that of the moral relevance of the victims to the perpetrators of violence. There are likely to be differences between groups with regard to the moral perceptions of the actors concerning the acts that they perform. A left-wing revolutionary group or, possibly to a lesser extent, a national liberation movement, may admit that killing and bombing are not good things *per se* and even that they are wrong in certain specific contexts and thus that they should be avoided in those contexts. However, they would argue that it is necessary to perform some evil in order to do good. Conversely, fascist or hate groups may not see their acts as necessarily wrong in themselves, in the sense that they see their targets as morally irrelevant, whether they be black, Jewish, communist or an abortion doctor.

To clarify further, the first such group might admit that all human life has value and that taking it is, in a perfect world, to be deplored. However, they would argue that certain contexts require the necessary and regrettable use of violence that results in death in order to achieve a situation that is of great benefit to the majority. The second set of groups might deny that all human life has equal value: some categories or races are subhuman, and thus morally irrelevant. This may also apply to those who defy the will of God by refusing to convert or by persisting in apostasy.

To refer to a potential third category, animal liberationists have used the slogan 'if we are trespassing, so were the soldiers who broke down the gates of Hitler's death camps; if we are thieves, so were the members of the underground railroad who freed the slaves of the South; and if we are vandals, so were those who destroyed forever the gas chambers of Buchanwald and Auschwitz'.[8] This indicates a clear willingness to extend the criteria of moral relevance beyond the human species.

Group Types and Justificatory Forms

A priori, I have identified six different sorts of violent groups that might be expected to exemplify one or other particular mode of justification, together with predictions of their likely justificatory form:

1. *Revolutionary left*: consequentialist justification as suggested above.
2. *Radical ecological*: largely consequentialist, but with the potential for a large dose of deontology in parts (for an extreme example, 'the human race is a destructive parasite on the planet, therefore we must be forced to conform to the ecological natural law').
3. *National liberation*: consequentialist in the main, perhaps elements of deontological justification with regard to the concept of national self-defence and the right to national self-determination.
4. *Religious Christian right*: specifically those engaged in campaigns of intimidation/assassination against abortion providers. The issue here is, do they do so because it results in fewer abortions (consequentialist) or because abortion providers are evil people who must be punished or who represent an affront to the will of God (deontological)?
5. *Secular right (fascist and race-hate groups)*: overlaps with 4 in terms of deontological inspiration. Violence will help to drive a particular target group out of the country, or put them in their (natural or divinely ordained) place, because white people/the Aryan race are superior/God's anointed people, and it is contrary to nature/God's will for races to intermingle.

6. *Islamic extremism*: the concept of *jihad* against the infidel appears, on one level, to be classically deontological.

It may be noted that this typology excludes at least two other potential distinct types: reactionary or pro-state terrorist groups, and millenarian groups such as Aum Shinrikyô. This has more to do with the definition of political violence/terrorism that has been used for the immediate purposes of this analysis than it has to do with any implication that such group's justifications are not amenable to analysis using this framework – on the contrary, they are. However, while not denying that reactionary groups which may be little more than an illegal, unofficial arm of the state may be 'terrorist' in a wider sense, I am currently only focusing on acts that are intended to influence directly state policy or individual action, rather than defend the status quo. For the moment – and perhaps contentiously – I am leaving aside entirely the possibility that reactionary/pro-state groups are (deontologically) pursuing their perceived duty to attain or preserve the good as they define it. Similarly, many millenarian groups' actions can be argued not to be 'political' in a strict interpretation of the term.

For the illustrative purposes of this paper I will be focusing only on four groups, representing one each of four of the six types outlined (national liberation, revolutionary left, religious Christian right and Islamic extremism). These are the Provisional Irish Republican Army (IRA), the Red Army Faction (RAF), violent anti-abortion activists and Osama bin Laden's al-Qaeda network. I will attempt a critical textual analysis of certain publications and statements released by such groups in order to parse them philosophically and assess them in terms of their ethical basis. There is a wealth of justificatory documentation available, so, because of space and time constraints, only a small fraction of the total possible literature will be examined.

The IRA

The present incarnation of the IRA, as other generations of the Republican Movement have before, sees itself as part of a tradition of resistance to British rule in Ireland. The rhetoric often stresses the notion of '800 years of rebellion' and the idea that every generation of Irish men and women has thrown up a valiant few who will not rest until the invader has been driven from the country's shores. In more recent times, rhetoric such as this has been largely toned down, probably in line with both modern propagandist trends and in recognition of political realities in Northern Ireland. However, the IRA remains in the classic, archetypal 'national liberation' mould of justification, and is interesting in the sense that – along with many of its contemporaries – it often mixed a Marxist analysis with its traditional justification, especially in the 1970s and early 1980s. The basic and traditional political position of the Republican Movement is as follows:

> Throughout history, the island of Ireland has been regarded as a single national unit. Prior to the Norman invasions from England in 1169, the Irish people were distinct from other nations, cultivating their own system of law, culture, language and political and social structures. Until 1921, the island of Ireland was governed as a single political unit as a colony of Britain. A combined political/military campaign by Irish nationalists between the years 1916 and 1921 forced the British government to consider its position. With the objective of 'protecting English interests with an economy of English lives' (Lord Birkenhead), the partition of Ireland was conceived. Partition was imposed on the Irish people by an act of parliament, the Government of Ireland Act 1920, passed in the British legislature. The consent of the Irish people was never sought and was never freely given. Proffered as a solution under the threat of 'immediate and terrible war' (Lloyd George, the then British prime minister), the act made provision for the creation of two states in Ireland: the Irish Free State (later to become known as the Republic of Ireland), containing 26 of Ireland's 32 counties; and Northern Ireland, containing the remaining six counties.[9]

This historical analysis serves a number of purposes. First, it seeks to establish a historical claim to Irish nationhood, with the existence of a unique language and culture. Second, it both emphasises the 800 years of occupation and alludes to a tradition of continued resistance. Third, its sets the basis for the contemporary Republican analysis of the conflict. That is, it stresses that partition was a coerced imposition on the Irish people that had the purpose of safeguarding British economic and military interests. Later in the passage (continued in note 9) it emphasizes the Irishness of the Unionist population and bemoans the fact that partition has served to blind unionists further to their true nationality.

Passages such as these have the purpose of identifying the existence of a historic Irish nation and hence the existence of a nation's *rights* – rights to independence, to self-determination and to resist external aggression. It is the primary purpose of the Republican Movement to vindicate these national rights. The constitution of the IRA used to refer explicitly to the organisation's elected leadership, representing the General Army Convention, as the only legitimate government of the Irish Republic. This legitimacy was traced back to the second Dáil (parliament), a separatist assembly established following elections in May 1921, and seen as the successor to the 'Provisional Government of the Irish Republic' proclaimed during the Easter Rising of 1916. The first Dáil had maintained that 'the existing state of war between Ireland and England can never be ended until Ireland is definitely evacuated by the armed forces of England'.[10] Traditional, and indeed old-fashioned, Republican ideology maintains that the second Dáil was never legally disestablished, and thus legitimate government of the Republic passed to those opposed to the Anglo-Irish Treaty, signed in December 1921, which established the Irish Free State and partition.

The current IRA constitution, known as *The Green Book*, does not explicitly make this claim. However, it states among the primary objectives of the organization that it is to 'guard the honour and uphold the sovereignty and unity of the Republic of Ireland'.[11] It is not the legal entity represented by the Irish government to which it is referring. Furthermore, the constitution states that 'The Army Council, only after [General Army] Convention, shall have power to delegate its powers to a government which is actively endeavouring to function as the *de facto* government of the Republic.'

The IRA's other objectives, as set out in the constitution, are to support the establishment of an Irish socialist republic based on the 1916 Proclamation; to support the establishment of, and uphold, a lawful government in sole and absolute control of the Republic; to secure and defend civil and religious liberties and equal rights and equal opportunities for all citizens; and to promote the revival of the Irish language as the everyday language of the people. Its means to these ends are to organize the IRA for victory; to build on a spirit of comradeship, to wage revolutionary armed struggle, and to encourage popular resistance, political mobilization and political action in support of these objectives.

The justification is based on a classic national self-defence scenario: the Irish people are a nation with rights to self-determination and self-defence. The legitimate authority of the Irish Republic does not reside with the collaborators with British rule in the Dublin government. Revolutionary armed struggle combined with popular political mobilization must be waged in order to secure a withdrawal of British forces and the establishment of a 32-county socialist republic.

An interesting feature of much of the literature produced by the Republican Movement in the 1970s and 1980s is the identification of the movement with the goals of the revolutionary left. In a 1980 interview, Seán Mac Stiofáin, a former chief of staff of the PIRA, explicitly called the IRA a revolutionary left-wing organization.[12] He further said that the armed struggle and the political struggle in Ireland were merely part of the one real struggle, 'the revolutionary struggle against capitalism, imperialism and racialism' – 'a revolutionary movement, if it *is* a revolutionary movement, will support revolutionary movements all over the world'.[13] However, the national self-defence perspective is never too far away:

> the nationally minded, the Irish-minded people of the North know that the IRA is their army, is the revolutionary army of the Irish people, and they know that many IRA volunteers have died fighting in defence of their areas. They know they will never be able to lead a normal, peaceful and happy life until the British imperialist presence has been removed from this country.[14]

The main justificatory form is largely consequentialist – 'we take up arms as a last resort in order to secure national self-determination, socialist democracy, peace and justice' – although there are quasi-theological elements that are rarely explicitly stated, represented in a subcultural rhetoric of punishing the invader and asserting the true legitimacy of the organization's position. Moreover, there is the implication that it is an Irish person's *duty* to resist British rule, which has a clear deontological basis. What this shows is the difficulty of disentangling the ethical justificatory positions in order to label definitively a justification as one or the other. In practice, most justifications of action will have elements of both consequentialism and deontology, although with different weights and emphases.

The RAF

The West German Red Army Faction is one of the archetypal revolutionary-left terrorist organizations. The premise behind their sort of political violence was not to overthrow the state themselves and thereupon institute a socialist state but, rather, through their actions, they wished to provoke the state into introducing draconian counter-measures against both the RAF and the wider left. In this they largely succeeded, and their rhetoric concerning the German 'police state' was not just hyperbole. But they failed in their primary purpose, which was the mobilization of the masses in reaction to this 'unmasking' of the coercive and oppressive nature of the state. The German government succeeded in sidelining the organization and isolating it from the broader left, and the populace regarded them largely as dangerous criminals rather than the revolutionary heroes they sought to be.

In one of their first communiqués, which appeared in April 1971 and was attributed to Ulrike Meinhof, they state that urban guerrilla warfare represents 'the only revolutionary method of intervention available to what are on the whole weak revolutionary forces':[15]

> To this extent the urban guerrilla is the logical consequence of the negation of parliamentary democracy long since perpetuated by its very own representatives; the only and inevitable response to emergency laws and the rule of the hand grenade; the readiness to fight

> with those same means the system has chosen to use in trying to eliminate its opponents. The urban guerrilla is based on a recognition of the facts instead of an apologia of the facts.
>
> The urban guerrilla can concretize verbal internationalism as the requisition of guns and money. He can blunt the state's weapon of a ban on communists by organizing an underground beyond the reach of the police. The urban guerrilla is a weapon in the class war. The urban guerrilla signifies armed struggle, necessary to the extent that that it is the police which makes indiscriminate use of firearms, exonerating class justice from guilt and burying our comrades alive unless we prevent them … The urban guerrilla's aim is to attack the state's apparatus of control at certain points and put them out of action, to destroy the myth of the system's omnipresence and invulnerability. The urban guerrilla presupposes the organization of an illegal apparatus, in other words apartments, weapons, ammunition, cars and papers.[16]

The statement further says that the group's original intention was to work closely with and within existing socialist groups in various contexts in grass-roots activism, alongside their armed struggle. However, this failed because of the level of police surveillance of these left-wing groups. Thus the RAF concluded that 'individuals cannot combine legal and illegal activity'.

As it stands so far, the justification is classically consequentialist. Given the weakness of the broader left and the anti-communist activities of the state, revolutionary violence is the only means available to advance their cause. There is also the sense that there is a justification based on self-defence here too, with implications of 'fighting back' against anti-left state action. However, this passage is, in the main, consequentialist, with a firm declaration of intent (to attack the state's apparatus of control) and the statement that violence is necessary in the absence of other avenues.

In a later pamphlet, there is trenchant criticism of the mainstream left for its lack of internationalism and unwillingness to engage with the RAF in a broader front: 'the only methods of intervention that come into her [the mainstream left's] mind are still only those that the working class developed in the era of competitive capitalism and parliamentarism'. To the RAF, the urban guerrilla represents a merging of national and international class struggle, and their violent acts are an opportunity to expose the structures of imperialist rule. They further state that there can only be progress in the class struggle if legal work is complemented by illegal work, and that the political propagandist work should include the possibility of urban guerrilla warfare.[17]

This statement exemplifies a similarly strong consequentialist basis. The authors argue that the repressive counter-measures they sought to provoke can no longer be kept secret, and furthermore the state has been forced to contravene its own laws in the process: 'they are forced to break with their own rules and appear as what they truly are: the enemy of the people'. The reaction of the state does not render the RAF's tactics inappropriate, they argue, even though they say that the working class as a whole is bearing the brunt of the state's counter-measures and that it has become extremely difficult 'to embed the guerrilla within the masses'.

> Resistance does not become something wrong just because of the lengthiness of the war. What do the comrades expect anyway in a country that has allowed Auschwitz to happen without any resistance? Whose working class has the history of the German working class and whose police the history of the SS?[18]

Though the statement has an explicitly consequentialist basis, there is an indication, through the use of a quote from Mao, that the victims of the RAF's violence may fit into different categories of moral relevance. The quote says that if one dies in the interests of the people, that death is 'weightier than the Tai mountain', but if one is paid by the fascists and dies for the exploiters and oppressors of the people, that death 'has less weight than a swan's feathers'. However, in their 1998 statement announcing the official disbandment of the RAF, they contradict this interpretation, stating that revolutionaries desire a world in which nobody has the right to decide whether another person lives or dies, and that attacking people in their capacity as functionaries of the state is 'a contradiction to the thoughts and feelings of all revolutionaries in the world – it contradicts their notion of liberation'.[19]

This use of the classic argument from necessity indicates that, while their victims were agents of the state, they nevertheless were morally autonomous individuals, and their right to life was only transgressed as a last resort: This is the argument that certain contexts require the necessary and regrettable use of violence that results in death in order to achieve a situation that is of great benefit to the majority.

Anti-Abortion Activists

A pro-choice website quotes the following from a programme for a 1996 banquet for anti-abortion militants: 'The just punishment for the capital crime of abortion, as with any murder, is death.'[20] While the veracity of this quote cannot be ascertained, there are many confirmed statements with the same tenor. A statement released by a group named Defensive Action before the trial of Michael Griffin, accused of the March 1993 killing of Dr David Gunn outside his Florida clinic, reads:

> We, the undersigned, declare the justice of taking all godly action necessary to defend innocent human life, including the use of force. We proclaim that whatever force is legitimate to defend the life of a born child is legitimate to defend the life of an unborn child. We assert that if Michael Griffin did indeed kill David Gunn, his use of lethal force was justifiable provided it was carried out for the purpose of defending the lives of unborn children. Therefore, he ought to be acquitted of the charges against him.[21]

The statement is interesting on a number of justificatory levels. First, the use of the term 'godly action' seems to imply that such actions have divine sanction or that they represent God's will. Second, it is the defence of *innocent* human life that is at issue. This makes clear the difference in the moral worth of the lives of innocents rather than the guilty. It also indicates how anti-abortionists can claim to be pro-life at the same time as ending or endangering the lives of medical practitioners: they are pro-*innocent* life, and the guilty must answer for their sins, with death if necessary. Third, there is the equation of the life of a born child with that of the unborn foetus. This has a clear basis in contemporary Christian theology. And fourth, the latter part of the statement indicates a consequentialist justification, in that the use of lethal force is justified if it serves to defend the lives of unborn children.

Another example represents an even clearer form of deontological justification. It is the closing declaration of a pamphlet entitled *When Life Hurts We Can Help … The Army of God: A How To Manual of means to disrupt and ultimately destroy Satan's power to kill our children, God's children*. The publication was found buried in the garden of a woman convicted of the assassination of an abortion provider in Kansas in 1993. The manual includes directions for harassing and destroying clinics, including instruction on arson, the making and detonation of home-made bombs, jamming telephones and clogging doors with glue:

> We, the remnant of God-fearing men and women of the United States of Amerika [sic], do officially declare war on the entire child-killing industry. After praying, fasting, and making continual supplication to God for your pagan, infidel souls – we then peacefully, passively presented our bodies in front of your death camps, begging you to stop the mass murdering of infants. Yet you hardened your already blackened, jaded hearts. We quietly accepted the resulting imprisonment and suffering of our passive resistance. Yet you mocked God and continued the Holocaust.
>
> No longer! All the options have expired. Our Most Dread Sovereign Lord God requires that whosoever sheds man's blood, by man shall his blood be shed. Not out of hatred of you, but out of love for the persons

> you exterminate, we are forced to take arms against you. Our life for yours – a simple equation. Dreadful. Sad. Reality, nonetheless. You shall not be tortured at our hands. Vengeance belongs to God only. However, execution is rarely gentle.[22]

This statement also has a number of elements. Primary among them is the dark Old Testament imagery of the wrath of a vengeful God who will punish the sinner. The implication is that God's will is at work, and that to kill an abortion provider is merely to send them early to God's eternal judgement. A second element is the argument that the decision to resort to violence was taken only after all other methods failed – praying, fasting, occupation and other modes of passive resistance. It was only after these failed that the resort to violence became necessary. A further point is the apparent willingness of the activists to submit to the judgement of the temporal, civil power, and accept their punishment accordingly. This draws an implicit distinction between earthly and divine justice. If temporal imprisonment is the price to be paid for carrying out the justice of God, so be it, for it is to God's justice that we ultimately answer, not to the laws made by corrupt, venal and weak politicians. Two more points are relevant. First is the reference to abortion providers as 'pagan', 'infidel' and 'heathen', with 'blackened, jaded hearts'. This reference serves to draw a distinction between the moral status of abortion providers and that of 'God-fearing' anti-abortion activists. It has certain parallels to the references of fascist and racist organization to 'heathen mud-races'. It also parallels certain racist and anti-Semitic statements made by Fr Paul Marx, the chairman of Human Life International.[23] This links to the second, perhaps minor, point: the idiosyncratic spelling of 'Amerika'. Certain racist and hate groups in the US often use a spelling that replaces the 'c' in 'America' with 'kkk', a well-known acronym.

There are many similar such justificatory statements available, most of which refer to the just punishment for murder being death and often refer to anti-abortion violence as being righteous. However, these examples will serve for our purposes.[24] These statements have a clear and overwhelming deontological character. Their justifications of violence are clearly based on the belief that it is their duty to carry out the justice of a vengeful God, as established by the Old Testament. To a large extent, at least in the extracts quoted, any consequentialist justification ('we do this to save lives in the long run') is of very secondary importance. Though it would be a logical consequence of their actions that abortion providers may be deterred, this is a minor part of their justification for the use of force. The justification seems to be primarily about dispensing divine justice and punishing sinners, and this is an archetypal deontological position.

Islamic Political Violence

Here the focus is on the sorts of justifications that are used by some Islamic extremist groups, specifically on the Qur'anic text-based scriptural interpretations that have been employed by Osama bin Laden in speeches, articles and interviews.

Most scripturally based forms of justification are deontological in structure. They are often based on a particularistic and anachronistic interpretation of canonical religious texts that does not or may not reflect the mainstream interpretation of the relevant religion. There are thus similarities in the manner in which certain groups choose, interpret and employ religious texts. The literal, fundamentalist and particularistic interpretation of certain Qur'anic texts has a direct analogy with the literal and fundamentalist interpretation of Christian texts employed by various white supremacist groups and militant anti-abortion groups.

The Basis for Contemporary Justifications of Islamic Violence

Formally, Islamic law prohibits violence except as official punishment for criminal transgressions, in personal self-defence, or in the case of formally declared legitimate war. 'Clandestine violence against defenceless victims' is condemned.[25] However, the Qur'an permits the use of force for two reasons: self-defence and the propagation of Islam. The term we tend to be familiar with is *jihad*. This is usually interpreted as meaning 'holy war'. While it can have this implication, its literal meaning is 'effort' or 'exertion'. This may include effort or exertion in war, but the meaning is not restricted to this. It may refer to day-to-day moral struggles, or to the attempt to convert non-believers through peaceful argument and persuasion, in ways that have nothing to do with the use of force.[26]

In one *sunna* (tradition of the prophet), Mohammed describes the use of force in battle as the minor *jihad*, and self-exertion in peaceful personal compliance with the dictates of Islam as the superior *jihad*. Likewise, another *sunna* reports that Mohammed said that the best form of *jihad* is to speak the truth in the face of an oppressive ruler.[27] That said, certain verses of the Qur'an apparently sanction the use of force against non-Muslims. It has been argued that such verses are based in the context of the time they were written: a context of insecurity and hostility between neighbouring peoples, a context where the very survival of Islam was paramount. The corollary position is that these verses, or strict interpretations of them, are not relevant today and should be open to reinterpretation by Muslim scholars.[28]

That said, the first Qur'anic verses that, in a literal interpretation, sanction *jihad* (in the sense of force) against non-Muslims are as follows:

> Fight in the cause of God those who fight you, but do not transgress the limits [initiate attack or aggression], for God does not love transgressors. And slay them wherever you catch them, and turn them out from where they have turned you out, for tumult and oppression are worse than slaughter; but fight them not at the Sacred Mosque [Mecca] unless they first fight you there; but if they fight you there slay them because that is the reward of the unbelievers. But if they cease, God is most forgiving … And fight them until there is no more tumult or oppression and there prevails faith in God; but if they cease, let there be no hostility except to those who practice oppression.[29]

Verses of chapter 9 of the Qur'an are, in this context, generally taken to contain the clearest permission for the use of force against non-Muslims and are believed to have superseded all previous verses that limit this use of force:

> [Once the period of grace – 4 months or until the end of a specified treaty – is over] then fight and slay the unbelievers wherever you find them, and seize them and beleaguer them, and lie in wait for them in every stratagem [of war]; but if they repent and establish regular prayers and pay *zaka* [Islamic alms and religious tax] then open the way for them, for God is most forgiving …[30]

A notable verse in this chapter refers to the treatment of 'people of the book' – Christians and Jews who have been enlightened by divine Biblical scriptures:

> Fight those People of the Book who do not believe in God or the Last Day, nor hold as forbidden what has been forbidden by God and His Apostle [Mohammed], nor acknowledge the Religion of truth until they pay *jizya* [poll tax] with willing submission, and feel themselves subdued.[31]

As an aside, various Qur'anic verses stress that Muslims should seek support from within the Muslim community, or *umma*, and should disassociate themselves from non-believers, not taking them as friends, helpers or supporters.[32] Similarly, Muslims should not take Jews and Christians as friends or allies, as they are friends and allies for each other. Any Muslim who turns to 'people of the book' for friendship or support becomes one of them.[33]

It has been argued that there is a clear progression with regard to Qur'anic sanction of the use of force against non-Muslims from using force for self-defence to using force in the propagation of Islam – moreover, these are the only circumstances in which the use of force is justified.[34] However, early

Muslim scholars developed the interpretative theory that Islam and unbelief cannot both exist in the world. There are many instances of Mohammed, and his succeeding caliphs, instructing Muslim armies to offer the enemy the opportunity to convert to Islam. If they converted, then no force was allowed to be used against them. If they refused to convert, but were Christians or Jews, then they were offered the choice of reaching an agreement with Islam wherein they would pay poll tax and submit to Muslim sovereignty, but retain the right to practice their religion and apply their personal laws. If this second option was rejected, then Muslims must use force: 'then seek help from God and combat them'.[35]

Leading founding scholars of *shari'a* (the interpretation of the Qur'an and of the deeds of Mohammed) spoke of a permanent state of war between the Islamic world and the non-Muslim world. Muslims may have to enter into peace treaties with non-Muslims if Muslim interests required it, but such treaties should only be of a temporary nature, to allow Muslims to resolve their internal differences or to prepare for the next period of conflict with non-Muslims.[36] Thus, whether through active fighting or by other means, the territory outside the jurisdiction of Islam must be brought within that jurisdiction.[37] The literal interpretation of this, combined with the injunction on individual Muslims to rectify – if possible – by direct private action whatever they perceive to be injustice or evil, seems to form the basis for the beliefs of militant proponents of the literal application of historical *shari'a*, or Islamic fundamentalists.[38]

The Example of al-Qaeda and Osama bin Laden

The justificatory form employed within bin Laden's speeches, articles and interviews is overwhelmingly deontological. The primary issues relate to the occupation, and thus desecration, of the lands of Islam's holiest shrines by non-believers. This includes the Israeli occupation of Jerusalem, and indeed the very existence of the State of Israel, and the presence of US troops in Saudi Arabia, the site of Mecca and Medina. These examples provide first-class bases for straightforward deontological motivations and justificatory structure. Another set of issues relates to the perceived oppression of Muslim people in, among other places, Iraq, Palestine, Somalia (through the abortive US mission there), Bosnia and Chechnya. These feed into the 'self-defence' aspect of the literal interpretation of *shari'a*. For example: 'Afghanistan, having raised the banner of Islam and started to seek to apply the *shari'a* of Islam, by the grace of God, has become a target of the crusader-Jewish alliance …'[39]

These two sets of issues are, by and large, interlinked in bin Laden's addresses. A representative quote is this, from May 1998:

> It does not worry us what America thinks. What worries us is pleasing Allah. The Americans impose themselves on everyone who believes in his religion and his rights. They accuse our children in Palestine of being terrorists. Those children that have no weapons and have not even reached maturity. At the same time they defend a country with its airplanes and tanks, and the state of the Jews, that has a policy to destroy the future of these children.[40]

Here bin Laden is saying that resistance to the Israeli occupation of Palestine, and opposition to America, Israel's perceived supporter, is a matter of divine will. The struggle is to vindicate Islam and religious rights. In another quote, from the same interview, he discusses his religious edict (*fatwa*) that called on all Muslims to kill Americans wherever and whenever they can:

> Allah ordered us in this religion to purify Muslim land of all non-believers, and especially the Arabian Peninsula where the Ke'Ba is. After WWII, the Americans became more aggressive and oppressive, especially in the Muslim world ... Each action will solicit a similar reaction. We must use such punishment to keep your evil away from Muslims, Muslim women and children.

The passage goes on to talk of the atomic bombing of Nagasaki, and the inability of these weapons to distinguish between civilians and military. It also refers to the 'co-operation between Christian and Zionist forces' in massacres of civilians in Lebanon, and to the effects of the 'American-led' economic sanctions in Iraq, before continuing:

> All this was done in the name of American interests. We believe that the biggest thieves and terrorists in the world are the Americans. The only way for us to fend off these assaults is to use similar means. We do not differentiate between those dressed in military uniforms and civilians: they are all targets in this *fatwa* ... The *fatwa* includes all who share or take part in killing of Muslims, assaulting holy places, or those who help the Jews occupy Muslim land.

These passages are employing the 'defence of Islam' position. There is no mention of a duty to propagate the religion of Islam beyond the boundaries of what is traditionally held to be Muslim land, though actions of self-defence are clearly sanctioned beyond this area. This echoes the interpretation of *shari'a* that says that it is a personal duty of all Muslims to rectify what they perceive as evil or injustice by direct personal action.[41]

In a classically deontological statement of motivation and justification, bin Laden responds to a question about him being seen as a terrorist leader in the West by invoking the will of God:

> We do not worry about what America says. We look at ourselves and our brethren as worshippers of Allah who created us to worship him and follow his books and prophets. I am one of Allah's worshippers. I worship Allah, which includes carrying out the *jihad* to raise Allah's word and evict the Americans from all Muslim land.[42]

And:

> We are sure of Allah's victory and our victory against the Americans and the Jews as promised by the prophet, peace be upon him: Judgement day shall not come until the Muslims fight the Jews, whereupon the Jews will hide behind trees and stones, and the tree and the stone will speak and say 'Muslim, behind me a Jew, come and kill him', except for the al-Ghargad tree, which is a Jewish plant.

The latter passage seems to suggest that conflict with the Jews is the will of Allah, is thus inevitable, and that victory is assured, as the very trees and rocks will turn against the Jews. Victory is assured against the US also, but for less magical reasons – namely, the righteous fury of the devout at its perceived desecration of Islamic holy sites:

> We are sure of our victory. Our battle with the Americans is larger than our battle with the Russians. The Americans made a very stupid mistake that no one has made before. They attacked the Muslim symbol, the Kibla, of 200 million people. The reaction by the Muslim scholars and the youth was very encouraging. We predict a black day for America and the end of the United States as united states, and will be separate states, and will retreat from our land and collect the bodies of its sons back to America. Allah willing.[43]

Analysing the Justifications

Returning to our theoretical issues, we can see three main points.

1. The justificatory form, as is the tendency with justifications based on religious texts, is overwhelmingly deontological. The publications and interviews are replete with statements that the perpetrators of violent acts are acting in accordance with the will of God, that it is their moral and religious duty to wage *jihad* against the infidel in order to preserve and defend Islam itself and to cleanse Islam's holy sites of the desecration that the Western presence represents. There is, however, little suggestion that *jihad* is to be waged in order to propagate Islam throughout the world. That said, certain interpretations of *shari'a* suggest a permanent state of conflict between the Islamic and non-Islamic worlds – treaties concluded

with non-Muslims are to be respected only as temporary measures to allow the Islamic world a breathing space to resolve its internal differences. Given that the brand of literal and anachronistic fundamentalism we have been discussing has many difficulties with regimes within the Islamic world, notably the Saudi regime, it is possible that, if these differences were resolved in the manner that the fundamentalists would favour, then their literal and anachronistic interpretation of *shari'a* could come into play.

2. A second-order consequentialist justification can be seen in certain passages. That is to say, they hint at a consequentialist *justificatory* structure. It is not to suggest that the *motivational* structure is anything other than deontological. The hints towards a second-order consequentialist justificatory structure relate primarily to deterrence: for every delay that the US makes in retreating from the Holy Sites, 'they will receive a new corpse from Muslim countries'.[44] If the Americans want to avoid this, and if they want to avoid having to explain and justify to their people why a US passenger aircraft, for example, has been shot down, then they should pull out of Saudi and stop their support for Israel. Straightforwardly stated, the position is that we are perpetrating particular acts in order to persuade you to undertake a certain form of action. This is a justification with a consequentialist form. The consequentialist goal is a concrete and distinct end state that could, conceivably, be achieved. However, in terms of the deontological motivational structure, there is an actual religious duty to attempt to achieve this end whether or not it is consequentially rational to do so and regardless of the possibility of actual success. There is a (deontological) bounden duty to attempt to achieve this consequentialist end state, even if it is apparent that the task is impossible.
3. With regard to the moral relevance of Islam's enemies, there is a clear sense that the lives of devout Muslims are worth more than those of infidels, even 'people of the book'. Indeed, there is the implication of an international Jewish conspiracy, quite similar to that propagated by neo-Nazi groups. Thus bin Laden says that Jews have the first word in American government, borne out if we look at the department of defense, the state department and the CIA. This is how the Jews 'use America to carry out their plans in the world and especially the Muslim world ... The presence of Americans in the Holy Land supports the Jews and gives them a safe back'. At a time when there are many homeless and poor in the US, 'we find the American government turning toward helping Israel in occupying our land ... The American government is throwing away the lives of Americans in Saudi Arabia for the interests of the Jews':

> So we tell the American people, and we tell the mothers of soldiers, and American mothers in general, if they value their lives and those of their children, find a nationalistic government that will look after their interests and not the interests of the Jews.[45]

With regard to Jewish people themselves, bin Laden gives a clear indication of how he sees their moral status:

> The Jews are a people who Allah cited in his holy book the Koran as those who attacked prophets with lies and killing, and attacked Mary and accused her of a great sin. They are a people who killed Allah's prophets – would they not kill, rape and steal from humans. They believe that all humans are created for their use, and found that the Americans are the best-created beings for that use …[46]

Conclusion

It can often be difficult to disentangle combined threads of consequentialist and deontological justifications. Most deontologically based statements that purport to justify violent acts will at least nod towards consequentialism, because any actual real-world end state that is desired is also a consequentialist end state – there is a consequence to be achieved. Another reason relates to the power of consequentialist rationality among those who may not share the justifier's deontological approach. Of the four sorts of groups examined, the RAF and the anti-abortionists held most consistently to one approach or the other, but perhaps the RAF were more consistently consequentialist than the anti-abortionists were consistently deontological. The anti-abortion justifications, though containing some consequentialist elements, were overwhelmingly deontologically inspired. That is to say that the deterrent aspect of their violence seemed to take second place to the 'vengeful or divine punishment' aspect. By contrast, the justifications for violence employed by the IRA and al-Qaeda were rather more of a mixed bag. The IRA were consequentialist on the whole, but it is hard to avoid elements of deontology when you are arguing in terms of the rights of a nation to self-defence and the right to punish aggression. Perhaps this is in the nature of national liberation movements in contrast to revolutionary left-wing groups. On the other hand, bin Laden's justificatory arguments are directly and obviously steeped in deontological religious duty, but include consequentialist end states that may or may not be actually attainable. However, regardless of their attainability, there is a bounden duty to strive for them.

NOTES

1. Nancy Davis, 'Contemporary Deontology', in Peter Singer (ed.), *A Companion to Ethics* (Oxford: Blackwell 1991) p.205.
2. Samuel Scheffler, 'Agent-centred Restrictions, Rationality, and the Virtues', in S. Scheffler (ed.), *Consequentialism and Its Critics* (Oxford: Oxford University Press 1988) p.244.
3. Ted Honderich, *Violence for Equality: Inquiries in Political Philosophy*, 3rd edn. (London: Routledge 1989) ch.3.
4. Philip Pettit, 'Consequentialism', in Singer (note 1) p.204.
5. Bernard Williams has some interesting things to say about individual squeamishness in the face of rationally prescribed consequentialist acts in his essay, 'Consequentialism and Integrity', in Scheffler (note 2) p.20ff.
6. Scheffler (note 2) pp.251–2. Scheffler argues that the persuasiveness of consequentialist accounts derives from the fact that they appear to embody a conception of rationality that we recognize from many diverse contexts, 'and whose power we have good independent reason to respect'. This form of rationality Scheffler calls a *maximizing rationality*, which has at its core the idea that, if one accepts the desirability of a certain goal being achieved, and if one has a choice between two alternatives, one of which is certain to accomplish the goal better than the other, then it is rational to chose the former option over the latter. The notion of a maximizing rationality is also central to rational choice theory.
7. This brings us to the consideration of 'satisficing' consequentialism, as discussed by Michael Slote, 'Satisficing Consequentialism', in P. Pettit (ed.), *Consequentialism*, International Research Library of Philosophy, vol.6 (Aldershot: Dartmouth 1993) p.352: 'could not someone who held that rightness depended solely on how good an act's consequences were also want to hold that less than the best was sometimes good enough, hold, in other words, that an act might qualify as morally right through having good enough consequences, even though better consequences could have been produced in the circumstances'. This is interesting in a number of ways. Importantly, it recognizes the process of goal attainment as dynamic, and it seeks to apply the common-sense, and indeed rational, consideration of the increasing marginal cost and/or diminishing marginal utility to this process. At some point, it seems plausibly to suggest, continued expenditure of time and effort at some given level of commitment is not worth it, as what has been achieved is good enough. It does not rule out continued efforts at a lower and less intense level of commitment. However, it raises many questions, particularly to do with the interpretation of 'the best that can be achieved'. Can we ever know what 'the best that can be achieved' really is, and how do we know when 'good enough' *is* good enough relative to 'the best'? Is there even a final 'best' endpoint, rather than just the continued incremental additions of extra achievement? Perhaps we can never know until after the fact, as in the *post hoc* justifications of 'actual consequence utilitarianism' (see Marcus Singer, 'Actual Consequence Utilitarianism', also in Pettit). Satisficing consequentialism, applied to the issue of the justifiability of political violence may, for example, dictate the earliest possible abandonment of revolutionary violence, and even revolutionary intent, in favour of reformism. But then, which sort of reforms are 'good enough' to warrant this? In response to Slote, Pettit argues that unless there are good, if non-conclusive, reasons for any one of which a wide-scope consequentialist might prefer a satisficing to a maximizing policy, satisficing is an irrational policy to pursue. This is to say that, in the absence of a determinate relationship between 'the best' and 'good enough', it is not rational to seek less rather than more. However, the issue of what can be said to constitute 'the best' in a dynamic process of attainment is still problematic.
8. Animal Liberation Front, *No Compromise: Animal Liberation Front and More*, http://nocompromise.org/alf/alf.html, accessed 24 May 1999.
9. This quote is taken from a Sinn Fein political education document entitled *Freedom*. It was published as a pamphlet in 1991. The version here was taken from the Sinn Fein website, www.sinnfein.ie, accessed 30 Aug. 2000. The document continues thus:

   Northern Ireland (the Six Counties) represented the greatest land area in which Irish unionists could maintain a majority. The partition line first proposed had encompassed the whole province of Ulster (nine counties). Unionists rejected this because they could not maintain a majority in such an enlarged area. The partition of Ireland was merely an innovation of the British government's tried and trusted colonial strategy of divide and rule, used throughout its former colonial empire. However, while the British government had the single objective of 'protecting English interests', its strategy for achieving this created deeper, more acute and more bitter multiple divisions in Irish society than those previously fostered, and which, until then, had helped sustain British rule in Ireland. Partition did not only physically divide the national territory of Ireland. It spawned the Civil War in 1922, which has moulded politics in the 26-County state ever since. It made more acute the divisions between nationalists and unionists in the Six-County state, and between the populations of the two states. Not least, it created real and lasting divisions among nationalists themselves. Increasingly, partition has generated the foolish and self-interested ostrich mentality in the power structures of the two statelets, which seeks piecemeal treatment of the symptoms, through coercion and censorship, instead of root-and-branch treatment of the problem. Throughout the 19th century and until partition in this century, the British government provided its colonial rule in Ireland with a cover of 'democracy'. Like other colonial powers in continental Europe, which 'integrated' their colonies into the imperialist state, Britain 'integrated' Ireland into the 'United Kingdom' through the *Act of Union (1801)*, which made provision for Irish representation at the British parliament. In the changed conditions of a full-blown struggle for independence in 1920, new means for 'protecting British interests' had to be found together with a new 'justification' for the continuing British presence which that necessitated. The 'wishes' of Irish unionists in North East Ireland have provided that 'justification' since partition.

10. Quoted in Sean Cronin, *Irish Nationalism: A History of Its Roots and Ideology* (Dublin: The Academy Press 1980) p.125.
11. *The Green Book* is published in full as an appendix to Martin Dillon, *The Dirty War* (London: Arrow 1990) pp.482–96.
12. Interview with Seán Mac Stiofáin, in the Revolutionary Communist Group, *Hands Off Ireland!* 10 (April 1980) pp.10–11. It is very likely that Mac Stiofáin's remarks were tailored towards the magazine's audience.
13. 'I, for one, regard the revolution in all these countries [Algeria, Cuba, Angola, Mozambique, Aden, among others] as one revolutionary struggle – the struggle against capitalism and its offspring – imperialism and racism. And the revolutionary in Ireland – his first duty is to promote the revolution in Ireland and by doing so he is helping the revolution all over the world. If only by good example! Revolutionary success in any part of the world is a success for all because it is going to encourage revolutionaries elsewhere to take action. So I regard our struggle in Ireland, the struggle of the Basque people, the struggle in Zimbabwe, in Southern Africa, in Southern America – anywhere in the world – as one struggle. Our victory will be their victory. Any defeat that any revolutionary movement suffers is a defeat for us all. And I'm quite sure that we will see more and more co-operation between revolutionary movements.' Mac Stiofáin, ibid. pp.14–15.
14. Mac Stiofáin, ibid. p.11.
15. Attributed to Ulrike Meinhof, *The Concept Urban Guerrilla*, 1971, an English language extract prepared by Richard Huffman. Many RAF statements in the original German are available on the Internet. The source for those referred to are from Richard Huffman's *This is Baader-Meinhof*, http://www.baader-meinhof.com, accessed 24 Aug. 2000. I would like to thank Marion Seibert and Heinz Brandenburg, Assistant Professor in the Department of Sociology and Political Science, Norwegian University of Science and Technology, Trondheim, for translating some of the statements.
16. Ibid.
17. Attributed to Ulrike Meinhof and Gudrun Ensslin, *The Urban Guerrilla and the Class Struggle*, c.1974, trans. by Heinz Brandenburg.
18. Ibid.
19. RAF statement on the organization's disbandment, April 1998. The statement is a long and often critical overview of the history of the RAF. In it they say that they are proud to have been part of a revolutionary attempt by a minority to resist the tendencies of capitalist society and contribute towards its overthrow. However, they are critical of some of the organization's past political strategies, particularly of what they see as the dominance of anti-imperialist over social revolutionary theory and praxis.

20. http://www.altculture.com/aentries/a/abortionxc.html, accessed 24 May 1999.
21. The undated Defensive Action statement and the list of 31 signatories to it can be found at http://www.cais.com/agm/main/statemen.htm, accessed 23 Aug. 1999. The veracity of the text is confirmed by newspaper reports, for example *The Irish Press*, 11 Nov. 1993.
22. Extract from the manual of the Army of God, reprinted in *Ms.*, May–June 1995.
23. Fr Marx's autobiography, *Confessions of a Pro-Life Missionary* (Human Life International 1988) has a chapter entitled 'Pro-Abortion Jews and the New Holocaust', which includes statements such as 'notice how many Jews led the infamous 1971 abortion planning meeting in Los Angeles, which I exposed', and 'note the large number of abortionist (consult the *Yellow Pages*) and pro-abortion medical professors who are Jewish'.
24. For a detailed analysis of the theological basis of anti-abortion militancy, I recommend two pamphlets. The first is by an anti-abortion activist, Rev. Paul Hill, entitled 'Should we defend born and unborn children with force?' (1994). It sets out his argument in favour of the use of force with copious Biblical quotation, and answers ten possible objections to his position. The second is by Tom Burghardt of the Bay Area Coalition for Our Reproductive Rights (BACORR), entitled 'The Crown Rights of King Jesus: A Brief Outline of Christian Reconstructionism'. Both papers can be obtained from BACORR, which is based in San Francisco.
25. Abdullahi Ahmed An-Na'im, 'Islamic Ambivalence to Political Violence: Islamic Law and International Terrorism', *German Yearbook of International Law* 31 (1988) p.307.
26. Ibid. p.325.
27. Ibid. p.325.
28. Ibid.
29. Verse 2:190-93 of the Qur'an, quoted in ibid. p.326.
30. Verse 9:5, quoted in ibid. p.327.
31. Verse 9:29, quoted in ibid. p.327.
32. Ibid. p.325. Cf. verses 3:28, 4:144, 8:72-3, 9:23 and 71, and 60:1.
33. Ibid. p.325.
34. Ibid. p.328.
35. Ibid. pp.328–9.
36. Ibid. p.330.
37. Ibid. p.331.
38. Ibid. p.333.
39. Remarks by Osama bin Laden in a December 1998 interview with ABC News, in the context of the then US cruise missile attacks on Afghanistan.
40. Interview with John Miller of ABC News, May 1998.
41. An-Na'im (note 25) p.333.
42. Bin Laden (note 39).
43. Ibid.
44. Ibid.
45. Ibid.
46. Ibid.

[19]

BORROKA—The Legitimation of Street Violence in the Political Discourse of Radical Basque Nationalists

HANSPETER VAN DEN BROEK

Amsterdam School for School Science Research
University of Amsterdam, Amsterdam, The Netherlands

The present article analyzes the discourse employed by the left-wing nationalist movement in Spain's Basque Country to legitimize the use of street violence for political ends. I distinguish four "faces" of legitimation ("ex ante" vs. "ex post," "for us" vs. "for others") and argue that in a situation of radicalization of politically inspired (terrorist) violence, the discourse developed to justify violent action is principally meant for the organization's own following, and less to communicate with the outside world. Basque militants claimed that their strategy of political and military radicalization in the 1990s had been responsible for recent political successes of their movement.

In 1992, the left-wing nationalist movement in the Basque Country experienced a serious setback when the entire leadership of ETA was arrested in the south of France. In the next few years, the so-called (and self-proclaimed) *Basque National Liberation Movement*,[1] or MLNV, forced on to the defense both militarily and politically, modified its strategy in order to regain its former strength. As a consequence of this change, ETA actions, though fewer than before, came to have a much greater impact on Basque (and Spanish) society. But it was above all the frequent riots, acts of sabotage, and other expressions of street violence in many towns and villages of the Spanish Basque Country which began to condition social life in the region.[2] In these violent actions, usually characterized by radical nationalists as expressions of the Basques' *popular struggle* ("herri borroka" in the Basque language) against Spanish oppression, the presence of teenagers (aged 14 to 20) was dominant.

In September 1998, the radical nationalist party coalition Herri Batasuna (HB) and two moderate nationalist parties, together with a number of smaller political parties and social movements, signed the Lizarra Agreement, in which they expressed their compromise to work jointly towards a solution of the conflict. A few days later, ETA declared a ceasefire. Although the ceasefire was revoked again in November 1999, for well over a year Basque society experienced a situation of relative peace: that is, no ETA actions against politicians, police, and military forces took place in this period. However, acts of sabotage, intimidation, and harassment by radical

Address correspondence to Hanspeter van den Broek, C/Padre Aller, 11-6°C 33012 Oviedo (Asturias), Spain. E-mail: hpvandenbroek@hotmail.com

The research project *Ekintza or the logic of violent action* is funded by the NWO, The Netherlands.

Basque youth still continued. The continuity of the *popular struggle*, which was also criticized by many HB supporters, frequently strained the collaboration among the nationalist parties.

Violent actions committed by militant nationalists were the subject of frequent articles in the regional and national press, whereas the mostly young protagonists became the object of sociological studies and political analyses. However, in these news reports and studies, seldom was an attempt made to bring to the fore the MLNV's definition of the current political situation in the Basque Country or to seriously analyze the discourse of left-wing nationalists explaining the background of the *popular struggle*. Nevertheless, as Patricia O'Connor observed, "more comprehension about acts of violence may come about if we learn to analyze carefully the discourse of those who victimize others."[3] And according to David E. Apter: "People do not commit political violence without discourse. ... The key to political violence is its legitimacy."[4] Indeed, the political discourse of the MLNV and its members in the second half of the 1990s was focused in no small measure on the legitimation of the intensification of street violence.

In the Basque case, radical nationalist discourse was not simply about justifying the use of violence against an outside enemy in order to achieve the liberation of the Basque people. Several factors made the picture more complex. In the first place, the Basque population's aversion for ETA had gradually increased during the course of the 1980s[5]; one sociological study claimed that a decade later ETA members were slightly more disliked in the Basque Country than neo-Nazis.[6] Basque people's opinions on the perpetrators of street violence were even more negative than those on ETA activists, which had much to do with the second circumstance: from 1994 until 1998, the so-called "popular struggle" for the Basque cause was principally aimed at Basque institutions (especially the Basque autonomous police force, the *Ertzaintza*) and members and party offices of moderate nationalist parties. Thirdly, although ETA kept a long-term ceasefire period from September 1998 onward, so as to facilitate negotiations between the MLNV and the Spanish Government, radical Basque youth continued to commit acts of street violence against Spanish interests.

Thus, the purpose of the present article is to analyze the political discourse used by the radical nationalist movement in the Basque Country to justify the radicalization of the *popular struggle* in the 1990s, in a situation of decreasing support for this type of violence among the movement's sympathizers. It is through such discourse that otherwise individual acts of violence are related to each other and given meaning.[7] This analysis should highlight the elements the fabric of legitimation of political violence in the Basque Country is made of. In his article on the conflict in Northern Ireland, Bairner provided the main elements which tend to recur in Republican discourse legitimizing the use of violence: arguments of self-defense, the doctrine of national self-determination, the idea of fighting a "just war," and Marxist-Leninist anti-imperialism.[8] We may expect that these elements, in a greater or less degree, also appear in the discourse of Basque left-nationalists who legitimize violence carried out by ETA or by radical youth.

However, considering the specific circumstances in the Basque Country in recent years (radicalization; ceasefire and cooperation of moderate and radical nationalists; break of truce and renewed radicalization), the following questions are appropriate:

1. In what terms does left-nationalist discourse explain the use of violence against the very people (Basque citizens, even fellow nationalists) whose interests radical nationalists claim to defend?

2. What rhetoric is employed to justify the continuation of acts of sabotage, intimidation, and the like in a period in which ETA respected a ceasefire?
3. How does left-wing nationalism account for the widespread aversion among Basques for those who allegedly struggle for the liberation of their territory?

I argue that the legitimation of the use of violence may take place both before (*ex ante*) and after (*ex post*) violent action is committed. At the same time, the messages of legitimation are aimed at two different audiences: at the activists and sympathizers of the radical nationalist movement, and at Basque society in general. We can thus distinguish what we might call "four faces of legitimation": the *ex ante* and *ex post* legitimation for internal utilization, and the *ex ante* and *ex post* legitimation for the outside world. We may expect the purposes of the discourse to be different in each of these cases.

So as to be able to answer the questions formulated before, the most relevant MLNV documents were analyzed: the document *Oldartzen*, which had been elaborated by the HB leadership[9] and laid the basis of the strategy to be followed by the left-nationalist movement in the second half of the 1990s; some internal writings of ETA that provided early evaluations of this strategy[10]; and a few internal documents of the MLNV youth organization Jarrai. Furthermore, interviews were done with 25 left-wing nationalists: three group interviews were carried out with a dozen youngsters who had been convicted or were awaiting trial for having participated in acts of street violence; the other interviews were done with individual members of a number of MLNV organizations, such as Herri Batasuna and Jarrai.[11] Finally, several members of other political parties, who had been victims of acts of street violence, were interviewed.

As María J. Funes correctly observed, the fact that ETA still exists, even after more than two decades of democratic rule in Spain, should be attributed mainly to "its social support from a qualitatively significant sector of Basque society"[12]; there is a network that actively supports those who commit violent activities, and there is another sector which does not provide direct support, but does not look unfavourably upon the activists and their actions either. Both sectors legitimize the violence used by ETA and the radical youth movement. The same author demonstrated, however, that the percentage of Basque people who accept the use of violence to achieve political ends has strongly declined in the last 20 years. At the same time, the number of people who openly manifest their opposition and even organize demonstrations against ETA violence has increased, especially since the mid-1990s. But Funes suggested that the attempt to politically and socially isolate the sectors close to ETA may well have led to the movement's "radicalizing its posture and diversifying its violent actions."[13]

Reinares found that former ETA activists justified the use of violence because of its alleged efficiency to achieve political goals[14]: the assassination of Franco's intended successor, Admiral Carrero Blanco, was believed to have hastened the decline of the autocratic regime; the continuity of ETA attacks in the period after Franco's death forced the Spanish government to declare amnesty for ETA prisoners; several bomb attacks and the killing of two engineers led to the closing down of the nuclear plant of Lemóniz, something that numerous appeals and demonstrations had not been able to bring about, and so on. ... By extrapolation, many left-wing nationalists were equally convinced that independence of the Basque Country could never be achieved without using violence.

Similar justifications can be found in José M. Mata's study on radical Basque nationalism,[15] which also highlights another frequently heard opinion: since the Franco era, when ETA was supported by a significant part of Basque society, the situation of oppression of Basque culture and political demands has not changed fundamentally. The author suggested that left-wing nationalist legitimation here becomes tautological: the political situation in the Basque Country has not changed, the 'proof' being that if it had, ETA would not exist today.

A sociological report edited at the request of the Basque Government and pretending to offer an analysis of the life-world of the perpetrators of street violence, does not present these radical youth as individuals capable of thinking and acting for themselves, but as victims of indoctrination and manipulation by ETA: although depicted as aggressors, "(t)hese violent youths themselves are victims of the totalitarian strategy they serve."[16] The motives of juveniles resorting to violent action are being depoliticized: "Many young people participate [in acts of violence] without any arguments nor political intention, even moved by a pitiful ludic conception of violence."[17]

Other authors, however, lay greater emphasis on the political aspects of street violence in the Basque Country. MacClancy, commenting on the struggles of left-wing nationalist demonstrators with the police, stated that "[t]he fight may have ritualistic elements: it is still a fight for political ends."[18] The movement has been able to develop quite an elaborate discourse on the national identity and political situation of the Basque people: "radical Basque nationalists have created an explanatory world-view with great interpretive extension."[19]

The question why conflicts between groups which are sociologically close (as in the Basque case, the moderate and radical branch of the nationalist "family") tend to be especially virulent is dealt with by Blok,[20] who suggested that the explanation should be found in threatened group identity. The identity of a group tends to be blurred most by the proximity of another group with similar features. People striving to preserve the identity of the group they belong to usually emphasize the (small) differences that exist between themselves and the members of groups that are close (either in ethnic, religious, social, or political terms), treating the latter as alien, inferior, and very often as arch-enemies. Although Blok illustrated the functioning of this principle with a great number of examples, we do not learn whether the arguments with which the protagonists themselves legitimize their indulging in collective "fratricides" also tally with this explanation.

Street Violence and its Protagonists

Up to the mid-1980s, the number of mortal victims of ETA oscillated between 30 and 40 a year and, after peaking in 1987, declined to some 20 a year by the end of the decade. Table 1 enables us to compare the numbers of lethal ETA actions in the 1990s with those of acts of street violence in towns and villages of the Basque Country. The table suggests that as for numbers, there was an inverse relationship between ETA attacks and the intensity of street violence. In 1992, Spain was the stage of two major international events, the Olympic Games in Barcelona and the Expo in Seville. In the knowledge that the attention of the world press would be focused on Spain for quite some time, ETA launched an offensive campaign the year before, which was aborted as a result of the detention of the organization's top leaders in March 1992. In subsequent years, ETA actions were fewer than they

Table 1. Number of ETA victims and acts of street violence (riots, sabotage, etc.) in the 1990s

	1990	1991	1992	1993	1994	1995	1996	1997	1998	1999
ETA victims	24	46	26	15	13	15	5	13	6	0
acts of street violence	294	305	552	428	287	924	1,113	971	489	344

Note: The last ETA attack before the ceasefire occurred in June 1998. (Sources: "Asociación de Víctimas del Terrorismo" (1998) URL http://www.avt.org/informacion/ ; Egin, *Euskadi 1997 Urtekaria* (San Sebastián: Orain, S.A., 1997) p. 86; *El País*, 10 April 2000.)

had been for the last 20-odd years, but the attacks would become more selective, causing greater impact on Basque (and Spanish) society. Several politicians, most of them Basque municipal councillors of the *Partido Popular* (Spain's governing party since 1996), were assassinated, and there were attempts to murder Prime Minister Aznar and King Juan Carlos. In addition, some of the longest kidnappings in ETA's history took place in this period.

As for actions of street violence, the peak in 1992 should probably be interpreted as the response of part of the MLNV followers to the detention of the head of ETA. In the course of 1994, the left-nationalist movement discussed the strategy to be followed in the second half of the decade. The following years saw a spectacular increase of violent incidents perpetrated by radical youth.

In former years, riots had usually taken place more incidentally, mainly following MLNV demonstrations in the provincial capitals Bilbao and San Sebastian, and the objects of aggression used to be banks, public transport, and members of the National Police. But after 1994, acts of youth violence were being perpetrated almost every weekend, in towns and villages all over the Basque Country.

The following (Table 2) gives an idea of the principal objects of urban guerrilla actions. The numbers are from my elaboration of the data presented in the 1996 yearbook of the left-nationalist newspaper *Egin* over the period January 1 to

Table 2. Objects of urban violence in the Basque Autonomous Region and Navarre (1 Jan.–31 Oct. 1996)

Objects of urban violence	Number of attacks suffered	% of total number of attacks
Banks and insurance companies	208	31.6
Public transport	75	11.4
Telefónica (company's cars, cabins)	57	8.7
Post Offices	19	2.9
Ertzaintza (Basque police force)	99	15.0
Other police forces	20	3.0
Political parties	56	8.5
Miscellaneous	124	18.8
Total	658	100

Note: *Telefónica* is Spain's national telephone company. (Source: Egin, *Euskadi 1996 Urtekaria* (San Sebastián: Orain, S.A., 1996) pp. 151–168; adapted.)

October 31, 1996. Though these numbers may not be entirely representative for other periods in the nineties, they quite accurately reflect which institutions and collectives most suffered the attacks of MLNV activists. These attacks were still for the most part directed against Spanish interests and capitalist symbols (note that the left-wing nationalist struggle is aimed at achieving an *independent* and *socialist* Basque Country), but in no small measure they also affected Basque institutions and citizens, principally property and members of the *Ertzaintza* (the Basque autonomous police force) and of the moderate nationalist parties.

Of the 56 acts of violence committed against political parties, 34 were directed against the moderate nationalist PNV (*Partido Nacionalista Vasco*, or Basque Nationalist Party), constituting 60.7 percent of all the attacks on political parties. These actions ranged from setting fire to party offices and cars of party members to throwing paint-bombs or Molotov cocktails at their houses. When responsibility was claimed for the actions against political parties, motives generally related to the supposed infringement of the rights of ETA prisoners (in 27 cases, = 48.2%), or to police repression (in 21 cases, = 37.5%).

As the Basque police force had been able to wind up several ETA commandos and was also involved in the repression of violent action perpetrated by left-wing nationalists, the MLNV accused the *Ertzaintza* of collaboration with Spain's "occupying forces." In the nineties, ETA killed a few police officers they held responsible for this policy, but also rank and file policemen were victims of harassment by MLNV followers.

The numbers in Table 2 do not reflect the incidents which often took place when demonstrations were held to demand the liberation of ETA hostages. The kidnappings in the years 1995–1997 were among the longest in the history of ETA and month after month, both massive demonstrations and small-scale concentrations were organized, usually several times a week, to claim the liberation of the hostages; many ordinary citizens used to wear a blue ribbon to express their support of this demand.[21] Soon, however, the MLNV started to organize counter-demonstrations in order to regain their domination of the streets, demanding "Freedom for the Basque Country" (*Euskal Herria Askatu*), the idea being that not only one or two persons, but the entire Basque nation was held hostage by the Spanish and French states. The participants in the anti-ETA demonstrations and people wearing blue ribbons often became victims of intimidation (with slogans like "The murderers wear blue ribbons," or "ETA kill them") and harassment by MLNV members who saw them as enemies of their cause. According to many political comments in those days, the so-called "Basque conflict" had gradually turned into a "conflict among Basques."

In the following sections we will analyze how the MLNV organizations which designed the strategy of radicalization in the early 1990s (ETA, Herri Batasuna, Jarrai) motivated the need for an intensification of the *people's struggle*, and what discourse MLNV members employed by the end of the decade to justify, in retrospect, the 'everyday violence' in previous years.

The Necessity of Intensifying the Struggle: *Ex Ante* Legitimation

Riots and acts of sabotage in the Basque Country have generally been subsumed under the heading of *kale borroka*—a Basque term which has become familiar in the Spanish media as well. The literal translation of *kale* is "street," whereas *borroka* should be translated as "struggle." But, according to MLNV respondents, it would be incorrect to simply translate *kale borroka* as street violence ("violencia callejera") or youth violence ("violencia juvenil"), as is generally done in the regional and national press. The interpretation in vogue within the MLNV is that *kale borroka* is the people's political struggle (predominantly acts of protest) developed outside the institutions, in the streets of the towns and villages of the Basque Country.[22]

In the words of a spokesman of Jarrai: "They [the media] reduce *kale borroka* to violence, but for us *kale borroka* is something which includes much more: sabotage, burning cash-dispensers, but also meetings or sticking up posters in the street... all this is *kale borroka* as well."[23] As the term *kale borroka* acquired increasingly negative associations in the course of the 1990s (the cult of throwing Molotov cocktails, accusations of using fascist methods, etc.), the expression was gradually abolished in favour of the broader designation *herri borroka* or popular struggle ("lucha popular" in Spanish).

As we have stipulated above, violence needs legitimation, not only *ex post* (meant to justify its use in the past) but also *ex ante* (especially to explain a change of strategy, like the intensification of actions or the modification of objectives). Such *ex ante* legitimation provides motivation to the political following and may, at the same time, be a warning to the enemy, anticipating and reinforcing the intimidation which emanates from violent action itself. The greater part of the MLNV's discourse of *ex ante* legitimation of political violence in the 1990s can be found in the documents *Oldartzen* and *Karramarro I* and *II*.[24] Basically, the line of argumentation was as follows: the Basque Country is deprived of truly democratic structures as it suffers the oppression of the Spanish and French states; the Basque people's struggle is defensive, meant to preserve their culture and their language and to regain their freedom and democratic rights; since non-violent options are ineffective, it is justified to resort to violence.

The MLNV documents indicated that the movement's members had become used to delegating the initiative of the political struggle to ETA, a practice that had to be corrected: henceforth, major involvement of the movement's political following would be required. By the end of 1996, an internal ETA document confirmed that this aim had been achieved: more and more "sectors" of society were becoming involved in *kale borroka*, counter-demonstrations of *Euskal Herria Askatu* (see above), and other forms of "popular struggle." The *kale borroka* was qualified as the "star" phenomenon of the current political situation; it had had its setbacks as well (youths who had been arrested and wounded), but "in the streets we are winning." The same document corroborated the MLNV's role in the development of *kale borroka*.

> ... left-wing patriotism does not just 'justify' what is happening, but somehow incites and pushes to take part in the KB [*kale borroka*] as well, thus giving protection to those who participate or are about to participate. ... KB [is seen] as a political phenomenon, ideologically well-founded and politically guided and supported.[25]

The movement is warned not to lose control of the phenomenon: "The pace and levels of KB should be completely in our hands."[26] Those who take part in *kale borroka* must be considered as MLNV activists; when they are arrested they should be assisted by the movement's lawyers and those who are sent to jail "should become part of the collective of political (i.e. ETA) prisoners."[27]

From these documents and the declarations of some of Herri Batasuna's leaders it may be concluded that the purpose of the intensification of the struggle and the major implication of the MLNV following was twofold. First, the idea was that the Spanish state should be forced to negotiate with ETA, and this might be realized through a combination of countless *kale borroka* actions and selective ETA attacks.

> ...the unquestionable truth is that [the Spanish state] WILL NEGOTIATE WITH ETA WHEN ETA WANTS. ... It is obvious that the process will start at the moment Euskadi Ta Askatasuna [ETA] decides it is convenient to declare a ceasefire. ... The new tactics of destabilizing the state and the massive response of patriotic youth in the streets will accumulate sufficient power to enable the Organization to announce a ceasefire, which will force the enemy to start the process.[28]

Second, the objective was to pressurize Basque society to the maximum, both its politicians and its citizens. This strategy became known as the "socialization of suffering." In the words of a member of the HB leadership: "Some of us have been putting up with this situation of violence for years; now it is other people's turn to go through this."[29] The central idea behind the radicalization of the *kale borroka* and similar forms of struggle seems to have been that a situation of continuous destruction, tension, and insecurity would make people accept *any* solution, if only violence came to an end—and that it would induce them to demand from their political leaders to do everything possible to reach a solution.[30]

But there were other factors as well which explain why the left-wing nationalist movement sought to emphasize the atmosphere of conflict and confrontation. It was seen as virtually the only way for the MLNV to get some media coverage. For its members it was a source of constant frustration that, for example, their many declarations, demonstrations, hunger strikes, and other actions, in favour of Basque prisoners were almost systematically ignored, not only by the Spanish media, but also on the Basque radio and television. As a document of the youth organization Jarrai explained: "In the society we live in, what does not appear on television does not exist. ... Our presence in those mass media is vital as well."[31]

This was one of the reasons why the MLNV used to organize counter-demonstrations claiming, "Freedom for the Basque Country" only a few steps away from demonstrations of pacifist organizations protesting against ETA actions, something which normally created an atmosphere of extreme tension. Television news bulletins invariably paid attention to these pacifist demonstrations, but from then on they also had to dedicate part of this information to the presence of MLNV activists.

Furthermore, the generalized atmosphere of political confrontation was thought to be beneficial for the internal functioning of the movement. The Jarrai document cited above was quite explicit about this:

> The popular movement has to generate conflict. It does not search for conflict, but if a movement really works in the right direction, it will bother those who dominate the established order and conflict will arise. It is in conflict, during the struggle, that consciousness increases and militancy arises.[32]

Not only was political consciousness expected to motivate people's participation in the struggle, but at the same time it was believed that a person's direct implication in actions would boost his or her ideological maturity[33] and lead to growing identification with the movement.

As for the potential objectives of popular struggle, institutions supposedly related to the Spanish state (from the police forces and judiciary to the banks and the press) were considered to be the principal enemies to be combated. But in the eyes of the MLNV, it was only because of the collaboration of the moderate nationalist parties PNV and EA and the *Ertzaintza*, the autonomous police force, that "state repression" of left-nationalist aspirations could be so effective. The PNV (*Partido Nacionalista Vasco* or "Basque Nationalist Party") was founded at the end of the Nineteenth century; since the 1979 Statute of Autonomy it has always occupied central positions in the different Basque Governments. EA (*Eusko Alkartasuna* or "Basque Alliance"), a smaller nationalist party of social-democratic tendency, has also been present in the regional governments since its separation from the PNV in the 1980s. The MLNV accused both parties of obstructing the realization of truly nationalist principles like independence and the territorial reunification of *Euskal Herria*.[34]

The *Oldartzen* document suggested that the Government in Madrid and the Basque Nationalist Party, in a perfect symbiotic relationship, depended on each other to curb left-wing nationalism:

> ...the PSOE[35] has intensified the State's repressive strategy by means of some new measures: ... international collaboration, ideological struggle annex intoxication, the direct implication of the PNV, the dirty war, the mass-media, repentance of prisoners, the instrumentalization of negotiation ... the *Partido Nacionalista Vasco* and the Spanish state develop a common strategic project against left-wing patriotism and the national project it defends. ... [The PNV] knows that the state needs its collaboration to neutralize our struggle.[36]

The *Ertzaintza* was understood to play a fundamental role in the belligerent policy of the PNV and the Spanish state against left-wing nationalism: "...the Ertzaintza, led by the PNV, has turned into a political and repressive instrument of the Spanish state."[37] In left-nationalist discourse, Basque policemen are addressed as *zipaioak*, comparing them with the native Indian police force (sepoys) under British colonial rule.

In *Karramarro 2*,[38] a slight change of attitude towards the *Partido Nacionalista Vasco* may be detected. According to the authors of the document, the PNV had modified its position somewhat as a result of the pressure exercised on the party, through actions of *kale borroka* against PNV party members and attacks of ETA against members of the *Ertzaintza;* therefore, "our political objective with respect to the PNV is that the party ceases to be an extra obstacle in our conflict with the Spanish state; we should not stigmatize the party as an eternal enemy."[39] There is a warning in the message: if *kale borroka* or ETA actions go too far, "we may reach a point of no return,"[40] which would make all future cooperation with the PNV impossible. The attacks would continue for two more years, but an ideological opening was made towards closer political relations in the future—which is what eventually occurred. However, the MLNV discourse concerning the *Ertzaintza* remained highly negative.

Hence, in the Basque Country of the 1990s, the MLNV's *ex ante*legitimation of political violence dealt with the reasons for the intensification and "toughening"[41] of the struggle, for the necessity of greater involvement of more of the movement's members (particularly youth), and for the selection of Basque objectives. Basque people were depicted as victims of Spain's policy violating their collective and personal rights and of the PNV's betrayal. But at the same time their resistance capacity was stressed. Indeed, the *Oldartzen* document emphasized the allegedly progressive attitude of the Basque people, a people which had remained faithful to the values of the left:

> This is the people that said no to the NATO, that develops initiatives and dynamics full of solidarity both at the international and internal level, that has the largest number of conscientious objectors, and that – through ETA—is capable of maintaining armed struggle in the heart of capitalism.[42]

The so-called Basque problem consisted of two related conflicts: a "national" conflict between the Spanish state and *Euskal Herria*, and a "social" (or class) conflict between nationalist forces moved by economic and power interests and the radical upholders of truly nationalist principles. As for the latter conflict, it was, according to MLNV discourse, not left-wing nationalism but the PNV that had first adopted a strategy of confrontation. If MLNV activists resorted to violence, it was only to respond to acts of aggression perpetrated by others; left-nationalist violent actions basically were of a defensive nature. Both the Herri Batasuna leadership and ETA considered the role of "patriotic youth" to be of particular significance in this struggle against oppression and betrayal. There was a growing number of Herri Batasuna followers and members of MLNV organizations who had ambiguous feelings about the political effectiveness or the moral acceptability of the *kale borroka* actions, but the *Karramarro 2* document contained a clear message for them: "s/he who practises *kale borroka* is an activist and that's that, and that is how s/he should be considered if s/he is arrested or sent to jail."[43]

In the following section I will bring to the fore how at the end of the 1990s, during the 14-month ceasefire of ETA, members of different MLNV organizations justified the radicalization of the "popular struggle" in former years and how they attempted to explain the continuity of the *kale borroka* in a period when ETA had provisionally ended its military actions.

Looking Back; *Ex Post* Legitimation

When MLNV members were asked to explain what being a nationalist meant to them, most of them would only briefly refer to a foregone Arcadia (e.g., the Kingdom of Navarre, in the Middle Ages, which comprised the greater part of the regions that today are considered to make up the Basque Country) or a future Utopia (a reunited, independent, and socialist *Euskal Herria*); but almost everyone claimed that their patriotic feelings could be attributed to the four decades of Franco dictatorship, with its severe oppression of Basque culture and language, and its present legacy of a "pseudo-democracy," with its denial of the Basques' right to self-determination and its harsh repression of "active" youth by the *Guardia Civil* and the National Police. In these interviews, MLNV members again emphasized the connivance of the Basque Nationalist Party (PNV) with Madrid's strategy of obstructing the realization of "truly patriotic" principles:

> They went to Madrid with the message: we keep radical independentism in check and in return you grant us the right to manage the Statute of Autonomy. ... But the PNV was not interested in completely finishing us off, for in Madrid they derive a political bonus from our existence: if left-wing patriotism, and ETA, did not exist, their political influence would be far less.[44]

It was because of the PNV's "betrayal" of the nationalist cause that its party members would be targeted as preferential objectives of *kale borroka* actions. The radicalization of the *kale borroka* may be seen as complementing the ETA strategy of attacking politicians. Although ETA had committed numerous attacks against members of the Spanish police forces and military until the 1990s, the state's policy on the Basque Country had not changed fundamentally. MLNV respondents suggested that this might have been the main reason why ETA decided to directly attack politicians of the two principal parties in Madrid: they were the ones who were held responsible for police action in the Basque Country, and who had designed or approved of the policy of dispersion of ETA prisoners in prisons all over Spain. As the Basque Nationalist Party legitimized and had even helped to execute the state's policy, "they had acquired such degree of responsibility that they would have to face the consequences. ... HB wanted to express that they could not deceive us, that for us the political responsibility of the PNV was very obvious."[45] And: "If someone on your side goes over to the enemy, it's even worse than if someone has always been an enemy."[46]

Both Jarrai spokespersons and *kale borroka* participants would demonstrate great zeal in denying any direct relationship between the MLNV's youth organization and acts of street violence.

> You have to dissociate Jarrai from the *kale borroka*. All these years, people have accused Jarrai of organizing the *kale borroka*, but if Jarrai justifies or approves of *kale borroka* actions, that does not mean we organize them or participate in them.[47]
>
> I was arrested together with more than a hundred other people, but only me and another guy were Jarrai members. Jarrai has never planned acts of sabotage; these actions are planned by the people who execute them.[48]

Within the MLNV, it was recognized that the intensification of *kale borroka* had been planned: "There was a sensation of impotence, of stagnation, which particularly made young people want to act. The idea was: if all these demonstrations of 50,000 people are of no use, we have to strike harder."[49] But respondents invariably assured that individual actions were the result of spontaneous initiatives and improvisation, predominantly motivated by a desire to respond to police repression.

> I can assure you that Herri Batasuna has no authorship over the *kale borroka*, and the same holds good for Jarrai - because the *kale borroka*

has no organized leadership. But there are certain sectors who believe that this type of popular response against structural violence exercised in *Euskal Herria* by the French and Spanish states is totally valid, and necessary.[50]

Young people who had participated in *kale borroka* actions emphasized that spontaneity was not the same as lack of political awareness. They rejected the suggestions in the Elzo Report[51] that many youth committed acts of violence under the influence of alcohol or drugs or for the mere pleasure of destroying things or frightening people. They did recognize that it had occurred that, in riots which had originated for political motives, people from outside the MLNV began to participate for the thrill of fighting with the police or because they had drunk too much.

> But these people never take part in acts of sabotage. These are planned actions, carried out by very small groups, three or four people. ... There are three things we have to observe. I would never carry out an act of sabotage with someone who has taken drugs or alcohol. Nor with someone who says he's not afraid, for such a person must be crazy: those who commit acts of sabotage are afraid. And third, they must be aware of the risk they're running: that they may be arrested and face a charge of 50 years imprisonment, as has happened to some of us.[52]
>
> You don't participate in *kale borroka* because you want to have some fun, and if you did, you'd be a fool. There are other ways of doing things, and if you get caught, you're only sentenced to one or two years. But if you do the same thing as part of the *kale borroka*, you may be sentenced to dozens of years in prison.[53]

MLNV members would stress that *kale borroka*, protagonized by radical youth, had also existed in the 1970s and 1980s, and some doubted whether the phenomenon had radicalized in the nineties. "I don't know if today's actions are more radical. ... But it's true that society finds them more difficult to accept, more difficult to assimilate."[54] It was recognized that even people who sympathized with left-wing nationalist ideas might have critical opinions on the *kale borroka*: "Few of our people raise their voice against ETA—because ETA... is ETA! But there are more people who criticize the *kale borroka*."[55] Nevertheless, people who had practised *kale borroka* affirmed that they had continued their struggle despite this criticism, because "we saw it enabled us to reach our objectives"[56]; after all, what they had in common with Herri Batasuna was a political project, not necessarily the methods of struggle.

Repeatedly, members of different MLNV organizations assured that political successes had been the result of the past strategy of straining the political situation.

- In the last three years, the process has progressed as the situation was getting more and more tense. ... The analysis of left-wing patriotism may be: when confrontation is getting more intense, it becomes easier to find a solution. ... In this country, things depend on gambles. We said: let's take a gamble on this [fomenting the confrontation]; if it works out well, we've won, and if it doesn't, they'll keep on giving it to us. Well, it looks as if we've won the wager. ... Most of the time, when confrontation is getting tougher and tougher, people say: we have to solve this.[57]

- I don't know if it was designed like that, but the purpose was that the PNV would modify its attitude—and they eventually did.[58]
- Without this process of increasing tension, these levels of confrontation in the last four years, without this struggle of left-wing patriotism—the *kale borroka* and other forms—the process we're going through at present would be inconceivable.[59]

In September 1998, after months of secret negotiations, the nationalist parties HB, PNV, and EA, together with a number of smaller parties and social organizations, signed the Lizarra Agreement; a few days later, ETA announced its ceasefire, which would last for fourteen months. The purpose of the aforementioned parties was to develop a policy which would turn the temporary ceasefire into permanent peace, solve the situation of ETA prisoners (their approach to the Basque Country, some sort of amnesty arrangement), and bring the Basque Country closer to sovereignty.

In the interpretation of the MLNV, the improved understanding among the parties that had signed the Lizarra Agreement, their commitment to achieve lasting peace and to meet certain fundamental demands of left-wing nationalism, could only in some measure be attributed to the negotiations among these parties in the course of 1998; in the end, however, these results should be seen as the outcome of the persistent struggle of radical nationalists.

Some sectors of the MLNV maintained this discourse of conflict and confrontation during the ceasefire period: also in a time of truce the popular struggle had to continue.

> At political level, there may have been some progress. But the prisoners are still being dispersed. The employers continue bleeding our youth, so there are still reasons to attack them; the banks are still there; the police continue repressing the youth, there still are detentions, tortures. ... If they keep on attacking you, you don't turn the other cheek all the time. So, people feel that nothing has changed and that we can't stop now, that we have to continue putting pressure on the government.[60]
>
> The *kale borroka* exists, because we live in a situation of war. I don't think this is a conflict—this is war. A small-scale war, maybe, if you refer to pistols, but as to politics, the war is incredible. ... We're at war and there are still people willing to risk their necks in order to solve this situation.[61]

The main objectives of the *kale borroka* in this period were state interests, banks, and the houses and cars of Basque municipal councillors of the two principal Spanish parties: the conservative *Partido Popular* then in power in Madrid, and the oppositional, social-democratic, PSOE. Participants in *kale borroka* actions claimed they attacked rank-and-file members of these Madrid-based parties "so that they put pressure on the people at the top—that they have to enter into negotiations."[62] From the point of view of the MLNV, the principal commitment of the Lizarra Agreement was the "national construction of *Euskal Herria*," while the main obsession of the Spanish state was believed to be the ruining of this project.

The MLNV maintained that during the ceasefire period the *kale borroka* was not nearly such a visible exponent of the so-called Basque conflict as all the forms of "structural violence" of which the Spanish state was responsible. And, again, the "didactic" elements of *kale borroka* actions were stressed:

> If they set fire to the car of a *Guardia Civil*, you should not ask: why did they do that?—but: why on earth are there still *Guardia Civiles* in *Euskal Herria*? And when they burn the car of the Minister of Education of Navarre, you should ask yourself: why is it that the autonomous government of Navarre still does not provide enough facilities to study *Euskara* [the Basque language]?[63]

The fact that the media paid much attention to the consequences of the *kale borroka* was seen as a strategic move of the state to avoid discussing the "real" problems. "Therefore, if we speak so much about the *kale borroka*, we're playing the state's game. If the PNV and EA ask Herri Batasuna to condemn the *kale borroka*, they should consider whose interests they're serving!"[64]

Since the end of the ceasefire period, ETA attacks and *kale borroka* actions have mainly been aimed at non-nationalist politicians and at representatives of other sectors the MLNV sees as enemies of their cause. At present, all (municipal and regional) PP and PSOE politicians in the Basque Country and many of them in the rest of Spain, as well as a great number of journalists, judges, even university lecturers, can only do their work under permanent police protection.

Summarizing: in the interviews, *kale borroka* actions were depicted as the Basque youth's response to "state repression," "structural violence" (bad working and housing conditions) and "the PNV's betrayal," and as acts of protest against the situation of ETA prisoners. Thus, although individual actions were claimed to have originated spontaneously, *kale borroka* activists were politically motivated. Attributing these actions to the planning and preparation of ETA or Jarrai was said to form part of the joint strategy of the state and the media to criminalize the politically engaged youth in the Basque Country, and the left-wing nationalist movement in general. In this way, the state's fascist methods of repression were being legitimized. According to MLNV members, this also explained the opposition of so many people against the movement's struggle: they were either active supporters of this state policy or victims of political manipulation.

While the *ex ante* explanations for the intensification of the kale borroka in MLNV documents and by the movement's spokespersons in the first half of the 1990s and the *ex post* discourse of legitimation of left-wing nationalists interviewed in 1998 and 1999 by and large overlapped, we see here a salient difference. The documents and spokespersons in the former period used to speak of the *kale borroka* in terms of planned, disciplined action and the necessity to control this type of violence. One Herri Batasuna spokesman recognized that left-wing nationalism had "mounted the attack" and that this had evoked "the repression we suffer."[65] Yet, during the ceasefire period, MLNV discourse did not make explicit mention of a strategic design behind the *kale borroka*. Herri Batasuna and Jarrai denied having any authority over the protagonists, emphasizing the "spontaneous" and "defensive" character of the struggle of radical youth. It is not unlikely that this change of discourse was meant to counteract the forceful reaction of police and judicature, which treated all acts of street violence in the Basque Country as part of one terrorist strategy.[66]

At the same time, the MLNV maintained that the Lizarra Agreement between all nationalist forces and the ETA ceasefire could only be attributed to the previous (*kale borroka*) pressure exercised on the PNV and EA. Part of the MLNV following regarded this as the ultimate legitimation of the strategy of radicalization. We note that martial discourse prevails: peace and negotiations were the result of struggle and confrontation. This maxim was extrapolated to the ceasefire period. If the strategy of intimidation and harassment of moderate nationalists had been successful in former years, the same strategy should now be continued—in spite of the ETA ceasefire—against members of non-nationalist parties, so as to force the Government in Madrid to grant the Basque Country the right to self-determination and to change its policy with respect to ETA's "political prisoners."[67] For the MLNV, the ceasefire period was not a period of stable peace, but should rather be seen as another stage in the process of "liberation" and "national construction."

Conclusions: The Four Faces of Legitimation

As Kotarba observed, "[t]he creation of deviance occurs within a normative framework."[68] The generally accepted norm in democratic society is that political ideas should be defended and put into practice by political means, that is in Parliament and Town Councils, through debate, persuasion, negotiations among parties, compromising, establishing majorities, and so on. Not by resorting to violence, not by imposing the will of one party onto the rest of society, not through intimidation, harassment, assassination, and destruction. Those who do so are labelled anti-democrats, terrorists, or criminals. For the left-wing nationalist movement in the Basque Country, this normative framework is not applicable to the Spanish state. For a start, it does not accept the premise that Spain is a democracy where the rights of regional minorities are respected. The factors which the MLNV perceives as conditioning the political climate of the Basque Country are: the "imposed division" of *Euskal Herria* in three separately administered regions (the Basque Autonomous Community, Navarre, and the French Basque region), the non-fulfilment by Madrid of the Statute of Autonomy (which regulates the transfer of political competences to the Basque Autonomous Community), lack of respect for the Basque culture and language, high unemployment rates and precarious job and housing facilities, manipulation by the "state media" of information about the Basque Country, the "occupation" of the centres of Basque towns at weekends by police forces, vigilance of left-nationalist bars, and the like. In this view, the democratic rhetoric of the advocates of the Constitution and the integrity of the Spanish state is only meant to conceal the true, oppressive, character of the system and the situation of "structural violence" suffered by the Basque region. For radical MLNV members, economic insecurity, social problems (like the high incidence of drug addiction among Basque youth), despair, and apathy are consciously created by the Spanish and French state with a view to annihilate the Basque Country's social fabric, its culture, and its language, and thus crush the people's nationalist aspirations. The radical nationalist movement considers that all forms of struggle, including the use of violence, are allowed to fight this pernicious state policy.

In this article, I have analyzed the discourse which MLNV organizations and members developed to legitimize the use of political violence, and I have argued that this legitimation may take place both before and after the violent acts are committed. But only part of the corresponding discourse of the organization responsible for these acts is meant to convince the outside world of the "inevitability" and "legitimacy" of the actions. Another, and perhaps the most important, part of the discourse is aimed at its own members and supporters: so as to provide them with arguments with which to parry external criticism, to meet expected internal opposition, and to silence dissident voices. We can distinguish four different types of discourse of legitimation: the *ex ante* and *ex post* discourse for "home consumption," and the *ex ante* and *ex post* discourse aimed at the general public; these are what I have denominated earlier the "four faces of legitimation."

The central concept in the *ex ante* discourse for internal use is undoubtedly "victimhood" (as in most contemporary emancipatory movements).[69] The Basque Country is depicted as a victim of the historical circumstances which led to the partition of *Euskal Herria* as a result of the constitution of the Spanish and French states and the domination of the two parts by these states; of the almost forty years of Franco repression in the twentieth century; and of the present democratic régime's refusal to recognize the Basque Country's right to self-determination. As non-violent strategies alone are insufficient to achieve freedom and democratic rights for the Basque Country, the use of violence is justified. Furthermore, the left-nationalist movement complained that its demonstrations, hunger strikes, and its political claims in general, were hardly reflected by the media. *Kale borroka* actions and counter-demonstrations against pacifist organizations were justified as being the only way for the movement to get media coverage. In addition—and this part of the discourse was also aimed at the rest of society, up till then it had been principally the left-nationalist movement and its activists who had suffered the consequences of the situation of violence; the time had come that the rest of society up until then experienced these consequences as well. The strategy was aimed at the socialization of suffering.

In the second half of the 1990s, the discourse of legitimation had to account for a number of circumstances which to a large extent conditioned the relation between the movement and the rest of Basque society:

a) actions of street violence (*kale borroka*) perpetrated by radical nationalist youth mainly affected Basque citizens, usually members of moderate nationalist parties;
b) *kale borroka* actions continued during the 14 months (from September 1998 till December 1999) that ETA respected a ceasefire; and
c) the use of political violence was increasingly more rejected by Basque society, and so were those who defended this option.

Attacks Against Moderate Nationalism

The legitimation of a struggle fought with methods which are not approved of by the majority of the population may nonetheless be effective if it can be made plausible that this struggle does not just serve partisan goals but aims at defending more "universal" values. If a just cause is defended by the wrong people or with wrong methods, many observers feel reluctant to censure the means or those who employ them. Since left-wing nationalists in the Basque Country claimed to be the most determined and consistent defenders of the sacred properties and principles of the Basque people (language, culture, territorial integrity...), for many years moderate nationalists, who condemned their methods, found it hard to criticize them too severely. Nationalists of diverging ideologies would affirm that for decades the moderate *Partido Nacionalista Vasco* had looked upon ETA and Herri Batasuna members as prodigal sons of the nationalist family. But this changed in the 1990s, when party offices and members of the PNV and *Eusko Alkartasuna* began to be systematically attacked by MLNV followers.

The MLNV's *ex ante* discourse, both for internal use and for the outside world, was that the moderate nationalist parties were to a large extent responsible for the current political situation. Left-wing nationalists had to do the dirty work on behalf of the liberation of *Euskal Herria*, while the other nationalist parties, particularly the PNV, merely defended the economic interests of their members and attempted to increase their hegemonic power in the Basque Autonomous Community. More severe was the accusation that moderate nationalism not only ignored the Basque cause, but actively obstructed the realization of the fundamental principles of sovereignty and territorial unification, while collaborating with the Spanish state to annihilate the left-nationalist movement; here, the Basque autonomous police force was suspected to have an important role. Hence, the moderate nationalist parties had betrayed the Basque people and the true defenders of the Basque fatherland. There were MLNV members who considered that being a traitor was much more despicable than being an enemy. The *Oldartzen* document stated in unambiguous terms what the left-nationalist movement thought of the PNV's implication in the state's repressive strategy as to left-wing patriotism; and the PNV understood quite well that this message implied both a warning and a threat.

By acting against the moderate nationalist parties PNV and EA, the MLNV managed to increase confrontation in the heart of Basque society. The political discourses employed in the movement's writings and by the MLNV members interviewed explained the rationale of this strategy as follows:

a. The attacks against PNV and EA offices and members were meant to make these parties pay for their aggression against the MLNV (political isolation and marginalization of Herri Batasuna, repression of radical nationalists by the *Ertzaintza*, etc.) and to convey that left-wing nationalism held these parties responsible for the suffering of the Basque people.
b. Counter-demonstrations against the anti-ETA demonstrations of pacifist groups, integrated by many moderate nationalists as well, had to demonstrate the "hypocrisy" of pacifists, who protested against the kidnapping by ETA of one individual, but had never raised their voices against the oppression of *Euskal Herria* or the violation of the rights of political (i.e., ETA) prisoners; moreover, these MLNV demonstrations affirmed once more that "the streets are ours."
c. Destruction and intimidation would put pressure on moderate nationalists, motivating them to convince their parties' leaderships of the necessity to come to some sort of agreement with the MLNV.
d. And this generalization and radicalization of street violence would turn the political confrontation into a personal experience for almost all people involved in the *kale borroka*, boosting their political consciousness.

The Continuity of Violence Despite the Ceasefire

The ceasefire period ETA announced in September 1999 would last for fourteen months. Throughout this period, however, *kale borroka* actions continued. Both Jarrai spokespersons and participants in acts of street violence argued that in spite of the ceasefire hardly anything had improved for Basque youth, who still suffered the consequences of repression, exploitation, and speculation. So there was no reason why the struggle against the institutions responsible for this situation (the police, the banks, employment agencies, state enterprises) should stop.

But left-wing nationalists would also use more political arguments to explain the continuation of the *kale borroka*. In their view, the ceasefire did not mean that the "Basque conflict" had been solved; thus, the ongoing *kale borroka* drew attention to the different manifestations of the conflict. Furthermore, among moderate and radical MLNV followers alike, there was a firm belief that the movement's strategy in former years of straining the situation in the Basque Country to the maximum had been effective: the pact of "democratic" parties meant to isolate and marginalize Herri Batasuna (a pact which had been in force for a decade and included the PNV and EA) had broken up; moderate and radical nationalist parties had signed the Lizarra Agreement, committing themselves to strive for the realization of basic nationalist demands and lasting peace. There were MLNV followers, particularly in Jarrai and among *kale borroka* youth, who claimed that this experience should be extrapolated to the ceasefire period: actions against state interests and representatives of "state parties" were still necessary so as to induce the Spanish Government to start negotiations on nationalist demands.

All this *ex post* discourse was principally meant for home consumption. Whereas the discourse meant, not so much to legitimize the actions of street violence, as to differentiate them from the left-nationalist organizations that were generally held to be responsible for them (Jarrai and Herri Batasuna)—claiming that acts of *kale borroka* were the spontaneous initiatives of those who committed them—was aimed at the rest of society (first and foremost at the judiciary and the media). On the other hand, left-wing nationalists would assure that the political motivations of the protagonists of these actions were entirely justified.

Coping with Growing Aversion

The aversion for the perpetrators of *kale borroka* actions was rather widespread in Basque society, and even among many Herri Batasuna members there was little sympathy for them. The *kale borroka* youth and those who supported them unconditionally were well aware of that and their discourse attempted to rationalize this opposition.

It was deemed logical that potential victims of acts of street violence, like PNV and EA municipal councillors, rejected the *kale borroka* and its protagonists, "because we make life difficult for them." The fact that this negative attitude towards the *kale borroka* also prevailed in the rest of society was attributed to the biased reporting on the Basque conflict by what MLNV members systematically qualified as "the state media." Average citizens were believed to be victims of manipulation by the media, which impeded their correct understanding of what the struggle of radical Basque youth really was about. Left-wing nationalism accused the media of criminalizing Basque youth by suggesting there existed an organic relationship between *kale borroka* participants and ETA; the media thus created a situation of moral panic, which enabled the state and judiciary to justify more repressive measures against radical adolescents (the application of anti-terrorist legislation), neutralizing the youth's justified demands.

The opposition from the rest of society was obviously not the MLNV's main concern. But the lack of support within its own circles caused the movement more worries. The *ex post* message to the following with ambiguous feelings about the *kale borroka* was that the participants in actions of street violence should be seen as true

Table 3. The four faces of legitimation

Discourse of legitimation	*ex ante*	*ex post*
for internal use	• explaining • inciting • removing doubts	• reiterating and demonstrating the justness, correctness, and effectiveness of the actions carried out • explaining the "didactics" of actions
for the outside world (incl. the "enemy")	• warning • intimidating • separating the enemy from the "public"	• explaining didactics reiterating identification of the enemy (identifying the victim as aggressor)

patriots and as activists of the left-nationalist movement (the suggestion being that, in this respect, they were not much different from ETA activists).

In the end, however, the loss of votes and the increase of critical voices within Herri Batasuna as a consequence of the strategy of radicalization were accepted, as long as this strategy was effective, that is, if it brought the solution to the conflict nearer. Left-wing nationalists recognized that the strategy had been a gamble, which they might just as well have lost. The official MLNV evaluation of this period was that the ETA ceasefire and the Lizarra Agreement (the pact of moderate and radical nationalists on behalf of "national construction") should eventually be attributed to the strategy of radicalization: "The purpose was that the PNV would modify its attitude—and they eventually did."[70] Hence, the efficacy of this strategy had been demonstrated.

Thus, the discourse of legitimation of violence has four faces, and the purposes of the discourse, which are different in each of these cases, are summarized in Table 3. We should stress the hypothetical character of the table; moreover, the compartments' contents may not always be mutually exclusive.

Legitimation and Radicalization

Terrorism cannot do without legitimation. It is my contention that the discourse aimed at justifying acts of violence is more than a mere exercise of cynicism on the part of the terrorists—it is an essential part of terrorist strategy. The terrorists' discourse gives meaning to individual acts of violence by putting them into an explanatory framework. The message conveyed is that these actions are not indiscriminate (and the victims not randomly chosen), but form part of a consciously designed strategy. A strategy aimed at both the achievement of immediate objectives (e.g., the government's willingness to negotiate with the movement) and the attainment of the "ultimate" political goals (in case of nationalist terrorism: territorial unification, independence, etc.). Thus, in so far as the discourse is aimed at the state apparatus and the political parties in power, it is one of intimidation and blackmail: "These are our demands and if you don't yield to them, our actions will continue and more and more of your people will become victims of our attacks." The "didactics" of the acts of violence are aimed at the general public, and, more in particular, at the organizations that the victims of these actions represent.

However, in the case of radicalization of the terrorist strategy the discourse may be more inward than outward bound. In the Basque Country, the left-nationalist movement has followed such a strategy of political and military radicalization since the early 1990s. Formerly, ETA actions had mainly affected members of the Spanish military and police forces, but in the nineties they were more and more directed against politicians, members of the *Ertzaintza*, representatives of the judiciary, businessmen, journalists, university lecturers, and others. At the same time, the *kale borroka* increased considerably, principally affecting politicians of moderate nationalist parties and participants in anti-ETA demonstrations; these acts of street violence also continued during the ETA ceasefire period. Many of the recent ETA and *kale borroka* actions were hardly understood by a great part of the MLNV following, and consequently, the didactics of these violent actions had to be explained principally within the movement itself. Every time ETA assassinated a politician or an *ertzaina*, or *kale borroka* youth attacked fellow nationalists, the discontent within left-wing nationalist circles was evident. According to one of the movement's dissidents: "It is highly significant that lately, ETA has had to explain its actions above all to members and sympathizers of the left-nationalist movement."[71]

In 1987, an ETA car-bomb exploded in the supermarket *Hipercor* in Barcelona, killing 21 people and injuring many more. This attack, ETA's most bloody and most indiscriminate action, caused such great consternation within the left-nationalist movement that the organization did not even try to justify it. Instead, ETA apologized for this action and qualified it as a "mistake"; the excuse given was that ETA had warned the police in advance, but that the police, intentionally, had waited too long in clearing the people out of the building, so as to provoke a great number of casualties which would discredit the organization. According to some observers, the action may have been a test case: if the left-nationalist following had accepted its consequences, such indiscriminate actions might have become a normal part of ETA's strategy. However, it had become clear that the members and sympathizers of the movement were 'not yet ready' for such actions.

Hence, I argue that for a terrorist organization involved in a strategy of radicalization, a discourse of legitimation is essential, and, in this case, this discourse is principally aimed at those who sympathize with the organization's goals. The movement which supports the terrorist organization can normally cope with internal criticism and the incidental exit of dissidents, but more disruptive tendencies, like splits within the movement or the massive desertion of activists, should be avoided. Hence, the failure to successfully legitimize violent actions that go *in crescendo* within the circles of its political following may make the organization reconsider its strategy of radicalization.

Notes

1. This denomination, *Movimiento para la Liberación Nacional Vasco* (MLNV), was adopted by the radical nationalist movement to establish parallels with the national liberation movements in other parts of the world (e.g., Algeria, Vietnam) and to convey the image of a guerrilla army with general and wide support within Basque society. In this conception, ETA is the MLNV's military branch, Herri Batasuna (HB) its political organization, and Jarrai its youth movement. (In recent years, and anticipating judicial attempts to

declare organizations belonging to the MLNV illegal, Herri Batasuna changed its name to "Euskal Herritarrok," then to "Batasuna," and, recently, to "Sozialista Abertzaleak," whereas Jarrai became "Haika," and, later, "Segi.")

2. For Basque nationalists, the Basque Country (or *Euskal Herria* in the Basque language) comprises the Basque Autonomous Community and the Foral Community of Navarre in Spain, and *Iparralde*, or the French Basque region, on the northern side of the Pyrenees. This is the region where historically the Basque language has been spoken and which both moderate and radical nationalists see as their Basque Fatherland; still, the region has never been a political subject in itself. The Basque Autonomous Community is made up of the provinces Guipúzcoa, Vizcaya, and Álava, and acquired its special status as a result of the Statute of Autonomy of 1979; the level of autonomous rule of the Basque Government and Parliament is generally assumed to be even higher than that of the German Länder. However, and unless stated otherwise, throughout the text I will use the expression "the Basque Country" to refer to the Basque region *in Spain*, as it is principally on Spanish soil that ETA activists and adherents have carried out their violent actions. (The Basque region in the south of France does not have a special status, but forms part of the Acquitaine department. Despite the fact that in radical nationalist discourse both the Spanish and the French State are qualified as the occupying enemy forces, for "practical" reasons, ETA actions have hardly ever taken place in France. For decades, ETA commandos considered the French Basque region a sanctuary where attacks could be prepared and where activists could find refuge after they had been carried out. Several times, I heard Spanish politicians and journalists complain that there seemed to exist some sort of tacit agreement between the French state and ETA which implied that the latter would not commit any terrorist attacks on French soil, as long as the *gendarmerie* left ETA undisturbed. However, this situation changed after 11 September 2001; since then, operations of French police forces against ETA members have been more frequent and successful.) For the good order, moderate and radical nationalist parties account for just over 50 percent of the votes in the Basque Autonomous Community, whereas support for Basque nationalism is about 10 percent in the province of Navarre and less than 5 percent in the Basque region in the south of France. Votes for Herri Batasuna have always oscillated around 15 percent in the Basque Autonomous Community.
3. Patricia O'Connor, "Introduction: Discourse of Violence," *Discourse & Society* 6/3 (1995) p.310.
4. David E. Apter, "Political Violence in Analytical Perspective," In D.E. Apter (ed.), *The Legitimation of Violence* (London: MacMillan Press Ltd., 1997) pp.2, 5.
5. Michael Wieviorka, "ETA and Basque Political Violence," in D.E. Apter (ed.), *The Legitimation of Violence* (London: MacMillan Press Ltd., 1997).
6. Javier Elzo, *Plan de actuación del Gobierno para el desarrollo de los valores democráticos y fomento de actitudes de solidaridad, tolerancia y responsabilidad en los adolescentes y jóvenes vascos* (Vitoria-Gasteiz: Eusko Jaurlaritza, 1996; internal document).
7. Apter (note 4) p.11.
8. Alan Bairner, "The battlefield of Ideas: The Legitimation of Political Violence in Northern Ireland." *European Journal of Political Research* 14 (1986) pp.637–640.
9. Herri Batasuna, *Oldartzen*, Documento definitivo, 1ª parte (1995; internal document).
10. ETA, "Ponencia general—Karramarro" *Zutabe*, 72 (1995; internal document); ETA, *Karramarro (2. zatia)* (1996; internal document).
11. Obviously, some of the left-wing nationalists I interviewed had more extremist views than others (Jarrai spokespersons and participants in acts of street violence were generally more radical than the average Herri Batasuna member), and not all respondents managed the same discursive resources (some militant youths, in particular, used rather rudimentary rhetoric). Radical nationalist youth generally distinguished themselves from other young people for their preference for revolutionary symbols (Che Guevara badges, T-shirts with slogans in favour of ETA prisoners) and their deep, often openly professed, respect for ETA.

12. María J. Funes, "Social Responses to Political Violence in the Basque Country: Peace Movements and Their Audience," *The Journal of Conflict Resolution* 42/4 (August 1998), p.495.
13. Ibid. p.507.
14. Fernando Reinares, *Patriotas de la muerte. Quiénes han militado en ETA y por qué* (Madrid: Grupo Santillana de Ediciones, S.A., 2001).
15. José Manuel Mata López, *El Nacionalismo Vasco Radical. Discurso, organización y expresiones* (Bilbao: Servicio Editorial de la Universidad del País Vasco, 1993).
16. Elzo (note 6) p.4.
17. Ibid. Similar depolitization occurs in Douglass and Zulaika's analysis of ETA violence as ritual action (William A. Douglass and Joseba Zulaika, "On the Interpretation of Terrorist Violence: ETA and the Basque Political Process," *Comparative Studies of Society and History* 32/2, 1990). Elsewhere, Zulaika affirms that youth participation in *kale borroka* actions respond to "rituals of manliness" (*El Diario Vasco*, 29 Sept. 1996).
18. Jeremy MacClancy, "At Play with Identity in the Basque Arena," in S. Macdonald (ed.), *Inside European Identities: Ethnography in Western Europe* (Oxford: Berg Publishers Ltd., 1993) p.94.
19. Ibid. p.87.
20. Anton Blok, "Het narcisme van kleine verschillen," *Amsterdams Sociologisch Tijdschrift*, 24/2 (1997).
21. For a good analysis of the history and strategies of the peace movements in the Basque Country, see María J. Funes, *La salida del silencio. Movilizaciones por la paz en Euskadi, 1986–1997* (Akal Ediciones, 1998).
22. Herri Batasuna (note 9) p.61.
23. Jarrai-1, V/99. The respondents are referred to by indicating the organization they belong to or are active in: HB = Herri Batasuna; Jarrai = the MLNV youth organization; KByth = youth who had participated in *kale borroka* actions; EHA = the movement *Euskal Herria Askatu*. Respondents are numbered according to the first time they were interviewed; also given are the month and year the interview was done: V/99 = May 1999.
24. Herri Batasuna (note 9); ETA (note 10).
25. ETA, *Karamarro (2. Zatia)* (note 10) p.16.
26. Ibid. p.19.
27. Ibid. p.18.
28. ETA, *Zutabe* (see note 10) in: Annex *Karramarro Txostenak, KAS alternatibatik Euskal Alternatiba Demokratikora eman beti hitza herriari;* emphasis in the original.
29. *Egin*, 1 Jan. 1996; cited in José Antonio Rekondo, *Bietan Jarrai. Guerra y Paz en las calles de Euskadi* (Bilbao: Aranalde, 1998) p.55.
30. Cf. also Rekondo (note 29) p.26.
31. Jarrai, *Los movimientos populares y nuestra actuación política*. Usurbilgo Jarraiko ikastaroak, batzar nazionala; Uda ikastaroak (1995, internal document) p.7.
32. Ibid. Emphasis in the original.
33. Ibid. p.8.
34. See note 2.
35. *Partido Socialista Obrero Español*, the Spanish social-democratic party in government in Madrid from 1982 until 1996, when it was displaced from power by the conservative *Partido Popular*. Since 14 March 2004, The PSOE has been in government again.
36. Herri Batasuna (note 9) pp.20–22.
37. Ibid. p.22.
38. ETA (note 10).
39. ETA, *Karramarro(2. zatia)* (note 10) p.8.
40. Ibid.
41. Rekondo (note 29) p.22.

42. Herri Batasuna (note 9) p.29.
43. ETA, *Karramarro 2* (note 10) p.18.
44. HB-6, X/99.
45. Ibid.
46. HB-5, IX/99.
47. Jarrai-3, VI/99.
48. KByth-1, X/98.
49. HB-5, IX/99.
50. HB-4, VIII/99.
51. Elzo (note 6).
52. KByth-1, X/98.
53. KByth-3, IX/99.
54. Jarrai-4, IX/99.
55. KByth-3, IX/99.
56. Ibid.
57. EHA-1, IX/99.
58. HB-5, IX/99.
59. Jarrai-1, V/99.
60. KByth-1, X/98.
61. Jarrai-4, IX/99.
62. Ibid.
63. Jarrai-1, V/99.
64. Ibid.
65. Cited in Rekondo (note 29) p.30.
66. In the late 1980s, one of the ETA leaders had designed this type of part-time juvenile terrorism with different goals in mind: it would compensate for the reduced operativeness of ETA; participants, most of them being minors, would receive relatively low punishments if arrested by the police; these violent acions would be useful training for those who desired to become full-fledged ETA members.
67. As a matter of fact, an MLNV document had already stated in 1997 that Basque youth had to be instructed on how to sustain the *kale borroka* on their own account in time of truce; see Rekondo (note 29) p.32.
68. J.A. Kotarba, "Labelling Theory and Everyday Deviance," in Jack D. Douglas et al., *Introduction to the Sociologies of Everyday Life* (Boston: Allyn and Bacon, Inc., 1980) p.90.
69. Cf. P. Arthur, '"Reading' Violence: Ireland," in D.E. Apter (ed.), *The Legitimation of Violence* (London: MacMillan Press Ltd., 1997).
70. HB-5, IX/99.
71. HB-7, v/2000.

Name Index